LANGUAGE DEVELOPMENT

Peter A. Reich

University of Toronto

PRENTICE-HALL, ENGLEWOOD CLIFFS, NEW JERSEY 07632

Library of Congress Cataloging-in-Publication Data

Reich, Peter A.
    Language development.

    Bibliography: p.
    Includes indexes.
    1. Language acquisition.   2. Language disorders in
children.   3. Language and languages—Study and teaching.
I. Title.
P118.R42   1986   401'.9   85-24453
ISBN   0-13-523069-1

Editorial/production supervision and interior design: Jeanne Hoeting
Cover design: Lundgren Graphics
Manufacturing buyer: Barbara Kelly Kittle

Printed in the United States of America

10 9 8 7 6 5 4 3 2 1

ISBN 0-13-523069-1   01

Prentice-Hall International (UK) Limited, *London*
Prentice-Hall of Australia Pty. Limited, *Sydney*
Prentice-Hall of Canada Inc., *Toronto*
Prentice-Hall Hispanoamericana, S.A., *Mexico*
Prentice-Hall of India Private Limited, *New Delhi*
Prentice-Hall of Japan, Inc., *Tokyo*
Prentice-Hall of Southeast Asia Pte. Ltd., *Singapore*
Editoria Prentice-Hall do Brasil, Ltda., *Rio de Janeiro*
Whitehall Books Limited, *Wellington, New Zealand*

DEDICATION

**To my children Quentin and Athena,
whose own language acquisition process
made the subject come alive
in a way that no amount of systematic research
and nonparental observation could.**

CONTENTS

PREFACE

When I first proposed to my department chairman to offer a course entirely devoted to language acquisition, he asked, "Is there enough material to cover a whole semester?" I replied that I thought that there was. Today that question seems ridiculous, for the field of language acquisition has blossomed, supporting two annual meetings, three journals, a growing number of textbooks, and an international society solely devoted to first language acquisition, and much more in the areas of second language learning and developmental language disorders.

I began with the intention of reading at least the abstract of everything written on the topic, but the literature explosion, plus a broadening definition of what constitutes the field has prevented me from coming close to that goal. Still, I was able to survey perhaps three thousand papers, and discuss in this book perhaps one thousand of them.

This book presents the lectures which I have been giving in my course, offered at the third year of university. Some of my students come in with a background in psychology; others with a background in linguistics; still others with a background in other sciences, such as human physiology. Some wish to become speech and language pathologists, teachers, or doctors. Many are drawn to the developmental area because they are parents or expect to become parents. Because of the diverse backgrounds of the students, I do not assume any specific knowledge; teaching the linguistics and psychology necessary to understand the language development findings as I go.

This book has some conventions designed to clarify the material and aid the student. The first place a technical term is defined, it appears in **boldface,** as does the reference to the definition in the index. Use of language in a way that I consider to be not quite right is indicated by single quotes, as, for example, when I use 'talk' to refer to deaf children learning to use sign language. Linguistic examples in the text are given in *italic*, except for direct quotes of particular incidents, which are given in double quotes. The meaning or translation of linguistic examples is given in double quotes. The phonetic representation, which appears in square brackets, follows the standard of the International Phonetic Alphabet as taught in most phonetics courses, except that the initial consonants in *char* and *jar* are represented as single symbols—[čɑɹ] and [ǰɑɹ]—instead as two symbols—[tʃɑɹ] and [dʒɑɹ]. The international standard becomes increasingly appropriate as more information about language acquisition comes from examples from languages other than English. My deviation is due to my belief that [č] and [ǰ] are each psychologically a single unit in English. Linguistic terms used in syntactic constructions, such as SUBJECT and OBJECT are given in large and small caps. Words in linguistic examples that are intonationally stressed are given in CAPITAL letters. The occasional word in text that I wish to stress is in ***boldface italic***.

There are many different ways an instructor may order the material in language acquisition. The order I use in the book is the order I have found is best for my classes. I have attempted, however, to insure that subsections of each chapter stand alone, so that other instructors may impose their own preferred order on the material. As a further aid to students, each chapter has a summary and suggestions for further study.

I have tried to write a text book that is enjoyable to read as well as comprehensive and accurate. For this reason I have tended to foreground children learing language and background the researchers who study them. Also, I have attempted to provide figures and illustrations that are enjoyable, yet appropriate.

Many people have helped me in my labors to produce this book. Particularly outstanding was the help given by Karen Hume, who spent several years helping on the project. Many of the graduate teaching assistants I have had in the course have helped by preparing lectures on material with which I had not been familiar. Term papers written by both granduate students and undergraduates aided me in my search for balance and completeness. I must thank Dianne Bond for her fine work on several of the figures and illustrations. The people at Prentice-Hall aided me by taking on the project before I was even expecting to turn it into a book—I thought I was just producing a more complete set of lecture notes—and encouraging me to complete it. They have been frustrated by my failure to meet their deadlines, but, lo, the work did eventually get done.

Finally, my thanks go to my wife Judith Bond, who helped see me through depression and despair at ever seeing the work completed, and who made useful critical comments on every part of the manuscript.

Peter A. Reich, 1985

ONE
INFANCY

infant /'infant/ [From Latin *infans, infantem*, adjective, "incapable of speech"; from *in-* "not" + *fans, fantem* present participle of *fari* "to speak"] A child in the first year of life.

DEVELOPMENTAL CONTEXT

Infancy is a time of great physical and cognitive change. The major motor developmental milestones are sitting, crawling, and walking. Infants are able to sit with support for an average of one minute at 0;3 or 0;4 (3 or 4 months), and without support at 0;7 or 0;8. By 0;9 they can sit for 10 minutes or more (Gesell & Amatruda 1941). They are able to crawl at about 0;7,23 (7 months 23 days—34 weeks) (Ames 1937), and stand while holding onto furniture about a month later. At 0;11 they can stand alone, and at about 1;1 (1 year 1 month) they can walk alone (Gesell et al. 1940).

Visual acuity and depth perception seem to be present at birth (Gibson & Walk 1960; K. Pratt 1946), and newborns appear to be able to track moving objects visually (Wickelgren 1969). For the first month or so infants appear to have a fixed focus set for about 20 centimeters away. By 0;2 they begin to be able to adjust their focus, until at 0;4 their ability is comparable to that of an adult (Haynes et al. 1965).

1

Cognitive development is generally described in terms of stages. The first year is considered to consist of four stages. In the first month development is limited to modification and elaboration of simple reflexes such as sucking. The second stage lasts from 0;1 to 0;4. During this period an infant will develop the ability to perform purposively certain simple behavioral sequences, such as thumb sucking, which it had first engaged in by accident. It also begins to anticipate that certain situations will lead to known outcomes, such as the fact that being placed in a certain position will lead to being fed.

The third stage runs from 0;4 to 0;10. During this period the infant will begin to engage in repetitive behavioral sequences involving objects in the environment. There is evidence that the infant begins to classify objects, in that it will behave one way to one set of objects and another way to other objects. During this stage some understanding of the nature of physical objects is acquired. For example, if a matchbox is dropped too fast for the infant to follow its fall, the infant will look for it at the right place—namely, on the floor directly below. This period marks an improvement in the ability of infants to remember for short periods the location of an object. At 0;8, when an object is hidden under one of two cloths, infants cannot find the object after being held back for only one second; by 1;0, 70% of infants can find it after being held back for seven seconds (Kagan et al. 1978).

The fourth stage runs from 0;10 to 1;0. During this stage one can get infants to engage in two-step processes, such as removing an obstacle to get to a toy. In general, if a desired object disappears, the infant will search for it (Ginsburg & Opper 1969: 26-57).

This background of other developmental milestones will help to put in context the findings that are the main concern of this chapter—the development of communication and other abilities relevant to the acquisition of language.

PRENATAL COMMUNICATION

For lo, as soon as the voice of thy salvation sounded in my ears, the babe in my womb leaped for joy.—Luke 1:44

Communication is possible even before birth. As early as the 12th week after conception, one can detect signs of unrest in a fetus following blows or pressure applied to the mother's abdomen. In the ear, the cochlea and sensory end-organs are apparently developed by the 24th week (Bast & Anson 1949; Ormerod 1960). By the 28th week the fetus is listening to outside noises, such as the mother's heartbeat, intestinal sounds, voice, and cough (Liley 1972; Wedenberg & Johansson 1970).

Certainly the ability of a fetus to hear outside sounds has always been obvious to most mothers. According to his mother, my son Quentin had clear preferences in music before he was born (see Clements 1977). However, it apparently was not until 1925 that this fact made its way into scientific journals. In that first study more than a third of the fetuses subjected to a loud sound produced detectable movements in response. Most often the fetus seemed to draw its whole body together (Peiper

1925). In a later study four mothers in the last 2½ months of pregnancy were each placed lying on their backs beneath a loudspeaker. Pure tones at various frequencies were sounded over the speaker. The fetuses' heartbeats increased immediately following the presentation of the tones over a wide range of frequencies (Bernard & Sontag 1947).

At this time the fetus has a well-developed nervous system and, if born, a good chance of survival. A 22-week-old fetus, born prematurely, has been heard to cry faintly on exposure to air (Minkowski 1922). There are even reports that infants cry while still in the womb (Illingworth 1955: 75). Such reports are found in ancient writings from Assyria, Babylonia, Greece, India, and Rome (Parviainen 1949). There are at least 125 cases of crying in the womb reported in writings from 1800 to 1947, including one case in which the infant is said to have cried two weeks before birth (King & Bourgeois 1947). Can an infant make a vocal sound when its lungs are filled with liquid? Current experts think not. For a cry to be heard before birth, the membranes must have ruptured and air must have entered the womb (Blair 1965; Ostwald 1972).

Even while fetuses are still in the womb, communication can be a two-way street. Mothers often report that their unborn child will kick them if they sit in a certain position. This is often a very successful way of getting the mother to sit in a different position, presumably more comfortable for the fetus. When this happened to the wife of a friend of mine, he proposed that it was never too early to impose some discipline on the unborn child. He suggested that the next time the baby complained by kicking, his wife should respond by poking the baby back. She tried this, and according to my friend, rapid learning ensued; the fetus stopped complaining. Whether or not you wish to believe that there was successful communication in the case of my friend's wife and her unborn child, there is experimental evidence that fetuses can learn. In one study 16 fetuses were taught to kick in response to a gentle vibrating sensation (Spelt 1948).

Some psychiatrists and psychotherapists believe fetuses can have memory of events that occurred before birth. One patient remembered hearing the muffled sounds of laughter, a carousel, and trumpets. His mother confirmed that she had attended a carnival in the final weeks of her pregnancy (Grof 1976). Canadian conductor Boris Brot was amazed to discover that he already knew a cello piece that he had never before encountered. Later his mother confirmed that she had repeatedly practiced this piece on her cello while she was pregnant with him (Verny & Kelly 1981: 22).

There are even reports of fetuses remembering speech. One afternoon a woman in Oklahoma City heard her two-year-old daughter chanting to herself, "Breathe in, breathe out, breathe in, breathe out." She claimed that these words were part of a prenatal exercise program she engaged in before her daughter was born. The mother ruled out the possibility that the daughter had heard it on television because the words came from a system used in Toronto; if the daughter had seen it on television, she would have picked up the American version, which used different words. The mother concluded that the daughter had remembered the exercises from two years earlier (Verny & Kelly 1981: 23, see also pp. 32-33). I am not impressed. It seems more likely to me that the daughter had heard the words on a television show not concerned with prenatal exercises. Some children's shows have exercise segments and it seems less farfetched to suggest that the girl heard the words in this context.

Whatever limited communication, muffled sounds, and vague memories may be a part of the life experience of a fetus, one cannot doubt that the possibilities for communication grow enormously with birth.

CRYING

Language is not imposed upon a silent creature. Whatever else a child may lack, it is certainly not the power of making a noise.—M. M. Lewis, *Infant Speech,* Harcourt, Brace, Jovanovich, 1936: 21

The birth cry

Generally the first thing an infant does when it is born is cry. Most observers consider the birth cry to be entirely physiological, relating to the establishment of normal respiration (McCarthy 1954: 505), although some philosophers and psychiatrists have thought otherwise (see Box 1.1). The ancient Romans believed that a spirit named Vagitanus induced the first cry (J. Ferguson 1970: 68). People who take the birth cry to be purely physiological seem to consider that first utterance to be unique, for "within a very few hours, the child's cry may be taken as a sign of discomfort" (M. M. Lewis 1936: 21). Recently this distinction has been called into question. Many now say that the birth cry is, like later crying, due to discomfort, which can be avoided if one takes steps to make the birth process less traumatic to the infant. Such steps include having the delivery take place in a darkened room, immediately immersing the baby in a bath at body temperature, and playing a record of heartbeats and other muffled body sounds (Murooka 1974). Advocates of this approach claim that infants treated in this way cry less or not at all.

If the infant's cry is abnormal, it is a signal to the doctor that something is wrong. Mongoloid children and children with neurological abnormalities have cries that differ from those of normal children in pitch, rhythm, accentual character, volume, and latency of cry following onset of stimulus (Michelsson & Wasz-Höckert 1980; Zeskind & Lester 1978). Unlike most other vocalization, crying is normally involuntary. Evidence in support of this comes from infants with brain lesions causing a paralysis of volitional facial muscles on one side. Such lesions do not affect the muscles of the face during crying (Illingworth 1955: 75).

Crying is not the only sound that newborns can make. Other sounds include coughs, sneezes, squeeks, burps, flatulence, and hiccups (Stark et al. 1975). Crying, however, is the most salient to both scientists and parents.

Different cries to different stimuli?

One controversy in this area seems to have been started over a century ago by Charles Darwin. He stated: "The noise of crying . . . is of course uttered in an instinctive manner, but serves to show that there is suffering. After a time the sound

BOX 1.1 *BABY'S FIRST CRY*

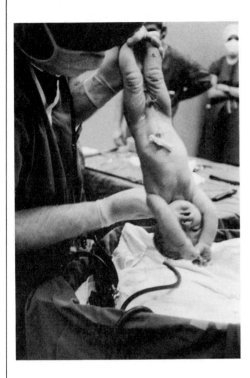

When we are born we cry that we are come
To this great stage of fools.—Shakespeare, *King Lear*

For a childe naturally neither laments nor cries so long as he doth abide in his mothers wombe.

And I have often observed that a childe neither cries, nor makes any noise, neither sighs, though he be halfe come forth, what paine or anguish soever he suffers in the passing. But as soon as he is born and sees the light (besides the alteration in the ayer which he finds) even very necessity and his owne feeling doe force and as it were wring from him cries and moanes, thereby to show in what he need be stands of helpe.—Jacques Guillemeau, 1609

The outcry that is heard from a child scarcely born has not the tone of lamentation, but of indignation and of aroused wrath; not because anything gives him pain, but because something frets him; presumably because he wants to move, and feels his inability to do it as a fetter that deprives him of his freedom.—Immanuel Kant, 1799

The first cry represents an overwhelming sense of inferiority at thus being suddenly confronted with reality without ever having had to deal with its problems.—Alfred Adler, 1946. © Routledge & Kegan Paul. Used by permission.

differs according to the cause, such as hunger or pain (Darwin 1877: 292). Are there different types of cries to different types of distress?

In one of the first experimental studies on the topic, infants 3 to 7 days old were induced to cry in response to four causes—hunger, fear, anger, and pain. Hunger was produced by delaying a normal feeding 15 to 30 minutes, fear by dropping the infant 30 to 60 centimeters towards a table, anger by holding it in a face-down position on a table for about 5 seconds, and pain by sticking a needle into its face 4 times in rapid succession (Sherman 1927). A group of listeners, consisting of college students, mothers, and nurses, was asked to guess the cause of the crying. The observers were not able to match the cries to the type of discomfort. Twenty years later a similar study obtained the same negative result (Aldrich et al. 1945).

These early studies were criticized for a number of reasons. One was that they tested infant cries in the first week of life. Many, including Darwin, argued that differentiation comes later.

In the mid 1960's the availability of the tape recorder as a research tool allowed for more highly controlled experimentation. In one study the cries of 80 infants were recorded during four different situations: at birth, prior to the noon feeding, when the child was vaccinated, and pleasure sounds when the baby was happy. Of the 320 'cries' thus obtained, 6 of each type were selected, "because they seemed, by an auditive analysis, to be typical of the four situations." Eighty trained nurses each listened to the 24 recordings thus obtained. They were able to select the correct cry 67% of the time. Another study found that experienced listeners were better than inexperienced listeners (Wasz-Höckert et al. 1968).

One can argue, however, that two of the four cry types used were irrelevant to the issue. Nobody ever claimed that happy sounds were the same as cries. And the difference between the birth cry and the cries of an older infant is also irrelevant to the issue. If just the confusion between pain and hunger cries is taken into account, one finds that observers are correct about 70% of the time, compared to a chance value of 50%. Unfortunately, since the cries used were not chosen at random, all that is proved is that the trained nurses tend to identify as a pain cry those cries chosen as typical pain cries by the experimenters, and similarly with the hunger cries.

Yet another experiment seemed necessary to resolve the issue. This time cries were elicited in three different situations—pain, loud noise, and 'hunger.' Pain was produced by snapping an elastic band against the infant's foot; the loud noise was produced by clapping two wooden blocks together once; the 'hunger' cry was produced by beginning to feed an infant at its normal feeding time and then halting the feeding after several seconds. 'Hunger' is in single quotes because one could argue that this cry results from frustration, not hunger directly. The experimenters isolated the first and third 15-second segments of each of the cries of each of eight 3-to 5-month-old infants, and played these segments to 18 mothers—the mothers of the 8 infants used, and 10 others. Again the findings indicated that mothers cannot distinguish the source of discomfort from the acoustic properties of their infant's cries (E. Müller et al. 1974).

(© **1977 by Lynn Johnston. Reprinted by permission of Meadowbrook Press and Simon & Schuster, Inc.**)

This result of the psychologists is not only contrary to the observations of Darwin, but also to the observations of most parents. How can such a discrepancy be resolved? There seem to be three factors involved.

The first factor is that there is, in fact, variation in the sound of infant cries, right from birth. Phoneticians who have analyzed infant cries instrumentally can

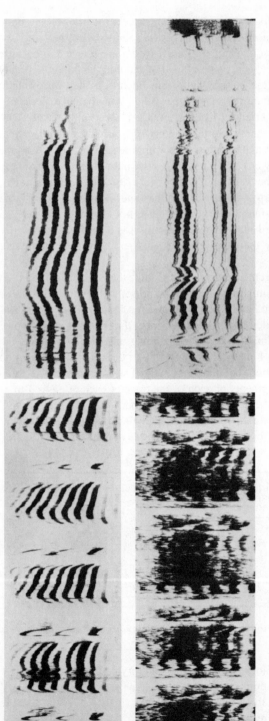

FIGURE 1.1
Sound spectrograms of five different cries. (From Wolff 1969.
©Tavistock Institute of Human Relations. Used by permission.)

distinguish the 'normal' cry (Figure 1.1a) from the louder and qualitatively different 'scream' (Figure 1.1b) (Lieberman 1967; Stark et al. 1975: 219).

One remarkable study involved recording all vocalizations of two infants continuously for their first five months of life. The main finding from all this data collection seems to be that there is a correlation between amplitude and duration. In other words, longer cries are louder than shorter cries (Sheppard & Lane 1968). Although phoneticians have found different cries, they have not tried to relate these differences to different causes.

The second factor is that most parents can guess the problem and correct it on the first try most of the time. If the cries are all the same, how can parents be so accurate? Often in naturally occurring situations, most of the information parents rely upon undoubtedly comes from the situation. Did the baby just fall? How long has it been since the last feeding? How long since diapering? Is it cold in the room, and has the baby come out of its blanket? Other cues can come from the infant. If when the baby is picked up, it begins **rooting** behavior—turning its head to the side in an instinctual search for its mother's nipple—the parent will not unreasonably assume that the baby is hungry. This knowledge of the situation is often enough to determine the cause.

The third factor is that although there are identifiable differences in infant cries, the experiments have been designed in such a way that these differences could not be observed by the subjects. For example, although the first experiment came out negative, it was set up only after extensive observation, some of which was also reported. In particular, if subjects were allowed to listen to cries for longer periods than were used in the experiment, they were more successful. A cry which was prolonged over two or three minutes, and which subsided and increased in intensity rhythmically was often correctly judged as that of hunger (Sherman 1927: 340). Similarly, unusually long and intermittent crying which subsided and then reoccurred with sudden intensity was judged as colic (Blanton 1917). A cry that was sharp, loud, and of short duration was usually judged as pain or anger. It appears that the time course of the crying coincides with the time course of the discomfort.

Thus although there are qualitative differences in cries, these differences do not appear to be related to differences in cause. Rather, there is a quantitative relationship between a cry and the intensity of the distress, and thus certain types of distress will be identifiable on the basis of changes in the intensity of crying when listened to over an extended period. Experimental studies that control for length and intensity will find no difference between cries.

An alternative explanation is that we have not been looking at the right variables. Instead of looking at vowel quality and intensity perhaps we should look at the number of pauses between bursts of crying. And instead of looking at hunger versus pain, we should be looking at discomfort of all types versus 'call' (the cry an infant produces when it realizes that the mother is not present, as indicated by appearing to look for her). Under these circumstances it is possible that at least statistical differences may exist (D'Odorico 1984).

Contagious crying

All nurses who have tended infants in hospital nurseries are aware of another fact about crying—it is contagious. When one infant starts to cry, others begin to cry, and soon most of the infants in the nursery are crying. Are the infants responding purely to the sound they hear, or are they responding more specifically to crying? In order to test this, 2½- to 3-day-old infants were subjected to one or more of six different auditory stimuli—silence, white noise (hissing) that varied in intensity in a way similar to the cry of a newborn infant, a synthetic cry produced on a speech synthesizer, the cry of a 5½-month-old, the cry of a newborn, and the infant's own previously recorded cry. The more the sound was like its own cry, the more likely was the infant to cry in response. Contagious crying was greater among female than male infants (Simner 1971).

Although one can argue that infants three-days-old have already learned to associate crying with discomfort, a later study on even younger infants (average age 34 hours) replicated the earlier results (Sagi & Hoffman 1976). Furthermore, I observed the same phenomenon in my own son less than an hour after birth, so I doubt any learning explanation. Rather it appears that there is an instinctual response of discomfort to the sound of an infant crying, which causes infants hearing crying to begin to cry themselves. If an instinctual response of discomfort to the sound of an infant cry survives to adulthood, one can see how it would have survival value for the species (Murray 1979).

Caregiver response to infant cries

Mothers in a maternity hospital claim that they are awakened in response to their own infants' cries, but not in response to the cries of other infants (Illingworth

1955). A systematic study appears to support these claims. By their infants' third day, awake mothers could pick out the cries of their own infants over those of four other infants 100% of the time. And when asleep they awoke to the cries of their own infants 95% of the time (Formby 1967). Parents of first-born children are more highly aroused by their infants' cries than are nonparents. However, by the time they are parents a second or third time, they are *less* aroused by the cry of their infants than are nonparents (Boukydis & Burgess 1982).

How should the caregiver respond when an infant cries? There is controversy both among parents and among researchers. Some researchers have found that infants of parents who responded more consistently and promptly to their cries in the first quarter of the first year cried less in the remainder of the year (Ainsworth & Bell 1977; S. Bell & Ainsworth 1972). Others feel that responding to an infant's cry is positive reinforcement of crying, and that parents would do better to refrain from reinforcing such behavior (Gewirtz & Boyd 1977).

(© 1977 by Lynn Johnston. Reprinted by permission of Meadowbrook Press and Simon & Schuster, Inc.)

The average American infant cries 117 minutes per day in the first eight days of life (Aldrich et al. 1945). In the first seven weeks the average is 135 minutes per day. The amount of crying per day declines slowly thereafter. Infants cry more often in the evening (Brazelton 1962). Mothers respond to their infants cries typically in three to four minutes after the onset of the crying, but some response can take as long as 30 minutes (S. Bell & Ainsworth 1972; Bernal 1972) and about one in six cries is ignored completely (Moss & Robson 1968). There is a correlation between excessive crying and child abuse. Which is the cause and which is the effect is a matter of debate (R. Bell 1968, 1971; Bennett 1971; Lamb 1977; Steele & Pollock 1968).

There are wide variations between cultures as to the amounts of crying and the speed of response to it (Mead & Newton 1967). Japanese mothers respond faster and their infants cry less (Caudill & Weinstein 1969). Infants in primitive hunter-gatherer cultures hardly ever cry. Their mothers respond within six seconds. In these cultures it is common for the mother to carry the baby in a sling all day. With this close contact she is often able to respond to her infants' fretting behavior prior to crying, and thus avoid cries altogether (Devore & Konner 1974).

Such rapid response is often not practical in our society. What should we do? Dr. Spock's advice to parents on this matter has rung true in my personal experi-ence: One need not worry about spoiling the infant by responding to its cries in the first month or two, but after 3 months the parent should become ''a little more suspicious'' and ''a little less tenderhearted'' (Spock 1957: 183; but see Thoman et al. 1977).

PERCEPTION OF SOUND

Properties of sound

Speech involves the medium of sound. Sound originates with an object that is vibrating—such as a loudspeaker, a tuning fork, or the human vocal cords. The vibrations cause the air molecules near the vibrating object alternatively to be closer together and farther apart. These condensations and rarefactions cause neighboring air molecules to do likewise. The local vibratory changes in air pressure spread out from the source at the rate of 331 meters per second at 0° C and normal sea level atmospheric pressure.

Sound varies on two dimensions (see Figure 1.2). One is the **intensity** of the variations in air pressure. The other is the **frequency** of these vibrations. Frequency is measured in **Hertz** (Hz), which is the number of cycles per second. If the air pressure associated with a particular tone reaches its maximum 60 times each second, it is said to be a 60 Hz tone.

FIGURE 1.2 Sound varies on two dimensions.

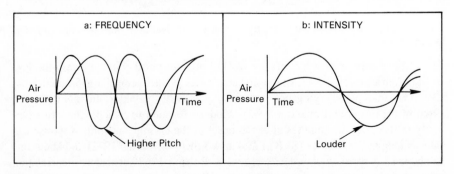

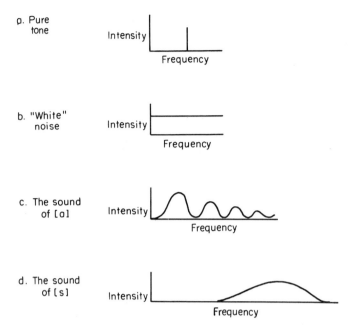

FIGURE 1.3   Spectrum: intensity by frequency.

Sounds are usually made up of more than one frequency at the same time. A pure tone is a sound which vibrates at only one frequency. The sound produced by a tuning fork is close to a pure tone. If sound is represented on a graph of intensity by frequency, the graph of a pure tone would be as shown in Figure 1.3a. Such a graph is called a **spectrum.** In a pure tone all of the intensity of the sound is concentrated at one frequency. At the other extreme is **white noise,** which is similar to the sound one hears when listening to a television set tuned to a channel on which no station is broadcasting. The spectrum of this sound is shown in Figure 1.3b. The intensity of the sound is equal at all frequencies. Different sounds have different spectra. The sound of the first vowel in *father* has a spectrum that looks something like Figure 1.3c. The spectrum for the sound of the initial consonant in *sob* looks something like that shown in Figure 1.3d.

The infant's perception of sound

As has already been mentioned, there is evidence that fetuses can hear sound, although some researchers believe that the fetus can only hear very loud sounds until some time after it is born, when the somewhat gelatinous liquid in the fetal middle ear drains out (Preyer 1888: 72-96). A great many techniques have been used to determine the sensitivity of newborns to sound. The earliest studies, dating back to the 1800's, used quivering of the eyelids, wrinkling of the forehead, head movements, screaming, and awakening from sleep as indications that the newborn heard the sound presented (K. Pratt 1946: 209). The first carefully controlled study, for example, used instrumentally recorded measures of body movements and breathing patterns in response to 10-second pure tones (Stubbs 1934).

The next question beyond the basic fact of hearing in the newborn is to find out how well developed the auditory sense is. Upon emergence from the womb is everything "one great blooming buzzing confusion," as suggested by William James (1890, I:488)? Apparently not. In fact, the neonate responds differently to sounds which are varied in a number of different ways.

Rate   The sound of a mother's heartbeat at 78 beats per minute is particularly soothing to newborns. On the other hand, the sound of a heartbeat galloping at 128 beats per minute is noticeably upsetting to them (Salk 1962).

Frequency   At least some newborns can discriminate frequencies. In one study 15 out of 50 newborns tested showed discrimination between two frequencies (400 Hz and 1000 Hz) (Bridger 1961). How can one tell that an infant can hear the difference between two tones? This study made use of the **orienting reflex.** This is a normal response by an infant to a novel stimulus. One of the properties of this reflex is a momentary deceleration of the rate of heartbeat, which can be measured. One presents a particular sound to an infant until its initial orienting reflex has died out, and then changes the sound. If there is an accompanying change of the infant's heart rate, one can say that the infant was able to perceive the difference between the two stimuli.

Although in this study the technique was successful with some of the newborns, many researchers find that this method leads to inconclusive results when applied to infants younger than two to four months (F. Graham & Jackson 1970; Morse 1974: 22). Nevertheless, the results of this study have been confirmed in studies using other measures. Following presentation of a novel stimulus, and after the initial heart rate deceleration, there is a heart rate acceleration. By monitoring this it was found that three- to five-day-old infants respond to a shift from a 500 Hz tone to a 2000 Hz tone (Stratton 1970). Another study obtained confirmation using measures of movement, respiration, and heart rate decrement, plus subjective observation by observers who were themselves unaware of when the sound was on (Bench 1969).

Intensity   Neonates can apparently also discriminate differences in intensity of sound. When presented with a white noise at varying intensities, neonates reacted differently to the different magnitudes, as measured by the magnitude of their startle responses and heart rate changes (Bench 1969; Steinschneider 1968; Steinschneider et al. 1966). Similar differential responses have been found to clicks (Barnet & Goodwin 1965) and to pure tones (Bartoshuk 1964).

Duration   Neonates differentially react to differences in duration of a signal. In the only study of this variable, the observer recorded the number of eye, head, limb, and whole body movements of neonates that occurred in a one-second period following the onset of stimuli lasting 0.05, 0.25, 0.5, and 1.0 second. Observer accuracy was checked by including periods in which the observer thought the neonate was hearing the sound, but in fact was not. The amount of reaction of the neonates to the stimuli increased greatly from the first day of life to the fifth day (Ling 1972). This study does not demonstrate that the infant can detect these differences, only that it reacts more to signals of longer duration. Since the observation period overlapped the stimulus presentation period, it could be that the infant reacts for as long as the stimulus is on and stops when the signal goes off.

Location Another ability that has been investigated in newborns is the ability to locate the direction from which a sound is coming. There is one report that a newborn only 10 minutes old would orient its eyes in the direction of a sound made by clicking a toy 'cricket' (Wertheimer 1961). However, a number of others have tried to replicate this finding and have failed. In one study the 'cricket' was used with 20 neonates with no correlation found (McGurk et al. 1977).

In another, very ingenious study, infants were placed in a soundproof room with a window, through which they could see their mother talking. In one condition the sound of the mother's voice came from a speaker located at the window; in the other condition the speaker was located to the right or left of the child. When the voice of the mother did not come from the same direction as her face, the children exhibited considerable distress (Aronson & Rosenbloom 1971). The infants in this study were 30 to 55 days old. However, again, other researchers have failed to replicate this result. Depending upon which study you read, infants first orient their eyes toward sound at between two and six months (2 months: Carpenter 1973; 3-5 months: Lyons-Ruth 1975; 4 months: Spelke 1976; 6 months: Chun et al. 1960).

One would think from these studies that a newborn infant cannot localize sound for the first few months, but a recent study indicates otherwise. Instead of watching for eye movements, in this new study they watched head-turning movements. Twelve infants whose ages ranged from two to seven days old were tested. The sound of a rattle was played through one of two speakers placed on either side of the infant's head. The infants turned their heads in the direction of the sound 74% of the time. This study selected for babies most likely not to have been born premature or drugged or injured during the birth process, and the investigators pointed out that the same results may not have been obtained by a less selected population. Nevertheless, it appears that infants can, in fact, localize sound, at least to the extent of determining whether it comes from 90 degrees to the right or 90 degrees to the left (Muir & Field 1979).

Thus neonates appear to be able to distinguish sounds that vary in intensity, frequency, rate, direction of source, and perhaps duration. Although this basic information is important as a foundation for what follows, from the point of view of language acquisition, it is more interesting to find out what abilities infants have at discriminating human speech.

PERCEPTION OF SPEECH

Speech sounds

The sound of speech is distinctively different from other sounds. The vowels are characterized by three or four peaks of intensity on the frequency spectrum, as shown in Figure 1.3c. These peaks are known as **formants.** The peak at the lowest frequency is called the first formant; the next higher frequency peak is the second formant; and so on. Different vowels have their first and second formants at different frequencies. Consonants either interrupt this pattern with silence or other sounds, or cause the formants of neighboring vowels to start or stop at different frequencies, or both.

An important characteristic of speech is that the sound is constantly changing with time. In order to represent this information graphically, phoneticians have developed **sound spectrographs,** machines which produce graphs of speech showing frequency, intensity, and time. Frequency is represented on the vertical axis, and time on the horizontal axis. Intensity is indicated by the degree of darkness of the point at each frequency and time. Figure 1.4 shows such a graph, which is called a **sound spectrogram.** The cry of young infants is distinctive from the speech of adults in that it may contain as many as eight formants, as opposed to four for adults (see Figure 1.1).

Given that human speech is acoustically quite distinctive, one can ask whether there are any built-in mechanisms for perceiving human speech. Although the evidence is still weak, there appear to be three types of evidence favoring such mechanisms:

1. The human voice begins to become more effective at quieting a crying baby than certain other sounds tested—bells, whistles, rattles—when the infant reaches approximately two weeks of age (Wolff 1969: 97).
2. Recently frame-by-frame analyses of motion pictures of neonates as young as one day old have been made. Such analyses appear to indicate that the seemingly random body movements made by neonates change direction in rhythm to the sound of the human voice to a significantly greater extent than they do to the sound of disconnected vowels or to tapping sounds (Condon & Sander 1974).
3. In most adults language is processed in the left half of the brain, while nonspeech sounds such as music are processed more in the right half. The cortical activity of infants as young as one week of age has been measured. There is greater activity on the left side in response to speech, and greater activity on the right side in response to the sound of a piano chord (Molfese et al. 1975).

Such early differential response to the human voice suggests that there may be an inborn ability to discriminate the sound patterns specific to the human species, just as birds appear to have built-in patterns to identify the calls of their own species (Marler & Hamilton 1966).

The next question that must be addressed is to what extent the perception of speech sounds is built in at birth. However, in order to address this issue easily it is best to introduce the notation used by linguists to describe the sounds of speech.

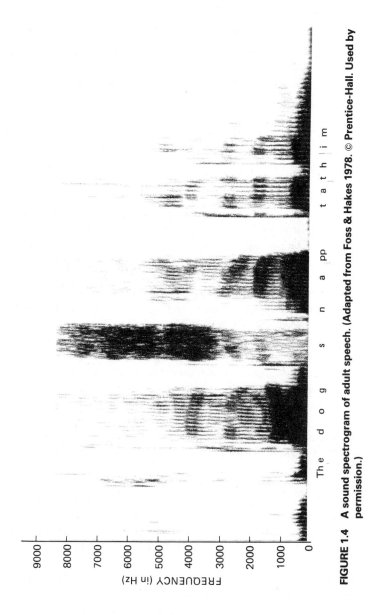

FREQUENCY (in Hz)

The d o g s n a pp a t a t h l i m

FIGURE 1.4 A sound spectrogram of adult speech. (Adapted from Foss & Hakes 1978. © Prentice-Hall. Used by permission.)

Phonetic notation

In order to refer to speech sounds with a minimum amount of confusion, phoneticians have developed a set of alphabetic symbols which represent most of the sounds of human speech. With only a couple of exceptions ([č] is used instead of [tʃ]; and [ǰ] is used instead of [dʒ]) the notation used in this book is that approved by the International Phonetic Association. The phonetic symbols which are used for describing the sounds made by speakers of Midwestern North American English are shown in Figure 1.5. Phonetic notation is indicated in text by surrounding it with square brackets.

With very few exceptions, each sound has a unique articulation—that is, there is only one way to arrange the vocal articulators in order to produce it (One exception is that there are two ways to place the tongue to produce [ɹ]). Thus speech sounds are generally categorized by the way they are articulated. The speech sounds of a language are usually organized in charts based on a few basic dimensions. When this is done, sounds that are similar to one another are placed near one another. In English the sounds are best described in terms of three dimensions: place of articulation, manner of articulation, and voicing.

Place of articulation refers to the point in the mouth at which there is the greatest constriction when that sound is being produced. For example, the greatest constriction for [b] is at the lips, for [d] it is at the ridge behind the upper front teeth, and for [g] it is at the back of the mouth. In Figure 1.5 the sounds are placed in columns lined up with the place in the mouth at which the greatest constriction occurs. Some sounds have two places of constriction, a primary and a secondary constriction. In this case the sounds are located in two columns, with the secondary constriction given in parentheses. Note that vowels that are called **front vowels** actually have their greatest constriction quite far back in the mouth; no farther forward than the constriction in the consonants in the word *king* [cɪŋ], while many **back vowels** in English also have lip rounding, which is a secondary constriction in the front of the mouth.

Many sounds have the same place of articulation as the [d] sound, but they differ in the **manner of articulation.** In a [d] the airstream is stopped completely, whereas in a [z] the constriction remains open, but narrow enough to cause a friction sound as the air passes through. In an [n], the air is stopped in the mouth, in the same place as in a [d], but it is allowed to escape through the nose by lowering the velum, a flap in the back of the mouth that can close the passage between the nose and mouth. In all, seven manners of articulation are used in producing Midwestern North American English consonants. The manner of articulation for the vowels varies from a relatively narrow constriction, called **high,** to a relatively open constriction, called **low.**

The third dimension, **voicing,** applies in English only to the stops, affricates, and fricatives. This dimension refers to whether or not the vocal cords are vibrating when the sound is being made.

Looked at from either an accoustic or an articulatory point of view, speech sounds can vary continuously along several dimensions. This continuity is not

PLACE OF ARTICULATION

EXAMPLES OF EACH OF THE ENGLISH SOUNDS

CONSONANTS

b	bib	n̩	barn
c	king	ɲ	king
č	chip	ŋ	Kong
d	did	p	pip
ḍ	drip	ɹ	rear
ð	Thy	s	sis
f	fife	ʃ	ship
g	goose	t	teat
h	hip	ṭ	trip
ɦ	ahead	ɾ	water
j	yes	θ	thigh
ǰ	gyp	v	vie
k	Kong	w	witch
l	lip	hw	which
ɫ	pill	ɸ	whew
m	mom	x	Bach
m̩	comfort	z	zip
n	non	ʒ	vision
		ʔ	uhuh

VOWELS

ɑ	bottle
æ	bat
aɪ	bite
aʊ	bout
eɪ	bait
ɛ	bet
ə	about
i	beet
ɪ	bit
oʊ	boat
ɔ	bought
ɔɪ	boy
ʊ	put
u	boot
ju	beauty
ʌ	but
ɨ	dishes
:	(lengthen preceding sound)

MANNER OF ARTICULATION

	VOICE	Bilabial	Labiodental	Dental	Alveolar	Retroflex	Palatoalveolar	Palatal	Velar	Glottal
Stops	vd	b			d	ḍ		ɟ	g	
	vl	p			t	ṭ		c	k	ʔ
Flap					ɾ					
Affricates	vd						ǰ			
	vl						č			
Fricatives	vd		v	ð	z		ʒ		ɣ	ɦ
	vl	ɸ	f	θ	s		ʃ		x	h
Nasals	vd	m	ɱ		n	ṇ		ɲ	ŋ	
Laterals	vd				l					
	vl				ɫ					
Semivowels		w			ɹ			j	(w)	

VOWELS	Bilabial	Front	Central	Back
High	(u)	i	ɨ	u
Mid	(o)	e ə	ɘ	o
Low	(ɔ)	ɛ æ	ʌ	ɔ ɑ

(Secondary points of constriction given in parens)

FIGURE 1.5 Chart of the most common English sounds.

19

obvious to native speakers. Rather, two speech sounds either appear to be identical or distinctively different. In other words, for any given language each speech sound is perceived by native speakers to belong to one of a small set of sound classes, known as **phonemes.** Depending upon the language, the number of phonemes ranges from about 10 to 70; English has about 40. Phonemes are indicated in text by surrounding them with slashes. Thus we can differentiate phonemes from particular pronunciations of them. For example, we can say that in Midwestern North America, the phoneme /r/ is pronounced [ɹ].

A particular phoneme may be pronounced differently depending upon where it is placed in a word and what sounds precede and follow it. In English the phoneme /k/ is pronounced in the same place in the mouth as the vowel that follows it, or, if it is word final, that precedes it. Thus depending upon the vowel, /k/ may be pronounced [c] or [k] or anywhere in between. Therefore in English [c] and [k] are two instances of the same phoneme. If a speaker used the [c] where a [k] normally appears, it would still sound like the same word, and a native speaker might not be able to tell the difference between the two sounds. To speakers of other languages—Arabic, for example—[c] and [k] are recognized as two separate phonemes; if used improperly, it would make the word sound like a different word, just as it does to us when a Chinese speaker appears to say *lice* instead of *rice* ([l] and [ɹ] are instances of the same phoneme in Chinese).

Because of these differences in phoneme categories in different languages, we know that at least some of the categorization of sounds is learned. However, some is also clearly built in.

Distinguishing speech sounds

Using several different methods, researchers can determine very precisely which speech sounds a young infant can discriminate. One such method is known as the **Non-Nutritive Sucking (NNS)** method (Siqueland & De Lucia 1969). A pacifier-type nipple is connected by a closed air line to an electrical pressure-measuring device. This device is used to control a stimulus—for example, it might turn on a tape recorder for a short period of time. If the stimulus is reinforcing—that is, if the infant likes to hear the sound—it will quickly learn to suck at a high rate, which keeps the stimulus continuously available. After a while the infant's sucking rate will go down. When it drops by a set amount—for example, by one third—the experimenter will switch from the sounds on one track of a tape to the sounds on a second track. If the infant detects a difference, the rate increases again; if the infant does not detect a difference, the rate will not increase. This method appears to be reliable as early as one month after birth, and is good to about four months. The problem with testing younger infants is that they tend to fall asleep when a pacifier is put in their mouths; the problem with older infants is that they lose interest in sucking. This technique and others have been used extensively to determine the extent of the infant's ability to distinguish different speech sounds.

Infants as young as one month have been found to be able to discriminate the following consonant pairs: [ma] from [pa], [pa] from [ba], [ba] from [ga], [ga]

Laboratory set up for non-nutritive sucking experiment.

D. Bond

from [dɑ], [dɑ] from [tɑ], [ɹɑ] from [lɑ], [sɑ] from [vɑ], [sɑ] from [ʃɑ], [ɑs] from [ɑːz], [ɑt] from [ɑːd], and [ɑːt] from [ɑːd] (Eilers & Minifie 1975; Eimas 1975a; Eimas et al. 1971; Morse 1972; Trehub & Rabinovitch 1972). Infants can also discriminate steady versus rising intonation (Morse 1972), stress on the first versus the second syllable, as in ['bɑbɑ] versus [bɑ'bɑ] (Spring & Dale 1977), and various vowel contrasts: [ɑ] from [i], [i] from [u], [pɑ] from [pi], [tɑ] from [ti], [pɑ] from [pu] (see Figure 1.6; Trehub 1973). Notice that the pairs of consonants tested in no way exhaust the number of pairs which could be tested. There are for English over 500 consonant pairs that could be tested in initial position. The consonants chosen for examination tend to differ from one another by only one dimension—either manner, place, or voicing (see Figure 1.5). Researchers seem to have assumed that if infants can differentiate consonants that differ on one dimension, then they can certainly differentiate consonant pairs that differ on more than one dimension, such as [kɑ] and [čɑ]. Studies of perceptual confusions in adults suggest that this is not a very safe assumption (G. Miller & Nicely 1955). It is also not clear that the ability to distinguish two consonants which are followed by one vowel implies that the same two consonants can be distinguished when followed by another vowel. Nor has it been shown that the ability to distinguish two consonants in initial position implies that they can be distinguished in final position or in medial position between two vowels. Similar remarks can be made about vowel contrasts. Nevertheless, it appears that infants can distinguish many phoneme contrasts.

With further testing the limitations of infants' discrimination abilities begin to appear. They apparently cannot discriminate [sɑ] from [zɑ], [fɑ] from [θɑ], [ɑːs] from [ɑːz], or [ɑt] from [ɑːt] (Eilers & Minifie 1975). And while infants can

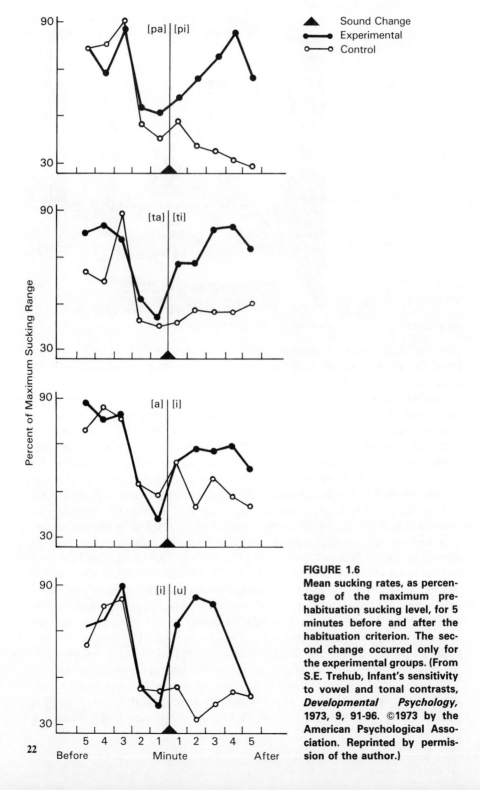

FIGURE 1.6
Mean sucking rates, as percentage of the maximum prehabituation sucking level, for 5 minutes before and after the habituation criterion. The second change occurred only for the experimental groups. (From S.E. Trehub, Infant's sensitivity to vowel and tonal contrasts, *Developmental Psychology*, 1973, 9, 91-96. ©1973 by the American Psychological Association. Reprinted by permission of the author.)

22

distinguish [ɑbɑ] from [ɑpɑ], they cannot distinguish [mɑpɑ] from [pɑmɑ] or [atɑpɑ] from [atɑbɑ] (Trehub 1973).

Since the NNS technique doesn't work with infants younger than one month, there is still the possibility that infants learn the phonemic distinctions in their first month of life. In order to eliminate this possibility, infants can be tested on contrasts that are not phonemically distinct in the language of their caregivers. This has been tested on two such contrasts. Infants apparently can discriminate between nasalized and nonnasalized vowels [pɑ̃] from [pɑ] (A nasalized vowel is one pronounced while the passage between the mouth and nose is open, and is indicated by the superscript tilde [˜]. In English the vowel in *man* is nasalized, while the vowel in *bad* is not.). Although this contrast is not phonemic in English, native English speakers can distinguish nasalized and nonnasalized vowels.

A more interesting case is the contrast between the two Czech phonemes [ʐ] and [r̝] Symbolized as ž and ř in Czech orthography, the former is similar to [ʒ] and the latter is a voiced retroflex trill. Although native speakers of Czech have no trouble discriminating these two sounds, they sound the same to English speakers. Nevertheless, infants from homes where Czech is not spoken can discriminate the two sounds (Trehub 1976). Another example of the same phenomenon is the already-mentioned fact that infants can discriminate between [ɹɑ] and [lɑ], while adult Japanese, whose language does not make this distinction, cannot (Eimas 1975b). It appears that part of learning a language involves losing the ability to make distinctions between sounds not important in one's own language, as well as gaining the ability to make some distinctions not present at birth. Although the number of contrasts tested is still relatively small, it appears that infants can distinguish at birth most of the contrasts that they will need for their language.

Some interesting findings have come from the use of a special device known as a **parallel resonance synthesizer.** This device does just the opposite of what a sound spectrograph does. It can take a sound spectrogram which has been hand painted and convert it into sound. Using this technique one can produce sets of human-like speech sounds that differ from one another by precisely specified amounts on any dimension. One such dimension is the starting frequency of the second formant. Changes in this aspect of the speech signal correspond to changes in the place of articulation for most consonants (A. Liberman et al. 1967).

Consider, for example, the distinction between [bæ] and [dæ]. In a naturally produced [bæ], the second formant rises to its steady-state value for [æ] (about 1700 Hz). In a naturally produced [dæ], it starts higher and falls to that value, as shown in Figure 1.7. The difference in the two starting values can be under 250 Hz. Infants

FIGURE 1.7
Sound spectrograms for [bæ] and [dɑ].

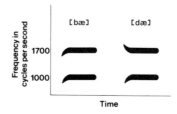

can detect this difference in naturally produced and artifically produced speech. If, however, the starting frequency for two artificial syllables is lowered so that the difference is the same (under 250 Hz), but in both cases there is now a rise to the steady-state value for [æ], infants can no longer detect the difference. Thus they behave categorically. Equal differences along an acoustic dimension—in this case, starting frequency—do not have equal distinctiveness in infant or adult perception (Eimas 1974). It is not just a case of detecting a rising versus a falling value for the second formant. When only the second formant is played, infants could discriminate both the original difference and the lowered version. When only the second formant is played, the sound does not sound like speech, but rather like bird chirps. Whatever is built in seems especially tuned to speech. Essentially the same experiment was run with the same results on the [ɹ] versus [l] distinction, which involves the direction of movement of the third formant (Eimas 1975b).

Probably the most studied dimension in speech perception is that of **Voice Onset Time (VOT)**. This is a measure of the difference between the time the oral articulator is opened and the time the vocal cords start vibrating. In initial position in English, this is the way voiced stops differ from their voiceless counterparts. In other words, this is the difference beween [b] and [p], [d] and [t], and [g] and [k]. In the case of the voiced consonants, voicing begins about 10 milliseconds (10 msec = 1/100 sec) after release of the lips (in the case of [b]) or tongue (in the cases of [d] and [g]). When voiceless consonants are being produced, voicing begins at about 100 msec after the release of the articulator. On sound spectrograms this shows up as a delay in the onset of the first formant relative to the other formants (see Figure 1.8). A negative VOT means that voicing begins before the release of the oral articulator. On sound spectrograms this appears as an onset of the first formant preceding onset of the other formants.

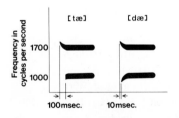

Figure 1.8
Voiced versus voiceless consonants.

In adult speakers of English the perceptual boundary between voiced and voiceless stops seems to be at about + 35 msec, the exact value depending upon which consonant pair is being studied (Lisker & Abramson 1970). When VOT is varied systematically by means of synthetically produced speech, one finds that young infants can discriminate the two sounds if the VOTs are on opposite sides of the + 35 msec boundary, but not if the two sounds have VOTs on the same side of the boundary, even if the two sounds are the same amount of VOT apart. Again it appears that the ability to perceive specific contrasts which are important to language is built in at birth (Eimas et al. 1971).

Although as far as we know this ability is useful only to humans, we are not the only animals with the 35 msec VOT discrimination boundary built in. It has also been found in chinchillas (see Figure 1.9; Kuhl & Miller 1975) and rhesus monkeys (Morse & Snowden 1975; Waters & Wilson 1976). Furthermore, categorical perception of music-like stimuli, presumably not necessary to language acquisition, has also been found in 2-month-old infants (Jusczyk et al. 1977).

FIGURE 1.9
Mean percentage of /d/ responses by chinchilla and human subjects to synthetic speech sounds constructed to approximate [tɑ] and [dɑ]. (From Kuhl & Miller 1975. © 1975 by the AAAS.)

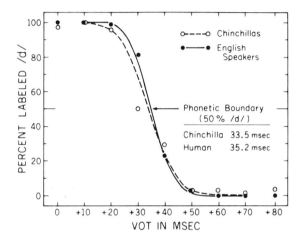

Scientists Kuhl and Miller discover that chinchillas can distinguish /t/ and /d/.

Some languages make a voiced-voiceless distinction at other places along the VOT continuum. The Thai language even makes a three-way distinction. Not only is there a perceived difference of consonants on either side of the +35 msec boundary, but there is another boundary in the range of −50 msec to −20 msec. (Eimas 1974, 1975a; Lisker & Abramson 1970).

Because of the Thai distinction, researchers have looked to see if this other VOT boundary is also identifiable by infants. The results are not as clear-cut as for the English boundary. There may be a boundary, but it is not as sharp as the +35 msec boundary.

Two studies taken together appear to suggest a specific age at which discrimination begins to tune to the native language. One study of children 0;4 to 0;6 of Spanish-speaking parents found that they failed to discriminate around the VOT that was the most relevant to their parents, suggesting that there was no learning going on in the first 6 months (Lasky et al. 1975). The other study was of children of Spanish-speaking parents who were 0;7. These children could make the distinction at the Spanish VOT better than a similar group of children of English-speaking parents, suggesting that discrimination begins to develop in the seventh month (Eilers et al. 1979a). However, the differences in results could also be due to differences in the method of testing, or in the sample populations used, or a number of other factors.

Another way to determine when learning of a language-appropriate contrast begins is to test infants from two separate language groups in one experiment. If a group is significantly better at discriminating a contrast in the language they are experiencing than the group which is not hearing that language, then one can surmise that learning has taken place. An experiment of this type tested to see whether Spanish-learning infants could distinguish the difference between the tapped and trilled **r.** This contrast is important to Spanish, but not to English. The stimuli used were the tap [ɑrá] versus the trilled [ɑrɑ́], in which the trill consisted of a double tap (as opposed to three or four taps). The second syllable was the one receiving primary stress. Spanish-learning infants were better than English-learning infants at the age tested, which was 0;6 to 0;8 (Eilers et al. 1982; see also D. Oller & Eilers 1983). This tells us that the process of learning has begun by this time, but a single experiment run on two or more different age groups would help to determine when the process begins.

Adults are supposed to lose the ability to make certain contrasts not used in their own languages. However, this loss has only recently been tested in an experiment which directly compared the performances of infants and adults using the same experimental procedure. Obviously, the nonnutritive sucking technique is not appropriate to adults. The technique that was used is known as the **Visually Reinforced Infant Speech Discrimination (VRISD) paradigm.** In this paradigm an infant is taught that whenever a change occurs in a sequence of auditory stimuli, a stuffed moving toy will appear in a box to the left. The experimenter plays the first stimulus repeatedly to the child until the child is alert and attending to some toys in front of it, and then switches to the contrasting stimulus. If the child notices the difference, it will look to the left, in expectation that the toy will appear. This paradigm can be used with only minor modifications with adults.

Differences in VOT on the [p-b] continuum were tested on English-learning 6-month olds and English-speaking adults. The adults were actually *better* at discriminating the VOT differences than were the infants, even those differences that were not relevant to English (Eilers et al. 1979b).

Finally, speech discrimination appears not to be only auditory. There appears to be a visual component. Infants 0;2,7 to 0;3,25 (10 to 16 weeks old) were presented with nursery rhymes under two conditions. In one condition the speech sounds were in synchrony with the lip movements, and in the other condition the speech sounds were not synchronous—they lagged behind the lip movements by 0.4 sec. Infants observing synchronous speech were attentive 85% of the time, but infants observing asynchronous speech only attended 66% of the time (Dodd 1979).

An interesting visual effect has been found in much older children. When children 3;0 to 5;0 were shown a person saying *ga* but heard that person saying *ba,* they reported that they thought the person said *da* 81% of the time (McGurk & McDonald 1976).

It appears as if infants are pretuned to many but not all of those contrasts which are important to natural language. To put it another way, human language has developed such that many of its contrasts are those that are easily perceived right from infancy. Development of speech perception seems to involve both learning to attend to new contrasts and learning to ignore other contrasts. In addition, perception of speech seems to be qualitatively different from perception of other types of sounds. The perception of speech seems to be categorical rather than continuous. That is, around certain points in objectively established continua infants are very good at making a distinction, while around other points they are either less good, or slower, or totally unable to make a distinction.

HAPPY SOUNDS

Λαλεῖν ἄριστος, ἀδυνατώτατος λέγειν. (In chatter excellent, but quite unable to speak.)—Eupolis, *Fragments,* No. 95.

The sophisticated ability to differentiate human speech sounds comes at a time when children are very limited as to what sounds they can produce. In this section we shall consider the next stage in the development of language production—happy sounds. Happy sounds first appear when the infant is between 0;1 and 0;2. At first the happy sounds are generally referred to as **cooing.** Cooing can be described as the production of clear vowels, often in relative isolation.

Early cooing is not affected by the environment. The cooing of deaf children is the same as that of children with normal hearing (Lenneberg et al. 1965). Many observers consider this cooing to be distinctively different from previous vocalization. One reason is that studies of the sounds of crying have found that for the most part crying and cooing make use of different sounds. The vast majority (78%) of crying consists of the vowel [æ] (Irwin & Curry 1941; Ringel & Kluppel 1964), whereas in early cooing, [ɪ], [ɛ], and [ʌ] account for over 90% of the vowels (Irwin 1948a, 1957: 411, 415).

Others suggest that cooing sounds may evolve from earlier cries, discomfort sounds, and vegetative sounds (Stark 1978; Stark et al. 1975). According to one such observer, cooing arises out of 'fake crying', which consists of long drawn-out moans of low pitch and intensity, and which develops in about the third week (Wolff 1969).

When the child is between 0;2 and 0;6, the nature of cooing gradually changes. Consonant-vowel patterns, such as [ʔɛ] or [gʌ], begin to appear. The variety of sounds infants can produce in early cooing is thought to be limited by the physical configuration of their mouths (see Figure 1.10) and the lack of voluntary control over the vocal articulators, especially the front of the tongue and lips (Lecours 1975; Stark 1979). It is also during this period that cooing begins to be affected by the environment. At 0;3, when an infant's belly is rubbed just after it makes a cooing sound, it is likely to coo again (Haugen & McIntire 1972). At this age children raised in families vocalize more than children raised in institutions (Brodbeck & Irwin 1946). The cooing of deaf children tends to diminish, although if mirrors are hung over their cribs, their vocalization will tend to be prolonged and even increased (Van Riper 1950: 18).

By the time the infant is 0;6, and lasting to approximately 1;0, the happy sounds begin to get yet more complex. Reduplication of syllables occurs, such as [pɑpɑ], [kɛkɛ], and [gigi]. When this begins to happen, the child is generally said to be in the **babbling** stage. During this stage greater numbers of clearly articulated vowels and consonants are formed, and occasionally more complex syllables—for example, of the form CVC (**C**onsonant **V**owel **C**onsonant), CCV, CCVC—appear. It is also during this time that intonation patterns similar to those of adult speech

FIGURE 1.10   Crossection of the head of a newborn infant and adult in midline. In the newborn, the tongue is relatively large, filling the mouth and resting on the lower lip. Only at the back is there room for adjustment when the mouth is closed. In the adult the tongue can assume a much larger variety of configurations when the mouth is closed.

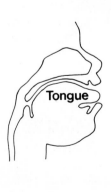
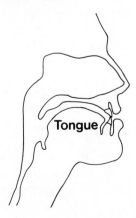

BOX 1.2 *ADULT BABBLING?*

Kupoy shandrey feelay soondrookooma shandrey lasa hoya takee
(from Samarin 1972: 77).

The above quotation is not in a foreign language, but in **glossolalia.** Glossolalia, or 'speaking in tongues', is a vocal art in which an individual speaks what is believed to be a language inspired by the Holy Spirit. It is common among Pentecostals, but is practiced by people of many other denominations. It is a practice going back at least to biblical times (for example, Corinthians 12:30, 14:1-33).

Speaking in tongues can be produced spontaneously by adults, though most people who have used it have previously been exposed to it. Syllables in glossolalia tend to involve relatively few consonant clusters, and less variety of speech sounds than occurs when not speaking in tongues. The most common speech sounds of people's native speech tend to be even more common in their glossolalia. Like babbling, there are usually no systematic relationships between the sounds and syntax, morphology, or meaning (Samarin 1972).

appear, making it seem as if the infant is speaking a foreign language (Delack 1976; Kaplan & Kaplan 1971; Tonkova-Yampol'skaya 1968).

At about 0;10 or 0;11 many children babble in 'sentences,' combining several incomprehensible 'words' and uttering them with declarative, interrogative, and exclamatory inflections. This conversational jargon overlaps the period of early speech (Shirley 1933). One can usually tell when children are babbling in this way because the jargon sentences are longer than the one-word utterances that may be occurring during the same period.

Sometimes one cannot be sure. Once my daughter Athena at this stage repeated several times most insistently, "Daddy, ['digo bu'maɪ]!" The fact of repetition, and the inclusion of the word *Daddy* suggested that she had something in mind, but the use of what appeared to be three words in a sentence, combined with the fact that no one could figure out what she was trying to say, suggest that it was jargon. When children are uttering such jargon, do they think they are saying something meaningful? Nobody knows.

There is no evidence that at this stage any meaning can be attached to the different intonation patterns which the child produces. However, a consistent variation in the average pitch of the infant's babbling also appears and does seem to vary in a consistent fashion. The infant seems to attempt to match the pitch of its speech to that of its parents. When the child babbles to its father, it babbles with a lower pitch than when it babbles to its mother, which in turn is lower than when it babbles to itself. This change does not occur when the child is crying (P. Lieberman 1967).

Down through the years there have been many studies on the relative order of the first occurrence of the different sounds of speech. Although there have been some contradictory reports (e.g., Murai 1960) one large-scale series of studies indicated that young infants produce back consonants such as [h], [k], [g], and [x]

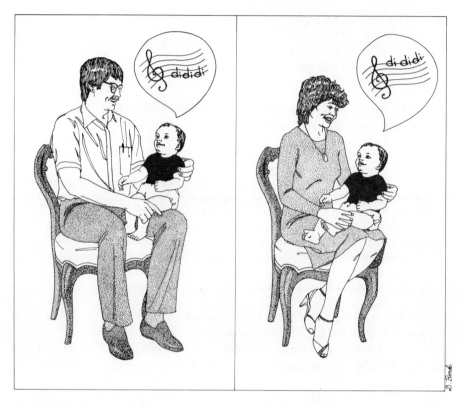

ILLUSTRATION 1.8   Child babbles differently to different parents.

before they produce mid and front consonants. For vowels, they produce front vowels earlier than back vowels. This may seem strange, but recall that front vowels such as [i] are really in the same position in the mouth as back consonants such as [c] or [ɟ]. In these studies [c] was not distinguished from [k] or [g] from [ɟ], thus it is likely that often the consonant and vowel in a syllable would be in the same position in the mouth, although the vowel would be termed front and the consonant back (Irwin 1947a).

Although the study of the sound pattern of babbling goes back several decades, one of the most extensive studies is relatively recent (D. Oller et al. 1976). This study analyzed the babbling of five children aged 0;6 through 0;9 and another five children aged 1;0 through 1;2. In both groups very few consonant clusters occurred; over 90% of the consonants appeared alone. In the younger group there were far more medial consonants than initial; in the older group they appeared in about equal numbers. In both groups there were considerably fewer final consonants than initial consonants. Initial stops were almost never aspirated—that is, they never had high VOTs. Final consonants were almost always voiceless. Initial stops were overwhelmingly preferred to initial fricatives or affricates (Irwin 1947b). On the other hand, final fricatives were preferred to final stops. Medial consonants [t, d, θ, ð, č, ǰ, n, s, z] were preferred over back consonants [ŋ, g, k, x, ʃ, ʒ] by both groups, but far more by the older group, suggesting that a study on much younger infants might have confirmed earlier claims that the first consonants tend to be back consonants (Irwin 1947a). There are serious problems of listener agreement in babbling, which suggests that at this stage findings should be taken with a grain of salt (see Stockman et al. 1981).

The interesting thing about almost all of these findings is that the same relationships and preferences found in babbling are also found in early meaningful speech, as will be discussed in the next chapter. Thus although many observers have emphasized that there is a significant discontinuity between babbling and early meaningful speech, careful consideration of sound preference data suggests that the discontinuity is less than was previously suspected.

A number of situational factors have been found to correlate with the rate of development of babbling. Children of business and clerical parents are somewhat more advanced in terms of the number of distinct phonemes uttered in babbling at various ages than children of 'blue collar' workers (Irwin 1957: 421) or institutionalized retarded children (Irwin 1942). On the other hand, no differences have been found between U.S. Negroes and Caucasians, between males and females, or between first-borns and later-borns (Chen 1942; Irwin 1948b, 1952).

The babbling of infants from different linguistic groups usually cannot be distinguished by students who are untrained in phonetics (K. Atkinson et al. 1970; Olney & Scholnick 1976). However, at 1;0 very slight differences have been noted in the frequencies of the vowels babbled by two groups of eight infants, one from Spanish-speaking homes and the other from English-speaking homes. The differences were in the direction predicted by vowel frequencies in the mother tongues (D. Oller & Eilers 1982). Also, if languages are different enough, identification does seem possible. One study comparing the babbling of French, Arabic, and Chinese infants found differences in intonation contours and whether the infants vocalized on both expiration and inspiration. These differences were distinctive enough for naive native speakers to guess the language of the infants' parents correctly more often than they would by chance (de Boysson-Bardies et al. 1984).

Nevertheless, it appears to be generally true that babbling, like crying, cooing, and early speech perception, is relatively independent of the language of the parents. In fact, one can find sounds and sound combinations in the infant's babbling which the same individual as an adult will find very hard to produce (for example, uvular *r* [ʁ]; Jesperson 1925: 106) or just will not use, such as syllabic nasals, bilabial trills, and labial-lingual consonants (D. Oller et al. 1976). However, if languages are distinctive enough, certain slight differences can be found, showing that there appears to be, in fact, slight progress toward the time when true language begins.

There is evidence that when the infant is in the babbling stage its neural connections in the areas of the brain most closely connected to speech are not yet mature enough to permit cortical control (Whitaker 1973). This would help to explain the apparent language independence of cooing and babbling.

INFANT-ADULT COMMUNICATION

Konrad Lorenz once suggested that if the very young of any species were unable to survive on their own at birth, they had better have some way of making sure that the caregiving needed for their survival was forthcoming (Lorenz 1952). In spite of the severe limitation on what a young infant can say and do, there is an enormous amount of communication between children and their caregivers right from the start. Most parents will tell you that their children had very different personalities right from birth, and research appears to back this up (Bennett 1971).

An incident that happened to this author will illustrate the specificity of information that can be conveyed by a very young infant. Shortly after the birth of Quentin, his mother and I interviewed people to take care of him while we were at work. One thing we did during the interviews was to hand him to the interviewees to see how they reacted to him. When we did this with one woman, herself the mother of two, I thought, "She is holding him wrong—but how do I know? I have been a parent for only a few weeks, and she has had much more experience than I." I didn't say anything. We hired her, and about a week later, she said to me, "You know, Quentin doesn't like to be held like a baby; he likes to be held upright!" When Quentin was cradled the way one is supposed to hold a baby, his limbs remained active—he didn't seem to relax. When he was held upright he was less active and would calmly look around. In general, the infant communicates by means of head and body movements and tone, by gaze, and by facial expressions, as well as by vocalization (D. Stern et al. 1975: 89).

Researchers have only recently begun to explore the connection between this early communication behavior and later language acquisition. Infants have been filmed while in the presence of speaking adults. These films have then been studied frame by frame. Those researchers are convinced that an infant's arm and leg movements, though seemingly random, are in fact coordinated with the rhythm of speech (Condon & Sander 1974). Attempts to repeat this study by others have failed to replicate the results, however.

In another study mothers of infants 0;2 and younger were instructed to 'chat' with their infants. Careful analysis of films of these interactions seems to show 'prespeech' activity in the infants, consisting of rudimentary speaking movements of the lips and tongue, characteristic changes of breathing, and distinctive hand-waving movements (Trevarthen 1974, 1979). Infants can also, at a very early age, imitate such movements. Axel Preyer was clearly able to imitate the pursing of the lips in his seventh month (Preyer 1888: 283).

There seem to be two distinct modes of infant-adult interaction. One type is **turn-taking,** in which the adult talks and the infant 'listens,' followed by periods in which the infant 'talks' and the adult 'listens' (Bateson 1975). In the second type of interaction, the caregiver and infant vocalize simultaneously. Although both occur in the behavior of all infants, simultaneous vocalization occurs about twice as much as turn-taking when the infant is 0;3 to 0;5. Simultaneous vocalization occurs most often when the infant is in a high state of arousal; turn-taking when the infant is only moderately aroused. This pattern continues through adulthood—when highly aroused, as in arguments, the parties involved are more likely to talk at the same time; a method of crowd arousal is unison chanting (D. Stern et al. 1975:96).

If you want to get an infant to babble at you, be sure to give it a turn. When Athena was about 1;0, if we babbled to her, she would babble back. However, Quentin, aged 5;2, couldn't get her to babble to him. "Why won't she babble with me?" he asked. I observed him with her, and the answer was obvious. "Because she is listening to you—you never stop talking! Talk to her, and then stop. Give her a chance to take her turn." He tried this, and the problem was solved.

One research project investigated when mothers and infants begin incidents of vocalization. While mothers vocalize more than infants, each is more likely to begin vocalizing if the other is vocalizing. Mothers stop vocalizing more often when their infants are not vocalizing than when they are (B. Anderson et al. 1977).

SUMMARY

This chapter has covered the developmental precursors of true language. Children are born with good visual acuity and depth perception. During infancy children develop significantly in their understanding of the nature of the physical universe and in their ability to move in it and to manipulate it. Infants are capable of hearing and learning even before birth. They appear to be born with sophisticated auditory discrimination abilities, which not only allow them to distinguish sounds by intensity, frequency, rate, and direction of source, but also allow them to distinguish a great many speech sounds in the relative isolation of a monosyllable.

The first communication from the infant to the adult is the cry. Differences in infant cries are not tied to differences in types of distress, but differences in the time course and severity of the distress do lead to corresponding differences in the time course and intensity of the cry. The sound of crying appears to be instinctively distressing, which fact, no doubt helps ensure the survival of the infant, and thus the species. However, after a few months the infant begins to cry on occasion merely for attention, and it appears best not to spoil the child by responding to all such cries. Babbling begins as simple monosyllabic cooing and develops into complex multisyllabic utterances, complete with intonation pattern.

Thus by the time they begin to develop their earliest abilities at comprehending and producing language, children are not starting with nothing, but rather they are equipped with sophisticated auditory, vocal, and cognitive abilities.

SUGGESTED FURTHER STUDY

BATES, ROBIN & G. MASSEY, Producers. (1976) *Benjamin* [Film/Videotape]. London: BBC Enterprises. Part of the British television series *Horizon* (in the U.S.: *Nova;* in Canada: *Vista*).

BULLOWA, MARGARET, ED. (1979) *Before speech: The beginning of interpersonal communication.* Cambridge, England: Cambridge University Press.

MORSE, P. A. (1974) Infant speech perception: A preliminary model and a review of the literature. In Richard L. Schiefelbusch & L. Lloyd, eds., *Language perspectives—Acquisition, retardation and intervention,* Baltimore, Md.: University Park Press, 1974, pp. 19-53.

MURRAY, A. D. (1979) Infant crying as an elicitor of parental behavior: An examination of two models. *Psychological Bulletin* **86,** 191-215.

TWO
THE DEVELOPMENT
OF WORDS

FIRST REFERENCE

An important feature of human language is the ability of a person to label an object so that it can be referred to when communicating with another person. The first such communication between caregiver and child is visual rather than spoken. There are apparently several stages of visual communication of reference that infants go through.

Visual reference

He speaketh not; and yet there lies
A conversation in his eyes.—Henry Wadsworth Longfellow, *The Hanging of the Crane*

The first stage involves gaze. In one study mothers were asked to teach their six-month-olds to take an object from behind a transparent barrier. When the child looked away from the task, the mother would attempt to redirect the child's attention back to the object by touching it, shaking it, or otherwise 'marking' it (Kaye 1976).

Not only does the mother attend to the infant's gaze; the infant attends to the mother's. As early as four months in some children and with high frequency by nine months, the infant looks in the same direction that an adult facing it looks. This ability to focus on the same object as the caregiver is thought to play an important role in naming—the infant knows what the caregiver is naming by looking at what the caregiver looks at (Bruner 1974/75; Scaife & Bruner 1975). Caregivers spontaneously begin to give things or show them to infants while simultaneously naming them when infants are three or four months old (Escalona 1973; see also Messer 1978). By six or seven months infants reciprocate by beginning to show things to adults (Collis 1977; Murphy & Messer 1977).

The second stage involves orienting toward an object. At about ten to twelve months children begin to recognize the names of objects. The evidence for this comes from playing the **where game.** Caregivers ask, "Where's the X?" When infants know what that X is, they will often turn toward the object. For instance, when at ten months Hilde Stern was asked, "Where is tick-tock?" she turned toward the clock (Stern & Stern 1928).

Gestural reference

There was speech in their dumbness, language in their very gesture.— William Shakespeare, *The Winter's Tale*

The next stage involves pointing. When infants are seven or eight months old, adults start to use pointing gestures to direct the infant's attention to objects. At about 10 to 14 months their charges figure out what pointing is all about. Before this age when someone points at something infants look at the pointing hand. After this age they look at the object being pointed to (Lempers et al. 1977). At about the same time they begin to use pointing themselves for reference purposes. Some infants go through an intermediate stage in which they reach for an object without extending their index finger any more than their other fingers (Scupin & Scupin 1907: 48). While there is some evidence of pointing behavior much earlier, this pointing is different in being a distinctively **communicative** act. For example, when Quentin was in the pointing stage, the first time we put mittens on him he immediately started pointing with his thumb. While he could have still pointed with his index finger inside the mitten, if he had, we couldn't have seen it. So he adjusted his signal to suit the circumstances. Other evidence of the communicative nature of pointing is that children will look to see if their caregiver is looking in the right direction. If not, they will do something to attract his or her attention and point again (Bates 1976a: 61).

At this early stage one can usually distinguish two types of reference gestures: **assertions** and **requests.** When Bubi Scupin at 12 months wanted to make an assertion, as if to say, "There is the object," he would extend one arm toward it. But if he wanted to make a request, as if to say, "Give that to me," he would extend both arms toward the object and extend his upper torso toward it as well (Scupin & Scupin 1907: 48; see also E. Bates 1976a; E. Bates et al. 1975; Bruner 1974/75; Dore 1973).

At this stage children develop other gestures as well, such as waving "bye-bye" or opening their mouths to signal that they want to eat. Such gestures taken in context can be surprisingly successful as a means of communication (see Carter 1978).

Some children stay in this stage for a long time before they begin to speak. Parents of such children may get worried and contact the family physician. More than one doctor has been known to respond that it is probably because they get everything they want by pointing. Although I can trace this notion back to 1919, ("Speech will not be acquired until there is a necessity for it."—Blanton & Blanton 1919) I suspect it goes much farther back than that. However, I know of no research which supports this 'old doctors' tale.' A child will talk when it is ready, and the best estimate of when that is likely to be is the age when the parents began to talk. The onset of speech probably relates more to maturation of the nerves and muscles needed for speech than to success at communicating by pointing (Lecours 1975). The caregiver who takes the 'old doctors' tale' to heart and pretends not to understand the child's gestural message will probably only make life more difficult for both until the child matures enough to talk.

Other evidence for the importance of the maturational component comes from anecdotal accounts concerning children of deaf parents. These children often begin to 'talk' in deaf sign language many months sooner than children of normal parents begin to speak. I have heard of cases of children as young as eight months producing two-'word' utterances in sign. Children of hearing parents usually don't reach this stage in speech until about 18 months or later. One explanation for this is simply that the motor coordination of the hands needed for children's sign language utterances develops sooner than the motor coordination needed for speech.

Vocal reference

The first vocal communication is, of course, crying. But crying does not provide a way to refer to specific objects in the environment, so it is not considered to be related to vocal reference. While babbling may be said to provide feedback to the child as to which motor acts result in which sounds, it, too, does not appear to be related to vocal reference. The first object-directed sounds usually come as a part of children's straining to reach toward objects beyond their grasp. These sounds accompany what we have labelled request gestures, so we shall call them **request sounds.** There appears to be a significant shift in the nature of vocalization when children switch from babbling to request sounds. By the time children reach this stage, their babbling has become quite complex. These sounds may involve fairly long sequences, and are usually produced without strain. In contrast to this, request sounds are typically short, simple, and strained (Tischler 1957: 247).

The first vocal reference seems to come as a result of a shift in function in these sounds from being request sounds to being assertion sounds. For example, one 8-month-old uttered *[da]*, *[dja dja]*, and *[hedai]* when straining to reach things. By 11 months this child used *[da da]* as a sound which accompanied pointing (Gutzmann 1911: 25). Although this can be called vocal reference, it is used generally, not selectively to refer to a particular object. It is used rather like the way adults use deictic words such as *this* and *that*.

IDIOMORPHIC LANGUAGE

The next stage is an interesting and, one can argue, important one. This is the stage when children begin to use different sounds to refer to different objects or actions. It is at this stage that we may say that children are beginning to use language. Interestingly, this first language is not one that children learn from caregivers; rather it is a language that children invent themselves and that their caregivers learn from them.

Some time around the first birthday most children develop one to twenty or so idiosyncratic words, whose meaning their caregivers eventually learn. Thus each child develops her or his unique little language.

There is no standard term for such idiosyncratic words. Werner & Kaplan (1963: 106) use the term **idiomorph,** which is the one adopted for this book. Other terms which have been used include vocable (C. Ferguson 1977a), phonetically consistent form (Dore et al. 1976), expression (Cruttenden 1979: 9), and quasi-words (Stoel-Gammon & Cooper 1984).

Origins of idiomorphs

These idiomorphs can come from several sources. Some probably come from straining sounds. Quentin at age 1;1 had an idiomorph *[ʔəˈhəʔ]*, which was accompanied by pointing. It meant "Give me the name of that object to which I am pointing." It became quite clear that this was the meaning, since he often pointed to objects whose name he comprehended (though he could not yet produce these names), and if one responded with anything other than the correct word, he would respond with a sharp whine *[e::]* and then repeat the question *[ʔəˈhəʔ]* until the correct answer was produced. Thus the first born of two professors began language by testing his parents. On the other hand, our daughter Athena's straining sound *[ʔʌʔ]* came to mean "Give me the food."

An interesting (though dated) use of a straining sound came from Günter Stern at 1;10. His straining sound, *ö-ö-ö,* came to mean "horse carriage." He was relating to the fact that the horse had to strain to pull the carriage (Stern & Stern 1928: 374). Hildegard Leopold retained the original deictic meaning to her straining sound. She arrived at two idiomorphs, both pronounced *[ʔə]*. When it was said in a high pitch it meant "See that!" When it was said with a rising intonation it meant "Give me that!" (Leopold 1939: 82).

A second origin of inspiration for idiomorphs comes from imitating sounds in the environment. Günter Stern had *r-r-r,* which meant "coffee grinder," and *s-s-s,* which referred to an indoor plant mist sprayer (Stern & Stern 1928: 374). Axel Preyer said *ling-dong-mang* for "church keys" (Preyer 1882: 291). Other examples from children in their first year: *didi-lip-didi-lip* for "keys" (the jingling noise) (Pavlovitch 1920: 15), *shüdde-shüdde* for "ball" (the sound of bouncing) (Meumann 1902: 11, 28), *nōt-nōt* for "walking" (the sound of shuffling) (C. Stern & Stern 1928: 378f), and *bu* for "thunder" (Leopold 1939: 140).

A third source for idiomorphs comes from self-imitation. Athena discovered that if she coughed when sitting at the dinner table, we would give her a drink, so she learned to give a fake cough to indicate "Give me drink." Similarly *achoo* came to mean "handkerchief." And from other children: *kx* for "tastes bad" (action of spitting out food) (Leopold 1939: 140), and a clicking or smacking sound for "Give me my pacifier" (Pavlovitch 1920: 28).

The origin of some idiomorphs has been attributed to physical depiction by the vocal organs. One child 1;6 rolled his tongue from back to front (the sound was described as *gollah*) to describe all rollable objects such as balls, coins, and rings (Kussmaul 1885: 49).

Finally, there are examples of idiomorphs whose origin is the one which will shortly dominate—idiomorphs based on imitation of adult speech. Some examples: *dididi* for "scolding" or "comfort," depending on voice quality (Leopold 1939: 140), *bugge-bugge* (Gutzmann 1911: 29), *blablab* (Guillaume 1927), and *degatte-degatte* (Lindner, cited in C. Stern & Stern 1928: 379) for "reading." An interesting related example was produced by Jacob, a two-year-old son of a friend of mine, a child otherwise well past the idiomorph stage. One day he said, "Can I have some A-B-C-D-E?" The family was mystified. Finally the 10-year-old daughter figured it out. Jacob wanted ice cream. Apparently the parents had on a number of occasions said to one another something like, "Should we let him have some I-C-E C-R-E-A-M?" Since the only such sequence he knew was *A-B-C-D-E,* that is what he used!

Meaning in idiomorphs

Once a child creates an idiomorph for a particular referent object, the range of meaning associated with that idiomorph will tend to grow. A typical example of this phenomenon involves the use of *fff* as an idiomorph which originally depicted "blowing out a match." From that, the meaning grew first to include "steam" and "smoke," then "chimney," then "funnel," and finally "flagpole" (Jesperson 1922: 183). We shall call this type of meaning change **chain association,** although it has also been called chained association (Werner 1948) and chain complex (Vygotsky 1934: 64). The different referents of such an idiomorph are not related to one another in a systematic way, but rather each extension of meaning is associated to a previously established meaning in a way that differs from step to step. In the case of *fff,* the first link is from an event to its sound and action; the second link is from one part of an image—the flame—to another part—smoke or steam; the third link is from the smoke of a different image to its source, a smokestack, and so on.

The grammar of idiomorphs

Although idiomorphs when they first appear are generally used as one-word utterances, they are often accompanied by gestures. Sometimes these combinations become rather complex. A. Wepner, aged 1;10, while sitting in the bathtub wanted her mother to put into the water a whistle that was on the rim of the tub. Her communication act consisted of three simultaneous parts: She grabbed her mother's hand and put it into the water; she looked at the whistle; and she said *f-f-f*.

In general, the ability of children to express ideas precedes by some time their ability to do this strictly by vocal means. Thus a person who looks only at the vocal component of early child language will miss much of the sophistication found at this stage. The reason children are so successful at communication at this stage is their ability to make effective use of context, glance, facial expression, gesture, and sound simultaneously.

Idiomorphic inflection

Not only do children develop their own idiosyncratic vocabulary, they also develop idiosyncratic inflections, which they may apply to their idiomorphs or to words learned from adults. For example, some children experiment with changing the vowel to modify the meaning. Gabelenz's grandchild had the idiomorph *lakell,* which meant "chair." But if it was a doll chair, he 'reduced' the vowels so that the idiomorph became *likill;* if it was an overstuffed chair, he 'enlarged' the vowels so that it became *lukull*. Likewise the word *papa* was "father," but *pupu* was "father when wearing a big fur coat" (Gabelenz, cited in C. Stern & Stern 1928).

Other children may change their intonation pattern. Günter Stern had a baby-talk word *psi,* which originally meant "flower," but evolved by chain associations to include "leaves," "trees," and "cherries." *Psi* was not an idiomorph, because it no doubt came from imitating adults holding up a flower and pretending to sneeze, a routine common several European cultures (baby-talk vocabulary is discussed in Chapter 3). However, Günter's inflection of this word was idiomorphic. When the inflection developed, his pronunciation had evolved to a more accurate representation of a sneeze: *ha-psi*. When uttered with a high peeping voice, it meant "small flower"; when uttered with a deep, long intonation, it meant "big tree" (C. Stern & Stern 1928: 242). Similarly, another child had the word *teinn* for "stone" (the adult word in German is *Stein*). When uttered in a high, thin, short tone with the lips tightly together, it meant "pebbles"; when uttered in a low, long tone with mouth and eyes wide open, it meant "rocks." The same child used this technique for other words as well (Neugebauer 1915: 299).

Although these examples come from children of German-speaking parents, Gabelenz's grandchild reinvented an inflectional technique used in semitic languages such as Arabic, while the other two children each independently reinvented a technique for vocabulary differentiation used in tone languages such as Chinese.

Transition to adult forms

Eventually idiomorphs disappear from the language of the developing child, having been replaced by the normal adult forms. However, the idiomorphic stage tends to overlap the onset of adult forms. Five different transition phenomena have been found to occur during this period of overlap.

One phenomenon is that children who are learning highly inflected languages sometimes apply the adult inflections to their idiomorphs. One Belgian child learning French began to inflect the idiomorph *bum,* meaning "to fall down and go boom," as the verb *bumer* (Grégoire 1937: 185). Similarly, a German child, aged 1;8, had an idiomorph *wieh,* meaning "to slide down a slide, whee," which he began to use with the German verb inflection, producing *wiehen* (Neugebauer 1915: 305). A final example comes from Hilda Stern at age 2;6. Her idiomorph *atze* (an imitation of the sound of tearing), which meant, "to tear a paper or cloth," appeared in this sentence: *Hab geatzt mund,* meaning, "[I] have torn off [the bread with my] mouth" (C. Stern & Stern 1928: 375).

The second phenomenon involves combining idiomorphs with other adult words to make compound words. The examples come from German-speaking situations. German is a language that makes extensive use of this type of construction, and German children begin to apply word building in their first year. One lad had *poch* ("hammer"—the sound of hitting something with a hammer). He invented *Pochmacher* for "worker"—literally, "one whose job it is to make the sound *poch*" (Ament 1899: 73ff). Another used *fui,* meaning "tastes bad," to make *fui-ordnung* for "disorder, mess"—literally, "bad tasting order" (Scupin & Scupin 1910: 242). Another lad turned *hap,* meaning "eat," into *hapman,* meaning "one who is eating" (Stumpf 1901: 387). And from the idiomorph *tinkeli,* meaning "piano playing," a lass produced *tinkele kommode* for "piano"—literally, "piano playing chest" (C. Stern & Stern 1928: 387).

The third phenomenon sometimes found in this period is the combination of the idiomorph with the adult form of the same word. Thus the child says *shu-shu-train, bah-sheep, muh-cow, didde-didde-clock,* and so forth (C. Stern & Stern 1928: 243).

The fourth phenomenon involves imitation. During this period some children, when asked to imitate an adult form, will reply with their idiomorphic form. Thus the following conversation:

Adult: Say "bottle."
Child: Huhu.
Adult: Say "ring."
Child: Dintz.
Adult: Say "shoes."
Child: Buph.
Adult: Say "spoon."
Child: Ta.

Such children clearly understand the adult forms. They simply prefer to use the well-rehearsed idiomorphs (C.Stern & Stern 1928: 242, 293).

The fifth phenomenon involves what is known as **code switching.** When talking to his mother, one child used the idiomorphic forms, but when talking to his father or others, he used the adult forms (Werner & Kaplan 1963: 109).

Significance of idiomorphs

Although the idiomorphic state is a relatively short, transitory stage, it may be a very significant one. With the discovery that chimpanzees and other higher primates can learn human sign language (see Chapter 7), there appears to be little or no qualitative difference between humans and other primates. If primates **can** learn to use a complex language, why didn't they ever do it on their own? Perhaps part of the answer lies in the idiomorphic stage. It is in this stage that we see in every child the creative spark, the ability to create language anew. In most children this creative spark is soon dominated by the language of their caregivers, but there are examples to suggest that, if given a chance, it would continue to develop.

Twins tend to test lower than normals on early tests of language development. Some now feel that the reason is not one of mental retardation, but rather that twins tend to develop their own private language, slowing down somewhat the acquisition of the language of their caregivers. Twins usually lose their unique language by the time they are 2;6 to 3;0. However, a speech and language pathologist has reported a case in San Diego of seven-year-old twins, thought to be retarded, who were continuing to use their private language. The condition of having developed a private language is known as **idioglossia** in the field of speech and language pathology.

Another case involves the recent discovery of Kangobai, a 55-year-old deaf man living on an island where, in the memory of its inhabitants, there had never before been a deaf person. When discovered, Kangobai was found to have a complex sign language, which he apparently had invented and taught to the people in contact with him, so that they could communicate with him (Kuschel 1973).

Kangobai's ability to create a new sign language is not unique. The parents of many deaf children purposely prevent their children from learning American Sign Language (see Chapter 6). Recently, six such children aged 1;6 to 4;0 have been studied, and they, too, had begun to create their own unique language to communicate with their parents (Goldin-Meadow 1982).

It appears that we all have within us the natural ability to create language. This ability appears to a limited extent in almost all of us in our idiomorphic language. Some people in unusual circumstances seem to go much farther than the rest of us in creating language. It does not seem to be too great a step to propose that it is this creative spark which is the basis of the origin of language in our species (see Hale 1887).

FIRST WORDS

It is between 0;8 and 1;5 that most children produce their first word (C. Bühler 1931). Just when this occurs is difficult to tell. It is only with consistent and spontaneous use with understanding that a word can be said to be acquired. The age at which the tenth word is acquired, generally around 1;3, is perhaps easier to

Kangobai, the only deaf-mute on Rennell, a tiny island in the Solomon Islands, who created his own sign language. He is shown here making his sign for "hill." (From Kuschel 1973: 14. (© Linstok Press. Used by permission.)

determine (Ka. Nelson 1973a), though that criterion will never seem as meaningful to eager parents.

Vocabulary growth

The first vocabulary changes in several ways. The prime fact, of course, is that new words are added as the child develops. Figure 2.1 shows the growth of vocabulary spontaneously produced by the child. Vocabulary has also been measured by counting the number of words comprehended. Words are clearly comprehended before they are spoken, and the number of words comprehended continues to be greater than the number of words produced all through language development and later life. Comprehension of the first word is approximately three months ahead of the production of the first word, and the gap grows. Comprehension of 50 words appears to occur five months before production of 50 words (Benedict 1979).

While vocabulary growth starts out slowly, literally one word at a time, a great spurt occurs between 1;6 and 3;0. After this period the number of words added levels off to about 500 words a year (see Figure 2.1) (M. E. Smith 1926).

What sets off this great spurt? W. Stern (1914) had the following explanation:

That first period of unconscious speech . . . as a rule, lasts for six months or a little more . . . . Then a decisive turn takes place . . . with the *awakening of a faint consciousness of the meaning of speech and the will to achieve it*. . . . Now the discovery is made that . . . *everything has a name*. This change has two evident symptoms: (1) In the child's suddenly awakened enquiry as to the names of things. (2) In the increase, often proceeding by leaps and bounds—of vocabulary.

Hilda Stern at 1;6 arrived at a period when the desire to find out the names of things "entirely usurped all her speech and thoughts." Günter Stern was at 1;7 when he began his "unwearied search for names." And Bubi Scupin was 1;10 when his parents recorded, "His joy in naming things is great. Today he stood in the middle of the room and said as he pointed to the several things: *lamp, the cupboard, the bassy* ("basket")" (W. Stern 1914: 46).

Perhaps the most famous illustration of this breakthrough is that of the deaf and blind girl Helen Keller, who grew to be seven years old before taking this crucial step. In the first month she was with Helen, her teacher, Anne Sullivan, succeeded in teaching her a few finger symbols by association with objects touched at the same time. But the breakthrough came at the beginning of the second month, when (as reported by Sullivan):

> We went to the pump . . . . As cold water poured out and filled the cup, I spelt *w-a-t-e-r* on her empty hand. The word . . . seemed to take her aback . . . . Quite a new light passed over her features. She spelt the word *w-a-t-e-r* several times, then crouching down touched the ground and asked its name, and in the same way pointed to the pump and the grating, then turning around suddenly she asked my name. All the way home she was most excited, and enquired the name of everything she touched, so that

FIGURE 2.1
Vocabulary growth by age. Based on M.E. Smith 1926, who elicited productive vocabulary by using objects, pictures, and questions. At any point in language acquisition, a child's comprehension vocabulary is greater. For example, at 6;0 a child's comprehension vocabulary has been estimated at 8000 words (Templin 1957).

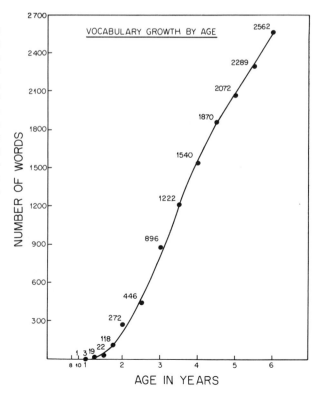

in the course of a few hours she had embodied thirty new words in her vocabulary (cited in Stern 1914: 46).

And in Helen Keller's own words:

> That living word awakened my soul, gave it light, hope, joy, set it free! . . . I left the well-house eager to learn. Everything had a name, and each name gave birth to a new thought (Keller 1903: 315).

Interestingly, this period is not simply one of continued vocabulary growth; some words also drop out. Naturally, as children learn the vocabulary of their caregivers' language, idiomorphs will drop out. But even words acquired from the adult language will drop out for extended periods. By the time Allison was 1;2, she had used a total of 25 words, but within any given one week period there were never more than 10 or 12 different words occurring with regularity. Many words, after having been used consistently for a while, dropped from use and did not reappear until several or many months later. At 1;2 Allison used *[gaja]* to mean "flower." Then the word disappeared for four months, and at 1;6 reappeared in a somewhat more accurate form—*[fawa]* (Bloom 1973: 41).

Why do words disappear? There appear to be a number of reasons (based on Leopold, as cited in McLaughlin 1978: 79):

1. **Idiomorphs.** Idiomorphs drop out as they are replaced by standard forms.
2. **Homophony.** If two words end up sounding alike due to the child's primitive phonology, one of them may drop.
3. **Phonological dissatisfaction.** If the child's best attempt to pronounce the word doesn't meet her or his standards, the word may be dropped. This will be discussed further shortly.
4. **Synonym competition.** Occasionally one synonym will supplant another.
5. **Change of interest.** The passing of winter may mean the dropping out of *snow;* the passing of a family epidemic may mean the loss of the word *measles.*
6. **Other.** Sometimes no reason can be found. The use of a word may be just a passing fancy.

Which words come first?

Most children learn to produce at least 50 words before they begin to put them together to form sentences of two or more words. This one-word stage of development is fairly lengthy, lasting up to 10 months or more. Most children acquire their first 50 words sometime between 1;3 and 2;0. Although the time it takes to acquire these words varies considerably, there is some consistency in what words they acquire. According to one study of 18 children, the majority of words are names for objects that move by themselves (*mama, dada, dog, cat, baby, car, truck, clock*) or that can be manipulated by the child (*juice, milk, cookie, shoe, sock, hat, ball*). Much less common are action words (*give, bye-bye, up*), modifiers (*dirty, mine, outside*), personal-social words (*yes, no, please*) and function words (*for, what*). Conspicuously absent are names for clothing that the child cannot easily manipulate (*diaper, pants*) and names for places or objects in the environment (*chair, tree, kitchen*) (Ka. Nelson 1973a).

"OF COURSE HE SAID 'ARF'... WHAT DID YOU EXPECT HIS FIRST WORD TO BE?"

(© **Bill Maul in Good Housekeeping. Used by permission.**)

There is considerable variation among children as to which words come first. The percentage of the first 50 words acquired by children that are common nouns varies from 26% to 71%, for example (Leonard & Fey 1979). Those children who acquire many common nouns at first have been termed **referential** and those who acquire other words first, such as *bye-bye, naughty,* and *want,* have been termed **expressive** (Ka. Nelson 1973a). Referential children seem to be more interested in communicating about objects, while expressive children seem to relate more to social interaction. When they reach 2;0, referential children have more extensive vocabularies than expressive children, but by age 2;6 the difference disappears (Ka. Nelson 1975). Similar variation has also been found among language delayed children (A. Weiss et al. 1983).

The labels expressive and referential do not imply that there are two distinct types of children; rather they are labels for opposite ends of a continuum. Children develop their vocabularies as a result of different interests on their part or on the part of their caregivers, but these differences do not appear to have any long-term effect, because by the middle of the second year the differences have evaporated.

What do children talk about?

Although one of the endearing things about children is that one never knows what they are likely to come up with, at this stage there is a certain amount of predictability as to what they are likely to comment on. The two basic motivations, which can be traced back to the pointing stage, are assertion and request. When a child reaches this stage, one can probably distinguish within these two categories a number of distinct subcategories. Within assertion, there is: naming for the sake of naming, naming when first noticed, pointing out when first noticed, indicating ownership when first noticed, commenting on change of appearance, and commenting on change of location. Within request, there is: request for others to act, request for oneself to act, and refusal. Table 2.1 gives examples of each type.

TABLE 2.1   Most Common Topics at the One-Word Stage

ASSERTIONS

Naming for the sake of naming:	Bubi (standing in the center of a room, pointing to objects): Lamp. Cupboard. Bassy.
First notice:	
Naming:	Child (sees flower): Fow.
Pointing out:	Child (sees balloon): See.
Possession:	Child (sees Father's slippers): Daddy.
Change of appearance:	Housekeeper: Look, Athena. Daddy cut the grass. Athena (looking and pointing): Allgone.
Change of location:	(Airplane flies by.) Child (points to it; tracks it): Airplane. (Leaf falls.) Child (points): Down.

REQUESTS:

For others to act:	Child (wanting to get parent to open jar): Open.
Self-command:	Child: Blow. (Then blows her own nose.)
Refusal:	Child: No!

Roles

One can describe any event in terms of the actions involved and the participants involved. Different participants may play different roles in the event. The two most basic roles are the **agent,** who performs the action, and the **affected,** which is the person or object acted upon. Among other, more marginal, roles are the **possessor** and the **location** (Halliday 1967a; C. Fillmore 1968).

At least for some children in the one-word stage there appears to be a developmental sequence in which roles are referred to. The sequence observed in one child was: First only the agent was named, then either agent or action, then affected was an added possibility, then possessor, then location (Greenfield & Smith 1976).

Thus it appears that each word uttered by a child in this stage has its own function and expresses a specific role in the event being communicated. Furthermore, each word appears to have its own sentence-like intonation pattern, and often accompanying gestures. The effect that this has on observers is to make it appear as if each word were really an entire sentence from which only one word had been uttered. Words in this stage, when viewed as whole sentences, are called **holophrases.** There is considerable controversy as to how much information actually exists in children's minds when they utter such holophrases. Some postulate complex hidden structure (e.g., Dore 1975; D. Ingram 1971), while others take a much more conservative approach (Bloom 1973; Jesperson 1922).

Meaning

"When I use a word," Humpty Dumpty said, in rather a scornful tone, "it means just what I choose it to mean—neither more nor less."

"The question is," said Alice, "whether you *can* make words mean so many different things."

"The question is," said Humpty Dumpty, "which is to be master—that's all."
—Lewis Carroll, *Through the Looking Glass*

When children acquire their very first words, the meaning and use of these words appear to be very restricted compared to the way an adult would use the same words. Allison Bloom at 0;9 used *car* only to refer to moving cars when seen from the living-room window, and not when seeing them at other times (Bloom 1973: 72). Wendy at 0;10 only used *hi* when she was in her crib and someone came into the room, but not elsewhere (Huttenlocher 1974: 341). Nigel went through a period when a number of words were used only for a specific communication function. *Cat* could only mean "Hello, cat," not "I want cat"; *syrup* could only mean "I want the syrup," not "There's the syrup"; and so on (Halliday 1975: 42).

Children first learning a word will hear it while watching a particular scene and may not know exactly what part of that scene is being referred to. In fact, they appear to behave as if that word applies only when that entire situation is repeated. Slowly, as they hear the word used in other contexts, they may begin to apply it more broadly.

I witnessed one very early example of this myself, when Quentin was 0;8. The example involved comprehension of the word *shoes*. When Quentin was in our bedroom, we would ask, "Where's the shoes?" In this situation he would crawl to his mother's closet and play with her shoes. At first the door had to be open, but this is probably because he hadn't learned to open doors. He soon learned this, and then could find the shoes even when the door was closed. What is interesting is that only the shoes in his mother's closet were *shoes*. When some of his mother's shoes were placed at point X (see illustration on next page), Quentin would crawl around them to get to the closet door, then open the door to get the shoes. Apparently the shoes at point X were not *shoes*. Similarly, when Quentin was placed in front of his father's open closet (at point Z), he would not stop to play with his father's shoes.

At approximately two-week intervals, the meaning of shoes expanded. At the next stage shoes in his father's closet were *shoes,* but not shoes on the bedroom floor. Then shoes on the bedroom floor were added, but not when they were worn. And finally shoes when they were being worn were included (P. Reich 1976).

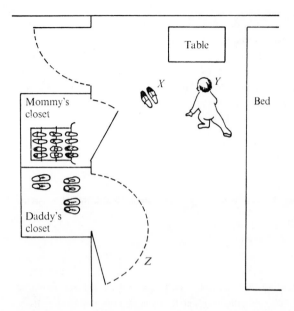

The layout of the bedroom.

This very early growth of word meaning is rarely observed but may be very important. This is because not only can children learn about the meanings of individual words, but they are probably also learning general **heuristics** about what is and is not important for word meaning. A heuristic is a strategy or procedure that is helpful for accomplishing some goal, but one which may not always work. Through early learning such as this children probably learn that location is irrelevant to word meaning. A shoe is a shoe, wherever it is found. Even the London Bridge is still the London Bridge after being moved to Arizona. This heuristic is very useful for learning most words, but it would tend to slow down the acquisition of place names, such as *kitchen*. As previously mentioned, place names are, in fact, learned late.

Another heuristic which is probably learned in this way very early is that color is unimportant. Shoes may be of any color; apples may be red, green, or yellow; wine may be clear, yellow, light or dark red; beer may even be green on St. Patrick's Day. Thus children learn to ignore color when they are trying to match words to the environment to discover what they mean. This explains why it is particularly late when children finally begin to learn their first color word (Rice 1978).

This early conservatism in the comprehension of words results in what is known as **underextension.** What this means is that the range of referents of a word for a child is narrower than for an adult. Quentin's original concept of *shoes* was much more limited than the adult conception.

Theoretically, there are seven possible relations between the child's range of meaning for a word and that of an adult (see Figure 2.2). The opposite of underextension is **overextension.** When this occurs the range of meaning is greater for the child than for an adult. Some children for a period use *mommy* to refer to all caregivers. This would be a case of overextension.

Another one of the possibilities is **overlap,** in which the range of referents is overextended in some areas and underextended in others. Dale's daughter at 2;0 used *muffin* to refer to blueberries and blueberry muffins, but not to other muffins (Dale 1976: 12).

Yet another of the seven possible relations is **mismatch,** in which the child's meaning for a word does not overlap that of the adult. Quentin during one period called the television set *TV Guide,* yet he emphatically denied that the program guide was a *TV Guide* or that the set was a *TV.* Another example: Children often first interpret *old* as if it meant ''big'' or ''tall,'' and *young* as if it meant ''small'' or ''short'' (Kuczaj & Lederberg 1977).

A possible relation that is probably quite rare is **identity,** in which the range of the child's word is exactly the same as that of the adult. Many observers have noted that the meaning of proper names does not become overextended. It appears that children even before they are 1;1 learn to categorize certain objects, such as people and dolls, as capable of taking a proper name that does not generalize (N. Katz et al. 1974).

Another possibility is that the child has a word which is not a part of the vocabulary of the adult. This is the case of the idiomorph. The final possibility is that the adult has a word that is not a part of the vocabulary of the child. This, of course is the case of a word which has not yet been learned. As can be seen by the above examples, all possibilities occur (Anglin 1977; P. Reich 1976).

Both in early comprehension and in early production, underextension appears to be the norm. However, use of words in production soon deviates from use in comprehension. Children start to produce words when referring to a greater range of objects than they seem to accept in comprehension situations. Some researchers have found no evidence of overgeneralization in comprehension, although in the same children at the same time there was evidence of overgeneralization in production (Fremgen & Fay 1980; Huttenlocher 1974: 354).

FIGURE 2.2
Seven possible relations of the child's word meaning to that of the adult.

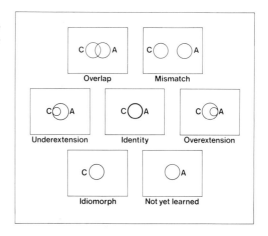

(Reprinted by permission: Tribune Media Services, Inc.)

Why should there be this difference between comprehension and production? One proposal is that children really know that the words they use don't quite fit, but they use them anyway because they have no better alternatives available. It is as if they reason thus: "I know that that thing is not a dog, but I don't know what else to call it, and it is like a dog, so I'll call it a dog" (Bloom 1973: 79). There is some evidence to support this. Some children, apparently, distinguish appropriate uses of a word from overextended uses of that same word by means of intonation. One child, for example, habitually called his father *Daddy,* and called other men *Daddy?* if they, like his father, wore mustaches (example provided by one of my students).

The growth of meaning in the very first words seems to be similar to the growth of meaning in idiomorphs. In one famous example a child learned the word *qua* ("quack") with reference to a scene of a duck swimming on a pond. While the original reference was to the whole situation, later use of the word gave evidence that the child associated *qua* with both the duck and the pond. On the one hand, the word meaning grew to include other liquids, such as milk in the baby's bottle. On the other hand, the meaning grew to include a representation of an eagle on a coin, then the coin itself, and finally coin-like objects such as buttons (Vygotsky 1934: 70). It appears that the meaning of *qua* grew from a vague reference simultaneously in two directions by chained association.

The word-referent relationship at this stage can vary considerably, both from the standard adult usage and among different children. For example, for some children *Mommy* seems to be a name for all women, and *Daddy* for all men. For other children *Mommy* names the mother, while *Daddy* appears to be the name for everyone else. But for Edmond Grégoire *mama* was how you call a parent who is absent and who you want to return, while *papa* was how you call a parent who is present (Grégoire 1937). Or consider the example from a two-year-old Russian girl:

Adult (picks up a stick):	What's this?
Child:	Paka. (*Palka* means "stick.")
Adult (throws stick into the air):	What's this?
Child:	T'ipka. (*Pitchka* means "bird.")
	(Twig lands in some water.)
Child:	Day ypka. (*Day rybku* means "Give [me the] fish.")

Thus the object changed its name three times in two minutes according to the function it was performing at the time (Shvachkin 1948: 93).

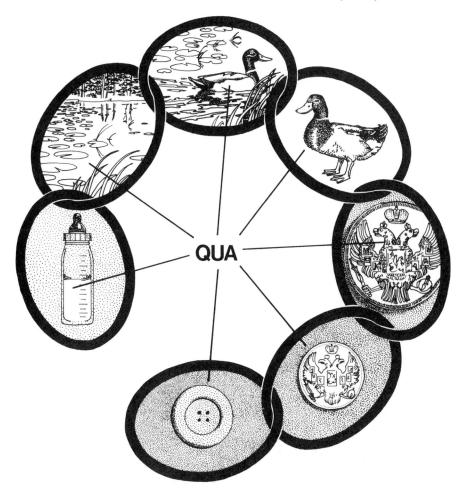

Chained association of meaning in one child's use of *qua*.

As the child acquires more vocabulary the meanings of newly acquired words begin to have an effect on the meanings of earlier acquired words. Consider this famous example of one child acquiring animal names, shown in Figure 2.3. The original idiomorph *tee* grows in its range of referents to include first "small dog" then "cow." At age 1;11,1 a new word, *goggie,* meaning "toy dog," appears. The next day the new word has captured part of the range of *tee*. No longer is "small dog" called *tee;* it has become a part of the range of *goggie*. At 1;11;24, the child names "horse" for the first time, by expanding the range of *tee*. The next day the child uses *hosh* for the first time. On this day only both *hosh* and *tee* are used for "horse." By the following day *hosh* has captured "horse" and *tee* is not used for this referent. The next day *pushi* captures "cat," leaving the idiomorph without its original referent. Slightly less than a month and a half later, the idiomorph is demolished completely with the advent of *mooka*. At the same time *hosh* is

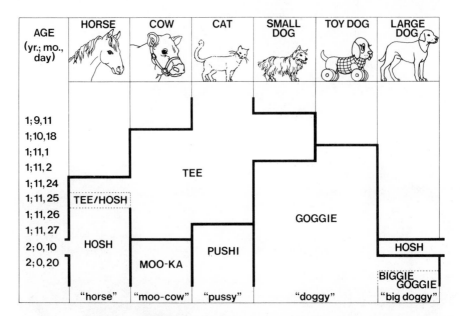

FIGURE 2.3   Effect of newly acquired words on the range of meaning of previously acquired words. (Based on M.M. Lewis 1957: 134, 1963: 51.)

expanded to include "large dog," but 10 days later *goggie* captures this new referent (M. M. Lewis 1963: 51).

This example illustrates several points about the development of word meaning. First, young children appear to be guided by a one-word-per-referent heuristic. If a new word comes in for a referent that is already named, the old name is almost always immediately replaced. The only exception in the example was the period when both *tee* and *hosh* are used for "horse," and that period only lasted a day. This appears to support the hypothesis that children know their use of a word is improper, and so continue to use it only until they acquire the correct words. A second point to note is that both expansion and contraction of a range of referents can occur at the same time. Although *goggie* had captured part of the range of *tee*, it still expanded to include "horse." A third point is that children during this period experiment on referents, trying one word, then switching to another if the first fails to do the job. Thus the child's first attempt to label the large dog as a *hosh* didn't work, so he switched to *goggie*, and finally to *biggie goggie*.

During this period children's use of words is still expanding to cover new, as yet unnamed, referents. Meanings are often still chain associations. It has been suggested that there are stages in the way meanings change. At about two years children are supposed to become much more conservative in their use of words. Rather than experiment in naming new referents, they appear to build their language by slowly accumulating instances on the basis of experience (Bloom 1973: 74).

This period, in turn, is supposed to be merely a transition to another period, which starts at around three years. At this time children appear to pick out some perceptually or functionally salient features of exemplar referents and use the same

THE FAMILY CIRCUS **By Bil Keane**

"Which is this, Mommy, a lasso, a lariat, a noose
or a rope?"

word to refer to any other objects they encounter with like features. The result of this is to overextend the semantic domain of many words. For example, they may use *truck* for any vehicle other than a car, or *dog* for any furry four-legged creature. Some observers find that overextension tends to be based on perceived similarities of function (Ka. Nelson 1973a, 1973b), while others find that it tends to be based on perceptual attributes such as shape, size, movement, sound, taste, and texture (E. Clark 1974: 112). Unlike earlier periods, during this period there is evidence of overextension in comprehension as well as production. The evidence that children extend the range of meanings in different ways as they go through different stages is, at present, slight (Ka. Nelson 1974: 269).

Later development of meaning is discussed in Chapter 4.

How words sound

Just as the meanings of children's first words are very different from those of adults, so also are the ways these words are pronounced. As discussed in the previous chapter, children are born with the ability to perceive many of the fine distinctions needed for speech. What is the status of their sound system at the time that they begin to produce their first words? It is useful to answer this question in three ways. First we shall consider perception of the speech sounds during this period, then the production of the first words, and finally the strategies children use to match their production abilities to their perception.

Perception of the first words The classic study of the early perception of word sounds involved 19 Russian children between the ages of 0;10 and 2;0

(Shvachkin 1948). These children were taught simple one-syllable names for a set of geometric shapes and unusual toys. The names were designed so that there would be pairs of names that differed only in one phoneme. The children were tested for their ability to distinguish one phoneme from another by being asked to find, fetch, or point to the appropriate object. This study yielded a number of important findings:

1. When children acquire the ability to distinguish between two phonemes within a word, this ability does not apply simultaneously in all positions in the word. Specifically, children can distinguish between two phonemes when they occur in initial position before they can distinguish them when they occur in final position.
2. Children can distinguish between words that differ by more than one phoneme before they can distinguish between words that differ by only one phoneme.
3. Children can distinguish between words that differ only in their vowels before they can distinguish words that differ only in their consonants.
4. Children can distinguish words that differ in the presence or absence of an initial consonant before they can distinguish words that each have a different initial consonant.
5. There appears to be a consistent pattern in the order in which particular contrasts become discriminable.
6. Children's phonemic perception appears to be complete by age 2;0.

Later research on children of English-speaking parents tends to support the general outlines of phonemic differentiation as described in the Russian study, but there is more individual variation in the acquisition patterns than originally thought (Garnica 1973; see Barton 1975 for a methodological criticism). Furthermore, the picture derived from the Russian study is of a whole class of sounds splitting into classes distinguishable from one another. More recent work suggests that the distinction proceeds more or less one phoneme pair at a time. Thus, for example, the ability to distinguish /b/ from /p/—Stage 10, according to Shvachkin (1948)— would not necessarily come at the same time as the ability to distinguish /d/ from /t/—also Stage 10. Finally, there is evidence that phoneme perception proceeds more slowly than Shvachkin thought. Children as old as 3;0 do not have complete phonemic perception (Edwards 1974).

The work just cited seems at first blush to contradict work cited in Chapter 1 on perception in newborns. In that work infants 0;1 to 0;4 demonstrate the ability to discriminate many of the phoneme pairs that children 0;10 to 2;0 appear to have to relearn. The most probable explanation is that the difference is due to differences in the requirements of the two tasks. In the infant studies the task was merely to demonstrate awareness that a change from one sound to another had just occurred. In the latter task children must compare the sequence of sounds just heard to similar sequences stored in memory. Furthermore, they must retrieve the referent with which that sequence had been associated. Clearly the later task involves much more than the earlier one (D. Ingram 1976: 24).

The sound of the first words   When the child first begins to talk, the variety of sounds produced actually decreases relative to the later stages of babbling. This should not be a surprising finding. The number of sounds which children can produce at random is bound to be greater than the number they can produce when aiming at a target—that is, when attempting to utter a particular sound.

What do the first words sound like? Table 2.2 gives phonetic descriptions of the first 25 word forms of four children. As can be seen, the number of different phonological building blocks which children start with when they first form words is quite limited. It is also different for every child. Among the consonants, only [b] is used by all four children. Among the vowels, only [a] is shared by all. The average number of different sounds is nine, split roughly equally between consonants and vowels. Among the consonants, stops are the most common, especially those made with the lips or with the tip of the tongue; [g] and [k], which are made with the back of the tongue, are rare. Other consonants include the fricatives, [n], and [h]. Among the vowels, the earliest typically appear to be [a], [i], and [u]. Different children appear to add to these in different ways. The syllable structure is also quite simple. The most likely syllable patterns at first are V, CV, VC, and CVCV, where the second syllable is the same as the first (*baba, dada, papa*). Before the 25th word form is produced, all children have produced more complex syllables, however.

When children are at the beginnings of their phonological development, their pronunciation of their first words will vary. One day when Athena was about to go for a walk, her nanny told her to "Say 'bye-bye'." She waved and said, "Dye-dye." I waved and said back, "Dye-dye." Athena waved again and said "Guy-guy." Thus it appears that at this time [b], [d], and [g] were all instances of one phoneme /b~d~g/.

Once a contrast is established—for example, between /b/ and /d~g/, one would expect that the two phonemes would be kept distinct in all words. This apparently is not true. Prior to the complete establishment of an /m/ versus /n/ contrast, one child had some words which were always pronounced with [m], some always with [n], and some which were pronounced sometimes with [m] and sometimes with [n] (Ferguson & Farwell 1975: 431).

As the child's phonology develops, it is usually the case that the pronunciation of any given word becomes more and more adultlike. However, in some cases, the pronunciation of individual words actually gets worse before it gets better. The most famous example of this comes from Hildegard Leopold's acquisition of *pretty*. Starting with an adultlike pronunciation at 0;10, it evolved over the following year as follows (Leopold 1939):

0;10	[pɹəti]
0;11	[pɹɪti]
1;0	[pɪ̩ti] (The mark under the ɹ indicates that that sound is the vowel of the syllable.)
1;1	[pɹiti], [pɹəti]
1;3	[pʃɪti]
1;4	[pwɪti], [pəti], [jɪti]
1;9	[bɪdi]

Children can be said to have **mastered** a sound if they can produce it in words always and only when needed. Children may regularly produce a sound before they

TABLE 2.2 First 25 Recorded Forms for Four Normal Children

JOAN VELTEN		DANIEL MENN		HILDEGARD LEOPOLD		JENNIKA INGRAM	
FORM	MEANING	FORM	MEANING	FORM	MEANING	FORM	MEANING
[ap]	up	[bab]	byebye	[prʌti]	pretty	[ba]	blanket
[ba]	bottle, bang	[bæ bæ]	byebye	[dɛu]	there	[babi]	blanket
[bas]	bus, box	[hæ]	hi	[duɪ]	there	[ba]	byebye
[baza]	put on	[ha]	hi	[de]	there	[baba]	byebye
[za]	that	[ōo]	no	[prʌti]	pretty	[da]	daddy
[da]	down	[no]	no	[dɛ]	there	[dada]	daddy
[at]	out	[nu]	no	[tak]	tick tock	[dadi]	daddy
[baba]	away	[hwow]	hello	[bu]	ball	[dat]	dot
[bat]	pocket	[gæ]	squirrel	[bu]	Blumen (flower)	[dati]	dot
[af]	Fuff (family cat)	[gow]	squirrel	[da]	da (there)	[haɪ]	hi
[faf]	Fuff	[o]	nose	[opa]	pa	[ma]	mommy
[bada]	put on	[i]	ear	[papa]	papa	[mami]	mommy
[bus]	push	[bu]	boot	[pi]	peep	[mama]	mommy
[uf]	dog	[njaɪ]	nice	[pip]	peep	[no]	no
[ba]	pie	[njaɪs]	nice	[pʌti]	pretty	[si]	see
[dat]	duck	[aʊ]	light	[ʃ]	sh	[siæt]	see that
[bap]	lamb	[gaɹ]	car	[tʊta]	tick tock	[da]	that
[am]	'M'	[jis]	cheese	[tatʌt]	tick tock	[hat]	hot
[an]	'N'	[iv]	Stevie	[ba]	ball	[haɪdi]	hi
[n]	in	[eg]	egg	[bu]	bimbam	[ap]	up
[da]	doll	[æp]	apple	[da]	da	[api]	up
[as]	'S'	[gʊs]	kiss	[dɛda]	Gertrude	[nodi]	no
[ul]	'O'	[ʌf]	up	[dədi]	Gertrude	[dodi]	no
[a]	'R'	[mæʊwf]	mouth	[ti]	kick	[noni]	no
[nas]	nice	[aʊ]	eye	[tʊtsa]	kritze (scrawls)		

Based on a table compiled by D. Ingram 1976: 17 from diary studies by Velten (1943), Menn (1971), Leopold (1947), and D. Ingram (1974a). The phonological representations have been altered and simplified to bring them into line with the system used in this book. © Edward Arnold Ltd. Used by permission.

have mastered it. Before Amahl Smith had mastered [θ] (the unvoiced *th* sound), he would say *fick* for "thick." On the other hand, he said *thick* for "sick." He could produce [θ], just not when he aimed for it (N. Smith 1973).

Children master the set of sounds that constitute their language more slowly than one might expect. Many sounds have not been mastered by 4;0 (Olmsted 1971: 246); the median age for the last sound to be mastered is 6;0, and 10% of children still have not mastered it by 8;6 (Sander 1972). Table 2.3 presents some additional details.

TABLE 2.3   Age of Acquisition of English Consonants[c]

CONSONANT	NOT ACQUIRED BY AGE 4[a]	MEDIAN AGE OF CUSTOMARY USAGE[b]	AGE AT WHICH 90% HAVE ACQUIRED SOUND[b]
p,m,n,h,w		1½	3
b		1½	4
k,g,d		2	4
t,ŋ	-t-,-ŋ-,-ŋ	2	6
f,j		2½	4
ɹ,l	-l-,-l	3	6
s		3	8
č,ʃ	č-,-č-	3½	7
z	z-,-z	4	7
ǰ	ǰ-,-ǰ	4	7
v		4	8
θ	θ-	4½	7
ð	ð-	5	8
ʒ	-ʒ-	6	8½

[a]From Olmsted 1971.
[b]From Sander 1972.
[c]Table adapted from D. Ingram 1976: 28–29. © Edward Arnold, Ltd. Used by permission.

Yet another phenomenon that has been noted as children are beginning to develop their phonology is **sound avoidance.** Many children at an early stage find themselves with the ability to produce a [b] but not a [p]. Some of these children appear to avoid using words that contain a [p] until they can pronounce them, at which time a large increase of words containing [p] may suddenly appear (C. Ferguson 1978; C. Ferguson & Farwell 1975: 433). This is a bit sad if one of the words is one's own name. For example, the [θ]-sound is one that is mastered quite late. Athena refused to pronouce her own name until she had mastered this sound. Avoidance of words containing sounds the child is not yet comfortable with has been confirmed in two experimental studies of a combined total of 26 normal children aged 1;0 to 1;10, and in 14 language-delayed children as well (Leonard et al. 1982; Schwartz & Leonard 1982).

Strategies for producing the first words

Why are children's pronunciations of their first words quite primitive? One possibility is that their articulation is limited by the undeveloped nature of their perception. The other is that their perception is much better than their production, and that their articulation is limited primarily by the undeveloped nature of their articulatory muscle control. The evidence clearly supports the latter explanation. Every parent and researcher has experienced an episode similar to this one:

> One of us, for instance, spoke to a child who called his inflated plastic fish a *fis*. In imitation of the child's pronunciation, the observer said: "This is your *fis?*" "No," said the child, "my *fis*." He continued to reject the adult's imitation until he was told, "That is your fish." "Yes," he said, "my *fis*" (Berko & Brown 1960: 531).

Clearly this child could distinguish [ʃ] from [s] in the speech of adults, and knew the proper pronunciation, even though he could not produce it.

Even though children may be able to hear a difference, they may not object when an adult purposely mispronounces a word in imitation. Consider this example:

Father:	What is a sirt?
Child:	(Immediately points to his shirt.)
Father:	What's a soo?
Child:	(Immediately points to shoe.)
Father:	What's a sip?
Child:	When you drink. (Imitates action.)
Father:	What else does sip mean?
Child (puzzled):	Zip?
Father:	No, it goes in the water.
Child:	A boat.
Father:	Say it.
Child:	No. I can only say *sip* (N. Smith 1973: 136-137).

This example illustrates three points. The first is that there are individual differences, and that this four-year old, unlike the one in the previous example, accepted mispronunciations which apparently he could perceive. The second point is that the child was aware that he could not pronounce the sound correctly, so it is not the case that he could hear the distinction when others produced it but not when he did. And the third point involves his reticence to utter a word that he knows he cannot pronounce correctly. It suggests that at least some words that are not in children's productive—active—vocabulary because of pronunciation difficulties are in their comprehension—passive—vocabulary.

The fact that some children are more reticent than others in using words that they know they can't pronounce correctly may be one cause of variation in the time a child first starts to speak. It may also explain why sometimes previously acquired words drop out of the vocabulary of a child for a period. Quentin was more conservative than Athena. He was slow at beginning to speak, but when he did start, his speech was easy to understand. This desire to be correct was evident even after he began to speak. Once Quentin, a Star Trek fan, tried to say *Mr. Spok*. All he could produce was *Mr. Spop*. He broke into tears when he found he couldn't say it properly. On the other hand, Athena was more concerned with doing things that she saw others doing than she was in doing them right. She began to speak early, but her phonology was much worse than that of her brother. (However, as noted above, she was conservative with respect to her own name.) Leopold noted similar differences between Hildegard and her younger sister Karla (Leopold 1939: 172).

Not only do children perceive phonological constructions that they cannot produce, they also appear able to recognize the adult pronunciation better than their own. When some children heard a tape recording of an adult saying a list of words, they were able to identify the words 94% of the time, whereas when listening to a tape recording of their own pronunciations of the same words, they succeeded only 47% of the time (Dodd 1975).

In general, phonemic perception is not complete before speech develops, but develops before the corresponding production contrasts develop. The sequence of development in production does not necessarily follow the sequence of development in perception. For example, /l/ and /r/ are sometimes acquired earlier than /w/ and /j/ in perception, but later in production (M. Edwards 1974).

Given that children hear greater complexity in words than they find they can produce, they do the best they can to imitate the adult forms that they hear. The details of what they do are now beginning to be understood.

When children first start to produce words, they probably develop separate articulatory routines for each word. The concept of the phoneme doesn't seem to be relevant yet, because similar sounds in different words are not yet related to one another (Cruttenden 1970; C. Ferguson & Farwell 1975; Moskowitz 1973). This point of view explains how a child could pronounce some words consistently with an [m] but produce others sometimes with an [n] and sometimes with an [m]. The [m] in one word is not yet related to the [m] in another word. Thus there is no reason to be surprised if there is more variation in the [m] of one word than there is in another.

Slowly a system emerges. When two or more words have sounds in common in the adult form, such as initial consonant clusters, those sounds begin to be pronounced consistently. The result of this may be that some words are pronounced more poorly than they had been previously. The advantages of an organized system seem to supercede earlier developed word-sized articulatory routines. This explains how a word like *pretty* could degenerate. Although pronounced less accurately, the change in pronunciation brings it into line with the systematic articulation system under development. This process of fitting already acquired forms to an emerging set of rules is known as **regularization.** We shall see later that this same sort of thing happens in other aspects of language acquisition as well as in phonology.

From time to time children focus on particular phonological problems. When they become aware of a particular difficulty they may take any of several possible actions. They may choose to avoid that sound or sound combination altogether. Or they may concentrate so hard on producing that unit or sequence that the result is a degradation of other parts of the words involved (C. Ferguson & Farwell 1975: 423). Occasionally it appears that some children become aware that two words that sound different when an adult pronounces them sound the same when they pro-

nounce them. In order to avoid homophones the children may deliberately differentiate the two pronunciations (D. Ingram 1975. Locke 1979 takes a more skeptical
view). Hildegard Leopold employed for this purpose normal voice versus whispering: *baba* when voiced meant "Papa"; when whispered, it meant "bye-bye"
(Leopold 1949a: 152). Hildegard also used vowel length to distinguish two words;
she pronounced *walk* as [wɔk] and *fork* as [wɔːk]. One little French boy named
Charles was compelled to change his own name in order to avoid homophony.
Chat, which he pronounced [ʒa], means "cat" in French. But [ʒa] was also the best
pronunciation he could manage for his own name. So that he could avoid calling
himself a cat, he changed his own name to [ʒaʒa] (Kaper 1959: 33).

Ultimately children arrive at a system which relates what they hear to what
they say. As they develop, the system changes, and during the process of such
changes particular sounds or combinations may be unstable. When this occurs,
these sounds may be pronounced with greater variation for awhile. Each child
seems to work out the details of phonology in a unique way. This is why the
caregivers of young children can understand their speech better than strangers, a
fact that has been verified experimentally (Weist & Kruppe 1977). Although each
child uses them differently, there are seven general processes which all children use
in constructing their own unique sound system.

(1) **Syllable deletion.** Especially in the early stages of phonological development, children will drop unstressed syllables. Thus *way* for "away" (N. Smith
1973), and *[æp]* for "apple" (Menn 1977). In three-syllable words in which the
stress is on the second syllable, the first syllable is the most likely candidate for
dropping. Thus *nana* for "banana," and *mado* for "tomato." If the stress is on the
first or third syllable, the second is most likely to be dropped. Thus *tephone* for
"telephone."

(2) **Syllable reduplication.** When children hear a two-syllable word, they
may not have the motor skill to produce a second syllable distinct from the first, but
apparently it is not too difficult to repeat the syllable just uttered, so sometimes they
resort to this strategy. Thus *baba* for "bottle"; and *fafa* for "father."

(3) **Deletion of sounds.** A very common type of deletion, especially in the
very early stage, is deletion of final consonants. Thus *da* for "dog"; and *ee* for
"eat." Dropping of initial consonants and consonant clusters also occurs,
especially if the stress is not on the first syllable. Thus *apposed* for "supposed"
(produced by Quentin), *ouette* for "brouette" (French for "wheelbarrow") (Greenlee 1974). Consonant clusters must be considerably more difficult for children to
produce than simple CV syllables, because children universally reduce consonant
clusters by dropping some of the consonants. For example, when a stop consonant
is combined with another consonant, typically the stop is retained and the other
sound drops. Thus *top* for "stop," *mik* for "milk," and *bing* for "bring" (N. Smith
1973). Occasionally the reverse will be the case—Quentin habitually said *sop* for
"stop."

(4) **Addition of sounds.** Occasionally a final consonant is avoided not by
dropping the consonant but by adding a vowel so that the consonant is no longer
final. Thus *piga* for "pig." Similarly a vowel may be added to break up a consonant
cluster. Thus *pulay* for "play." This is relatively rare in child language, but very

common when nonnative speakers attempt a combination not in their native phonology.

(5) **Substitution of sounds.** Certain sounds appear to be easier for children to make in certain syllable positions. There is a tendency for final consonants to become unvoiced, for example. Thus *bak* for "bag." Children who do this have invented a phonological process that is a part of standard adult German and other languages. Another tendency is for initial fricatives and affricates to become stops (C. Ferguson 1978). The stops made are generally in the same position in the mouth as the target fricatives and affricates. It is as if children know where to put their tongue or lips; they just don't have the motor control, so they end up overshooting the tongue or lip height to produce the corresponding stop. Thus *deebra* for "zebra," *tued* for "shoes," and *doot* for "juice" (N. Smith 1973). There is also a tendency for final nasals to be replaced by the corresponding stops. Thus *pad* for "pan," and *cub* for "come." The liquids [ɹ] and [l] must be relatively hard to pronounce, because most children go through a fairly long stage replacing these with either [w] or [j]—the initial sound in "yes." Thus *wabbit* for "rabbit," and *yizzee* for "Lizzie." For many children it appears that consonants pronounced in the front of the mouth are easier than their counterparts further back. Thus *sue* for "shoe," and *tea* for "key." This process is called **fronting.** A common substitution process for vowels is for many different vowels all to be pronounced as some neutral vowel. Thus *but* for "boat," and *bub* for "bib" (D. Ingram 1976: 43; "bib" example from speech of Athena).

(6) **Assimilation of sounds.** The substitution processes described above happen without regard to other sounds in the word. Another type of phonological process is the change of a sound so that it sounds more like another sound in the same word. This is known as **assimilation.** Assimilation can be categorized in two different ways. One way is to split examples into two groups, depending on whether the earlier sound causes the later sound to change, or the later sound causes the earlier sound to change. The former is known as **progressive assimilation,** and the latter is known as **regressive assimilation.** (D. Ingram 1976: 35). Another way of categorizing assimilation is in terms of the types and relationships of the two sounds involved. This yields five categories: consonant cluster (CC—two consecutive consonants), consonant-consonant (C-C—two consonants separated by a vowel), consonant-vowel (CV), vowel consonant (VC), and vowel-vowel (V-V—two vowels separated by a consonant). These two categorizations yield a total of ten different types of assimilation.

First, consider *fweet* for "sweet." This is an example of regressive CC assimilation. The initial fricative [s], made with the tongue, has been replaced by the fricative [f], which is made with the lower lip. This means that both parts of the initial consonant cluster are made with the lips. Since the second sound has caused the first to change, it is an example of regressive assimilation.

An interesting case of such regressive CC assimilation occurred in the early speech of Quentin. It involved the initial consonant clusters [sn-] and [sm-]. In place of the [s] in these clusters, he produced voiceless nasal fricatives. Fricatives are made by narrowing the air passage somewhere in the mouth and increasing the flow of air through the narrowed passage by increasing the pressure from the chest. If you close the passage through the mouth but open it through the nose, the mouth is in the position for a nasal. If you now increase the flow of air without starting the vocal cords vibrating, just as you would do with an [s-], you can produce a friction sound through the nose—sort of a snort, but not explosive in nature. Depending upon whether this is made with the mouth in the [m] position or the [n] position, we shall symbolize these as [m̥] or [n̥]. Thus Quentin said *[m̥mɑɔ]* for "small" and *[n̥now]* for "snow." When the movement of the articulators in the mouth is described in this much detail, the reason that children tend to make use of assimilation becomes clear. It is that assimilated clusters involve less complex articulatory movements. It is simpler to say *[n̥o ɑ]* than it is to say *[sno ɑ]*.

If one considers a word-final consonant to be part of a consonant cluster consisting of that consonant followed by silence, then one can consider final consonant devoicing to be another instance of regressive CC assimilation (D. Ingram 1976: 35).

Consonant-consonant assimilation (C-C) is very common in child language. This refers to assimilation of two consonants separated by a vowel. *Goggie* is an example of regressive C-C assimilation, since the [d] was changed to be more like the following [g]. On the other hand, *noinie* for "noisy" is a case of progressive C-C assimilation, because the -*s*- (actually [-z-]) was changed to be more like the earlier [n].

Both types of consonant-vowel (CV) assimilation have been observed in children's speech; *[wɔk]* for *look* [lɔk] is an example of regressive CV assimilation. Specifically, it demonstrates the replacement of the initial consonant by the corresponding bilabial before a vowel that involves lip rounding (Carter 1978: 319). On the other hand, *Bü [by]* ([y] is the phonetic symbol for a vowel in which the mouth is in the [i] position, but the lips are rounded as they are when producing [u]) for "bee" *[bi]* would be an example of progressive CV assimilation, in which the lip rounding for the [b] was carried onto the following vowel (based on Leopold 1939: 37).

Both types of vowel-consonant assimilation (VC) have also been observed in children's speech. *Nick* for "neck" is a form of regressive VC assimilation. The tongue is raised from the [ɛ] position when followed by a [k], which requires the tongue to be raised. An example of progressive VC assimilation would be *soak* for "soap," in which the backness of the vowel carries onto the following consonant. Progressive CV and VC assimilation have been reported only rarely (Leopold 1939).

The final type of assimilation is vowel-vowel assimilation. *Naw Yawk* for "New York" is an example of regressive V-V assimilation; the first vowel is changed to agree with the second vowel (Leopold 1947). Similarly, *apa* for "apple" is an example of progressive V-V assimilation. The second vowel, which is unstressed, is changed to agree the with the stressed vowel. Children who engage in V-V assimilation are reinventing a phonological process known as **vowel harmony,** which is a part of the phonology of adult Turkish and other languages.

(7) **Reversal of sounds.** In producing their first words children often get the sounds out of their proper sequence. Three that occurred in the speech of Quentin were *aminal* for "animal," *navilla* for "vanilla," and *cinnamon* for "synonym." These each involve reversals of consonants from different parts of words. Another common reversal takes place within the same consonant cluster: *ax [æks]* for *ask [æsk]*. Sometimes children appear to adopt a consistent strategy for reversal. Some children tend to reorder those words in which the initial consonant is farther back in the mouth than the final consonant, so that all words end up being pronounced with their consonants in front-to-back order. Thus *puck* for "cup," because [p] is more frontal than [k] (D. Ingram 1974b). This may be common, but it is not universal (Menn 1975). For example, Quentin's *navilla* is a case in which the adult pronunciation is front-to-back, so that the reversal took the consonants out of that order.

(8) **Multiple processes.** The examples given above almost all involve a single phonological process. However, the most common situation, especially on the very first words, is that the words undergo more than one phonological process at the same time. In fact, it is so hard to find cases of specific processes operating in isolation that many of the examples given above had to be modified from what was actually said in order to give a pure case. More typical are such examples as *[bɔdɔ]* for "pudding" (three processes operating), *[pʌsʌ]* for "fish" (four processes operating), and even *[bap]* for "lamb" (seven processes operating) (D. Ingram 1976: 44).

Protomorphs?

One researcher, observing the development of a child named David over the period of 1;0 to 1;4, claimed to have discovered a previously unreported phenomenon. She claimed that David started out with a set of eight 'sensorimotor morphemes,' each consisting of an undifferentiated class of similar-sounding utterances marked as a single class not only by their sound similarity but also by the similarity of the accompaning gestures and goals, as perceived by the observer. Over time, these original morphemes each differentiated into two classes, both phonologically and semantically, and many branches differentiated still further, until each original morpheme had split into a set of relatively unrelated morphemes. Thus each original morpheme was the grandparent, or **protomorph,** of a family of morphemes. For example, one protomorph consisted of all syllables with the alveolar initial sounds [l-] and [d-]. The vowel that followed was quite variable. This class of sounds was accompanied by pointing to or holding out an object, and the perceived goal of the child was to draw the listener's attention to the object. This initial protomorph was hypothesized to split into an *l*-branch and a *d*-branch. The *l*-branch ultimately split into *[lʌ]* "look," *[læ]* "glass," and *[əlæoɷ]* "clown." The *d*-branch ultimately split into *[doɷ]* "dog," *[diz]* "these," *[dɪs]* "this," *[di]* "the," *[dæt]* "that," and *[dæɪ]* "there" (Carter 1978).

Due to the primitive nature of David's phonology, however, it is not clear whether the child starts out with one protomorph, as proposed, or several morphemes which just happen to start out homophonous. More objective criteria, applied to more than one child, are needed before I can accept the existence of protomorphs which evolve in tandem phonologically and semantically.

CONVERSATIONS

Even at the one-word stage, children can engage in true conversations in which two or more individuals verbally interact according to the rules of conversational interaction. Among other things, in a conversation the speaker must first obtain the listener's attention; the listener must signal in some way that he or she is giving that attention; the speaker then attempts to impart information to the listener; the listener must signal understanding or lack thereof; and the speaker must take this into account. Children at the one-word stage show evidence of learning some of what is required for the roles of both speaker and listener.

One distinction that is useful in studying conversational interaction is the **given-new** distinction (Halliday 1967b). **Given** information is information that has already occurred in the conversation; **new** information is that which has not. In adult language, each utterance by a speaker generally consists of some given information and some new information. One way of looking at this is that information is stored in a listener's head in some network-like structure. In order to add information to this structure the speaker must first locate that part of the listener's information store to which the new information is to be added. The second step is to add that information. The given portion does the locating; the new portion does the adding.

We shall consider three aspects of communication at the one-word stage in terms of the given-new distinction. The first aspect concerns the **initiation of conversation.** What does the child choose to talk about? Apparently children choose to talk about what is new to themselves. Consider the following examples (Greenfield & Smith 1976):

> A child is playing with his toy bear on the floor when he notices a block lying under the edge of the sofa. He points to it and says *Block.*

> A child is standing at the basin holding a piece of soap in her hands. As her mother turns on the tap, she says *Hot.*

> A child comes into the room, looks at one of the lights that happens to be on, and says *Light.*

In children in the one-word stage, initiation of communication appears often to be a response to a new stimulus, irrespective of whether it is new from the point of view of the speaker.

The second aspect concerns **communication response.** How do children at the one-word stage respond to questions? There appear to be two possibilities. If they understand the question and know an answer for it, they will respond appropriately, giving new information. For example (Greenfield & Smith 1976):

Mother: What do you want?
 Nicky: Shovel.

Mother: Do you want some milk?
 Nicky: Nana ("banana").

When the question is not understood or when children don't have an answer, they may respond quite differently, giving old information instead (the first report of this that I have found is in Preyer 1889: 147-148). Compare the first response with the second, both made by Allison at 1;4,21 (Bloom 1973: 163-166):

Mother: Where's the rabbit?
 Allison: Gone.

Mother: Where's dada?
 Allison: Dada.

In the first example Allison displays understanding of the question by producing an appropriate answer for it. In the other example, Allison apparently doesn't know the answer, so she responds by repeating given information—namely, the last word of the question.

The third use of given-new analysis in conversation at the one-word stage concerns communication of lack of understanding by the listener. The following example was observed in Brenda, aged 1;3 (Scollon 1974):

Brenda: Fan (looking at the electric fan).
 Mother: (No response.)

Brenda: Fan.
Mother: Hm?
Brenda: Fan.
Mother: Bathroom?
Brenda: Fan.
Mother: Fan! Yeah.
Brenda: Cool!
Mother: Cool, yeah. Fan makes you cool.

Notice that Brenda continued to repeat her remark until she was sure she had communicated, as evidenced by the fact that her mother responded with given information. Even though she is operating at the one-word stage, she seems to make use of the two steps in the process of imparting information to a listener. Looked at in this light, perhaps one can interpret Allison's given response to her mother's question as intending to convey something like "I don't have an answer to your question, but keep talking."

SUMMARY

The acquisition by children of their first words can be seen as an important and complex step in the process of learning to talk. First reference progresses from interaction involving gaze and body orientation, through gesture, to vocal communication. The first vocal reference consists of a mini-language which children teach to their caregivers. Around the first year children begin to learn the words of adult language. The meanings and uses given these words are at first very narrow, but their scope gradually broadens, guided by some early learned heuristics, which, while generally helpful, seem to make certain content areas more difficult to learn. Each word acquires a range of different meanings, which may be related to each other by chains of associations or by similarities of functional or perceptual attributes. This range of meanings may overlap, or be broader, narrower, or completely different from the range of meanings covered by the same word as the adult understands it. Only rarely will the child and adult versions be identical. Likewise the pronunciation of the first words differs considerably from adult pronunciation. While each child develops through a series of unique sets of pronunciations, these sets can be viewed as varying combinations of seven basic phonological processes. In spite of the primitive nature of the sound and meaning systems of this early language, children at the one-word stage already seem to be able to utilize some of the basic principles of conversational interaction. In the next chapter we follow children through their next great accomplishment—learning to put words together.

SUGGESTED FURTHER STUDY

BATES, ELIZABETH (1976) *Language and context: The acquisition of pragmatics.* New York: Academic Press.

GREENFIELD, PATRICIA & J. SMITH (1976)   *The structure of communication in early language development*. New York: Academic Press.

INGRAM, DAVID (1976)   *Phonological disability in children*. London: Edward Arnold.

LOCK, ANDREW (1980)   *The guided reinvention of language*. New York: Academic Press.

NELSON, KATHERINE (1973)   Structure and strategy in learning to talk. *Monographs of the Society for Research in Child Development* **38,** serial 149.

WERNER, HEINZ & B. KAPLAN (1963)   *Symbol formation*. New York: John Wiley.

THREE
PUTTING WORDS TOGETHER

TRANSITION TO TWO-WORD SENTENCES

He speaks one word nonsense and two that have nothing in them.—Thomas Fuller, *Gnomologia,* No. 2025.

About seven months after children utter their first words, they begin to put them together to form sentences (average is based on the following children: 5 mo.: Günther Stern, Togel's son; 5½ mo.: Gherogov's son I; 6 mo.: Gherogov's son II; 7 mo.: Hilda Stern, Idelberge's son; 7½ mo.: Ament's niece, Eva Stern; 8½ mo.: Lindner's son; 12 mo.: Preyer's son. Based on C. Stern & Stern 1907: excerpt p. 93). Careful observation of children during this initial onset period has revealed that there are several transition phenomena which may occur.

Comprehension of multiword commands

Children in the one-word stage appear to their parents to be able to comprehend utterances of two or more words. However, appearances can be deceiving. Several researchers have argued that children are probably only responding to a single word and perceiving the remainder of the message through the context (Bloom 1973, 1974; R. Clark et al. 1974).

Two studies appear to support the view of parents. Two children in the one-word stage were found to be able to respond appropriately to commands of the form *Give me your bottle* in which each of the roles was varied: the action (*give, show*), the indirect object (*me, mother*), the owner (*your, the baby's*), and the object (*bottle, toy*) (Huttenlocher 1974). Twelve other children in the one-word stage were instructed to respond to two-word commands, consisting of an action (*tickle, love* ["hug"], *smell, kiss*) followed by an object (*doggie, mommy, bottle, book, keys*). All children correctly obeyed at least a third of the instructions. On the average, children responded correctly 58% of the time (Sachs & Truswell 1976). Thus children appear to be able to combine the meanings of sequences of words into a single correct coherent response. However, neither of these studies used commands that required knowledge of syntax. This is because for each command there was only one possible way the meanings of the words could be combined to arrive at an instruction that the child could execute in that situation.

Another study that investigated this question suggested that children do not use syntax. In this study children were given commands in the correct order and in two scrambled orders. Children in the one-word stage and even beyond responded equally well to the commands regardless of the word order, whereas children whose language was more fluent responded significantly better when the order was syntactically correct (Whetstone & Friedlander 1973). Unfortunately, this study does not prove that children don't have knowledge of syntax; only that they don't seem to be affected if the order of words heard is out of the ordinary.

A better study would be one that involved utterances that required one to attend to syntax in order to differentiate between two different interpretations. Syntax would be needed, for example, to correctly differentiate *Doggie kick* from *Kick doggie,* or *Give mommy baby's drink* from *Give baby mommy's drink.* Unfortunately, this experiment has not yet been performed.

Dummy forms

A second type of transition phenomenon is the occurrence at this stage of **dummy forms.** Dummy forms are defined by two properties:

1. They are variable phonologically.
2. They have no obvious referents.

These units sometimes consist of a single sound. One infant habitually inserted one of a set of five different vowel sounds ([ə], [a], [i] [ɪ], and [æ]) before a word, thus extending the utterance phonologically, but adding no detectable meaning. Thus the child said "[ə] more" and "[i] ball."

Other children develop more complex dummy units. One child developed a dummy form consisting of a consonant followed by a vowel, but other than this structure, there were no obvious constraints. This child produced "[dæ] bottle," "[mʌ] bottle," "[tɛ] bottle," and "[wə] bottle." Again, there was no obvious referent (Dore et al. 1976: 21).

Empty forms

A related phenomenon is the occurrence of **empty forms.** An empty form is like a dummy form in that it has no discernable meaning, but differs in that it has a stable phonological form. An example of an empty form is [wɪdə], which Allison used in a wide diversity of situations. Again it seems to extend a sentence beyond one word phonologically, without adding any perceptible meaning. Thus Allison said: *mama [wɪdə], dada [wɪdə], uh oh [wɪdə],* and *no [wɪdə]* (Bloom 1973: 35). Another child had a similar empty form, in this case *[ɪdi]* (Menyuk 1969).

For an observer to decide that a word has been produced by a child, she or he must match the phonological form the child produced with some adult word. If the child's form is a reasonable reduction of some adult word phonologically, and if it is reasonable to say that the child wished to convey an approximation of that meaning, then the observer says that that word has been uttered. If the observer cannot think of a word close enough to the child's form then she or he may postulate that it is a dummy or empty form. But it may be that the observer just didn't figure out what the child meant to say. According to one researcher, this may be the case for Allison's [wɪdə]. This person suggested that [wɪdə] might have been Allison's way of saying "Allison," much modified by the application of a total of 8 phonological rules common to children in this stage (D. Ingram 1978:273-274). I tend to doubt this analysis, because one of the rules involves deletion of the first syllable of *Allison*—the one with the primary stress in the adult form. In my experience this syllable would be the least likely to go. But the criticism still stands that the existence of these forms is based solely on negative evidence—on the inability of observers to figure out what the child might be saying.

Reduplications

Another type of transition phenomenon is two-word sentences in which a single word is repeated twice within a single intonation pattern. Thus a child looked out of a window, and, seeing a single car pass by, uttered *Car car* (Dore et al. 1976: 22). This, too, has the effect of sounding like a longer utterance without carrying any additional meaning. It reminds one of syllable reduplication within words so that they more closely match the rhythm of the word attempted (see Chapter 2).

Pseudophrases

During this stage one can also find what appear to be two-word sentences, but which appear not to be so from the point of view of the child. For example, one child had the sentence *No more.* Although that child had both *no* and *more* in its vocabulary, neither of the two words ever appeared in combination with other words to form sentences, such as *No house* or *Want more.* A more reasonable explanation is not that the independent form *no* combined with the independent form *more,* but rather that *No more* was learned as a single indivisible unit. Thus in spite of its appearance to an adult, *No more* is probably best considered to be a one-word sentence from the point of view of the child.

Partially bound word sequences

Many children go through a state in which they produce what subjectively appear to be two or more successive single-word utterances which belong together in terms of the meaning expressed (Dore 1975; Guillaume 1927; Rodgon 1976). For example, Allison at 1;7 took a pot from the shelf in the stove and 'stirred' with her hand, saying, "Cook. Baby." The adult present responded, "Is the baby cooking?" Allison replied, "Pot. Meat" (Bloom 1973: 41). It is as if children find that they have two roles that they wish to express about a particular event, but possessing no sentence syntax adequate to bring the two roles together, they express them by means of a sequence of two one-word sentences.

These utterances have been considered to consist of sequences of single words rather than the first two-word utterances. Three properties mark words that are bound together as a phrase or sentence unit: There are no distinct pauses between the words; they share an overall intonation contour which is marked by a fall on the last word of the utterance; and nonfinal words are shortened relative to final words and single word utterances.

A phonetic study of these partially bound words in three children has found that although they are separated by distinct pauses of between 400 and 1100 msec, and thus sound subjectively like separate utterances, they share an overall intonation contour (see Table 3.1), and the nonfinal words are shortened (see Table 3.2) (Branigan 1979). Thus there is evidence that these words are bound together and should be considered true two-word utterances.

Bloom has reported that at this stage there was no consistent order to Allison's partially bound word sequences. However, in one study of 65 successive one-word utterances produced by children looking at pictures, they do appear to order these

TABLE 3.1 Mean Fundamental Frequency Level at the Ends of Words in Three Utterance Types

	SINGLE FINAL	SUCCESSIVE NON FINAL	SUCCESSIVE FINAL	MULTIPLE NON FINAL	MULTIPLE FINAL
Jonathan	196	215	190	232	192
Benjamin	198	237	207	260	202
David	188	254	197	237	187

Adapted from Branigan 1979: Table 1. © Cambridge University Press. Used by permission.

TABLE 3.2 Mean Duration in msec of Monosyllabic Words in Isolation and Non Final Words in Two Other Utterance Types

	SINGLE	SUCCESSIVE	MULTIPLE
Jonathan	458	401	196
Benjamin	521	400	305
David	678	353	300

Adapted from Branigan 1979: Table 3. © Cambridge University Press. Used by permission.

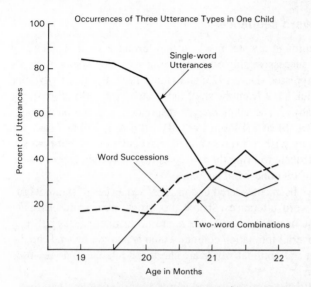

FIGURE 3.1   **Relative proportions of single-word utterances, word succes-
sions and two-word combinations in one child. (From Garman
1979: 187, based on Branigan 1976)**

sequences in a more consistent manner than would be accounted for by chance
(Horton 1976). Furthermore, Branigan, who had access to Bloom's tapes, has
reported that such partially bound word sequences continued to occur in Allison's
speech after she had begun to use syntax (see Figure 3.1). Thus the use of partially
bound sequences does not seem to be due solely to lack of syntax. The reason for
their occurrence, especially after regular utterances of two words and longer are
uttered, remains a mystery.

   Thus there are six phenomena associated with the transition to two-word
sentences: early comprehension, dummy forms, empty forms, word reduplications,
pseudophrases, and partially bound word sequences. Within any one child one may
find some or all of these phenomena. In fact, in cases in which more than one of
these occur in the same child, one can sometimes find examples of combinations
within the same sentence. Thus *[ə wɪdə]*, a dummy form followed by an empty
form, occurred several times in Allison's speech (Bloom 1973: 35). Similarly, *[ə]
book book*, a dummy form followed by a word reduplication, occurred in the speech
of another child (Dore et al. 1976: 22).

SENTENCE LENGTH

Finally each child arrives at his or her first two-word sentence. The age of occurrence of the first two-word sentence appears to range from 1;3 to 2, with a mean age
of 17½ months (National Society . . . 1929). The children on whom these figures
are based were not systematically selected from the general population, so it is
likely that the range is, in fact, considerably broader, particularly in the upper limit.

   From this point onward, children's sentences grow in complexity continuously until maturity. A relatively objective measure of this growth is a count of the number of words in a sentence. Figure 3.2 charts this growth from age 1½ to age 9½, as collected from four studies, named on the figure. One possibility for differences in results between the study by Davis and that by Templin may be differences in child-rearing practices in the decades in which the studies took place (McCarthy 1954: 545). Other explanations may involve differences in sampling procedures and differences in the responsiveness of the adult listener.

FIGURE 3.2
Growth of sentence length in words with age.

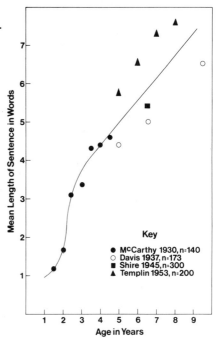

Roger Brown with (l. to r.) Eve, Adam, and Sarah.

In the 1960's, the distinguished Harvard psychologist Roger Brown began an intensive longitudinal study of three children, whom he named Adam, Eve, and Sarah. When comparing the language development of these three children, he found that they developed their language at different chronological ages and at different rates, as shown in Figure 3.3. However, he found that they each went through roughly the same sequence of stages. He also found that he needed a relatively objective quantitative measure which would help him relate the development of one child to that of another.

Instead of using the mean length of utterance in words, he chose mean length of utterance in morphemes, which he felt would be a more sensitive measure. **Morpheme** is a term used by linguists to describe the minimum unit of speech to which one can ascribe a distinct meaning or function. A single word may be a morpheme, but often a word will consist of more than one morpheme. For example, *sudden* is a single morpheme, but *suddenly* consists of two morphemes—*sudden* and *-ly,* a morpheme that has the function of making an adverb out of an adjective. Similarly, *rearrangements* consists of four morphemes—*re- arrange -ment -s.* Occasionally a morpheme may consist of more than one typographic word. One example is *um pa pa,* as in *The band specializes in um pa pa music.*

What might constitute a morpheme for an adult may not be a morpheme for a child. For an adult, *outside* would consist of two morphemes, *out* and *side.* But a child may learn the word before she or he learns an independent meaning for either

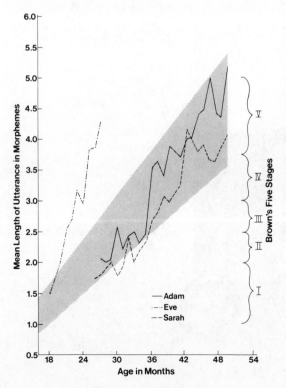

FIGURE 3.3
Growth in mean length of utterance in morphemes with age. The shaded portion represents the middle 68% of 123 middle-class children in Madison, Wisconsin. The three jagged lines show the MLUs of Adam, Eve, and Sarah, the three children studied by Roger Brown and his students. (Adapted from J. Miller & Chapman 1979, cited in J. Miller 1981 [©PRO-ED Inc. Used by permission.] and from R. Brown et al. 1969 [©University of Minnesota Press. Used by permission.]

of its parts. For such children *outside* consists of one morpheme. Because extensive evidence is needed to determine whether a word consists of one morpheme or two in the linguistic system of the child, Brown developed some relatively arbitrary rules of thumb for counting morphemes. These rules are given in Box 3.1 (R. Brown et al. 1969; R. Brown 1973: 54; see Crystal 1974: 294-300 for a criticism of Brown's rules).

BOX 3.1 *RULES FOR CALCULATING MEAN LENGTH OF UTTERANCE*

> 1. Start with the second page of the transcription unless that page involves a recitation of some kind. In this latter case start with the first recitation-free stretch. Count the first 100 utterances satisfying the following rules.
> 2. Only fully transcribed utterances are used. Portions of utterances containing transcription uncertainties are used.
> 3. Include all exact utterance repetitions. Stuttering is marked as repeated efforts at a single word; count the word once in the most complete form produced. Where a word is repeated for emphasis or the like (*no, no, no*) count each occurrence.
> 4. Do not count such fillers as *mm* or *oh*, but do count *no, yeah,* and *hi.*
> 5. All compound words (two or more free morphemes), proper names, and ritualized reduplications count as single words so long as there is no evidence that the constituent morphemes function as such for the child. Examples: *birthday, racketyboom, choo-choo, quack-quack, night-night, pocketbook, see-saw.*
> 6. Count as one morpheme all irregular past tense verbs (*got, did, went, saw*). Justification is that there is no evidence that the child relates these to present forms.
> 7. Count as one morpheme all diminutives (*doggie, mommie*) so long as children do not seem to use the suffix productively. Diminutives are the standard forms used by young children.
> Count as separate morphemes all auxiliaries (*is, have, will, can, must, would*). Catenatives such as *gonna, wanna,* and *hafta* are counted as single morphemes rather than as *going to, want to,* and *have to,* because they function as single units for the children. Count as separate morphemes all inflections, for example, possessive [-s], plural [-s], third person singular [-s], progressive [-ɪŋ].
>
> Adapted from Brown 1973: 54. © 1973 Harvard University Press. Reprinted by permission.

Consider the following example:

> Daddy coming. Hi, car. Daddy car comed. Two car outside. It getting dark. Allgone outside. Bye-bye outside.

According to Roger Brown's rules, this sample of seven sentences would have the following sentence lengths in morphemes: 3, 2, 4, 3, 4, 2, 2. The suffixes *-ing* and *-ed* are treated as separate morphemes. On the other hand, *allgone* is treated as one morpheme if, as we have assumed here, neither *all* nor *gone* appear separately. The mean length of utterance in morphemes is computed by dividing the total number of morphemes (20) by the number of sentences (7). This yields a mean length of 2.86.

Using this measure Brown divided the speech samples of his children somewhat arbitrarily into five stages. Table 3.3 gives these stages. He and his students

TABLE 3.3   Brown's Five Stages

STAGE	APPROX. MLU	TYPICAL AGE
I	1.75	22 mos
II	2.25	28 mos
III	2.75	32 mos
IV	3.50	41 mos
V	4.00	45 mos

then wrote grammars for each of the three children in each of the five stages. Analyses of these sample utterances have resulted in many articles and papers, and have provided a useful foundation on which the study of the syntax of the utterances of young children has been largely based. Because of the importance of the work of Brown and his students, mean length of utterance, or MLU for short, is generally taken to be mean length of utterance in morphemes as defined by Brown's rules of thumb.

CHARACTERIZATIONS OF EARLY SENTENCES

Productivity

One of the most striking facts about child language is its productivity. By this is meant that it is clear quite early that children do not put words together only if they have heard those words in combination before, not even when they first begin to put words together. Rather we find that children often produce utterances which they have never heard before. When a child looks out of the window, finds that it is dark, and utters, *Allgone outside* (Braine 1963a), we know that the child did not come up with that utterance by imitating an utterance that was made by an adult, but rather by learning some general principles of word combination and applying them to the vocabulary he knew. This is one of the basic facts that makes the study of children's language so interesting, and also makes it such a challenging task for the researcher.

Telegraphic speech

Another way that early child language has been characterized is that early sentences appear to be very much like telegrams. Because telegraph companies often charge by the word, when one sends a telegram one tries to eliminate as many of the words as possible while still retaining the essence of what must be communicated.

Suppose, for example, one wishes to communicate: *My wallet has been stolen. Therefore I need money. Please send me $500 in care of American Express Copenhagen.* The telegram would look something like this: *Wallet stolen. Send $500 American Express Copenhagen.* The words that are retained are content words, such as nouns and verbs; the words that are lost are most often function words, such as pronouns (*I, me*), articles (*a, the*), prepositions (*in, of*), conjunctions (*and, but*) and verbal auxiliaries (*have, be, may*). Early child language appears to be very similar. In general, content words such as nouns and verbs are uttered, while other words are not.

As a general characterization, the term telegraphic speech seems quite apt, but one should be cautioned from taking the analogy too literally. For one thing, children tend to omit inflections, such as the plural ending on nouns, the past tense and perfect tense endings on verbs, or the -*s* that appears on verbs when they are used with third-person singular subjects in the present tense. These inflections are retained by adults in telegrams, as the telegraph companies don't charge extra for them.

Another difference is that not all function words are omitted. There are three types of function words which are likely to be used quite early in children's speech. The first is personal pronouns, especially first and second person (*I, me,* and *you*) and their possessive adjectives (*my, mine, your, yours*). Unlike many function words, these words have relatively clear referents, and are useful to communicate some of the basic roles in discourse, such as agent and affected, and the concept of objects belonging to individuals, which occurs quite early. The acquisition of these terms is discussed in more detail in Chapter 4.

A second class of function words used quite early is the demonstrative pronouns *this* and *that*. These pronouns serve a function in adult speech that corresponds to children's first referential utterances (see Chapter 2), and thus are among the first words used. These words, too, can be used to refer to the basic roles children first communicate. They are also discussed in more detail in Chapter 4.

A third class is verb particles, such as *up* in *get up, down* in *put down, off* in *take off,* or *on* in *put on.* Often the particles are used in place of the entire verb-particle unit instead of the verb alone, as might be expected. There are at least three reasons why this happens. One is that such particles often convey the main stress in the sentence. When a caregiver says *Let me pick you up,* the main sentence stress is on the *up.* A second reason is that such words are often the last word in a sentence. There is reason to believe that the last word is more salient than other words in a sentence. The third reason is that the verbs such as *get, put,* and *take* often have very general and vague meanings, which are probably difficult for the child to extract, whereas the meanings of *up, down, off,* and so on, are easier to understand. The use of a verb particle in place of the verb is especially noticeable in children who are learning German, which makes much greater use of verb-particle constructions than does English (Park 1970a).

Another trap in the telegraphic speech analogy is that in composing a telegram adults start with a complete utterance and eliminate function words. One can take the analogy too literally and suggest that children have more developed syntax than they show, but due to limited memory children express only part of the syntactic form they have available to them. Most observers now believe that children use telegraphic speech because they have not mastered the other parts of the syntax rather than because of any memory limitations.

The aptness of the characterization of early speech as telegraphic remains, though modified by the above caveats, and applies not only to English, but to early speech in other languages as well. If one measures development in terms of the percentage of function morphemes present, one finds a consistent picture across languages. In English the percentage is in the 6% to 16% range (R. Brown 1973: 78); in Finnish it has been measured at 3% to 10% (Bowerman 1973a). Similar findings have been reported for French (Grégoire 1937: 84), German (Park 1970a), Hebrew (Bar-Adon 1971), Japanese (McNeill 1966a), Korean (Park 1970b), Luo (Blount 1969), Mandarin (Chao 1951), Russian (Slobin 1966), Samoan (Kernan 1969), and Swedish (Rydin 1971). Thus as a global impression of early child speech, its description as telegraphic appears both apt and universal.

Pivot/open speech

The first people to study the two-word stage found that there appeared to be a consistent pattern to these early sentences. This pattern has come to be known as a **pivot grammar** (Braine 1963a). Although the child may have a vocabulary of 50 or more words, the first two-word sentences seemed to be such that one of the words usually seemed to come from a very small set of words. These were termed **pivot words.** The other word in the sentence came from the remaining words in the child's vocabulary. This larger set of words was known as the **open class set.**

Several characteristics have been proposed to distinguish pivot words from open class words (see van der Geest 1974: 16-24 for a comparison of different versions of the pivot/open distinction):

1. Pivot words are more frequent than open class words.
2. The pivot class has only a few members.
3. Pivot words always occur in the same position in the sentence—some only occur initially; others only finally.
4. Pivot words do not occur by themselves as one-word sentences.
5. A two-word sentence never consists of two pivot words.
6. Each pivot word can be combined with any open class word.
7. Nouns and verbs tend to be in the open class.

One of the first children looked at from this point of view was Andrew. During the first five months of speech Andrew's two-word sentences seemed to fit the notion of pivot/open class sentences (Braine 1963a: 5). They included the sentences shown in Table 3.4. A pivot/open description of such sentences would be that *all, more,* and *off* are pivot words, while all the remaining words are in the open class. The first two pivots occur only in initial position; the third occurs only in final position.

TABLE 3.4 Some of Andrew's pivot/open sentences.

all broke	more car	boot off
all clean	more cereal	light off
all dressed	more hot	pants off
all fix	more high	shoe off
all through	more sing	water off

Initially a number of researchers felt that a pivot/open framework fit early child language well (Braine 1963a; R. Brown & Fraser 1963; Jenkins & Palermo 1964; McNeill 1966a; W. Miller & Ervin 1964; Slobin 1970). However, later research has indicated that the pivot/open distinction does not hold up as a description of early sentence-forming behavior (e.g., Blount 1969; Kernan 1969; Park 1970a, 1970b; Rydin 1971). For example, when five Dutch children were studied from the pivot/open point of view, it was found that most of the characteristics distinguishing pivot words tended to be violated or useless (Van der Geest 1974: 33-50).

Table 3.5 shows the 14 most frequent words in the speech of Hester in her first six months of speech. For each word are provided its English translation, frequency of occurrence in the samples, part of speech, and whether it occurs in each of three syntactic positions: alone as a one-word sentence, in initial position, and in second position.

TABLE 3.5   Hester's 14 Most Frequent Words

WORD	TRANSLATION	FREQUENCY	PART OF SPEECH	POSITION IN SENTENCE		
				ALONE	FIRST	SECOND
pakken	take	30	verb	yes	yes	yes
Hester	Hester	27	noun	yes	yes	yes
daar	there	24	adverb	yes	yes	yes
ditte	this	18	pronoun	yes	yes	yes
koeke	cake	17	noun	yes	yes	yes
maken	make	16	verb	no	yes	yes
eten	eat	15	verb	yes	yes	yes
deze	this	14	pronoun	yes	yes	yes
open	open	14	adjective	yes	yes	yes
mama	mommy	13	noun	yes	yes	yes
ook	also	11	adverb	no	yes	yes
in	in	11	preposi- tion	yes	no	yes
is	is	10	copula	no	yes	yes
zitten	sit	10	verb	yes	yes	yes

Compiled from van der Geest—1974: 36, 38.

This table demonstrates some of the problems with the pivot/open framework. There is no sharp boundary between high frequency and low frequency words; rather, it is a smoothly declining curve. Pivots are supposed to occur in one or the other position in a two-word sentence, but not in both; nor should they occur as one-word utterances. Over half of the 14 most frequent are nouns and verbs, which are supposed to be in the lower-frequency open class.

Those characteristics which are not refuted by Hester's utterances can be refuted by studying the utterances of other children. Evie was one of the first children analyzed in this framework (R. Brown & Fraser 1963). In her pivot class are the words *see, that,* and *'s* (probably meaning "it is"). Yet Evie says *See that,* thus violating characteristics 3 and 5. And there is no evidence supporting the notion that *see* or *'s* can precede any of the verbs in the open class, as would be required by characteristic 6.

It is clear that the pivot/open framework doesn't fit all children. If the data of the original pivot/open framework children were reanalyzed, it would very likely be found that it never fit anybody very well (Bloom 1970; Bowerman 1973a; van der Geest 1974). As Roger Brown said, "All this makes one suspect that none of the children . . . , not even Gregory, Andrew, and Steven [the children studied originally by Braine] really had a pivot grammar" (R. Brown 1973: 101).

More detailed analyses of sentence form have led to more sophisticated insights into early multi-word sentence structure, and it is to these that we now turn our attention.

TWO-WORD UTTERANCES

Word order

Although the notion of a pivot/open stage in child speech can be rejected, one frequent finding about word order is that for most children it is fixed. English-speaking children at the two-word stage almost always put the subject of the sentence before the verb, and the verb before the object, for example.

Adult English has a relatively fixed word order. That is, if the order is changed, often so is the meaning changed. Thus *Fathers enjoy babies* means something quite different from *Babies enjoy fathers*. Many other languages have a much freer word order. Usually this is because the syntactic information that is in English conveyed by word order is in these other languages conveyed by suffixes or other word inflections.

How do children learning these freer word order languages handle word order? In general, they appear to adopt a relatively strict word order, just as do children learning English. Generally it is the word order that is most frequent in the speech of their parents. Across the languages studied thus far, SUBJECT—VERB—OBJECT (SVO) seems to be the order adapted most often.

But there are exceptions. One child learning Russian first started with a SUBJECT—OBJECT—VERB (SOV) order, then later switched to a SVO order. Rina, a Finnish child, used a consistent SVO order, while Seppo, another Finnish child, varied sentence order frequently (Bowerman 1973a). In one study, three children learning German actually used a wider range of word orders than was acceptable in adult German (Park, as cited in R. Brown 1973).

Even in English occasionally a child will go through a stage of relatively free word order. This apparently happened to Gregory during the month following his second birthday (Braine 1971). This **groping pattern** can be described as follows (Braine 1976: 11): It occurs when a child tries to express a particular meaning combination never attempted in a multiword utterance; it only involves a few word combinations; and it is produced haltingly—that is, with repetitions and hesitations. Sometimes it is even produced in a 'circular' fashion: Braine's son Jonathan at two years produced: *In there . . . old apple . . . in there . . . old apple.* Another example was: *All wet . . . mommy . . . all wet* (" . . . " indicates hesitation).

Functions and roles

The analysis of word order involves putting words into categories and comparing utterances to see if words in similar categories appear in the same position in different sentences. In the previous section the categories SUBJECT, VERB, and OBJECT were used. But are these the most appropriate categories? A more careful analysis not only involves looking at such syntactic categories, but also involves looking at different functions expressed by these early utterances, and the roles used by children to express them.

Unfortunately, no one is sure how best to classify these functions and roles. First consider functions. Different observers of child language have arrived at different lists (R. Brown 1970a: 220; 1973: 166ff; H. Clark & Clark 1977: 315; Dale 1976: 40; Slobin 1970: 178-179). The lists vary as to whether they are intended to list all types observed or just most, as to whether evidence for the type occurs in more than one language, and as to how detailed the observer wishes to make the categories. Table 3.6 gives such a list in hierarchical form. One can talk about two functional categories (**Assertion** and **Request**), five categories, and so on up to 20 or more.

TABLE 3.6 Categorization of Utterance Types

Assertion	
Comment on object	
Nomination	*That car.*
Notice	*See boy.*
Presence	
First notice	*Hi belt.*
Denial of presence	*No wet. Not hungry.*
Disappearance	*Byebye hot. Allgone outside.*
Recurrence	*More green. 'Nother dog.*
Description	
Attributive	*Pretty dress. Big train.*
Possessive	*Mommy sock. My shoe. For daddy.*
Locative	*Sweater chair.*
Classificatory	*Mommy lady.*
Two objects	*Kimmy Phil.*
Comment on event	
Agent-action	*Eve read.*
Action-affected	*Put book.*
Agent-affected	*Mommy sock.*
Action-location	*Walk street.*
Action-instrument	*Sweep broom.*
Action-comitative	*Go mommy. ("Go with mommy.")*
Experiencer-experience	*Kimmy see.*
Request	
For action	
Provide object	*Want gum.*
Repeat event	*More taxi.*
For information	*Where ball?*
Refusal	*No more.*

There is evidence for the major dichotomy—between assertions and requests—in the speech of a few children. Nigel at 1;7 and for several months thereafter produced all requests with a rising tone, and all assertions with a falling tone (Halliday 1975: 46). Another child made a similar distinction in the use of the word *that*. Used with one intonation *that* was a request for the name of the object pointed to; with another intonation it was used as an assertion (Griffiths 1974). Aside from this limited evidence, the categorization has been based on the intuition of the observer rather than on inference from distributional or other data. The choice of categories is thus quite controversial.

The same is true for roles. When a child says *Boy kick*, should the utterance be described as AGENT—ACTION or as ANIMATE-BEING—MOVEMENT? Do all verbs of action constitute one category in the mind of the child, or are there separate categories for whole body movement—such as *slide, go,* and *ride*—and part body movement—such as *hit, kick,* and *touch?* The categories used by the child to generate sentences may differ from adult categories in the same way that child meanings may differ from adult meanings. Relative to adult categories, the child's category may theoretically be identical, more specific, more general, overlapping, entirely non-overlapping, non-existent, or totally unrelated to any adult class. How might one determine which of these possibilities actually occurs in language development?

A particularly careful analysis of this question was performed by Braine on the utterances of his son Jonathan at age two. Among other patterns, he found a consistent ATTRIBUTE—OBJECT formation for a number of different attributes. As shown in Table 3.7, Jonathan used *big, little, hot, blue, red, hurt,* and *old* consistently, but not *wet*. This suggests that Jonathan was not making use of a general framework of ATTRIBUTE—OBJECT, but rather either learning sentence patterns on a word-by-word basis, or at least using much narrower categories—perhaps SIZE—OBJECT, COLOR—OBJECT, and so on (Braine 1976: 33-35).

One child, Eva, has been reported to have developed early syntax such that

TABLE 3.7   Some of Jonathan's Attribute-Object Sentences

big shell	little shell	hot sand	hurt Andrew
big hot	little wet	hot ball	hurt fly
big water	little water	blue shirt	hurt knee
big step	little step	red balloon	hurt plane
big jump	little split	old cookie	hurt hand
big tobacco	little hurt	old apple	blue stick
all wet . . water . . all wet			
all wet pants			
all wet . . mommy . . all wet			
daddy all wet daddy all wet			
all wet ball			
shirt wet			
wet nose			
shoe wet			
wet diaper			

From Braine—1976: 34.

each word had its own possibilities of occurrence. Thus each word formed its own unique class (Bowerman 1976, 1982: 333).

Order of emergence

Do all children acquire different sentence types in the same developmental sequence? The answer seems to be that general trends can be found, but one can also find some children who have a different order of acquisition. The general sequence of acquisition proceeds roughly as follows (Bloom et al. 1975a: 95-96; Braine 1976; Leonard 1976: 113):

1. Expressions of reference.
   That car.
2. Expressions of events.
   Eva read.
3. Expressions of attribution, location, and possession.
   Big water.
   Stick car.
   Andrew book.
4. Expressions of experiencing and instrument.
   Kimmy see.
   Eat fork.

Stress pattern

In two-word utterances one of the two words is almost always stressed more than the other (Wieman 1976). One factor that seems to determine which word gets the greater stress is information focus. In Chapter 2 it was pointed out that even at the one-word stage children appear to understand how to apply the distinction between given and new information to control a conversation. In two-word utterances this distinction explains many decisions as to which word to stress. In utterances in which one word is given information and the other is new information, it is the new information which receives the greater stress. This is illustrated in a pair of examples from the speech of one child. Though the sentence forms are similar and both are answers to questions, the child varies the stress to place it on that which is new (Griffiths 1974).

Adult: Which is baby?
Child: THAT baby.

Adult: What's this?
Child: That MUMMY'S.

New information is almost always last in the sentence, but there are exceptions. For example, when a question is answered, the answer may follow the order of the question (Wieman 1976: 285):

Mother: What's in the street?
David [2;1]: FIRE TRUCK street.

And when a sentence is built up in stages, the new information may not be last (Wieman 1976: 286):

Seth [1;9]:   BALL. NICE ball. ORANGE ball.

When both words in a sentence are new, or both are given, other aspects of the utterance determine which word is stressed. There appears to be a precedence order:

1st: New information; contrasting information.
2nd: LOCATIVE; POSSESSIVE.
3rd: NOUN OBJECT.
4th: ACTION.
5th: PRONOUN OBJECT.
Last: AGENT.

Whichever word in a two-word utterance is higher on the above list, that word receives the greater stress. Here are some examples:

ACTION—LOCATIVE	Goes HERE.
POSSESSIVE—OBJECT	ELEPHANT'S foot.
ACTION—NOUN OBJECT	Hit BALL.
ACTION—PRONOUN OBJECT	KICK it.
AGENT—ACTION	Mommy FALL.

In spite of the new use to which the given-new distinction is put, children at the two-word stage continue to make use of given as a signal to continue, just as they did at the one-word stage (E. Keenan 1974a):

David (2;9. Alarm clock rings.):   Oh oh oh, bell.
Toby (David's twin brother):   Bell.
David: Bell. It's Mommy's.
Toby: (mumbles)
David: Was Mommy's alarm clock.
Toby: (no response)
David: Was Mommy's alarm clock.
Toby: Alarm clock.
David: Yeah. Goes ding dong. Ding dong.

A memory limitation?

One researcher, Lois Bloom (1970: 70-74), noted that the early speech of Kathryn (when her MLU was 1.32) contained sentences of three types: AGENT—ACTION; ACTION—OBJECT; and AGENT—OBJECT. It appeared as if Kathryn had the ability to make use of the sentence frame AGENT—ACTION—OBJECT, but that she never used it. Bloom suggested that such three-item sentences existed in the mind of the child, but that only two of the items were produced. If Kathryn mentally understood the three-item sentence frame, why didn't she use it? One possibility is that a child just beginning to produce two-word utterances has memory limitations that require reducing sentences to two words.

There are problems with this explanation. For one thing, Kathryn can produce three- and four-word sentences. The following sentences were all produced by Kathryn at this stage (Bloom 1970: 46-49, 70, 75-77):

Me show Mommy.
[Ma]chine make noise.
Man ride a bus.
Kathryn want raisin.
I comb pigtail.
Mommy do it.
Mommy throw it away.
Two sheep sit down.
Make him sit down.
Many shirts hot.
No pocket in there.
Where the spider?

If there is a memory limitation, how can she produce these three- and four-word sentences?

Furthermore, the memory explanation does not predict which word in the three-item string will not be produced. One can, however, find patterns in the missing words. Consider these examples:

Mommy [ə] muffin man ("Mommy, sing Muffin Man").
Wendy cottage cheese ("Wendy [is] eat[ing] cottage cheese")

In both cases the missing word was not produced in any other utterance of the child (Kathryn had *ate* in her vocabulary, but not *eat*—Bloom 1970: 246-247). This suggests that the child describes action not in her vocabulary by expressing that portion of the sentence whose vocabulary she knows. That this strategy is at least sometimes successful is shown by the fact that the above two sentences could be interpreted by her listeners. Thus one reason words are missing is that the child doesn't yet know them.

Next, consider these:

Helping squish ("I helping squish").
Touch milk ("I touch milk").

Another component often missing is a name for herself when she is the agent of the sentence. This is not a case of not knowing a name for herself, because she in fact has two ways of referring to herself when she is indicating possession—*Kathryn* and *Baby* (Bloom 1970:58):

> Kathryn raisin ("These are Kathryn's raisins").
> Baby raisin ("These are Baby's raisins").

The sentence frame calls for the first person pronoun *I*, however. If she has not mastered *I*, but she knows that calling herself by a name isn't appropriate, then one strategy for her to adopt is to delete a reference to herself when she is the agent.

Another strategy can be used to explain these examples:

> More raisin ("I want more raisins").
> Mommy push ("I want Mommy to push").

Though gestures are not usually described in Bloom's book, I suspect that "I want" is obvious from some gesture, such as an outstretched hand, or from a pleading intonation. Thus to say *I want* is redundant. At four years old my daughter still reverted at times to this form of baby talk when she wanted something, in spite of our attempts to discourage it by pretending not to understand, and not rewarding her until she said *Please may I have* . . .

Many of the remaining examples of missing items can be described as given information—places where adults would use pronouns:

> Mommy diaper. Fold up. ("Mommy, you have a diaper. *You* are folding it up.")
> Mommy sock. [də] dirty. ("Mommy has the socks. *They* are dirty.")

Kathryn: Jocelyn cheek. ("Look at Jocelyn's cheek")
Mother: What happened to Jocelyn cheek?
Kathryn: [ə] cry. ("*She* cried.")

It appears that rather than being due to memory limitations, the shortness of early utterances may be due to lack of knowledge of specific verbs and pronouns, and other linguistic reasons (Bloom recognizes the inadequacy of her 1970 proposal; see Bloom et al. 1975b; Bloom 1984).

Along the same lines is another study which explored the question of why, after children have acquired facility for multiword sentences, they still continue to use many one-word utterances. It appears that part of the answer lies in the concept of change of focus. When children happen upon an object not noticed or used immediately previously, or an act newly begun, they tend to begin talking on the new topic by producing a one-word sentence naming the object or act (Leonard & Schwartz 1978).

THE EMERGENCE OF LONGER SENTENCES

The use of sentences that are longer than two words follows quickly after the first use of two-word sentences. Occasional three- and even four-word sentences appear even when the child's MLU is only 1.33. An MLU of 1.33 occurs when two-thirds of the utterances are one-word sentences and one third are two-word sentences. Thus children have hardly moved out of the one-word stage when they begin to put together longer sentences. The most common types of three-word sentences are given in Table 3.8, roughly in the order of their frequency. Within the list are general types. Numbers 1, 2, and 4 are sentences involving three roles in an event. The others involve two roles, with one of the roles expanded into a two-word phrase.

TABLE 3.8   The Most Common Types of Early Three-Word Sentences

TYPE	EXAMPLE
1. agent-action-object	Mommy eat cookie.
2. agent-action-locative	Mommy sit chair.
3. demonstrative-entity (2)	That big ball.
4. action-object-locative	See doggie window.
5. action-object (2)	Watch pretty bird.
6. agent (2)-locative	Dirty doggie stuck.
7. entity (2)-locative	Kathryn raisin pocket.

Based on Brown—1973: 174-175.

When sentences contain more than two words, one can begin to ask whether these sentences have any **hierarchical structure.** In other words, is there any evidence that two of the three words are more closely bound together than either is to the third word?

Most linguists find reasons for claiming that adult sentences have hierarchical structure. For example, in a sentence like *Mommy ate cookies,* the verb *eat* is considered closer to *cookie* than to *Mommy.* This point of view can be diagrammed as shown in Figure 3.4.

How might one determine whether there is any evidence supporting such a structure in children? If ACTION—OBJECT is more tightly bound than AGENT—ACTION, one might expect to find more of the former among children's two-word sentences (McNeill 1970). For some children this seems to be the case (Bloom 1970; Brown 1973), but for others the reverse is true (Bowerman 1973a, 1973b).

FIGURE 3.4   Hierarchical structure postulated for Mommy eat cookie.

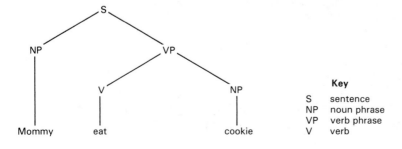

Key
S   sentence
NP   noun phrase
VP   verb phrase
V   verb

Other suggestive evidence might come from what has been called **buildup.** In buildup, a child utters a sentence, then repeats it in an expanded form:

> Ate cake. Mommy ate cake.

If buildup tended to be in complete constituent units, this would constitute evidence in favor of hierarchical structure. In buildup, predicates tend to appear as complete units (Braine 1971), but there are exceptions (Bowerman 1973b: 204)—see Table 3.9. Although there is some support for the notion of hierarchical order in children's three-word sentences, it is not very persuasive.

Another idea contained in the diagram in Figure 3.4 is the notion that both AGENT and OBJECT are expressable by the same set of syntactic constructions— namely, the set known as NOUN PHRASE. While this may be true for adult speakers, it is not true for children at this stage. For them, the set of noun phrases that can be agent is different from the set that can be object; modifiers are much more likely to appear in object noun phrases than in subject noun phrases, for example (R. Brown et al. 1969). Thus it appears that a sentence like *Mommy ate cake,* though a possible utterance for both adult and child, has a quite different structure when uttered by an adult than it does when uttered by a child.

TABLE 3.9   Buildup Sequences—Evidence Regarding Hierarchical Structure

SUPPORTING HIERARCHICAL STRUCTURE

Chair. Pussy cat chair.
Go nursery. Lucy go nursery.
Kristin. Kristin sit chair.

COUNTEREXAMPLES

This belongs. This belongs there.
Kendall innere. Kendall innere bed.
Kendall pick up. Daddy pick up. Kendall. Mommy pick up Kendall.

Based on Bowerman—1973b: 204. This interpretation of the data differs from hers, however.

LANGUAGE ADDRESSED TO CHILDREN

> Have you ever noticed that when grownups talk to babies
> They talk in the strangest language you have ever heard?
> Babies seem to like it and they understand each word.
> —Sandy Offenheim, song lyric from the album *Are We There Yet?* © 1978, Berandol Music Ltd., Toronto.

In 1965 Noam Chomsky commented that children learn language in spite of the very complex relationship between grammatical structure and meaning, and in spite of the fact that most language is riddled with speech disfluencies and speech errors. Shortly thereafter, one of his colleagues speculated that "the language environment of the child does not differ in any systematic way from that of an adult'' (Fodor 1966:126). These remarks are partly responsible for the development of a research topic that has seen a vast amount of work in recent years (Tannock 1980 lists 290 references). The topic concerns the language addressed to children.

The language acquisition task, while still an amazing accomplishment, might not be so impossible a task if the language that the child hears is significantly different from the language heard between adults. And the facts are that the language of adults is significantly different when speaking to children. It differs in practically every aspect which has been looked at.

The basic finding is that mothers, fathers, older children, child care workers, and others in contact with children talk differently to them. This style of talking has been called motherese, parentese, baby talk, child-directed talk, and A-C speech. I shall use the abbreviation **ACL** for **Adult-to-Child Language,** and contrast this with **AAL,** which stands for **Adult-to-Adult Language.**

General properties of ACL

Length   ACL is shorter than AAL. The length of ACL utterances varies with the age of the child. As can be seen in Figure 3.5, before the child shows much evidence of comprehension of speech, the MLU in words of mothers is about 4.2. Once the child begins to comprehend, the rate drops to about 3.6 (Sherrod et al. 1977; however, a rate drop was not obtained by Kaye 1980), and apparently stays there until the child is two years old or so, when it begins to rise again (Phillips 1973; Snow 1972a). The actual values at particular ages vary with the task.

FIGURE 3.5
Mothers' speech adjustment to their children as a function of age.

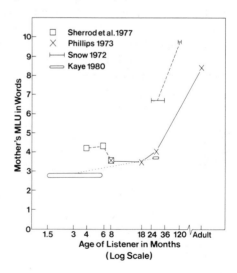

Once the child starts talking, the length of the mother's utterances can be compared with that of the child. Figure 3.6 demonstrates the strong correlation that exists between children's linguistic ability and the speech addressed to them. This has also been found in aspects of the mother's speech other than MLU (Bellinger 1980). Thus it appears that caregivers 'fine tune' their speech to their children.

As Figure 3.6 shows, ACL appears always to be a little ahead of the speech of the child being addressed (e.g., Cross & Morris 1980; Gleitman et al. 1984; Moerk 1974). The relationship does not always come out as nicely as it did in the study in the figure, however. In another study of 15 mothers with their one- to two-year olds, the mothers' ACL correlated better with age than with the child's MLU (Newport 1976).

Rate   ACL is slower than AAL. In one study of 10 lower-class black mothers the rate averaged 34 words per minute (wpm) as opposed to 61 wpm for AAL (Ringler 1978). A comparable study of 8 well-educated white mothers yielded 34-68 wpm, as opposed to 100-140 wpm for AAL (Remick 1976). Some of the slowness is due to pauses between utterances. Some involves the fact that utterance-final syllables tend to be pronounced more slowly than other syllables, and in short utterances the final syllable is a greater proportion of the utterance. There is evidence, however, that even within the utterance the rate of ACL is slower than AAL. One study of ACL to 26-month olds clocked ACL at 4.7 syllables per second within utterances, compared to AAL at 5.2 syllables per second (Drach 1969). The rate of speech also increases with age, as Figure 3.7 shows. This study was based on 32 adults, eight addressing children at each of four ages (Fraser & Roberts 1975). The rate used also depends considerably upon the task occupying the attention of the adult-child pair.

It may also depend upon how much experience the speaker has had with young children. Another study involved making up a story and telling it first to a 22-month old, then to an adult. Most of the subjects were students; none were parents. The rate was computed by counting the number of words in the first minute of the speech sample. The rate spoken to the child was 132 wpm; to the adult, 170 wpm (Sachs et al. 1976: 243). The fact that the rate to the child was faster than in similar situations in other experiments probably had to do with the lack of previous experi-

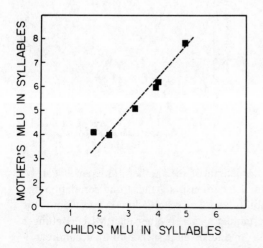

FIGURE 3.6
Mothers' speech adjustment to their children as a function of MLU. (Based on data from Moerk 1974: 106).

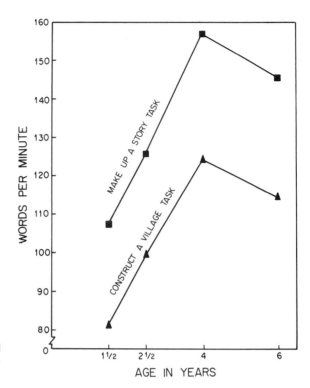

FIGURE 3.7
Rate of adult-to-child
speech. (Based on data from
Fraser & Roberts 1975.)

ence, coupled with the fact that there was no time to interact with the child before the rate was taken.

Error rate   Another striking finding is that essentially all ACL is well-formed and error-free. The error rate has been found to be as low as one in 1500 utterances (Newport 1976).

Enunciation   A number of researchers have reported that the enunciation of ACL is clearer than that of AAL. For example, the differences in voice onset time between voiced and unvoiced initial stop consonants is greater, thus making them more distinct from one another (The VOT of unvoiced stops is increased; the VOT of voiced stops does not change). ACL tends to have distinct pauses between sentences, whereas AAL does not (Drach 1969; Newport 1976; Sachs et al. 1976). The intonation pattern is greatly exaggerated. The fundamental frequency is higher; when rises and falls occur, they are more extreme (Garnica 1977; Jacobson et al. 1983; Remick 1976; Sachs et al. 1976: 243). In general, ACL is reported to be easier to transcribe than AAL (Broen 1972; Remick 1976; Newport et al. 1977).

The increased intelligibility of speech to children has recently been called into question by a study conducted in Edinburgh (Bard & Anderson 1983). In this study parents were recorded talking to their children and to the experimenter. When matched words were isolated and evaluated as to their intelligibility, it appeared that those words uttered to the children were slightly *less* intelligible than the same words spoken to the investigator. When the effect was broken down by sex of the speaker and listener, it was found to be due entirely to mothers speaking to their sons.

Does the evidence justify the conclusion? The result is based on a group of just three mothers; we are not told if the effect applied to all three—indeed, it might have been due to just one mother. The point that is out of line in the results for mothers of boys is not a lower intelligibility of words when spoken to their sons, but a higher intelligibility of the same words when spoken to the experimenter. The parents were described as speaking "various local varieties of British English." An alternative hypothesis that would also explain the result is that one or a few mothers were careful to adjust their dialect to one more closely corresponding to that of the experimenter. The intelligibility was determined by asking a group of undergraduates to identify each word in isolation. If we assume that the majority of undergraduates had dialects similar to that of the experimenter, it is not difficult to believe that they would find words spoken in their dialect more intelligible than words spoken in the mother's own dialect. Because of the limited numbers of adults used and the possible dialect problems, I would require replication before believing the result.

However, the technique of isolating words and measuring their intelligibility appears to be a promising one, and the experiment does seem to indicate that the findings of more careful enunciation may actually have been in error.

Vocabulary   ACL contains between 20 and 60 distinct vocabulary items not used in AAL. While the number of such terms varies from one language to another, the particular objects and actions so lexicalized are similar across languages (see, e.g., Austerlitz 1956; Kelkar 1964; Voegelin & Robinett 1954). The following list gives a sample of English ACL words and their adult equivalents:

pussy	cat
bow-bow	dog
wee-wee	urinate
poo-poo	defecate
night-night	sleep
boo-boo	hurts
piggy-back	carry on back
yucky	dirty

In addition, ACL contains modifications of adult forms of other words:

mommy	mother
doggie	dog
kitty	kitten

This special vocabulary usually includes names for family members, animals, body parts and functions, basic evaluation terms, and games and toys. The modifications of existing words tend to be associated with endearment (lovers may use the same terms) and small size (*Suzie* refers to a smaller person than does *Susan*). Though there are exceptions, these words tend to be simpler phonologically. Consonant clusters tend to be simpler than in AAL, and there tends to be reduplication of consonants, syllable parts, or whole syllables (Casagrande 1948; C. Ferguson 1964, 1977b).

Meaning Semantic differences between ACL and AAL have also been found. When caregivers talk to 13-month-olds, they tend to name objects not the way they would to adults, but rather in ways that they feel are more appropriate to their children. Thus they call a stuffed leopard a *kitty-cat,* a toy van a *car,* and a round candle a *ball.* In other words, they tend to overextend the range of these words. This is true, apparently, even for words that the child has not yet used.

Interestingly, this finding appears not to be true of caregivers talking to 9-month-olds. One explanation for this is that 9-month-olds do not act that differently to different toys. Whether it is a toy leopard, a toy van, or a candle, their reaction to it is to pick it up, put it in their mouths, and shake it. By the time they are 13 months old, they react differently to different classes of objects. They hug stuffed animals, push toy vehicles, and throw round objects. Caregivers appear to be responding to the child's categorization of objects by different action routines by using words in an overextended manner. But caregivers do not overextend a word to cover all objects the child might react to similarly. They do not call a stuffed dog a *kitty-cat,* an airplane a *car,* or a frisbee a *ball* (Mervis & Mervis 1982). If children go through a phase where they overextend some words, it may not be entirely due to the imperfect nature of their acquisition strategy; rather, it might be due to the fact that they are accurately reflecting the ACL they hear.

Syntax Many syntactic differences have been reported. Many utterances consist of single words uttered in isolation (Broen 1972; Snow 1971, 1972a). Sentence subjects and verb auxiliaries are much simpler or completely deleted (e.g., Moerk 1972; Ka. Nelson 1973a). Pronouns, modifiers, and function words are rare (Phillips 1970), and there are fewer coordinate and subordinate clauses (Drach 1969; Phillips 1973; Shatz & Gelman 1973). Certain sentence types are more frequent in ACL: imperatives and questions, for example. And among the different types of questions, tutorial questions—questions to which the speaker already knows the answer—are more frequent (Blount 1972).

Content The content of ACL differs as well. There is less variety of words used, and the topic discussed usually concerns the here and now—events that have just happened or are still taking place, and objects currently in the presence of the child (Philips 1973).

The functions of ACL also differ. Adults order children about a great deal. Also, there is a greater frequency of utterances produced for the purpose of pointing objects out (Newport 1976).

One study of language addressed to older children—children in the range of four to eight years—found most of ACL to be ''basically a language of socialization'' (J. Gleason 1973: 16). It told the child ''what to do, what to think, and how to feel.'' In particular, four characteristics of ACL content seemed to be dominant:

1. Although the language was not rich in actual imperatives, implied imperatives abounded:

Mother: Do you want to take your own plate off the table?

2. The conversation spelled out dangers of situations:

Mother (putting plate before child):   Hot! Hot!

3. In conversations with children, parents typically supplied the entire context, leaving very little room for the child to deflect the conversation:

Mother: How was school today? Did you go to assembly?
  Child: Yes.
Mother: Did the preschoolers go to assembly?
Mother: Did you stay for the whole assembly or just part of it?

The child hardly had more to do than say *yes* or *no*.

4. Adults in conversations with a child often do not express their own true feelings; rather, they seem to be telling the child how she or he ought to feel:

Adult: Hey, wow! That's almost full to the *top!*

This sort of exaggerated response clearly does not reflect the opinion of the speaker.

Factor interactions?   Just about every feature of ACL that has been studied has turned out to be different from AAL. When an adult switches to ACL, a great amount of adjustment happens simultaneously. Probably too much. Much of what happens is very likely a byproduct of other, more basic, factors. For example, do adults separately adjust the voice onset time of their initial voiceless stops, or does this happen naturally as a result of a slower speech rate and/or shorter sentences and/or bright intonation? Do adults specifically delete modifiers and subordinate clauses, yielding a shorter MLU as a byproduct, or does the causality go the other way—does imposing a shorter MLU force the syntactic changes? These are empirically testable questions. For example, one could compare VOTs in ACL with those in AAL in which the tempo is forced to match that of ACL. One could also compare VOTs in ACL with those in AAL to people who are hard of hearing. Unfortunately, research sorting out which variables are primary and which are byproducts of other variables has not yet been done.

Types of ACL Interactions

Quantitative measures such as length and rate do not in themselves convey what is really taking place in ACL. Another way to look at these interactions is to categorize them by interaction types.

Self-repetition   Approximately one-third of ACL consists of self-repetition (Benedict 1975; Friedlander et al. 1972; Kobashigawa 1969; Newport 1976). Here is a sample sequence (Snow 1972a: 562):

> Put the red truck in the box now . . . . The red truck . . . . No, the RED truck . . . . In the box . . . . The red truck in the box.

As is undoubtedly the case in this example, self-repetitions occur most often when children fail to respond appropriately (Cross 1975; Gleason 1977). The original utterance is broken into smaller parts and then recombined. Apparently these smaller parts are easier to comprehend, because this strategy is often effective in getting the child to do what the adult wants.

On the face of it, self-repetition has properties which appear to be useful from a language acquisition point of view. Long sentences are broken into shorter segments, which make them easier to comprehend. The short fragments tend to be phrases; thus, this activity may contribute to the child's learning of phrase structure. This behavior also provides several examples of particular words, giving the child more opportunity to learn them. By maintaining the same topic over several successive utterances, adults provide children with a longer period of time with which to comprehend the meaning. They also provide feedback as to when the comprehension is correct. When the child picks up the red truck, repetition of that phrase ceases, signalling that the object now in the child's hand is, indeed, a red truck.

Expansion   Another very common form of interaction is adult expansion of the preceding child utterance. Here are two examples (R. Brown & Bellugi 1964):

Child: Baby high chair.
Adult: Baby is in the high chair.

Child: Eve lunch.
Adult: Eve is having lunch.

Middle-class parents expand their children's utterances twice as often as lower-class parents (Snow et al. 1976). One can also see how this adult behavior could facilitate language development in children. Children are provided in each context with a model of what their intended utterance should have been.

Reponses to expansion   Children's responses to expansions have also been categorized. A very common response is to repeat the same utterance once more, perhaps in slightly different form. Three possibilities, with examples of each, follow:

Unexpanded imitation

Child: Just like cowboy.
Parent: Oh, just like the cowboy's.
Child: Just like cowboy.

Expanded imitation

Child: Pick 'mato.
Parent: Picking tomatoes up?
Child: Pick 'mato up.

Reduced imitation

Child: Play piano.
Parent: Playing piano.
Child: Piano.

There appear to be individual differences among children in their responses to parental expansions. Adam rarely responded with reduced imitation; Eve was least likely to respond with unexpanded imitation. Among the three response categories, both Adam and Eve responded with expanded imitation about half of the time. This behavior probably reinforces the adults' expansion behavior. Many adult expansions are produced with a rising intonation, signalling a question. When they are, this is known as a **request for clarification.** Such requests increase the likelihood of communication success. They also give children information as to what is missing, and inform them that what they said wasn't clear enough to be understood the way they said it.

Tutorial questions   One of the most common ways for a caregiver to initiate a conversation with a child is to ask that child a question for which the caregiver knows the answer (Howe 1980: 93):

Mother (to son looking at book):   What's he doing before he goes to bed?
Ian (1;11):   He doing teeth.

For some caregivers such questions are used in more than half of the caregiver-initiated conversations. It has been suggested that children with caregivers who do this a lot have better developed language as a result (Howe 1980), but the correlational evidence used to support this contention does not exclude other explanations, such as that parents of children who are more linguistically advanced are more likely to make heavier use of this form.

Prompt questions   One way to ask a question is to ask it using declarative word order but with a question intonation:

Goldilocks has been sitting where?

Such a question has been called a **prompt question** (Bellugi 1971:98). Adults use prompt questions in at least two types of adult-child interaction—**echoing** and **constituent prompting.**

Echoing occurs when the adult understands part but not all of the child's utterance. The appropriate question word is inserted in place of the unclear portion of the utterance:

Child: I going owa nah.
Adult: You're going where?

Constituent prompting comes most often in response to a lack of response to a previous question phrased in a normal question order (R. Brown et al. 1969):

Adult: What do you want?
Child: (No answer.)
Adult: You want what?

The adult has phrased the question in a way which helps children to know how to phrase the answer.

Overt teaching   All parents, of course, occasionally engage in various forms of overt language teaching, in which a particular response is specifically elicited. Three types have been noted (Friedlander et al. 1972):

Directed mimicry
Say "Bye-bye."

Overt correction
No, it's a "bottle."

Prompting
Thank you. (Nudge). Thank you.

In prompting the caregiver says what the child should say, perhaps accompanied by a little nudge, either physical or intonational.

Discourse modelling   Discourse modelling occurs particularly in ACL to very young infants. The adults do not expect a response, so they provide it themselves, thus carrying out the roles of both speaker and hearer (Ervin-Tripp 1973: 264).

Adult: Where's doggy? There's the doggy.

Extension   Extension (Howe 1980) and modelling (Cazden 1965) are terms used to describe a conversation in which the adult continues on the same topic as the previous utterance of the child without imitating it (Howe 1980: 84-85):

Kevin (1;8): Dolly
Mother: Isn't that beautiful!

Yvonne (1;10):   It rabbit.
Mother: He's got his eyes blindfolded, hasn't he?

Acknowledgement   When the child is talking, the adult will insert *Uh huh* or something similar at pauses as a communication maintenance strategy, just as the adult does in AAL. When children arrive at the nonstop-talking stage, parents become very adept at inserting *uh huh* at pauses without even listening to what the child is saying. This rude but sanity-preserving behavior fools the child for some months.

Who uses ACL?

Just about everybody uses ACL. Most of the studies have involved white middle-class American mothers, of course, but many other groups have been studied, with similar results. These groups include: American Blacks (Drach 1969); different social classes; different language communities and cultures (Blount 1972; C. Ferguson 1964; Rūke-Dravina 1977), including deaf parents to deaf children (Cicourel & Boese 1972); fathers; other adults (Gleason 1975; Sachs et al. 1976); and even older children (Shatz & Gelman 1973).

Fathers   Not all groups behave exactly alike, however. Although fathers' ACL is similar to that of mothers, there appear to be some differences. Fathers give their children fewer turns to talk, and tend to use a more extensive vocabulary (J. Gleason 1975). They also use more commands and threats, and are generally more directive (J. Gleason 1975; Malone & Guy 1982). French-speaking fathers in Quebec City use fewer requests for action or stopping some action (Rondal 1980). They also produce more attentional utterances, correct their children's utterances less, and produce more requests for clarification. The study of French-speaking fathers, and two of English-speaking fathers, found that they had shorter MLUs (Malone & Guy 1982; McLaughlin et al. 1983; Rondal 1980); however, other studies have not found MLU differences (Blount & Padgug 1976; J. Gleason 1975; Golnikoff & Ames 1979).

Other studies found that fathers produce a higher proportion of *Wh-* questions, while mothers produce a higher proportion of *yes/no* questions (J. Gleason & Weintraub 1978; McLaughlin et al. 1983. These question types are defined in Chapter 4). Another study obtained exactly the opposite result (Malone & Guy 1982). Still other studies found no differences between the two groups on the types of questions asked (Blount & Padgug 1976; Golinkoff & Ames 1979; Hummel 1982).

Another finding is that mothers tune the MLU and other aspects of their language to the linguistic abilities of their children more accurately than do fathers (McLaughlin et al. 1983).

One might expect that whatever differences there are in the speech of fathers to children as compared to the speech of mothers to children might be due to the amount of time spent with the children. One study compared male and female day-care workers with mothers and fathers, and found fewer differences in the speech of the daycare workers than they did in the speech of the parents. This research was based on only a very few subjects, so the results are quite tentative (J. Gleason 1975).

Another study designed to test this hypothesized that fathers who spent more time with their children would use language more like that of mothers than fathers who spent relatively little time with children. This study found no differences between the two types of fathers, however (Hummel 1982).

Other social classes   Other differences have been found based on social class. Dutch middle class mothers differ from their lower-class counterparts in several ways. Middle-class mothers use more deictic noun phrases (such as *See that birdie!*), fewer modal verbs (such as *can* or *must*), fewer imperatives (such as *Come here!*), and more interrogatives (such as *What's this?*) (Snow et al. 1976). But again, the overwhelming finding is that in most ways the ACL is similar in different social classes.

ACL to other children   What happens to the language of an adult to a child when an older child is present? On the average, first-born children and those who are an only child appear to end up better off in language and intelligence than their later-born siblings (McCarthy 1954: 588-589). Could some of this be due to changes in the way caregivers talk to two-year olds alone compared to when they talk to them in the presence of older siblings? In one experimental situation mothers were found to use almost the same language to their younger child alone that they used when both of their children were present, suggesting that in this circumstance they tended to talk to the level of their younger child. There were some differences, but there was no control condition of a mother talking to two same-aged children, so one cannot determine whether the differences were due to the basic fact of one more child or the fact that the other child was older. One finding that does seem clear is that older siblings tend to dominate, answering the mother's questions in this study about two-thirds of the time. In question-answering situations younger children tended to give more imitative answers when with their older sibling. No doubt most such imitation was of their older sibling's answers (Wellen 1985).

Although limited, this study brings to our attention the fact that in a great many homes children must compete for the attention of their caregivers with other siblings, and that this may have important effects on their language experience. Further studies could shed light on the relation of differential experience of first- and later-born children and their language development.

Other cultures   Similarities outweigh differences in the use of ACL in different cultures, as well (e.g., Snow et al. 1979), but occasional differences have been reported. One difference is variation in attitude toward public use of baby talk.

North American caregivers are often embarrassed when other adults overhear them using baby talk. No such embarrassment exists within Arab culture. Both cultures feel it is more appropriate for women than men, however. Also, in North American society there seems to be an attitude that too much use of baby talk is not good for a child. There is no evidence to support this. It is at least as reasonable to suggest that caregivers who refuse to use ACL may retard their children's language development (C. Ferguson 1964: 112, 114).

(© **1977 by Lynn Johnston. Reprinted by permission of Meadowbrook Press and Simon & Schuster, Inc.)**

In Papua, New Guinea, Kaluli parents believe that using ACL when talking to children is a bad idea. An anthropologist who lived among the Kaluli people for several years has claimed that they don't use it (Schieffelin 1980). They may not have a separate baby talk vocabulary, or they may not admit to using ACL to an anthropologist outsider, but I don't believe that Kaluli parents don't make some adjustments, such as shorter sentences or clearer enunciation. Kaluli parents also believe that children should not eat pigeons, a staple of the adult Kaluli diet, because if they do they will not learn to talk, only coo!

Why do people use ACL?

The ability to communicate with a child is something that an adult must learn. Adults who have had recent contact with children are better able to understand children's speech than adults who have had no recent contact (Weist & Stebbins 1972).

For the greatest deviation of ACL from AAL to occur, the child must be present. Mothers talking to real children use greater simplification than when they are instructed to talk into a tape recorder as if they were talking to real children (Snow 1972a). Thus simplification depends partly upon feedback to the mother from the child.

What is the nature of that feedback? For one thing, children are more attentive to simpler speech. For children between 0;9 and 1;6 a package of automated equipment can be brought into the home and attached to the infant's playpen or crib (Friedlander 1968, 1970). This system has two large omnidirectional switches which the infant can operate. They are placed so that the infant can reach only one switch at a time. Each switch will turn on one track of a two-track tape recording for as long as the switch is being displaced by the infant. The two tracks contain materials which differ from one another in whatever attribute is being investigated. The equipment is left with a family over a period lasting several weeks. Using this equipment, it has been found that:

1. Children generally prefer bright intonation to flat intonation.
2. Children generally prefer material which repeats itself after 20 seconds to material that repeats itself after 4 minutes.
3. Children prefer their mother's voice to that of a stranger, all other variables being equal.
4. Children prefer a stranger's voice with bright intonation over their mother's voice with a flat intonation.
5. After several days children often switch their preferences; presumably they get bored with their previously preferred material.

Similar results have also been obtained under laboratory conditions (Spring 1974). In one study two- and three-year olds listened to a taped story, half of which was in ACL and the other half in AAL. Observers rated the children's attention. The children were more attentive to the ACL half (Snow 1972b). A study of the detailed interaction between child and adult has turned up the finding that adults shorten their utterances immediately after specific signals of noncomprehension on the part of the child (Bohannon & Marquis 1977).

Speech to children, while simplified, tends to be more complex than the speech of the children to whom it is directed. Children respond appropriately more often to speech above their productive level than to speech at their productive level (Shipley et al. 1969). This is evidence that children's comprehension tends to precede their production, but also that they can signal to adults when their speech is too simple.

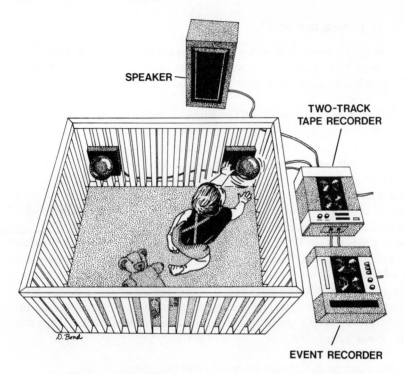

SPEAKER

TWO-TRACK
TAPE RECORDER

EVENT RECORDER

At first, such signalling involves attention and displaying understanding; later it can be more explicit:

Caregiver: Be sure to look before you cross the street.
Child: Okay, okay. I know how to cross the street.

This angry negative feedback eventually teaches the caregiver to address the child in a different style:

Caregiver: Be careful—the traffic is very heavy.

The feedback need not be angry for the child to convey the message. The following sequence occurred between Quentin and myself as we were walking through the fine china department of a department store:

Me: Be careful. Lots of thing in this department break easily.
Quentin: You mean this is the *fragile* department.

Thus overt correction is a second way children, especially older children, signal to their parents that they are using the wrong level of ACL.

The effect of ACL

What is the effect of all the differences between ACL and AAL? It is certainly plausible that the simplifications described make it easier for children to learn to talk; people have further argued that they are essential to language acquisition.

What evidence is there to support such proposals? The evidence accumulated thus far is slim. The best evidence on the matter has already been discussed. If adults talk to children in AAL, the children tend not to attend. We *assume* that children will learn less language when they are not attending to it. One could not, of course, subject a child to an environment free of ACL, but one can test various aspects of ACL and compare their relative efficacy. Since there are differences in ACL among individuals and groups, one can explore which variations correlate with most rapid language learning. Or one can experimentally elevate some feature of AAL and note the results, if any, on the course of acquisition. Both of these procedures have been employed.

A study using the correlational approach involved 15 middle-class mothers and their children aged 1;0 to 2;3. Two two-hour sessions were recorded six months apart. Individual differences of the mothers were compared with individual differences in *improvement* of their children on various language measures over the six-month period. Children whose mothers use a greater number of *yes/no* questions and deixis (pointing out) utterances seem to develop language at a faster pace, whereas children whose mothers use a greater number of imperatives do more poorly. Extension seems to be positively correlated; too much repetition seems to be negatively correlated (Newport et al. 1977: 129).

With correlational studies one is never sure of the causal relation. Do imperatives slow acquisition, or is it that slow language learners tend to be more active and get into situations requiring imperatives? Does repetition slow language progress, or do children who are slow learners tend to induce repetition by their higher rate of not understanding the first time? Perhaps the parent is less tuned to the child's level of understanding and uses more words that the child doesn't know or utterances that are too long. The child fails to respond so the parent repeats. In this situation repetition is a side issue, whereas the real issue may involve vocabulary and syntax selection problems. For such reasons as these, experimental studies are ultimately undertaken.

The classical experimental approach to this problem involved 12 black children 2;4 to 2;6 in a Boston day-care center. The children were sorted into four matched groups of three children each according to age, talkativeness, and MLU. From each group one child was assigned to each of the three conditions: expansion, extension, and control. For 40 minutes a day the four children assigned to the expansion group were placed in a separate room with an adult who behaved somewhat peculiarly. Everything each child said was expanded. The extension group spent 40 minutes with an adult who extended each utterance of each child. The control group children got some time in the special room, but no special linguistic treatment. Several measures of language development were taken before and after the 12-week experimental period. There were no meaningful differences between the expansion and the control groups. The children in the extension group were marginally better, however (Cazden 1972).

Before we count out expansion in favor of extension, we should consider the fact that there were dialect differences between the black children and the white tutors. In normal situations adults expand perhaps one-fourth of their children's utterances. When 100% of the utterances are expanded, it is bound to be true that some of the expansions will be misinterpretations, especially given the cultural and dialect difference. And many of the expansions are likely to have been different from expansions that black adults would have made, again due to dialect differences.

In a similar study of 27 white middle-class children aged 2;8 to 3;4, expansion came out better. Under the expansion condition, sentence fragments were recast as complete sentences, and complete sentences were recast in another form, using the same vocabulary. Thus *The baby fell down* might receive the response *The baby did fall down, didn't she?* Under the extension condition, the topic was continued, but the content words of the children's sentences were specifically excluded. A control group received no special experience. After 11 weeks with two 20-minute sessions per week, the expansion group came out better than the control group. The extension group appeared to be marginally better than the control group, though the difference was not statistically significant (Ke. Nelson et al. 1973).

Thus it appears that changes in the ACL that children hear for a small proportion of their time results in small improvements in their language development after a few weeks. The possibility exists that by training some children's primary caregivers in some of the ACL techniques that seem to have a positive influence on language development, major improvements in language skills might be realized in these children.

SUMMARY

Children begin putting words together into longer utterances about seven months after uttering their first word. Their first comprehension of multiword utterances appears to be based purely on the meanings of the words and not at all on the word order. The earliest utterances produced that are longer than a word are sometimes a word combined with other syllables that appear to add no meaning. Soon after real two-word utterances appear, children are able to produce still longer utterances. The mean length of a child's utterances has turned out to be a useful indicator of a child's syntactic development.

Early characterizations of two-word utterances emphasized their productivity, their likeness to telegraphic language, and what appeared to be a strategy of forming utterances by combining one of a small set of highly frequent words (pivots) with one of a large set of lower frequency words (open class). More recent studies of these early combinations have looked at fixed versus variable word order, early expression of different functions and roles, and the use of stress pattern.

An area of considerable interest is the fact that caregivers of children at this stage use language that differs significantly from normal adult-to-adult language (AAL). This adult-to-child language (ACL) is shorter, slower, more clearly pronounced, and more error-free than AAL. Differences have been found in specific vocabulary items, object naming, syntax, and content. Caregiver-child exchanges have been categorized into a number of different types, some of which have been studied in detail to determine whether purposely increasing their frequency can hasten the progress of language learning. ACL is used by mothers, fathers, older children, and child care workers, by lower class individuals as well as middle class individuals, and in most languages and cultures. It appears to be universal because children prefer it and express this preference by paying more attention when spoken to in this manner.

SUGGESTED FURTHER STUDY

BLOOM, LOIS (1973)   *One word at a time*. The Hague: Mouton.

BRAINE, M.D. (1976)   Children's first word combinations. *Monographs of the Society for Research in Child Development* **41,** Serial 164, 1-104.

DEPAULO, B.M. & J.D. BONVILLIAN (1978)   The effect on language development of the special characteristics of speech addressed to children. *Journal of Psycholinguistic Research* **7,** 189-211.

RODGON, MARIS M. (1976)   *Single word usage, cognitive development and the beginnings of combinatorial speech*. Cambridge University Press.

SNOW, CATHERINE E. & C. A. FERGUSON, EDS. (1977)   *Talking to children: Language input and acquisition*. Cambridge University Press.

VAN DER GEEST, TON (1974)   *Evaluations of theories on child grammars*. The Hague: Mouton.

FOUR
LATER DEVELOPMENT

With patient inattention hear him prate.—George Meredith, *Bellerophon*, St. 4.

THE QUANTITY OF LANGUAGE

The total amount of adult speech that children between the ages of two and three and a half hear is about one million words. They produce half a million words themselves (Suppes et al. 1974). Since the amount heard is from all sources, by the time they are three, children are talking at least as much as adults.

Children do not require another person to be present in order to have someone to talk to. In one study the speech of three normal and three autistic four-year olds

Gasoline Alley (Reprinted by permission: Tribune Media Services, Inc.)

was recorded when they were in a room by themselves. The researchers found out that the children continued to talk over extended periods of time. They concluded that speech is "self reinforcing" (Lovaas et al. 1977).

It may even be that children talk more when they are alone than they do in the presence of others. One study of infants found that in an active waking state they vocalized less in the presence of their mothers than when alone (Jones & Moss 1971).

COMPLEX SYNTACTIC CONSTRUCTIONS

Who climbs the grammar tree distinctly knows
Where Noun, and Verb, and Participle grows.—John Dryden, tr., *Juvenal's Satires,*
Sat. vi, 1.583 (1693)

As the child's ability to produce longer sentences grows, the variety and complexity of the sentences grow as well. In order to follow the developmental course of the child at this stage, it is best to specialize, and to look at the blossoming of particular syntactic constructions. In this section we shall explore the growth of a few of the more important types of construction.

Negation

No, no, no. No, no, no.
No no no no no no no no, no, no, no, no.
No, no, no. No, no, no.
No no no no no no no no, no!—Sandy Tobias Offenheim, song lyric from the album *Are We There Yet?* ©1978 Berandol Music. By permission.

Negation is a term used to refer to the use of negative morphemes in language. These include words such as *no, not,* and the CB term *negatory;* prefixes such as *un-* as in *unloved, dis-* as in *disappear,* and *non-* as in *nonsense,* the suffix *-n't* as in *isn't, can't,* and *don't;* as well as words closely associated with negative constructions, such as *hardly* and *any.*

Its uses There are many uses to which negation can be put. (Bloom 1970: 171-174; Bloom & Lahey 1978: 188-192) Three categories of uses are **nonpresence, rejection,** and **denial.**

Nonpresence. Nonpresence is used to describe four related concepts: **nonexistence** and **disappearance** of objects, and **nonoccurrence** and **cessation** of events. Here are examples of each:

Nonexistence:

Child (looking at picture of a barefoot Pooh):   No shoes.

Disappearance:

Child (looking out window at night):   Allgone outside.

Nonoccurrence:

Kathryn (unable to turn a screw):   No turn.

Cessation:

Gia (stuck in tree; Bloom frees her):   No more stuck.

Rejection. Rejection is used to refer both to **simple rejection,** in which the child objects to some object or action, and to the related concept of **prohibition,** which carries with it the notion that an act is forbidden by authority:

Simple rejection:

Kathryn (pushing away worn soap; wanting new soap):   No dirty soap.

Prohibition:

Child (to younger sibling):   Don't play with matches (Belkin 1975).

Denial. Denial involves negating the truth of a statement made by someone else:

Mother (offering car to Kathryn):   There's the truck.
                            Kathryn: No truck.

The development of different uses   Rejection is probably the first form of negation an infant expresses. A parent hands little Meagan over to a friend to hold. She begins to cry, and does not stop until the friend returns her to her caregiver.

When she is a little older, she learns to use gestures and actions to indicate rejection. When she has had enough strained carrots, she manages to grab her dish and throw it onto the floor. Less violently, when she is handed a toy she doesn't wish to play with, she pushes it away.

Some children are more subtle. When he was nine months old, Nigel would signal "I don't want that" by touching the object lightly, whereas if he wanted something, he would grasp it firmly (Halliday 1975: 61).

Denial can also appear early—even before the first word. At about nine months my son Quentin signalled denial by uttering his idiomorph [e::] with falling intonation and a sour expression on his face. This would occur when he would ask for an object to be named and I would give the wrong answer. His [eːː] would signal that he denied the truth of my statement.

Some of the most complete records of the early development of negation are those of Allison (Bloom 1973: 90). At 10 months Allison began to use *away* to signal a request for the removal of an object. Three days after this use first appeared, she began to use *away* to comment on an object's disappearance. From 11 to 14 months, Allison used [nənənənənə] accompanied by appropriate gestures and emphasis to express protest at something—at 14 months she began to use *no* instead. At the same time she began to use *no* in the prohibition sense. She would look at or touch forbidden objects and say *no*.

At this time she also acquired a new word for expressing disappearance: *allgone*. In the context of food she used this exclusively; in other contexts she would sometimes use *allgone* and sometimes use *away*.

At 15 months Allison began to use *no* to express nonoccurrence. She would look at a picture of something, name it if she knew the name, and then turn it over and say *no*. She would do this with pictures wherever they occurred—on book covers, cereal boxes, or elsewhere.

Yet another word, which she learned at 13 months, was *stop*. This was her comment on the cessation of a noise or activity; in this stage she did not use this word as a request.

Similar development has been found at the same stage in children learning other languages (R. Brown 1973: 117). Thus while still at the one-word stage children have been found to express a number of different forms of negation: rejection, disappearance, prohibition, nonoccurrence, and denial.

Given all the various types of negation that children express at the one-word stage, one would expect to find at least these types to occur in longer sentences as soon as the child reaches that stage. But according to one researcher (Bloom 1970: 170-220), this is not what happens. At the multiword stage nonexistence occurs first (*No pocket.*). Second, rejection is added to the child's repertoire (*No dirty soap.*). And later still denial is added (*No truck.*). A similar sequence occurred in the acquisition of Japanese by one child (McNeill & McNeill 1968).

Why should there be such an acquisition sequence? Children seem to have mastered all three ideas semantically at the one-word stage or earlier. Syntactically they all appear to be of equal difficulty. Perhaps rejection is so successfully accomplished with a single-word utterance that there is less need for elaboration for this use than with nonpresence. This would account for multiword nonpresence utterances coming in before multiword rejection utterances. And one can argue that the later appearance of denial is due to greater complication of the situation in that the referent (''car'' in the *No truck* example) must be compared with the speech act of another person (*truck*) (Bloom & Lahey 1978: 190; McNeill & McNeill 1968). Since my son could do this in the idiomorphic stage, this argument does not convince me. In any case, it is not certain that every child follows the same acquisition sequence; in this regard there is information only about three English-speaking children and one Japanese-speaking child.

Whatever may be true in general, in the three English-speaking children it was found that not only did the three categories of negation begin to be expressed in multiword sentences in a set sequence, but also these sentences began to be elaborated in the same sequence. Thus nonpresence sentences began to include more elaborate negation markers, such as *can't, doesn't,* and *not* before similar elaboration occurred with denial (Bloom & Lahey 1978: 191).

Syntactic development   When negation first occurs with a verb (MLU approximately 1.75 morphemes), it most often occurs in first position:

> No want stand head.
> No sit there.
> No the sun shining.
> No Lois do it.

The occurrence of *no* before the subject of a sentence, as in the last two examples, has been a matter of some interest. Adult sentences are negated by placing the negative element after the subject:

> The sun isn't shining.
> Lois didn't do it.

One study concluded that early negative sentences are produced by affixing the negative element to the front of the affirmative sentence, rather than in its normal adult slot (Klima & Bellugi 1966). However, researcher Lois Bloom has argued that in NEGATIVE-SUBJECT-VERB sentences, what children really mean corresponds to these adult sentences:

> No, the sun *is* shining.
> No, I want *Lois* to do it.

Thus in these sentences the *no* is referring to something previously said or implied, and the sentence parts are in the normal adult order after all. One thing which confuses observers is that, unlike adults, children often fail to pause between the negative element and what follows (Bloom & Lahey 1978: 191).

Perhaps most of the early sentences may be explained in this way, but not all. The context for one of the above sentences has been published (Klima & Bellugi 1966: 193—reprint: 342):

Adult: Well, is the sun shining?
Child: No the sun shining.
Adult: Oh, the sun's not shining?

It is hard to explain this other than to assume it means

> No, the sun isn't shining.

However, in such contexts adults would most likely produce both *no* and *isn't.* Thus the simplest hypothesis to explain this sentence is that the child's *no* is modelled on the adult *no,* rather than coming from the negative element *-n't* by order reversal.

Although there does not seem to be order reversal as originally hypothesized, at this stage it does seem to be true that negative elements appear only as the first word of an utterance, or occasionally as the last word—*Wear mitten no*—but never within.

As speech develops, children reach a stage (MLU approximately 2.25) at which this restriction no longer holds:

> That no fish school.
> I no taste them.
> There no squirrels.

During this stage *can't* and *don't* also first appear:

> Don't leave me.
> I don't sit on Cromer coffee.
> I can't catch you.

Nevertheless the earlier form still occurs:

> No pinch me.

In a still later stage (MLU between 3.4 and 3.9) use of *no* within a clause is replaced by *not,* and the child makes use of additional forms:

> It's not cold.
> Ask me if I not made mistake.
> Paul didn't laugh.
> Donna won't let go.

These utterances still deviate from adult forms in several ways. Forms of the verb *to be* (*am, is, are, was, were, will be*) are often, though not always, absent:

> This not ice cream.
> I not crying.
> I not see you anymore.

but:

> That was not me.

Another common deviation at this stage is that they occasionally produce double tense markings:

> I didn't caught it.
> I didn't did it.

A third common deviation is that double negatives will occur:

> No one didn't come in.

In adult English, where affirmative sentences use *some,* negative sentences use *any:*

> I want something.
> I don't want anything.

This distinction is learned quite late, so a fourth deviation one finds at this stage is the use of *some* where *any* is needed:

> I didn't see something.

Children appear to go through similar stages in other languages as well (French: de Boysson-Bardies 1972; German: Grimm 1973; Italian: Antinucci & Volterra 1975, Volterra 1972).

Questions

Question types   In order to appreciate what children accomplish in learning to understand and ask questions, consider what they must learn. There are three types of questions: *yes-no* **questions,** *wh-* **questions,** and **quoted questions.**

Yes-no questions. The most common type of question is probably the *yes-no* **question.** These are questions that call upon the addressee to respond to *yes* or *no:*

> Is the lady of the house at home?
> Had they remembered to feed the fish?
> Can Don raise the money in time?
> Tomorrow will the postal workers be going on strike?
> Sir, am I on the list?

These questions bear an interesting relation to their corresponding declarative sentences. Certain verbs are known as **auxiliary verbs.** One or more of these verbs may precede the main verb and modify the tense or other aspects of the verb. Among these verbs may be found various forms of the verbs *be, have, can, may,* and others. When such an auxiliary occurs in a declarative sentence, the corresponding *yes-no* question is formed with the first auxiliary immediately preceding rather than following the sentence subject. Compare the questions above with their declarative counterparts below:

> The lady of the house is at home.
> They had remembered to feed the fish.
> Don can raise the money in time.
> Tomorrow the postal workers will be going on strike.
> Sir, I am on the list.

There are several complications to this simple relationship. Consider declarative sentences that don't contain an auxiliary:

The giant ate the parson.

The corresponding *yes-no* question contains a form of the auxiliary *do,* which takes the tense marker, in the usual auxiliary slot:

Did the giant eat the parson?

A second complication concerns when *be, do,* and *have* are the main verbs of the sentence. *Be* behaves like an auxiliary, *do* does not, and *have* does in Britain but not in North America:

He is here.
Is he here?
He did it.
Did he do it?
He has the book.
Does he have the book? (North America)
Has he the book? (Britain)

Another complication concerns certain words that cannot appear in both declaratives and questions:

She has forgotten something.
But: Has she forgotten anything?

Have they gone yet?
But not: They have gone yet.

Had she ever been sick?
But not: She had ever been sick.

She has hardly slept a wink.
But not: Has she hardly slept a wink?

Yet another complication is that sometimes a *yes-no* question takes the same form as the declarative except with a question intonation.

Mel still wants to get married?
The tiger is still chained up?

Even when a *yes-no* question is cast in its more common form, in normal rapid speech the initial auxiliary may be only barely pronounced, or not at all.

[mɑɪ] going too? (Am I going too?)
[jə] want it? (Do you want it?)
[dðeɪ] get lost? (Did they get lost?)

The story is more complex still. One can also ask a *yes-no* question and simultaneously express one's belief as to what answer is expected. This is done by means of what have been called **tag questions:**

You are going, aren't you? (Expects *Yes*)
You aren't going, are you? (Expects *No*)

A way of expressing an even more complex expectation is to ask a **negative question,** which uses a negative morpheme but is not related to the usual meanings of negation:

Aren't you going? (Originally expected *Yes*, but now not so sure)

Closely related are **truncated questions:**

I'm going. Are you?
I'm going. Aren't you? (Expects *Yes*)

Wh- **questions.** The other major type of question consists of those which require other than *yes* or *no* answers. These are the question-word questions. Since most of the English question words contain *w* and *h* (*who, whom, whose, what, where, when, why, how, how much, how many*), these questions have come to be known as *wh-* **questions.**

Goldilocks has been sitting on my chair.
Who has been sitting on my chair?
Where has Goldilocks been sitting?

Goldilocks sat on my chair.
Where did Goldilocks sit?
Whose chair did Goldilocks sit on?

When these questions are compared with their corresponding declarative form, the outstanding feature is that if the question word is not the subject, the part of the sentence involving the question word is placed before the subject, rather than in the location it occupies in the declarative. In these cases—but not when the question word is the subject—the same placement of the first auxiliary—or the insertion of a form of *do*—that occurs in *yes-no* questions also occurs in *wh-* questions.

Again, an option open to an English speaker is to produce *wh-* questions in declarative word order but with question intonation. Questions in this form are sometimes known as **prompt questions** (Bellugi 1971: 98) or **occasional questions** (J. de Villiers & de Villiers 1978: 105).

Goldilocks has been sitting where?
Goldilocks sat on whose chair?

Quoted questions. As if this were not enough, there are also **quoted questions,** and these can be either **direct** or **indirect:**

Direct: Ask her, "What time is it?"
Indirect: Ask her what time it is.

Direct: Ask her, "Will you go out today?"
Indirect: Ask her whether she will go out today.

Given all this complexity and more (R. Stockwell et al. 1973: 600-631), it should not be surprising that it takes years for children to learn how to handle questions in their adult forms, and that there are many steps along the way.

Their development **Being asked.** As soon as children are born they are talked to, and a high proportion, 25% to 60%, of the utterances addressed to them are in the form of questions (Remick 1976; Sachs et al. 1976; Snow 1978: 257. However, caregivers appear to ask more questions when they realize their interaction is being taped; see Graves 1980). The conversational interaction between two children and their respective mothers was recorded at 3, 7, 12, and 18 months. Neither the amount of conversation nor the percentage of it devoted to asking the child questions seemed to change over the 15 month interval. When the children were 3 months old, of course, they had essentially no language skills, and so, in general, did not answer the questions asked. This did not concern their mothers, who would answer the questions themselves or accept a glance, gesture, smile, coo, or even a burp as an appropriate answer:

Mother: What's that funny thing? Can you see it? A TV camera, do you reckon? Hmm?

The two girls were named Ann and Mary. As Figure 4.1 shows, Ann's mother was able to phrase her questions with such ingenuity that almost one-eighth of the time her three-month old could be considered to have made an appropriate response!

Differences in the topics of the questions with age were also noted. At 3 months the topic was often determined by the direction of the child's gaze, or by other activity of the child. At 7 and 12 months the mother attempted to focus the child on what she, the mother, was doing. By 18 months, the questions were more often either specifically tutorial or else genuine requests for information (Snow 1978).

Learning to answer. True question-answering behavior begins as soon as the caregivers are aware that their children know the meaning of a word. Once the children reach that stage, their caregivers begin to play the *where* game (Huttenlocher 1974: 342):

Mother: Where is the cookie?
Wendy: (Looks around; picks up cookie; takes a bite; puts it down.)

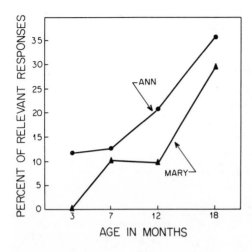

FIGURE 4.1
Children's responses to adult questions
(Based on Snow 1978: 258.)

When children realize that the caregiver wants them to signify a referent in response to *where,* and then do so, the first successful conscious question-answering behavior has taken place.

The first thing a child must learn is that when a question is asked, it is appropriate to respond. One unnamed lad—we shall call him Caesar—seems to have learned this lesson for questions in general at around 1;6. At 1;5 Caesar responded to 59% of the questions his mother directed to him, whereas at 1;6 this had increased to 75% (Tamir 1980; see also Crosby 1976).

Learning to give a response to an utterance bearing a question intonation is only the first step. Understanding what is wanted and providing an appropriate response is more complicated. This ability appears to grow gradually. Caesar's ability to give an appropriate response grew slowly during the four month period he was studied. At 1;4 he responded appropriately only 8% of the time; by 1;7 he was responding appropriately 36% of the time.

It is interesting to look at which questions are easiest for a child to answer. Although one may make a good case for the proposition that *wh-* questions are syntactically more complex than *yes-no* questions, there is evidence that young children may have more difficulty answering *yes-no* questions than *where* or *What do you want?* questions. A correct answer to a *where* question involves a point to a named referent; a correct answer to a *What do you want?* question involves naming a physical object, or simply pointing to it if it is present. But a correct answer to a *yes-no* question involves either mastering the abstract words *yes* and *no* or their equivalents *uh huh* and *uh uh,* or mastering the equivalent head movements—**nod** for *yes* and **shake** for *no.*

Consider this exchange with Marshall, aged 1;7 (Steffensen 1978: 234):

Marshall: (Reaches for bottle; then takes adult by the hand.)
   Adult: What do you want?
Marshall: Bottle.

Adult: You want the bottle?
Marshall: No. (Then takes adult by the hand, reaches for the bottle). Want bottle.

Marshall said *no* but obviously meant *yes* (I believe the first report of this is in Preyer 1889: 82). In general during the period 1;5 to 2;2 Marshall knew, presumably by the question intonation and lack of a *wh-* word, that a question was being asked that required a *yes* or *no* response. To such questions he correctly responded *uh uh* or *no* or *uh huh* or *yes,* but during this period these answers were apparently not related to his wishes; his negative responses appeared to be contradicted by other actions or verbalizations, as in the above example, about two thirds of the time. Similar confusion appeared when, at about 1;7, he started using head nods and shakes.

Another child in the same stage also failed to understand *yes-no* questions. His response to such questions was to repeat the last part of the question:

Adult: You want a wiener?
Jackson: Want wiener.
Adult: Jackson, would you like some milk instead?
Jackson: Milk instead.
Adult: Is that your coat, Jackson?
Jackson: Your coat.
Adult: Shall I cut your meat?
Jackson: Meat.

Thus Jackson knew that a response was required, and not really understanding what to do, adopted a strategy that was sometimes successful in satisfying the adult (as in the first example), though at other times the strategy worked less well (as in the last example).

As in the cases of Jackson and Marshall, Caesar also appeared better able to handle *what* questions than *yes-no* questions (Tamir 1980: 415).

Learning how to ask. Let us turn now to the problem of learning how to ask questions. The first question asked by the child is often the child's idiomorph for "What is the name for that?":

Nigel: [ædyda] (Halliday 1975: 44).
Quentin: [ʔəhəʔ]

At this stage this behavior can just as well be described as a request rather than a question. That is, it can be also interpreted as "I want the name of that." The main difference is that this is the first request for a specific verbal response (recall that at a much earlier age infants appear to request general verbal interaction through gesture, lip movements, eye contact, and vocalization).

At the one-word stage asking questions seems to be rare. Halliday reported that at this stage Nigel could ask for the name of something, first with his idiomorph, and later with *What's that,* but apparently he never asked any other question (Halliday 1975: 31, 49; see also Savić 1975).

As children reach the two-word stage, they begin to produce questions (Bell-ugi 1965; Klima & Bellugi 1966). As Figure 4.2 shows, the frequency with which they ask questions increases until about five years of age, when it begins to decline. A general finding regarding the acquisition of *wh-* questions is that questions involv-ing *what, where,* and *who* precede *why, how,* and *when,* which in turn precede *which* and *whose* (Bloom et al. 1982; R. Brown 1968; Labov & Labov 1978; M.M. Lewis 1938; M.E. Smith 1933). This sequence has also been found in second language acquisition (e.g., Felix 1976; Lightbown 1978).

When one looks at the acquisition of questions in finer detail, one finds a great amount of variability as to the sequence in which different question types are learned (Ervin-Tripp 1970a: 89). Thus the sequence described below should be considered to be typical, but in any particular child it will vary.

The first question at the two-word stage is likely to be the same one asked idiomorphically:

What that?

Thereafter it is likely that *where* questions will appear:

Where Mommy boot?
Where horse go?
Where Daddy going?

This is not surprising, given that *where* questions are the most frequent questions put to children (R. Brown et al. 1969; Savić 1975). At first blush, these questions may seem more complex than they really are. In fact, the first *where* questions are

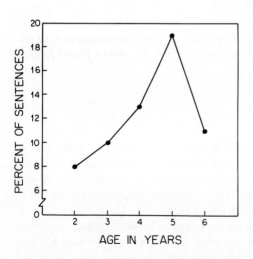

FIGURE 4.2
Percent of children's sentences that are questions.

"Why do I keep asking questions, dad?"

limited to a few simple sentence frames, into which a noun phrase (NP) can be slotted:

> Where (NP)?
> Where (NP) going?

At about the same time *yes-no* questions first appear:

> Sit chair?
> Mommy eggnog?
> No ear?

Syntactically these questions are quite simple. They are produced with exactly the same word order as their declarative counterparts, except with the rising question intonation.

Perhaps the next question type to come in is the *what-doing* question:

> What cowboy doing?

Like *where-going* questions, this use of *what* is limited to a simple framework:

> What (NP) doing?

One girl, Laura (2;7) appears to have been observed in the stage after she had acquired *where* but before she had acquired *what-doing*. Apparently she understood simple *where* questions, but also gave location answers to *what-doing* questions—that is, she behaved as if the two types meant the same thing (Ervin-Tripp 1970a: 84). Children who produce *what-doing* questions don't necessarily understand the use of *what* in other sentence frames:

Mother: What did you hit?
 Child: Hit.

Mother: What did you do?
 Child: Head.

Mother: What are you writing?
 Child: Arm.

One child at about this stage could understand *what-doing* questions and simple *who* questions, but when asked more complex *who* questions, answered as if *who* meant the same thing as *what, what-doing,* or *where* (Ervin-Tripp 1970a: 84-85):

 Adult: What's Tommy doing?
Carol (2;6): Putting shoes.

 Adult: Who's that?
 Carol: Paul.

 Adult: Who's eating?
 Carol: Meat.

 Adult: Who's watching Daddy?
 Carol: Shaving.

 Adult: Who put it in? Who put the car in?
 Carol: In that hole.

In the last three examples, it appears that Carol recognizes that *who* is a question word, but not knowing its meaning, she looks for a missing participant slot in the sentence and fills it in as her answer (This interpretation has been supported by Tyack & Ingram 1977 in a study of 100 children, and by Winzemer 1980 in a study of 20 children).

Somewhere about this time, when the child's MLU is about 1.8 to 2.0 morphemes, another question comes in:

Why?

At this stage children do not understand *why* in the adult sense of asking for a cause. Rather they discover that if they say *why?*, the other person will continue talking. For one trying to learn a language, it's a good way to collect data!

As the MLU reaches the 2.3 to 2.9 level, the range of possible questions increases. A new question introducer emerges—*D'you want:*

D'you want its turn?
D'you want me get it?

At this stage questions involving *what* and *where* involve more syntactic variation:

> Where me sleep?
> What the dollie have?
> What soldier marching?

What questions are now usually understood:

Mother: What d'you need?
   Child: Need some chocolate.
Mother: What d'you hear?
   Child: Hear a duck.

Similarly, *who* questions begin to be understood:

Mother: Who are you peeking at?
   Child: Peeking at Ursula.
Mother: Who do you love?
   Child: Mommy, you. I love fishie, too.

At this stage children produce complex *why* and also *why not* questions, although they still don't understand their causal meaning (R. Brown et al. 1969):

Mother: I see a seal.
   Child: Why you see a seal?
Mother: You can't dance.
   Child: Why not me can't dance?

Not much change has occurred in *yes-no* questions at this stage. The sentences are a bit longer, and questions containing *can't* are now used:

> You can't fix it?

As the child's language develops to the point where the MLU ranges from 3.4 to 3.6 morphemes, the English auxiliaries begin to appear before the subject in questions. A topic currently in dispute is whether the development of 'inverted' word order first occurs in *yes-no* questions and later generalizes to *wh-* questions. That is, is there a stage in which the child consistently produces inverted *yes-no* questions and noninverted *wh-* questions? Thus:

> Can I have a piece of paper?
> What he can ride in?

Initial studies of Adam, Eve, and Sarah suggested that there is such a stage (Klima & Bellugi 1966). However, a more recent study of 21 children found no such stage (D. Ingram & Tyack 1979), and a still more recent study of 18 children found only one child in the hypothesized stage, but also found six children who had inversion in *wh-* questions ***before*** inversion in *yes-no* questions (Erreich 1980). It appears that the inversion of the auxiliary can be established at different times in the two questions types, and that which type appears first varies from child to child.

Also at about this stage, *when* and *how* questions begin to be used:

How they can't talk?
When me want it?

Just as in the case of negation, there are still a number of other grammatical details to be worked out. Sometimes there is double tense marking:

Did I caught it?
What did you doed?

There can also be problems marking number:

Does lions walk?
Where were I?

And case (*me* versus *I*) can be a problem:

Why me going?

Entering the scene very late are tags and tag questions, at least for North American children. This should not be surprising, since the frequency of usage is low. Indeed, the frequency in North America may well be declining (Compare M.E. Smith 1933 with Tyack & Ingram 1977).

Acquisition of tag question production appears to take place in four steps. The first step is, of course, not to attempt a tag. The second is to use one tag expression in all circumstances:

Adult: Are those Kermit the Frog slippers?
Robin (2;10):   Yes, there is.

In the next stage, when the tag appears on a question, the negative is missing (R. Brown & Hanlon 1970: repr. 187):

He'll catch cold, will he?
This is Boston, is it?

Finally the complete form of the tag appears:

We had a ball, didn't we?

The age at which the complete form appears has been set at 4 years in a Boston study (R. Brown & Hanlon 1970), but has still not appeared in 45% of 12-

and 14-year olds in Toronto (Dennis et al. 1982). This difference may be due to several factors: the relative intelligences of the two subject groups; the passage of more than a decade during which the use of this construction may have declined further; the fact that in Canadian English there is extensive use of *eh?* as a tag, which has replaced the use of the 'standard' tag in most colloquial conversation.

Where they occur, one can argue that tag questions involve negation, *do*-insertion, and other linguistic constructions which are needed in other, simpler constructions. Since these other constructions are simpler, one might expect that they are learned before tag questions. Indeed, they are learned earlier, but since they are also more frequent in parent talk to children, frequency seems to be a simpler explanation than relative complexity.

Other languages. Question acquisition seems to follow a similar path of development in other languages. Two studies, however, have turned up interesting differences.

In English, *yes-no* questions can be produced quite easily, by superimposing question intonation over a declarative sentence form. *Yes-no* questions are among the first questions asked by English-learning children. On the other hand, Finnish does not mark questions by means of intonation. *Yes-no* questions are formed by adding a suffix to the verb and placing the verb first in the sentence. This more difficult signalling system seems to explain why two Finnish children, Seppo and Rina, could not produce *yes-no* questions until later in their development (Bowerman 1973a: 153).

The other study involves negative questions. There are two different ways a language can specify how one should answer a negative question. One can respond to the underlying affirmative statement, or one can compare one's own intent with the truth value of the negative form of the underlying statement. English prescribes the former; Japanese prescribes the latter, as shown in Table 4.1 (Akiyama 1979: 488). In theory, the English system is simpler. Is it learned sooner?

The development of these responses was studied in monolingual English, monolingual Japanese, and bilingual English-Japanese children. The English system was learned earlier. (It is interesting to note that English used to have a system which took both types of information into account, as shown in Table 4.2 [Pope 1973].) Modern English abandoned the rule requiring agreement with the question form).

The use of bilingual children to compare the relative difficulty of two different language structures is an interesting technique. If bilingual children learn a con-

TABLE 4.1 Responses to "Aren't You Going?"

LANGUAGES	INTENTION	ANSWER
English	I am going.	Yes
	I'm not going.	No
Japanese	I am going.	No
	I'm not going.	Yes

Adapted from Akiyama, 1979. © Academic Press. Used by permission.

TABLE 4.2   The 16th Century English Question-Answering System

QUESTION	INTENTION	ANSWER
Are you going?	I am going.	Yea
	I'm not going.	Nay
Aren't you going?	I am going.	Yes
	I'm not going.	No

struction in one language but not in the other, it suggests that the difference must be due to differences in the languages, not to cultural or other differences.

Passives

Because the passive construction has played a central role in linguistic theory over the last quarter century (since N. Chomsky 1957), its development has been charted by a number of researchers. When studying acquisition, it is useful to classify passives into two types—**short passives** and **full passives.** Short passives are sometimes called **truncated passives,** but I shall refrain from using this term, as it implies that they are derived by truncating full passives, a highly debatable premise. Here are some examples of each:

Short passives:

My bat was stolen.
It got broken.

Full passives:

The dog was chased by the girl.
The lawn was mowed by Sharon.
The lamp was broken by (*or* with) the ball.

The most common reason to use the passive construction in English is to express that something happened when you don't know or don't want to tell who did it. Thus most passives are in the agentless short form. Full passives do not seem to occur in the free speech of children (Harwood 1959) or in adult speech addressed to children (R. Brown 1973: 358).

The fact that full passives don't appear in children's free speech doesn't necessarily mean that children can't produce them—it may mean that the situations in which children would find the full passive construction most appropriate are extremely rare. One researcher managed to obtain full passives from children as young as two years, by having them view pictures, some of which showed events in which only the participant affected by the action was colored, thus focussing attention on that participant (Horgan 1978: 66).

One can argue that in the speech of children at least some short passives are more closely related to predicate adjective sentences such as

Brian was happy.

than to full passives (Bowey 1982; Watt 1970). Children tend to use short passives sooner (Braine 1971; Harwood 1959) and tend to use the two types to convey different types of information. The subjects of children's short passives are almost all inanimate objects, whereas the same is not true for full passives. Furthermore, the verbs used in the two types tend to be different. The verbs of short passives are more likely to describe states—*got broken, got lost, was left*—than actions—*got killed, got hit, was crashed* (Horgan 1978: 68). On the other hand, in one experiment that only studied the acquisition of the passive of action words, the short and full passives appeared to be acquired roughly at the same time (Maratsos & Abramovitch 1975). Thus it appears that stative verbs form the first passives, which are in the short form and modelled on the predicate adjective construction, and action verb passives appear later, simultaneously in full and short form.

Even when full passives appear, if one categorizes full passives into different types, one finds that there is a slower acquisition sequence than one might expect. A **reversible passive** is a passive sentence which would still make sense if one reversed the roles of the two participants.

The dog is chased by the girl.

is a reversible passive, because

The girl is chased by the dog.

also makes sense. On the other hand,

The lawn is mowed by Susan.

is a **nonreversible passive,** because

Susan is mowed by the lawn.

does not make sense.

The category of nonreversible passives can be further subdivided into **agentive nonreversible** and **instrumental nonreversible** passives.

The lawn is mowed by Susan.

is an agentive passive, because Sharon performed the action.

The lamp was broken by the ball.

is an instrumental passive, because someone unnamed performed the action using the ball as the instrument.

It appears that children don't produce agentive nonreversible passives until they are nine years or older, whereas children begin to use the full passive at four years or younger. Some of these younger children begin by using only reversible passives, while others begin by using only nonreversible instrumental passives. In experiments, most passives produced by children in the two- to four-year-old range are semantically reversed. Children would say, for example:

The cat was chased by the girl.

when the picture they were describing showed

The girl was chased by the cat.

In one study no child under 11 years old produced both reversible and nonreversible passives (Horgan 1978. See also Baldie 1976; Hayhurst 1967; Slobin 1968). Compared to adult speech, the set of events which children can express in the passive remains limited for a very long time.

Since passives appear so rarely in child speech, much of the research on their acquisition has been explored by means of comprehension experiments. Such experiments either involve having the child select one of two pictures (Fraser et al. 1963; Lovell & Dixon 1965) or take the form of a game in which the child is given some stuffed animals or other toys and is asked to act out the sentences spoken by the experimenter. For example, what do children who are given the following sentences do?

Make the horse be kissed by the cow.

If most children make the cow kiss the horse, then one assumes that they understand the passive. If most children make the horse kiss the cow, then one assumes that they are interpreting the sentence as if it were an active. If half respond one way and half respond the other, they are considered to be responding randomly—that is, without making use of syntactic cues.

The picture that emerges from such studies is something like this (J. de Villiers & de Villiers 1973a: 335;): Children whose utterances have MLUs in the 1.0 to 1.5 range (ages generally between 1;7 and 2;0) show no evidence of comprehending the participant roles in reversible active and passive sentences. About a third of these children make themselves the agent of the action—they will kiss the cow. Another 15% refuse to do the task. Among those who use both participants when acting out the sentence, about half match the participants to the correct roles and half reverse them—they respond at chance level.

Children with MLUs above 1.5 interpret actives with about 85% accuracy, while passives remain at chance level. This means that although they don't understand the passive, children do recognize the different syntactic markers that mark the passive and use them to differentiate the active from the passive.

There appears to be a period (MLUs in the 3.0 to 3.5 range) when children perform significantly worse than chance on passives, as can be seen in Figure 4.3. During this period they appear to treat passives as if the passive markers were not there. They interpret the noun before the verb as the agent and the noun after it as affected. This strategy has come to be known as the NVN strategy (Bever 1970: 305). The period in which children use this strategy has been identified in three studies (Bever 1970; J. de Villiers & de Villiers 1973a; Maratsos 1974a).

It has been claimed that some children develop the ability to comprehend the passive correctly, then temporarily reject the correct analysis to adopt the NVN strategy. I am not convinced that this occurs. In the study shown in Figure 4.3 there is no evidence to support this claim. The two studies that seem to support it are both flawed. In one study (Bever 1970) no statistical analysis was reported, and in the other study (Maratsos 1974a) the criterion for understanding the passive was very weak. To pass, the child had to act out correctly two out of three sentences. Under this criterion a child making use of both toys but assigning roles randomly has a 50% chance of passing. I would have preferred a much stricter criterion for comprehension.

Thus it appears that some children go through a NVN-strategy stage; how many is not known, and whether some come to handle the passive correctly before this stage is still open. A clearer picture would be obtained in a longitudinal study, in which the sequence of events could be followed for individual children.

Another strategy for understanding passives has been explored in a study that systematically varied the types of agent and affected (Lempert 1978). The two types

FIGURE 4.3
Development of comprehension of reversible actives and passives.

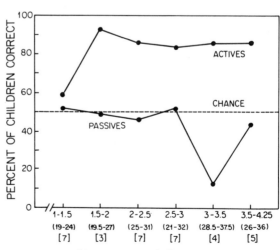

MLU ; (Age in months) ; [Number of children]

were animate—*Goofy®*, *the horse*—and inanimate—*the car, the ball*. The most common type of agent is animate (A), and the most common type of affected is inanimate (I). Since in a passive sentence the affected is subject and the agent is the object of the preposition, this would lead to sentences of this type (labelled I-A):

The car is pushed by Goofy.®

The least common is probably the reverse (labelled A-I):

Goofy® is pushed by the car.

One might expect that young children would find I-A passives easier than A-I passives, but, as shown in Table 4.3, the reverse seems to be the case. Although our expectations are contradicted, nevertheless, children do respond differently to passive sentences that differ in the semantic nature of their participants (see also A. Sinclair et al. 1971, Strohner & Nelson 1974).

Thus young children take both syntactic and semantic factors into account when trying to comprehend a passive utterance. This has been found to be true for English and for other languages in which the acquisition of the passive has been studied (French: H. Sinclair & Ferreiro 1970; Swiss-German: Caprez et al. 1971). Support can also be found in an experimental study of adults learning an artificial language. When given a chance to do so, the subjects looked for semantic regularities before attending to syntactic regularities (Mori & Moeser 1983).

Most of the research on the acquisition of the passive construction in English has involved those which use the auxiliary *be*. However, children at all ages are far more prone to use *get* as the auxiliary passive marker. They are also better at comprehension and imitation tasks when the passive marker is *get* (F. Harris & Flora 1982). Given this fact, one would hope that more future studies of the passive would include the *get* form.

TABLE 4.3 Comprehension of Passive with Different Participant Types

	SENTENCE	PERCENT CORRECT BY AGE			
TYPE	EXAMPLE	3;0	4;0	4;6	5;0
A-I*	Goofy is hit by the ball.	90%	77%	77%	87%
A-A	Goofy is chased by Donald Duck.	63%	63%	73%	87%
I-I	The truck is pushed by the car.	63%	63%	70%	80%
I-A	The truck is bumped by the horse.	27%	50%	57%	87%

*A-I means the first noun is ANIMATE and the second noun is INANIMATE. Based on Lempert 1978.

Comprehension versus production

One of the most interesting aspects of the acquisition of complex syntactic constructions is that children sometimes can produce them correctly before they have much success at comprehending them. This has been found in a study of children's ability to handle active sentences containing animate and inanimate subjects and objects (Chapman & Miller 1975).

Another area of syntax for which this is true is number agreement between the verb and its subject noun:

The sheep is jumping.
The sheep are jumping.

In most sentences in English the number of the subject is determinable from the ending on the subject noun. In some sentences it can be determined by both the noun ending and the ending on the verb or its auxiliary. In a few sentences, such as those above, it can be determined only by the verb or auxiliary ending. It turns out that children learn to produce the correct noun-verb number agreement *before* they can make use of the number markings on the verb alone in a comprehension test (Keeney & Wolfe 1972). Here again the ability to produce a correct construction precedes the ability to use the information it encodes for comprehension.

These two areas, however, are very likely the exception rather than the rule. In general, people have believed that comprehension of any given construction should appear earlier than production of that construction. Indeed, early studies seemed to support this (Fraser et al. 1963). Later studies, however, pointed out that biases built into the experiments probably influenced the results (Baird 1972; Fernald 1972). It turns out to be very difficult to produce a convincing study to determine the relative onset times for comprehension and production of particular utterance types. Nevertheless, it is probably true that for most constructions comprehension either precedes or co-occurs with production. The fact that there are known to be exceptions demonstrates that the two processes are not necessarily tied to each other developmentally.

Complex sentences

Complex sentences are sentences which contain more than one verb, not counting auxiliaries. Here is a simple example:

I wanna go home.

First occurrence   The first complex sentences to appear occur at MLU 3.5 to 4.0, at around two years of age. The first type of complex sentence is generally the **object complement** construction, in which the object of a sentence is a construction including another verb. The above example is such a sentence. Certain verbs—*wanna, like, let,* and *lookit,* for example—commonly take verbal constructions. Generally, if the child has produced any four word sentences at all, this type of construction will appear within a month of the first use of one of these verbs (Limber 1973: 175-176).

Subjects can also be verbal constructions:

That she likes him surprises me.

but these do not appear until much later. Just as in the case of simple sentences discussed in Chapter 3, the noun phrase is expanded first in the object noun phrase, and only later in the subject noun phrase.

In the case of *I wanna go home,* the agent of the second verb is the agent of the first, but right from the first use of such constructions, this is not necessary (Limber 1973: 177; additional examples in R. Brown 1973: 21):

> Watch me draw circles.
> I see you sit down.
> Lookit a boy play ball.

Shortly after the appearance of object complement constructions, two other types appear: conjunctive constructions and *wh-* constructions.

Conjunctions   Before the appearance of the first conjunctions, two parallel sentences may be juxtaposed:

> (At 2;0): You lookit that book: I lookit this book (Limber 1973: 181).

But true conjunction begins with the first use of a conjunction—often *and*:

> (At 2;8): He was stuck and I got him out (Limber 1973: 181).
> We went up in Foxboro and there were slides.
> No, you have some and I have some (Brown 1973: 26).

Conjoining parts of sentences seem to begin at the same time as conjoining whole sentences:

> (At 2;8) He still has milk and spaghetti.
> (At 2;10) I went to the aquarium and saw the fish (Limber 1973: 181).

Evidence that a child understands the meaning of sentences containing conjoined parts can sometimes be obtained by playing an imitation game with a child (Slobin & Welsh 1968: 492-493).

> **Adult:**   The pencil and some paper are here.
> **Echo (2;3):**   Some pencil here and some paper here.
>
> **Adult:**   The pussy eats bread and the pussy runs fast.
> **Echo (2;4):**   Pussy eat bread and he run fast.

These examples show that the child understood and could make use of the semantic relationships implied by conjoining sentence parts.

Appearing shortly after *and* are other conjunctions: *and then, because, so, when, if, or, but,* and *while* in no particular order, but with *before* and *after* coming in later (Cromer 1968). Similar development has been found in German, Turkish, and Italian (Clancy et al. 1976). Here are some examples of early use of conjunctions in English:

> (At 2;6) I do pull it the way he hafta do that so he doesn't, so the big boy doesn't come out.
>
> (At 2;10) I want this doll because she's big.
>
> (At 2;10) When I was a little girl I used to go "geek-geek" like that; but now I can go "This is a chair" (Limber 1973: 181).
>
> I'll hurt my brother if I scratched her.
>
> If they put him in between, he wants to go there (Menyuk 1969: 92-93).

Wh- clauses   The first *wh-* clauses are used adverbially (Limber 1973: 180; additional examples in R. Brown 1973: 22):

> Do it how I do it.
> Can I do it when we go home?

Verbs which take questions as complements appear at the same time (Limber 1973: 180):

> I remember where is it.
> I show you how to do it.

Wh- clauses that are **relative clauses**—that modify a noun—appear later. The first relative clauses are attached to abstract adverbial nouns (Limber 1973: 181):

> I show you the place we went.
> That's the way Mommy talks.

The next relative clauses to appear modify 'empty' nouns:

> That's the one I want.
> Show Mommy the thing you made.
> I got everything what you got (Menyuk 1969: 96).

Finally, relative clauses begin to appear on common nouns:

> Now where's a pencil I can use? (R. Brown 1973: 23)

Last to come in are sentences using *which,* no doubt due to its lower frequency.

The first relative clauses children use appear at the end of sentences. Much more difficult to master are relative clauses that modify other than the last noun, and thus interrupt the main clause and are surrounded by it. Young children neither produce these nor do they understand them, as becomes evident in imitation tests:

Adult: The boy the book hit was crying.
Echo (2;5):   Boy, the book was crying.

Adult: The house the boy hit was big.
Echo: Boyhouse was big.

Adult: The boy the chair hit was dirty.
Echo: Boy hit the chair was dirty (Slobin & Welsh 1968: 494-495).

A number of experimental studies have probed children's understanding of embedded relative clauses such as these. Children appear to behave one way in some of the experiments and another way in others (S. Aller 1977; Bowerman 1979; H. Brown 1971; Cook 1973; J. de Villiers et al. 1979; Gaer 1969; A. Gordon 1972; Hakuta 1976b; Lahey 1974; Sheldon 1974; M.D. Smith 1974; Solan & Roeper 1978; Tavakolian 1977). Suffice it to say that the children have considerable difficulty understanding these sentences.

The minimum distance principle   One of the most interesting areas of research on complex sentences involves the acquisition of a particular class of object complement sentences—those that violate the **minimum distance principle (MDP)** (Rosenbaum 1967). According to this principle, when the verb in a complement clause is missing a subject, the participant that is taken to be the subject is the noun phrase in the main clause most closely preceding the complement verb. Consider these sentences:

Tanya wanted to go.
Henry wanted Judy to return.
Jason told Sasha what to do.

The subject of *go* is *Tanya;* of *return* is *Judy;* and of *do* is *Sasha.* In each case the subject is the nearest preceding noun phrase in the main clause. However, certain verbs and adjectives, when in the main clause of such a sentence, require a violation of the MDP for their interpretation. Compare the implied subjects of the complement verb in each of these sentence groups:

Roger is eager to please.
Roger is easy to please.

Arthur told Jean to leave soon.
Arthur promised Jean to leave soon.

David told Jack what to do.
David asked Jack what to do.

Naomi asked to wear it.
Naomi asked Rebecca to wear it.
Naomi asked Rebecca what to wear.

Note that the first sentence in each set is correctly interpretable using the MDP, whereas the last is not. The crucial difference in the first three sentence pairs is the particular verb or predicate adjective used. The last set illustrates the fact that *ask* is more complex. When an infinitive complement is used, *ask* is usually interpreted as a polite form of *tell,* and like *tell* it follows the MDP. In the case of the presence of the recipient of the message—*Rebecca* in the second sentence of the group—it could be interpreted as asking for permission, in which case it violates the MDP. Thus the second sentence is ambiguous. There is no ambiguity when the complement is a *wh-* clause. In this case *ask* really means "to query," and in this meaning it violates the MDP.

It turns out that children are very slow to learn constructions that violate the MDP.

First, consider *easy* and *hard.* The child is shown a doll on which is tied a blindfold (C. Chomsky 1969: 30-31):

Experimenter:	Is this doll easy to see or hard to see?
Peter (6;9):	Hard to see.
Ex.:	Why?
Peter:	'Cause she got a blindfold.
Ex.:	Will you make her easy to see.
Peter:	(Removes blindfold)
Ex.:	Will you explain what you did.
Peter:	I punched her. (An accurate description)
Ex.:	How did that make her easier to see?
Peter:	It punched off the blindfold.

It is clear from this protocol that Peter is interpreting the sentence to mean that the doll is to do the seeing. Of 40 children ranging in ages from 5;0 to 10;0, 14 children, including Peter, failed this task (C. Chomsky 1969: 27).

The age at which children catch on in this task seems to be about seven years old. Of those children tested who were under seven, only 31% succeeded, whereas of those seven or older, 88% succeeded. The improvement is charted in Figure 4.4.

Some have argued that the presence of the blindfold, which is, in fact, irrelevant to the correct answer, seduces children into giving the wrong answer, and that children really acquire this construction at an earlier age than was thought. Therefore other, less deceptive, tasks have been devised.

One study had Linus, Lucy, and Charlie Brown dolls playing hide-and-seek (Kessel 1970). Children were shown two of these dolls and given sentences such as:

Lucy was easy to find.

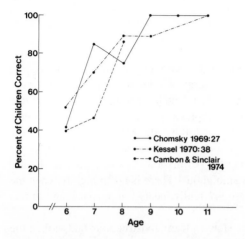

FIGURE 4.4
Acquisition of *easy to X* in three studies.

The questions asked were: *Who is hiding?* and *Who is seeking?* As Figure 4.4 shows, children acquired the construction in this case at roughly the same rate as in the blindfold task.

Another study involved acting out with stuffed animals these two sentences (Cromer 1970):

> The duck is glad to bite. Show me that.
> The duck is fun to bite. Show me that.

In this case it appears that the construction was mastered a bit earlier, at around 6;7 (Cromer 1970: 401). The results were given in mental age rather than chronological age and were not broken down on a year-by-year basis, so they cannot be plotted on Figure 4.4.

A similar study of the French counterpart—*facile*—yielded similar results, which are also plotted in Figure 4.4.

Considering the last three mentioned studies together, one can conclude that whatever is determining the slight differences in the age of acquisition, the blindfold does not appear to have had much of an effect (Morsbach & Steele 1976 claim to have demonstrated the 'trick' effect of the blindfold strongly, but my interpretation of their data is that when presented in sequence with two situational interpretations of a word, children will tend to be consistent and interpret the word in the second situation the same way they did in the first).

Once children master the *easy/eager* distinction, they can apply it to newly created words (Cromer 1970: 400):

Experimenter: See? Someone gave this dog a bone. And so he's feeling very risp. Now show me: The wolf is risp to bite.

Experimenter: This cat climbed up and picked a rose. And he found that chewing the rose was larsp. Now show me: The rose is larsp to bite.

Most children who correctly handled *easy* could perform these tasks correctly.

Consider now the problem of the word *promise*. Bozo and Donald dolls sit on a table. The experimenter says:

Bozo promises Donald to hop up and down. Make him hop.

Young children will make Donald hop, as predicted by the MDP; older children make Bozo hop. As Figure 4.5 shows, this task appears to be harder than *easy* is.

Also difficult to master is *ask*. Though it is a more common word than either *easy* or *promise* (Thorndike & Lorge 1944), its difficulty is probably due to the complex way its two different meanings and syntax interact, as has already been described.

By five years old, children correctly interpret *ask* when it is used as a request (C. Chomsky 1969: 52-53):

Experimenter: Suppose Donald Duck asks to go first. What does he say?

Eric (5;2):   Can I go first?
   Ex.:   Suppose Mickey asks Donald to go first. What does he say?
Peter (5;2):   You wanna go in line first?

**FIGURE 4.5   Acquisition of complement constructions in 40
                children. (Based on C. Chomsky 1969.)**

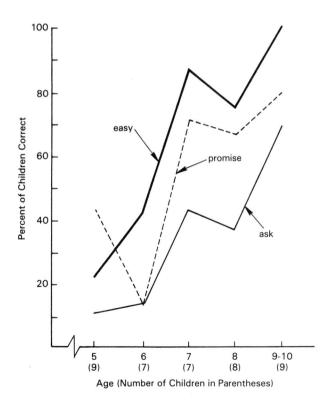

This second construction is ambiguous; the interpretation given by Peter is the most likely, but the other meaning occasionally will occur in an advanced child:

Experimenter: If you ask Kim to leave the room, who's going to go out? What do you say to her?
Warren (9;7):   May I go out of the room?

The acquisition of the question meaning of *ask* comes more slowly and in stages. The first such construction to appear is *ask* (PERSON) *who* or *ask* (PERSON) *what,* where the subject of the *wh-* clause is given:

Before:

Experimenter: Ask Eric who his teacher is.
Christine (5;1):   Miss Turner.

After:

Experimenter: Ask Peter what color this tray is.
Laurie (6;6):   What color's it?

The next construction to be acquired is *ask* (PERSON) (NP):

Before:

Experimenter: Ask Peter the color of the doll's house.
Laurie (6;6):   Red.

After:

Experimenter: Ask Joanne her last name.
Laura (6;5):   What's your last name?

Next children begin to realize that the *ask* (PERSON) *what to* (VERB) construction involves the question form of *ask,* but they fail to realize that it violates the MDP:

Before:

Experimenter: Ask Joanne what to feed the doll.
Laura (6;5):   The hot dog.

After:

Experimenter: Ask Lynn what to feed the dog.
Stephen (8;8):   What do you wanna feed the dog?

Finally, at about 8;7 or so (see Figure 4.5), children come to realize that *ask* violates the MDP:

Experimenter: Ask Kim what to feed the doll.
Warren (9;7): What should I feed the doll?

Similar results have been obtained in a study of monolingual Lebanese-Arabic-speaking children (Aller et al. 1979).

Slight differences in experimental method seem to lead to large differences in reported age of acquisition of *ask* constructions. One study found essentially complete acquisition by eight years (Kessel 1970: 34. People wishing to try this on children will appreciate the stimulus pictures in the appendix of this monograph), while another recorded only 35% success at this age and even at age 19 found only 68% success (Kramer et al. 1972: 125).

Although many of the errors children make can be accounted for by the MDP, this does not necessarily imply that children use the MDP to decide on the subject of the complement verb. In fact, this is not the case. It was demonstrated by asking four- and five-year olds to act out several complement sentences, including two in which the main verb was passive (Maratsos 1974b):

The bear is told by the elephant to get in.
The daddy is asked by the mommy to get in.
The monkey promises the dog to jump off.

If children were using the MDP, they should incorrectly make the elephant and the mommy get in the car. Those children who understood the passive—that is, those who knew who was talking to whom—also chose the correct participant as agent of the complement verb. However, many of these same children still gave the wrong response to *promise*. Thus the strategy that children actually use is not a simple word-order strategy, as is the NVN strategy, but rather appears to be more semantically based. When an addressee is specified, that addressee is taken to be the agent of the complement verb.

The other half of this strategy, one suspects, would be: When the addressee is not specified, the speaker is taken to be the agent of the complement verb. This was also tested on two constructions:

John asks to sit down.
John tells to sit down.

Children had no trouble with the first sentence, as one would predict. But what about the second? Although it is ungrammatical, adults will interpret this sentence to mean that the unnamed listener should do the sitting. Some children assigned that role to John, as the semantic principle would predict, but about two-thirds behaved like adults and assigned it to the unnamed listener. Thus whatever the semantic strategy children use, it did not lead them astray on the second sentence.

From this research we must conclude that acquisition of complex systactic constructions continues at least into the early school years and may even continue into early adulthood. By this time the strategies children use, though still sometimes incorrect, appear to be more semantically based.

MORPHOLOGY

Twas brillig and the slithy toves
Did gyre and gimble in the wabe—Lewis Carroll, *Through the Looking Glass*

Morphology is the term used to describe the system of word building in language. The smallest unit of speech that has a separately identifiable meaning is known as a **morpheme.** Some morphemes are also words. For example, *witch* is a morpheme that is also a word. But many morphemes cannot stand alone as words. The plural morpheme in English is an example. Thus *witches* is a single word made up of two morphemes: *witch* and *-es.* Occasionally a single morpheme is written as two or more words; *um pa pa* as in *I like to listen to um pa pa music* is an example.

Segmentation problems

One of the tasks a child must accomplish is to break up the stream of speech into morphemes and to assign the correct meaning to each morpheme. This is the problem of **segmentation.** Young children often make mistakes in segmentation. The three most common mistakes are **undersegmentation, oversegmentation,** and **missegmentation.**

Undersegmentation   Undersegmentation describes the situation in which the child doesn't break the stream of speech into enough segments. For example, when Athena was about two, she would sometimes come up to me, stand on tiptoe, arms up, and say, "Carryyou!" What she should have said, of course, was, "Carry me!" but she did not realize that *carryyou* as in *Do you want me to carry you?* consisted of two morphemes (see Bloom et al. 1975a: 20, R. Brown 1973: 390-398).

Verbs with separate particles, such as *stand up,* are sometimes treated as a single unit. Evidence for this comes from misapplication of the verb endings. One of the children studied at Harvard said, "Look how she standups" (Cazden 1968: 236). Another child, Susan, said *standupped* (W. Miller & Ervin 1964: 26).

A similar example occurred when Athena was 3;8. The following conversation took place:

Athena: Why should I do it?
Mother: Do it because I say so!
Athena: "Sayso!" That mean you're mad!

One student of mine remembered being surprised when at age three she learned to read and found out that *this morning* was two words rather than one.

Another person learned the following hymn in church: *Low in the gravy lay Jesus, my savior*. He remembers being surprised to find out that it was, in fact: *Low in the grave he lay, Jesus, my savior*. Yet another student of mine reported that a relative as a child misinterpreted the hymn line *Gladly the cross I'd bear* as *Gladly, the cross-eyed bear*.

Oversegmentation   More common, perhaps, is the occurrence of over-segmentation. This describes the situation in which the child breaks up an utterance into too many parts. For example, Athena at about three saw her mother doing some gardening. She came up to her and said, "I want gard too, Mommy." She had considered the *-en* an inflection that should be stripped off to yield the basic morpheme. Later I heard another example:

Athena: (Pointing to a spot on her leg.) What's this Daddy?
Me: That's a bruise.
Athena: Look, Daddy. Here's another bru!''

Another case of oversegmentation occurred when one small boy tried to recite the alphabet, and ended with (Tanz 1980:52):

. . . U, V, double me, X, Y, Z.

And yet another example (Kuczaj 1978):

A.K. (5;2):   Ben's hicking up. He's hicking up.
Adult: What?
A.K.:   He's got the hiccups.

Family Circus (© 1980 The Register and Tribune Syndicate, Inc.
Used by permission.)

THE FAMILY CIRCUS®   **By Bil Keane**

"Now, remember — I want you to behave."
"Don't worry, Mommy, I'll be REAL 'haive'."

Finally, from another child, five years old, came this (Hockett 1967: 115):

Father: Don't interrupt.
 Child: Daddy, you're interring up!

Compare the last two examples with *stand up* in the previous section. No wonder children get confused!

Missegmentation Missegmentation involves placing the morpheme boundaries at the wrong places in an utterance, as is illustrated by this example (Gleitman et al. 1972):

> Mommy, is it "an adult" or "a nadult"?

Missegmentation most often occurs in long memorized routines such as the American Pledge of Allegiance or in hymns, anthems, or other songs. The most famous example of this is the purposefully misleading song (Drake, Hoffman & Livington 1943. Used by permission):

> Mairzy doats and doazy doats and little lamzy divy.
> A kiddelee divy, too, wooden chew.

"Keep out! Keep out! K-E-E-P O-U-T."

Herman (© Universal Press Syndicate. Used by permission.)

which, as some of us old-timers will recall, actually says:

> Mares eat oats and does eat oats and little lambs eat ivy.
> A kid'll eat ivy, too, wouldn't you?

Categorization problems

In addition to segmentation problems, children make a number of categorization errors. Three types of errors of this nature are **miscategorization, undercategorization,** and **overapplication.**

Miscategorization   Occasionally it appears that children place morphemes in the wrong morphological or syntactic class. This often comes to light when children use an inappropriate inflection with that word. One morning Athena, at 2;7, came into our bedroom and proclaimed:

> Mommy, time to get up now. It stops darking out.

Another child, 2;6, while scribbling on a piece of paper, said (E. Clark 1980: 16):

> I'm darking the sky.

In both of these examples, the adjective *dark* has been given a verb ending. Similar errors have been reported in the children studied at Harvard:

> Let me have somes.

This example puts a noun ending on a pronoun. Similarly,

> Dat greens.

This example puts a noun ending on an adjective.

One of the earliest reported cases of this was a German child who used *messen* as a verb meaning "to cut," based on the noun *Messer,* meaning "knife" (Preyer 1888). This involved putting a verb ending on a noun.

A **lexical gap** is a concept or idea for which a person doesn't have a word. Many miscategorizations appear to be purposeful attempts to fill lexical gaps. Here are some examples (first two from E. Clark 1980; others from Kuczaj 1978):

EB (2;8):   (After roaring with claws outstretched at a towel.) I monstered that towel.
CB (3;11):   (Putting crackers in her soup.) I'm crackering my soup.
HK (3;6):   (Observing rain and thunder.) Why is it weathering?
JW (5;7):   (Hitting a ball with a stick.) I'm sticking it.
JW (5;7):   (Putting a shirt on a doll.) I'm shirting my man.
AK (5;1):   (Referring to dancing in a ballet.) She's ballerening.

Since in such cases the children usually also used the words in question correctly in other contexts, this type of miscategorization is usually really overextension of syntactic use combined with appropriate morphological inflection for that overextended use.

Undercategorization   The greatest number of miscategorizations involves more subtle subcategories. This is perhaps better described as **undercategorization.** Here are three examples:

> Going put some sugars.

This shows confusion of the distinction between **mass nouns,** which don't take plurals, and **count nouns,** which do (see also Slobin 1966: 140).

> I seeing Fraser.

This shows confusion of the distinction between **process verbs,** which can take the progressive aspect *-ing* ending, and **stative verbs,** which cannot (some of the senses of *see* are process and can take the *-ing*—for example, *seeing* in the sense of dating, or making regular visits, as to a psychiatrist).

> I falled that down.

This shows confusion of the distinction between **transitive** and **intransitive** verbs.

Overapplication   Some morphemes can only appear combined with a few other morphemes. The morpheme *cran-* occurs in only a few words: *cranberry* and those recently invented blended juice products, *Cranapple,*® *Crangrape,*® and *Crantastic.*® Another type of error young children can make is to overextend the use of a limited-use morpheme. This example occurred when Athena was 3;9:

Me: (Supervising Athena getting dressed.) I think you've got your underpants on backwards.
Athena: Yes, I think so.
Me: You'd better take them off and put them on frontwards.
Athena: (Taking them off and turning them around.) Is this the rightwards?

The following example was produced by the daughter, 1;9, of a colleague:

Judith: Somebody's at the door.
Mother: There's nobody at the door.
Judith: There's yesbody at the door.

Allomorphs

When two different forms have the same meaning, they are considered different **allomorphs** of the same morpheme. For example, *she* is the third-person singular feminine pronoun in subject position, while *her* is the third person singular feminine pronoun in object position. We say that *she* and *her* are two allomorphs of the same morpheme, and that they are in alternation with one another. This is sometimes written: /she~her/. Which allomorph is used depends upon the context. The context that determines which allomorph is used can be syntactic, morphological, or phonological. The above example is syntactic, because subject and object are syntactic categories.

When a particular allomorph is chosen depending on which morpheme it is appended to, the context is morphological. Consider the morpheme /un-~non-/. Which allomorph occurs depends upon which morpheme it is attached to: *unkind, unfortunate, unsound,* but *nonexistent, nonstop, nonnuclear.*

For some morphemes, which allomorph is used is **phonologically conditioned**—that is, it is determined by some aspect of the phonological structure of a neighboring morpheme. The conditioning environment may precede or follow the morpheme. For example, the indefinite article, /a~an/, is a morpheme the allomorph of which is determined by the initial sound of the following word. On the other hand, in the case of the possessive suffix, /-s~-z~-əz/, the choice of allomorph is determined by the final sound of the preceding morpheme.

Since the acquisition of the latter alternation has been studied extensively, it is useful to describe it in detail. The rule is as follows: If the immediately preceding sound is any one of /s,z,ʃ,ʒ,č,ǰ/, choose /-əz/. If the immediately preceding sound is not one of the above but is any other unvoiced consonant, choose /-s/. If the immediately preceding sound is none of the above, chose /-z/. Thus *Butch's* is pronounced /bɑčəz/, *Rick's* is pronounced /ɹɪks/, and *Ted's* is pronounced /tɛdz/. The only exceptions to this rule are the possessive forms of the personal pronouns: *my, your, her, our, their.*

Two other morphemes are almost identical in form to the possessive. One is the **concord** element—the ending appended to main verbs taking a singular subject, provided they are in the present tense and the verb phrase contains no auxiliaries. Thus *Roger washes* /-əz/, *Roger wakes* /-s/, and *Roger wades* /-z/. The other similar morpheme is the plural. Thus *dishes* /-əz/, *plates* /-s/, and *spoons* /-z/. The plural morpheme, however, has many other allomorphs, which are **morphologically conditioned**—that is, there are many other forms that are used with specific words or very small classes of words: /-en/ for *oxen;* /-ren/ for *children;* /-∅/ (the null form) for *sheep, fish;* /-ɛ-/ (replacing the vowel in the root) for *men,* to list just a few.

Acquisition of morphological variation

How do children learn the plural forms and other morphological rules? One possibility is that children learn the plural form of each word by rote. They know how to form the plural of a particular word only after they have heard someone else use that word in the plural. A good way to test for this is to give children words they have never used before and to ask them to form utterances requiring that the plural form be used. The best way to ensure that the words are new to the child is to invent new words and new objects or actions for the new words to refer to.

Jean Berko Gleason with picture of Wug.

The most famous study of this type is the Wug Test, named after its first item, a birdlike creature called a *wug* (Berko 1958). This test consists of 27 items. They test for the plural, the progressive verb suffix (/-ing/), the past tense, the possessive, the comparative and superlative endings for adjectives (/-er/ and /-est/), and a few compound word formations. The first item on the test is *This is a wug. Now there is another one. There are two of them. There are two _____.*

This test and various improved versions of it have been used many times on many populations. The result has been a much clearer view of the steps children go through in the acquisition of morphology.

The first finding is that the test can be done. Adults can, for example, pluralize nonsense syllables consistently, and they are in general agreement with one another as to how the plural should be formed. Thus we can reject the notion that people only use a plural of any particular word after they have heard someone else use that word in the plural.

The next finding is that the acquisition of morphology in English is relatively late. Although children use words that are made up of more than one morpheme almost from the time that they begin to speak, it appears that their ability to sort the rotely learned forms into a system of rules doesn't begin much before four years. While many of the basics are learned by age seven, additional constructions are still being learned up to age eleven and beyond. And some of the exceptions to the rules are never learned by a large proportion of the population—for example, that *phenomena* is the plural of *phenomenon*. There appear to be no differences in the rate of acquisition of morphology between boys and girls (Berko 1958: 364).

We shall now consider the case of the plural in detail. Children can be found to go through several steps in the acquisition of this morpheme:

1. At first no plurals are used. In general, when children don't know an inflection, they leave it off.

2. There follows an awareness by children of the singular/plural distinction and the notion that it is marked by others and should be marked by them, but they don't know how to mark the plural in the adult way. In one improvement on the Wug Test, the sentence *There are two _____* was replaced by the question *Now what do you see?* When this was done, it was discovered that children often respond by appending a number to the name: *I see five hesh* (Anisfeld & Tucker 1968). Since the original test always gave the number as part of the unfinished sentence, this stage was not discovered until the later study.

3. In a comprehension task young children are able to recognize plurality in words that take /-əz/ before they can recognize plurality in words that take /-z/ or /-s/ (see Figure 4.6). This is somewhat mysterious, since /-əz/ has the lowest frequency of the three regular forms. It is probably due to the fact that it is easier to perceive when a root is lengthened by a whole syllable than by a single phoneme.

Why would this matter? Before they learn the correct forms of the plural, children learning English seem to have a strategy that if they have heard two forms of a noun, that form which is the longest is the one that refers to the plural. When asked to choose whether the plural of *wafk* was *waf* or *wafkit*, 98% of the children chose the longer form (Anisfeld & Tucker 1968).

4. When children start producing plurals, they appear to learn the plurals of a few words. They correctly use the plural on these words, but don't generalize to other words or to nonsense syllables. Children in this stage will correctly pluralize *glass* to *glasses,* but will continue to give *tass* as the plural of *tass.*

5. The first pluralization to be used on nonsense syllables occurs on those syllables that end in a stop consonant. The correct form will be an /-s/ if the preceding consonant is unvoiced, and /-z/ if it is voiced. The probable reason that

FIGURE 4.6
Acquisition of the regular English plural allomorphs (Based on Anisfeld & Tucker's 1968 study of 18 kindergarteners [mean age 5;6]).

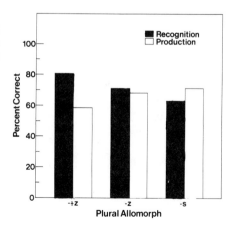

this subset of plurals is acquired earlier is that it obeys a general phonological rule. In English all consonant clusters consisting of two stops or a stop and a fricative are either entirely voiced or entirely unvoiced. Thus [st, ts, sk, ks, sp, ps, pt, kt] are all acceptable, but [sd, ds, sg, gs, sb, bs, bt, gt] are not.

6. When a word ends in a vowel, phonologically it is acceptable to add either an /-s/ or a /-z/. Thus the rule in English that nouns ending in vowels—such as *tree, superhero,* and *zebra*—take /-z/ in the plural is a much less general rule, even though it applies to plural, possessive, and concord. It should not be surprising, then, that /-z/ after vowels is acquired later than after stop consonants.

7. Later still is the appearance of /-əz/ on invented words. Why so late? Perhaps because this plural allomorph has relatively low frequency in English.

8. Once the regular rules are learned, exceptions and irregularities have to be learned or relearned (the latter is explained below). Thus a next stage is to learn that, for example, *leaf* becomes *leaves.*

9. Later still, exceptions to the exceptions must be learned. Quentin was eight before he realized that although the plural of *leaf* was *leaves,* the hockey team is known as the *Toronto Maple Leafs,* not the *Toronto Maple Leaves.*

The above description suggests that children attend to phonological features—such as voiced or unvoiced—of the final consonants of the words they are attempting to pluralize. One plausible alternate hypothesis is that they model their inflection of the new word after a known word that rhymes with it—that is, they model it after a word with the same vowel and final consonant(s). Thus they say *wugs* ([wʌgz]) because they already know that the plural of *rug* is *rugs* ([ɹʌgz]).

Wug with pictures of Jean Berko Gleason.

Certainly in the case of adults this is part of the story. Almost all verbs which end in *-ing* (/-ɪŋ/) have irregular past tenses—*sing, sang; ring, rang; fling, flung; sting,stung; wring, wrung; bring, brought.* When adults were asked to produce the past tense of *bing,* half said either *bang* or *bung;* when asked to produce the past of *gling,* three-quarters said *glang* or *glung* (Berko 1958: 368).

However, this strategy does not seem to be used by children. In a more systematic test of plurals, half of the nonsense words had no real-word rhymes at all, yet the children behaved no differently on these than they did on the other half that did have real-word rhymes (Derwing & Baker 1977: 99-100). And only 4 of the 172 responses of children to *bing* and *gling* were influenced by the irregularity of rhyming words (Berko 1958: 368). On the contrary, as will be described in the next section, children are more likely to regularize the irregular words than to use them as models.

Just because children have acquired the ability to produce a plural doesn't mean that they will pluralize the word in all the contexts that require it. As shown in Figure 4.7, children are more likely to pluralize correctly when required by other words within the same noun phrase, such as *some* in the phrase *some crayons,* than they are when agreement is required with a word that lies outside of the noun phrase boundary, as is the case between the subject *those* and the predicate nominative *crayons* in the sentence *Those my crayons.*

FIGURE 4.7
Use of plural in two contexts. Shaded bars show correct use when plural is otherwise marked within the noun phrase; light bars show correct use when plural is otherwise marked outside of the noun phrase.

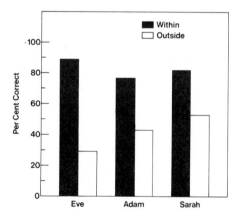

The constructions of the possessive and plural morphemes in English are very similar; in fact, they are identical for the vast majority of nouns. Thus it is not surprising that the course of acquisition is very similar for these two constructions. Nevertheless, these two morphemes are not usually acquired in lock step. Statistically, plurals are acquired ahead of possessives (Derwing & Baker 1979: 212), but this is a trend, not an absolute. Adam and Sarah acquired plurals before possessives; Eve acquired them at the same time (Cazden 1968: 227). Other children acquired possessives first (e.g., Leopold 1949a: 84). Among children studied in Berko's original study, plural preceded possessive for *wug* (*wugs,* 91% correct; *wug's,* 84% correct), but possessive preceded plural for *niz* (*nizzes,* 28% correct; *niz's,* 49% correct) (Berko 1958: 365 & 369).

The acquisition of the past tense morpheme proceeds along lines similar to the acquisition of the plural morpheme. A great many other morphemes have been charted developmentally, also with very similar patterns of development.

Overregularization

Once children learn general morphological rules, not only do they apply these rules to nonsense syllables, as in the Wug Test, they also sometimes apply them to words which take irregular forms. This can actually lead to a temporary worsening of this aspect of language. For example, most verbs in English take the regular past tense—/-d/, /-t/, or /-əd/, depending upon the phonological form of the preceding sound, similar to that described for the plural. However, many of the most common verbs have irregular past tense forms. Because they are so common, children learn many of these irregular forms before they have learned the general rule.

Interestingly, when the general rule is learned, children will often stop using the previously learned irregular form and instead produce a regularized version. Thus a child who had been using the correct past tense of *sing*—namely, *sang*—may start using the form *singed* (/sɪŋd/) instead. Before the correct irregular form is again learned, some children have been known to produce forms that combine the irregular and the regular form. In the case of *sing,* this would be *sanged.* Thus children may proceed through as many as five steps in the acquisition of some inflections. Table 4.4 lists the five steps and gives examples of each of these steps for three different inflections. Although probably every child overregularizes somewhat, each child may do it on a different set of words. Furthermore, overregularization of one inflection doesn't necessarily occur at the same time as overregularization of another inflection.

When do overregularizations begin to appear? Adam began overregularizing when he was producing plurals in 68% of the places where he should have pluralized; Eve began overregularizing at 86%; but Sarah did not begin until 98% (Cazden 1968: 228).

One day when Quentin was three years old I overheard him listening to a television program about the cactus plant. He said something to me in which he used the plural form *cacti.* I thought that was quite sophisticated, so later I attempted to elicit this behavior in front of his mother:

Me: Suppose I have one cactus and then I get another. What would I have now?
Quentin: Two cactuses.
Me: (Trying again.) What would I have if I had lots of them?
Quentin: You would have lots of cacti.

TABLE 4.4   Steps in the Acquisition of Irregular Inflections

		EXAMPLES		
STEP	DESCRIPTION	NOUN	VERB	ADJ
1	No inflection	man	go	bad
2	Adult form	men	went	worse
3	Overregularization	mans	goed	badder
4	Transition	mens	wented	worser
5	Adult form	men	went	worse

When faced with competition of a normal plural rule and an unusual form, he had resolved the conflict by postulating an additional distinction. Although I don't know exactly what the basis was for Quentin's distinction, it appears to be similar to the dual/plural distinction described in the next section. This is another example of children creating a system which is not in use in their language, but is used in other languages.

Inflection in other languages

Studies of inflectional development in English cover only the tip of the iceberg. Inflection in many languages is far more complex, and thus the task of development is more difficult.

Plural Pity the child who must learn the plural in Egyptian Arabic. Not only are there **singular** and **plural** forms, there is also a **dual** form—a form to indicate exactly two items. The plural form applies to three to ten items; more than ten is marked by the singular. Furthermore, there is a distinction between **counted** and **collected** nouns. Thus there is one form to indicate a collection of individual houses and another form to indicate a group of houses. Most important, unlike English, in which the vast majority of nouns have regular plurals, in Egyptian Arabic the class of regular nouns is small, and most nouns fall into a large number of fairly irregular classes. With all this complexity it is not surprising that Egyptian children as old as 15 continue to make errors in pluralizing even familiar nouns (Omar 1973).

Declension, gender, and case In many languages whole classes of nouns take different sets of endings. All nouns taking the same set of inflections are said to form a particular declension. Latin, for example, has five declensions. Within each declension the endings often differ depending upon their syntactic use. In English the only remnant we have of this is in the pronouns—*I, me, my, mine; who, whom, whose;* and so on. The different forms are said to be in different cases. Furthermore, each case of each declension may be different, depending on number, which, as already described, can be far more complex than simply singular or plural. Related to declension but not identical to it is gender, which determines which endings must be placed on pronouns, articles, adjectives, and/or verbs when they must agree with the nouns. Latin, Russian, and German have three genders; French, Hebrew, and Hindi have two genders; and worse yet, Lamba, a Bantu language, and Fulani, a Niger-Congo language, each have about a dozen genders (H. Gleason 1961: 227 and personal communication)! Complicating an already complex situation is the fact that particular inflections may mark more than one case, different cases and numbers in different declensions, and so on. Similar if not greater complexities occur with verbs and other parts of speech.

How all this complexity interacts has been a topic of a number of studies. Consider the case of Dainis, a boy learning Latvian (Rūķe-Draviņa 1959). The first use of case endings appeared at 1;7, with rapid development beginning at 1;11. By this time he had over 600 words in his vocabulary, and sentences up to 6 words long were common. Differentiation into different cases preceded differentiation on the basis of number, and individual cases appeared first in the singular, then in the plural. When case endings began to be elaborated in the plural, their progress was more rapid, the way having been paved by earlier development of the singular system.

The system of verb inflection came later. Marking for tense preceded marking for person (first, second, or third). Marking for number coincided with development of the personal pronouns. The development of verbal inflection was still under development at age four, when the study ended.

The basic insight from this case study is that inflections appear to be acquired earlier in languages in which inflection is more pervasive. Acquisition of inflection is really just beginning in English at age four, while for at least this one Latvian boy it is already well advanced.

Let us turn to an example from Russian. One case in Russian is the **instrumental.** In the Russian equivalent of the sentence *Ivan opened the door with a key,* the noun *key* would be in the instrumental case. Russian nouns have three declensions, each associated most strongly with one of the three genders. (The association of case to gender is not perfect, and there are exceptions, which lead to acquisition difficulties. See Popova 1958: 272.) Masculine and neuter nouns are marked by *-om* in the instrumental singular; feminine nouns are marked by *-oy*.

The development of these Russian case endings by a boy named Zhenya demonstrates an interesting interaction of form and function in influencing the course of development. Zhenya began to inflect for case before he marked for gender. Thus he would choose one inflectional ending to mark nouns in a particular case, without regard to the declension to which they belonged. But which would he choose? From 2;1 to 2;4 he used *-om* for all nouns; from 2;5 to 3;0 he used *-oy* exclusively; thereafter he used the two forms correctly for their respective noun classes.

How can one interpret this behavior? Three facts seem relevant. The most frequent noun class is the feminine. The suffix *-oy* not only marks feminine instrumental singular nouns, in adjectives it also marks three cases in the feminine and one in the masculine. In contrast, *-om* marks only one other case—the masculine and neuter prepositional. Presumably Zhenya figured out the meaning of the ending with fewer different meanings first, and thus chose it over a more frequent but more ambiguous alternative (Gvozdev 1948, 1949).

Accusative is the case name used for the direct object of sentences, and possibly other uses, such as the object of some or all prepositions. The ending Zhenya chose for the Russian accusative singular illustrates another factor that appears to influence acquisition sequence. There are four different accusative markers: *-ø* (no ending), *-u, -a,* and *-o.* The most frequent marker is no ending; *-u* is second. But *-u* was chosen, presumably because it was less ambiguous than no ending. Thus there is a preference to mark a case with some ending rather than a null ending, even if that is the most frequent ending. (Similar cases are found in

Dutch: Snow et al. 1980; and in Serbo-Croatian: Mikeš & Vlahović 1966; Pavlovitch 1920.)

The *-om* ending that Zhenya chose for the instrumental was masculine; the *-u* ending that he chose for the accusative was feminine. Apparently Zhenya chose each case ending separately on its merits rather than selecting one gender and using it for all cases (Gvozdev 1948, 1949). Zhenya's course of acquisition was not unique; similar results were found in large-scale studies of gender of both nouns (Zakharova 1958) and past tense verbs, which are also inflected for gender (Popova 1958).

Certain cases are used often or exclusively with prepositions in many languages, such as German, Russian, and Serbo-Croatian. In general, children begin marking the inflection before using the preposition (Gvozdev 1949; Mikeš 1967; Mikeš & Vlahović 1966; Pavlovitch 1920). A particularly clear demonstration of this was observed in two girls in Northern Yugoslavia, who learned Hungarian and Serbo-Croatian simultaneously. In Hungarian, noun inflections include locative information, which in Serbo-Croatian is contained in prepositions. For example, the meaning of the English prepositions *into, onto, out of,* and *on top of* is contained in the noun endings in Serbo-Croatian. The same girls that were expressing locative information via inflections in Hungarian were not expressing it in Serbo-Croatian. It is clear that these girls had differentiated the appropriate concepts; it was the form of expression that they had not yet mastered (Mikeš 1967; Mikeš & Vlahović 1966). Apparently, all other things being equal, suffixes are easier to acquire than prepositions.

To a native speaker of English learning French or other languages involving gender, mastering gender is perhaps the most frustrating part of the task because of the apparent arbitrariness of classification. Children learning gender languages do not seem to encounter the same difficulty (e.g., Park 1971; C. Stern & Stern 1928). Although it has been noted that there is a correlation between the last syllable of the root of the noun and its gender, authors of French grammars conclude that this factor is of limited value and generally unreliable as an indicator of gender (Byrne & Churchill 1950; Grevisse 1964; Sonet & Shortliffe 1954, as cited by Tucker et al. 1968: 313).

Do French-speaking children make use of the correlational information in deciding on gender? To answer this an experiment was conducted involving 402 children in grades 4 through 7 in Montreal. The experimenters invented words by combining 3 initial syllables with 14 final syllables. The students heard the pseudowords pronounced on a tape, and half also saw the words printed on an answer sheet. They were asked to indicate whether the word should go with an adjective with a masculine ending or an adjective with a feminine ending. The final syllables from which the words were constructed were such that the percent of masculine real words containing them varied from 100% to 0%. One of the initial syllables appeared in real words that were mostly masculine; another, mostly feminine; and the third appeared roughly equally in both.

TABLE 4.5   French Gender Estimation

ENDING	PERCENT THAT ARE MASCULINE IN DICTIONARY	PERCENT WHO GUESS MASCULINE WHEN INITIAL SYLLABLE IS		
		AMBIGUOUS (FEUILL-)	MASCULINE (DÉB-)	FEMININE (FLOR-)
-ais	100	70	90	82
-air	100	73	92	86
-illon	98	91	96	87
-eur	95	96	96	96
-oi	94	71	93	79
-oie	76	44	82	23
-eure	56	61	65	32
-oire	54	42	60	56
-é	35	60	77	59
-stion	13	28	22	30
-ée	8	9	18	6
-aie	0	67	36	20
-ssion	0	26	17	17
-(a)tion	0	11	17	13

Based on Table 1 of Tucker et al. 1968. © Academic Press. Used by permission.

As Table 4.5 shows, the students relied heavily on the tendency for the second syllable to be of one gender or the other in making their decision. They also seemed to attend to the gender frequency of the first syllable, although to a lesser extent. In learning new vocabulary French-speaking children may be relying partly on gender frequencies of similar sounding words. To the extent that the new words fit the statistical pattern, the gender can be learned faster (Tucker et al. 1968. Although this section has discussed only noun inflections, verb inflections have also been studied; see, e.g., Simões & Stoel-Gammon 1979).

Compound words

In English many words have been formed by compounding two or more roots. Such words include *doghouse, classroom, homework, moviegoer, mailbox, mainland, thermometer, flagship, milestone,* and *sunrise.*

Creating compounds   **English.** On the original Wug Test children were asked several questions that were designed to elicit compounding:

What would you call a man who zibbed for a living?
What would you call a house a wug lived in?

While all adults would call the man a *zibber,* only 11% of the children did. The house was called a *wughouse* by 58% of adults, but by a much smaller percentage of the children—18% of first graders, for example.

Children as young as two years old do produce word compounds spontaneously. They appear to do it when they want to make finer categorical distinctions than the current state of their vocabulary would allow. One two-year old, for example, used *plate-egg* for "fried egg" and *cup-egg* for "soft-boiled egg." Similarly, another two-year old distinguished *house-smoke* from *car-smoke* (E. Clarke 1980; E. Clarke et al. 1985). For "one who does X" in English, adults coin the word *Xer*—for example, *helper, pipe fitter, street sweeper.* In a few cases, *Xman* is used, such as *fireman, policeman.* Some children as young as two years old have been observed spontaneously creating new compounds such as *fixman* ("auto mechanic") and *gardenman* ("gardener").

By 2;6 to 3;0 some children will coin a compound on demand. When asked what they would call "someone who sweeps things," some would respond *sweepman.* The youngest tend to use *Xman* for "one who does X," while older children tend to prefer the form preferred by adults—*Xer.* Occasionally a child will produce a form using both endings—*kickerman* ("someone who kicks things"). Since this double marking occurs only very rarely in adult English—for example, in *fisherman*—it is unlikely that children model such double markings after words that they have heard; more likely, when children do this it is a self-invented double marker like *worser* or *wented.*

If you ask young children to name an object, they tend to give a compound word in which the second root comes from the experimenter's definition. Thus "machine for throwing things" becomes *rock-machine;* "thing for eating with" becomes *eating thing* (E. Clark 1980).

The choice of *man* or *thing* by younger children instead of *-er* may be due to the fact that *-er* is more ambiguous, since it occurs on comparative adjectives (*shorter*) and on other words in which the "one who" meaning doesn't seem to apply (*mother, father, sister, brother*).

German. Word compounding is much more prevalent in German than it is in English. The German language is notorious for its lengthy compounds such as *Sonntagnachmittagspaziergang,* which means "Sunday afternoon stroll," and is formed from *Sonntag* ("Sunday") plus *nachmittag* ("afternoon") plus *spaziergang* ("stroll"). Each of these parts is itself a compound: *Sonn-tag* ("sun day"), *nach-mid-tag* ("after mid day"), and *spazier-gang* ("stroll going").

German children have been reported to use compound words as early as 1;10—for example *bilde-buche,* (for *bilderbuch* "picture book"). By 2;6 German children are creating new words to express concepts for which they have no word: *brennlicht* ("burning light"), for *stern* ("star"). By the time they are between the ages of four and six, they are creating many new words in this way (C. Stern & Stern 1907).

Most of the information we have on word compounding still comes from observational studies. It is to be hoped that a clearer picture of the course of its development will arise out of experimental research in this area, some of which had just begun at the time of writing this book.

Etymology   The children in the original Wug study were also asked questions such as *Why do you think Thanksgiving is called "Thanksgiving"?* Adults would generally give an answer that takes into account both parts of the word (Berko 1958):

Adult: Thanksgiving is called "Thanksgiving" because the pilgrims *gave thanks.*

Only 13% of children's responses were of this nature. Most responded giving a salient feature of the thing named:

Child: A blackboard is called a "blackboard" because you write on it.

The youngest children often gave no answers at all; and 23% of them gave an identity response:

Child: A blackboard is called a "blackboard" because it is a blackboard.

Of the older children only 9% gave such an identity response.

It is very rare that one finds naturally occurring awareness of word etymology. One occurrence that has been reported: Panagl's daughter at age 5;0 wondered why "Italian" in German is *italienisch* and not *italisch,* since "Bulgarian" is *bulgarisch* (Panagl 1977).

WORD MEANING

In Chapter 2 the development of meaning in the first words was discussed. Learning the meanings of words that refer to simple acts and concrete objects is a major accomplishment, but only the beginning. Natural language words can encode some marvelously complex concepts, some of which take children quite a long time to master. Two particular categories of words which tend to be mastered late are **shifters** and **relationals.**

Shifters

There exist in natural language a number of words whose referents change depending upon who is the speaker and where and when he or she is speaking. One can find these **shifters** in almost all parts of speech. Among the nouns, kinship terms—when used as names or parts of names—are shifters, because one speaker's *daddy* is not the same person as another speaker's *daddy.* Also, *home* for one speaker is not necessarily *home* for another speaker. Pronouns—*I, me, my, mine, you, your, yours*—shift their reference depending upon who is speaking, and likewise *this* and *that,* depending upon the relative locations of the speaker and referent.

Similar location information is required to handle verbs such as *come* and *go,* and *bring* and *take* properly. And the same event would be described in different tenses, aspects, and moods, depending upon the relation of the event to the present, to other events being discussed, and a number of other factors. Among the adverbs, *here* and *there* can refer to the same place, depending upon the location of the speaker. And a really tough distinction to learn is *yesterday* versus *tomorrow*. Finally, two of the most complicated shifters are the articles *a* and *the* (Jesperson 1922).

Pronouns   Adults speaking to very young children tend to avoid pronouns:

Mother: Is baby tired?
Mother: Mommy give baby a hug.

This has been reported for English, Japanese, Marathi, Romanian (C. Ferguson 1977b) and Serbo-Croatian (Jocić 1976). Presumably adults do this because they do not expect very young children to be able to understand pronouns. Not surprisingly, the first self-reference of some, though not all, children is to use *baby* or their own names (Huxley 1970).

Redundant use of both the pronoun and the noun has been reported by several observers:

> I Douglas pick up big cards on floor (Huxley 1970: 148).
> Fix it choo-choo train (Bloom et al. 1975a: 20).
> Mommy get it ladder (R. Brown 1973: 86).

In the case of the second and third examples, one interpretation is that *fix-it* and *get-it* are examples of undersegmentation; however, this interpretation cannot explain the first example.

Using the first person as subject involves two grammatical differences from using third person—use of the pronoun *I,* and using the correct verbal auxiliary *I am* as opposed to *Douglas is.* One step in the progression toward correct pronoun usage in the case of Douglas was to produce his name as subject, but to put the auxiliary into the first person:

Douglas (3;1):   Douglas am Douglas Scott Brown (Huxley 1970).

The first pronoun children appear to use is *I.* This first use is almost always correct (E. Clark 1978: 99). With the introduction of the use of *you,* things get more complex. While most children apparently figure out that *I* refers to the speaker and *you* refers to the listener, some children go through a period in which *I* refers to the adult, and *you* refers to the child:

Nigel (to his mother):   You want Mummy red toothbrush (meaning "I want"; Halliday 1975).
Mother: What did you hurt?
Adam (2;6):   Hurt your elbow (meaning "my elbow"; Tanz 1980: 52).

This has also been reported by others for children learning English (Cooley 1908; Sharpless 1974; Shipley & Shipley 1969; Sully 1896), Danish (Jesperson 1922), Dutch (van der Geest 1975), and Serbian (Savić 1974). This improper use may last from four to six months.

Another pronoun confusion has been noted in a situation involving the relaying of questions:

Experimenter (to subject):   Ask Tom where my bicycle is.
Subject (to Tom):   Where is your bicycle? (Tanz 1980: 67)

Here the switch is made between *I* and *you* in a situation in which it is inappropriate—the correct form, of course, would have been *Where is her bicycle?*

Most children have mastered the correct usages of first and second person pronouns by the age of 3;3; however, the age of mastery for autistic and other problem children may be later (Rimland 1964; Tanz 1980: 57-60). Thus, at least for some children, the shifting nature of the first person and second person pronoun use causes some trouble for a few months.

Mastery of third person pronouns comes even later. Children over five years old still make mistakes in carefully controlled comprehension tests. While children quickly learn the gender distinction between *he, him,* and *his* and *she, her* and *hers,* they are slower at learning that the addressee—normally addressed *you*—cannot also be addressed by a third person pronoun of the appropriate gender (Brener 1983).

This and that; here and there   The pronouns *this* and *that* and their corresponding adverbs *here* and *there* are used to point out objects in the environment. This is a very important aspect of child language, and one of these terms— most often *that*—almost always appears among the first 50 words (Braunwald 1978: 493; Ka. Nelson 1973a: 120-127). These terms are common in children's early two-word utterances, not only in English (Bellugi & Brown 1964; Braine 1976), but also in Chinese, Danish, Finnish (Bowerman 1973a), French, German (C. Stern & Stern 1928), Hebrew (Braine 1976), Italian (E. Bates 1976a), Japanese, Korean (Park 1970b), Quechua, Samoan (Kernan 1969), and Swedish (Lange & Larsson 1973). Two or more of the terms are usually present by the time children reach 2;6 (for example, Bateman 1914; W. Boyd 1914; Grant 1915; Nice 1915).

In spite of the early beginnings of the use of these terms, the acquisition of the distinctions between *this* and *that* and *here* and *there* takes a considerable amount of time. The major distinction is that the first of each pair refers to objects near the speaker, and the second refers to distant objects. This distinction is not made in free speech by young children, nor is it made by their mothers when talking to them (Wales 1974: 244, citing findings by Cross).

If young children make use of more than one term, but are not making a distinction between near and far objects, what distinctions do they make? Some children have been reported to use *this* or *here* to refer to 'new' objects—objects which they are beginning to or want to play with—and *that* or *there* to refer to objects they are finished playing with (Griffiths 1974; Wales 1979: 244).

The development of the near/far contrast in these words has been studied in several experiments (Charney 1979; E. Clark & Sengul 1978; P. deVilliers & deVilliers 1974; Tanz 1980; Wales 1974, 1979; Webb & Abrahamson 1976). Most of the experiments involve a situation similar to this one: A child is seated at a table on which are placed two identical objects. One object is placed near him or her and the other is placed farther away. In some conditions the adult sits near the child, and in other conditions the adult sits across the table nearer the object that is farther away from the child. Tasks are required of the child, such as *Make the dog over here/there hop.* or *Make this/that dog hop.* Variations on the task have included separating the two objects by a barrier, and making the two objects equidistant from the child but different distances from the adult.

One finding is that although one would think that the distinction between *here* and *there* is the same as that between *this* and *that,* it is not true that the two distinctions are acquired at the same time. In general, *here/there* is acquired before *this/that* (E. Clark & Sengul 1978: 468; Wales 1979: 245).

A second finding is that it is a difficult task. Even at seven years old only 30% of children tested have mastered the contrasts in all situations (Wales 1979: 245).

Finally, it has been found that children who have not completely mastered the distinction employ a number of different strategies. Among those who do not distinguish between the words, some will always pick the nearest object, no matter what is said. Others will manipulate each toy in alternation. Still others will choose the toy apparently at random. Among children who behave differently to the two words, but who have not completely mastered the distinction, some will always behave correctly when the speaker is beside them, but will behave inconsistently when the speaker is sitting across from them. Others will behave correctly when the speaker is sitting across from them, but will behave inconsistently when the speaker is sitting beside them (E. Clark & Sengul 1978; Wales 1979).

Thus what appears to an adult to be a single consistent distinction is acquired by children quite slowly, word by word and case by case.

Come and go; bring and take   Whether one uses the verb *come* as opposed to *go,* and similarly *bring* as opposed to *take,* is, like *this* and *that, here* and *there,* determined by the location of the speaker and the listener. In its primary meaning, *go* is used to indicate motion from one location to another. *Come* is used if the goal of the motion is the location of the speaker either at the time referred to or the time the utterance is produced, or if the goal is the home base of either the speaker or the listener (C. Fillmore 1971). In spontaneous speech children use these terms appropriately as young as age two (Bloom et al. 1975b; Macrae 1976). In more demanding experimental tasks, the mastery of these terms appears to be highly dependent on the particular situation. In one situation almost all children appeared to have mastered the *come/go* distinction by four years old; in a second situation, it was only at seven years that over 90% of the responses were correct (Richards 1976:

660); in a separate experiment mastery was not accomplished by 20% of the children at age nine (E. Clark & Garnica 1974). *Bring* and *take* tend to be acquired slightly later than *come* and *go* (E. Clark & Garnica 1974; M. Richards 1976).

A and the   One of the most complicated contrasts a child has to master is the contrast between the two articles *a* and *the*. It is so difficult in English that the author of one psycholinguistics textbook, herself a native speaker of Korean who has lived in an English-speaking environment for many years, confesses that she never has mastered it (Taylor 1976: ix).

Basically, *the* is used when the object referred to is a specific object in the mind of the speaker and when the noun used and/or the context would allow the listener to identify that referent uniquely. It may be unique because there is only one—*the moon;* it may be unique because of specification in a prior utterance—*That a jeep. I put some in the jeep* (Uttered by Adam—R. Brown 1973: 352); or it may be unique because of a prior or concurrent gesture—*Sit in the chair there* (accompanied by pointing).

If the referent is specific for the speaker but not specific for the listener, *a* is the appropriate article—*I bought a dress today.* Likewise if the referent is not specific for either speaker or listener—*Let's go to a movie.* The indefinite article *a* is also used in categorization statements to mean "a specific instance of the category," as in *That's a tree* or *It's a boy.*

The complete story of the articles in English is even more complex (R. Brown 1973: 340-356; Christopherson 1939; Maratsos 1976: 1-13; Warden 1977; Zehler & Brewer 1982), but this account will do for our purposes.

The overall pattern of acquisition appears to be as follows. In early 'telegraphic' speech articles are generally not used (R. Brown & Fraser 1963; W. Miller & Ervin 1966). By the age of 17 months, girls, but not boys, have been shown to have one of the uses of *a*. This was determined in a study in which children were shown two dolls. In one condition the experimenter would say about one of the dolls "This is a *zav*" or "This is *zav*" (or some other nonsense syllable). When we state that an object is an example of a set of objects we use *a* (*This is a girl.*); when we state a name for a particular object, we don't use *a* (*This is Nancy.*). When the children were asked to do something with *zav,* girls who had been given *zav* as a category name chose each of the two dolls about half of the time; girls who had been given *zav* as a proper name were much more likely to choose the particular doll so named. Boys did not show this effect, perhaps because the dolls were 'girl-oriented' toys. When the same task was tried with two blocks rather than two dolls, neither sex made a distinction between *zav* and *a zav.* Dolls can be given proper names, but blocks cannot, so the children ignored the fact that *a* was missing and treated *zav* as a name for the set of objects rather than as a proper name for one of them (N. Katz et al. 1974).

One of the things that children learn quite early is what types of objects can have proper names and what types cannot. Dale tells this story about his daughter when she was two. One day when he was wearing only his bathing suit, she looked at him and said something unintelligible. Based mostly on the direction of her gaze, he responded, "Yes, my tummy is hairy." She looked at him thoughtfully for a moment and replied, "My tummy doesn't have a name."

When children first begin to use *a* consistently, they master the categorization distinction first (Emslie & Stevenson 1981). By the age of 2;8 the use of *a* is well established, but the correct use of *the* is rare. Generally *a* is not used in utterances where *the* should be used; rather, no article is used in these places.

Slowly the use of *the* appears. The most common error children make appears to be to use *the* when the referent is specific to them but not to the listener:

Sarah: The cat's dead.
Mother: What cat?

Other errors involve using *a* when *the* is appropriate, either because it is specified by the situation:

Eve: I don't like a crust.
Mother: I know you don't like the crust.

or because it has been specified by a prior utterance (R. Brown 1973: 354; Dunlea 1978; Zehler & Brewer 1982).

In order to make correct use of *a* and *the*, the speaker must understand, among other things, what information is available to the listener. Even three-year olds are surprisingly nonegocentric in that they can take the point of view of the speaker into account (Maratsos 1974c), but children as old as nine (Warden 1976) and even adults, occasionally make errors of this type.

Another role of *a* is to introduce a count noun—as opposed to *any* or *some*, which introduce mass nouns. Compare *Do you know what a "latt" is?* with *Have you ever seen any "latt?"* The first question informs one that the latt is an object with well-defined boundaries—if you saw more, you could **count** the number of latts. The second indicates that the latt is a **mass** of something without clear boundaries—if you saw some you would say you saw *some latt;* if others saw more they would still say they saw *some latt.* Most four-year olds have enough knowledge of this aspect of *a* versus *any* or *some* to select the correct picture from a set that includes one picture of a count noun thing and another of a mass noun thing (R. Brown 1957. See also Garton 1983; Karmiloff-Smith 1979).

Relationals

Teacher: Draw a square *above* the ball.
Child: (Draws square around the picture of the ball.)
Teacher: That's not *above*, that's *around*.
Child: No, it's not. It's a square (J.L. Bond 1983, personal communication).

Another category of words that children appear to master late is **relationals.** These are words that express relations between two or more objects or events. They often exist in antonymous pairs. Such words include *more* and *less, big* and *little, large* and *small,* and *before* and *after.*

One of the first pairs of relational adjectives to appear is *big* and *little,* appearing in the vocabularies of most children before they are three years old (Su. Carey 1978b: 278-279). An object is *big* or *little* depending on how it compares to a typical example of such objects. A little chair is bigger, for instance, than a big shoe.

Eight two-year olds who had *big* and *little* in their vocabularies were tested for their understanding that *big* or *little* is relative to the typical example. The objects were shoes, chairs, paper bags, and other similar items. All but one child either were perfect or missed only one out of seven items. There were no more errors on *little* than on *big* (Su. Carey & Potter 1976).

It is also true that the same object may be *big* in one context and *little* in another. A shot glass is normally considered a little glass, but when compared to eating implements in a tea set designed for dolls, it is *big.* Two- to three-year olds generally cannot handle this switch due to context, and call the shot glass a *little glass,* even when the experimenter asks, "For *these dolls* is this a big glass or a little glass?" Four-year olds, however, shifted with context, as adults do (Su. Carey n.d.; for a similar study of Italian, see Bates & Rankin 1979).

Two aspects of the acquisition of relational adjectives have especially attracted the interest of researchers. One aspect concerns the order in which different adjective pairs are acquired; the other concerns the order of acquisition of the two adjectives in each pair. Among the dimensional adjectives, the first pairs to be acquired are *big/little* and *large/small.* Slightly later are *long/short* and *tall/short,* followed by *high/low, thick/thin, wide/narrow,* and *deep/shallow,* in that order (Bartlett 1974, 1976; Su. Carey & Considine 1973; E. Clark 1972; Eilers et al. 1974; Tashiro 1971; Wales & Campbell 1970).

There are two points of view as to why such a consistent acquisition sequence is found. One is that it is due to the degree of specificity and relative importance of the dimensions referred to. *Big/little* and *large/small* are most general and do not specify particular dimensions, so they are learned first. Among the terms that specify a dimension, length and height are more perceptually salient, so the adjective pairs which refer to them appear next (Bierwisch 1967; E. Clark 1972, 1973a, H. Clark 1973). The other point of view is that the order is not necessarily due to semantic complexity or perceptual salience, at least not directly. Rather, it is due to the relative frequencies of the words in adult and child speech (Su. Carey & Considine 1973). Of course, the relative frequencies are probably due, in turn, to the fact that it is more often appropriate to indicate size without specifying dimension; or if dimension is specified, it is more often of interest to indicate the size of the perceptually more salient dimension.

The other major aspect that has attracted interest is the sequence in which the two antonymous adjectives of each pair are acquired. A number of researchers have found that children perform more accurately for one adjective of the pair than the other. While this has been found for many adjectives, most of the research has centered around the pair *more/less*.

More appears earlier in the spontaneous speech of most children (Bloom 1970; Braine 1963a; R. Brown & Fraser 1963). For example, *more*, but not *less*, was found in the recorded spontaneous speech of 15 children aged 3;6 to 5;0. (Donaldson & Wales 1970). When children of this age are tested for comprehension of *more* and *less*, they often appear to behave as if in their understanding *less* means the same as *more*. In one study children 3;5 to 4;0 were shown pictures of two apple trees bearing various numbers of apples. They were asked, "Which tree has more apples?" or "Which tree has less apples?" Many of the children responded in both cases as if the question had been "Which has more?" (Donaldson & Balfour 1968; Donaldson & Wales 1970). This study has been replicated and extended. A substantial minority of children even as old as five years perform the action requested on the object containing *more,* even if the instruction is to give the experimenter the cup with less candy and thus keep the cup with more candy (Palermo 1973, 1974).

These results have been interpreted to mean that children go through a stage in which to them the meaning of *less* is identical to the meaning of *more*. An alternative explanation is that the children who showed this effect may not have understood the meaning of either word; rather they simply attended to displays with greater perceptual salience—namely, those with more of the substance being attended to (E. Clark 1973b; Holland & Palermo 1975; Huttenlocher 1974).

This alternative has been tested. In one study children were given the tasks cited above, but they were also given another instruction: *Here is a pile of zebras; and here is a pile of zebras; point to one of them.* It was found that children 3;6 to 4;2 were just as likely to point to the larger pile when asked merely to point to *one of them* as they were when asked a question using either *more* or *less* (Trehub & Abramovitch 1978; see also Su. Carey 1978a, 1982; Wannemacher & Ryan 1978). Thus it appears not to be true that children go through a stage when they think that *less* means what adults mean by *more.*

The corresponding hypothesis in spatial adjectives is that the negative version of other dimensional adjective pairs is first learned as its opposite. Thus *short* is supposed to first mean *tall; thin* is supposed to first mean *thick,* and so forth. Similar response biases have been found in studies of these adjective pairs (Eilers et al. 1974), and the general finding is that the hypothesis is not true of these adjectives either (Bartlett 1976; Brewer & Stone 1975; Townsend 1974, 1976; Townsend & Erb 1975).

The comparable hypothesis has also been explored in the acquisition of spatial adjectives, such as *in, on,* and *under* (E. Clark 1973b), *front, back,* and *side* (L. Harris & Strommen 1972; Kuczaj & Maratsos 1975; Tanz 1980), and *in front of* and *behind* (Cox 1977). Again, the results do not support the hypothesis (Grieve et al. 1977; Wilcox & Palermo 1974).

The development of understanding of some adjectives does not follow the normal course of increasing improvement. While three-year olds appear to be able to understand correctly *big* as referring to global size, and *long* as referring to one dimension, it appears that four- and five-year olds treat *big* as synonymous with *long* or *high* (Maratsos 1973a).

The acquisition of temporal as well as spatial relations has been studied extensively. Several predictions concerning the acquisition sequence have been made. One theory predicted that understanding of simultaneous reference—*at the same time*—should precede understanding of sequential reference, and that *before* should precede *after*. It also predicts that there should be a stage when *before* and *after* are synonymous, both meaning "before." Another suggestion is that young children tend to apply an order-of-mention strategy. According to this strategy sentences of the form

The elephant jumps before the dog sits down.

are easier to understand than

Before the dog sits down, the elephant jumps.

because the order of occurrence of the two events corresponds to the order of mention in the former sentence but not in the latter (E. Clark 1971).

Some of these predictions have received support; others have not. The notion of simultaneity does seem to be acquired before *before* and *after*. Children in the age range 4;1 to 5;0 have been found to be able to comprehend *at the same time* better than *before* and *after* (Munro & Wales 1982). This result does not apply to all expressions of simultaneity—*while* has been found to be more difficult than *before* or *after* (Feagans 1980a).

The proposal that *before* is acquired earlier than *after* has received support from a number of studies (Bever 1970; Coker 1978; Hatch 1971; H. Johnson 1975). However, other studies found that *after* is sometimes acquired earlier than *before* (Barrie-Blackley 1973; Coker & Legum 1974; Feagans 1980b; Trosborg 1982).

A recent study appears to support the notion that *before* and *after* are acquired at the same time. In this study one group of children was instructed to "Make the girl go to the stroller *before* (*after*) you make the boy go to the stroller." Another group was shown an event and then asked "When did the girl get to the stroller? *Before* (*After*) the boy got to the stroller?" The usual difference turned up in the first group of children, but there was no difference in the second group. This suggests that the relative failure to respond appropriately to *after* was due not to differences in comprehension of the two words, but rather to the heuristics employed by children in comprehending complex sentences (Goodz 1982). This interpretation is supported by a study of children's ability to imitate sentences, which shows that children as old as 6;6 still have not mastered the syntactic structures involved in using *before* and *after* to connect two clauses in a compound sentence (Tibbits 1980).

Similarly, the prediction that there is a stage in which *after* is interpreted as *before* has not been supported by experimental research (Amidon & Carey 1972; Coker 1978; French & Brown 1977).

Whether young children make use of the order-of-mention strategy appears to be a function of the particular experimental situation. A number of studies have reported that children use this strategy (E. Clark 1971; Coker 1978; Ferreiro & Sinclair 1971; French & Brown 1977; H. Johnson 1975; Kavanaugh 1979; Weil & Stenning 1978), but other strategies have also been reported (Amidon 1976; Amidon & Carey 1972; Bever 1970; Coker 1978; Weil & Stenning 1978).

Kinship terms

I'm My Own Grandpa.—Title of song by Dwight Latham & Moe Jaffe

Kinship terms are words that refer to relatives in terms of their relationship to one another. In English these terms include *mother, father, sister, nephew, cousin, grandmother, uncle, brother-in-law,* and *step-sister.* Although *Mommy* and *Daddy* or their equivalents are among the first words which most children learn, they are not true kinship terms, but rather proper names for particular people. The original study of the acquisition of kinship terms was done on the words *brother* and *sister* (Piaget 1928). This work has been replicated (Elkind 1962) and extended to other kinship terms by a number of other researchers (Chambers & Tavuchis 1976; Danziger 1957; Haviland & E. Clark 1974).

In the first stage children will respond to a question such as *What is an uncle?* by naming one of their uncles. In this stage *uncle* is simply a part of some people's names. In the second stage *brother* is simply a boy, *sister* is a girl. Adults cannot be brothers or sisters. Children in the third stage realize that there must be two children in the family in order for there to be a brother or sister, but they do not understand that the relationship is reciprocal—that if one has a brother or sister, one is a brother or sister. In the final stage, children finally fully understand the meaning of all the major kinship terms.

It turns out that children do not begin to understand kinship terms until age 4 or so, and complete understanding of the system comes as late as 10 years or older.

Children can be at different stages for different words. Thus a child may be in the third stage for *brother* and *sister* but still be in the first for *aunt* and *uncle.* At age seven, girls have better understanding of kinship terms than boys, but by age nine both sexes are equal in ability. Terms for the nuclear family—*mother, father, sister, brother*—tend to be acquired earliest; *aunt, uncle, cousin, niece,* and *nephew* are acquired quite late. In between are *son, daughter, parent, grandmother, granddaughter,* and *grandson.* It would be interesting to compare these findings with similar studies in cultures in which the extended family is the customary living group—where, for example, the grandmother is the children's primary caregiver.

In general, the acquisition of shifters and relationals has been found to be quite complex. Children don't reach full understanding of many of these words until well after the age of five. Some have suggested that children acquire the meanings of these words one feature at a time. This analysis sometimes predicts the sequence that actually occurs, but just as often it does not. Rather, researchers have had to look for their explanations not at the general-feature theories of meaning but at heuristics that children attempt in their effort to understand what they hear. There appear to be many such heuristics, and they often apply to one or just a few words. Alas, such behavior is not as easily described as it would be if children behaved as researchers have predicted.

CHILDREN'S CONVERSATIONS

Having covered the development of words and sentences, it is appropriate to turn our attention to how children use these words and sentences in conversations.

Conversation types

One can classify discourse in terms of the degree to which it has the properties we associate with normal socialized conversation. We shall consider a number of examples that show different levels of socialization.

Lev: (Sitting alone at a table.) I want to do that drawing, there. . . . I want to draw something, I do. I shall need a big piece of paper to do it (Piaget 1923: 37).

This is an example of a child's **monologue.** The child is talking to himself, and doesn't seem to have the desire for or interest in interacting with anyone else. This type of monologue has been called **self-guidance.** We all have what is known as **inner speech** (Vygotsky 1934), the voice we hear in our minds when we are thinking. Before children learn to produce this inner speech internally, they utter it aloud. Children in this stage appear to use this speech to help them focus their attention on a task. Hence the term self-guidance. Evidence in support of this interpretation comes from studies that find that the more difficult the task a child is faced with, the greater the amount of this type of monologue is produced (Flavell et al. 1966; Vygotsky & Luria 1930. For a pragmatic analysis of monologue, see Gallagher & Craig 1978).

Not all monologue is self-guidance. Another type has been termed **affect expressive monologue.** This would describe periods when children sing, chat, repeat real and nonsense words, engage in verbal fantasy, and comment on their feelings (Klein 1963).

Affect expressive monologue dominates a subclass of monologues known as **presleep monologue.** The most extensive study of this type of behavior was done on Anthony Weir when he was between 2;4 and 2;6. His mother left a microphone in his crib and turned on a tape recorder when she put him to bed. Here are two samples of what she heard (see also Box):

Find it. With juice. Drink it. Juice. That's the right way. Right way. Where you going? I'm going. Shoe fixed. Talk to Mommy. Shoe fixed. See Antho. Anthony. Good night. See morrow morning. Shoe fixed. Shoe fixed. Shoe fixed. Shoe fixed. Fix it. Fix it. Fix it. Shoe fixed. It took it. Bring it back. Took them. Took it down. Took it down. Took it down. Took it down. He took it. He took it. I'm going. Yellow one. Another one. Another one. Take a book. Another book. A phone call. Phone call

BOX 4.1

So—here I am in the dark alone,
There's nobody here to see;
   I think to myself,
   I play to myself
And nobody knows what I say to myself;
Here I am in the dark alone,
   What is it going to be?
I can think whatever I like to think,
I can play whatever I like to play,
I can laugh whatever I like to laugh,
   There's nobody here but me.

I'm talking to a rabbit . . .
   I'm talking to the sun . . .
I think I am a hundred—
   I'm one.
I'm lying in a forest . . .
   I'm lying in a cave . . .
I'm talking to a Dragon . . .
   I'm BRAVE.
I'm lying on my left side . . .
   I'm lying on my right . . .
I'll play a lot tomorrow . . .

. . . .
I'll think a lot tomorrow . . .

. . . .
I'll laugh . . .
      a lot . . .

        tomorrow . . .
        (*Heigh-ho!*)
         Goodnight.

Excerpt from "In the Dark" in *Now We Are Six*, by A.A.
Milne, pp. 99-101. © 1927 by E.P. Dutton, renewed 1955
by A.A. Milne. Reprinted by permission of Methuen Children's Books (London), E.P. Dutton, a division of New
American Library (New York), and McClelland & Stewart
(Toronto).

book. This phone call book. This phone call book. This phone call book. This is the.
This is the. Book. Another phone call book. This is light. One light. This is light on it
(Weir 1962: 131-132).

   Alice (calling). Mommy (calling). Mommy (calling). Mommy (calling). Mommy's
too weak. Alice strong. Alice too weak. Daddy's too weak. Mommy's too weak. Too
weak with Barbara. Be careful Barbara. Barbara can broke. Careful broke the /rami/.
Careful broke Anthony. Careful broke it. Careful broke it. Careful broke the. Broke
the finger. Broke the Bobo. Broke the vacuum clean. The broke. /begi phu/. Get
some broke. Broke the. Alice broke the baby fruit. Alice almost dropped. It's David
fruit. Look. Look. All right. Lady. Mama (Weir 1962: 135-136).

A careful analysis of these monologues revealed four different types of discourse phenomena:

1. **Buildup.** In the case of a buildup, Anthony would utter a word or phrase, then immediately repeat it in an expanded form:

> Sit down.
> Sit down on the blanket (Weir 1962: 82).

2. **Breakdown.** In this type the second sentence is a shorter version of the first:

> Anthony jump out again.
> Anthony jump (Weir 1962: 82).

3. **Completion.** Here a complete sentence is uttered, yet the next utterance appears to be a continuation of the thought expressed in the previous sentence:

> Look at those pineapple.
> In a pretty box (Weir 1962: 83).

In adult speech the two utterances would have been expressed in one sentence.

4. **Quotation.** Many of Anthony's longer sentences—six or seven words— were recognized by his mother as having been repetitions or close approximations of sentences he had heard others say that day:

> Anthony wants to talk to Daddy (Weir 1962: 84).

While most normal waking child language can be said to express emotion, opinion, or reference, most of Anthony's presleep monologues seemed to involve language play. This included both phonological and grammatical play.

Phonological play. Phonological play included alliteration, rhyming, and rhythm play:

> Bink.
> Let Bobo bink.
> Bink ben bink.
> Blue kink (Weir 1962: 105).

Grammatical play. Grammatical play appears in the form of successive substitutions of words into sentence slots. This behavior bears a striking resemblance to the grammatical and lexical exercises in textbooks for self-instruction in foreign languages (Jakobson 1962: 19):

What color.
What color blanket.
What color mop.
What color glass (Weir 1962: 109).

A more advanced type of conversation is the **collective monologue.** When children are in the presence of other children, they may attend to one another to the extent that they will take turns talking. However, in collective monologue the content of the utterances of each child shows no evidence of being affected by the remarks of the other children:

Pie (6;5): Where could we make another tunnel? Ah, here Eun?
Eun (4;11): Look at my pretty frock (Piaget 1923: 76).

The next level of sophistication we might term **associated monologue.** In this type of interaction the children attend to one another to the extent that they are all talking on the same topic. In the example cited below, the children are drawing, and each is talking about her or his own picture. Other than the fact that all are talking about the content of their pictures, there is no evidence of communication interaction:

Lev (5;11): It begins with Goldilocks. I'm writing the story of the three bears. The daddy bear is dead. Only the daddy was too ill.
Gen (5;11): I used to live at Salève. I lived in a little house and you had to take the funicular railway to go and buy things.
Geo (6;0): I can't do the bear.
Li (6;10): That's not Goldilocks.
Lev: I haven't got curls (Piaget 1923: 77).

Drabble (© 1981 United Feature Syndicate. Used by permission.)

Another step toward socialized speech is seen in **collaboration** (Piaget 1923: 79-83). As opposed to the types just discussed, in collaboration one can find that a child's remark will be affected not just by the general situation under discussion, but by the previous remark made by the other child. It will be affected by it, but not necessarily be a direct response to it:

Arn (5;9):   It's awfully funny at the circus when the wheels (of the tricycle) have come off.

Lev (5;11):   Do you remember when the gymnastic man but who couldn't do gymnastics, fell down? (Piaget 1923: 80)

Slightly more socialized is a type of conversation that has been labelled **repetition** or **echolalia** (Piaget 1923: 34). Since these terms have each come to be used with other meanings elsewhere in the field of language acquisition, I prefer the term we used in our house: **copycat talk.** Little children, especially younger siblings, want to participate in a conversation, but in fact have nothing to say. Whatever another child might say, they will repeat (Piaget 1923: 35):

Jac: (To Ez.) Look, Ez, your pants are showing.

Pie: (From another part of the room.) My pants are showing, and my shirt, too. (This wasn't true.)

Such comments have no content; they have no bearing on truth. They are made for the sole purpose of feeling a part of the conversation. They are more socialized than the previous type because the second child attends to the previous remark and makes a direct response to it.

Athena went through a stage in which copycat talk was quite often used. During this period she drove her brother and parents to distraction. Quentin got to the point that he wouldn't venture an opinion or comment in Athena's presence until after she had commented.

Yet another step toward completely socialized speech can be seen in children's quarrelling. Such children are attending to what the others are saying; they are responding to it; and they are also expressing their own thoughts.

Most children's arguments are begun as a response to two types of remarks (examples from Brenneis & Lein 1977):

Derogatory remark:
I got my math done before you did.
You're dumb.

Possession assertion:
That's mine.
Gimme that ball.

The most primitive response is the **flat contradiction:**

Ez: You're going to marry me.
Pie: No, I won't marry you.
Ez: Oh yes, you'll marry me.
Pie: No.
Ez: Yes (Piaget 1923: 46).

One child makes a statement and the other states the opposite. The first repeats his or her remark. The second does likewise. Like a poorly written computer program that gets into an infinite loop, in which it performs the same operation repeatedly until it runs out of time or until an operator stops it, flat contradiction quarrelling goes on indefinitely. One such exchange went on for an incredible 45 conversational turns (Keenan 1974b: 180-181). Not infrequently, it will continue until it degenerates into a physical fight or crying, until an adult or older child intervenes, or some combination of the above.

The way out of this loop is to introduce some variation. Among children whose arguments have gone beyond the flat contradiction stage, quite a few different argument tactics have been observed. These include (examples from Brenneis & Lein 1977; their categories have been modified somewhat):

Stylistic variation:

James: I can climb higher than you.
Mike: No you can't.
James: Un huh.
Mike (Drawn out): Nooo sirrr.
James (Drawn out): Unnn hunhhhh.
Mike (Quickly): Nosir.
James (Quickly): Unhuh.
Mike: Cannot, Can't, can't, can't can't.
James: I can, I can, I can, I can.
Mike: No you can't.
James: Uh huh.
Mike: (Drawn out) Nooo youuu caan't.
James: (Drawn out) Unnnnn-hunhhh.

In this example Mike is purposely varying his style, while James is purposely copying Mike's style.

Content variation:

Dave: I'll bust your brains out.

Jim:　I'll tear yours out first.
Dave:　I'll knock your teeth down your throat.
Jim:　I'll punch your head off.

Escalation:

Ann:　I can lift up our whole family.
Joey:　I can lift the whole world with one finger.
Ann:　Well, I can lift up the whole universe.

Drabble (© 1983 United Feature Syndicate. Used by permission.)

Instantiation:
(To the argument, ''I'm stronger than you.'') I can lift up this school.

Giving a reason:
I had it first.

Demand for proof:
How do you know?

Stating disbelief:
I bet you can't.

Ironic bribe:
I'll give you a dollar if you can.

Command:
Don't say that.

Threat:
I'm going to tell the teacher on you.

Insult:
You dummy.

BOX 4-2 *THE MAGIC MAN ARGUMENT*

Joey *All right, I can lift*
up this school.
What can you lift
up?

Ann *I can lift up our*
whole family. I bet
you can't lift that
up with one finger.

Joey *I can lift the whole*
world up with one
finger.

Ann *Well, I can lift up*
the whole universe.
So why don't you
just be quiet about
that?

Joey *Yeah-you too. I*
can . . .

Ann *I bet you wouldn't*
dare go near the
sun.

Joey *I can pick up*
everything, catch
the world, catch the
sun, catch Jupiter,
catch everything,
and with one finger.

Ann *Even if you touched*
the sun, you'd burn
up.

Joey *If I'd touch the*
world, then the
world'd touch the
sun.

Ann *Then everybody'd*
burn up on the
world.

Joey *So what?*

Ann *I'd throw you up on*
the world and you'd
burn up too.

Joey *No, I'd be fine, I'm*
a magic man.

Ann *Oh, you're not a*

magic man.

Whynsha be quiet
about that? You
• *don't even have a*
magic hat or a
magic book like all
magic men have.

Joey *Yes, I do. You*
never saw it before
you came over.

Ann *I sneaked over to*
your house
yesterday and I
sneaked through
your whole house
and closets and
everything and I
couldn't find that
magic hat.

Joey *Well, I gave it to*
my friend.

Ann *Well, that means*
you're not a magic
man anymore.

Joey *No. I gave it to my*
friend to protect
them cause I knew
you were coming
over.

Ann *Oh, you did not.*

Joey *Because you called*
my mother up and
my mother said you
were coming over.

Ann *Yeah, but I didn't*
say when.

Joey *Ah, she knows.*
She's magic too.
My whole family's
magic.

Ann *Ah, now I couldn't*
find your whole
family's magic hats.

Joey *I gave them to my,*
to my friend.

Ann *And I went over to*
your friend's.

Joey *So what?*

Ann *I checked his whole*
house through. That
means you're just
telling lies. You're
not magic.

Joey *All right. If you*
want to say that, I
can lift up
everybody in the
whole world.

Ann *You cannot.*

Joey *Yes, on my finger.*
They could stand on
each others' heads.

Ann *Your finger'd*
break.

Joey *No it wouldn't.*

Ann *I could lift up a*
boulder with one
toenail.

Joey *I could lift up a*
boulder with
nothing.

Both *(Laughter)*

Ann *How could you lift*
it up with nothing?
It would come down
and smash your
head open.

Joey *I could lift it up*
with a little teeny
whittle piece of dirt
. . . with my finger
under it.

Ann *You are crazy*
today. Now you
aren't magic and
you don't have any
friend that's
keeping your magic
hat either.

Joey *So you just be*
quiet.

From Brenneis & Lein 1977: 62-64. © Academic Press. Used by permission.

Ironic praise:
You are smart.

Indifference:
So what?

Nonword taunts:
Nyeeh-nyeeh.

A type of talk that doesn't quite fit in the degree-of-socialization scheme is **imaginative dialogue** (Kohlberg et al. 1968 refer to this as **vocalized self dialogue**). This speech is monologue in that it is not directed at any real person present, but in form it is dialogue in that the child pretends to be carrying on a conversation with one or more other parties. The child speaks for all parties to the conversation.

B (pretend baby): I don't want to.
A (pretend adult): Try to.
         B: I am trying.
         A: Try to do it.
         B: I don't want to.
         A: Sure you do. You try.
         B: I never get to do it.
         A: You will do it. Sit up here.
         B: I don't want to.
         A: Try it, baby. Have to try.
         B: Okay (Pickert 1982).

This imaginative dialogue was uttered by Mary Alice (4;3) as a part of a presleep monologue. Such imaginary dialogues constituted from 55% to 100% of Mary Alice's presleep monologues. Such speech accounted for approximately 30% of Anthony Weir's presleep monologues (Pickert 1982: 8). Strictly speaking, imaginary dialogues are monologues, but they demonstrate the children's facility at socialized speech, and so are, theoretically, more advanced.

Developmental changes in discourse

Private speech   Self guidance, affect expressive, presleep, collective, and associated monologues can be considered to be different types of **private speech**—speech which is not addressed or adapted to a listener and which is carried on with apparent satisfaction in the absence of any sign of understanding by a listener (Kohlberg et al. 1968, following Piaget). The renowned epistemologist Jean Piaget claimed that the speech of young children contains as much as 39% private speech (Piaget 1923: 56) and that the proportion declines with age—for example: 40% at age two; 33% at age three; 26% at age four (M.E. Smith 1935a). Piaget related this behavior to other behavior he observed in children, claiming that it was part of a general pattern in which children are very egocentric at first and slowly became socialized. Thus private speech is also known as **egocentric speech.**

Piaget's claims have been investigated in a number of other studies. Some studies support Piaget's figures—for example: 31% private speech at age four; 18% at age six (Kohlberg et al. 1968: 714), while other studies, even by the same researchers (Kohlberg et al. 1968: 717), find a much lower incidence. For example, one study found private speech to average just 3.6% and to decline slightly with age (McCarthy 1930), and another found it to average less than 1% with no age trend (Davis 1937).

A number of factors explain this large discrepancy. There appears to be a considerably higher percentage of private speech in a situation in which children are playing with their peers than when they are talking to adults (McCarthy 1929). The original study involved the former situation; some of the later studies involved the latter. Children also appear to engage in less private speech the more children there are in the group (Williams & Mattson 1942). The situation seems to be an important factor. Piaget's original study was done in a preschool which particularly emphasized working alone (W. Stern, cited in C. Bühler 1931). This would explain the relatively higher result obtained by Piaget. However, other situational differences are harder to explain (for example, between the two studies by Kohlberg et al. 1968).

Another important factor is variations in the definition of private speech used. Piaget's definitions are not clear enough to be used directly; some interpretation is required (McCarthy 1954: 564). Also, his original examples for the different types don't correspond with his definitions for those types. Some researchers used the definitions (McCarthy 1930); others used the examples (M. E. Smith, cited by McCarthy 1954:566); still others developed their own definitions (Fisher 1934). Also, Piaget's general definition of private speech seems to cover more material than the sum of the subtypes proposed. Those who attempted to replicate the original study using the subtypes have tended to find less private speech than those who have used a global definition. In later research some studies have supported Piaget's view, but many others have not. It appears that Piaget's observations that young children make very high use of private speech is not a robust finding. (See McCarthy 1954: 562-574 for further discussion.)

Developmental changes in the nature of private speech have been found, however. In one study children between 3 and 7 were left alone in an observation room with a puzzle and drawing tasks, and their private speech was recorded. While the amount of audible private speech declined with age, the percent of audible private speech which can be described as self-guidance increased. Interestingly, the total amount of private speech did not decline during this period; rather, the amount of inaudible mumbling increased as the amount of audible speech declined (Klein 1963). This study was extended to children up to 10 years of age. As children get older their private speech eventually diminishes. It does not necessarily disappear; a large proportion of adults admit that they sometimes speak to themselves when alone (Flavell et al. 1963, 1966).

Socialized speech   More recent studies have revealed that even very young children are more adept at conversational interaction than studies focussing on their communication failures seem to suggest. When a preschool child (aged 3;6 to 5;6 and from an upper middle-class family) was placed with another child of the same sex and similar age in a room full of toys, 62% of all utterances produced a definite response from the other child, an additional 23% were attended to, and only 15% failed to be attended to. Twenty-four pairs of children were tested. Most of the children's language was clear, grammatically well formed, and well adapted to the listener's perspective. Clarity was important—of the five percent of utterances that were not clear, approximately 80% were not attended to. These figures did not change with age over the age range tested (Mueller 1972).

Similar results were obtained in another study. This study differed from the previous one mainly in that the pairs of children knew each other. The children were regarded as engaging in joint language or play activities 66% of the time they spent together (roughly 15 minutes). About 60% of the utterances were attended to by the other child. Children in the age range 3;6 to 4;4 tended to engage in slightly shorter exchanges than children whose ages ranged from 4;6 to 5;0. Five out of 12 pairs of the other children engaged in at least one verbal exchange 12 or more units long. Such a sequence would consist of one child talking, the second one responding in a relevant way, the first one responding to the second's remark, and so on for 12 or more utterances. Only 1 of 6 of the younger pairs had an exchange this long (Garvey & Hogan 1973).

Considerable conversational competence has been found in even younger children. For example, when the conversation between a pair of twins, Toby and David, aged 2;9, was analyzed, only 7% of the conversational turns could be classified as private speech. Even sound play similar to that found in presleep monologues was socialized in that the two twins took turns repeating phonologically similar or identical strings. Some of the exchanges appeared to be quite long—up to 45 conversational turns. Many exchanges were longer than most of the exchanges reported in the previously mentioned study of older children. Some of this may be due to less stringent requirements for what constitutes a continuation, but some may be due to the fact that the twins knew each other so well (Keenan 1974b).

The natural communication of young children playing in groups has also been studied. Two groups of children, one consisting of four children (mean age 2;5), the other of six children (mean age 2;6), were videotaped, and all cases in which the communicator's intent was to point out, show, or display a referent were analyzed. The children succeeded in engaging other listeners 80% of the time, and reacted differently depending on whether the listener understood, didn't understand, or didn't pay attention. They also were observed to tailor their messages to the needs of the listener (Wellman & Lempers 1977).

If two-year olds have such socialized speech, what about even younger children? A study of three boys playing together at age 1;10 and again at 2;6 finally turned up a developmental difference. At 1;10 only 27% of the boys' utterances received a verbal response from their peers. By 2;6 their interactions had improved to the point where 64% received a verbal response. During this period speakers learned to select message content more appropriate to the listener, and to look more at the listener as they spoke (Mueller et al 1977).

In order to carry on a conversation, when one speaker makes a remark, the other speaker gives a response which adds something new but on the same topic:

> **Adult:** I'm gonna build a high house.
> **Kathryn** (2;2,2):   I wanta build a high house too.

This is called a **contingent response.** A more primitive response is one which is on the same topic, but in which nothing new is added. This is called an **imitative response:**

> **Adult:** She might pinch her fingers.
> **Peter** (1;11,1):   Pinch her fingers.

A response which does not continue the topic of the previous remark is called a **noncontingent response:**

> **Adult:** All right, put the light on.
> **Eric** (2;1,1):   Cookie.

As Figure 4.8 shows, the ability to carry on a conversation, as measured by the proportion of contingent responses, increases greatly during the second year (Bloom et al. 1976). The crucial period for development of this skill appears to be in the period just after children have turned two (see also Wellman & Lempers 1977).

Having established the basically social nature of preschool children's conversations, researchers have turned to more detailed investigation into the structure of the conversational interactions. Preschoolers (3;6 to 5;7) have been found to be surprisingly sophisticated in their use of various forms of direct and indirect requests and in their responses to them (Garvey 1975). Another area of sophistication appears in the ability of children (2;10 to 5;7) to respond appropriately to different types of contingent queries. A **contingent query** is an attempt by a listener for a clarification of the previous remark of the speaker.

There are several types. One of the most common is the **nonspecific request for repetition:**

Harlan (2;3):   Want d'you policeman?
     Adult: Hm?
  Harlan: Want . . . want d'you policeman? (W. Miller & Ervin 1964)

Another type is the **specific request for repetition:**

Harlan: I go boom boom.
  Adult: What'd you go?
Harlan: I went boom.

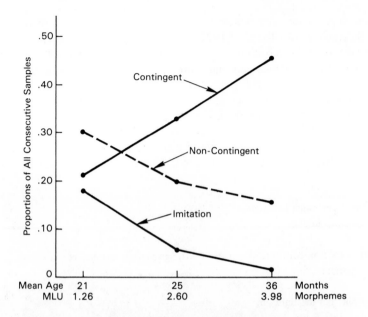

FIGURE 4.8   Distribution of three discourse types in four children.
(Adapted from Bloom et al. 1976: 527).

A third type is the **specific request for confirmation:**

> **Child** (2;0):   [mouka]
>   **Adult:**   Motor car?
>   **Child:**   No.
>   **Adult:**   Moo-cow?
>   **Child:**   [muka] (M.M. Lewis 1936)

At age two children apparently not only know how to respond to such queries; they know how to use them:

> **Adam** (2;2):   Radio.
>   **Mother:**   No, that's a tape recorder.
>   **Adam:**   Tape corder?
>   **Mother:**   Yes, tape recorder (From a transcript by R. Brown, cited by Garvey 1977:
>   79).

Another type is the **specific request for elaboration:**

> **Child:**   She got it.
> **Adult:**   What. [falling intonation]
> **Child:**   The book.

Note that this type may differ from the nonspecific request for repetition only by intonation pattern (Garvey & BenDebba 1978):

Child: She got it.
Adult: What? [rising intonation]
Child: She got it.

In conversations between two preschool children, contingent queries are used extensively. Such queries are responded to appropriately between two-thirds and three-quarters of the time, depending on the type of query. Three-year olds are just as adept at contingent queries as four- and five-year olds (Garvey 1977; see also Spilton & Lee 1977).

Another important conversational skill is the ability to take turns. There have been several studies of turn-taking in the conversations of children aged 1;3 to 9;6, but at all ages tested children seem to understand how to take turns, and no developmental trends were observed (Berninger & Garvey 1981; Craig & Gallagher 1982; Ervin-Tripp 1979; J. Fine 1978; Gallagher & Craig 1982; Garvey & Berninger 1981).

Indirect speech acts

In normal adult conversation, much of what is communicated is accomplished by means of **indirect speech acts** (Searle 1975). An indirect speech act is an utterance in which a speaker communicates more to the listener than she or he actually says. In doing so, the speaker relies on a large body of conventions within the language and culture, plus the listener's ability to make inferences based on knowledge of the situation and the listener's desires.

Bridging   A simple type of indirect speech act is **bridging.** Speakers are bridging when they leave logical gaps that the listener must bridge in order to understand. Consider the following example:

Horace got some picnic supplies out of the car. The beer was warm.

In order to make sense of the second sentence, a listener must add the information that beer was included among the picnic supplies (H. Clark & Clark 1977: 97; H. Clark & Haviland 1977; Haviland & H. Clark 1974).

I know of no systematic studies of bridging in children, but some examples from my own experience show that explicit learning must take place, and that the ability to handle bridging when necessary is not complete at age four.

Athena (2;6): What are you doing, Mom?
Mother: I'm calling the stores to see if they have some things.
Athena: But stores not talking, Mommy.
Mother: I'm calling the *people* at the stores to see if they have some things.
Athena: Oh.

In this first example a bridge must be built to understand the antecedent of the pronoun *they*. My daughter was considerate enough to comment explicitly when the normal linguistic analysis led to an unreasonable conclusion.

> (The family is preparing to leave for a holiday.)
> **Mother:** Now I'm packed.
> **Athena** (3;6): No you're not; you're walking.

This example, which was not meant by Athena to be a joke, demonstrates the fact that people often substitute a personal pronoun for a possessive noun phrase as the subject of a verb. In this case *I* was substituted for *my things*. This abbreviation is then normally uncoded by the listener and thus goes unnoticed, except when a naive child calls attention to it.

> **Grandmother** (talking to Athena on the telephone):   What are you doing?
> **Athena** (2;6):   Talking on the telephone.

Here the question makes sense and thus is answered straightforwardly. What the child must learn is that when speakers ask questions the answer to which is clearly known to them, they often are using a polite or abbreviated way of asking for some other information. In this case the question intended was something like *What activity were you engaged in which was interrupted by this phone call?* When one thinks about this problem one is surprised, not that children fail to bridge here, but that they don't fail more often. For such questions are used by adults not only to seek information, but also to test the child's knowledge—**tutorial questions,** such as *What color is this?* (Holzman 1972 refers to these as **test questions;** Dore 1977 calls them **examination questions.**) Adults also use them, as in the next example, to make polite requests.

> **Child** (approx. 4 yrs.):   (Answering the telephone.) Hello.
> **Adult:** Is your mother there?
> **Child:** Yes.
>   (Long pause.)
> **Adult:** Please tell her to come to the phone.
> **Child:** Okay. (Calling) Mommy!

Nestlings (© 1982 Warren Clements. Used by permission.)

Politeness A very large source of indirectness relates to politeness. In ordinary conversation, cultural rules of politeness make it rude to utter straightforward imperatives. Thus we say *Don't you think it's a little chilly in here?* when what we mean is *I want you to turn up the heat in this place*. Politeness is the most frequent motivation for indirectness in requests (Ervin-Tripp 1976).

Children who are quite young can understand and use indirect requests. Even in the conversations of pairs of children 3;6 to 4;4 one can find several types of indirectness. Rather than ordering the other child to do something, the speaker asks a question. For example, the speaker asks (Garvey 1975; see also Reeder 1980; Shatz 1978b):

> If the other is **able to perform** the act: *Can you take the baby?*
> If the other **wants to perform** the act: *Wanta get on my new car?*
> If the other **will perform** the act: *Will you put this hammer in for me?*
> If the other **has a reason not to perform** the act: *Why don't you tickle me?*

Other indirect requests appear in the form of statements or commands:

> Statement of **need:** *I need that pencil.*
> Statement of **desire:** *I want a purse.*
> Statement that other **must perform** the act: *You have to call.*
> Command other to **remember to perform** the act: *Don't forget to smoke your pipe.*
> Command other to **attribute ownership** to self: *Pretend fishy was mine.*

In all of the cases just cited, the other child did, in fact, perform the act desired by the speaker. The use of indirect requests is still a very small proportion of requests at this age. The mean number of indirect requests per 15 minute interaction was 1.25, compared to 22.5 direct requests. In an older group of children studied (aged 4;7 to 4;7½), the number of indirect requests was higher; the mean number per interaction was 2.17, compared to 17.1 direct requests (similar results were obtained in: S. James & Seebach 1982; Wilkinson et al. 1982).

In all of the examples except the last, one might reasonably assume that in most of the instances of sentences of that form the child had previously heard, the intended message was also a request to perform an act. How many times is the child likely to have heard the construction, *Why don't you X?*, in which the communication intent was to obtain information as to the reason the listener doesn't do X? Such occurrences are probably quite rare. Thus when young children use such constructions, they do not need to reinterpret the literal meaning; rather it is the case that the so-called indirect use is the only one they know.

Though the intent of such utterances is not revealed by the syntax, caregivers regularly use indirect forms even when their children are just beginning to leave the one-word stage, and their children rarely misinterpret them (Holzman 1972). The reason is that the intent is conveyed redundantly through situation or gesture. One study of mothers' directives to their two-year-old children found that 87% to 100% of the interactions contained other cues as to the meaning of the directives (Shatz 1978a).

Children are probably quite old before they become consciously aware that the literal meaning is different from the indirect request. How old is not known, but Quentin was 10 years old before he discovered the strategy of responding to the literal meaning of an indirect speech act in order to—very temporarily—avoid performing the act:

Me: It's time to go to bed.
Quentin: (Making no motions toward going to bed.) That's interesting.
Me: Quentin!!
Quentin: (Moving very slowly.) Okay, okay.

The *Pretend fishy was mine* example is more indirect. The intended goal was to get the listener to let go of the fish, which the listener in fact did. This example is more indirect than the others because the intended goal does not form a part of the utterance (see Ackerman 1978; Newcomb & Zaslow 1981).

Additional cases of more indirect requests have been noted:

Turkish child (2;8):   (Pretending to iron clothes.) This one is finished, too (Aksu 1973).

The intended message was to have the adult hand the child new clothes to iron. Four-year olds often request adults to intercede by citing violations to rules:

Jason's trying to take my stuff (O'Connell 1974).

They also seek help by drawing attention to their own incapacities:

Daddy, I can't get this out (O'Connell 1974).

And even more indirectly still (seeking help to clean up):

I'm sorry. My room's too messed up (Mitchell-Kernan, cited by Ervin-Tripp 1977).

Even more obliquely:

Child (3;6):   We haven't had any candy for a long time (Ervin-Tripp 1977: 177).

Such oblique requests are among the last to be acquired by children (Aksu 1973).

The comprehension of 20 different types of directives has been experimentally investigated for children between four and seven (nursery school to grade 2). For some types of sentences, even the youngest children tested responded correctly most of the time. This was true for, for example:

You should color the circle blue.
Please color the circle blue.
I'll be happy if you color the circle blue.

For the other types of sentences, children showed significant improvement during the age range tested. Such sentences included:

The circle doesn't need to be colored blue.
Can you color the circle blue?
Must you color the circle blue?
Why not color the circle blue?

By grade 2 children were responding correctly at least 80% of the time for all but one of the directives:

I'll be happy unless you color the circle blue.

This one had climbed to only 42% for the oldest group (Carrell 1981).

The development of the use and recognition of different levels of politeness has also been studied in an Italian study. Sixty children between the ages of three and seven were each separately introduced to a hand puppet named Signora Rossi. The children were told that if they asked, Signora Rossi would give them a piece of candy. The children asked the Signora, who then whispered to the experimenter. The experimenter then told the children, "Signora Rossi wants to give you a nice piece of candy, but she likes children to ask very, very nicely. Could you ask her again even nicer?" In response to the second request, the child then received a piece of candy.

In a second task the child was asked for a piece of candy by two puppets and had to decide which puppet asked most nicely. One puppet would say, for example, "I want a piece of candy," while the other would say, "I would like a piece of candy."

Most of the youngest children in the study were unable to change their request form, though they could tell that a soft intonation was better than a harsh one, and that using *please* was better than not using it. Older children could choose successfully between more complex politeness forms, even though the polite versions of their own requests were more primitive. The most complex politeness forms were not correctly distinguished until age six or so (E. Bates 1974, 1976a, 1976b). The use of an increasing variety of types of directives has been found in other studies as well (see, e.g., B. Read & Cherry 1978).

A particularly interesting example of the relationship between what is actually said and what is intended to be communicated is the following:

Athena (5;3):   I'm cold.
         Me: Well, what do you think you can do about it?
    Athena: I'm please cold.

Athena's initial remark was an indirect way of requesting her father to get her a sweater. My reply was an indirect way of telling her that she could get the sweater herself. However, Athena's interpretation of my indirect remark was that she had not asked politely enough, and so she tried to increase the politeness of the request by adding *please*. Another similar example occurred almost two years later:

Athena (7;2):   I didn't get any applesauce, please.

Syntactically, these uses of *please* cannot appear in a declarative. In order to explain why she put them there one must refer not to the syntactic or semantic form of the message, but to the underlying intention.

Children must learn to make inferences from utterances other than politeness forms as well. When told that the cereal is hot and not to eat it now, one can generally make the assumption that one is expected to eat it later, when it has cooled. A statement not to do X often allows an inference to do Y. The acquisition of this type of inference has been explored experimentally. Fifty-five children aged 2;0 to 6;1 were each individually seated at a table and given three tasks. In one task two dolls, one of an adult female, the other of an adult male, were placed before the child. The child was then told, "Don't give me the mommy doll." The other two tasks were similar: "Don't color the circle red," and "Don't put the green block in the cup."

There appear to be three stages of responses. The two youngest children did what they were told not to do. Perhaps the expectation that they were going to be told what to do in the situation overwhelmed their incipient understanding of the *don't*. Among the next 30 youngest (aged 2;4 to 4;6), 77% were literally obedient and did nothing for at least 45 seconds. On the other hand, 92% of the 25 oldest children made the inference and performed the other task: They handed over the daddy doll; they colored the circle blue; and they put the yellow block in the cup. An interesting sex difference appeared: 73% of the girls asked first whether they could do the alternate task, whereas only 27% of the boys did (Eson & Shapiro 1982; see also Hildyard & Olson 1978).

In contrast to the previously mentioned conversational abilities, more subtle skills appear not to develop completely until much later. These skills include being sensitive to different discourse rules in different contexts, and the ability to convey a message successfully.

Different discourse rules in different contexts   The rules of how to conduct a conversation include, among other things, how to initiate a conversation. These conversational rules differ in different situations. Most people are not aware that such differences exist, but their existence is demonstrated by children who apply the right rules to the wrong context. For example, the following telephone conversation took place between me and Mark, a four-year-old friend of my son:

    Me: Hello?
    Mark: Hello.
              (Long period of silence.)
    Me: Who is this?
    Mark: Mark.

Me: What do you want, Mark?
Mark: Can Quentin come and play?

When two people meet in person, one person will say *hello;* the other will respond *hello;* then it is up to the first speaker to continue the conversation. However, in a telephone conversation it is the responsibility of the second speaker to immediately continue the conversation: *Hello. May I speak to Quentin?* Mark was merely applying the discourse grammar of normal face-to-face interaction when he responded *hello* and then waited for me to talk.

Now consider this telephone conversation, which was the first time Athena called her mother at work:

Mother: Hello?
Athena: Hello.
             (Pause.)
Mother: Athena?
Athena: Hi, Mommy.
Mother: Did you call me by yourself?
Athena: I called you three times! The first time I got oo-oo-oo (imitation of sound resulting from incorrectly dialed number). The second time I forgot what to say!

In order to reach her mother at work, Athena had to ask a switchboard operator for *Professor Reich.* Since this is not the normal way a child refers to her mother, she was unable to get past the operator, so she became flustered and hung up. Readers of this book may recall a similar experience the first time a phone call they had placed was answered by a machine advising them to *leave a message at the sound of the tone.*

Code switching

A related conversational skill that children must learn is to use different varieties of speaking in different social situations. This is known as **code switching.** The earliest example of code switching is perhaps babbling at different pitches to father and mother (Lieberman 1967). Another example of early code switching occurs when a child talks or babbles happily to its parents, but falls silent when in the presence of strangers. Preschoolers whine to their parents but not to strangers (J. Gleason 1973).

A much more sophisticated form of code switching is the ability to use simpler language when talking to younger children. When talking to two-year olds, four-year olds use shorter, simpler sentences than with peers or adults, and more utterances intended to gain the listener's attention. This is true of four-year olds whether or not they have younger brothers or sisters (Shatz & Gelman 1973). Children also speak differently when talking to adults than they do when talking to other children (Martlew et al. 1978; Sachs & Devlin 1976; Weeks 1971).

Communication of information

Another way of studying children's conversations is to look at them from the perspective of their ability to convey information. Young children are less successful at imparting information to others than are their older counterparts. The growth of the child's ability to take into account the perspective and knowledge of the listener has been investigated in a number of studies. Piaget (1923: Ch. 3) explored this by giving one child some information and asking that child to tell it to another child who was not present at the original telling. He used three one-paragraph stories and two explanations of how a simple object worked (a tap and a syringe). He tested 10 pairs of six-year olds and 15 pairs of seven-year olds. The speakers often failed to communicate many of the essential details of the stories or explanations. They communicated slightly more of the content of the stories than of the explanations, but their explanations were understood slightly better by the listeners. The seven-year olds were slightly better than the six-year olds. The greatest problem noted was that the speakers failed to specify the people and objects being referred to, and used pronouns and demonstrative adjectives (*this, that*) instead. Piaget claimed that this was due to egocentrism; the speakers appear not to be able to distinguish what the listener knows compared to what they themselves know.

Egocentrism also seems to explain the behavior of children in another study. Children were asked to describe one of a set of cards so that a listener could identify the card. When asked to explain why communication had failed in this type of experiment, five- and six-year olds blamed the listeners on the grounds that they chose the wrong card. On the other hand, seven- to eleven-year-olds realized that the speaker could be at fault (Robinson & Robinson 1977a, 1977b).

An alternative explanation involves the development of the ability to perceive ambiguity. In a task in which children listen to a message and then are asked an ambiguous question, their ability to perceive the ambiguity increases greatly between ages five and nine (Bearison & Levey 1977). If they cannot perceive ambiguity when listening to others, one cannot attribute to egocentrism the fact that they cannot perceive it in their own speech, either.

In fact, children as young as three do take their listener into account. When three-year olds talked with an adult about some tasks they had mutually performed a week earlier, they talked in a more abbreviated fashion than when asked to discuss the same tasks with an adult who had not been present (Menig-Peterson 1975). A similar result was obtained when children three- to-five years old talked to a blind-folded listener, compared with others talking to a sighted listener (Maratsos 1973b; see also Meissner & Apthorp 1976).

Another study involved children explaining a board game to a listener who could not see the board. Four- to six-year olds were more disorganized in their descriptions than six- to nine-year olds. The younger children do not systematically start with a description of the game board, whereas the older children are careful to set the context (M. Pratt et al. 1977).

It appears that the problems that young children have with communication derives at least partially not from the egocentric nature of children, as Piaget suggested, but simply from a lack of skill at communicating information.

The ability to communicate successfully develops slowly and continuously. This was illustrated in a stack-the-blocks task. In this task two children were seated at a table which had a screen between them so they could not see one another. Each side of the table contained a set of blocks. Each block had a picture on it. The speaker's blocks were arranged in a stack. It was the task of the speaker to communicate this sequence so that the listener could construct an identical stack.

When the blocks had pictures of circus animals on them, the nursery school children tested had no problem; but when the pictures on the blocks were more abstract, such as those shown in Figure 4.9, the nursery schoolers failed miserably. The names used by three-year-old speakers could not be correctly interpreted by their listeners (see Table 4.6; Glucksberg et al. 1966). The ability of children to perform this task improves with age, but they do not reach adult levels of success until they are 11 or 12 years old (Glucksberg & Krauss 1967). Performance also can be improved by modelling the appropriate behavior in this situation (Whitehurst & Merkur 1977).

At more complex communication tasks one may continue to improve well into adulthood. However successful or unsuccessful you may feel this book to be at communicating, I can assure you that my writing is better now than it was when I was a graduate student. Actors, playwrights, journalists, politicians, and others whose occupations involve communication can confirm that one can continually improve through adulthood at these crafts.

FIGURE 4.9   **Abstract figures on the blocks task. (From Glucksberg et al. 1966. ©Academic Press. Used by permission.)**

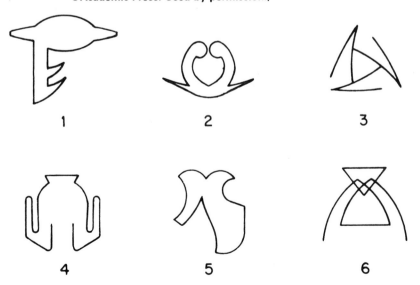

TABLE 4.6   Responses in the Blocks Communication Task

FIGURE NUMBER	SUBJECT 1	SUBJECT 2	SUBJECT 3	SUBJECT 4	SUBJECT 5
1	Man's legs	Airplane	Drape holder	Zebra	Flying saucer
2	Mother's hat	Ring	Keyhole	Lion	Snake
3	Somebody running	Eagle	Throwing sticks	Strip-stripe	Wire
4	Daddy's shirt	Milk jug	Shoe hole	Coffee pot	Dog
5	Another Daddy's shirt	Bird	Dress hole	Dress	Knife
6	Mother's dress	Ideal	Digger hole	Caterpillar	Ghost

From Glucksberg et. al. 1966. © Academic Press. Used by permission.

The success of communication also depends, of course, on the communication ability of the listener. The percentage of listeners who ask for additional information increases with age (Alvy 1968), and the ability of the listener to request specific information from the speaker improves dramatically at about age 9. Girls are more likely than boys to ask questions when the message is ambiguous (Ironsmith & Whitehurst 1978; see also C. Patterson & Kister 1981).

Listener skills have also been shown to improve with training (Cosgrove & Patterson 1977, 1978). Both four- and seven-year olds have been found to readily reformulate a message when asked to do so (Peterson et al. 1972). The form of the request is especially important. Both four- and seven-year olds fail to reformulate when confronted by nonverbal facial expressions of noncomprehension. Seven-year olds reformulate in response to implicit requests such as *I don't understand,* but four-year olds require explicit commands to say it another way. Apparently the four-year olds recognize the implicit statement as a request for help, but they don't know what kind of help to give. (An extensive list of references to referential communication research may be found in W. Dickson 1981b, 1982.)

Another type of communication skill is the ability to comfort someone in distress. A slow and continuous improvement in this ability, as measured by the number, variety, and degree of sophistication of the strategies employed, has been found in children ranging in age from 5 to 14 or more. A small, but statistically significant, difference was noted in the responses of the boys as opposed to the girls tested. The girls were slightly more skilled than the boys on this task (Burleson 1982).

LANGUAGE PLAY

One of the most salient aspects of child language in the middle and late childhood years is language play. Language play does not begin during this period, of course. Language play begins even before language itself begins—at the onset of cooing. Later, language in the crib and other monologue language behavior can also be described as a type of language play. However, it is in middle and late childhood that language play really blossoms. This behavior is rich enough to be considered a linguistic culture in its own right. It includes special vocabulary and discourse rules, and it provides utterances to accompany many aspects of child behavior. As children reach adulthood they cease making use of this rich cultural heritage. Language play demonstrates the role of children in both maintaining the language of the past and creating the language of the future.

Types of language play

Any categorization of different types of language play is arbitrary; the purpose is setting out such a categorization is to demonstrate the variety of pervasiveness of such activity.

Play with language form   The first type of play with language is play with language form. This begins as phonological play, emphasizing sound to the exclusion of syntax or semantics (Helmers 1965; Sanches & Kirshenblatt-Gimblett 1976: 95; Shultz & Pilon 1973). This first occurs with babbling, but resurfaces in middle childhood in a wide variety of forms.

Secret languages. The most universal form of play with language form may well be the use of secret languages. The variety of possibilities is endless (see, for example, R. Price & Price 1976; Sherzer 1976). They include:

Pig Latin:

Owhay oday ouyay oday? ("How do you do?")

Bebop Talk:

Hob-a-pob-pob-y bob-i-rob-tob-hob-dob-a-yob ("Happy birthday").

Gibberish:

[sɪθəgaɪ kɪθəga lɪθəgoɔ jɪθəgi] ("Psychology").

Talking backward:

Talking backward has been reported as a type of secret language play in a number of different cultures (Chrisman 1893; Conklin 1956—Tagalog; Sherzer 1970—Cuna). It is fairly rare in English. I certainly never ran into it as a child, but the occasional child will acquire the skill. Such people occasionally show up on late night television interview shows. One such person has recently been studied intensively (Cowan & Leavitt 1982; Cowan et al. 1982). Although he was an adult when studied, his ability is reported to go back at least to when he was in fourth grade. This individual retained normal word order, and, usually the normal intonation pattern both within the word and in the sentence. Within the word the order of phonemes would be reversed. He could repeat what he heard with a time lag of between two and five words. His reversals were accurate enough to sound like a distorted version of English when played backward on a tape recorder.

The reversals differed from true phonemic reversal in several respects. Here are three examples: vowel glides were not reversed—[ɑʊ] did not become [ʊɑ], for example; initial /h/ was not pronounced when, on reversal, it became final /h/; and words ending in [ʊŋ] were pronounced [gɪnɪ] or [gənɪ] rather than [ŋɪ].

Here is a list of a few of the recorded reversals:

ambergris	[sʌɹgɹɛbmæ]
gathering	[gɪnʊɹəðæg]
number	[ɹɛbmʌn]
pounds	[dzɪnɑʊp]
project	[tkɛjɑrp]
wheelbarrow	[oʊɹæbliju]

The detailed linguistic analysis of this man's speech showed an ability at phonological analysis that was remarkably sophisticated for someone who was untrained. However, the most sophisticated backwards talker ever was probably the famous linguist Y.R. Chao, who could talk backward in five languages. He could take long memorized passages and utter them into a tape recorder such that, when the tape was played backward, the entire passage came out sounding as if it had been produced normally.

Cockney rhyming slang. Closely related to secret languages is Cockney rhyming slang, in which many nouns are replaced by set phrases which rhyme with the words they replace:

> I was taking the cherry 'og for a ball o' chalk up the frog and toad the other night, when I met a China plate o' mine. We 'ad a few dicky birds an' then 'e suggested we 'ad a tumble down the sink together ("I was taking the dog for a walk up the road the other night, when I met a mate of mine. We had a few words and then he suggested we had a drink together."—Espy 1971: 80).

Tongue twisters. Another quite different form of language play is the tongue twister. It may be a simple phrase, such as:

> Rubber baby buggy bumpers.

Or it may be considerably more involved, as is this one from Great Britain:

> There's no need to light a night light
> On a light night like tonight
> For a night light's a slight light
> On a light night like tonight (Opie & Opie 1959: 30).

Tangle talk. Even more involved language play is tangle talk, which consists of entire monologues which children memorize and recite to one another:

> Ladles and jellyspoons:
> I stand upon this speech to make a platform. The train I arrived in has not yet come, so I took a bus and walked. I come before you to stand behind you and tell you something

I know nothing about. (Heard in Toronto, 1983. Examples not otherwise cited have been observed by myself or my students.)

Puns. Punning is a very sophisticated linguistic behavior. It is an activity which children with language problems often cannot appreciate. Two stages in the development of punning are the ability to appreciate them and the ability to make them up on the spot. With the ability to appreciate them comes the spread of riddles such as this one through the community of children (for more detail, see Shultz 1974; Sutton-Smith 1976):

Q. What do you call a bunch of idiots who sing, drink Tab, and eat apples?
A. The Moron Tab 'n' Apple Choir.

The ability to make up puns on the spot seems to come around puberty. Indeed, among some groups of teen-agers, a sport of competitive punning occurs, in which each bad pun provokes a worse one in response. This is not unlike escalation in children's quarrelling, described earlier in this chapter.

Related sorts of verbal dueling have been reported in other cultures as well. One interesting report comes from an area of Mexico where the people speak the Chamula dialect of Tzotzil. Here adolescent males alternate remarks, each of which should differ from the previous by a very few phonemes—preferably only one. The remarks generally have sexual content. The person who can not think of a comeback loses the exchange (Gossen 1976).

Naive spelling. Occasionally preschool children will start writing messages without the benefit of adult help with spelling. Only a small number of children engage in this type of language play, but the messages produced by those who do can be very interesting because of the inventiveness of the spelling displayed.

When writing English without the benefit of memorized spellings, the would-be literate child runs into numerous problems due to the lack of a one-to-one relationship between English sounds and alphabetic characters. One study of such naive spelling found a high degree of similarity among the over 20 children studied (C. Read 1971, 1975).

Let us turn first to the way such children treat the vowels. At least some children appear to go through two stages. At first they base their spelling on the pronunciation of the vowel letters of the alphabet. It is relatively straightforward to pronounce the so-called 'long' vowels, since the names of the vowel letters use these pronunciations:

FAS	face
DA	day
LADE	lady
FEL	feel
LIK	like
TIGR	tiger
BOT	boat
JOK	joke
UNITD	united

The more interesting question is how such children spell words with the so-called 'short' vowels:

PAN	pen
LAFFT	left
FLEPR	Flipper
EGLIOW	igloo
BICS	box
GIT	got

In order to explain what such children do in these cases, it is important to remember that in English the long vowels are phonetically glides. Thus *a* is pronounced [ɛɪ], *e* is [ʮi], and *i* is [ɑɪ]. Now consider the child who is trying to represent a word pronounced [pɛn]. The [ɛ] sound is the first part of the sound of the letter *a,* so the child uses this, and spells *pen* as *PAN.* The same reasoning explains why the other words in the above list were spelled as shown.

This way of analyzing the glides into their parts does not help the child to find a way to represent the short *a* ([æ]) as in a word like *cat.* Phonologically, two sounds that the naive speller can represent are close to [æ]. They are [ɛ], which the child spells with an *a,* and [ɑ], which the child spells with an *i.* Two different phonological theories predict which letter the child will actually pick. Jakobson's theory predicts that height of the vowel should be more salient to a child than degree of backness. If this is the case then [æ] should appear to the child to be more distinctively different from [ɛ] than it is from [ɑ]. By this reasoning children should represent [æ] the same way they represent [ɑ]; namely with an *i.* Thus Jakobson's theory predicts that children would write *KIT* for *cat.*

On the other hand, the theory of Chomsky & Halle (1968) predicts that the place of articulation (degree of backness) is more salient. Thus children should prefer to represent [æ] the same way they represent [ɛ], since the two sounds have the same degree of backness. Since children represent [ɛ] with the letter *a,* it follows that they would write *KAT* for *cat.* It happens that in fact children write *KAT.* Thus one can argue that Chomsky & Halle's theory is confirmed. The major flaw in such reasoning is that children may use an *a* for the much simpler reason that it is the vowel adults use to represent that sound, and that children simply pick up this fact from reading or asking an older person. However, supporting evidence can be found in the way these children handle [ŋ], which will be described below.

Some naive spellers go through a second stage in handling the vowels. Children who do this learn to associate the vowel letters with the sound of their associated short vowel sounds. Thus *a* is associated with the [æ] sound; *e* is associated with the [ɛ] sound, *i* is associated with the [ʮ] sound; *o* is associated with the [ɑ], and *u* is associated with the [ʌ] sound.

This naive rule makes it easy to spell words which contain short vowels:

LAP	lap
LEG	leg
LIP	lip
LOTS	lots

However, now the problem is how to spell words containing a long vowel. If *a* represents [æ], *e* represents [ɛ], and *I* represents [ɩ], then how do children represent long *a* [ɛɩ], long *e* [ɩi], and long *i* [ɑɩ]? Since the first part of the long *a* glide is the sound of a short *e*, they use *e;* similarly, since the first part of the long *e* glide is the sound of a short *i*, they use *i*. Thus:

TEBL	table
PLEY	play
FRONTIR	frontier

Some interesting points arise from the way naive spellers handle consonants, as well. For example, before they are taught how to spell the [ʃ] and [č] (also representable as [tʃ]) sounds as *sh* and *ch* respectively, they may find those sounds in the letter *h*, pronounced [ɛɩtʃ], and thus use that letter, as in:

FEHEG   fishing

Another point involves the fact that in English the liquids can sometimes be used as entire syllables. Adults learn that every syllable must contain a vowel, and thus insert one. Children, unencumbered by such prejudices, tell it as it is:

TIGR	tiger
LITL	little
SODNLY	suddenly

In the initial consonant clusters *tr-* and *dr-* the *t* and *d* are affricated, and thus sound not unlike [č] and [ǰ] respectively. This fact is recorded faithfully by naive spellers in such words as:

CHRIBLS	troubles
JRAGIN	dragon

Naive spellers have another problem when it comes to representing the sound [ŋ]. As in the case of stage-one naive spellers representing [æ], there are two representable sounds relatively close to the problem sound. The sound [g] differs in manner but not in position; the sound [n] differs in place—degree of backness—but not in manner. As in the case of [æ], children prefer to represent [ŋ] by a sound that is identical in place, even though differing in manner. Thus they use the letter *g:*

GOWEG	going
SOWEMEG	swimming

Nasals before stop consonants in English have as their major phonetic effect the nasalization of the vowel, rather than existence as a separate speech segment. This fact explains why naive spellers tend not to represent the nasal in such cases:

NUBRS	numbers
WOTET	want it
AGRE	angry

Although this type of language play is relatively rare, it shows that children can perform phonological analyses with an agility that exceeds that of most adults, whose abilities have been adulterated by knowledge of their unphonetic spelling system.

Performatives   A second broad category of language play is the performative. A performative is something one says to accompany some action. In early childhood, waving *bye-bye* and saying it would be an example. Among the most common language-action combinations in the middle childhood years are jumping rope to chants, playing hand-clapping games, counting out, pulling petals off flowers, and ball bouncing. Children learn from other children the rhymes and chants along with the actions themselves.

Jump rope rhymes:

Apples, peaches, pears, and plums.
Tell me when your birthday comes.
January
February
. . .
First
Second
Third
. . . (Milberg 1976: 107)

Susie and Johnny sitting in a tree.
K-I-S-S-I-N-G
First comes love, then comes marriage,
Then comes Katy in a baby carriage. (The name, given here as "Katy" indicates the
  next person to jump into the rope.)

(Rope begins moving back and forth with the jumper jumping over it.)
Blue bells, cockle shells,
Eevy ivy over!
(Rope begins going over the skipper's head.)
My mother sent me to the store
And this is what she sent me for:
Salt, eggs, vinegar, mustard, peppers!
(Rope turners start turning the rope very fast. *Peppers* is the technical term for turning
  a jump rope very fast.)
1,2,3, . . . (until jumper misses—heard in Toronto, 1980. See also Milberg 1976: 82).

I'm a little Dutch girl dressed in blue.
These are the things I like to do.
Salute to the captain, curtsy to the queen,
And turn my back on the mean old king.
(Appropriate actions while jumping accompany the last two lines.—Milberg 1976:
  105.)

Hand clapping.

First child:	Zing zang zoom.
	My heart goes shaboom!
	Who stole the cookies from the cookie jar?
	Was it you, number one?
Second child:	Who me?
First child:	Yes you!
Second child:	Couldn't be.
First child:	Then who?
	Was it you, number two?
	. . . (and so on).

Lucy had a steamboat, steamboat had a bell,
Steamboat went to heaven and Lucy went to
Hello operator, give me number nine,
If you disconnect me, I'll chop off your
Behind the 'frigerator, there was a piece of glass,
And if you don't like it, you can just
Ask me no more questions, tell me no more lies,
The boys are in the bathroom, pulling down their
Flies are in the garbage, bees are in the park,
Boys and girls are kissing in the dark, dark, dark.
Ask me no more question, tell me no more lies.
A man got hit with a bottle of pop, right between the eyes (Milberg 1976: 241-242).

Counting out. These performatives are uttered while pointing consecutively to different individual items of a set of people or objects. The object or individual pointed to when the rhyme ends is eliminated, and the rhyme begins again until all but one have been eliminated.

One potato, two potato,
Three potato, four,
Five potato, six potato,
Seven potato, more.

Eeny, meany, miny, mo.
Catch a tiger by the toe.
If he hollers, let him go.
My mother says you are out.

Pulling petals off flowers.

He loves me,
He loves me not,
He loves me,
He loves me not.

. . .

One petal is pulled off the flower for each line, until the last petal is removed, at which time it is determined whether he loves her or not. This is just the tip of the fortune-telling iceberg. There are many other ways, the most common of which is perhaps jump rope games in which the answer is determined by when the child finally misses and stops the rope.

Ball bouncing sayings. These are uttered while simultaneously bouncing a ball. Each stressed syllable is said to the bounce of the ball.

> 1, 2, 3, O'Leary.
> Lost my ball in the city dairy.
> If you find it, give it to Mary.
> 1, 2, 3, O'Leary
> A, my name is Alice,
> My husband's name is Albert,
> We come from Alabama,
> And we sell apples.
> B, my name is Barbara,
> My husband's name is Barry,
> . . . (and so on) (Milberg 1976).

Technical terms   Being a child has something in common with being a member of a profession: a set of technical terms which one member uses to talk to other members of the same group. There appear to be two major categories of such terms—game terms and descriptives.

Game terms: It, gotcha, rock, scissors, paper, snooger, peppers.

Descriptives: Nurd, silly billy, monkey's uncle, townies ("people who live in a university town who are not university students"), gurbies ("tourists"), browner, cat's pajamas, square, fluffy, decent, bad ("good"). Many additional such terms will be given in the appropriate sections below.

'Legal' customs   Just as in the adult world, the child's world runs more smoothly because of the linguistic customs for handling contracts and other similar 'legal' matters.

Truth. The adult *I swear to tell the truth, the whole truth, and nothing but the truth* has at least three children's counterparts:

1. Cross my heart and hope to die If I ever tell a lie.
2. I bet you it's true.
3. Scout's honor.

Secrecy. The adult world, especially the governmental sector, has its secrecy oaths, which are mirrored in the child world by:

> Cross my heart and hope to die.

Lock my lips and throw away the key (Opie & Opie 1959: 141).

Commerce. Apparently in Britain they seal a bargain with a pinkie shake, saying:

> Ring a ring a pinkie.
> Ring a ring a bell.
> If ye brake the bargain
> Ye'll go to hell (Opie & Opie 1959: 131-132).

In North America, it appears to be simpler:

> Spit on it.

A subset of commercial transactions is the swap, which is sealed by uttering:

> No call backs (heard in Toronto, 1980).

> No backsies.

> Stamp it.
> Double lock it.
> No erasing (Opie & Opie 1959: 132).

And what would commerce be without ownership?

> Finders keepers,
> Losers weepers.

In cases of doubt, who gets it first? Depending upon dialect region, the child who first shouts:

> Dibs.

> I borrows.

> Stamp it.

Truce. If only adults could reach truces as easily as children can, simply by uttering:

> Olly olly oxon free.

> 1, 2, 3, home free.

> Uncle.

> Times.

> You're it, and I quit (Opie & Opie 1959: 149).

THE FAR SIDE   By GARY LARSON

© Chronicle Features, 1984

"Dibs."

The Far Side (Reprinted by permission of Chronicle Features, San Francisco.)

    Rules of the road. No legal system would be complete without at least one rule of the road:

> Step on a crack, break your mother's back.
> Step on a line, break your mother's spine.

    Taunts   The world of childhood differs from that of the adult in the social acceptability of the taunt. There appears to be a taunt for practically every occasion.

Cheating:
Cheaters never prosper!

Lying:
Liar, liar, pants on fire.
Nose as long as a telephone wire.

Becoming 'it':
Richard's it. Prickle stick.
Can't get over arithmetic.

Failed attempt to hit:
Missed me, missed me.
Now you gotta kiss me.

Blabbing:
12 and 12 is 24,
So shut your mouth and say no more.

Seeking information:
That's for me to know and for you to find out.

Name calling. This language behavior seems to occupy enormous amounts of energy of prepubescent boys, especially. One can insult others on the basis of physical characteristics—*fat lips, gimpy, four eyes, tin grin*—mental characteristics—*clunkhead, dummy, jerk, lunchbucket, spaz, nitwit, dip*—ethnic origin, color of clothing, lack of courage, and/or their name. One of my criteria for naming my own children was to choose names for which there were no jeers. I didn't want them to suffer the agony I went through because of my own name:

Peter, Peter, pumpkin eater.
Had a wife and couldn't keep her.

For Better or for Worse (© 1977 by Lynn Johnston. Reprinted by permission of Meadowbrook Press and Simon & Schuster, Inc.)

This section would not be complete without recording some responses to name calling:

Sticks and stones may break my bones,
But names will never hurt me.

Takes one to know one.

Twinkle, twinkle, little star.
What you say is what you are.

Accidental rhyming:
You're a poet and you don't know it, but your feet show it, 'cause they're Longfellows.

Telling an old joke:
Ha ha ha, hee hee hee.
Elephant's eggs in a rhubarb tree (Opie & Opie 1959: 53).

Trickery:
I made you look, you dirty crook.
You stole your mother's pocketbook.

Crooked answers:
Q. What time is it?
A. Half past the second freckle.

Etiquette   While obnoxious taunts abound in child speech, it is not without
its etiquette.

Saying the same thing at the same time:
Jinx (sometimes accompanied by locking pinkies).

Begging:
Pretty please with sugar on it.

Animal Crackers (Reprinted by permission: Tribune Media Services, Inc.)

Table manners. The first rhyme is for saying grace; the second is for burping;
the third is obvious:

Over the teeth
Around the gums
Look out stomach
Here it comes!

Excuse me for my ignorance;
It wasn't very smart.
But if it came out the other end,
It would have been a fart.

Mable, Mable, strong and able.
Get your elbows off the table.
This is not a horse's stable.
But a respectable dining table (from my childhood. A slightly different version is
    found in Abrahams 1969: #323).

Asking someone to leave:

Be like a banana and split.

Be like dandruff and flake off.

Be like a bee and buzz off.

Take a long walk off a short pier (Knapp & Knapp 1976: 64).

Saying good-bye:

First child: See you later alligator.

Second child: After awhile, crocodile.

Saying good night:

Good night, sleep tight,

Don't let the bedbugs bite.

If they do, take a shoe

And beat them 'til they're black and blue.

Now I lay me down to sleep,

A bag of apples at my feet.

If I die before I wake,

You'll know it was a stomach ache (Knapp & Knapp 1976: 171).

Commemorating special days:

Happy birthday to you.

You belong in a zoo.

You look like a monkey,

And you smell like one, too (Knapp & Knapp 1976: 223).

Trick or treat, smell my feet,

Give me something good to eat.

No more pencils, no more books,

No more teacher's dirty looks.

Fine arts: No culture is worthy of the name without a tradition in the fine arts, and childish culture, extending into college years, has it in abundance.

Songs:

(To the tune of Bye, Bye Blackbird)

Oh, I have lost my underwear.

I don't care. I'll go bare.

Bye, bye, long johns.

They were very good to me;

Tickled me; hee hee hee!

Bye, bye, long johns . . .

Great big gobs of greasy, grimy, gopher guts,

Mutilated monkey meat,

Little birdies' dirty feet,

Top it all off with pulverized vulture beaks.

Oops! I forgot my spoon (Milberg 1976: 137).

Cheers. Almost every school has a cheer or two. The following comes from my alma mater, and hasn't changed since I attended, even though the last line has been rendered obsolete by the electronic chip.

e^x dudx ("E to the X, D U, D X")
$e^{\ x}$ dx ("E to the X, D X")
cosine, secant, tangent, sine
3.14159 ("3 point 1 4 1 5 9")
vdu + udv ("V D U plus U D V")
Slip stick, slide rule, M.I.T.

Literature. The fine arts would be incomplete without consideration of the written word, such as the signature book messages, also available for signing yearbooks:

When you are old and out of shape,
Remember girdles are $2.98

I wish you luck, I wish you plenty.
I wish you a husband before you are 20.

And finally, we pay homage to graffiti, a fine art that has been traced back to the dawn of humanity. The two examples I choose to represent that genre here are not quite so ancient:

I would rather have a bottle in front of me than a frontal lobotomy.

The above example can be found in washrooms from Toronto, Canada, to Sydney, Australia. It also appears as a song performed by Randy Hanzlick, M.D. (Dr. Rock); I do not know which came first, but I saw the graffito years before I heard the song.

Sign over a men's urinal: Stand closer. It's not as big as you think.

Some general characteristics

The preceding sections attempt merely to give examples of different types of children's language play sayings, rhymes, and chants. Compilations attempting completeness have filled numerous books. In this section, we will look at this material from a broader perspective.

Oral tradition One thing that is supposed to mark an advanced civilization is the development of a written form of language. Before this stage all culture must be transmitted orally, handed down from one generation to the next, whereas after this stage the oral modality is eclipsed by tablets, scrolls, books, records, films, microfiches, videotapes, laser disks, floppy disks, ROM microchips, and so on. But the fact remains that there is an enormously rich culture within our society that is still handed down from generation to generation in the oral tradition. The rhymes, chants, songs, and special vocabulary of childhood are still handed down from generation to generation in the oral tradition.

Continuity In spite of the evanescent form of cultural transmission, a surprising amount of the material has remained relatively unchanged for long periods of time. The Opies compared verses recorded in London in 1916 with their own collection in 1956 and found that 78% of the poems on the 40-year-old list were still in use in 1956. Furthermore, some stories, poems, and jokes can be traced back hundreds of years, to as early as the 16th century (Opie & Opie 1959: 10-11):

1725:
Now he acts the Grenadier,
Calling for a pot of beer:
Where's his money? He's forgot:
Get him gone, a drunken sot.

1907:
Eenty, teenty, tuppeny bun,
Pitching tatties doon the lum;
Who's there? John Blair.
What does he want? A bottle of beer.
Where's your money? I forgot.
Go downstairs, you drunken sot.

1916:
Rat a tat tat, who is that?
Only grandma's pussy cat.
What do you want?
A pint of milk.
Where's your money?
In my pocket.
Where is your pocket?
I forgot it.
O you silly pussy cat.

1950:
Mickey Mouse[1]
In a public house
Drinking pints of beer.
Where's your money?
In my pocket.
Where's your pocket?
I forgot it.
Please walk out.

1952:

A pig walked into a public house
And asked for a drink of beer.
Where's your money, sir?
In my pocket, sir.
Where's your pocket, sir?
In my jacket, sir.
Where's your jacket, sir?
I forgot it, sir.
Please walk out.

Universality   Many rhymes span the English-speaking world. One can find essentially identical poems in Britain, Australia, the USA, and Canada. This lore is also universal in another respect. It is known and transmitted by children in all social classes and in both urban and rural environments.

Rapid transmission   One property of this lore is that it is capable on occasion of spreading extraordinarily rapidly. For example, on November 25, 1936, King Edward the VIII provoked a constitutional crisis when he made public his intention to marry the divorcee Wallis Simpson. On the 10th of December he abdicated. By the 20th of December, just 10 days later, all over England children were singing:

Hark the herald angels sing
Mrs. Simpson's pinched our King.

As the Opies put it: "Many an advertising executive with a six-figure budget at his disposal might envy such crowd penetration" (Opie & Opie 1959: 6).

Another example involves the ballad of Davy Crockett, which came out early in 1956. Within six months a child-lore version with only slight variations had spread from Sydney, Australia:

Reared on a paddle-pop in Joe's café,
The dirtiest dump in the USA,
Poisoned his mother with DDT,
And shot his father with a .303.
Davy, Davy Crockett, The man who is no good.

to Swansea, England:

Born on a table top in Joe's Café,
Dirtiest place in the USA,
Polished off his father when he was only three,
Polished off his mother with DDT.
Davy, Davy Crocket, King of the Wild Frontier.

School children appear to employ transworld couriers (Opie & Opie 1969: 7).

Origin   The origin of most rhymes and verses is unknown. Those that are known are often relics of once-famous songs, professionally written. For example, Harry Hunter wrote this lyric in 1875 (Opie & Opie 1959: 13):

> I saw Esau sawing wood
> And Esau saw I saw him
> Though Esau saw I saw him saw
> Still Esau went on sawing.

Regional variation   Many terms used in childhood have regional variants, so there are identifiable dialect areas just as in adult language. One such term which has been investigated by the Opies is the term a child uses to claim first place. In my own childhood the word was *dibs*. Throughout northern England the term is apparently *bags* or *baggy*. However, in Kircaldy it's *Chucks me first;* in Ruthin it's *Cogs I first go;* in Headington it's *Touch wood bags I first;* in the East End of London it's *Me squits;* in Enfield it's *Lardie;* and in northern England, depending upon region, it is one of these: *furry, fuggy, foggy, feggy, ferry, fog, fogs, firsy,* or *fussy* (Opie & Opie 1959: 138-139).

We find that children in middle childhood live in a culture only partly disseminated by their parents and teachers. A very robust oral culture, spread from child to

FIGURE 4.10
Dialect map of distribution of precedence term in northern England (From Opie & Opie 1959: 139. © Oxford University Press. Used by permission.)

child, thrives, even in this age of mass media. (This is not to deny the power of the mass media. One day I was walking down the street with my three-year-old son, when suddenly he said, "To be, or not to be. That is the question." "Where did you hear that?" I asked. "Bugs Bunny said it on television," was his reply.)

SUMMARY

The development of certain syntactic constructions has been studied in detail. These constructions include negation, question, passive, object complement, and conjunctive sentences. In each case progress has been found to proceed in a slow, orderly progression of small steps; in a few cases the process is not complete until as late as 10 years old. The development of morphology also proceeds slowly and over a long period. Early problems of segmentation and categorization give way to problems of inflection, morphological variation, and irregular forms, especially in highly inflected languages. In the area of word meaning, research interest has been particularly keen on the acquisition of shifters and relationals. On the discourse level, it has been found that as children mature, greater proportions of their utterances are more highly socialized and more successful at communication of complex information. Middle and late childhood also brings an explosion of different types of language play.

SUGGESTED FURTHER STUDY

BATES, E. (1976) Pragmatics and sociolinguistics in child language. In Donald M. Morehead & A.E. Morehead, eds., *Normal and deficient child language.* Baltimore: University Park Press, 1976, 411-463.

BROWN, ROGER (1973) *A first language: The early stages.* Cambridge, Mass.: Harvard University Press.

FLETCHER, PAUL & M. GARMAN, Eds. (1979) *Language acquisition: Studies in first language development.* Cambridge: Cambridge University Press. See especially Chapters 11 through 16, written by Derwing & Baker; Maratsos; Wales; Fletcher; Bowerman; Karmiloff-Smith.

KOHLBERG, L., J. YAEGER, & E. HJERTHOLM (1968) Private speech: Four studies and a review of theories. *Child Development* **39,** 691-736.

OPIE, IONA & P. OPIE (1959) *The lore and language of schoolchildren.* Oxford: Oxford University Press.

REES, N.S. (1978) Pragmatics of language. In Richard L. Schiefelbusch, ed., *Bases of language intervention.* Baltimore: University Park Press, 1978, 191-268.

NOTES

[1]Mickey Mouse is, of course, a cartoon character controlled by, indeed symbolizing, Walt Disney, Inc. The use of this name in this way must have upset company executives, who carefully guard against its cartoon characters being associated with the use of alcoholic beverages.

FIVE
ACQUISITION OF MORE THAN ONE LANGUAGE

BILINGUALISM IN THE WORLD

Quot linguas calles, tot homines vales. [You are worth as many men as you know languages.]—Attributed to Charles V (Holy Roman Emperor, 1500-1558) by Goethe, *Spruche est in Prosa,* 1819.

We have room for but one language here and that is the English language, for we intend to see that the crucible turns our people out as Americans and not as dwellers in a polyglot boarding house.—Theodore Roosevelt, Jan. 3, 1919 (Morison 1954: 1422).

A **bilingual** is a person who can speak two languages. A person who can speak more than two languages is a **multilingual** or **polyglot.**

What percentage of the world's population can speak and understand more than one language? To the best of my knowledge, nobody has hazarded a guess in print, though I have heard fellow academics make verbal estimates ranging from 25% to 80%. There are many problems which make it difficult to compute such a figure with any degree of accuracy. Many countries have no census information, and of those that have it, each country's census asks different questions. However, four countries account for almost half of the world's population—China, India, the USSR, and the USA—and there are figures, or at least estimates, of bilingualism in these countries. Extrapolating from these figures (jumping in where others have feared to tread), I have come up with an estimate for the world's population. I figure that between 45% and 50% of the world's population, or roughly two billion (2 000 000 000) people, are bilingual.[1] Some details are given in Box 5.

Furthermore, many people can speak more than two languages. Several members of the family of refugees from Vietnam that I helped to sponsor to Canada could speak five languages. Unfortunately, neither English nor French were included among the five. Now they speak varying degrees of English as well, and one is learning French. According to the Guinness *Book of Records,* the most accomplished living polyglot is probably Georges Schmidt, a translator for the United Nations, who can speak 30 languages fluently and can translate 36 others.

BOX 5.1 *WORLD BILINGUALISM*

	China	India	USSR	USA	Total
Percent of world's population[a]	20.8	15.4	6.5	5.4	48.1
Percent of country's population that is bilingual	40[b]	80[c]	18.2[d]	17.1[e]	47.3

Other interesting estimates:
    In the USA it is on the increase.[f]
    In Canada (1971): 24.4%.[g]
    In the United Kingdom: Under 5%, but in Wales 21% speak Welsh.[h]
    In Australia and New Zealand: Very low.[i]
    In South Africa (1960): 73%.[j]
    In Israel (1961): Aged 15+: 62.7%. Aged 2–14: 36%.[k]
    Countries with the least bilingualism: Iceland, Portugal, Western Samoa (practically nil).[m]
    Countries with the most bilingualism: Bolivia, Paraguay, Peru (approx. 85% +).[n]

Many of the above figures concern mother tongue only, and do not include languages learned through schooling and travel. In some countries this figure can be quite high. For example, there are very few people in Denmark whose mother tongue is not Danish, but 11 years of English is required in the schools, and many films and TV programs are in English with Danish subtitles. Furthermore most Danes living near the German border seem to have some facility with German. Thus mother tongue figures would be quite low, while actual bilingualism appears to be quite high.

Based on figures or estimates given in the following sources:
[a]McWhirter 1978 [b]Fincher 1978. [c]Khubcandrani 1978. [d]Lewis 1978.
[e]Kloss & McConnell 1978. v.2. p. 10. [f]Ibid. p. 12. [g]deVries & Vallee 1980.
[h]Central Office of Info. 1981. [i]Benton 1978. [j]Mackey 1967. [k]Bachi 1974.
[m]Kloss & McConnell 1979 v. 3. p. 29. [n]Ibid, p. 12.

A second language comes to be acquired in various ways. Two general categories are natural and formal. **Natural bilingualism** occurs in children when the two parents speak different languages in the home, or when a family has emigrated to an area that speaks a different language. If a family emigrates after a first language is established, the acquisition can be said to be **sequential,** otherwise the acquisition can be said to be **simultaneous** (Vihman & McLaughlin 1982). In many countries a dominant language is used throughout the country and by the media, while at the same time many different local languages are used by families who live in the country. In such situations a large percentage of the population may be bilingual. **Formal learning** is what goes on in schools. There are many different types of formal language programs, including traditional, immersion, submersion, and mixed. We shall discuss each of these in turn.

SIMULTANEOUSLY ACQUIRED LANGUAGES

Case histories

The earliest case in which a child's acquisition of two languages was reported in detail is that of Louis Ronjat (Ronjat 1913). Louis's father was French and his mother was German; he grew up in France. Before he was born his parents were advised by a linguist colleague never to switch languages when speaking to him. Taking this advice, his father always spoke French to him and his mother always spoke German. Louis learned to distinguish between the two languages before he reached two. When he learned a new word he would try using it with French and German pronunciation. Within a week he would assign the word either to "Mamma's box or Papa's box," and thereafter there was no confusion between the two languages.

After some initial confusion, each new person in the household, such as a nurse or a servant, would be identified as French or German, and would thereafter be addressed in the appropriate language. Initially Louis favored his mother's language, but soon the other language caught up and the two languages developed at the same pace. His progress in each language appeared to be in the normal range for monolingual speakers. His fluent bilingualism continued through his teens, when he was reported as preferring French, his school language, in technical matters, and German for literary self-expression (Vildomec 1963: 25).

A similar case history involves Duchan, the son of a Serbian linguist and his wife, who grew up in France spending a great deal of time with a French-speaking friend of the family from 13 months on. In this case, too, the caregivers were each careful to speak only one language to the child. Duchan's acquisition matched that of Louis—for example, he, too, ceased confusing the two languages by the age of two (Pavlovitch 1920).

Greater language mixing is reported in children whose caregivers are not as strict about keeping the two languages separate. This was true in one reported case of eight children born in China to English-speaking missionaries (M. E. Smith

1935b). The parents spoke both English and Chinese to the children; all others spoke Chinese to them. Considerable language mixing occurred. The two languages were confused up to age three; on the average the eight children stopped producing mixed-language sentences at about 3;3. The age that most observers cite for the separation of two languages seems to be somewhere between three and five (Elwert 1960; Geissler 1938; Imedadze 1960; Rūķe-Draviņa 1967). The separation age varies with each child, of course, but it also depends upon the observer's definition of separation (McLaughlin 1978: 96).

The most complete diary study of a child's language acquisition is Werner Leopold's four-volume analysis of the development of his daughter Hildegard (Leopold 1939, 1947, 1949a, 1949b). Hildegard was spoken to in German by her father and in English by her mother. She was raised in a suburb of Chicago, except for a short visit to Germany at the end of her first year and a seven month stay there when she was five. Hildegard and her younger sister Karla did not appear to be aware of dealing with two languages until the beginning of their third year. Only at the end of their third year did the active separation of the two languages begin. Thus Hildegard's language separation was quite late, and her ability at German, though good enough to win an award in Chicago (Leopold 1949b: ix), never reached native speaker competence. Perhaps this is because, unlike Louis and Duchan, her mother spoke the language of the community, leaving the burden of contact with the other language solely on her father, who probably was able to spend far less time with her than her mother.

Bilingual and multilingual language development has been studied in a large number of language combinations.[2] Although one can find considerable variation in these case studies, a fairly consistent picture emerges. Neither the rate nor the success of acquisition seems to be affected by whether the languages the child is acquiring are related, such as French and English, or from entirely different language families, such as English and Garo, English and Japanese, or Georgian and Russian.

In their second year many bilingual children appear to have impaired language development, but by age four all who have not moved to a new language environment recently appear to have normal native ability in the language of the street plus ability that ranges from good to native in whatever languages are spoken in the home, depending on the degree of contact they have with the language.

The course of acquisition does seem to run more smoothly if each person in contact with the child sticks rather strictly to only one language. Lacking this, there is much greater language mixing. One study reported that at age two years 60% of the child's sentences contained words of both languages (Tabouret-Keller 1962).

Language interference

Language mixing, or **interference,** occurs at all levels of language organization, but much more at some levels than others. The least interference occurs at the phonological level. A number of children studied seemed to have little or no phonological interference. In other words, they appeared to have no noticeable accent (von Raffler-Engel 1965; Metraux 1965; Oksaar 1970; Pavlovitch 1920; Ronjat 1913: 16; Totten 1960). I am a little hesitant about accepting reports of no phonological interference. Most of these reports are diary studies made by parents of the children being studied, who have moved to a place where the language of the region is not their first language. Even though these parents may be trained linguists, it is possible that, not being native speakers of the language of the street, the parents did not themselves notice the interference.

Other children were found to use parts of the phonological system of one language when speaking the other. Stephen Burling, raised after 1;4 in a Garo-speaking community by English-speaking parents, used the Garo consonant system when speaking English (Burling 1959). Two children learning Swedish and Latvian and the one learning Swedish and Polish sometimes used Swedish intonation when speaking their other languages. They also tended to use the uvular [ʀ] of Swedish in place of the rolled apical [r] of Latvian and Polish. Similarly, Hildegard appears to have preferred [ʀ] to [ɹ] of midwestern American English (Leopold 1947). Similar cross-language replacements were found in the consonant [l] in the above-named cases and in Takahiro, a little boy learning Japanese and English (Itoh & Hatch 1978).

When the corresponding sounds in two languages are differentially difficult to acquire there is often a period when the easier phoneme is used in both languages (Leopold 1947; Murrell 1966; Rūķe-Draviņa 1965). Alternatively, words that the child finds difficult to pronounce may be avoided in that language but not in the other (Celce-Murcia 1978), a phenomenon that we noted earlier in monolingual children.

Children learning related languages occasionally 'fuse' the pronunciations of the word in the two languages, producing a word intermediate in sound between its two pronunciations. For example, one girl learning Swedish and English merged the Swedish *bussen* with the English *bus* to produce an intermediate-sounding *basen* (Murrell 1966).

If the two languages are equally strong, the period of confusion is relatively short (Pavlovitch 1920), whereas if one language is dominant, substitution of some of its sounds into the other language is likely to occur. Thus Stephen at first spoke English with a Garo accent (Burling 1959).

It is probably a safe generalization to conclude that most but not all children do have some mixing of the phonological systems of their two languages for a period of a year or so after they begin to speak. Once resolution comes, both languages can be spoken with phonological accuracy indistinguishable from that of native speakers the same age. Indeed, there is even a report of children whose mother spoke native French and whose father spoke French with an American accent. The children spoke French without an accent to their mother and French with an American accent to their father (von Raffler-Engel 1965).

On other than the phonological level, initial interference between the two languages is universally reported. In vocabulary, bilingual children, like their monolingually raised counterparts, initially adopt a strategy of one word per referent. Thus in Hildegard *nein* and *no* coexisted briefly, but *no* won out and *nein* dropped out. Similarly, *eye* beat out *Auge* and *away* beat out *Weg*. On the other hand, *mehr* submerged *more* and *Haar* won out over *hair*.

Occasionally one well-established word would after a time be superceded by the word in the other language. In Hildegard's case this usually involved shifts from German to the increasingly dominant English—*Augenblick* was replaced by *wait,* for example; but occasional shifts were in the other direction—*mitten* to *Handshuh,* for example. Once bilingual children realize that they are speaking two languages they begin to learn the words from both languages simultaneously. Indeed, when they learn a new word in one language, they may specifically ask for its name in the other (Ronjat 1913).

When the two languages are related, children may attempt to convert a word they know in one language to a word in another language by pronouncing it according to the phonology of the other language. When she was 3;6, Hildegard converted *candle* to *Kandl* by changing the vowel sound to its German equivalent (Leopold 1947). This has also been noticed in other bilingual children (Murrell 1966; Rūķe-Draviņa 1967; von Raffler-Engel 1965).

Interference is also reported in children's early syntax. It appears that many children go through three stages in the separation of their two languages. Up to their second year, the language they have is treated as one language with a single syntax and vocabulary. During this period utterances containing vocabulary from both languages are common. For a short period after that, children sort the vocabulary into two languages, but they use the same syntax for both sets of vocabulary. For example, the child learning Russian and Georgian first expressed the subject-object relation in Georgian by analogy to Russian (Imedadze 1960). Initially the two Italian-German children developed a single syntax which was different from either language (Volterra & Taeschner 1978). Finally, in balanced bilinguals, both lexicon and syntax become differentiated and each language is used in its own appropriate contexts (Mikeš 1967; Rūķe-Draviņa 1967; von Raffler-Engel 1965).

When the acquisition of specific syntactic constructions is studied, the pattern that seems to emerge in balanced bilinguals is this: (1) The syntax that is acquired first is that which is common to both languages. This has been noted, for example, in a study of *yes-no* questions by French-English children (Swain 1971). (2) If a particular semantic relation is represented with syntax of equal complexity in both languages, the syntactic constructions will be acquired at the same time. This seemed to be the case when the Georgian-Russian children acquired the use of the genitive (possessive) and instrumentals of both languages in lock step. Both languages express these relations in essentially the same way (Imedadze 1960, 1967). (3) If one language is more complex than the other in its syntactic representation of a semantic relation, the easier syntactic construction will develop first. This seems to explain why Hungarian-Serbo-Croatian children acquire the locatives sooner in Hungarian than in Serbo-Croatian. The construction is more complex in Serbo-Croatian (Mikeš 1967; Mikeš & Vlahović 1966). Similarly, if one language requires a semantically more complicated response in a particular situation than another language, the response that is semantically more complex will be mastered later. This appears to be the case in what is required to answer negative questions in English and Japanese. The English system is easier, and children bilingual in both languages tend to master it first (Akiyama 1979. See Chapter 4 for further discussion of this study).

The story is similar in morphology. Hildegard went through a stage when she would use English words in German sentences but adapt them by giving them German inflections—for instance, *pouren, geyawnt, monthe*. Similarly, a boy learning English and Italian often attached Italian endings to English words (von Raffler-Engel 1965). And another attached Estonian endings to Swedish verb forms in Estonian sentences (Oksaar 1970).

SUCCESSIVELY ACQUIRED LANGUAGES

When a family moves to a region that speaks a different language before a child's first language is established, the child will usually learn two languages simultaneously—the language of the street and the language of the home—and will do so without loss or difficulty. But what if the family moves after considerable acquisition of the first language has already taken place? This is the case of sequential acquisition. The line between simultaneous and sequential acquisition is an arbitrary one; following McLaughlin (1977, 1978), we will say that if acquisition of one of the languages begins after the third birthday the acquisition is sequential.

Case histories

As with simultaneous acquisition, our knowledge relies heavily on case studies, although recent papers tend to be more systematic and to be concerned with more specific issues. Also like simultaneous acquisition, studies have involved many different language pairs.[3] The basic finding is that, as with simultaneous acquisition, children succeed at the task.

The speed with which children who are thrust into a new language environment will catch up with their monolingual peers in their new language is impressive. Volz's child was in an almost completely monolingual Malaysian environment for his first three years. At 3;1 he moved to a monolingual German environment. By 4;0 his German was approximately equal to that of monolingual German children the same age (Volz, as cited in Stern & Stern 1907). Eva Kenyeres was 6;6 when her family moved from Hungary to Geneva. Within 10 months she was able to speak French as well as her same-age peers, according to her mother (Kenyeres 1938). A six-year-old Spanish refugee ended up in Belgium, where she acquired French and Flemish. By the age of eight she had scored two years *above* the mean for her age on tests of French language skills. Two other children, one three and the other four, seemed to require one year to switch from Italian to Dutch (Francescato 1969).

Switching was not so easy for an American three-year-old child relocated to Paris. Although he went to a French nursery school for eight hours each day, he heard only English in the home. After one year he was one year behind his peers in his French. Nevertheless, it appears that a typical child younger than seven can successfully switch languages within a year.

Is acquisition the same the second time?

Does the acquisition proceed the same way as it does for the first language, or is the process different? Some observers have concluded the former (e.g., Dato 1970; Ervin-Tripp 1974; Francescato 1969; Milon 1974; Ravem 1978), others the latter (e.g., Cancino et al. 1974, 1975; Kenyeres 1938; Politzer 1974; Tits 1948). There are several reasons for these differences of opinion.

One reason is that different children may use different strategies for learning their second language; some may learn it the same way they learn their first language and others may learn it differently. During the first three months in a French environment Eva consciously worked at the language task by translating French into Hungarian, by rehearsing French forms when playing alone with dolls, for example, and by consciously exploring rules for French gender (Kenyeres 1938). Six months after being thrust into a German environment, Volz's son went through a three-month period of discouragement and relative silence, after which he began to speak more, though with considerable effort at first (Volz, cited in Stern & Stern 1907). On the other hand, Francescato's two children did not seem to consciously compare their second language with their first (Francescato 1969). Some of these differences reported may relate to age: Francescato's children were three and four; Eva was 6;6. However, some of the differences are simply due to differences in the personalities of the individual children.

A second reason that opinions differ is that different observers may have different threshholds for concluding that two acquisition sequences are different. In general, the opinions one way or the other have been due to subjective impressions. Most observers who conclude that acquisition is similar admit to some differences. The most pervasive one is speed of acquisition. Also, most children at least briefly borrow features from their first language. Rune and Reidun Ravem occasionally borrowed Norwegian forms while learning English (Ravem 1978). Other children occasionally used English forms while learning French (Ervin-Tripp 1974).

On the other hand, many observers conclude that the processes are similar because in many other instances children seem to go through the same sequence of development in their second language as their monolingual peers do, even though using analogy with their second language might have actually helped them. A seven-year-old Japanese boy learning negation went through the same stages that English-speaking children did, even though one might have expected to see occurrences of sentences with the negative after the verb—*I want not,* for example—because that is the Japanese order (Milon 1974).

There is a similar finding involving the acquisition of questions by two English children learning French. They went through a strategy of putting the question word first, but otherwise using the standard declarative word order, a stage monolingual children go through, even though the French invert the word order just as the English do, and thus modelling the French on the English would actually have helped them (Ervin-Tripp 1974).

The same phenomenon was noted in seven English-speaking children, aged 4;1 to 6;6, learning Spanish. If they had modelled their Spanish questions on English, they would have inverted subject and auxiliary, but they did not. Spanish questions also have inverted order, so again it would have been beneficial for the children to have followed the English order. These children also learned the Spanish person-number, tense, and other elements of the auxiliary in the same sequence as Spanish monolingual children (Dato 1970, 1978). Similarly, 21 English-speaking children learning Welsh appeared to use noun phrase constructions that reflect Welsh rather than English word order (Price 1968).

Many observers who have concluded that the acquisition process is different may have simply been employing stricter criteria for similarity. One project involved eliciting English speech samples from 151 Spanish-speaking children in three locations: in California; in Tijuana, a Mexican city just across the border from San Diego; and in New York City. The order of acquisition of 11 English function morphemes was compared with the order noted in a study of monolingual English speakers (R. Brown 1973). The orders in the three native Spanish groups were very similar to each other but different from that of the native English monolinguals (Dulay & Burt 1973).

One might conclude that the first language, Spanish, was influencing the sequence of development of the second language function morphemes. However, another study by the same researchers tends to discredit this proposal. They compared the order of acquisition of the same 11 English morphemes by 50 additional Spanish-speaking children with 55 Chinese-speaking children. The Chinese and Spanish groups were almost identical and again differed from English (Dulay & Burt 1974). Such a result cannot be due to similarities in the way Spanish and Chinese handle function words, because they are not at all similar. A more reasonable conclusion is that the acquisition sequence by native monolinguals is influenced by semantic factors—that is, by the sequence of acquisition of the semantic concepts underlying the function morphemes.

One can assume that those learning English as a second language have already acquired most or all of the underlying semantic concepts, and that the resulting sequence is due to some other factor or factors, such as the frequency at which the different function morphemes are heard. Strictly speaking, the sequences of development differ, but one can also argue that the acquisition strategies for the first and second languages are identical; it is just differences in conceptual knowledge which account for the different sequences found. Thus Kenyeres (1938) argued that Eva's second language acquisition was different because she employed the cognitive framework of a child of her age, but others would argue that this is not a difference in language acquisition strategies, and therefore not evidence to consider first and second language acquisition to be different.

A third reason that opinions differ is that observers of second language acquisition may have a false impression of normal variability in normal language acquisition, because many findings in monolingual language acquisition have been based on observations of only a small number of children. One such case involves the acquisition of questions in six Spanish speakers learning English. Two were five-year olds, two were adolescents, and two were adults. In none of these speakers did subject-auxiliary inversion in *yes-no* questions precede inversion in *wh-* questions (Cancino et al. 1974, 1975). The researchers concluded that this represents a difference between second and first language learners, because first language learners were supposed to invert in *yes-no* questions first (Klima & Bellugi 1966). But, as has been discussed in Chapter 4, later research (Erreich 1980; D. Ingram & Tyack 1979) found that many monolingual children behave exactly the way the six Spanish speakers did, and begin to invert the two types simultaneously.

Language forgetting

What effect does the new language environment have on the children's first language? Unless doggedly maintained in the home environment, the first language is apparently forgotten. And it appears that it doesn't take long, either. Stephen stopped using Garo almost immediately upon moving from the area where Garo was spoken, when he found his Garo was not being understood. Within six months he was having trouble remembering even the simplest and best learned Garo words, such as the names for body parts (Burling 1959). The Spanish refugee in Belgium declared on the 93rd day after her move that she did not know Spanish anymore. At age five Hildegard spent one month with relatives in Hamburg. At the end of this stay she could not speak English (Leopold 1956-57: 249). After seven months in Geneva, Eva was pronouncing her first language, Hungarian, with a French accent, and she spoke French in her dreams (Kenyeres 1938: 338-339).

One cannot blame the second language for causing a child to forget the first language. Rather one must blame disuse of the first language. Evidence in support of this comes from four reported cases in which a person who had normal language ability became totally isolated from the company of other humans for extended periods of time.

The first such person was the inspiration for Defoe's *Robinson Crusoe* (1719). In 1704 Alexander Selkirk, a 28-year-old Scottish sailor, was marooned on the island of Juan Fernández, off the coast of Chile, for attempting a mutiny. He was left a chest of supplies, which included a Bible and other books. He remained there until he was found four years and four months later by a Captain Woodes Rogers, who wrote in his diary: "At first coming on board us, he had so much forgot his language for want of use that we could scarce understand him, for he seemed to speak his words by halves." Selkirk later told an interviewer that he regularly recited prayers aloud "in order to keep up the facilities of speech." In spite of that, according to Rogers, he had "almost entirely forgotten the secret of articulating intelligible sounds. . . . If he had not had books, or if his exile had lasted two or three years more," he would have lost all ability to speak (Rogers 1712; Lane 1976: 197; Lane & Pillard 1978: 75-76).

The second case, not as well documented, is that of an eight-year-old girl who got separated from her camping group during a snowstorm in the Pyrenees. She was captured eight years later, identified, and institutionalized. She had lost all speech; she never recovered it (Leroy 1776, cited in Lane 1976: 178-179).

The third case is much more recent. In approximately 1935 Sidi Mohamed, a 15-year old who had been living with a flock of ostriches since he was 5 or 6 years old, was captured by three ostrich hunters and returned to civilization. When captured, he was "almost a deaf mute," but recovered his language well enough to write about his time in the wild (Monod 1945).

The fourth case occurred in 1963 at Saint Brévin, France. A young boy, Yves Cheneau, was found in a cellar by his uncle and some gendarmes. He had been imprisoned there for 18 months. According to his uncle, when he was shown a cat and a cow and asked what they were, he could no longer give their names. According to a newspaper reporter who visited him in the hospital later, he no longer knew how to speak (Malson 1972: 56).

In the second case, the loss of speech and the lack of progress at reacquiring it could be explained by brain damage due to exposure to the harsh elements in the wild. This doesn't seem to have been a factor in the other three cases; these appear to be bona fide examples of language forgetting due purely to disuse.

Even in adults there can be a surprising amount of language degeneration. A former student of mine reported that his brother, a native speaker of Moroccan Arabic, at the age of 24 went to university in France, where he spoke no Arabic. Three years later he attempted to return to Morocco to visit his parents. He was stopped at the border by Moroccan immigration officers, who didn't believe he could be a Moroccan because he had lost his ability to speak Arabic.

That an unused language tends to be forgotten is well established. How completely it is forgotten is another matter, however. Volz reported that when his son had forgotten all Malaysian, he still used the sounds and intonations of Malaysian when speaking nonsense gibbersh (Volz as cited in Stern & Stern 1907).

One can find evidence that disused languages are not forgotten by studying cases of aphasia in bilinguals and multilinguals. In most cases of brain damage, all of the patients' languages are equally affected, and all recover equally (Charlton 1964; Hécaen et al. 1971; L'Hermitte et al. 1966; Nair & Virmani 1973). However, in a few cases there is differential recovery.[4] In some of these cases a language that hadn't been spoken for some years was recovered first. One case involved a German who immigrated to the United States at the age of 10. After that time he had no exposure to German. At age 16 he had a migraine attack, after which he found himself thinking in German for 10 minutes (Dreifuss 1961).

And then there is the case of the professor who, when his son was 15 months to 3 years old, read to him three 20-line selections of Greek poetry daily. He read each selection for three months, after which he changed the selections. In total, 21 selections were read. The boy had no knowledge of Greek or the meaning of the passages. When the boy was 8, 14, and 18 years old, he was tested to see how fast he could memorize Greek selections from the same poems. At age 8 he was 30%

faster on passages he had heard as a baby; at age 14 he was 8% faster; by age 18 there was no difference (Burtt 1941). Apparently even a superficial contact with another language can have a very long-term effect.

It appears that children entering a new language environment need only about a year to learn the new language. Different children employ different strategies—for example, some children make more use of their first language than others in learning their second—but the major surprise is that such little use is made of the first language even when such use would be beneficial. Although the sequence of acquisition of a second language varies in some aspects from that of the first, the processes of learning the two languages seem to be more similar than different.

LANGUAGE TEACHING

Some traditional approaches

In the first half of this century second language instruction in the United States consisted of courses in high school. Enrollment in these courses was usually optional, and those who enrolled were those who aspired to college or university, most of which required foreign language courses for entrance.

The traditional method was to emphasize, especially in the first year of such courses, reading, grammar, and vocabulary. The medium of instruction was primarily English. Dissatisfied with the degree of success of the traditional method, educators began to look to new methods of instruction.

World War II took Americans into countries where the natives spoke esoteric languages such as Burmese. It became necessary to teach members of the Armed Forces some oral skills in these languages as rapidly as possible. The reading of Burmese shop and road signs was useful, but an ability to read the literature of the language was not needed. The **audiolingual approach** and the language laboratory were born of this necessity.

The audiolingual approach[5] makes heavy use of intensive drills in listening and speaking through memorized dialogues and pattern drills. Only later are reading and writing skills developed. The foreign language is used as much as possible as the medium of instruction, but English is used occasionally for explanations of structure and some teaching of meaning. Materials are constructed so that grammar can be deduced rather than directly taught, although the latter is also used somewhat (Donoghue 1968).

The comparative merits of audiolingual (AL) and traditional (T) instruction were evaluated in a two-year study of beginning students of German. At the end of the two years, these were the results: AL and T were equal on listening, reading, and English-to-German translation; AL was far superior to T in speaking; but T was superior to AL in writing and far superior to AL in German-to-English translation (Scherer & Wertheimer 1964). Thus neither method is clearly superior. Which you prefer depends rather on what you deem most important.

The increasing availability of the tape recorder in the 1960's made the language laboratory possible. At least as first used, language laboratories turned out not to be very useful. Passive listening to tapes in a language laboratory is apparently not an effective means of learning. Shown to be more effective was a system of discrimination training, in which the student must decide which of two pronunciations of a word is correct, and then receives feedback (Mace & Keisler 1965). Controlled studies of the effectiveness of the language laboratories as actually used in schools in the 1960's found that they were either a not particularly effective method of instruction (Carroll 1967; Scherer & Wertheimer 1964) or they were actually detrimental to language learning (Keating 1963).

New technologies and numerous variants of the traditional method of instruction seem able to produce after three or four years of instruction, a certain proportion of students who are not totally lost when faced with the task of communicating with native speakers of some other language. Still, one would hope for better.

Languages in the elementary schools

Based partly on the belief in the existence of a critical period for language learning (see Chapter 7), and supported by U.S. Government and foundation funding, educators began to teach Foreign Languages in Elementary Schools (commonly referred to as FLES). This idea initially met with some resistance:

> Several investigators . . . would like to introduce foreign languages . . . even into nursery schools and the very first classes of elementary schools. Some of these investigators have no doubt had very little first-hand experience as school teachers. . . . Such policies may be justified in exceptional circumstances, . . . but under normal conditions they are hardly desirable. . . . Changes as adventurous as those suggested . . . are likely to shatter the school system and increase difficulties (Vildomec 1963: 51).

However, research seems to indicate that adding FLES to the school curriculum does not detract from other subjects (Leino & Haak 1963). In fact, children in FLES programs actually appear to gain in other subjects, especially reading (O. Gordon et al. 1963; C. Johnson et al. 1963; Lopato 1963). Furthermore, when they get to high school, FLES students elect to take foreign languages more often; and those who do take languages in high school receive grades that average 10% higher than those of students of similar ability who have not gone through a FLES program (Donoghue 1968; Vocolo 1967). Another benefit is that FLES students end up with a more positive attitude toward the people who speak the language they study. This positive attitude does not generalize to people who speak languages other than the one studied, however (Riestra & Johnson 1964). The overall gains from FLES appear to be positive (Pillet 1968), but it is also fair to say that they have been modest. The fact that grades were 10% higher in high school does not mean that FLES programs have produced a generation of bilingual children.

Peanuts (© 1978 United Feature Syndicate. Used by permission.)

Immersion

Total immersion   A method of teaching a foreign language that is apparently more successful is **total immersion.** In total immersion, schooling is provided in a language not native to the children by a teacher who is a native speaker of the classroom language but is bilingual, so that she or he understands the children when they speak in their native language.

Total immersion programs most commonly have involved teaching French to English-speaking children in North America, especially in Canada. We shall describe the program as a French immersion program, though, as we shall see, there are similar programs involving other languages. In the first years the teacher speaks only in French. Generally in kindergarten and the first half of grade one the children are permitted to speak English, although their use of French is highly encouraged. After this period, the children are expected to use French for all communication in the classroom. Slowly some English is introduced into the curriculum. As originally set up, this began with 90 minutes of English language arts, beginning in the second grade. The amount of English instruction was gradually increased, until in the seventh grade English and French were each used about half the time. Both the first and second languages are used for regular curriculum instruction. Mathematics may be taught entirely in French, while science may be taught entirely in English, for example.

Immersion programs are intended for children who speak the majority-group language, whose parents support the acquisition of the second language not for the purpose of forsaking the first language, but rather as a positive addition to the child's knowledge (Genesee 1983).

History and progress. The program was originated in 1965 in St. Lambert, a suburb of Montreal, at the request of English-speaking parents who were dissatisfied with the ability of the English language school system to teach French, the dominant language in the Province of Quebec. Since 1965, total immersion French programs have spread across Canada and have become the method of education chosen by a substantial minority of English-speaking parents. The program is most popular in Quebec and in Canada's capitol, Ottawa, where the ability to speak both official languages is important for advancement in federal employment. In Ottawa 40% of English-speaking parents are sending their children to French immersion kindergarten. In Toronto approximately 10% of senior kindergarten enrollment in the public school system is in the French immersion stream. In those neighborhood schools that have an immersion stream, the typical enrollment is much higher— approximately two-thirds of senior kindergarten pupils are entering the French stream. This is partly due to housing patterns. Many people who want to enroll their child in French immersion move to those neighborhoods serviced by a local school with a French immersion stream. But it also suggests that many more parents would send their children to French immersion if it were available in the neighborhood school. (Children attending French immersion programs who do not live near a school that offers it are bussed.)

How did an originally small experiment turn into a major alternative form of education in larger Canadian cities from coast to coast in just 10 years? The answer lies in research. Total immersion French has been extensively and carefully researched since it began. There are now over 200 research reports on it, and the results have been predominantly favorable (Swain, personal communication; see Swain 1976 for list of 114 references). It is to this research that we now turn our attention.

English skills. On tests of English reading ability, immersion children as a group lag behind matched controls (students in the normal English stream) up through second or third grade (Lambert & Tucker 1972). Once one hour a day of English language skills is introduced into the curriculum, immersion children catch up to their English educated counterparts within a year or less. It doesn't seem to matter whether this instruction begins in second, third, or fourth grade (Genesee 1979; Genesee & Stanley 1976; Swain 1974). They do not appear to catch up so quickly in tests of English language rules and English spelling. On the other hand, they never fall behind on skills of listening to or speaking English (Lambert & Tucker 1972), and even appear to be superior on some communication tasks (Genesee et al. 1975).

French skills. Immersion students become far more adept at French than do Anglophone (English speaking) students who have gone through a traditional French teaching program. The interesting comparison is between immersion students and native Francophones (French speakers). Immersion students appear to equal their native Francophone peers in French reading and listening comprehension, and in their ability to communicate ideas in French (Bruck et al. 1976; Swain & Lapkin 1982). However, they never reach native competence in the grammatical constructions they use in speech. Rather, they develop a 'classroom dialect' in which can be found examples of literal translations of English idioms and word order. Their pronunciation is also not quite the same as that of natives. These problems with the language do not seem to occur when individual children are placed in classrooms with many native speakers (Macnamara et al. 1976). This alternative was once popular in Quebec, where the majority of the population speaks French, but is currently forbidden by law (H. Edwards & Smyth 1976: 531). In any case, it is impractical in most other areas of Canada. In Toronto, for example, French is the mother tongue of only 1.1% of the school population, considerably fewer than those in the immersion stream.[6]

Other areas. No deficit has been found in other subjects. For example, they equalled their peers in computational and problem solving arithmetic tests both in English and in French, and on tests of science and social-studies skills (Bruck et al. 1976, Lambert & Tucker 1972; Swain et al. 1973). They also equalled their peers on intelligence tests and on measures of cognitive flexibility. Immersion children have also been given attitude tests. Their attitudes toward themselves were normal. Montreal immersion students considered themselves to be both English and French Canadians without psychological conflict.

Children in French immersion programs have tended to be the elite. Most parents who choose to send their children to immersion programs are socioeconomically upper middle class or higher. Children with below normal I.Q.s or with language or learning disabilities have generally been underrepresented. However, the evidence available indicates that working-class children, those with lower I.Q., and even children with disabilities, do as well in immersion as one could expect them to perform in the regular stream (Genesee 1976).

One area of concern is acceptance of immersion students by their Francophone peers. Apparently, immersion teenagers are not completely accepted. There appear to be several reasons for this. One is that early immersion classes used teachers who spoke Parisian French, the dialect that has the highest prestige, rather than teachers who spoke the native Quebec dialect. The result is that although the French of immersion students was imperfect, the Parisian dialect they spoke sounded haughty to their Francophone peers. More recently established immersion programs have used speakers of Quebec French. Another reason is that immersion students do not learn the complete range of language registers that native Francophoes make use of. They know the classroom middle-class teacher-to-student dialect, and the broadcast dialect they hear on TV, but not the current teenage slang (Genesee 1978; Tucker 1977).

Other reasons are sociological. The Anglophone community in Quebec, especially where the immersion programs originated, tend to be upper-middle-class and upper-class children, while the majority of Francophones tend to be middle- or lower-class. Since Francophones perceive French in Quebec to be a threatened language[7] anyone known to be fluent in English may tend to evoke feelings of inferiority, even if they are speaking fluent French. Thus some problems getting along with Francophones are probably related to class and sociological factors only indirectly related to language fluency.

Other immersion alternatives   Various alternatives to total immersion programs have been implemented and researched. One such alternative is **early partial immersion.** Early partial immersion begins in kindergarten or first grade and consists of a day split equally into French and English. In one such program over one thousand students took math, music, and French language arts in French, and the rest of their subjects in English. These children also suffered no long-term deficits in English language arts or content subjects. On the other hand, these children were by the end of grade 4 no better at English language skills than were their total immersion peers (Genese 1983; Swain & Lapkin 1982). Their understanding of spoken French was better than that of children taught in traditional French programs, but not as good as that of total immersion children. Partial immersion children had learned French as well as total immersion children when the children were compared not by year in school but by number of hours of exposure to French. Thus partial immersion students at the end of the second year were equal to total immersion students at the end of their first year. Though not as good as total immersion, partial is better than traditional French, and more likely to be accepted by many parents (Barik & Swain 1974, 1975, 1976a; H. Edwards & Smyth 1976).

A second alternative has been implemented in a few Ontario schools—**intermediate** or **delayed immersion,** which is similar to early total immersion except that it starts at the third or fourth grade. It was started under the apparently false assumption that if children were placed in total immersion earlier their English language arts skills would suffer. Research on this alternative has not yet been published, but parents, teachers, trustees, and administrators seem happy with it (H. Edwards & Smyth 1976; Genesee 1983).

A third alternative, in effect in parts of Quebec and Ontario, is **late immersion,** a one- or two-year immersion program starting in the sixth grade or later. These students make good progress in French, are not hurt in English or other subjects, and develop a more positive attitude toward the French language and culture (Barik & Swain 1976a; H. Edwards & Smyth 1976; Genesee 1981; Genesee et al. 1977). Their French is not as good as that of children who start immersion earlier (Barik & Swain 1976b; Barik et al. 1976; Connors et al. 1978; J. Oller & Redding 1971; Swain 1974).

A fourth alternative—**mixed languages**—is practiced at the J.F. Kennedy School in Berlin. Here half the students are German speakers and most of the remaining half are English speakers, though most are bilingual to a certain extent when they enter. Half of the teaching is in German and the other half is in English. The students appear to make substantial progress in the two languages without suffering any deficit in other subjects (Mackey 1972). Mixed language schools have also been successfully implemented in South Africa (English & Afrikaans—Malherbe 1978).

A fifth alternative is the **alternate days approach,** in which two languages are used as the language of instruction on alternate days. This has been used in Montreal, in South Africa, and in the Philippines with good results (Tucker et al. 1970).

In general, it appears that all forms of immersion are better than the traditional language instruction. The degree of facility with the immersion language is determined primarily by the number of contact hours with that language (Genesee 1983; Swain & Lapkin 1982). Since no other subjects suffer, there seems to be no valid reason to start immersion later than kindergarten, since this offers maximum exposure to the immersion language.

Double immersion   If immersion in one language is good, perhaps immersion in two languages is better. Two private Jewish schools in Montreal have developed a program in which Anglophone students take half their day in French and half in Hebrew. Research shows the students suffer no losses in English and make great gains in both French and Hebrew (Genesee & Lambert 1983; Genesee et al. 1976).

Immersion in the United States   Although well established in Canada, immersion education for native English speakers is just beginning to appear in the United States. French immersion programs are operating in Plattsburgh, New York (Samuels & Griffone 1979), San Diego, California (San Diego . . . 1982), Silver Spring, Maryland (a suburb of Washington, D.C.), and Cambridge, Massachusetts. Both Spanish and French immersion programs are operating in Culver City, California. The Culver City program is being extensively researched; the results appear in almost every way to be comparable to the Canadian experience (Boyd 1975; A. Cohen 1976a). Residents of Milwaukee, Wisconsin, have the most options that I have been able to find. There one can take one's schooling immersed in French, Spanish, German, and, of course, English (Lauerman 1981).

Programs serving language minorities

The story of bilingual education in the United States is not as encouraging as that in Canada. In order to understand why, it is useful to distinguish three distinct language goals: **language shift, language maintenance** (Fishman et al. 1966), and **language enrichment.** The goal of French immersion in Canada has been language enrichment, by adding knowledge of the other official language. In the United States the other two goals predominate. Many immigrants want their children to learn English so that they can succeed in the dominant English-speaking culture.

Accepting the "melting-pot" philosophy, they do not expect their grandchildren to know their language. This is the goal of language shift. Many immigrants from Mexico, the Caribbean, and Europe feel this way. On the other hand, other individuals wish to preserve their heritage and transmit it to further generations. This goal, language maintenance, is sought by many American Indians, Chinese, people of French origin in northern New England and Louisiana, and some Spanish-speaking groups in the Southwest. It is also sought by many immigrant groups in Canada.

Language shift   The goal of most bilingual programs in the United States is language shift. Federal government support of bilingual education specifically prohibits using federal funds to teach a foreign language to English-speaking children (von Maltitz 1975: 5).

If one's goal is acculturating non-English-speaking children, what is the best way to go about this? Judging by Canada's immersion experience, one might suppose that the best program would be no program at all. Simply place the children in classes where they receive all their instruction in English. This method, known as **submersion,** is the primary method of language shift in China (Fincher 1978), Belgium (Bustamante et al. 1978), New Zealand and Australia (Benton 1978), Sweden (Skutnabb-Kangas & Toukmaa 1976), and many other countries. Although this is the method by which the parents or grandparents of many Americans entered the melting pot, research and experience suggest that this method is not very effective.

Why not? There are several differences between submersion and immersion programs. First, in immersion all children begin at the same level of competence— nil, whereas in submersion children begin at different levels. In such classrooms the teacher often is using language far above the level of many of the pupils. Second, in immersion the teacher is bilingual, whereas in most cases of submersion the teacher does not know the language of the child. In immersion classes the teacher speaks to the children in French right from the first day of kindergarten, but the children speak back to her only in English. This continues until the middle of the first grade, when the teacher informs the children that from that time on, they have to answer in French. Because the teachers are bilingual, there is no problem of understanding during the initial period. Third, in immersion, second language learning does not imply replacement of the mother tongue or loss of cultural identity. In submersion the mother tongue is often deprecated. If experiences such as those shown in Box 5.2 are at all common, it is not surprising that such experiences lead to learning difficulties and behavior problems. Finally, in immersion classes children are praised for their use of the second language, whereas in submersion children are more likely to find their grammar corrected (Swain 1978).

In the famous case of *Lau* v. *Nichols,* the United States Supreme Court decreed that submersion was inadequate (see Box 5.3). A number of alternatives have been implemented as a result of the Lau decision and subsequent supporting legislation and court decisions. During part of the school day foreign language pupils may be pulled out of their classes for language instruction from teachers of English as a Second Language (ESL). Or they may be given teachers who are

BOX 5.2 *SUBMERSION FROM THE PERSPECTIVE OF TWO STUDENTS*

School is where it starts, and school can be a frightful experience for most Chicano children. It was for me. The subtle prejudice and the not-so-subtle arrogance of Anglos came at me at a very early age, although it took many years to realize and comprehend what took place. The SPEAK ENGLISH signs in every hall and doorway, and the unmitigated efforts of the Anglo teachers to eradicate the Spanish language, coupled with their demands for behavioral changes, clearly pointed out to me that I was not acceptable. . . . The association between being different and being inferior was difficult to resist, and it tortured me for many years.

—Antonio Gomez, 1968

Sitting in a classroom with about 33 English-speaking kids and staring at words on a blackboard that to me were as foreign as Egyptian hieroglyphics is one of my early recollections of school. The teacher had come up to my desk and bent over putting her face close to mine. "My name is Mrs. Newman," she said as if the exaggerating mouthing of her words would make me understand their meaning. I nodded yes because I felt that was what she wanted me to do. But she just threw up her hands in a gesture of despair, and touched her fingers to her head to signify to the class that I was dense. Whereupon all 33 classmates fell into gales of laughter. From that day on school became an ordeal I was forced to endure.

—Alma Bagù, 1969

bilingual and can communicate in their mother tongue. Or they may be placed in a transition program, which may involve teaching children in their mother tongue for the first two years or so, and then switching to English. Alternatively, they may be taught in the mother tongue for part of the day and English the rest of the day. In this case the percent of the day in English rises as the children get older, until it reaches 100% (A. Cohen 1976b: 85).

Transition programs exist not only in the United States, but also in Paraguay, the Philippines, India, Canada, Cameroon, Nigeria, China, the Soviet Union, the Union of South Africa, Ireland, and many other countries (P. Engle 1975; Tucker & Gray 1980). In Paraguay children are initially instructed mostly in their native Guarani, with some time devoted to Spanish. As the children get older the amount of time devoted to Spanish is increased (Rubin 1968). In the Philippines all children are instructed in their mother tongue for the first two years, and in English for the remainder (Engle 1975). In India over 200 languages are spoken. Eighty of these are used as the medium of instruction at different stages of education. Most are used for the first four years, after which the students are switched to a major language (Khubchandani 1978). In Toronto, Canada, there is experimentation in the use of the mother tongue for kindergarten students of Italian and Chinese heritage at the beginning of the school year, with the teacher gradually switching to English by the end of the year. In the United States transition programs are supported by federal funds ($150 million in 1979), and in many states by state funds[8] as well as local school taxes. In the academic year 1978-1979 there were 567 federally funded projects involving 58 languages (Tucker & Gray 1980). Considering the extent of use of these programs and the amount of money spent on them, the research evaluating them is surprisingly scarce.

Two studies in the Philippines were designed to determine the effects of initial instruction in the mother tongue followed by shift to English. In the first study the experimental group received instruction in Hiligaynon, the mother tongue of the children, for the first and second grades, and in English thereafter. The control group received instruction in English from the start. At the end of the fourth and sixth years the experimental group (the group with less English instruction) was *superior* in language and either equal or superior in reading, arithmetic, and social studies. The second study was designed to determine the best age for switching from Pilipino, the mother tongue, to English as the medium of instruction. The choices tested were first, third, and fifth grades. The conclusion was that the longer the contact with English, the better were the English language skills of the students (Ramos et al. 1967). This second study apparently contradicted the first one.

Mexico was the site of another well-known study, which compared direct teaching in Spanish with an Indian native language approach. There were three types of schools. Two taught in Spanish, one run by the federal government and the other run by a state government. The third, run by the National Indiginest Institute (INI) taught in the mother tongue of the children and slowly introduced Spanish. The test instrument was a Spanish reading test developed specifically so that the test items would be relevant to the Indian children. The test was administered to all children the teachers felt understood enough Spanish to attempt the test. A greater percentage of children in the INI schools were able to take the test, and those that took the test did better than children from the state and federal schools (Engle 1975; Modiano 1968; 1973). This study seems to agree with the first Philippine study.

BOX 5.3 *LAU* VERSUS *NICHOLS*

Title VI of the United States Civil Rights Act of 1964 states that "No person in the United States shall, on the ground of race, color, or national origin, be excluded from participation in, be denied benefits of, or be subjected to discrimination under any program or activity receiving Federal financial assistance."

In the case of *Lau* v. *Nichols*, parents of children who spoke Chinese but not English argued that their children were not receiving equal educational opportunity, because they could not understand their teachers. They asked the court to order special help, such as instruction in English by bilingual teachers. The San Francisco Unified School District argued that all it need do to be in compliance with the act is provide the same facilities, textbooks, and curriculum to all.

On January 21, 1974, the U.S. Supreme Court ruled unanimously that school systems that do not provide "meaningful education" for non-English-speaking pupils are in violation of the act. A meaningful education was considered "effectively foreclosed" in this case due to the language barrier.

Lau v. *Nichols* 414 U.S. 563.—Cited by Teitelbaum & Hiller 1977. See this source for a review of legal cases following this decision.

A fourth study, this one of Quechua Indians in Peru, appears to support submersion, thus agreeing with the second Philippine study (Pozzi-Escot 1972).

The four studies just cited found group differences. The first and third seem to support transition programs; the second and fourth seem to support the submersion approach. Most other studies seem to show no difference. These other studies include one in the Philippines (Tucker et al. 1970), one in South Africa (Bovet 1932), and one in Ireland (Macnamara 1966).

What can one make of these contradictory results? One interpretation is that whatever effect the choice of program has for the ultimate success of students, other factors, not adequately controlled for in the studies cited above, are probably more important. This interpretation is supported by a study of children finishing second grade in Uganda. This study found that the most important factors determining success were the social class of the parents and whether the setting was urban or rural, not the initial language of instruction (Ladefoged et al. 1968).

Improvement on reading tests may not be the best measure of success of a bilingual program. Perhaps more important is a measure used to study a program in Peru. This study found that more children who started schooling in their mother tongue stayed in school past the age mandated by law (Gudschinsky 1971).

In the United States there have been only a few controlled studies of the effects of bilingual transition programs.[9] One survey of these reports found that of a total of 66 findings 58% were positive, 47% were neutral, and only 1% were unfavorable (Dulay & Burt 1978). It appears that when they are of high quality, bilingual programs in the United States are superior to programs that place non-native-speaking children in the mainstream.

If I had to make a decision as to which program to recommend to parents and school boards, I would choose a mother tongue transition program, not just because the students will do better on language tests a few years later, but because by adapting the system to the language and culture of the community, the government is saying to the minority group that it cares about them and respects their language and culture. In the long run this could pay dividends far above any improvement on reading tests.

Language maintenance   Language maintenance as a goal is not supported by the United States federal government, and with the exception of Hebrew taught in Jewish private schools, has become practically nonexistent in that country. The situation is different in Canada. Whereas the "melting pot"[10] philosophy prevails in the United States, in Canada the metaphor is the "Canadian mosaic."[11] Language and cultural differences are encouraged as a way of developing a more interesting society. The practical result of this philosophical difference is the encouragement of language maintenance by means of **heritage language programs.** Under these programs students optionally enroll for the program of their choice. Attendance generally involves a longer school day. During the added time the language and culture of the ethnic group is taught. In Toronto, for example, 28 languages are offered under this program, including Estonian, Gujerati, Macedonian, and Ojibwa. This program is attended by approximately 16% of elementary school students.

SUMMARY

Approximately two billion people speak more than one language. Many people acquire more than one language when they first learn to speak. If in the presence of a child, one caregiver always uses one language and another always uses a second language, the child's two languages will be separate from one another at about two years, but if the caregivers each speak more than one language in the child's presence, he or she will not achieve language separation until about 3;3. Language interference can occur at all levels—phonological, vocabulary use, syntax, and morphology. It occurs most often when one language is dominant.

When children who already are in the midst of acquiring one language are thrust into a new language environment, they usually are able to become as fluent as their peers in the new language within one year. Unless it continues to be used, the first language can apparently be lost very quickly. Whether the acquisition process is the same or different for a second language is a controversy that seems based mostly on how different the learning must be in order to be considered different. There are differences in the sequences in which certain vocabulary and constructions are acquired, but these are usually relatively superficial.

Traditional second language teaching in North America has not been very successful. Dissatisfaction with traditional methods has led to experimentation with new techniques and technologies. These include the audiolingual method, the language laboratory, elementary school instruction, and immersion. By far the most successful is immersion, in which the second language is used as the medium of instruction for all or a large part of the school day. Although students do not come out of such programs sounding like native speakers, they do come out fluent in the second language, and with no detriment to skills in the first language or other subjects.

When the goal of the educational system is to help language minority children adapt to the dominant language, a number of different alternatives have been tried. The little research that has been done appears to offer some support for using the students' native language in the first few years of teaching.

SUGGESTED FURTHER STUDY.

GENESEE, F. (1983)   Bilingual education of majority-language children: The immersion experiments in review. *Applied Psycholinguistics* **4,** 1-46.
HATCH, EVELYN M. (1978)   *Second language acquisition: A book of readings.* Rowley, Mass.: Newbury House.
MCLAUGHLIN, BARRY (1978)   *Second-language acquisition in childhood.* New York: John Wiley.

NOTES

[1]Given the extent of the phenomenon, it is interesting to note how little is said about it in textbooks on the psychology of language or language acquisition. Bilingualism is not mentioned in Aitchison 1976; Bloom & Lahey 1978; R. Brown 1973; Cairns & Cairns 1976; H. Clark & Clark 1977;

Cruttenden 1979; Dale 1976; Deese 1970; Fodor et al. 1974; Glucksberg & Danks 1974; Greene 1972; Herriot 1970; Slobin 1979. It is only briefly mentioned in Carroll 1964; J. de Villiers & de Villiers 1978; DeVito 1970; Elliott 1981; Hörman 1971; Menyuk 1971. More substantial coverage can be found in Holzman 1983; Houston 1972; Kess 1976; Owens 1984; Paivio & Begg 1981; Taylor 1976.

[2]Bilingual: Bulgarian-German (Emrich 1938); Chinese-English (M.E. Smith 1935b); Czech-English (Bubenik 1978); English-French (Celce-Murcia 1978; Metraux 1965); English-Garo [a Tibeto-Berman language] (Burling 1959); English-German (Leopold 1939, 1947, 1949a, 1949b); English-Italian (von-Raffler-Engel 1965; Kessler 1972); English-Japanese (Hakuto 1975; Itoh & Hatch 1978); English-Mexican Spanish (Carrow 1971); English-Swedish (Totten 1960); Estonian-Swedish (Oksaar 1970); Georgian [a Caucasian language]-Russian (Imedadze 1960, 1967); German-Italian (Volterra & Taeshner 1978); German-Russian (Hoyer & Hoyer 1924); Hungarian-Serbo-Croatian (Mikeš 1967; Mikeš & Vlahović 1966); Latvian-Swedish (Rūķe-Draviņa 1965, 1967); Polish-Swedish (Zaręba 1953). Multilingual: English-Finnish-Swedish (Murrell 1966); four languages (Geissler 1938).

[3]English-Dutch (Snow et al. 1980; English-French (Valette 1964); English-Spanish (Dato 1970, 1971); German-English (Wode 1976); Hungarian-French (Kenyeres 1938); Italian-Dutch (Francescato 1969); Japanese-English (Milon 1974; Hakuta 1974a, 1974b, 1975, 1976a); Malaysian-German (Voltz, cited in Stern & Stern 1907); Norwegian-English (Ravem 1968, 1974, 1978); Spanish-English (Cancino et al. 1975; L. Fillmore 1976; Hernandez, cited by Ervin-Tripp 1970b); Spanish-French (Tits 1948); Swedish-Finnish (Malmberg 1945); Vietnamese-English (Kessler & Idar 1977). These studies cover language switching from the lower cutoff of three years to adolescence and adulthood.

[4]These cases tend to dominate the literature on the topic, since they are more interesting. See Albert & Obler 1978; Paradis 1977.

[5]Also referred to as the army method, the aural-oral method, the natural method, and the New Key.

[6]French is the ninth most frequent mother tongue of school students in Toronto, after English (48%), Portuguese (15%), Italian (13%), Greek (5%), Chinese (5%), Spanish (2%), Polish (1.5%), and Ukranian (1.4%). These figures are based on Deosaran et al. 1976, and on Metropolitan . . . 1981.

[7]Recent research indicates that this is very likely a false perception.

[8]See von Maltitz 1975: 123-147 for a review on a state-by-state basis.

[9]Troike 1978; unfortunately most are unpublished; some exceptions are: A. Cohen & Laosa 1976; Lambert et al. 1975; Plante 1977; Rosier & Farella 1976.

[10]This term first appeared as the title of a play by Israel Zangwill in 1909.

[11]This term first appeared as the title of survey of emmigrants to Canada (Foster 1926), though the 'mosaic' metaphor appeared earlier (Hayward 1922) and became more widely disseminated as the result of a later book (Gibbon 1938).

SIX
CHILDREN WITH PROBLEMS

Unfortunately, not all children learn their language or languages in as straightforward a manner as the children described in previous chapters. It is often possible to identify a physical cause for such problems; this chapter is organized by type of cause. First we will consider children with problems due to sensory deficits such as deafness and blindness. Then we will consider children with physical disabilities, such as malformations of the mouth and cerebral palsy. Finally we will look at children whose problems seem to originate in the cognitive and language areas of the brain.

HEARING IMPAIRMENT

Suppose that we had no voice or tongue and wanted to indicate objects to one another. Should we not, like the deaf and dumb, make signs with the hands, head, and the rest of the body?—Socrates, in Plato, *Cratylus*

Hearing problems severe enough to affect speech occur in approximately 760 000 children in the United States.[1] Although there is a wide range of individual differences, young adults with normal hearing can perceive frequencies from about 20 cycles per second to 20 000 cycles per second (Newby 1972: 8). The range most important to speech is between 500 and 5000 cycles per second.[2] Figure 6.1 gives

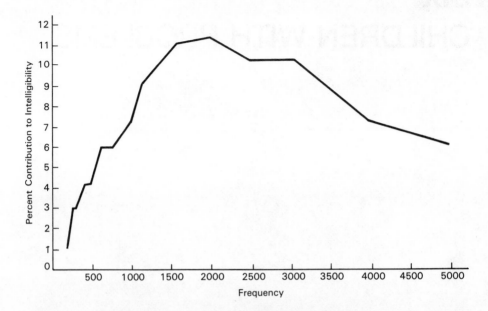

FIGURE 6.1.   Contribution to intelligibility of different frequencies in the speech range. (Based on American National Standards Institute 1969.)

an estimate of the relative importance of different frequencies to speech understanding.

Audiologists measure hearing loss by several methods. Tones at different frequencies are presented through earphones to each ear separately. Either the people tested are asked to indicate when they hear the tone, or the ability to hear is measured by detecting a response to tones in the auditory nerves. The responses are usually plotted on an **audiogram**—a line graph that records the hearing for each ear at various frequencies. The amplitude is plotted as decibels (dB) greater than that needed in a person of normal hearing. Sample audiograms are shown in Figure 6.2.

The amount of hearing loss ranges from 0 to perhaps 110 dB. Above this level, ordinary skin will detect vibrations. If a child responds as well to sound played through earphones placed on the knees as to sound played to the ears, one can assume that there is no residual hearing.

People are generally considered to be deaf when the loss is so severe that they cannot understand speech even with a hearing aid. The measurable degree of loss necessary for this to be true varies considerably from individual to individual. Some children may be functionally deaf who have a loss of 65 dB when tested wearing hearing aids, while others may function as hard of hearing even though they have a loss of 85 dB or more when tested wearing hearing aids.

The amount of hearing loss is often different at different frequencies. The loss may be flat—that is, it may be the same degree of deafness at different frequencies; but it may not be. Another common pattern consists of some hearing at the low frequencies, becoming less at higher frequencies. Such a person may have some

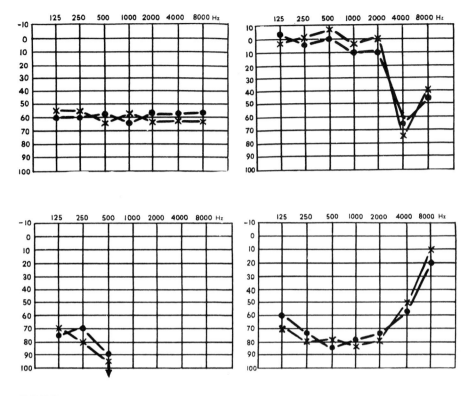

FIGURE 6.2. Audiograms for four different types of congenital hearing loss. Crosses are values for the left ear; dots are values for the right ear. (From Ballantyne 1977: 146, 156-157. © Longman Group Limited. Used by permission.)

hearing for vowels, but no ability to hear consonants. A person who has a relatively mild loss in this pattern may be able to discriminate all consonants except [s] versus [ʃ], which differ auditorily only in the high frequencies.

Causes

Hearing impairment in children can be due to a number of different causes. Approximately 50% of hearing loss is inherited.[3] There are more than 50 different types of inherited hearing loss (Konigsmark 1972a, 1972b; Rose et al. 1977: 33). About 11% of hearing impaired children have at least one parent who is hearing impaired (Rawlings 1973). The remaining 89% have hearing parents. Similarly, most deaf parents have children with normal hearing.

Deafness may also be due to ear infections or to any condition that can cause brain damage. If a woman contracts rubella (German measles) during the first three months of pregnancy, the infant may be born deaf (and/or blind and/or mentally retarded). A young child may become deaf as a result of contracting meningitis or some other illness that results in a high fever. Occasionally a side reaction to some drugs will cause deafness. In the case of 30% of deaf individuals, the cause is not known (D. Moores 1982: 96). For example, a colleague of mine has a pair of identical twin daughters. One is normal; the other was born with a number of deformities, including improperly formed ears, which leaves her deaf.

Communication options

What are the communication options for training deaf children? There are a number of different approaches. Not all of the options described below will be available in every community.

Auditory training   Also known as the **aural method,** auditory training is intended to make the most of residual hearing. It discourages reliance on **speechreading** (the more commonly used term is **lipreading,** but professionals do not like it as well) or forms of communication involving the hands—**manual communication.** An emphasis is placed on beginning training as soon as the loss occurs or is discovered. This method appears to have been used in ancient Rome as far back as 530 AD by Juventius Celsus (Peet 1851: 136).

Some amazing successes have come out of this program—profoundly deaf children who end up behaving as if they were merely hard of hearing. However, this method appears not to succeed with other children; and unfortunately, one cannot predict who will succeed and who will not.

The oral method   Children whose hearing is too limited to succeed in normal schools or in classes for the hard of hearing will be sent to schools for the deaf. Until recently many such schools used the oral method, also called the **oral-aural, oral only,** or **pure oral** method (D. Moores 1974: 399). The origination of the oral method is attributed to Samuel Heinicke (1729-1748), but the spread of the oral method can be attributed to two other German teachers, John Baptist Graser (1766-1841) and Frederick Moritz Hill (1805-1874) (J. Gordon 1885). Under the oral method teachers are expected to enunciate very clearly, even exaggerating—for example, sticking the tongue out when pronouncing words containing [θ] or [ð]. Teachers wear a microphone that transmits the sound of their voices to the child's own or special classroom hearing aids. The child is expected to make use of any residual hearing and also of speechreading. No manual communication is used.

Advocates of this approach argue that manual communication should not be used because it would tend to isolate the individual, since most hearing people don't know sign language. Because this is an oral world, deaf children should be forced to learn spoken English (or whatever language the community speaks). If deaf children are allowed to use manual communication, they will, it is argued, be less motivated to learn and use English.[4] Some educators even argue that spoken language is the medium of thought, and if deaf people never learn to speak, they will never be able to engage in any high level thinking.[5] This approach is not as common as it once was, but it is still used in 35% of classes for the deaf in North America (Jordan et al. 1979: 352), and is the approach of such highly regarded schools as the Clarke

PEANUTS
(© 1978 UNITED FEATURE SYNDICATE.
USED BY PERMISSION.)

School in Northampton, Massachusetts, and the Lexington School for the Deaf in New York City.

Cued speech   For people who are so deaf that they obtain little or no information from the sound of speech, speechreading is of limited use, since most of the information needed to distinguish the different sounds involves movement of articulators that cannot be seen. For example, *me* and *be* look exactly alike—the only difference is that when *be* is spoken the velum is raised to close off the passage of air through the nose. Cued speech involves using the hand to signal what the invisible articulators are doing. This system is apparently similar to handwritten systems used in Europe in the 19th century (D. Moores 1974: 398).

In cued speech the location of the hand relative to the face signals information as to which vowel is being used. It doesn't specify the vowel completely, however. The user is expected to differentiate whether the lips are more than normally open, relaxed, or rounded. These two sources of information completely specify the vowel. For example, if the hand is near the larynx and the lips are open, the vowel is [æ]; if the lips are relaxed the vowel is [ʊ]; if the lips are rounded the vowel is [o] (see Figure 6.3).

The shape of the hand cues the consonant immediately preceding the vowel. Again, in order to completely specify the vowel one must attend also to information from the lips and tongue. For example, when the index finger is extended and the thumb is out, the consonant could be [l], [ʃ], or [w], depending upon whether the tip of the tongue drops from the roof of the mouth ([l]), the blade of the tongue drops from the roof of the mouth ([ʃ]), or the lips are rounded ([w]), as illustrated in Figure 6.3 (Cornett 1967; 1969).

This method is used in only 0.2% of classes for the deaf, but is used as a supplementary method for another 2% of classes (Jordan et al. 1979: 352). Evalua-

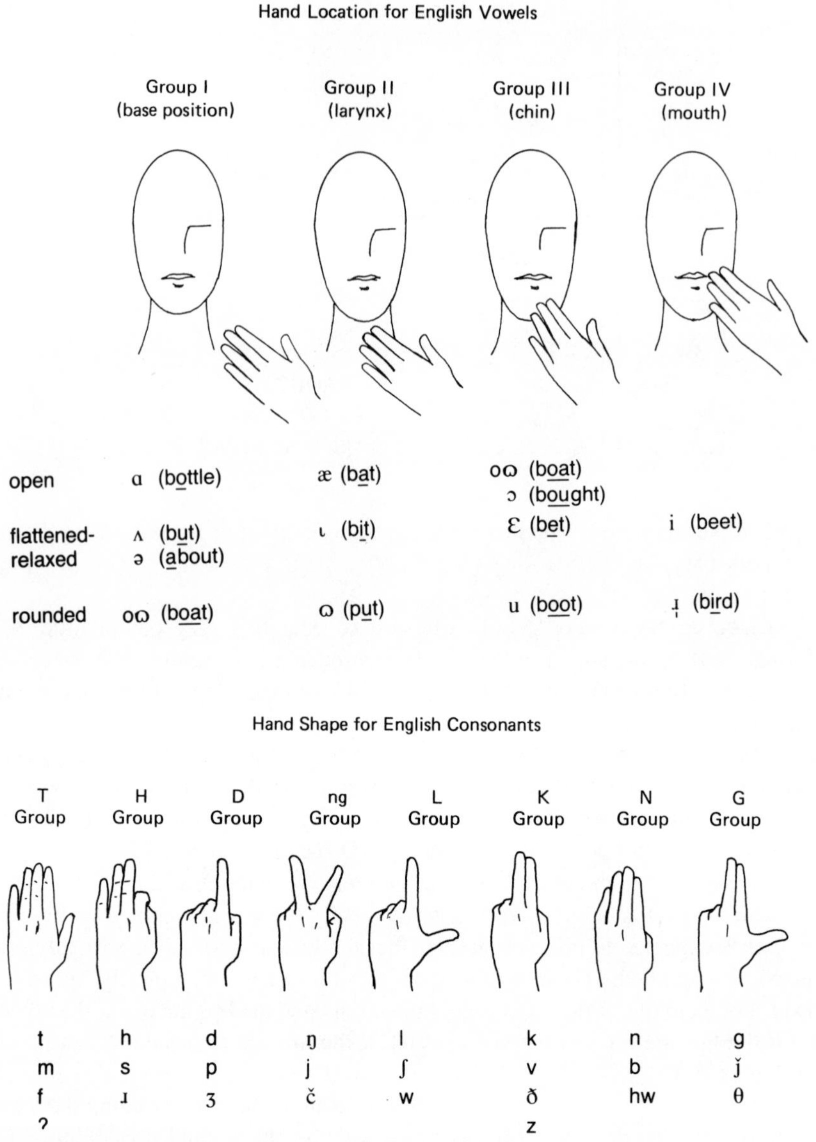

Hand Location for English Vowels

Group I (base position)	Group II (larynx)	Group III (chin)	Group IV (mouth)

open	ɑ (bottle)	æ (bat)	oω (boat) ɔ (bought)	
flattened-relaxed	ʌ (but) ə (about)	ɩ (bit)	ɛ (bet)	i (beet)
rounded	oω (boat)	ω (put)	u (boot)	ɪ (bird)

Hand Shape for English Consonants

T Group	H Group	D Group	ng Group	L Group	K Group	N Group	G Group

t	h	d	ŋ	l	k	n	g
m	s	p	j	ʃ	v	b	ǰ
f	ɹ	ʒ	č	w	ð	hw	θ
ʔ					z		

FIGURE 6.3. Hand location and shapes used in Cued Speech.

tions of its effectiveness indicate that, with proper training, it can be an effective method of communication.[6]

The Rochester method   Some educators who find the oral approach inadequate have adopted the Rochester method, which is also known as Visible English (P. Reich & Bick 1976, 1977), and in the Soviet Union as Neo-Oralism. This approach involves using the methods of the oralists, but augments these methods with **fingerspelling.** In this system words are spelled by placing the hand in a sequence of configurations, each one standing for a particular letter. Figures 6.4 and 6.5 show the North American one-handed alphabet and the British two-handed system. The manual alphabet was first used for instructional purposes in the sixteenth century by Pablo Ponce de Leon (1520-1584), a Benedictine monk in Valladolid, Spain (Peet 1851: 141). Educators using this method are supposed to fingerspell everything they say.

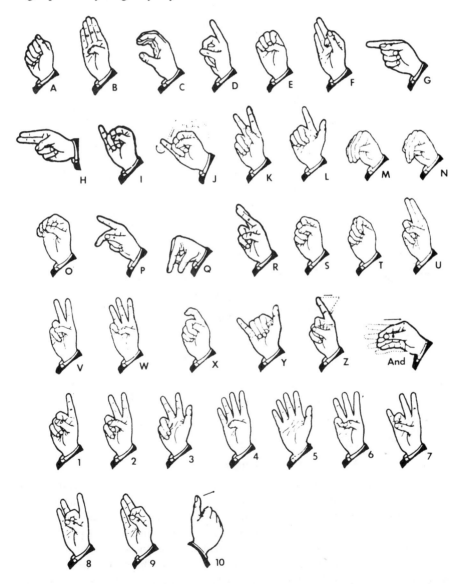

FIGURE 6.4. The North American one-handed fingerspelling alphabet.

QUICK SIGNS
YES — ONE TAP
NO — TWO TAPS

FIGURE 6.5. The British two-handed fingerspelling alphabet.

The Rochester method differs from cued speech in two ways: First, the entire message is theoretically on the hands, so that students are not forced to make use of speechreading; and second, cued speech is based on the sounds of speech, while the Rochester method is based on spelling. Thus, *their* and *there* would be produced the same way in cued speech, but spelled differently in the Rochester method. On the other hand *read* in the present tense ([ɹid] and *read* in the past tense ([ɹɛd]) are different in cued speech but the same in fingerspelling. Educators who use the Rochester method prefer it because they believe the resulting manual signal is more like spoken English than is the signal used in total communication (see below). The Rochester method is used in the preschool in Rochester, New York; a Russian alphabet version is the method chosen for use in the Soviet Union (Morozova 1954; see Figure 6.6).

FIGURE 6.6.   The Russian language fingerspelling alphabet. (From Gerankina 1972.)

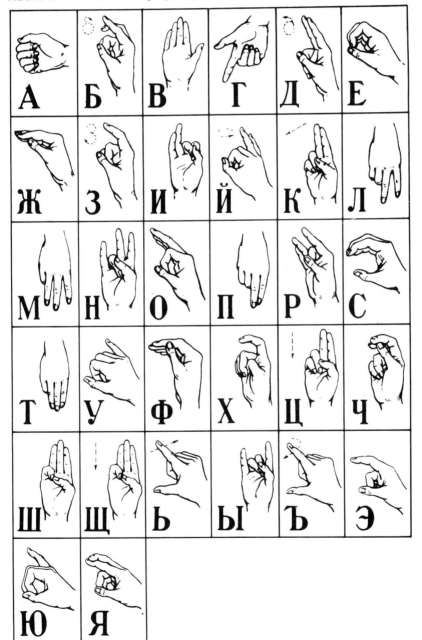

Total communication   In approximately 65% of the classes for the deaf in North America, teachers use the speech techniques of oral method teachers, augmented with a form of sign language and with fingerspelling. This approach is most often known as **total communication,** though it is also referred to as the **simultaneous method.**[7]

The sign language used most often in total-communication classrooms is not the sign language used by most deaf people when they talk to one another. Rather, it is generally a system based on such signs but augmented and modified such that there is supposed to be a one-to-one relationship between signs and spoken words (or spoken morphemes, in some systems). For example, while deaf sign language has one sign for the verb *to be,* the sign language used by most total-communication teachers has separate signs for each of its different allomorphs: *am, is, are, was, were, will be,* and so on. Teachers using total communication are supposed to sign every word or morpheme they say.

Several systems of signed English, sometimes referred to as manual English (e.g., Brasel & Quigley 1977), are used extensively. Unfortunately, two have been given the same acronym, SEE. One is Seeing Essential English (Washburn 1971), and the other is Signing Exact English (Gustason et al. 1972). A third is known as Siglish (Bornstein & Saulnier 1983). Some schools adopt one or the other of these systems; others have no policy preference; still others develop their own systems based on these sources and American Sign Language (see below). While the systems developed in these schools may not be the same as those used elsewhere, educators often try to be consistent among all classes in the same school by maintaining files of signs used in that school.

Advocates of total communication argue that communication, not speech, is what is vital in education. Any mode that communicates should be permitted.

Sign language   Throughout recorded history, deaf people have used sign language to communicate among themselves and with hearing people who have bothered to learn their language. The first use of sign language in instruction is attributed to Abbé Carlos Miguel de l'Epée (1712-1789) (McClure 1969).

There are many different sign languages, which in general are no more intelligible to a user of another sign language than a French speaker would be to a monolingual English speaker. However, experienced deaf travellers can establish communication with users of other sign languages much more easily than can speakers of two oral languages (Battison & Jordan 1976; Jordan & Battison 1976). Deaf people accomplish this by using gestures and mime along with their signs. Nevertheless, international conventions of deaf people require the services of a number of simultaneous interpreters, one for each language (Stokoe 1972: 11).

Sign language, like other languages, is a medium for the transmission of its own culture (Gannon 1981; Klima et al. 1979). Sign language has its own jokes, puns, and higher forms of culture, such as the plays presented by the National Theatre for the Deaf. Advocates of the use of sign language in the schools argue that it is a legitimate language, and that deaf people should not be denied their cultural heritage. In many schools for the deaf some teachers are themselves deaf. Some of these teachers use sign language when communicating with their classes.

Especially in recent years, the structure of sign languages from many different countries have been studied.[8] Nevertheless, most research on sign language, and especially on its acquisition, has been on **American Sign Language,** or ASL for short (also known as Ameslan—Fant 1972). Although some authorities continue to doubt that ASL is a full-fledged language, most researchers, viewing the increasing complexity that recent analyses are revealing (for example, Battison 1978; Fischer & Gough 1978; Klima & Bellugi 1979; H. Lane & Grosjean 1980; Siple 1978— especially the papers by Liddell and by Supalla & Newport therein; Stokoe 1980), are willing to consider it a language. Although its status as a language has been rising among linguists, at this point very few argue that it should be the exclusive form of communication in elementary and secondary school classrooms.

Which system is best in the classroom?

Although controversy has surrounded the use of communication systems almost since the dawn of deaf education, very few comparative studies have been carried out. One early study surveyed 43 day and residential programs and concluded that students at the Rochester School for the Deaf attained the highest achievement (Day et al. 1928).

A series of Soviet studies conducted in the 1950s supported the contention that neo-oralism (the use of fingerspelling) was superior to oral-only programs (D. Moores 1982: 244).

In the United States one extensive project compared the Rochester method with the oral method. After four years of instruction, children educated via the Rochester method were superior in one of two measures of speechreading, in five of seven measures of reading, and in three of five measures of written language. The oral group was superior only in one of five measures of written language (Quigley 1969).

In another study Rochester method students were compared with matched classes of total-communication students. After five years Rochester-method students were superior on all subtests of the Stanford Achievement Test, in some measures of syntactic ability (but not vocabulary), and, of course, in fingerspelling. There were no differences in measures of speech and speechreading. The younger the age at which children were introduced to fingerspelling, the greater the improvement was, compared to their matched total-communication peers (D. Moores & Quigley 1967).

Another study, this one an extensive investigation of children in seven different preschool programs, compared children in oral, Rochester, and total-communication settings. Children who were exposed to sign at an early age were actually superior at speechreading than children in oral-only programs. Children exposed to fingerspelling were equal to or worse than children in the oral-only groups (D. Moores et al. 1973).

The Illinois School for the Deaf has separate departments using total communication, the oral method, and auditory training. A comparative study of students in these three departments suggested that the comprehension of students in all three programs of fingerspelled messages was better than their comprehension of comparable signed messages (E. Johnson 1948).

On the other hand, a more recent study of students at the Arizona State School for the Deaf found that comprehension of information via total communication was superior to that via the Rochester method (Klopping 1972).

Another comparative study concentrated on college students—students at Gallaudet College in Washington, D.C., the only liberal arts college for the deaf in North America. In this study students were presented with material in one of three manual forms—fingerspelling, signed English, and ASL. The best comprehension was with signed English. ASL came in second, and fingerspelling came in last (Higgins 1973).

Proponents of the Rochester method over total communication have expressed concern that when the manual component is based on sign language, the manual signal, like ASL, would tend to lack function words, and that there would not be a one-to-one correspondence between English and signs. In one study that specifically looked at the manual component in two total-communication schools and two Rochester-method schools, it was found that, in fact, the reverse was true. The fingerspelling of classroom teachers tended to be very inaccurate. For example, the word *you* in the sample studied was never spelled correctly. Rather, it was spelled *U, YU, YSU, Y, YO, A, YS,* or *I.* But *you* was not the only word spelled sometimes as *I.* Also sometimes spelled this way were *I, is, they,* and *yes.* Similarly, all the following list were spelled at least once as *Y: you, is, they, your,* and *I.* In contrast, the manual component in total-communication classrooms was much more likely to be present and unambiguous (P. Reich & Bick 1976, 1977).

One subset of the deaf population tends to have much more contact with ASL than others—this is deaf children of deaf parents. Such children have been compared in a large number of studies to matched hearing impaired peers from homes with hearing parents. The findings almost invariably favor children of deaf parents. More such children go on to college—38% compared with 9% (Stevenson 1964), and they are superior on measures of written language (Brasel & Quigley 1977; Meadow 1966; Stuckless & Birch 1966; Vernon & Koh 1970), reading (Stuckless & Birch 1966; Vernon & Koh 1970), speechreading (Stuckless & Birch 1966; Vernon & Kon 1970; but no difference in Quigley & Frisina 1961), academic achievement (Brasel & Quigley 1977; but no difference in Quigley & Frisina 1961), vocabulary (Quigley & Frisina 1961), and six specific syntactic structures (Brasel & Quigley 1977). When speech intelligibility was measured, the results usually showed no difference (Meadow 1966; Stuckless & Birch 1966; Vernon & Koh 1970), but in one study speech was poorer in children of deaf parents (Quigley & Frisina 1961). Another area in which the two groups have been studied is that of psychosocial development. Two studies found no difference (Stuckless & Birch 1966; Vernon & Koh 1970), but a third found that children of deaf parents were more mature, responsible, independent, sociable, and popular. They were more willing to communicate with strangers, and in general more able to react appropriately in social situations (Meadow 1966).

There are essentially no differences between deaf children of deaf parents and deaf children of hearing parents at the college level. The only significant difference is that the latter are, as a group, slightly *better* at speech perception and speech intelligibility (Parasnis 1983). One should not conclude from this that the advantage of deaf children of deaf parents disappears as they grow older. One must take into account the different rates of college attendance. What we can conclude is that the advantage is such that the top 38% of deaf children of deaf parents are comparable to the top 9% of deaf children of hearing parents.

To sum up, it appears that manually augmented strategies of teaching are superior to oral-only methods. Among the different manual alternatives, total communication appears to come out slightly superior to the Rochester method, with essentially no data comparing these alternatives with cued speech or ASL. Children of deaf parents, who experience relatively normal communication within the family, do considerably better than children of hearing parents, in spite of the many other advantages hearing parents have to offer.

All this having been said, it is true nevertheless that even the system that appears best—total communication—is a long way from providing an education comparable to that of the normal hearing child. Most deaf children still achieve far below their hearing peers. Furthermore, they are often isolated from normal school life. Even today, almost half of deaf children attend residential schools, and thus may spend only weekends and holidays with their parents. Even deaf children who attend special schools and classes near their home have only limited interaction with hearing children. This, combined with their poor communication skills, deprives them of normal opportunities to develop socially.

Educators continue to explore additional alternatives to alleviate these problems. One alternative being investigated is **mainstreaming**—placing deaf children in regular classrooms with normal peers. Some deaf children have always been effectively mainstreamed. However, with the advent of earlier diagnosis, better hearing aids, and earlier and more effective intervention, this is possible for more such children. Mainstreamed children may require intensive support services, including speech and language training, interpreters, tutors, and note takers. Fully implemented, such a system is not necessarily less costly than maintaining separate facilities for deaf children. Research on mainstreaming generally shows that children do better academically, but may be socially isolated and experience personal problems as a result. Today, mainstreaming has generally been attempted only with the highest functioning deaf pupils, and so direct comparisons are not possible (C. Reich et al. 1977).

The use of interpreters in classrooms mirrors other aspects of a deaf person's life. In many of their more important contacts with hearing people, such as in courtroom appearances, visits to a doctor, and interviews with welfare workers, the deaf will take along or be supplied with interpreters, much as would anybody else whose native language was not English. Interpreters will simultaneously sign and silently mouth what is being uttered by the speaker. Registered interpreters can use signed English, fingerspelling, or ASL, depending upon the needs of their clients. One study of hearing impaired students in Minneapolis found that on a comprehension task the use of an interpreter was considerably better than the oral approach, but not quite as good as the use of total communication—that is, where the people imparting the information were doing their own simultaneous interpreting (Newell 1978).

The approach that seems the most reasonable is to make several alternatives available so that differing needs of different hearing impaired children can be met. However, where this has been done, manual communication methods have generally been reserved for children who were deemed to be oral failures (D. Moores 1974: 406). A better position would be to start children on total communication and to drop the manual component for those who make sufficient progress in auditory training or speechreading such that they feel that they can do without. In some sense this is the natural approach, since, as discussed in Chapters 1 and 2, before they learn to speak, children with normal hearing tend to make extensive use of gestures, some of which drop out as their ability to communicate via speech improves.

The various options described above all are intended to help students whose hearing loss is so severe that they cannot understand speech even with a hearing aid. One would generally not expect a child with a mild to moderate loss to be using total communication or be in a residential setting. Such children may be able to attend regular classes. Other children may be placed in special classes for hearing impaired students located in regular schools, with integration into regular classes for some subjects.

Acquisition of sign language

Since most deaf children have hearing parents and thus do not learn ASL at home, they normally learn it from the other deaf children when they get to school. However, the minority of deaf children with deaf parents learn ASL under conditions similar to those of hearing children learning spoken language. A number of such children have been studied for the purposes of comparing ASL acquisition with that of spoken language. In most respects acquisition of ASL parallels that of spoken language, but there are some slight differences, as we shall see.

As has already been mentioned in Chapter 1, deaf children engage in cooing as much as do hearing children. However, it has been claimed that babbling falls off in deaf children after six months, presumably due to the lack of auditory feedback (Lenneberg 1967: 140). It has also been claimed that mirrors hung over the cribs of deaf babies prolong and increase their vocalization (Van Riper 1950: 18, 1963: 79). However, the former claim appears not be be based on published research,[9] nor have I found any citation to published research on the second claim.

The manual equivalent of babbling, at 0;3 to 0;10, has been reported.[10] The manual equivalent of happy sounds begin at a younger age, but one cannot say that there is a difference here, because all infants wave their arms about. Should this be considered cooing? Perhaps if there were statistical evidence that infants 0;3 to 0;6 of deaf parents wave their arms more than similarly aged infants of hearing parents, one could argue that this excess was cooing. However, this study has not been done.

The first word (sign) generally appears sooner in ASL than in speaking children. The first sign has been reported as being at 0;5 or 0;6, compared with 1;0 in normal children. Two-sign utterances have been reported in children as young as eight months. Two reasons for such early acquisition have been given. One is the iconic nature of many signs. The ASL signs meaning "cry," "drink," "eat," "fight," and "sleep" (see Figure 6.7) all resemble the actual actions and thus can be figured out and used by children at an earlier age, so the argument goes (but see below). The other reason involves the relative rates of maturation of neuromuscular control of the hands and of the vocal apparatus (D. Moores 1974: 395). After all, normal children often begin to comprehend words four months before they begin to speak.

The first signs appear to be of the same types that have been reported for acquisition of vocal language—for example, signs for things that move or that can be handled by the child.

FIGURE 6.7.
Some signs that resemble the actions that they represent.

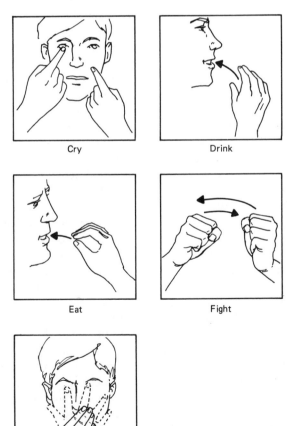

Cry

Drink

Eat

Fight

Sleep

Just as the first vocal words are pronounced inaccurately, so the first signs are less than perfect imitations of the adult version. There are four major aspects to the making of any ASL sign: the shape of the hand, the location of the hand, the movement of the hand, and the orientation of the hand. These four aspects are illustrated in Figure 6.8. Children first learning ASL will generally get some of these aspects right but make mistakes on others.

Figure 6.9 shows some examples of this. Children sometimes will make the sign in the wrong orientation. For example, the sign meaning "shoes" is made by bringing the two fists together, making contact at the side of the hands. One child brought the fists together so that the knuckles made contact instead. Or they might make the sign in the wrong place. For example, the sign for "dirty" is made by bringing the hand, palm downward to the bottom of the chin and wiggling the fingers. One child made it by putting the hand in the mouth instead. Or they might use the wrong hand shape. The sign for "telephone" is made by putting the knuckles of the fist against the cheek with the thumb outstretched to the ear and the baby finger outstretched to the mouth. One child made this sign with only the fist, with neither the thumb nor the baby finger outstretched. Or they might use the wrong movement. The sign for "cat" is made by using the thumb and forefinger of each hand to stroke an imaginary cat's whiskers on one's own face. The motion starts under the nose and moves downward rather than outward (Bellugi 1982).

Phonological mistakes generally involve simplification, such as dropping phonemes from the word or making phonemes within a word more like each other. Of the four aspects of signs, it is logically impossible to leave one out. For example, the hand may not be in the right orientation, but it cannot help being in some orientation. Can one say there is simplification of signs as there is simplification of words? Although not as extensive as in the case of phonology, there is some evidence of this. Specifically, of 18 different hand shapes used in making signs to one child, he always used only 9. Similarly, of 17 different locations for signs, he used only 10 (Bellugi 1982; McIntire 1977).

Just as one can argue that there are phonological-like errors, so there are similarities in how children alter the meanings of words. For example, Ann at age 1;4 used the sign for "dog" (Figure 6.10a) for all animate objects that did not resemble her parents. Similarly, she used the sign for "smell" (Figure 6.10b) to mean "Want to go to the bathroom," "Want that flower," and "Please change my diaper" (H. Schlesinger & Meadow 1972: 60-61).

In one area of the acquisition of meaning, one would suspect that deaf children would find it easier than hearing children. This is the acquisition of the signs corresponding to the personal pronouns *me* and *you*. The problem, as described in Chapter 4, is that the person referred to by *me* for one member of the conversation is *you* for the other. One would expect deaf children learning ASL not to have any problems with these pronouns, because "me" is expressed by pointing to oneself (Figure 6.10c) and "you" is expressed by pointing to the person or persons being talked to (Figure 6.10d). Thus ASL uses the obvious natural gestures. Yet deaf

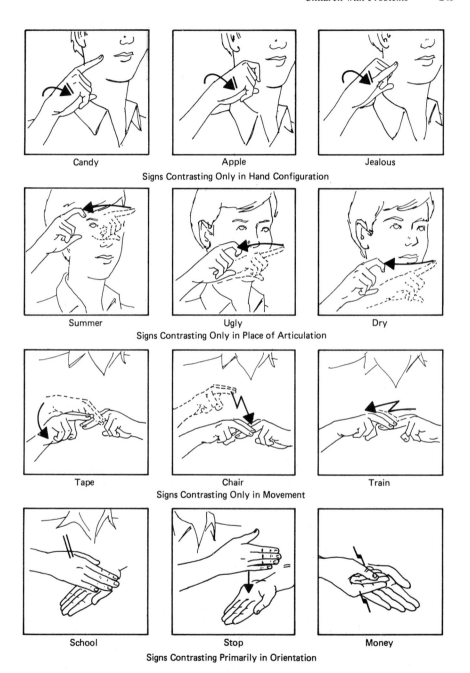

Candy　　　　　　Apple　　　　　　Jealous

Signs Contrasting Only in Hand Configuration

Summer　　　　　　Ugly　　　　　　Dry

Signs Contrasting Only in Place of Articulation

Tape　　　　　　Chair　　　　　　Train

Signs Contrasting Only in Movement

School　　　　　　Stop　　　　　　Money

Signs Contrasting Primarily in Orientation

FIGURE 6.8.　Minimal contrasts illustrating the four major hand formation parameters.

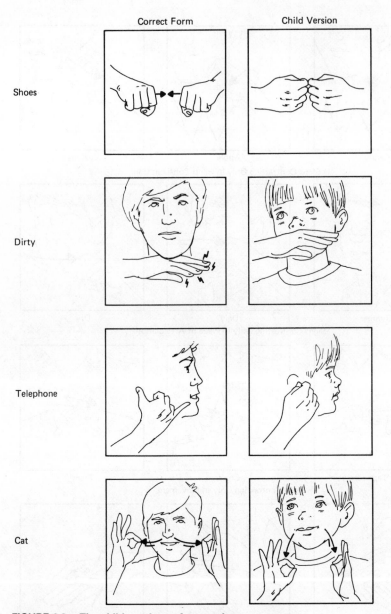

FIGURE 6.9.   The child versions of some signs.

parents sign utterances such as *Want Mommy help Jane?* instead of *Want me help you?* just as hearing parents do in spoken languages.

Why do parents do this? Because deaf children make the same comprehension errors, mixing up the pronouns, that hearing children do (Bellugi & Klima 1982). Deaf children learning sign language apparently acquire it as an arbitrary signal system, just as hearing children acquire speech. It may be true that infants acquire

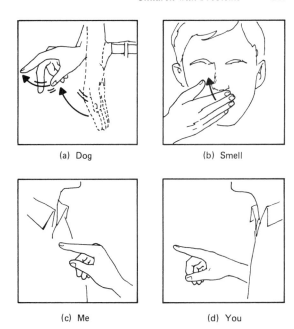

(a) Dog

(b) Smell

(c) Me

(d) You

FIGURE 6.10.
Four signs in which children's variations in meaning have been reported.

their first signs sooner because of ASL's iconicity, but once the acquisition process starts, the iconicity doesn't seem to help as much as one might expect.

Children who acquire ASL tend to produce their first two sign utterances several months earlier than children learning to speak. Extensive longitudinal studies have been done on the acquisition of multiple sign utterances, but they will not be reported further here because the results can be summarized simply: except where noted above, the acquisition of sign language, from first word to complex utterances, parallels the normal acquisition of spoken language (Collins-Ahlgren 1975; Livingston 1983; Prinz & Prinz 1979, 1981; H. Schlesinger 1972).

Hearing children of deaf parents

Quite a few researchers have looked at hearing children of deaf parents to see what if any, problems arise. The answer, essentially, is that in most cases no problems arise. Such children acquire language much as bilingual children do. For example, when a child named Davey had acquired his first ten words, some were signs, some were English words, and only in one case did he have both a word and a sign for the same concept (Holmes & Holmes 1980). This pattern is the same as that which has been reported for bilingual children (see Chapter 5).

Another example reminiscent of bilingual acquisition occurred in one child studied, who for a while used the ASL method of expressing plurality (repeating the sign) when speaking. Thus he said *gum-gum* when meaning more than one piece of gum (Prinz & Prinz 1981). The use of a single syntax for both ASL and speech has been reported in other studies as well (Sachs et al. 1981; Todd 1975; Todd & Aitchison 1980).

In normal bilingual acquisition there is often a period in which the phonologies of the two languages affect one another. When one of the languages is sign language, there is no evidence of delay or deficit of articulation of the spoken language (Mayberry 1976).

Even before they have much contact with other children in the neighborhood, hearing children of deaf parents appear to develop good speech with as little as two hours per week of contact with hearing speakers plus exposure to television (Schiff & Ventry 1976). Exposure to television alone is inadequate, however (Ervin-Tripp 1973: 262, 1978: 77). Occasionally a child is so isolated that he or she needs professional intervention to develop normal speech (Critchley 1967; Sachs et al. 1981). A child named Robin is said to have actually made it to age 6;0 knowing so little English that he was assumed to be deaf. Once it was discovered that he could hear, he was transferred to a normal grade-one class, where he quickly learned to speak (Vernon 1974: 222).

Anecdotally, one hears of hearing children of deaf parents having psychosocial problems other than language problems. Some feel that this is due to unusual adult responsibilities placed upon them by their parents—for example, to interpret for their parents in contacts with hearing people. Whatever problems occur are probably similar to the problems faced by children of parents who have moved to an area where a different language is spoken. They tend to prefer the culture of the neighborhood rather than that of their parents, which often leads to conflict.

VISUAL IMPAIRMENT

Children who are born blind or become blind at a very young age seem to learn to speak with little difficulty. One might expect that the lack of visual stimulation might retard comprehension and thus retard acquisition of certain words or structures. But if one believes that the other senses would tend to be improved to compensate for the missing sense, one might suspect that some aspects of language might develop earlier—for example, phonological accuracy. One may also argue that the blind person might use more language to compensate for a reduction in the amount of nonverbal communication that can be conveyed.

There has in fact been very little comparative research to study these issues. The most extensive information comes from one longitudinal study of ten congenitally blind children, aged 1;8 to 2;6. The children's behavior was compared to earlier-developed standards for normally sighted children (Bayley 1969). The medians for the blind children were not greatly different from those of normal children on three early measures: listens selectively to familiar words, responds to verbal request, and produces sentences of two words (see Figure 6.11). The language lags tend to disappear by the time the blind child reaches the age of five or so (Fraiberg 1977: 225).

There is some evidence that blind people may develop slightly heightened auditory ability. One study of 25 grade eight blind students found that they were superior to normals on an auditory embeddedness test. In such a test a series of

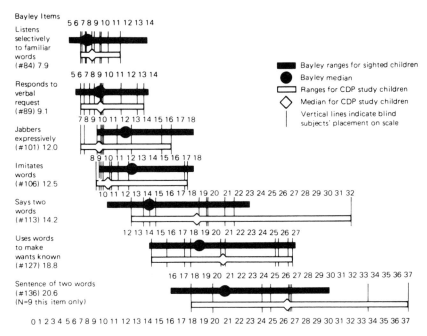

FIGURE 6.11. Language milestones of blind versus sighted children. (From Fraiberg 1977: 225. © Selma Fraiberg. Permission granted by Louis Fraiberg.)

tones is presented. The person taking it is then asked whether a set of tones was embedded within the longer series. Blind children also score above average on a subtest of the WISC (Wechsler Intelligence Scale for Children—Wechsler 1952) which measures **digit span**—how long a sequence of numbers the child can hear and repeat back. Blind children seem also to be superior at sentence repetition tasks (J. G. Gilbert & Rubin 1965: 239).

On the other hand, blind children tend to score lower on vocabulary, similarities, and comprehension subtests of intelligence tests (J. G. Gilbert & Rubin 1965: 240; K. Hopkins & McGuire 1966: 69-72; Tillman 1967: 67-70). Some of this deficit is due to questions that are inherently inappropriate for blind children— for example, they had difficulty obtaining any points for their answers to this question on a comprehension test: *What should you do if you see a train approaching a broken track?* (J. G. Gilbert & Rubin 1965: 240).

However, much of the deficit is clearly real. One area that apparently gives many blind children more problems than their sighted peers is the personal pronouns (McGuire & Meyers 1971: 140). Delay in acquisition appears to range from at least six months to as much as three years or more (Fraiberg & Adelson 1973: 544-547).

With regard to vocabulary, the blind are often said to engage in **verbalism** (Cutsforth 1932). Verbalism is defined as the use of words "not verified by concrete experience" (Cutsforth 1951: 48). For example, when blind people talk about *green grass* or a *foggy day,* one might say that they are using terms which they cannot possibly really understand because they cannot experience the concepts directly. It has been claimed that verbalism causes cognitive problems for the blind.

This notion has generated a fair amount of research and comment (e.g., Demott 1972; Dokecki 1966; Harley 1963; Santin & Simmons 1977), but it appears to me to be a red herring. We talk about ultraviolet and infrared as being colors even though we can no more see them than a blind person can see red or violet. Most words are learned not through direct sensory experience but through hearing them used by others. We should not be surprised if blind children use some words in inappropriate ways, because their notion of those concepts are less well developed than would be the case if they were sighted. We should not be surprised, but also we should not be concerned. As blind children get older, their concepts become more like those of their sighted peers, and in any case, there is no evidence of any relationship between amount of verbalism and cognitive or personal adjustment problems (Dokecki 1966; Harley 1963).

The greatest language problem for the blind is, of course, reading and writing. Since 1829 the solution to this problem has traditionally been the use of **Braille**—a system of written communication consisting of sequences of two by three matrices of dots—named after Louis Braille, its inventor (see Fig. 6.12). Braille is produced on heavy paper by means of a special Braille typewriter or a template and stylus for writing by hand. The typewriter or stylus produce raised dots that can be read by feel.

There are 63 possible combinations of dots, plus the blank space, and each combination represents a letter, a punctuation mark, or other character. Some combinations have more than one meaning, depending upon context. For example, *a* also stands for *1*, *b* for *2*, and so on. As well as the letters of the alphabet, a few common words and letter combinations are represented. The words include *and*, *for*, *of*, and *the*. The letter combinations include *ch*, *sh*, *th*, *st*, *ed*, *er*, and *ing*. People who read and write advanced Braille make use of a system of abbreviations, which allows shorter rendering of large numbers of words. The system is quite complex, allowing one to represent fractions, Roman numerals, italics, capital letters, accent marks, umlauts, diaeresis, and more (British National . . . 1971).

Braille is quite expensive to produce, and the finished product takes up a great deal of space. A recent invention is paperless Braille, in which the information is recorded on a magnetic tape casette. A casette recorder is attached to a line of Braille cells. As the tape is played, reeds within the Braille cells pop up to produce a line of 'print' at a time (E. Brown 1978).

The use of Braille takes considerable training and is of sufficient difficulty that not all blind people can learn it. Even when it is mastered, reading is three times slower than normal reading (Foulke et al. 1962). Another reading device, available since 1971, is the Optacon. This device can be used to scan print. It converts each letter to a tactile image. Its main advantage is that one can use it with most printed material. However, it cannot be used to read handwriting or fine print. Like Braille, it must be read letter by letter, so reading rates are low—30 to 60 words per minute (Goldfish & Taylor 1974).

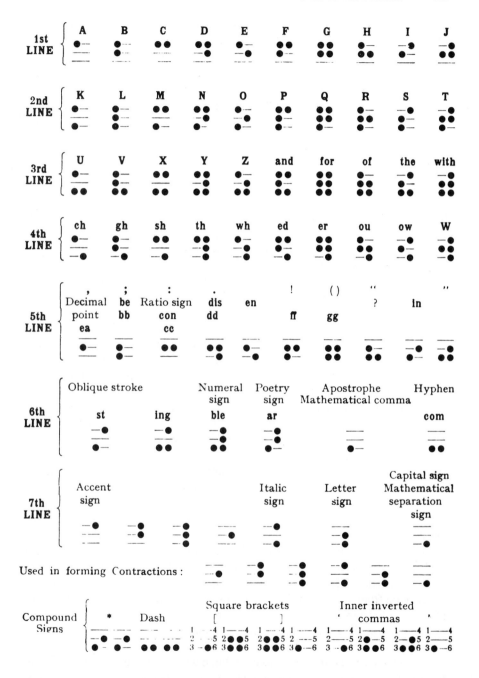

FIGURE 6.12. The Braille alphabet. (From British National Uniform Type Committee 1971. Used by permission of the Royal National Institute for the Blind, London, England.)

More sophisticated still (and more expensive) is the Kurzweil Reading Machine. This machine can scan most styles of type and can read the material aloud. It also can convert to Braille for those who are deaf as well as blind.

The problem of reading is slowly being overcome by technology. Computer technology is changing so fast that the last few paragraphs may have become obsolete before this book was published. My crystal ball says that in the not-too-distant future there will be an inexpensive, portable, battery-charged device that will be able to read printed material aloud. Although there are not enough blind people to warrant developing such a device, it could be marketed for preschool children as well.

DEAF AND BLIND

Thankfully, very few individuals are both deaf and blind. Estimates for the United States in 1975 placed the number at 4600 children (Committee . . . 1975); in Canada there are perhaps 200 children.[11] Thus the population is relatively small compared to other disabilities; this fact accounts for the comparatively little interest in deaf-blind children by researchers.

Deaf-blindness can result from a number of causes, including several genetic conditions, of which the most common is Usher's syndrome. Children with this syndrome are born deaf and gradually lose their sight, generally in their teens. Because they have their sight during their school years, they acquire language similar to other deaf children; thus by the time they have become blind, they have usually acquired a reasonable facility at manual communication (Vernon 1973).

Deaf-blindness can also result from conditions during pregnancy, such as rubella and blood-incompatibility problems, and conditions during the birth process, such as prematurity, active herpes in the birth canal, and other types of birth trauma. Rubella has been found to be the most common cause in the U.S. but not in Canada. Other causes can occur after birth. These include meningitis and scarlet fever.

The education of deaf-blind children has paralleled that of deaf children. In the last century instruction tended to be through a form of fingerspelling. More recently the pendulum swung to a method known as the **Tadoma method** (Norton et al. 1977; Reed et al. 1978, 1982a, 1982b). This is basically equivalent to the oral method. Residual hearing and vision are emphasized, combined with obtaining information from lip and tongue movements, vocal vibrations, and nasal air flow by placing the hand in a certain way on the speaker's face and larynx to pick up these cues. Now schools are switching to a form of total communication—signed English combined with fingerspelling.

No matter what method is used, children who are prelingually deaf and blind almost never acquire much language facility; even less are they likely to learn to speak (Industrial . . . 1959). In general the prognosis for such children is extremely poor, although there have been some outstanding exceptions, the most famous of which are Joseph Widd, Laura Bridgman, Helen Keller, and Robert Smithdas.

Joseph Widd was born deaf and became completely blind by age two. He learned the manual alphabet, and by adulthood had "acquired a store of scripture knowledge that would put to shame many of his more favored fellow creatures" (Widd 1886: 74).

Laura Bridgman was deafened and blinded at around the age of three due to scarlet fever. She acquired quite good language skills, though as an adult she never spoke. Of course, she must have started with some language skills acquired before the age of three (Lamson 1881: 13; Tilney 1929).

Helen Keller, undoubtedly the most famous due to the successful play about her (W. Gibson 1957), acquired her condition as a result of illness at 1;7. She wrote two books (Keller 1903, 1908) and learned to speak.

Robert Smithdas, deaf and blind since childhood, is the only such individual to have earned a masters degree—in Rehabilitation, from New York University. Smithdas is also a published poet (Salmon 1970).

Unfortunately, these four are the exceptions; most people who are pre-lingually deaf and blind never acquire more than a very rudimentary means of communication and ultimately end up in protected environments or institutional settings.

PHYSICAL PROBLEMS

Malformations

Between 75 000 and 120 000 school-aged children in the United States suffer speech difficulties due to physical problems with the articulatory apparatus (based on ASHA 1952; Pronovost 1951). Perhaps half of these children are born with a gap in the roof of the mouth, which opens into the nasal cavity. This condition, known as a **cleft palate,** can be a relatively small fissure or a complete opening from the lip to the back of the mouth. The speech of a child with a cleft palate is said to be hypernasal. Normally the connection between the nose and the mouth is closed during speech, except when the nasal consonants [m], [n], and [ŋ] are being pro-duced, but if there is a gap that the child cannot close, then some or all of the stops, affricates, and fricatives will be impossible to produce. Such conditions are treated surgically with a fair amount of success. Sometimes an artificial palate is worn, closing the gap. Speech therapy is also often useful.

Between 25% and 60% of children with cleft palates also suffer from a degree of hearing loss. This is often caused by intermittent occurrence of middle ear disease (Harrison & Philips 1971; Paradise et al. 1969). Children with cleft palate conditions also tend to become self-conscious and to withdraw from communication situations. It is probably due to this and to problems of hearing loss that cleft palate children tend to perform poorly on tests of language ability (Goodstein 1961; Lamb et al. 1972; Richman 1976; R. Smith & McWilliams 1968).

Children with **Down's syndrome,** a chromosomal abnormality causing men-tal retardation, are often born with certain oral problems that make clear articulation difficult. These include an overly large tongue, over which they have less muscle control than normal children, and an inability to close off the passage from the nose to the mouth, resulting in cleft-palate-like speech.

Other physical problems include malformations of and growths on the vocal cords. These can lead to abnormally high voice, hoarseness, or ability only to whisper. Sometimes these physical problems can be due to abuse; simply shouting, screaming, cheering, or talking too much can lead to vocal nodules and polyps, which may have to be removed surgically. A more benign treatment is to stop the abusive behavior. But as a parent of a child who has had this problem, I can attest that it is very difficult, if not impossible, to get a child to stop shouting.

Muscle control problems

The other major set of physical problems involves muscle control, which limits the ability to communicate by speech due to poor neural control of the speech articulators. The most common cause is **cerebral palsy.**

Cerebral palsy (CP) is the name given to damage to one or more parts of the brain that control muscle movement that occurs at or around the time of birth. This brain damage is most often caused by lack of oxygen due to prolonged labor, but also occurs due to prematurity, Rh incompatability, and fetal infections (Rutherford 1956). The degree of the problem can range from very mild to so severe that no meaningful communication is possible vocally. Speech therapy can help in the mild to moderate cases; for more severely affected children, more radical solutions are necessary.

One such solution is for the child to point to words or pictures to communicate. Such children are usually confined to wheelchairs, and the words or pictures are placed on lap trays attached to their chairs. Such solutions have their limitations. Pointing to words works only with children old enough to read; pointing to pictures can convey primitive needs and desires, such as wanting toilet, food, drink, sleep, or TV, but it hardly qualifies as a system that allows general communication.

One system that solves both of these problems is **Blissymbolics.** Blissymbolics is a pictographic language system invented by Charles Bliss. A refugee from Hitler's concentration camps, Bliss escaped to Shanghai, where he learned the Chinese writing system, in which each symbol stands for an idea rather than a sound. The various Chinese languages, such as Mandarin and Cantonese, are as different as French and German, and yet the country was united by a single writing system. If one couldn't communicate orally to someone from another part of China, one could communicate in writing. Bliss had the goal of developing a simple ideographic writing system that could be used by people of all languages, so that the world could be united as China was united, and so that there would no longer be any need for war (Bliss 1965).

Needless to say, the world did not beat a path to his door. Bliss's symbol system went unnoticed until it was discovered in 1971 by Shirley McNaughton at the Ontario Crippled Children's Centre in Toronto. Blissymbolics answered the communication needs of cerebral palsied children. It is a complete language system, and thus can be used for general conversation, and yet the symbols are simple enough to be learned by children too young to learn to read alphabetic writing (Archer 1977). Figure 6.13 gives a 100-symbol Blissymbolics display suitable for a child with cerebral palsy. Ultimately there evolved in Toronto the Blissymbolics Communication Institute, which adapts Bliss's symbols for use by children and which teaches the system in workshops and publishes materials such as stamps for making up symbol displays, dictionaries (Hehner 1980), and instruction books (McDonald 1980; see also Helfman 1981).

There are now perhaps 25 000 people who communicate using Blissymbols in Canada, the United States, Sweden, France, Israel, Australia, New Zealand, Denmark, Norway, and elsewhere. It turns out that perhaps only one-fourth of the users have CP. The majority of the remainder are severely mentally retarded. It is also being used by people with muscular dystrophy, multiple sclerosis, aphasia, and other disabilities (Kirby 1978; V. Land & Samples 1981; Saya 1978).

Some CP Blissymbol users ultimately improve their speech enough to leave Blissymbolics; some switch to word lists or other methods as they grow older; some continue to use Blissymbolics.

The usefulness of Blissymbolics in home settings seems well established. Parents and siblings take an active interest in the system and, of course, in the child. Under these circumstances Blissymbolics seems quite effective. The usefulness of Blissymbolics seems considerably more limited for users living in a residential setting, such as the Central Wisconsin Center for the Developmentally Handicapped. A study of seven Blissymbol users living in this setting found that they rarely used their communication board in spontaneous classroom interactions, and that the use of a communication board did not increase the likelihood of message success with teachers, ward personnel, and students who had not been trained on the system (Calculator & Dollaghan 1982). A later study of a quadriplegic in a nursing home indicated that proper training on a symbolic communication board and inservice training to staff and residents of the nursing home both significantly facilitated communication. The in-service training consisted only of a voluntary half-hour session (Calculator & Luchko 1983).

Many children with cerebral palsy do not have enough muscle control to point to symbols on a lap board. For such individuals a variety of accessing devices are created to suit their individual needs. These include computerized displays with a cursor that points to a symbol on the display. The cursor can be moved by operating any of various types of switches depending upon the muscle control of the user. There are also head pointers, and systems for indicating symbols through eye movement signals. Now on the market are **Voice Output Communication Aids,** or **VOCAs** for short, which can be used to produce synthetic speech. The displays on these devices can be used with words or with Blissymbols.

Another type of disability, relatively rare, is the **Moebius syndrome.** Children born with this condition cannot move their facial or oral muscles (A. Schaffer & Avery 1977). I saw one such person, a teenager, make very effective use of a VOCA to express himself at a conference. Unlike most people with cerebral palsy, his manual dexterity was not affected, so he could communicate relatively rapidly with the device, though still much more slowly than with normal speech.

FIGURE 6.13. A 100-symbol Blissymbolics display. (Blissymbols used herein derived from the symbols described in the work, *Semantography*, original copyright © C.K. Bliss 1949; Blissymbolics Communication Institute, Exclusive licensee, 1962.)

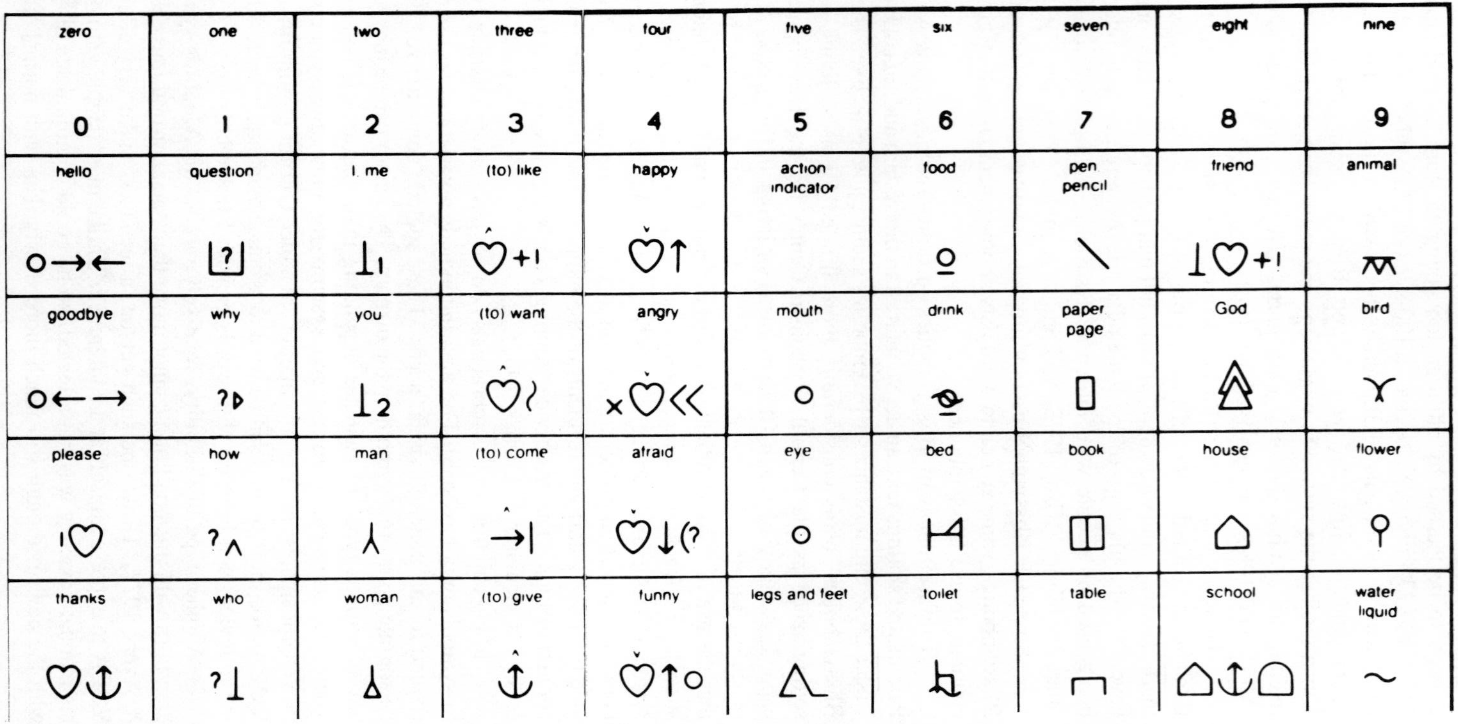

zero	one	two	three	four	five	six	seven	eight	nine
0	1	2	3	4	5	6	7	8	9
hello	question	I me	(to) like	happy	action indicator	food	pen pencil	friend	animal
goodbye	why	you	(to) want	angry	mouth	drink	paper page	God	bird
please	how	man	(to) come	afraid	eye	bed	book	house	flower
thanks	who	woman	(to) give	funny	legs and feet	toilet	table	school	water liquid

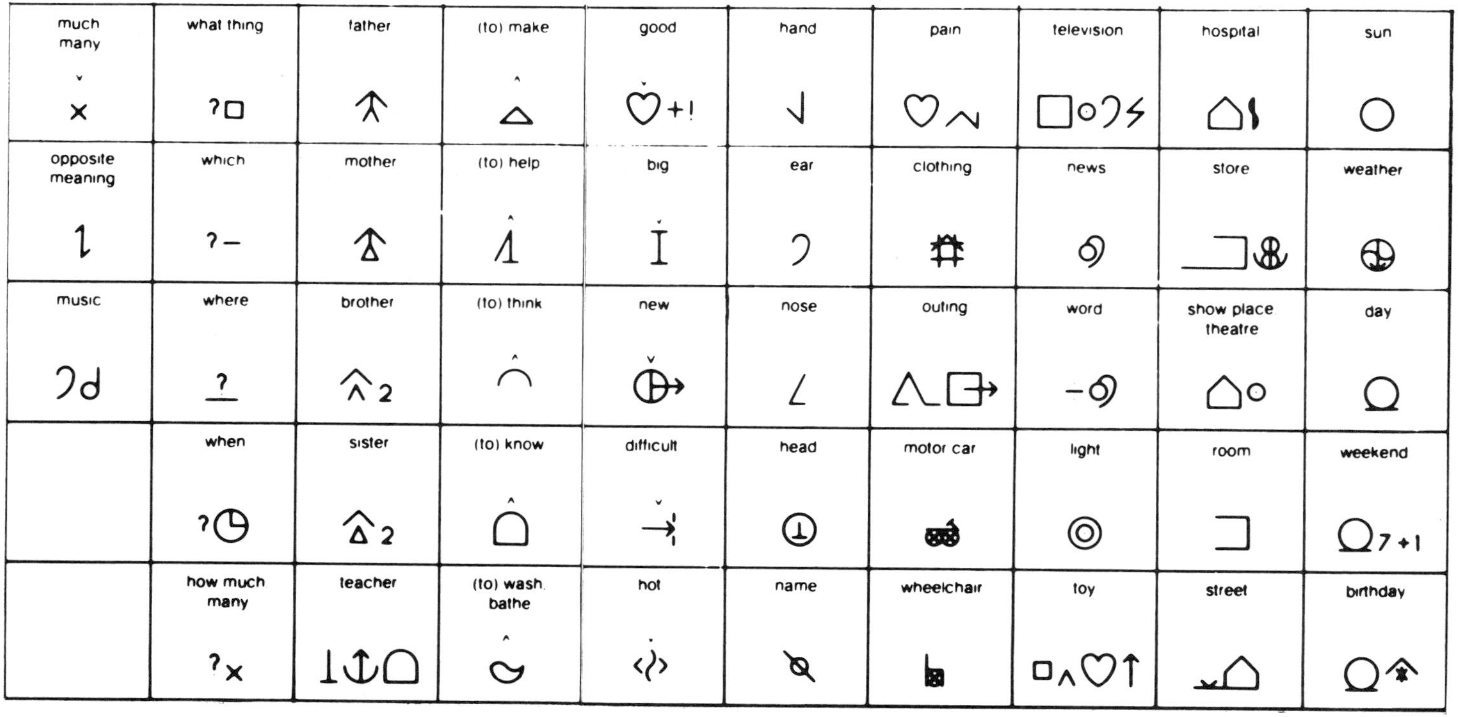

Blissymbol chart (labels):

sun	weather	day	weekend	birthday
hospital	store	show place theatre	room	street
television	news	word	light	toy
pain	clothing	outing	motor car	wheelchair
hand	ear	nose	head	name
good	big	new	difficult	hot
(to) make	(to) help	(to) think	(to) know	(to) wash bathe
father	mother	brother	sister	teacher
what thing	which	where	when	how much many
much many	opposite meaning	music		

257

A similar disability, also quite rare, is congenital **anarthria.** Children with this problem can laugh and cry and make other vocalizations, and have no difficulties chewing, swallowing, sucking, blowing, or licking, but they do not have the ability to voluntarily produce speech sounds. There is no problem with comprehension (Lenneberg 1962; 1964; 1967; 305-309). Such children would also be prime candidates for a VOCA.

Finally, two related conditions that appear to result in unusual language are **spina bifida** and **hydrocephalus.** Spina bifida is a congenital malformation of the spinal cord. Hydrocephalus is a buildup of spinal fluid in the brain due to improper circulation. It is usually relieved by surgically implanting a shunt, which provides an outlet for the fluid. Hydrocephalus often occurs with spina bifida. Children with these conditions have been said to be fluent—even superfluent—talkers, but a research study of this question has not found any support for this suggestion. These children do, however, make an unusual number of inappropriate responses in conversations (Fleming 1968). Some spina bifida children may also have some perceptual problems, which may make reading difficult (Association . . . n.d.).

AUTISM

Its nature

Autism, a condition that affects perhaps 16 000 children in the United States (Lotter 1966), was described as a separate syndrome in 1943 (Kanner 1943). Before that time children displaying what have come to be called autistic characteristics were diagnosed as mentally retarded or childhood schizophrenics. Unlike schizophrenics, autistic children show no evidence of delusions or hallucinations. Unlike mentally retarded children, they show normal development of manipulative skills and may show normal or even abnormally high skill at solving puzzles or other tasks.

What does characterize autistic children is a cluster of traits, many but not all of which will be present in any given child. Autistic children tend to be socially unresponsive. Even when they are infants, they do not respond to the presence of their mothers or other people as normal children do. They avoid eye contact and seem to prefer to be left alone. On the other hand, they may become fascinated with particular physical objects. Indeed, their behavior with respect to these objects may become obsessive. They may spin a bottle or line up cars or blocks for hours at a time, and may become upset if this behavior is interrupted. Other children may display repetitive behavior unrelated to objects, such as flapping their hands above their heads. Such behavior may even be self-destructive, such as hitting oneself or butting one's head against a wall or other object.

Another characteristic is excessive anxiety when required to deviate from an established routine. Such things as a change in clothing, food, or arrangement of furniture, leads to panic. One teenager, Mia (not her real name), recalled of her childhood, ''Once I established a ritual, it was not to be broken. Breaking a ritual would mean I would have to do something different. That would be a change, and I couldn't handle being surprised'' (Kohn 1979).

Another characteristic is abnormal response to sights and sounds. Some children have an ability to ignore voices and other sounds in the environment to such an extent that they may be diagnosed as deaf, and yet they may respond to a few sounds that are meaningful to them—the rustling of a candy wrapper or the faint sound of a distant fire engine siren. It has been reported that while normal infants tend to move their limbs in synchrony to speech sounds, autistic infants tend not to display the same syncrony, and if they do, they tend to give multiple responses, as if the sounds they hear echo in their minds (Condon 1975; Condon & Sandor 1974). This finding is somewhat questionable, as attempts to replicate it have failed (Oxman et al. 1978a).

Similar problems also occur with visual perception. Children who do not appear to see most objects in their environment may spot a sugar-coated cornflake six meters away (Lovaas et al. 1971). Mia recalled, ''It was hard to draw a table then. I would draw it all over the place because that was the way I saw it. Colors and sounds were sensations to me. I'd try to avoid certain sounds because they'd make me nervous, and 'play pretties' (caress and speak) with colors that I liked. . . . I see colors differently now. They're just colors'' (Kohl 1979).

One of the prime symptoms of autism is abnormal language development. About half of all autistic children develop at least some meaningful speech; the rest remain essentially mute. Even if they test as having normal hearing, many behave as if the sounds they hear are so jumbled that recognition is impossible (Kanner 1943; Lovaas et al. 1973; Rimland 1964; Rutter & Lockyer 1967).

Many autistic children have other problems as well. Half are retarded; about one in six develops epilepsy in adolescence; others are deaf; some display poor motor coordination (Bram et al. 1977)—for example, an inability to walk with their feet flat on the floor. Anyone who has dealt with autistic children knows that those who are so designated do not at all constitute a homogeneous group.

Some have thought that autism was a psychiatric problem caused by incorrect parental interaction, but there appears to be no empirical support for this view. For example, one would expect, if autism were a parental problem, that siblings would be more likely to be autistic as well, but such is not the case. Autism is now thought to be a disorder caused by brain damage, even if such damage cannot be identified by current clinical techniques. The damage appears to involve processing perceptual information from sights and sounds, especially sounds.

For those autistic children who learn to speak, the process is abnormal and clearly different from the process in, for example, mentally retarded children. The acquisition of the first words is often significantly delayed. More important, the vocabulary often doesn't grow the way it would in other children. New words might appear, but old words would be forgotten, so that the net result is a plateau of a few words (DeMeyer 1979). Some autistic children begin to speak and then lose all speech. Some of these children regain their speech; others do not (Usuda & Koizumi 1981). Development of articulation appears to be delayed but normal (Bartolucci et al. 1976; Fay & Butler 1968; Pronovost et al. 1966).

The most salient feature that distinguishes autistic speech is **echolalia**—the ritual repeating of words or whole sentences. All children, and even adults, tend to repeat words or phrases that they are just learning. However, some autistic children go far beyond this. They behave in parrot-like fashion, repeating whole sentences in response to a stimulus as if the sentence were unanalyzable into smaller components. For example, one five-year-old boy, when he wanted to signal "no," said *Don't throw the dog off the balcony.* It turns out that when he was two his mother had used that sentence in an appropriate context (the dog was a stuffed animal), and the child had stored and used it unanalyzed ever since (Kanner 1946). Another example: A child, waiting to go out, stands at a door and says *Do you want to go out?* Such utterances are repeated with uncanny accuracy of intonation.

These children do not appear to go through a telegraphic state, but rather use complete sentences right from the start (Simon 1975). It is as if the child, once having learned the routine of a complete utterance, rigidly adheres to it rather than varying it and trying out parts, which activity helps to sort out the meanings of the parts from the meaning of the whole. There has also been some suggestion that autistic children have difficulty attending to more than one sensory modality at a time (Lovaas et al. 1971). While attending to a long linguistic string with enough concentration to memorize it, the child fails to relate it to enough of the context to associate it to anything but a very vague and general meaning.

Some autistic children, not as severely affected, also produce spontaneous speech. Various difficulties have been reported, including use of idiomorphs, telegraphic speech, confusion of the pronouns *I* and *you,* incorrect use of question tags, and word and sentence order confusions (Frith 1972; Ricks & Wing 1975; Wing 1969, 1971). The degree of language delay has been reported to be significantly greater than that for mentally retarded children (Pierce & Bartolucci 1977).

Therapy

Since one of the traits of autistic children is their resistance to change, treatment of this disability has turned out to be difficult. Although there are a few cases in which claims have been made of complete or almost complete recovery, often involving herculean efforts on the part of parents and therapists (e.g., Kaufman 1975), the prognosis is not favorable. In a 1956 follow-up study of 63 autistic children at adolescence, 46 had not emerged from autism to any great extent, and many even got worse; 14 were able to attend regular classes in school at the appropriate age level, but were still deviant enough in their interpersonal interactions to cause problems; and only 3 were functioning well academically and socially, though even these were still considered odd.

The lack of useful speech by five years of age almost certainly guaranteed continued autism at adolescence; all but one of the 17 people in the latter two categories had begun meaningful speech by that age. Of those who had started speaking, half still ended up autistic in adolescence (Eisenberg 1956).

Most modern therapy involves the use of operant conditioning techniques, reinforcing the child's appropriate vocalization with bits of food or other rewards.

While this appears to have had some success with verbal autistic children, there has been no success with those who are mute (Lovaas 1966; Lovaas et al. 1973; E. Wolf & Ruttenberg 1967; M. Wolf et al. 1964).

Recently a variant of operant conditioning has been tried. Instead of attempting to develop speech directly, the method has been used to teach deaf sign language. The result of these programs is that many mute autistic children develop meaningful communication with other human beings for the first time. A reduced amount of self-destructive behavior has been noted in some children, and some meaningful verbalization has also occurred (Bonvillian & Nelson 1976, 1978; Fulwiler & Fouts 1976; Konstantareas et al. 1977a, 1977b; A. Miller & Miller 1973; Oxman et al. 1978b; Webster et al. 1973, 1975).

This appears to be a minor breakthrough rather than a major cure. Most of the graduates of the early sign language programs, like other autistic children, are ending up in institutional settings or protected environments. However, it is probably true that if they end up in settings where sign language communication is encouraged, the quality of their life is better than it otherwise would have been.

MENTAL RETARDATION

There is a very large population of mentally retarded. In the United States there are 1.2 million mentally retarded children, of whom 1.02 million, with IQs in the 50 to 70 range, are referred to as educable mentally retarded, 138 000, with IQs in the 20 to 49 range, are trainable mentally retarded, and 42 000, with IQs below 20, are custodial mentally retarded (President's Panel . . . 1962).

Children may lag behind normal children in mental development for many reasons. These include genetically determined metabolic deficiencies such as phenylketonuria or histidinemia, chromosomal abnormalities such as Down's syndrome (mongolism), brain damage due to birth problems, Rh incompatibility, encephalitis or other diseases, or just inherited retardation—retarded parents tend to have retarded children. All will be labelled mentally retarded.

Language acquisition in the retarded

There have now been quite a few studies of language acquisition in mentally retarded children. Many researchers have looked at Down's syndrome children separately; specific studies of other types are rare and involve very few children; otherwise, cause of retardation has not been considered. Practically no longitudinal studies have been conducted. One reason is that it takes too long—one year of development in a Down's child may be equivalent to only one month of development or less in a normal child (Dooley 1976).

Measures of language development have run from the rather primitive, such as using the categories 'mostly babble,' 'mostly words,' 'primitive phrases,' and 'sentences' (Lenneberg et al. 1964), to the quite detailed, such as producing grammars of the children's speech (Lackner 1968). The general finding is that the course of language development in mentally retarded children, whatever the cause of the retardation, is the same as in normals, only it is slower and, depending on the severity of retardation, may never reach normal adult levels (however, acquisition above age 22 has not been studied, to my knowledge).

One exception to the general finding is that Down's children tend to have greater articulation difficulty than would be predicted either by their slower developmental course or by malformations of the mouth and tongue. This was explored in a study which compared the speech of 10 Down's children with normal children and non-Down's retarded children matched for mental age and social background (Dodd 1974). While the phonological errors of the non-Down's children matched those of the normal children, some of the errors of Down's children appeared to be different. These included: perseveration—*denten* for "dentist"; stuttering and metathesis—*meta-meta-meto* for "tomato"; drastic consonant deletion—ɛ-ɛ for "elephant"; and inconsistent sound substitutions—any of [m], [f], [ʃ], [n], or [č] for [p] in the same child. This problem appears to be similar to mild cases of apraxia, a speech disorder associated with damage to a part of **Broca's area,** an area in the left front quadrant of the brain associated with language. Others have suggested that it might be related to known abnormalities of the **cerebellum,** an area in the lower back of the brain known to be related to motor performance (Cromer 1974: 256).

As far as I am concerned, no other studies have come up with convincing evidence of any differences other than rate between mentally retarded and normal children in language acquisition. Other differences have been reported, however. One study found that two Down's children tended to make heavy use of unanalyzed sentences such as *Here it is,* and *I got it* (Dooley 1976). However, recently this has also been found to be a strategy used extensively by some normal children (Galligan 1981).

Another reported difference involved the ability of retarded children to generalize the use of morphological endings to nonsense syllables on a Wug Test (Berko 1958; see Chapter 4). Retarded children tended to perform much more poorly at the task than their mental ages would predict (Lovell & Bradbury 1967; Newfield & Schlanger 1968). However, in later studies it was found that while the children didn't respond correctly in the test task, they occasionally used the nonsense words with their correct endings in spontaneous conversation (Dever & Gardner 1970). It now appears that the differences may be due to a reluctance on the part of retarded children in testing situations to try to use strategies that are available to them in less stressful contexts (Bradbury & Lunzer 1972). The difference turns out to involve social interaction skills rather than language development.

Let us consider one more reported difference. Retarded children, normal children, and adults were asked to figure out which of two puppets—a duck and a wolf—was the agent of the final verb in sentences such as *The duck is easy to bite* or *The duck is eager to bite.* The problem was to choose the right puppet in the case of a nonsense word: *The duck is risp to bite.* The correct answer could theoretically be figured out from information which had been given in a previously presented sentence—either *I am always risp to read to you,* or *Reading to you is risp.* The former sentence should tip one off that *risp* is like *eager;* the latter, that *risp* is like *easy.*

The task was successfully mastered by neither normal nor retarded children, nor even by normal adults. Young normal children, normal adults, and retardates tended to choose the named animal to do the biting; 10 out of 43 more advanced normal children chose another strategy—always choosing the other animal (Cromer 1974, 1975). The only thing I would conclude from this study is that in test situations involving impossible tasks, older normal children are more likely to give a perverse response than retarded children or normal adults. This again seems to say more about behavior in test situations than about language behavior.

Outweighing these and other questionable studies claiming a difference between retarded and normal children are many other studies concluding that the sequence and strategies of language acquisition are delayed but similar. These include studies of language milestones—onset of babbling, first word, and so on (Karlin & Stazzulla 1952; Lenneberg et al. 1964); phonological development (Bricker & Bricker 1972; B. Smith & Stoel-Gammon 1983); development of the use of different relations in early two-word utterances (Coggins 1976; Dooley 1976); syntactic development (J. T. Graham & Graham 1971; Lackner 1968); and morphological development (Dever & Gardner 1970; Lovell & Dixon 1967; Newfield & Schlanger 1968).

Therapy

Some profoundly retarded children remain without language in spite of the best efforts of special educators and speech and language pathologists. For such children various forms of visual communication have been used with some success. Profoundly retarded children have learned to use Blissymbolics and deaf sign language on at least a primitive level, for example.

Another method that has been used with some success with this population is Amer-Ind Gestural Code (Skelly 1979). Long before Europeans arrived in North America, different tribes of American Indians were using a manual sign language to communicate with one another for trading purposes. The various tribes spoke hundreds of different, mutually unintelligible languages. The American Indian Sign Language, however, was widespread across the continent. One of its properties was said to be its ease of learning, because of the iconicity of its signs. When Europeans arrived, the Indians taught it to them, and this was the language used in most Indian-colonial communications.

Madge Skelly, a speech and language pathologist and full-blooded Indian who had learned the system from her grandfather, decided to try it out on some particularly intractable cases—first on a patient who, due to cancer surgery, had no oral articulators, and then on some severely retarded patients, who she thought might be able to learn some signs because of their iconicity. It is now in use in a number of places throughout North America.

Skelly claims the system she is teaching patients is more iconic and therefore easier for a profoundly retarded person to learn than deaf sign language. **Transparency** of a sign is the term used to describe the degree to which that sign can be guessed by untrained observers. Skelly estimated the transparency of Amer-Ind in the neighborhood of 80% (Skelly 1979; Skelly et al. 1975). Independent researchers have found the transparency of Amer-Ind to be between 42% and 50% (Daniloff et al. 1983). Although Amer-Ind's transparency is not as great as originally thought, it does seem to be superior to that of ASL, which has been measured to be in the 10-30% range (Fristoe & Lloyd 1979; Hoemann 1975; Klima & Bellugi 1979; Luftig & Lloyd 1981). There are only about 200 signs in the Amer-Ind system used by Skelly and others, and each sign covers a wider semantic domain than the equivalent ASL sign; thus a person guessing the meaning of an Amer-Ind sign may be credited as correct for reasons other than the sign's iconicity. However, such explanations probably cannot account for the transparency differences completely. Some Amer-Ind signs have been lined up with their corresponding signs in ASL and Blissymbolics in Figure 6.14. On the basis of this sample, based mostly on the availability of symbols existing for each meaning in the three systems illustrated, it does appear that Amer-Ind signs may be more iconic than their counterparts in the other two systems.

DELAYED LANGUAGE

Many children referred to a speech and language pathologist are not deaf, not autistic, have no identifiable neural damage, and check out within the normal range on nonverbal IQ tests, yet in their language behavior they show a developmental lag of a year or more. Such children are said to have delayed language or speech. There are perhaps 120 000 such children in the United States (Berry & Eisenson 1956). About 15% of cases referred to speech clinics are of this nature (Van Riper 1972: 50); two-thirds are boys (Silva 1980: 775).

Since one criterion for inclusion in this category is that the child doesn't fall in any other category, it should not be surprising that children so labelled may be very different from one another (Morehead 1975) and may indeed have very different prognoses (Hall & Tomblin 1978). About 35% of language-delayed children are equally delayed in their receptive and expressive language abilities. Another 35% show significantly greater delay in comprehension than in expression; 29% show greater delay in expression (Silva 1980: 773). For many language-delayed children brain damage is the most probable cause, even though EEGs turn up nothing. Some of these children behave like adults with one or another type of speech or language disorder known to be due to brain damage. For example, when a little child has good comprehension but difficulty both speaking and performing voluntary oral motor acts, such as sticking his tongue in his cheek on command (a condition known as **apraxia**), a lesion in the motor cortex is the most likely explanation.

Other children may be delayed due to apparent family psychological problems. If these can be alleviated, the child's language may return to normal fairly rapidly.

Still other children may be marked as delayed because they have changed languages or due to dialect differences. Although they can benefit from additional help, these children have no serious problem and the prognosis for them is at least as favorable as for other members of their ethnic group.

Many language-delayed children will continue to have problems in school and may later be labelled as learning disabled (Aram & Nation 1980; Hall & Tomblin 1978). However, this need not be the case. One of my better university students reported that she didn't start to talk until she was five, but once she got going, she was fine.

Because the language of these children may never attain normal adult levels, the use of the term *delay* is somewhat misleading. Many other terms have been used, all of which have drawbacks: *childhood aphasia* (C. Weiss & Lillywhite 1981), *developmental dysphasia, developmental aphasia* (Eisenson 1972), *dyslogia* (Eisenson 1972: 60), *congenital aphasia, developmental language disorder* (Aram & Nation 1975), *language impaired* (Prinz & Ferrier 1983), and *the developmental speech disorder syndrome* (T. Ingram 1972). The terms involving the words *aphasia* and *dysphasia* suggest the breakdown of an already intact system, or brain damage, which in many childhood cases has yet to be confirmed. The other terms tend to imply inclusion of autistic children and mentally retarded children, which many practitioners would like to keep separate. Probably the best term is *language retardation* (Rutter 1972), but *retardation* evokes such strong reactions in parents that clinicians tend to shy away from its use. For want of anything better, therefore, we shall stick to the term *language delay*.

When children are classified as language-delayed, is their language merely delayed, or is it deviant? Many speech and language pathologists and researchers say that it is deviant. What is generally meant by this is that not only is the language of such children not up to the language of normal children their age, but also it does not correspond to the language of a normal child at any age.

Whether this is true or not is not easy to determine objectively. Unlike echolalic autistic children, language-delayed children do not engage in bizarre language behavior. Rather, particular errors ascribed to language-delayed children are ones that are also found in normal children. Such errors include misuse of indefinite pronouns (*someone, anything, nobody*), personal pronouns (*I, me, you*), auxiliary verbs (*do, can, may*), and the copula (*am, is, are, was*), as well as improper word order (*Where Mommy is?*) (Leonard 1972; Menyuk & Looney 1972). We shall consider a number of studies in order to evaluate the evidence for considering delayed language as deviant.

One study in which language deviance is claimed involved comparing the grammar of 10 normal and 10 delayed children matched on chronological age, sex, IQ, and socioeconomic status (SES) (Menyuk 1964). The language of the normal children was better developed than that of the language-delayed children. The language of the five oldest children in the delayed group (aged four to six) was then compared with the language of the five youngest children in the normal group (aged

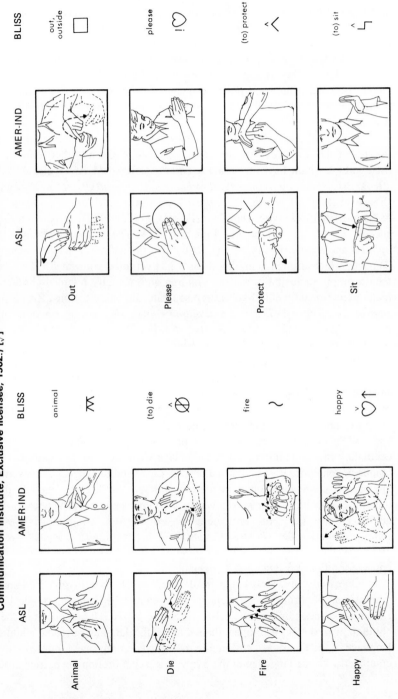

FIGURE 6.14. The ASL, Amer-Ind, and Bliss signs corresponding to some common English words ASL signs are described in many sources—e.g., Riekehoff 1978; Amer–Ind in Skelly, 1979; Blissymbols in Hechner 1980. (Blissymbols used herein derived from the symbols described in the work, *Semantography*, original copyright © C.K. Bliss 1949; Blissymbolics Communication Institute, Exclusive licensee, 1962.) [✓]

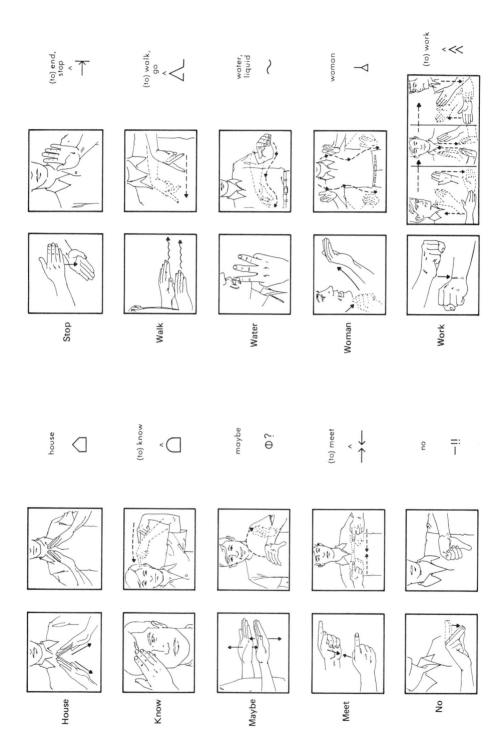

(to) end, stop

(to) walk, go

water, liquid

woman

(to) work

Stop

Walk

Water

Woman

Work

house

(to) know

maybe

(to) meet

no

House

Know

Maybe

Meet

No

three to four). The nonadult forms used by the older language-delayed children tended to involve word omissions (*This green, Put the hat*), whereas the nonadult forms used by the younger normals tended to involve redundancies (*The barber cut off his hair off; She splashted herself*). Since this is the same kind of difference that has been found between younger and older normal children (Menyuk 1963a), it does not constitute evidence for language deviance.

This same study also found that the ability to repeat a sentence uttered by the investigator was correlated with sentence length in the language-delayed children but not in the control population or in other studies of normal children (Menyuk 1963b). Obviously the ability to repeat a sentence is correlated with its length in normal children and adults. When no correlation is found in a particular study, it is simply because the range of sentence lengths is not great enough. Thus this reported difference does not constitute evidence for language deviance.

This study also compared the language collected in a longitudinal study of one two-year old to the language of language-delayed children. The basic finding reported is that by age three the language of this one normal child had exceeded the language of even the oldest language-delayed child studied. Again, I see no evidence of language deviance.

A second study claiming deviance (Menyuk & Looney 1972) compared 13 delayed children to 13 normal children with similar scores on a vocabulary test—the Peabody Picture Vocabulary Test (PPVT—Dunn 1959). The language-delayed children were enrolled in a hospital language therapy program; thus they presumably were drawn from the general population. The control group children came from a college nursery school program. These children probably came from parents of higher SES and educational attainment; they certainly were precocious in their language, as their scores on the PPVT were 1.3 years above their chronological age.

The delayed children performed more poorly at imitating sentences, in ways that indicated that they had poorer control of the syntax tested. What can we conclude from this? We can conclude that language ability as measured by a vocabulary test is not necessarily correlated with language ability as measured by a sentence imitation test. But is this due to the factor of language delay or is it due to the precociousness of the control group? We cannot tell from this study.

In another, more carefully controlled study, nine language-delayed children were matched to nine controls on chronological age, PPVT scores, and SES. Children were asked to make up a story for each of a series of 10 pictures that they were shown. The first sentence of each story was analyzed syntactically and morphologically. There were no significant differences in the number of children using any given type of linguistic structure, but there were differences between the two groups in the frequencies with which the different structures were used (Leonard 1972). In other words, no qualitative differences were apparent, but there were clear quantitative differences. This study suggests that the qualitative results of the previously discussed study were most likely due to SES differences between the two groups rather than due to the factor of language delay.

Another study that claimed a qualitative difference compared only one delayed child with one normal (Lee 1966). Some structures found in the normal child were not found in the language-delayed child, but there were differences in the way the language was elicited from the two children, which could account for the results (Bloom 1967).

Probably the most important variable to match a control group to is mean length of utterance (MLU), since this measure is known to correlate with syntactic development. In one study thus controlled, language samples were collected from 15 language-delayed and 15 normal children while they were engaged in spontaneous interactions with an adult, in structured play, and in elicitation using a picture book. Five aspects of syntactic and morphological development were studied. Although minor differences were noted in the frequency of occurrence of some infrequently occurring sentence types, the basic conclusion was that the language of language-delayed children was not qualitatively different. The explanation of the minor differences was that language-delayed children do not seem to use the linguistic systems that they have mastered as creatively as do normal children (Morehead & Ingram 1973).

Language use was the focus of another study that controlled for MLU. This study looked at what language-delayed children say when their previous remark is not understood. Twelve language-delayed and 18 normal children were recorded in conversation with the experimenter. Twenty times in each conversation the experimenter pretended not to understand the child's utterance, by responding "What?"

Both groups of children responded by repeating their previous utterance about one-fifth of the time, revising their previous utterance about three-quarters of the time, and failing to respond the remainder of the time. However, the two groups differed in the types of revisions. Language-delayed children more or less equally split their revisions among phonetic change, expansion, and reduction, whereas in normals the ratios of these three types of responses varied with linguistic ability, as measured by MLU (Gallagher 1977; Gallagher & Darnton 1978). Interpolating the data on normals, it appears that language-delayed children throughout the range of MLUs tested—approximately 1.6 to 3.1—behaved roughly the way normal children aged 1;10 do.

It is claimed that this represents a qualitative difference, but it appears to me that the only thing one can conclude is that the rate of change of revision behavior

BOX 6.1

Speech therapist:	Draw a picture of some food.
Child:	(Draws a roundish red blob.)
Therapist:	What is it?
Child:	Hufa.
Therapist:	What?
Child:	Hufa.
Therapist:	Say it another way.
Child:	(Whispering in therapist's ear) Hufa.[1]

[1] J.L. Bond, personal communication.

does not vary in lock step with syntactic development as measured by MLU. The independent development of syntax and semantics on the one hand, and pragmatics on the other, is most clearly found in a boy named John, whose ability at 3;3 at syntax and semantics was in the low normal range, but whose ability at pragmatics was practically nonexistent (Blank et al. 1979).

Revision behavior is just one aspect of pragmatics, the study of people's ability to communicate their intentions through speech acts. Ten other speech acts were investigated in another study of language-delayed children. The ten speech acts were acknowledging, answering, describing, interjecting, practicing, protesting, repeating, requesting action, requesting answer, and self-expressing. The relative frequency of the different types of speech acts among 20 language-delayed children, who were around four years old, was not significantly different from that of a control group approximately 1½ years younger but matched on MLU (approximately 3.0—Rom & Bliss 1981). This study appears to support the contention that language-delayed children are delayed but not qualitatively different in their pragmatic development.

The same seems to apply to the ability of language-delayed children to perceive differences in emotion based on nonverbal vocal cues. Although less accurate than normal children, language-delayed children are not different in the pattern of mistakes that they make (Courtright & Courtright 1983).

Similarly, language-delayed children do not appear to differ from normal children in the amount or type of inappropriate word extensions (K. Chapman et al. 1983). And finally, a study that looked at the sequence of development of eight morphemes found that the acquisition sequence was the same as in normal children (Johnston & Schery 1976).

What can one conclude from all these studies? It appears that when children are matched on MLU, a syntactic measure, there are no qualitative differences in the speech of language-delayed children. However, there are quantitative differences. Language-delayed children do not appear to use the structures they have knowledge of to best advantage. Also, syntactic knowledge appears to proceed independently of development of vocabulary and development of revision behavior. For example, the language of some language-delayed children can be spotted because of the use of advanced vocabulary in overly primitive syntax. The language of language-delayed children is different, but the differences are due to vocabulary and use rather than due to differences in language acquisition strategies.

STUTTERING

The speech of children who stutter differs from that of normal children in that even though they know precisely what they want to say, they find that the normal flow of their speech is interrupted by an involuntary stoppage, or **block,** due to an apparent inability to produce the next sound, and/or by repetition or prolongation of sounds, syllables, words, or phrases.

Stuttering is a problem that affects about 400 000 children in the United States (Bloodstein 1975: 72). About 41% of cases referred to a speech clinic involve this problem (Van Riper 1972: 50).

Causes and influencing factors

There is evidence that stuttering is partially caused by genetic factors. In a study in which 250 stutterers were matched with 250 nonstutterers on age, sex, and social status, it was found that 69% of the stutterers had at least one family member who stuttered, whereas only 16% of the control group did. Relatives included parents, siblings, grandparents, and more distant relatives (Wepman 1939a, 1939b. This figure is consistent with some more recent results, such as Yairi 1983, but others have not found such high numbers. See Porfert & Rosenfield 1978; Sheehan & Costley 1977). In another study 204 stutterers and an equal number of nonstutterers were asked about family members. The stutterers named 210 other stutterers in their families; the normals named only 37 (West et al. 1939). Most stutterers had no contact with their stuttering relatives, so direct learning can be ruled out, but in such a study one cannot rule out behavioral causes, such as family attitudes toward speech fluency. Such causes may also account for the results.

If you stutter, what is the likelihood that your child will? For men who have ever stuttered the figures are 9% for their daughters and 22% for their sons. For women the figures are 17% for their daughters and 36% for their sons (Andrews et al. 1983: 228).

Clearer evidence as to the genetic nature of stuttering comes from comparative studies of stuttering in fraternal and identical twins. When 30 pairs of fraternal twins at least one of whose members stuttered were compared to 10 pairs of identical twins in which at least one twin stuttered, the finding was strikingly in favor of a genetic influence. In only two of the fraternal pairs did both twins stutter, while in the case of identical twins, both stuttered in 9 out of 10 cases (S. Nelson et al. 1945). Two studies have replicated these results. In one both twins stuttered in 8 out of 9 cases of identical twins, and in 1 out of 25 cases of fraternal twins (Seeman, reported in Luchsinger 1959). In the other replication both twins stuttered in 10 out of 17 pairs of identical twins, but in only 2 out of 13 same sex nonidentical twins (Howie 1976, 1981).

It is hard to interpret these twin studies except to conclude that there is a genetic predisposition to stutter. Yet why are there some pairs of identical twins in which only one stutters? Identical twins share not only heredity, but also environment. What causes the difference is still a mystery.

The search for other medical factors has been extensive, mostly with negative results. Left-handed children are no more likely to be stutterers than are normal children (W. Johnson & King 1942; Spadino 1941), and the same is true of children with other articulation disorders (Winitz 1969). The evidence is mixed on children with visual handicaps. One study found no difference (Weinberg 1964), while another one found more stutterers in this group (Okada 1969).

Neither high intelligence nor high social class confer immunity: Aesop, Aristotle, Charles I, Churchill, Darwin, Demosthenes, and George VI were all stutterers (Taylor 1976: 339). There is some evidence, however, that gifted children are less likely to be stutterers (Terman & Oden 1947, 1959). Middle- and upper-class children may be slightly more likely to stutter (Morgenstern 1956), though most studies find no social class differences (Andrews & Harris 1964; Schindler 1955).

Approximately one-third of institutionalized Down's syndrome children have been said to show stuttering symptoms (Preus 1972). Other mentally retarded children also appear more likely to be labelled as stutterers than normal children (e.g., Chapman & Cooper 1973; Schaeffer & Shearer 1968). These studies are somewhat suspect, since the amount of stuttering found ranges from 2% (Karlin & Strazzula 1952) to 20% (Schlanger 1953). Furthermore, two studies found no difference (Martyn et al. 1969; Sheehan et al. 1968), and it has been argued that the earlier studies reported as stutterers people who should have been diagnosed as having articulatory inadequacies and other speech and language problems (Sheehan & Costley 1977). A clearer result would have been obtained if the children had been matched with normals with the same mental age so that the same definitions of stuttering could be applied to both. However, this was not done in any of these studies.

There appear to be no differences between stutterers and nonstutterers in birth weight (Berry 1938b; W. Johnson & Assoc. 1959: 50), age of parents (Andrews & Harris 1964: 52; W. Johnson & Assoc. 1959: 75; Morgenstern 1956), nonspeech breathing movements (Kurshev 1968; W. Moore 1938), heart rate, sinus arrhythmia, blood pressure, metabolism (Hill 1944; McCrosky 1957; Ritzman 1943; Walker & Walker 1973), body chemistry (J. Anderson & Whealdon 1941; Karlin & Sobel 1940; Laczkowski 1965), or physical development (Andrews & Harris 1964; Berry 1938b; W. Johnson & Assoc. 1959; Milisen & Johnson 1936).

There is some evidence of differences in the electrical activity of the brain. In order for there to be a properly controlled study in this area, not only must there be a matched control group, but also the person reading the electroencephalograms (EEGs) must not know which came from stutterers and which came from controls. Two such carefully controlled studies found no differences (Andrews & Harris 1964: 101; J.K. Graham 1966), but a third, applying more recent techniques, found that the EEGs of the stutterers were clearly abnormal, but not as much so as the EEGs of epileptics (Sayles 1971). There is also evidence that children who experience epilepsy, cerebral palsy, and similar neurological abnormalities are more likely to stutter (Bohme 1968; R. Ingram 1963). Deaf children are less likely to stutter (Backus 1938; Harms & Malone 1939).

Boys are more likely to stutter than girls, and the ratio increases with age. The ratio is roughly 1.4 to 1 among preschool stutterers (Glasner & Rosenthal 1957), 3.1 to 1 in grade 1, and 5.5 to 1 by grades 11 and 12 (White House . . . 1931). This increase is apparently due to more new cases of stuttering in older boys rather than to differential rates of recovery (West 1931).

There is also some evidence that children who are twins are slightly more likely to stutter than nontwins (Berry 1938a; Graf 1955; S. Nelson et al. 1945).

Whatever biological factors may be involved in stuttering, environment is thought to play a large part in determining whether a child will become a stutterer. One type of evidence for this comes from the incidence of stuttering in different cultures. While the incidence runs about 1% in North America, Europe, and Japan, information provided by anthropologists about other groups suggests that it may be different in other cultures. The claim is made that in some tribes of North American Indians and tribes in New Guinea, British Guiana (now Guyana), Borneo, Malaya, and India—stuttering is nonexistent or at least extremely rare, and indeed, the languages of those cultures have no word for it (Bullen 1945; W. Johnson 1944; Snidecor 1947). On the other hand, in a few cultures—such as the Ibo and Idoma of West Africa—there is reported to be a higher incidence of stuttering (Morgenstern 1953). In these societies public speaking is highly regarded and disfluencies are ridiculed (Bloodstein 1975: 92-98; W. Johnson et al. 1967: 244ff).

These claims should be taken with a grain of salt. In some tribes if an anthropologist is not completely accepted by the tribe, its members will hide any perceived weaknesses. This is why, some researchers believe, there were no reports of knowing anybody so afflicted, and even denial that there was a word for stuttering. In fact, other anthropologists have found in the same tribes studied earlier both stutterers and many expressions to describe stutterers and stuttering (Lemert 1953; Zimmermann et al. 1983).

A second type of evidence on environmental influence comes from the widespread impression among American clinicians that the incidence of stuttering has been declining over the last several decades. This is often attributed to a more relaxed attitude toward child rearing, promulgated by Dr. Spock (1957) through his popular manual on child care. General impressions of clinicians are notoriously unreliable, and although they are suggestive, they are no substitute for systematic research.

A third type of evidence comes from research on parental attitudes. Some North American researchers have felt that parents of stutterers tend to impose somewhat higher standards of behavior on their children and to be highly critical, highly anxious, and perfectionistic (W. Johnson & Assoc. 1959; Moncur 1952). However, other researchers have reinterpreted the same data and concluded that parents of stutterers are in fact more submissive (Quarrington 1974). This interpretation is supported by research in England, where it has been found that mothers of stutterers tend to have lower intelligence, poorer work and school records, poorer housing, and a less unified family life (Andrews & Harris 1964).

Yet another type of evidence comes from a 1940 case study of a family in Iowa. About 385 of the family members were stutterers (Gray 1940). Following identification of this family, advice about speech disfluencies was given to parents of the stutterers. A follow-up study 20 years later reported that only 1 of the 44 people in the next generation was a stutterer (W. Johnson 1961). However, one can also make a case that the findings concerning this family could be interpreted as strongly supportive of hereditary patterns in stuttering (Sheehan & Costley 1977).

Stutterers have been studied extensively for differences on psychological measures as well. Stutterers apparently differ from normals on a number of traits. The average verbal and nonverbal IQ scores have been reported to be five points lower for stutterers than for normals (Andrews & Harris 1964: 94; Okasha et al. 1974; Schindler 1955), however, the earlier mentioned apparent misdiagnosis of other speech and language disorders as stuttering among the mentally retarded may have biased these results. Stutterers come out slightly below normals on tests measuring self-reliance and social skills (Prins 1972; Wingate 1962). For example, five- to nine-year-old stutterers show more anxiety about being separated from their mothers than normal children (Wyatt 1958, 1969).

Stutterers have been tested on a number of psychoanalytic traits, such as oral and anal eroticism, obsessive-compulsive traits, hostility and aggression, body image, and guilt. Usually stutterers have turned out not to differ from their nonstuttering peers (Bloodstein 1975: 157-164).

In the few cases in which differences have been noted between stutterers and normals, these differences have been slight, and may be caused by the stuttering behavior rather than being the cause of it. For example, if stutterers are shy about using new words or long words because of fear of stuttering on them, this might reduce their knowledge of the meanings of such words enough to account for the slight differences in language and intelligence scores. Similarly, children who tend to stutter would naturally be shyer in social situations and thus come out lower on tests of social skills. In the last few decades a number of theories have been proposed claiming that stuttering is due to various psychoanalytic causes, but objectively collected evidence does not support any of them.

From factors related to stuttering, we shall now shift our attention to the stuttering behavior itself.

Stuttering behavior

Adult stutterers can anticipate when they are about to block or stutter on a word (W. Johnson & Solomon 1937; Knott et al. 1937; Milisen 1938; Van Riper 1936). It has been argued that it is the anticipation that triggers the stutter, but three facts appear to refute this proposal. The first is that not all stutters are anticipated. When an unanticipated stutter occurs, the stutterer may actually give a reaction of surprise (Van Riper 1936). The second is that some stutterers seem completely unable to predict their blockages (Milisen 1938). The third is that many children appear not to be able to predict when they will block (F. Silverman & Williams 1972). Only 38% of 8- to 9-year olds reported that they could sometimes tell when they were about to block; the figure is 45% of 10- and 11-year-olds; 62% of 12- to 13-year olds, and 71% of 14- to 16-year olds (Bloodstein 1960). Thus it appears that the ability to anticipate a block is learned after years of experience with stuttering, and is not the cause of it.

Stutterers are also very consistent in where they block. When asked to read the same passage more than once, they are likely to block on many of the same words. The agreement between two successive readings for a typical stutterer is about 65% (e.g., W. Johnson & Knott 1937; Siedel et al. 1973). This consistency remains, though diminished to 49%, when the two readings are done four weeks apart (Stefankiewicz & Bloodstein 1974). Consistency is also found in preschool and school-age stutterers (Neelly & Timmons 1967; Williams et al. 1969), and indeed, in disfluencies of normal children (Bloodstein et al. 1965).

The probability of stuttering at a particular place appears to be strongly predictable from the properties of the text. Within a word over 90% of stutters occur in the initial sound of the word (Hahn 1942; W. Johnson & Brown 1935). Most of the rest occur on the first sound of a syllable. Among words more than one syllable long there is also a tendency to stutter on the accented syllable (S. Brown 1938; Hejna 1972). Most stutterers tend to block on particular sounds (W. Johnson & Brown 1935); however, different stutterers block on different sounds. No one sound is appreciably more difficult than any other among stutterers in general, but consonants as a whole appear to be more difficult than vowels (Quarrington et al. 1962; Soderberg 1962; Taylor 1966).

Obviously, learned fears of particular sounds are important determinants. No physiological theory would account for the fact that some stutterers stutter on words beginning with the letter *f* but do not stutter on words with the same initial sound but beginning with the letters *ph*. Similarly, other stutterers may have no difficulty with words beginning with *f* but block on words beginning with *p*, including words that begin with *ph*.

Word position in a sentence also is relevant. In general, the closer a word is to the start of a sentence, the more likely it is to be stuttered (S. Brown 1938; Quarrington 1965). This is also true for phonemic clauses (Taylor 1966. A phonemic clause is a unit of an utterance spoken with a single intonation contour), and even random sequences of words (Conway & Quarrington 1963).

There also tends to be more stuttering on content words—nouns, verbs, adjectives, and adverbs—than on function words—articles, prepositions, and conjunctions (e.g., S. Brown 1937; Danzger & Halpern 1973)—especially when the stutter occurs on words in other than initial position (Soderberg 1967).

Word length is also relevant. Longer words tend to be stuttered more often than shorter words, all other things being equal (e.g., S. Brown & Moren 1942; F. Silverman 1972; Wingate 1967). This has been found to be true not only in situations involving reading passages, but also for spontaneous speech (Lanyon 1969).

The four factors of word position, word length, word type, and sound type have been found to be important predictors of place of stuttering in school children as well as adults (Williams et al. 1969).

Another relevant factor is word frequency. All other things, such as word length, being equal, the less frequent a word is in the language, the more likely a stutterer is to block on it (Danzger & Halpern 1973; I. Schlesinger et al. 1966; Soderberg 1966). Studies finding this result have not completely controlled for other factors. However, this factor does appear to be independent of word length (Soderberg 1971) and sentence position (Quarrington 1965).

A final property of the text that affects stuttering involves particular words. Just as particular sounds are feared and stuttered on by different stutterers, so many stutterers will have particular words that cause them trouble. Often this may be such things as their name, address, and telephone number, which are feared partly because they cannot be avoided by substituting synonyms (Hamre & Wingate 1973; Van Riper 1972: 269-270).

The frequency of stuttering tends to vary due to several factors, most of which can be described as affecting the amount of anxiety that the speaker is feeling. For example, the greater the communication pressure, the greater the tendency to stutter. The evidence in support of this comes from many different types of data. Words when read in a meaningful passage are more likely to be stuttered than those same words when read in a list or nonsense passage (Eisenson & Horowitz 1945). Stutterers find that they are very much more fluent when they are alone (e.g., Hood 1975; Langová & Šváb 1973; Quinn 1971) or when talking to infants and pets. Conversely, they may block severely if they are asked to repeat something by a listener who didn't understand the message the first time (Bloodstein 1975: 217).

Stutterers also tend to be fluent when reading a passage in unison with another person (Andrews et al. 1982; W. Johnson & Rosen 1937). This effect is reduced if, although the stutterer is reading in unison, he or she is reading into a microphone that is supposed to be transmitting to a person in another room only what he or she is saying (Eisenson & Wells 1942).

Just as adults are more critical listeners than infants and thus more likely to evoke stuttering, so some adult listeners cause more stuttering than others, presumably because they cause more anxiety. Stutterers stutter more to people they consider hard to talk to (Porter 1939) and even to their pictures (Berwick 1955). Among the people stutterers apparently consider hard to talk to are formally dressed faculty members, as opposed to fellow students (Sheehan et al. 1967). Conversely, stutterers have less trouble communicating with people of lower status, such as younger people or underlings at work.

Stuttering also increases with the size of the audience (Porter 1939; Siegel & Haugen 1964; Steer & Johnson 1936). In one study stutterers thought the audience was continually evaluating them through a device that the stutterers could monitor. When they thought the audience was reacting unfavorably, their stuttering increased; when they thought the audience was reacting favorably, their stuttering decreased (Hansen 1956).

When stutterers get together one might expect that their stuttering would get better, since their audience would be more understanding. Not so, according to a colleague of mine who stutters. It gets worse, because each stutterer wants to appear less disfluent than the others, and the resulting pressure to communicate more fluently makes things worse!

Almost any way of communicating that involves a distraction reduces stuttering: speaking in a fake accent, whispering, speaking in a voice that is much higher or lower pitched than normal (W. Johnson & Rosen 1937; Ramig & Adams 1980), speaking in time to a metronome (e.g., Andrews et al. 1982; Trotter & Silverman 1974), when walking on all fours (Geniesse 1935), when playing the piano, when dancing (Barber 1940), and on and on. However, if a stutterer talks with an accent or engages in other distracting behavior so long that it becomes second nature, the stuttering will no longer be suppressed (Bloodstein 1975: 228).

The ability of distracting movement to ease a stuttering block until that movement becomes habitual is thought to be the mechanism whereby many stutterers acquire body tics, eye blinks, head movements, facial grimaces, and other actions of this nature. Stutterers may discover that if they jerk their heads they can get past a stuttering block. Once this becomes habitual it is no longer effective, so additional and/or more violent jerks are necessary. In the case of my previously mentioned colleague, his head movements became so violent that he had to take off his glasses before he tried to speak. If he didn't, his glasses would fly off and be shattered. When he hit a stuttering block, his movements made him look as if he were having an epileptic seizure.

Onset

The earliest age of onset of stuttering is generally around 18 months, the time children begin to speak in sentences longer than a single word. A child may begin to stutter at any age, but the mean age of onset is about 3;6, and the incidence of onset declines each year from 18 months on (Andrews & Harris 1964: 113; Bloodstein 1975: 73-77; W. Johnson & Assoc. 1959. Yairi 1983 reported a mean age of onset of 2;4). Most stutterers begin to stutter without apparent cause, but acquired stuttering can begin in a previously fluent speaker after brain damage, both in children (Bohme 1968) and in adults (Andrews et al. 1982; Donnan 1979; Helm et al. 1978; Rosebek et al. 1978).

Although the incidence of stuttering is about 1% of the population, perhaps 10% of all children at some time are considered by their parents to have stuttered (S. Dickson 1971). Most recover spontaneously within a few months. About 79% recover by the time they are teenagers (Andrews & Harris 1964; Sheehan & Martyn 1970), and of the remainder, some recovery continues at older ages (Shames & Beames 1956). At least half of adults who consider themselves to have recovered report that they still have an occasional tendency to stutter. This is particularly likely among those who recover late (Shearer & Williams 1965; Wingate 1964).

Early stuttering

There is little evidence that the disfluencies found in children who are labelled as stutterers differ from those in children not so labelled, except, that on the average they have more of them. A study of 68 male children and an equal number of controls found that children labelled as stutterers averaged about 9 times as many sound and syllable repetitions, 4 times as many word repetitions, 10 times as many sound prolongations, twice as many phrase repetitions, and 3 times as many broken words (see Table 6.1). When they had repetitions, normals mostly repeated once or twice, whereas stutterers sometimes repeated three times or more. There were no significant differences in the number of interjections, broken words, or incomplete phrases. Although these differences are substantial, the distributions overlapped. It turned out that 20% of the nonstutterers spoke with more disfluencies than 30% of the stutterers. Thus whether a child's disfluencies are labelled as stuttering depends partly on the standards for fluency set by parents (W. Johnson & Assoc. 1959: 205-220).

TABLE 6.1:   Mean Number of Disfluencies Per 100 Words

	STUTTERERS	NONSTUTTERERS
Sound and syllable repetitions	5.44	.61
Word repetitions	4.28	1.07
Prolonged sounds	1.67	.16
Phrase repetitions	1.14	.61
Broken words	.12	.04

From W. Johnson & Associates 1959: 210. © University of Minnesota Press. Used by permission.

The stuttering of preschoolers has been said to differ from later stuttering both in the absence of struggle behaviors and in its patterns of occurrence in utterances. Recently it has been found that a few stutterers produce struggle behaviors from the start (Van Riper 1971; Yairi 1983). In early stuttering almost all stutters occur on the first word of a sentence; they occur more often on pronouns and conjunctions than on other parts of speech, and they usually involve the repetition of whole syllables or whole words (Bloodstein & Gantwerk 1967; Yairi 1983). This pattern is the same in the disfluencies of nonstuttering preschoolers (Helmreich & Bloodstein 1973; E.-M. Silverman 1974).

In summary, it appears that people vary greatly in their ability to speak fluently, and this ability is partially genetically determined. Many, though not all, children who are particularly disfluent get labelled as stutterers. Most recover spontaneously, but some, perhaps partially due to overly strict demands for fluency by their parents, become worse, adding frustration, struggle, and sometimes body tics to their disfluency. It should be added that this last group can be helped considerably with modern speech rehabilitation techniques. Although it may not be possible to reduce the amount of disfluency to normal levels—indeed, a number of the experts in the field are themselves not completely 'cured' stutterers—much of the disfluency and most of the overlaid struggle behaviors can usually be eliminated.

SUMMARY

Not all children acquire language with the same ease that normal children do. Deaf children often require special communication training. Several different methods are in use. While different methods may be appropriate for different children, the total communication method is the most used, and seems marginally superior to other approaches. Deaf children of deaf parents acquire sign language in very much the same way that hearing children acquire their first language. Hearing children of deaf parents acquire sign language and speech in very much the same way that other children in contact with two languages become bilingual.

The biggest language problem for blind people is reading. The traditional solution is to make use of the Braille system. This system is beginning to be augmented by print-reading machines and other high-tech devices. Those who are deaf and blind from an early age, with a few well-known exceptions, rarely acquire much language facility, despite the best efforts of teachers who use manual communication and other methods to try to teach language.

Other children have physical problems that result in speech and language difficulties. Children born with cleft palates, or tongue or vocal cord abnormalities may be helped by surgery and speech therapy. More difficult to treat are severe muscle-control problems such as cerebral palsy. For some such children, Blissymbolics and/or voice output communication aids may be useful. Some autistic children may be helped through the use of sign language.

The sequence of language acquisition has been studied in mentally retarded and language-delayed children to determine how it differs from that of normal children. The sequences appear to differ very little, though the acquisition of vocabulary, syntax, and pragmatics can proceed at different rates.

Stuttering appears to involve a pathologically greater use of language disfluency behaviors. Fluency varies with the nature of the text being spoken and the degree of stress in the situation. It is usually possible to ameliorate stuttering with treatment, but total cure is much more difficult.

SUGGESTED FURTHER STUDY

ANDREWS, G., A. CRAIG, A.M. FEYER, S. HODDINOTT, P. HOWIE, & M. NEILSON (1983) Stuttering: A review of research findings and theories circa 1982. *Journal of Speech and Hearing Disorders* **48,** 226-247. See also the comments on this paper that follows on pages 247-263.

FRAIBERG, SELMA (1977) *Insights from the blind: Comparative studies of blind and sighted infants.* New York: Meridan.

LAHEY, MARGARET, ed. (1978) Readings in childhood language disorders. New York: John Wiley.

MCDONALD, EUGENE T. (1980) *Teaching and using Blissymbolics.* Toronto: Blissymbolics Communication Institute.

MOORES, DONALD F. (1982) *Educating the deaf: Psychology, principles, and practices.* 2nd ed. Boston: Houghton Mifflin.

SCHIEFELBUSCH, RICHARD L. & L.L. LLOYD, EDS. (1974) *Language perspectives—Acquisition, retardation, and intervention.* Baltimore: University Park Press.

NOTES

[1]Pronovost 1951. In this chapter the figures given for the various handicaps are based on an estimate that there are 40 000 000 school-aged children in the United States.

[2]American National . . . 1969. Ling & Ling (1978: 116) place the upper limit at 8000 cycles per second.

[3]Genetic factors have been held responsible in anywhere from 5% to 65% of the cases studied (Bergstorm et al. 1971; Bordley & Hardy 1951; K. Brown 1969; Danish & Levitan 1967; Danish et al. 1963; L. Hopkins 1954; Pellegrini 1967; Proctor & Proctor 1967; Sank & Kallman 1963; Whetnall & Fry 1964). The wide range is due partly to the fact that many examiners label deafness as genetic when the etiology is unknown, and partly to differences in how far in a family tree researchers have looked for other cases of hearing loss.

[4]For example, Ling 1977; J. Miller 1970. These arguments can be traced back as far as 1880. See D. Moores 1982: 73.

[5]This argument comes from Aristotle. See D. Moores 1982: 31.

[6]Clarke & Ling 1976; Ling & Clarke 1975; Nicholls & Ling 1982. For additional comments and criticisms of this method, see D. Moores 1969a, 1969b.

[7]Some people differentiate between the two. Such people view total communication as an educational philosophy in which different methodologies would be used when appropriate (D. Moores 1974: 400).

[8]For example, Brazil (Hoemann et al. 1981), China (Yau 1977); Denmark (Hansen 1975; Sorenson 1975); southern France (Sallagoïty 1975); Great Britain (Woll et al. 1981); Israel (Namir & Schlesinger 1978; I. Schlesinger 1971; Japan (Peng 1974); New Guinea (Kendon 1980); Providence Island (Washabaugh et al. 1978); and Taiwan (W. Smith 1976; Stokoe 1980).

[9]See J.H. Gilbert 1982 for discussion.

[10]J. Moores 1980; H. Schlesinger & Meadow 1972. Fischer 1974: 24 says it occurs but cites no data.

[11]My extrapolation from 1980 Ontario figures. Since Canada has roughly one-tenth the population of the United States, there is a discrepancy in these figures. Any or all of several explanations could apply. Some possibilities: The definitions of who is deaf and blind may differ; government-supported medical care in Canada leads to fewer cases; more Canadian cases are misdiagnosed. See Csapo & Clarke 1974.

SEVEN
HOW DO THEY DO IT?

How do children accomplish the amazing task of learning their languages? How indeed. Although more and more detail about what happens is being accumulated, how the human mind is structured to accomplish this task is still mostly a matter of speculation and philosophical argument. This chapter surveys various positions taken by theoreticians on this issue, and then attempts to evaluate some of the arguments and data that are relevant to those positions.

THEORETICAL POSITIONS

Language is built in

The most extreme position taken by contemporary theorists is probably that of Noam Chomsky. Language acquisition is a fundamental part of the theoretical underpinnings for his theory of language, known as **transformational grammar.**

Chomsky is impressed with the enormous complexity of natural language (N. Chomsky 1975: 4). Children acquire language so rapidly that they cannot possibly have enough data to have learned it by any general learning principles (N. Chomsky 1975: 10). Not only is language enormously complex, but the data is flawed, in that much of natural speech shows numerous false starts, deviations from rules, changes of plan in mid course, and so forth (N. Chomsky 1965: 4, 200 fn 14). Chomsky

NOAM CHOMSKY

concludes that humans cannot possibly learn the nature of language from other humans; rather they use "highly restricted principles that guide the construction of grammar" (N. Chomsky 1975: 11). Thus, "learning is only a matter of filling in detail within a structure that is innate" (N. Chomsky 1975: 39). The linguistic formulas necessary for language are inborn; only a relatively few variables must be set, the values of which determine whether the syntax will end up being that of English, Eskimo, Chinese, or whatever.

The linguistic rules and the principles to modify them are species specific. They exist only in humans, which is why only human beings have language (N. Chomsky 1975: 11, 40). They are also task specific. The rules and principles have as their sole purpose the learning of language. They are not related to other cognitive abilities.

The way to make progress in understanding language learning is to develop better theories of **innate universals;** that is, of what constitutes the linguistic rules and principles (N. Chomsky 1975: 207). One cannot accomplish this merely by studying children acquiring language. Indeed, observations of early language may be "quite misleading" (N. Chomsky 1975: 53). Rather, an in-depth knowledge of the nature of the system being learned must logically precede development of a theory of language acquisition (N. Chomsky 1964: last paragraph; 1975: 197). One need not look at many different languages to determine linguistic universals; one can accomplish this by thinking about the nature of complex syntactic constructions in English, since "a single language can provide strong evidence for conclusions regarding universal grammar" (N. Chomsky 1967: 437).

For Chomsky, understanding how language works constitutes a major step toward understanding the nature of the human mind. Thus linguistics is a branch of cognitive psychology (N. Chomsky 1967: 434, 1968: 58ff, 1975: 36), or, since according to him it is almost all built in genetically, of biology (N. Chomsky 1975: 123).

Language learning rules are built in

Other theorists would not go so far as to postulate that a large part of the grammar is built in. Rather, they would say that children are born with certain specific language learning rules or strategies. These rules or strategies, when applied to the language children learn, allow them to construct a grammar for their language.

For example, it has been proposed (Fodor 1966) that children might have a built-in rule that allows them to relate utterances in different constituent orders. Such a rule would help children make the connection between *He called Jerry up* and *He called up Jerry,* or between *Andrew ate the sandwich* and *The sandwich was eaten by Andrew.*

Another proposal (Braine 1963b. See also Bever, et al. 1965a, 1965b; Braine 1965; I. Schlesinger 1967) of this type was that children make use of a language learning rule called **contextual generalization.** What this means is that children hearing a word in a particular linguistic context will tend to use that word in the same position in another context.

Another language-specific strategy proposed is the NVN strategy (Bever 1970). A child using this strategy, upon encountering a noun followed by a verb followed by another noun, will interpret the sequence as an actor-action-affected sequence (See Chapter 4). This strategy is the most famous of a number of similar strategies proposed by the same author.

A strategy that has been proposed to account for children's word order in languages that have relatively free word order is that they build up an impression of the relative frequencies of the different word orders used by their caregivers and match these frequencies in their own speech (Bowerman 1973a: 159-167; Ervin-Tripp 1973: 278-279).

The most frequently cited set of strategies comes from Dan Slobin (1971a, 1973, 1978). These include: pay attention to the ends of words; pay attention to the order of words and morphemes; avoid interruption or rearrangement of linguistic units; and avoid exceptions. More general proposals are discussed later in this chapter.

General learning rules are used
to learn language

Still other theorists argue that postulating language-specific learning rules is not necessary. Rather, language learning is just an instance, albeit a complex one, of the general learning principles that are used in other cognitive learning tasks as well. People who have taken this view include such eminent scholars as B. F. Skinner and Jean Piaget.[1]

The approaches of Skinner and Piaget have little in common except that they look at language acquisition in terms of general principles of learning and development. In the United States Skinner, Osgood, Mowrer, Staats, Palermo, and many others have looked at language from an approach known in psychology as **learning theory.** In this approach learning is considered to take place as a result of the organism being rewarded or reinforced in some way. Reinforcement can involve basic drives such as hunger, thirst, pain, or sex, or it can come from secondary sources, such as money, tokens, or other things that have been associated with or can lead to satisfaction of these basic drives. In the presence of reinforcement, a connection or associative link will be retained between some sensory stimulus and a behavior of the organism. If a rat is hungry and happens to press a bar as a result of random activity, and if that action is quickly followed by presentation of some food, that rat will quickly learn to press the bar when it is hungry. Through years of experience, associations are built up between words and their referents, and between words and other words, and the language is learned. Learning theory advocates argue that the same principles that apply to other types of learned behavior can account for language learning.[2]

An entirely different approach was taken in Europe by Jean Piaget and his associates. This approach has become very influential in the area of developmental psychology. Piaget felt that as children develop they go through several stages in the organization of their intellectual development—sensorimotor (birth to 2 years); preoperational (2 to 7 years); concrete operational (7 to 11 years); and formal operational (11 years and up). Each stage represents a basically different way of understanding the world, and children in any but the last stage will not be able to solve certain types of problems because their cognitive organization is simply not adequate to handle them.[3] People who study child language in this perspective look for links between cognitive development and the development of various aspects of language.

ARGUMENTS FOR THE DIFFERENT APPROACHES

A strong argument in favor of the general-learning-rules approach is the principle known as **Occam's Razor.** The 12th century philosopher William of Occam stated: "Entia praeter necessitatem non sunt multiplicanda." (Entities are not to be multiplied beyond necessity.) Widely accepted as a principle of science ever since, it means that if two theories account for a phenomenon equally well, that theory which is simpler is better. If it is possible to account for language learning with the same principles that account for other types of learning, that is a better theory than one which must postulate separate rules for language and for other learning.

Thus it is incumbent upon Chomsky and other advocates of special learning principles for language to argue that language is a special case. A number of such arguments have been put forward. We shall consider a few.

Arguments for language-specific learning principles

Argument I: Uniqueness Whereas other animals, particularly other primates, have relatively high-level cognitive abilities, only human beings have language. Thus language is distinct from general cognition.

Certainly when this argument was debated in the 17th century by Descartes and his peers (see N. Chomsky 1966, 1968: 1-20, 1975: 40), a good case could be made for this on the basis of the then available empirical evidence. However, in light of current evidence, the case is much less clear.

In June 1966 Allen and Beatrice Gardner began raising a female chimpanzee named Washoe in their home. They communicated with her by means of American Sign Language (ASL). By 1969 it had become clear that they had achieved success at establishing a human language in a nonhuman animal far beyond anything that had been done before (R. & B. Gardner 1969).

Since that time research with language in chimpanzees and other primates has taken three forms. The Gardners and others (e.g., Fouts et al. 1984; F. Patterson & Linden 1981; Temerlin 1975; Terrace 1979) have used relatively normal child-rearing techniques. Others have used a specially constructed plastic chip language, in which the chips are placed in columns on a vertical surface (D. Premack 1976). The third group has used Yerkish, another arbitrary symbol language. Yerkish is 'understood' by a computer, which can automatically respond to many of the chimpanzee's wishes. The computer requires correct word order. The sentences communicated by the chimpanzee or its trainer are displayed in a horizontal line, left to right, as in normal English orthography (e.g., Rumbaugh 1977).

From left to right: Washoe using sign language, Sarah using her plastic chip language, and Lana using Yerkish on her computer.

Whether or not this research demonstrates that chimpanzees and other primates can acquire language is still very much a matter of debate (e.g., Miles 1978; Savage-Rumbaugh et al. 1980; Sebeok & Umiker-Sebeok 1980; Seidenberg & Petitto 1979; Terrace et al. 1980). Chimpanzees can acquire a productive vocabulary of over 130 words (R. & B. Gardner 1972) and perhaps substantially more. They can use this vocabulary in syntactically ordered sequences and make use of word ordering in their understanding of the roles of the different constituents. They have been observed talking to themselves, asking questions, using their language to obtain food and tools, and to express other needs and desires. They have used it to communicate with other chimps and have taught it to young chimps.

The most advanced language acquired by chimpanzees is still quite primitive by the standards of normal human adults. However, when one compares films of chimpanzees learning sign language (Campbell-Jones 1974; R. & B. Gardner 1973; B. & R. Gardner 1974) with those of autistic children learning sign language (Webster et al. 1975), it appears that some chimpanzees are better sign language learners than some autistic children.

Some have claimed that this is not language because chimps have not yet been shown to have mastered some of the more complex aspects of language, such as clause embedding (Limber 1977). But neither do young children. Others have applied statistical criteria so stringent that if applied to children they might result in the conclusion that children don't have language (e.g., Terrace et al. 1980. See B. & R. Gardner 1980: 357).

Still others have pointed to differences between some chimpanzees and what was thought to be true about children. For example, Washoe, the first chimpanzee studied by the Gardners, used freer word order than is often found in children learning English. However, adult ASL has freer word order than English. More recent reports of children learning languages with freer word order (e.g., Bowerman 1973a) show that some of these children also use variable word order.[4]

Others have focussed on flaws in the reporting of research—especially of selecting anecdotal examples of meaningful sign combinations without referring to the much larger corpus of sign combinations produced, most of which may have been meaningless (Seidenberg & Petitto 1979). Clearly, more complete recording and analysis would be useful.

Another problem of editing relates to the problem of free word order just discussed. All of the primate researchers have noted long strings such as *Me banana you banana me you give* (Limber 1977; Seidenberg & Petitto 1979; Terrace et al. 1980). This looks very different from normal child speech, and maybe it is, but it is not unknown in children. Compare the above with *Sofa sit you sit you sit couch,* uttered by a child named Gia (Bloom et al. 1975a: 55). When my daughter was between three and five and even older, she often started sentences several times before producing what she intended. In speech one can tell from intonation that a false start is being restarted, but it is not clear that the same kind of information is objectively identifiable in sign language. It is clear that chimpanzees can and do produce syntactically correct sentences in Yerkish, as required by their demanding computer conversation partner, and when they make a false start they mark it by the

Yerkish symbol for end of sentence. Whether there is anything more going on here than simple repetition is not clear.

All in all, it appears that chimpanzees raised in a relatively humanlike language environment acquire a language in a way practically indistinguishable from human children, except that it is acquired at a much slower pace.

The ultimate level of language acquired is much lower, but so is the level of chimpanzee problem-solving ability. Thus the possibility still remains that language ability is part of general cognitive ability, and that it has not developed to any degree of sophistication in other animals mainly because it requires higher cognitive ability than is present in most species.

Argument Ia   *If animals had the ability to use language they would do so, given the enormous selective advantage even minimal linguistic skills would convey* (N. Chomsky 1975: 40).

While chimpanzees appear to have the ability to use language, they may not have the ability to invent it. Thus when taught a language they can handle, they use it and even pass it on to their offspring, but they never had one in the wild because they did not have the capacity to invent it.

It is also still possible that chimpanzees and other animals do have more sophisticated languages than we are aware of, simply because we have not been looking at the right medium. Recent research on gestures of chimpanzees in the wild seems to suggest that they make greater use of gestural communication in natural situations than we had previously suspected (Menzel 1973, 1975, 1978).

Argument Ib   *"Suppose that there is a general theory of learning that applies to rats as well as humans, and that humans differ from rats simply in that they make use of its mechanisms more rapidly, fully, and effectively . . . . We would then conclude that humans must be as far superior to rats in maze-running ability as they are in ability to acquire language. But this is grossly false . . . . [Therefore] the human ability to learn language involves a special faculty . . . . [Otherwise] we would expect other organisms that are comparable to humans in these other domains . . . to have comparable language acquisition ability as well"* (N. Chomsky 1975: 158-159).

This argument fails to take into account ceiling and floor effects. On a task that is too easy or too hard, differences among subjects will disappear. For example, if the task is to stand up, I am probably just as good as the best tennis athletes. Just because they would wipe me out on a tennis court does not mean that they have different muscles in addition to the ones I have. It is just that the task is not challenging enough to turn up a difference. This is a ceiling effect. If the task is too hard—to jump over the Grand Canyon, for example—the athlete and I would do equally well: We would both fail. This is a floor effect. The fact that humans and rats do equally well at mazes but not at language says nothing about special language abilities. It only says that running mazes is so easy that a difference between the two species does not show up. It is a case of a ceiling effect. Higher cognitive ability confers no advantage, just as the superior condition of the athlete's muscles doesn't show up in the low-level task of standing up.[5] Thus it is safe to reject argument Ib as faulty reasoning.

Ceiling and floor effects have led others besides Chomsky astray. Two experiments discussed in Chapter 6 demonstrate these effects. In the section on mental retardation an experiment attempted to get subjects to determine the type of adjective *risp* was in *The duck is risp to bite* by giving as clues either the sentence *Reading to you is risp* or the sentence *I'm always risp to read to you* (Cromer 1974, 1975). Neither mentally retarded children nor normal children nor adults could figure out and make use of the grammatical principle involved. This is a floor effect. The task was too hard even for normal adults.

Ceiling effects can also make two groups appear to be more different that they actually are. In the section on language delay, a study found a correlation between length of sentences and ability to repeat them for delayed children but not for normal children (Menyuk 1963b). This is a ceiling effect. The test sentences were too easy for the normal children. More difficult test sentences undoubtedly would have shown the same correlation for normals that was found for delayed children.

Argument II: Neurological separation   Language is different from other higher cognitive functions because it makes use of distinct areas of the brain.[6]

It is true that certain areas of the brain are associated with speech and language. Injury to these areas is highly correlated with language pathology. Furthermore, there exist children and adults who score within the normal range on nonverbal intelligence tests and yet who have language handicaps, and vice versa (see the language delay section of Chapter 6).

However, there is no one area which is necessarily and exclusively involved in language disturbances in all individuals, nor is there any evidence of differences in the neurological organization of the areas associated with language as compared to other areas of the brain (Lenneberg 1967: 61). Even if one assumes that language is located in specialized areas in the brain, it does not follow that different learning principles would be involved. Different parts of the body can behave in very similar ways. A primitive example of this is reflex jerks obtainable by striking the elbows or knees. An example more related to language: One can argue that the same principles that explain why some sentences are more likely to produce slips of the tongue— 'tongue twisters'—than others also explain why some instrument panels—for example in an automobile or an aircraft cockpit—are more likely to result in human error than others. Similarly, all the basic processes that result in phonological alternation—pronunciation of the same sounds in slightly different ways depending upon preceding and following sounds—can be seen to occur in fingerspelling (P. Reich 1975).

Argument III: Critical period   The presence of a critical period for language acquisition—and the lack of one for general learning—suggests that language learning is a special, isolated biological trait (N. Chomsky 1965; 206 fn 32; Lenneberg 1967: 158).

We shall review the evidence for a critical period later in this chapter. Suffice it to say here that the evidence currently available does not support the existence of a critical period, and thus argument III is rendered invalid.

Argument IV: Speed   *The amount of information learned is just too much to be acquired in such a short time* (N. Chomsky 1959: 171).

How short is a short time? Children have approximately 20 000 waking hours between six months and five years in which to learn language.[7] This may not seem to be very much time to a theoretician who has spent decades discovering complex relations among sentence types. However, it is not necessarily true that such complex relations exist in the minds of adults or children. They may exist in the language as a whole not because they exist in the brains of each of its users, but as a result of slow change through analogy with similar forms (Bever et al. 1976; Householder 1971: 61-80). The evidence stated in Chapter 4 supports a view that, rather than learning general rules of the type proposed by linguists, children first learn structures for particular sentence types in one specific situation, then later learn to use that form in other situations. The process, to most people who study the acquisition of language in great detail, looks possible without invoking built-in universal grammars. Each step seems to be a simple small step from the previous step. No great cognitive leaps based on other than available data ever seem necessary.

Argument V: Consistency   *Language learning must be a biologically built-in process because children everywhere go through the same steps in learning it.*

Although there is more variety than was once thought, there does seem to be remarkable consistency. Even differences in language delayed and retarded children are more in time frame than qualitative. One can argue, however, that this is due to the nature of the language being learned, rather than to a biological ontogenesis. Where differences exist in relative difficulty of expressing similar propositions in different languages, corresponding differences in acquisition have been noted.[8]

Argument VI: Universals   *There are some features that all languages have in common in spite of the fact that the people speaking them live in environments that have nothing in common. This is evidence that some aspects of language are built in* (K. Katz 1966: 272).

But as different as the environment of the Eskimo is from that of the Bantu, we all live in an environment in which the basic laws of physics, chemistry, and psychology apply. Most of us can see, hear, touch, love, hate, and feel other similar sensations and emotions. If all languages have the equivalent of nouns and verbs, is it because that language structure is built into us at birth, or is it because we share a universe in which there are human emotions and sensations, and physical objects, and actions such as the movement of one object relative to another (Sinclair 1971: 123)?

Argument VII: No good alternatives The advocates of a learning theory or cognitive approach have not come up with a theory adequate to explain language acquisition, though they have tried for years (N. Chomsky 1975: 19-20).

True. Learning theory is inadequate not just for language learning but for learning in general. Learning theorists have not come up with an adequate theory to explain any but the most primitive types of learning. This does not mean that one could not do so. It means only that the task of psychology is not complete. This argument cuts both ways. It is also true that the linguists have not come up with an adequate alternative (see Fodor et al. 1974: 468-483).

Argument VIII: Robustness Language acquisition is remarkably robust. It is learned by practically all humans, even the mentally retarded. Children are raised in all sorts of difficult and pathological situations. The middle class parents who sit down with their children and patiently teach them the names for objects are a small minority. The adult who gives explicit grammatical information is practically nonexistent in first language acquisition. And yet the child learns the language. No other learned behavior is so universally acquired. The development of language appears to be more like biological development such as the onset of puberty than like learned behavior (N. Chomsky 1965: 200 fn 14).

This is a most impressive argument. One flaw lies in the belief that language is the only cognitive behavior universally acquired. Research in the Piagetian framework reveals the enormity of what there is to be learned in the world—things that seem so obvious to adults that they are not even aware that they have to be learned. Consider the example of object permanence. This is the concept that when an object moves from point A to a hidden point B, one should not expect it to reappear at point A, but rather even if it is behind a screen, it is still at point B. Piaget showed that children are not born with this concept, but only acquire it later. But all do eventually acquire it. One can argue in fact that there is an enormous amount of information about the world which is acquired by as many children as acquire language (Sinclair 1971). Still, language does appear to be more complex an acquisition than any other cognitive ability acquired with this degree of success.

The other point that can be made is that the contexts do not seem to be as diverse as was once thought. Almost all children appear to be able to control their caregivers so that much of the language they receive is specially tuned to their needs (see Chapter 3). Children who have been in contact with language only through the TV do not learn the language (see Chapter 6). This demonstrates that this special adult-to-child language is necessary.[9] Impressive though argument VIII is, it does not prove that special knowledge of language is biologically built in.

A biological analogue

Although the arguments given in favor of special built-in language knowledge can all be refuted, this does not mean, therefore, that such special knowledge does not exist. There does exist at least one close analog in zoology. The white-crowned sparrow has been shown to learn its song. When raised in isolation it does not acquire it. It acquires its own song if it hears it during a certain critical period, but it will not acquire the song of other species. It is not the case that it does not acquire the song of other species because it cannot produce it; it cannot produce its own song during this critical period either. Nor is it true that it can acquire only one song. Birds of this species have different dialects and any bird of the species can acquire any dialect, just as any human can acquire any human language (Marler 1970). It is as if these birds are born with a template that will accept any song of their own species but not any other. This seems to be a very close analogue to that proposed by Chomsky for humans (Marler 1977).

Furthermore, at the level of infant speech perception, special built-in mechanisms have been found which seem useful for language acquisition. The [t] versus [d] contrast is one example. These special built-in mechanisms cannot be used to explain why only humans have language, however, because they have been found in other species as well.

The arguments in context

Chomsky engages in extensive argumentation because he believes his is the only tenable position for a person interested in language to take. Modern advocates of specific language-learning rules and of the general cognitive rule approach to language learning do not engage in such lengthy argumentation. This is probably due mainly to two reasons. In arguments between rationalists, such as Chomsky, and empiricists, one can expect more philosophical argumentation from the former. The latter, being empiricists, feel that more is to be gained in empirical pursuits— namely, in running studies and collecting data. The other reason is that in most of psychology truces have been declared between different schools of thought. It is now felt by many that different theoretical approaches lead to different insights. A priori, there appears to be no way to determine which approach will be more successful. Ultimately all current theories will be found to be inadequate and will be superceded anyway. Therefore, the best philosophy is to live and let live, and to try to learn not only from one's own approach, but from following the work of colleagues working within other frameworks as well.

THE CRITICAL PERIOD HYPOTHESIS

Many people believe there is a critical period in childhood when language can be learned, and that it is much more difficult or impossible to learn a language after this critical period. This notion is especially pertinent to second language acquisition, because of the common observation that when a family changes to a region in which a different language is spoken, it seems to be so much easier for the children to learn the new language than it is for the parents. By saying that there is a critical period for language acquisition, people are claiming that there is a biological reason for this difference.

What is the evidence to support this proposal? In biology the concept of a critical period is an important one. Biologists define a critical period as a period in the course of development of an organism during which it is sensitive to particular influences, and after or before which it is insensitive to those same influences.

In embryology, this notion applies to the susceptibility of the fetus during certain periods to rubella or to drugs such as thalidomide. In postnatal development one finds a critical period for the conversion of a larval female bee to a queen bee through the feeding of the royal jelly (Wigglesworth 1953).

Behavioral influences can also be subject to a critical period. A well-known example is imprinting in birds. During a limited period only, a young bird or other animal will become attached to its mother (Lorenz 1952).

A closer analogy to the problem of a critical period for language acquisition is found in the acquisition of song in some species of birds. In order for a white-crowned sparrow to be able to produce the proper song as an adult, it must hear that song in the first 10 to 50 days of its life. There is partial learning if the song is presented between 50 and 100 days, but if it is presented only before 10 days or after 100 days, there is no learning (Marler 1970).

A critical period is demonstrated in animals by conducting experiments in which the individual is deprived of the proposed influence for the proposed critical period. It is, of course, unethical to perform such experiments on human subjects. Thus it is far more difficult to demonstrate critical periods in humans. One way to collect such evidence is to correlate case histories of infants with specific disorders. In this way the effect of rubella and thalidomide on human embryos was found.

There has been some suggestion of a critical period for human vision. This arose as a result of the development of a new procedure for operating on patients with congenital cataracts. When the procedure was first perfected, many older patients were operated on and thus given the ability to see at a late age. It first appeared that such people never had trouble learning colors, but had great difficulty learning shapes (Hebb 1949: 29, based on von Senden 1932). However, later reexamination of the evidence appears to have cast doubt on this suggestion (Wertheimer 1951; see also Pokrovskii 1953).

A similar proposal has been made with respect to auditory perception (Fry & Whetnell 1954). The claim is that after the third year there is a decline in the ability of children to perceive foreign language speech sound distinctions.

Likewise, a 'readiness-to-speak' period at about 12 to 18 months has been proposed (Stinchfield & Young 1938). The claim was that speech acquired after this period is more likely to be defective. However, as is generally the problem with correlational findings, there is difficulty determining which is cause and which is effect. Did late acquisition cause language problems or did language problems cause late acquisition? I prefer the latter interpretation.

In addition to the above, critical periods for aspects of human social development have been proposed by many psychoanalytically oriented writers (e.g., Bowlby 1960; Erikson 1959; R. White 1960).

Evidence concerning bird song shows that there can be a critical period for complex language-like behavior. Evidence supporting the notion of a critical period for sensory or other behavioral development in humans would be encouraging. However, it appears that this evidence is not very convincing. Nevertheless, the possibility exists, and its probability is strongly supported by the frustration felt by most adults trying to learn a new language. Let us now consider evidence more directly connected with language development in humans. Advocates of a critical period have turned for supporting evidence to studies of brain damage in children, isolated children, and immigrants. We shall consider each of these in turn.

Brain damage in children

The adult human brain is known to be **lateralized.** That is, certain functions are known to be handled by structures on the left side of the brain and other functions are handled by structures on the right side of the brain. In at least 90% of adults language resides mostly in the left half of the brain (Basser 1962: 430). On the other hand, musical ability, especially memory for tone and timbre, is handled by the right half of the brain (H. Gordon 1974: 126). This lateralization is said to increase throughout childhood until it reaches adult levels at puberty. The completion of lateralization is supposed to result in a loss of cerebral plasticity, and this cerebral plasticity is believed to be necessary to learn a language easily (Lenneberg 1967: 176).

What is the evidence on lateralization? There are three main types of evidence:

1. Effect of damage to one side of the brain.
2. Results from tests on normal subjects.
3. Transfer.

We will consider each of these types of evidence.

Unilateral lesions   A lesion is any abnormal change in the structure of a body tissue due to disease or injury. A **unilateral lesion** is a lesion that involves only one side of the body—either the left side or the right side, but not both. Table 7.1 summarizes three studies based on case histories of people with unilateral brain lesions after the onset of speech. Aphasia—loss or impairment of language due to

TABLE 7.1   Speech Disfluency Resulting From Unilateral Lesions After Onset of Speech

STUDY	AGE RANGE OF PATIENTS	NUMBER OF PATIENTS	PERCENT WITH RIGHT LESSONS
Basser 1962	1;3-5;11	18[a]	39%
Alajounaine & Lhermitte 1965	6-15	32	0%
Russell & Espir 1961	adult	205	3%

Adapted from Krashen 1973: 65 © Language Learning. Used by permission. [a]Two cases have been removed from this sample as usually reported, because their ages of onset were over 5;11.

brain lesions—in patients over six years old seems almost never to be due to right hemisphere lesions. The same does not seem to be true for children under six.

Let us look in more detail at the study involving children under six. Motor control of the right half of the body is controlled by the left half of the brain and vice versa. Injury to the motor center of one side of the brain will result in **hemiplegia**— paralysis of all or part of the face, arm, and leg on the other side of the body. The study looked at the speech ability of children who had just suffered acute onset of hemiplegia. Table 7.2 summarizes the findings with respect to those hemiplegics under six years of age. From the figures one can see that 11 out of 13 (85%) children affected by hemiplegia to the right side of their body—lesions in the left half of their brains—also suffered problems with language. But only 7 out of 14 (50%) of children affected by hemiplegia to the left side of their body suffered problems with language as well.

How shall we interpret these findings? The notion that increasing lateralization occurs until puberty is not supported. If there is increasing lateralization at all, it appears to be complete before age six (Krashen 1973). Chapter 6 cites cases of children who easily learned a language after age five, so there doesn't seem to be much relation between increasing lateralization and ease of language learning.

Indeed, it is not even clear that there is evidence for increasing lateralization between birth and age six in this study. If there were, one would expect that among those who had right hemisphere lesions, the average age of onset of those who experience no language disfluency would be greater than the average age of onset of those who did have language problems. In fact, there was no difference.[10] Furthermore, of the seven children who had right hemisphere lesions and language disturbance, four of the case histories are given in the original article. In three of the cases hemiplegia followed unexplained loss of consciousness, and the fourth followed a case of measles and whooping cough (Basser 1962: 434-5). If the hemiplegia had been diagnosed as due to a wound, tumor, or disease known to affect only one side of the brain,[11] then we could say that the speech problem was due to damage on the right side. But this is not the case in any of the four histories for which detail is provided. Therefore, in none of the four case histories can additional damage to the left side of the brain be ruled out as the cause of the language problem. This study provides no real evidence that language isn't lateralized in the left hemisphere right from the start.

TABLE 7.2 Lesions After Onset of Speech and Before the Age of Six

SPEECH AFTER CATASTROPHE	SIDE WITH LESION	
	LEFT	RIGHT
Normal	2	7
Disturbed	11	7

Data from Basser 1962; figure based on Lenneberg 1967:151, with 3 cases involving children over age 6 removed, in response to criticisms of Lenneberg's analysis in Krashen 1973.

Tests on normal subjects   There are several methods to determine later-ality in normal subjects. One involves measuring the difference in electrical response of the two sides of the brain in response to a stimulus. One particularly relevant study tested the response of infants, children, and adults to words, sylla-bles, and mechanical stimuli—a piano chord and a burst of noise. The infants ranged from 1 week to 10 months, the children ranged from 4 years to 11 years, and the adults ranged from 23 years to 29 years.

Figure 7.1 presents the results in terms of **R-value,** a measure of the dif-ference in the amplitude of response between the two sides of the brain. When the R-value is greater than 0.5, there is greater response on the left side of the brain than on the right side. There was no evidence of increasing laterality of response to language with age. This was true both between the groups, as shown in the figure, and within groups as well. The latency—the length of time between the presentation of the stimulus and the response—declined with age, but the degree of laterality did not change (Molfese et al. 1975).

The most commonly used method of investigating laterality is **dichotic listen-ing,** in which different material is presented simultaneously to each ear, and dif-ferences in response or error rate are noted. A few studies have found age-related differences (e.g., Bryden 1970; Bryden & Allard 1978), but most have found no change with age (e.g., Berlin et al. 1973; Bever 1971; Geffner & Dorman 1976; Goodglass 1973; Kimura 1963, 1967. For further discussion see Kinsbourne 1980; Krashen 1975; Schnitzer 1978).

There is additional evidence that newborn babies already are lateralized for language. In the adult brain, areas in the left half related to speech are larger than the corresponding areas in the right half (Geschwind & Levitsky 1968). Similar differences have been found in postmortem examinations of the brains of newborn infants and of fetuses as much as two months prior to normal term (Wada et al. 1975; Witelson & Pallie 1973).

It appears that the evidence from studies of normal subjects predominantly fails to support the idea that language becomes increasingly lateralized as the child matures.

FIGURE 7.1.
Infant, children, and adult group median *R*-values for the speech syllables, words, and mechanical stimuli. (From Molfese et al. 1975: 361.) Aca-demic Press. Used by permis-sion.

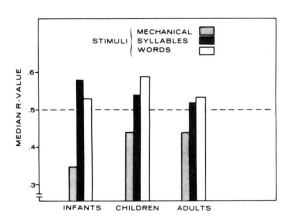

Transfer   If language is normally lateralized, what happens when there is extensive damage to the normal speech areas on the left side of the brain? Can the right hemisphere take over the job normally done by the left? The ability of one hemisphere to take on the functions of the other is known as **transfer** (Krashen 1973: 67). It is generally felt that the brains of children have greater plasticity than the brains of adults. Plasticity has been considered to be inversely related to increasing laterality, but the nonexistence of changes in degree of laterality does not preclude the possibility of changes in the plasticity of the brain. It has been proposed that plasticity is necessary for the natural and accent-free acquisition of a language (Lenneberg 1967; Scovel 1969).

Some of the best data concerning the ability of the right hemisphere to take over language function comes from studying the effects of **left hemispherectomy,** the removal of almost all of the left half of the brain. This operation is often performed on children with acute infantile hemiplegia accompanied by continuing seizures that do not respond to anticonvulsant drugs (Menkes 1980: 267). The operation completely eliminates or substantially reduces seizures in 82% of the children (Wilson 1970). Children operated on under the age of six appear to acquire or reacquire language completely (Basser 1962; H. White 1961). Obviously in such cases the right hemisphere must have taken over. In contrast, adults who have undergone this operation due to later acquired brain damage apparently never completely recover language (Hillier 1954; A. Smith 1966). There is very little evidence on children over five, but what evidence there is suggests that language recovery is usually not complete (Gardiner et al. 1955; Lansdell 1969; H. White 1961).

Similar evidence comes from studies of children recovering from aphasia. When there is recovery, it could be that language returns to the left side, which has recovered, or it could be that language has transferred to the right side. There is a test one can perform to determine which is true. It is known as the Wada test, and consists of injecting sodium amytal, an anesthetic, to half the brain at a time (Milner et al. 1964: 367-368). One investigator found that of five children who experienced and recovered from aphasia, language had transferred to the right hemisphere in the three children under six, but not in the two older children, aged seven and eight (Rasmussen 1964.) Unfortunately, risks associated with the Wada test preclude its use except for clinical diagnostic purposes (Milner et al. 1964: 370-371).

It was originally thought that if brain damage occurred at an early enough age, the other hemisphere could take over with no language deficit. Recent research at Toronto's Hospital for Sick Children indicates that this happy result is not quite true (Dennis & Kohn 1975). The research involves a long term follow-up study of nine patients who suffered acute hemiplegia at birth or within the first 18 months. All had severe seizures and ultimately underwent surgery to remove the diseased half of the brain. Four had the right half removed (RHR); five had the left removed (LHR). The two groups were closely matched. All but two patients were between 6;11 and 20;0 when the surgery was performed. The remaining two were operated on at five months. Results of the Wada test before surgery, if performed, were not reported, but based on other case histories (Milner et al. 1964: 369), the language had probably developed in the undiseased half of the brain originally.

A sensitive test of syntactic ability was administered to both groups. It measured speed and accuracy of comprehension of active, passive, negative, and passive-negative sentences. Compared to RHR subjects, LHR subjects were less correct on passive and passive-negative sentences. They were also slower in responding to passive sentences. These differences were very slight but statistically reliable. Apparently the right hemisphere is not quite as successful at handling language as the left half, though the difference is so slight as to be unobservable except through carefully controlled, sensitive testing (for a more complete review, see Moscovitch 1977).

Thus there appears to be a critical period for the transfer of language to the other hemisphere. Although the evidence is limited and the findings controversial, the upper date for this plasticity appears to be around the sixth birthday. Since the critical period for natural language acquisition is generally considered to be around puberty, if there is such a period, it seems not be related to the critical period for transfer of language to the other hemisphere.

Isolated children

Come on, poor babe!
Some powerful spirit instruct the kites and ravens
To be thy nurses! Wolves and bears, they say,
Casting their savageness aside have done
Like offices of pity.—Shakespeare, *Winter's Tale,* Act 2, scene 3.

The experimental approach to a critical period for language acquisition would be to isolate children from language to see if they can learn it. Obviously, modern morality prevents us from performing this experiment, but throughout recorded history there have been cases of isolated children.

BOX 7.1 *THE NATURAL LANGUAGE EXPERIMENTS*

For centuries it was believed that if children were raised in an environment in which no language was spoken, they would naturally speak the most ancient of tongues. Various monarchs tried the experiment. Psammetichus—also known as Psametik I— a pharoah of Egypt in the seventh century B.C., isolated two infants under the care of a shepherd, who was ordered to remain silent, in order to see whether they would speak Phrygian or Egyptian. Two years later the children uttered "becos," which was determined to be the Phrygian word for "bread." Thereafter the Egyptians admitted that Phrygian was the more ancient language.

—Herodotus, 5th century B.C., Book 2, Paragraph 3

Holy Roman Emperor Frederick II of Hohenstaufen tried the same experiment in the 13th century to settle a controversy as to whether such children would speak Hebrew, Latin, Arabic, or the language of their parents. Unfortunately, the children died.

—Salimbene 13th C.

Box 7.1 Continued

> In the 15th century, James IV, King of Scots, repeated the experiment with more successful results. He claimed that his children "spak very guid Ebrew."
>
> —Cited in Fromkin et al. 1974: 82 fn3
>
> The most recent attempt appears to have been made by one of the Mogul emperors of India sometime between 1526 and 1785. Unfortunately, the only reference I have access to which cites this fact does not inform us as to the outcome.
>
> —Müller 1877: 395, who cites Hervas 1785: 147ff.

On at least four occasions children have been isolated purposely by monarchs for 'scientific' purposes (see Box), but the isolated children we shall be concerned with are the so-called **feral children** and **attic/dungeon** children.

Homo ferus, which is Latin for "wild man," was listed by Linnaeus in 1758 as a subdivision of the genus Homo Sapiens. He described homo ferus as walking on all fours, mute, and covered with hair. Down through the ages there have been reports of children abandoned by their parents or carried off by animals, and a few of these have survived and been later brought back to civilization. The literature on such children spans recorded history. In classical mythology Thyro was raised by cows, Zeus by a goat, and Romulus and Remus, the founders or Rome, by a she-wolf. One can find German accounts of wild forest men, Persian accounts of bear teachers, Japanese accounts of nursing monkeys, and a Dutch story about a maiden washed ashore from the sea (Malson 1972).

The number of historically recorded cases of isolated children now numbers in the 60s (see Table 7.3). Linnaeus's description as covered with hair seems not accurate, but most such children do appear to walk on all fours and to be mute. From the point of view of a critical period for language development, the last fact is most important. As can be seen in Table 7.3, these children have been discovered at ages ranging from 2 to 30, with the mean being about 11½ years. This presumably is close to the critical age to learn a first language, and most did not. However, of the nonmarginal, nondiscredited cases listed in the table, nine did learn at least some language; one even became at least partly bilingual in Slovakian and German. Five who did not learn to speak did learn sign language; one learned to read and write; another learned to imitate gestures. Of those who learned to speak and whose ages at discovery are reported, the mean age at discovery is 13;1. The mean age of those who never learned to speak is 11;3. Thus it is not true that the younger they were when they were discovered, the more likely it was that they would learn language. In most cases, the language of those children who learned to speak was primitive and never attained adult standards (Bettelheim 1959; Malson 1972; Singh & Zingg 1942).

It is a sad fact that there are cases of children not living in the wild who nevertheless have been raised without language in attics or dungeons (see the table). All four for which reliable reports exist did learn to speak.

The case of Genie is the most recent and most systematically studied. Genie was 13½ in November 1970, when she was discovered and removed from the custody of her parents. They had kept her strapped up and confined in an attic room for 11½ years, and they had never spoken to her except for an occasional growl. Nor was there any radio or TV in the house for her to hear.

Although 13½ at discovery, she appeared to be hardly older than half that age, due to lack of adequate food. When discovered, she had no language. Although she had not reached puberty due to malnourishment, her chronological age presumably put her past the critical period for language acquisition. Her language and cognitive development have been studied extensively by linguists, psychologists, and others. The most complete report of her language development describes that development through the first four years following her return to the normal world (Curtiss 1977).

Genie's developmental course has been relatively normal. She began to produce single words spontaneously almost five months after her emergence. Her earliest words were monosyllables in which she tended to reduce initial consonant clusters and reduce or delete final consonant clusters. Her comprehension of consonant distinctions appeared to be superior to her ability to produce them.

Within about three months Genie had acquired a vocabulary of 200 words, at which time she began making two-word combinations expressing ATTRIBUTE-ENTITY, AGENT-ACTION, and ACTION-AFFECTED. Soon after, she began combining these into three-word sentences. Compared to normal children, her cognitive development appeared to be progressing faster than her linguistic development. Probably for this reason certain aspects of language tended to come in sooner. These included color terms and *wh-* words, which were all acquired more or less at the

BOX 7.2 *TARZAN, MOWGLI, AND THE CUB SCOUTS*

Mowgli was uneasy, because he had never been under a roof before. . . . "What is the good of a man," he said to himself at last, "if he does not understand man's talk? Now I am as silly and dumb as a man would be with us in the jungle. I must learn their talk."

—Rudyard Kipling, *The Jungle Book,* 1894, ch. 3.

The two most famous feral children in fiction must be Tarzan and Mowgli. Mowgli was a boy raised by wolves in Kipling's *The Jungle Book.* Kipling is thought to have based his story of Mowgli on Dina Sanicher, the wolf-boy of the Sikandra orphanage (Mandelbaum 1943: 26). This tale is the basis of the names and customs of Cub Scouts around the world. Each meeting the Cubs drop to all fours, in the fashion of feral children, and pledge allegiance to Akela, the Old Wolf who leads the pack.

Eighteen years after publication of *The Jungle Book,* the first story of Tarzan appeared (Burroughs 1912). Edgar Rice Burroughs based his tales on the story of Romulus and Remus and on Kipling's Mowgli (Porges 1975: 129).

TABLE 7.3 Feral and Attic/Dungeon Children[a]

ACQUIRED SOME LANGUAGE	NO LANGUAGE	LANGUAGE ABILITY UNKNOWN
FERAL CHILDREN	FERAL CHILDREN	FERAL CHILDREN
1344 Wetteravian wolf-boy 12	1344 Hesse wolf-boy 7	1767 Bear girl of Hungary 18
16?? Denmark bear-boy 14	16?? Jean de Liege 21	185? Bankipur child 10
1694 2nd Lithuanian bear-boy 10[b]	1661 1st Lithuanian bear-boy 12	185? Captain Egerton's child
1731 Wild girl of Chalons	1672 Irish sheep-boy 16	185? Overdyke wolf-child
1767 Mlle LeBlanc, Songi girl 10	1680 Bamberger calf-boy	1858 Shahjejanpur child 6
1767 Karpfen bear-girl 18	1694 3rd Lithuanian bear-boy 12	1872 2nd Sikandra wolf-child 10
1767 Tomko of Zips, Hungary[c]	1717 Pyrenees man 30	1876 2nd Lucknow child
180? Clemens, Overdyke pig-boy	1717 Pyrenees girl 16	1891 Skiron, the Pindus boy
1860 Sultampur child 4	1784 Wild man of Kronstadt 24	1893 Batzipur boy 14
1920 Kamala of Midnapore 8[d]	182? Salzburg swine-woman 22	189? Justedal snow-hen 12
1933 Tarzancito of El Salvador 6[e]	1849 2nd Sultanpoor wolf-boy 9	1910 1st leopard-boy
	1851 1st Lucknow child 10[n]	1916 Satna wolf-boy
ATTIC/DUNGEON CHILDREN	1858 Shahjejanpur wolf-man 20	1920 Indian panther-child
1828 Kaspar Hauser 17	1867 Dina Sanichar, Sikandra wolf-boy 6	1923 Jackal-girl
1937 Anna of Pennsylvania 5	1887 Jalpaiguri bear-girl 3	1933 Jhansi wolf-child
1938 Isabelle of Ohio 6	1920 Amala of Midnapore 2[p]	193? Indian wolf-child
1970 Genie 13	1927 Maiwana wolf-boy 10	193? Casamance child
	1946 Syrian gazelle child 12	193? Assicia of Liberia

300

MARGINAL LANGUAGE

FERAL CHILDREN

1717 Cranenburg girl 18[f]
1724 Peter of Hanover 13[g]
1799 Victor of Aveyron 11[h]
1843 Hasunpoor wolf-boy 12[i]
1943 1st Sultanpoor wolf-boy 12[g,k]
1847 Chandour wolf-boy 9[g]
1937 Mt. Olympus bear-girl 9[g,m]

CLEAR FAKES[q]

FERAL CHILDREN

1903 Lucas, the baboon-boy 13
1959 Parasram, the Agra wolf-boy 6
1974 John, the Berundi monkey-boy

193? 2nd leopard child 8
1954 Ramu, the Lucknow wolf-boy 12
1960 Mauritanian gazelle-child 6
1961 Teheran ape-child 14
1970 Two wild children in Lebanon?

ATTIC/DUNGEON CHILDREN

19?? Patrick, the chicken-boy 7
1963 Yves Cheneau

---

[a]Each entry gives date of discovery, name, and estimated age at discovery, where reported. This table was compiled from: Armen 1971; Briffault 1927; Curtiss 1977; Demaison 1953; H. Lane & Pillard 1978; Maclean 1978; Malson 1972; Mandelbaum 1943; Ogburn 1959; Singh & Zingg 1942; Zingg 1940. [b]Speech described as being in a hoarse and inhuman tone. [c]Became marginally bilingual—spoke Slovak, understood German, but persisted in using invented language of his own. [d]Had learned 50 words before death at age 17. [e]Completely recovered from wild behavior in three years. [f]Unintelligible speech. [g]Learned to imitate gestures. [h]Learned sign language. [i]Learned to read and write but not to speak. [k]Never spoke until a few minutes before death, when he said "it ached," and asked for a drink of water. [m]Understood "come" and "go." [n]Spoke one word—"Aboodeea"—the name of a girl who had treated him kindly. [p]Died within a year of return to civilization. [q]Many or most cases of feral children have been questioned at some time.

same time, which differs from the normal sequence. Furthermore, there did not seem to be a period during which there were overextensions and underextensions in her use of words, as tends to happen with young children. Like normal children she went through a stage in which she tended to use the NVN strategy, and in which she confused *before* and *after, front* and *back,* and *over* and *under* (see Chapter 4).

After four years her language seemed not to be quite as good as that of a normal four-year-old, especially the auxiliaries and inflections. Judging by the most recent samples of utterances given for her, sentences about 5 to 7 morphemes long seem to be typical, though there are examples up to 10 morphemes in length (Curtiss 1977):

> At school teacher give block (p. 174).
> Father hurt Genie cry long time ago (p. 160).
> Mama not have baby grow up (p. 160).
> M. say not lift my leg in dentist chair (p. 174).
> Mr. W. say put face in big swimming pool (p. 159).

Her language, though deviant, was not greatly so, and it continued to develop during the period she was being observed. Neurological and other testing indicated that her language was developing in the right hemisphere. It is not known whether this was due to isolation, malnourishment, beatings by her father, or an acute illness she was known to have contracted when she was 14 months old (Curtiss 1977: 4).

What can we conclude from Genie and the other cases of isolated children? Isolation in wolves' dens and jungles is clearly not conducive to normal language development. It also appears to be worse than isolation in attics and dungeons. But such cases do not offer us conclusive proof with regard to the critical period hypothesis. Certainly most isolated children end up with a severe language handicap. Is this because the critical period has passed, as in birds, or is this due to brain damage caused by malnourishment, exposure, or some other reason during or before the period of isolation? Genie's language really was quite good, all things considered. Since she started language acquisition at 13½, is she a counterexample to the critical period hypothesis, or should we ignore her chronological age and take her physical developmental age, which was only 7 or 8 when discovered? Although the known cases of isolated children do not resolve the issue, let us hope that no more cases such as these turn up. It is far better that we should resolve the issue of a critical period by other means, or even not at all.

What about language isolation without abuse or exposure? Such can occur in the case of the deaf. In spite of years of schooling, many deaf children never acquire any usable facility at English. In some schools for the deaf the use of sign language is actively suppressed (see Chapter 6), and some children appear to have no effective language for some time. About half of the graduates of one such school did not learn sign language until after puberty (P. Reich & Reich 1974: 70). Many of these had acquired some facility at English, but of this group were undoubtedly some for whom sign language was effectively their first language. On the other hand, there are some cases of unschooled deaf people who were not taught sign language until adulthood, and who were not able to acquire it at that time either. Still, in the case of sign language, it appears to be true that it can be acquired by some individuals as a first language after puberty.

Then there is the case of Helen Keller, who was deaf and blind. If there is a critical period for first language acquisition, it must surely be after age seven, the age when her breakthrough came (see Chapter 2). No one can doubt that she went on to learn language most effectively, and though her ability to enunciate clearly remained impaired, it was better than that of a great many other deaf people.

To summarize, while most reported cases do not contradict the notion of a critical period for first language acquisition, a few cases do seem to be real counter examples. One would not expect any counter examples to a truly biologically based limitation. No female bees become queens without the properly timed application of royal jelly, and no white-crowned sparrows learn their song if they haven't heard it before 100 days. While it is too strong to say that a critical period is disproved by language isolation cases, it is fair to state that the arguments favoring a critical period are not helped by the existence of such counter examples.

Acquisition of a second language in adulthood

Whatever is true about development of laterality and cases of extreme isolation, the impression remains that it is significantly easier for the child to acquire language than it is for an adult, and that in fact, an adult never completely succeeds, but is always left with an accent, at the very least. This impression even appears as a part of an important Supreme Court decision (see Box 7.3).

Does the evidence bear out the impression? There is not as much evidence on adult acquisition as one would like. There is some, however, which we will now consider.

Are children faster at acquiring language than adults? One estimate puts the amount of exposure needed for a child to acquire competence for a language at the six-year-old level at 9000 hours. Contrasting with this is an estimate by the U.S. Army Language School in California. According to them, 1300 hours is sufficient for an adult to attain near-native competence in Vietnamese (Burke 1974; see also J. Asher 1972 for a similar estimate).

Psychological studies seem to bear out the conclusion that increasing age may actually make acquisition easier rather than harder. Fourth grade children have been found to be better than third grade children at learning Japanese as a second language (Grider et al. 1961). Swiss children learning French starting in fifth grade made faster progress than children starting in fourth grade (U. Bühler 1972). Among children aged four to nine learning a second language in a natural milieu, the older children learned the language faster than the younger children (Ervin-Tripp 1974). And of three age groups of Americans learning Dutch in Holland, the adolescents acquired the second language more readily than either the younger children or the adults (Snow & Hoefnagel-Höhle 1978). Thus the available evidence indicates that adults can learn languages faster than children, rather than vice versa.

Adults may learn languages faster, but it may in some other sense be harder for them to do it. If second languages are harder to learn after puberty, one might expect that after that age people who immigrate to a new country would be less

BOX 7.3 *MEYER* VERSUS *STATE OF NEBRASKA*

"No person shall . . . teach any subject to any person in any language other than the English language. Languages other than the English language may be taught as language only after a pupil shall have . . . passed the eighth grade. . . ."

—Excerpt from the Siman Act
Nebraska Legislature, April 1919

On May 25, 1920, Robert T. Meyer was arrested for teaching German to a 10-year-old boy. The case reached the United States Supreme Court, which ruled on June 4, 1923, that all anti-foreign-language statutes were in violation of the 14th Amendment, which prohibits states from depriving persons of life, liberty, or property without due process of law.

The majority decision stated:

"No emergency has arisen which renders knowledge by a child of some language other than English so clearly harmful as to justify its inhibition. . . . It is well-known that proficiency in a foreign language seldom comes to one not instructed at an early age and experience shows that this is not injurious to the health, morals, or understanding of the ordinary child."

Oliver Wendell Holmes, one of two dissenting judges, admitted that youth is a time when familiarity with a language is established, but if a child otherwise hears only a foreign language spoken at home, he was "not prepared to say that it is unreasonable to provide that in his early years he shall hear and speak only English at school."

Meyer v. *State of Nebraska*, 262 U.S. 390, 43 S. Ct. 625, 67 L. Ed. 1042, 29 A.L.R. 1446. Cited by Donoghue 1968: 349-351 and 359 fn 19. See this source for additional interesting historical background.

---

likely to use that country's language. Census data on the use of Hebrew by immigrants to Israel indicates that the age of immigration at which there is a lower use of Hebrew is not puberty but around age 30 (Braine 1971, citing statistics in Bachi 1956). This evidence at least does not seem to support the contention that languages are harder to learn after puberty.

If languages are not harder to learn after puberty, perhaps at least they are learned differently—that is, using different cognitive abilities and strategies. If this were true, one would expect children and adults in the process of acquiring language to make different types of errors on tests of language ability. The reasoning is that if different strategies and abilities were used, adults would master some aspects while children would master other aspects.

This proposal does not seem to be borne out empirically. Twenty foreign adults and 24 English-speaking children aged 2;11 to 4;9 were shown a picture and read a sentence describing that picture. They were then asked to repeat the sentence and sometimes to answer a comprehension question. The stimulus materials tested various aspects of the relative clause (see Chapter 4). Overall the children performed more poorly: they scored 8% correct, while the adults scored 26% correct. All this means is that a slightly older group of children should have been used as a control group. The important finding is that both groups made the same types of errors—thus it appears that language acquisition processes in the two groups are similar (Cook 1973). Two other studies investigated how adults learning English handle object complement constructions (see Chapter 4). Non-native adults seem to go through the same stages that native English-speaking children go through (Cook 1973; d'Anglejan & Tucker 1975). Studies on other aspects of English have also found that patterns of accuracy do not differ with age (N. Bailey et al. 1974; Fathman 1975; Krashen et al. 1976; Larsen-Freeman 1976). It appears that not only are children not superior to adults at learning a second language, but also that the two groups appear to learn the second language in the same way.

In an effort to salvage one last shred of the critical-period hypothesis, let us look at the empirical evidence in the area of pronunciation accuracy. Even if adults under controlled conditions are better language learners than children, surely it must be true that children are more likely to produce the sounds of the language more accurately—that is, with less of an accent. Apparently, under controlled conditions not even this is true. English-speaking junior high and college groups are superior to elementary school children at learning German pronunciation (Olson & Samuels 1973), older Finnish-speaking children are more accurate at learning unfamiliar phonological sequences than their younger peers (Kuusinen & Salin 1971), and American adults are able to learn Japanese words faster and better than American five-year-olds (Weber-Olsen & Ruder 1980). Thus people who have passed puberty appear to be better than young children at learning pronunciation.

As new research comes along, we should be prepared to change our position, but it does appear that there is no support of the critical period hypothesis in any of its various interpretations.

This does not imply that adult immigrants are as fast as their children at acquiring the new language. Anyone in contact with any immigrant family knows that the children do learn the language faster than their parents. But it does mean that the reason for this is not biological. Undoubtedly, it is social. Both the quantity and the quality of the language experience of children are radically different from that of adults.

Children immediately enter an environment in which all their same age peers speak the new language. If they are old enough to go to school, the same is true at school. They are completely submerged in the new language—they hear large amounts of it in context daily. On the other hand, the older members of the family have a very different language experience. Some members, particularly mothers and grandparents, may remain at home and thus receive very little input in the new language. Those family members who do go to work usually find jobs in which little verbal communication is necessary, or else in which the supervisor and other workers speak their native language.

Even if the adults go to school before they move into the labor force, they will not be submerged in the new language, but most likely end up in classes in which none of the students knows the new language. All too often the teacher drills them on sentence patterns completely out of context. Even when the teacher provides an optimal learning experience, it simply doesn't compare in amount of language heard by a child who is the only person in the class who is not a native speaker of English. The amount of contact children have with the new language usually is far greater than that of their parents.

This fact alone could account for the speed with which children pick up the new language, but not with the differences in accent. Here the difference is most likely peer pressure. Children below puberty exert enormous pressure to make the pronunciation of their foreign-born peers conform to their own. I have heard this myself while living in a neighborhood that contained many immigrants. I have heard children laugh at mispronounced words and have seen children studiously practice pronunciation to avoid being laughed at in the future.

Indeed, I have experienced this myself, not with a different language, but with a different dialect. The first time I left my native dialect region of Chicago was to attend a Boy Scout Jamboree. Boys from other parts of North America would come up to me and other members of my troup and ask us to say the name of the capital of the U.S. When we said [wɔɹʃɪŋtən] they would double up with laughter at the appearance of the [ɹ] in the middle of the word. I can still remember practicing hard to change the pronunciation of this and other words that marked my dialect.

Adults, on the other hand, never correct the language of a foreign-born peer. It just isn't polite to do so. And certainly doubling up with laughter is unthinkable. Thus adults receive neither the feedback nor the motivation to perfect their pronunciation that children get. On the other hand, when it is a matter of life and death for adults to master a language so completely that there is no evidence of a foreign accent, apparently they can do so. This is known to occur in schools that train people to be spies in foreign countries.

Clearly there are both quantitative and qualitative differences in the language experiences of adults and children learning a second language. Many observers now feel that it is these social factors, rather than a biological critical period, that explains the differences in second language learning experienced by children and adults (J. Asher 1972; Hildreth 1958; Lambert 1967; Macnamara 1974; McLaughlin 1978; Schumann 1975; Smyth et al. 1975; Titone 1973).

SOME SPECIFIC-TO-LANGUAGE LEARNING PRINCIPLES

The Derivational Theory of Complexity

In the early 1960s people interested in language acquisition began to explore what appeared to be an intriguing possibility concerning the development of syntax: The sequence of development of different types of sentences might be predicted by the amount of complexity involved in generating the different sentences by means of grammatical rules postulated by linguists.

In the late 1950's Noam Chomsky developed a framework for the study of language structure known as **transformational grammar.** He proposed that the job of a linguist should be to develop a formal mathematical notation that could be used to define the set of sentences in a natural language.

His basic initial contribution was to bring together and apply to a substantial subset of English structure three major notions. One was the notion of **constituent structure.** Linguists had for some time noted that the words in adult sentences seemed to fall naturally into clusters, or word phrases, and these word phrases in turn seemed to be combined to form larger units such as clauses. It happens that complex algebraic formulas tend to have a similar structure, which is often indicated by the use of parentheses. Chomsky learned that mathematicians had developed a method of defining the set of all well-formed formulas. Chomsky's second contribution was to apply this idea to linguistics. In the mathematical system one started with a single symbol and built up more complex formulas from simpler ones by a sequence of steps, each involving replacing a single symbol by a sequence of symbols. This method had two advantages: (1) An infinite set of formulas could be rigorously described by a finite set of replacement rules; and, of particular interest to the linguist, (2) the sequence of symbol replacements followed the constituent structure of the formulas.

But natural language was more complex than mathematical well-formed formulas. This is where the third notion became useful. Linguists had noted that some sentence types differed from other sentence types in very consistent ways. For example, a declarative statement and its corresponding *yes/no* question differ primarily in the placement of the verb auxiliary. Consider these two sentences:

The hunters were shooting at ducks.
Were the hunters shooting at ducks?

One can define a mathematically precise rule that derives the second sentence from the first by reordering the words of the declarative. If one writes a rule that refers not to specific words, but to the grammatical classes of which these words and phrases are instances, then one can write a precise rule that will apply to all questions and their declarative counterparts. Such a rule is known as a **transformation.**

(By permission of Johnny Hart and News Group Chicago, Inc.)

Other sentence types may be built up the same way from these derived sentences. Consider this sequence:

The hunters were shooting at what.
Were the hunters shooting at what?
What were the hunters shooting at?

One may say that *wh-* questions are generated by further rearranging the constituents of *yes/no* questions. Thus there may be several steps in the derivation of a particular sentence type.

This process of rearrangement presumably simplifies the problem of defining the set of all sentences. One now defines the set of all simple declarative sentences, and then generates all other sentence types by a sequence of steps, each involving rearranging and merging simpler structures. Indeed, the relations among a very large number of sentence types have now been described in precise detail by means of such transformational rules (e.g., see Stockwell et al. 1973).

At this point we take a giant leap. Why is it possible to describe a language so successfully in this way? Might it not be that such a generative system is successful because a system closely analogous to this system is stored in the mind of each native speaker? And if so, might it not be possible that children learn derivationally simpler sentence forms before their derivationally more complex counterparts? This last leap, taken not by linguists but by psychologists interested in language acquisition, is a theory in itself.

This theory has come to be known as the **Derivational Theory of Complexity (DTC).**[12] Studies motivated by this theory focus on the sequence of acquisition of some set of syntactic constructions for which a grammar has been developed by linguists. According to the DTC, a construction that requires the interaction of two rules will be acquired after constructions that require each of the rules individually (Roeper et al. 1981: 35).

A second type of evidence supports the DTC. Children often produce constructions that do not correspond to any utterances adults produce. If some of these utterances correspond to what the grammar would produce if it were lacking some of its rules, this is taken to support the DTC. Evidence of this type is stronger support for the DTC, because evidence of the first type can also be attributed to other factors, such as frequency (see Su. Carey 1982: 362).

Many of the early observations of the development of syntax were conducted within this framework. For example, when early studies of the acquisition of negation turned up the fact that the negation element appeared first—*No the sun shining.*—this was taken as support for the DTC. At that time the grammar being expounded by linguists generated negative sentences by producing a negative element followed by an affirmative sentence. This phenomenon was supporting evidence of the second type. Later research suggested more satisfying explanations of this phenomenon (see Chapter 4). And since the particular grammar on which this evidence was based was changed so that negatives were no longer derived in this manner, this construction is no longer considered support for the DTC.

Another case in which evidence of the second type was claimed occurred in the acquisition of *wh-* questions by Adam (R. Brown 1968). Adam produced sentences like *When they are leaving?* at the same time that he produced sentences like *Are they leaving?* It appeared that he had the grammar necessary to produce *When are they leaving?* but could not produce it because it implied applying more linguistic complexity to one sentence than he was capable of. However, at least as many children master these two types of questions in the other sequence: They produce *When are they leaving?* at the same time they produce *They are leaving?* (see Chapter 4). This sequence of acquisition directly contradicts predictions made by the DTC, so this theory is not successful in this area of syntax either.

Children appear to acquire tag questions late (see Chapter 4), which would be predicted by the DTC, but a simpler and just as predictive explanation is that they acquire them late because these constructions occur with low frequency in ACL.

Versions of transformational grammar prior to 1977 generated sentences such as *The red beads and brown beads are here* from two separate sentences: *The red beads are here* and *The brown beads are here.* When children are asked to repeat compound sentences such as the one above, they sometimes will produce derivationally simpler sentences instead: *Brown beads here and a red beads here* (Slobin & Welsh 1968). However, in spontaneous speech there is no evidence to support the contention that full sentences precede the deleted forms (J. de Villiers et al. 1976).

The story is similar in other areas of syntax. Early versions of transformational theory derived *the red car* from *the car is red; Noah wants to play* from *Noah wants Noah to play; Washoe was tickled* from *Washoe was tickled by someone; Santa gave the baby a present* from *Santa gave a present to the baby; That's Daddy's* from *That's Daddy's hat* (or some other noun). In the first case, both constructions appear at the same time, with no clear preference between the two. In the other four cases, the order of derivational complexity is the opposite of the order of acquisition (Cazden 1968; Maratsos 1978).

The DTC has also been applied to the acquisition of morphological inflections. The morphemes studied were the present progressive *-ing* in *Arthur is drinking;* the present tense verb inflection marking a third person singular subject (*-s* in *Arthur drinks*), and one of its irregular forms (*has* in *Arthur has money*); the past tense, in both its regular (*-ed* in *E.T. phoned home*) and irregular forms (*E.T. went home*); the regular plural (*-s* in *Turtles meet.*); the prepositions *in* and *on;* the articles *the* and *a;* the verb *to be* as an auxiliary (*is* in *The water is running*) and as the copula (*is* in *The water is cold*), both in positions in which it can be contracted (*The water's cold*) and in positions in which it cannot (*Is it cold?*).

These 14 morphemes were analyzed for their syntactic and semantic complexity. Morpheme A is more complex than B if it involves anything that is involved in B plus something else. On this basis the contractible auxiliary is considered more complex than the present progressive, and five other orderings based on syntactic rules are also specified. Similarly, nine predictions are made on the basis of semantic complexity.

The acquisition sequence followed the predictions based on both syntactic and semantic complexity (R. Brown 1973). This acquisition sequence has been confirmed in other studies of normal children (J. de Villiers & de Villiers 1973b) and language delayed children (Johnston & Schery 1976). Such considerations predict the acquisition sequence better than frequency of occurrence of the form in ACL.

A different sort of test of the DTC involves requests for clarification. When a statement is not understood the listener may ask for clarification by asking *What?* The DTC would predict that if a person was not understood the first time, she or he might recast the statement in a derivationally simpler form. Thus exchanges like the following would be predicted:

A. Everyone had fun who went to the party.
B. What?
A. Everyone who went to the party had fun.

This was tried on children aged 6 to 10 and on adults. For the sentences tested the recasting was more often than not in the predicted direction, more so for some of the sentences than for others (Valian et al. 1976; Valian & Wales 1976). However, it has been argued that such a result is highly dependent on the particular sentences chosen, and that other sentences might give the opposite result (J. de Villiers & de Villiers 1978: 114-115).

What can we conclude about the DTC? Clearly, when it was based on the transformational grammars of the period, the theory failed. But most now believe that the grammars of the period were wrong. There are many ways to express the syntactic and semantic relationships among language units. The transformational grammars of the 1960s are not the only way. Later grammars within the transformational tradition, and other grammars from other schools of linguistics, such as systemic theory (Halliday & Martin 1981), stratificational grammar (Lockwood 1972), or tagmemic theory (Pike & Pike 1980) might well make other predictions as to complexity.[13]

For any such DTC to work, no matter what grammatical framework it is based on, all children must acquire the different related forms in the same order. If some children acquire such related constructions in one order and other children acquire them in another order, the whole concept of the DTC predicting an acquisition sequence is strongly called into question. The more we study children's acquisition of complex constructions, the more variety we find in the order of acquisition of such constructions. This variety in turn makes it seem less likely that there is any validity to the concept of DTC.

What if it turns out not to be successful at all? There are at least two possibilities. One is that children don't learn constructions by means of rules at all, but rather by analogy with other already-learned constructions (Hockett 1968: 93). The other is that children go through intermediate stages in which their grammars are very different looking from those of adults—not just a partially completed version, but different in basic organization. These two proposals are not mutually exclusive; both may be true. At this stage there is very little evidence that can help us evaluate the usefulness of either of these two points of view.

Semantic Feature Acquisition Hypothesis

Another influential theory of language acquisition is the **Semantic Feature Acquisition Hypothesis (SFH).**[14] The SFH assumes that the meaning of a word consists of a set of semantic features (E. Clark 1973a: 74). For example, the meaning of *boy* consists of the features *human, male,* and *immature.* The SFH asserts that when children first acquire the meaning of a word they may acquire only some of its semantic features, then as they accumulate additional experience with the word they slowly add additional features to their representation of its meaning. For example, the meaning of *brother* contains the meaning of *boy* plus one or more features that convey the meaning "has sibling." As mentioned in Chapter 4, Piaget (1928) and others found that children in fact do go through a stage in which they treat the word *brother* as if it had the same meaning as *boy.*

Several predictions arise out of the SFH. One is that children should go through a stage in which pairs of antonyms should be synonomous in the mind of the child. Thus *less* should mean the same thing as *more.* This prediction follows from the fact that *less* and *more* share all their components of meaning with the exception of polarity, *more* having positive polarity and *less* having negative polarity. As described in Chapter 4, early experiments in support of this have been followed by others that give different results and demonstrate that the findings of the earlier studies resulted from other causes, such as response biases.

When the meaning of a word has fewer semantic features than it should, the range of meaning of that word should be overextended in children's use. If the word *doggie* has the meaning *furry animal,* then one would expect the child to use the word to refer to *cats, horses,* and other mammals. And, as described in Chapter 2, they do. However, also described in that chapter were examples of underextension, overlap, and mismatch, which are not accounted for by the SFH.

The consensus that is emerging is that the SFH is inadequate (e.g. M. Atkinson 1982; Barrett 1978; Su. Carey 1978b; Richards 1979). Various adjustments to the SFH have been proposed (e.g.: missing features and haphazard examples—Su. Carey 1978b; the notion of partial overextensions—E. Clark 1977), but these will not be considered here due to space limitations.

Functional Core Hypothesis

Several alternatives to the SFH have received some acceptance. One related point of view is the **Functional Core Hypothesis (FCH)** (Ka. Nelson 1973b, 1974, 1975, 1979). This differs from the SFH in several respects.

One difference concerns the nature of the internal categories the child starts with. Three possibilities are **concepts, instances,** and **attributes.** Consider the case of *ball.* Before children have learned the word, they have undoubtedly encountered instances of balls. The other two are more problematic. Have they also developed a general concept of a ball? Have they developed—or are they born with—a set of attributes that could be assembled to arrive at a meaning or partial meaning of the word *ball?* The SFH appears to assume that children have a store of attributes from which they may construct meaning. Such attributes are not required by the FCH. Rather, it suggests that without benefit of language, but purely on the cognitive level, children develop the concept of a ball. Thus, at least at the beginning, children match words to their concepts. This is quite different from the approach in which the theoretical goal is to explain how the child forms concepts to fit words.

The concepts that are formed are the result of similar experiences with different instances. In the case of balls, the basic activities—rolling, throwing, bouncing—can be found in objects that can vary considerably as to color, shape, size, texture, location, who else is involved in the activity, and more. Thus the core of the concept is the function to which the object can be put. In other words, the child already has a concept that certain objects appear to have as their purpose the function of rolling, throwing, and bouncing; learning the word merely involves associating the sound sequence to the concept of the object as an additional property. This is not to deny that perceptual features play a role; rather it is argued that while concepts are formed on the basis of function, they are generalized on the basis of form. Thus the FCH asserts that there is a separate conceptual level to which word forms are attached.

This hypothesis seems better able to explain underextension of meaning, learning of a concept based on a single example, and the ability to learn a word in a noncontrastive setting—for example, learning *doggie* without knowing any contrastive words such as *kitty, moo-cow,* or *horsie.*

Prototype and Fuzzy-Set Semantics

An approach that looks promising, though quite different from those previously described, is **Prototype and Fuzzy-Set Semantics.** Three notions are important to this approach: prototypicality, fuzziness, and variability.

Prototypicality   Though any given word may denote a large class of referents, a particular narrow subcategory seems more central to the category than other members of the class. This narrow subcategory is said to be the prototypical case. Thus a hammer is probably the prototypical tool; a robin is probably the prototypical bird; an apple is the prototypical fruit; a Coke® is the prototypical soft drink.

Prototypicality can be determined by asking subjects, "Give me an example of X." The most frequent response is the prototypical one. Subjects shown a set of examples of a concept tend to agree on which is the most typical one. Thus a prototypical cup is made of porcelain, has one handle, has a circular cross section, curves inward toward its base, holds perhaps 250 ml of liquid when filled to about 1 cm below its rim, rests on a saucer, and so forth. A less typical cup would be one made of Styrofoam® or spandex.

Prototypicality predicts speed of reaction time to true-false questions of the type, "A chicken is a bird." Prototypical examples are also learned first (M. Atkinson 1982: 59-67; E. Bates & MacWhinney 1982; Rosch 1973).

Fuzziness   Fuzziness refers to the fact that there are often referents that differ considerably from the prototypical instances of any word. Such examples may be referred to by one name by one person and by another name by another person. One can create objects halfway between a cup and a bowl, for example, in the sense that about half of the subjects would call the object a cup, and the other half would call it a bowl.

Variability   What is and is not a cup depends upon the context: With mashed potatoes in it, it will be called a bowl; with coffee in it, it will be called a cup (Labov 1973). There is some suggestion that children become more flexible with respect to variability as they get older (E. Anderson 1975), but the evidence on which this suggestion is based is not yet very strong.

The strongest support for prototypicality comes from a longitudinal study of Eva and Christie Bowerman. Their mother recorded the early uses of many of their first words in such a way that the growth of meaning of these words could be analyzed. This growth of word meaning was looked at from the point of view of chain complexes, Semantic Feature Theory, and the Functional Core Hypothesis. Although examples could be found to fit aspects of each of these approaches, one of the most common ways of developing meaning was to extend the meaning from a prototype, which was usually the first learned and most frequently occurring use.

Consider the development of Eva's use of the word *kick*. The prototypical act consisted of kicking a ball with her foot so that the ball was propelled forward. One can argue that three aspects of this prototypical act are important to the understanding of Eva's extensions of the word: (a) a waving limb, (b) a sudden sharp contact, and (c) an object propelled. Eva's extensions included kicking a floor fan with her foot (a and b), watching a moth fluttering on a table (a), just before throwing something (a and c), making a ball roll by bumping it with the front wheel of her kiddiecar (b and c), and pushing teddy bear's stomach against Christy's chest (b).

Unlike a chain complex, all the uses of the word seem to share at least partial meaning with a single prototypical use. And unlike what would be predicted by featural models, no single set of features, perceptual or functional, can be found to be common to all the uses (Bowerman 1978).

Although developmental research within this framework is still scarce, I suspect it will be found that in general children first learn the prototypical examples of a word, and as they grow older, continuing through their teens and twenties, at least, they come to be increasingly accepting of the uses of words to denote atypical and metaphorical examples. They probably become more and more flexible in terms of adjusting the boundary between two words depending upon context (see also Caramazza & Berndt 1978; Coleman & Kay 1981).

A SPECIFIC-TO-LANGUAGE THEORY
OF PHONOLOGICAL ACQUISITION

One very ambitious attempt to predict the sequence of phonological development was proposed by Roman Jakobson (pronounced *ya-kob-son*) (1939, 1941; Jakobson & Halle 1956: ch. 4). Jakobson's theory was based on three propositions:

Proposition 1: The chronological sequence of phonological development follows the same principles in all children, no matter what language they are learning.

Proposition 2: Language is learned not one phoneme at a time, but in terms of contrasts. In other words, children learn to differentiate whole categories of sounds at once. They do not learn to distinguish /b/ from other voiced stops /d~g/ in isolation; rather, at the same time, they learn to distinguish /v/ from /z/, and /m/ from /n~ŋ/. They learn to distinguish the whole class of labial consonants from the class of lingual consonants.

These first two propositions appear to be shared with Shvachkin (1948), whose work was discussed in Chapter 2, although Shvachkin was apparently unaware of Jakobson's earlier papers. In any case, Jakobson goes considerably beyond Shvachkin in his third proposition:

Proposition 3: Given knowledge of the phonological systems of all the languages spoken around the world, one can predict the sequence of phonological development based on three principles:

Principle 1: **Universality.** Certain contrasts occur in all or nearly all languages of the world. Such contrasts include oral versus nasal consonants (/b/ vs. /m/), labial versus lingual consonants (/b/ vs. /d/), and stops versus fricatives (/b/ vs. /v/). These contrasts are acquired first.

ROMAN JAKOBSON

Principle 2: **Implication** (also called the Principle of Irreversible Solidarity). It is apparently true for all languages that if some types of consonants are present, then other types will also exist in that language, whereas the reverse is not true. For example, in English we have both affricates such as *j* (/ǰ/) and *ch* (/č/) and fricatives such as the *z* in *azure* (/ʒ/) and *sh* (/ʃ/). All languages that have affricates also have fricatives, but not all languages that have fricatives have affricates. Thus the presence of affricates in a language implies the presence of fricatives. The implication principle states that the implied phoneme type will be acquired before the implier. Thus in this example fricatives will be acquired before affricates.

Principle 3: **Rarity.** Contrasts that occur in only a small proportion of the languages of the word will be acquired relatively late. Examples would include the Czech contrast /z̧/ and /ʈ/ discussed in Chapter 1, and clicks, a class of phonemes that occur within words only in certain African languages.

Taken together, these three principles allow one to predict the sequence in which phonological contrasts will develop in any particular language. Figure 7.2 shows the sequence predicted for the acquisition of Russian.

Jakobson's daring theory has generated a fairly large body of research testing various aspects of the predictions made. We shall consider each of the three propositions separately.

The first proposition predicts a high degree of invariance in the order in which phonemes are acquired. Just as in the case of phoneme perception, evidence collected on the development of phoneme production shows much greater variation than should be expected. In one study of 16 children acquiring /w/, /r/, /l/, and /j/, it was found that while there were some similarities among the children in the acquisition of these sounds, 10 of the 16 had unique acquisition patterns (M. Edwards 1974: 217; counter examples are also noted by C. Ferguson & Farwell 1975). Such individual differences are the reason families of young children can understand their speech better than strangers can, a fact that has, incidentally, been verified under experimental conditions (Weist & Kruppe 1977).

The second proposition involves contrasts. The evidence on this point is mixed. Sometimes children behave as if they were acquiring whole contrasts at once, and sometimes they don't. Stephen Burling acquired the contrast between voiced and unvoiced stops "so rapidly as to be almost datable to the day" (Burling 1959: 182). On the other hand, Mackie at 2;2 had acquired the voiced/voiceless contrast in the stops /p/ vs. /b/ and /t/ vs. /d/, the stop/ fricative contrast in /p/ vs. /f/ and /t/ vs. /s/, and the labial/lingual contrast in /p/ vs. /b/ and /t/ vs. /d/, the stop/ fricative contrast /p/ vs. /f/ and /t/ vs. /s/, and the labial/lingual contrast in /p/ vs. /t/ and /b/ vs. /d/. According to proposition 2, he should have been able to produce /v/ and /z/ correctly, but he could not. In Mackie's case a contrast did not necessarily spread rapidly throughout the system to all relevant sounds (Moskowitz 1970: 431, based on data from Albright & Albright 1956). Overall, the greater weight of evidence appears to be against this proposition.

The preponderance of evidence collected in response to Jakobson's theory concerns the third proposition. This proposition, when elaborated, produces very specific predictions as to the order of development of phonemic contrasts.

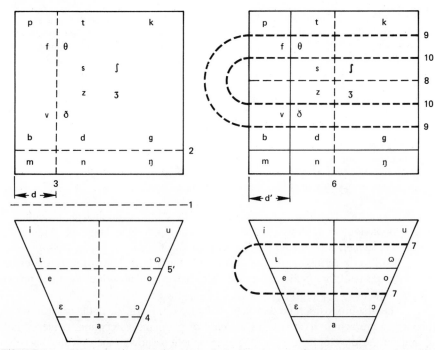

FIGURE 7.2.   Stages in the development of phonology according to Jakobson. Stage 1: the child starts with a distinction between vowel and consonant, thus having only two phonemes. Stage 2: the nasals are differentiated from the other consonants, yielding two consonant phonemes. Stage 3: the labial consonants are differentiated from other consonants, yielding four consonant phonemes. Stage 4: the low vowel is differentiated from other vowels, giving two vowel phonemes. Stage 5: there are two possibilities—front vowels may be differentiated from back vowels (5), or high from mid (5'). In either case the child goes through a stage where there are three vowel phonemes—either /a/, /i/, and /u/, or /a/, and /i/. Whichever differentiation takes place first, presumably the other occurs shortly thereafter. Stage 6: dental consonants are differentiated from those farther back. Stage 7: the remaining vowels are differentiated. Stage 8: voiceless consonants are differentiated from voiced. Stage 8: stops are differentiated from fricatives. Stage 10: sibilants are differentiated from other fricatives. (Based on Blache 1978; Jakobson 1941.)

It is one thing to record when a child becomes able to produce a specific sound consistently; it is quite another matter to collect the evidence necessary to demonstrate that the child has a phonemic contrast. Sufficient evidence for the /p/ vs. /b/ contrast, for example, would be that the child consistently produces *bye* and *pie* where appropriate, and never confuses the /p/ and /b/ elsewhere. Unfortunately, children generally do not have in their early vocabulary such pairs of words as *bye* and *pie,* which differ in only one sound.

To the extent that convincing evidence has been brought to bear on this proposition, it appears that the developmental sequence predicted by Jakobson is followed in general outline, but not in specific detail. For example, Jakobson's theory predicts that /w/ and /h/ should be acquired late, but Leopold's daughter acquired them quite early (Leopold 1947). In another reported case the oral/nasal distinction (*mama* vs. *papa*) was not the first, as Jakobson predicted, but the third (Velten 1943). Many other researchers have also reported counter examples (e.g., Braine 1971; C. Ferguson & Garnica 1975; D. Ingram 1976: 17ff; Olmsted 1971: 48).

Even though contrary evidence has been uncovered concerning all aspects of Jakobson's theory, it is still interesting because the basic fact remains: There is a correlation between developmental sequence and frequency of occurrence in languages of the world. If we accept this basic correlation as valid, why should it be true?

The most probable explanation involves four steps. First, it is highly likely that certain contrasts are inherently easier to produce. Second, those distinctions that are easier to produce are more likely to be acquired earlier. Third, those contrasts that are acquired earlier are most stable and thus least likely to disappear as a language undergoes phonological change. And finally, if over a period of time many languages each undergo phonological changes that are random but influenced by relative psychological stability, then there should result a correlation between order of acquisition of a contrast and the number of languages in the world that have that contrast.

One limitation of both Jakobson's theory and most of the empirical work that followed from it seems to be a lack of appreciation of the importance to acquisition of position of a sound in a word. Almost all empirical work has concentrated on the acquisition of initial consonants; acquisition of consonants in medial and final position has been relatively neglected. In general, phonemes are perceived and pronounced differently in different positions in the syllable. For example, in English the difference most perceptually salient between /t/ and /d/ in initial position is that the /t/ is produced with aspiration—that is, an audible puff of air follows the release of the stop (light a match and hold it in front of your mouth when saying *do, do, do, too, too, too*)—while the /d/ is not. On the other hand, the greatest difference between a /t/ and a /d/ in final position is that when a syllable is produced with a final /t/, the preceding vowel—and semivowel if present—is shorter. Com-

FIGURE 7.3.
Mackie's incomplete contrast.

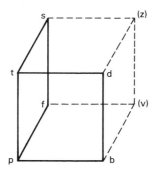

Established contrast

－－－－ Expected contrast

pare *cad* vs. *cat, card* vs. *cart,* and *canned* vs. *can't.* Generally there is no difference in aspiration between final /t/ and final /d/.

The acquisition of consonants in initial, medial, and final positions in the word has been studied. One study of 100 children found at least three different sequences of acquisition of phonemes in different positions: initial-medial-final (/d-/ then /-d-/ then /-d/), initial-final-medial (/t-/ then /-t/ then /-t-/), and medial-final-initial (/-z-/ then /-z/ then /z-/) (Olmsted 1971: 204). Furthermore, different contrasts are apparently not acquired in the same order in medial and final position as in initial position, as might be expected from Jakobson's theory.

Further problems have also been uncovered in the Jakobson approach. Here are three of them:

Problem 1: When children are at the beginnings of their phonological development, their pronunciations of their first words will vary. This is in keeping with Jakobson's model. But once a contrast is established—for example, between /b/ and /d~g/—one would expect that the two phonemes would be kept distinct in all words. This is apparently not true. Prior to the complete establishment of an /m/ vs. /n/ contrast, one child had some words that were always pronounced with [m], some always with [n], and some that were pronounced sometimes with [m] and sometimes with [n].

It appears that not only do children not acquire contrasts across whole classes of phonemes at once, nor acquire a phoneme in all word positions at once, they don't even seem to acquire all instances of a particular phoneme in a particular word position at the same time. Rather, at least in some cases, individual sounds can be acquired on a word-by-word basis (C. Ferguson & Farwell 1975: 431; see also Cruttenden 1970).

Problem 2: Jakobson's theory predicts gradual improvement in the pronunciation of words until they finally match adult forms. A metaphor that seems appropriate is that of a lens slowly bringing a scene more and more into focus. However, the development changes in the word *pretty* that occurred in Hildegard Leopold's early speech (see Chapter 2) demonstrate that this view of phonological development is not altogether correct. A better metaphor might be the debugging of a computer program. Slowly the program does more and more of what you want it to do, but in the process there are times when it appears to be temporarily worse.

Problem 3: The phenomenon of sound avoidance discussed in Chapter 2, in which children avoid using words that contain certain sounds, is also not predicted or explained by Jakobson's theory.

While it can be said that the work of Jakobson has been extremely important in generating research on the development of phoneme perception, it now seems clear that this point of view does not tell the whole story. The Jakobson picture is one of a relatively passive organism subjected to data which has a clear and obvious organization to it. As the organism develops, its picture of the data comes more and more into focus.

It turns out that both the organization of the data and the relative passivity of the organism can be questioned. The organization of sounds into contrasting subsets is not inherent in the data, but imposed upon it by linguists. While some contrasts are fairly straightforward, such as nasal versus non-nasal, other contrasts are considerably more problematic. Even the voiced/voiceless distinction is not straightforward in the case of word-final versions of the stops. Some problems in understanding the acquisition process are undoubtedly due to this. However, the more fundamental limitation is in picturing the child in a relatively passive role. Rather, it now appears necessary to consider the child an active participant in the learning process—a problem-solving organism, discovering problems and devising strategies to cope with them.

LANGUAGE LEARNING AS A PART OF GENERAL LEARNING THEORY

Although in the last couple of decades there has been a bias against viewing language acquisition in general learning theory terms, the failure of arguments in favor of a special language-specific mechanism suggests that we should look more carefully at language acquisition as an instance of learning in general. We shall do this by considering in the language context several types of behavior that learning theories find interesting.

Practice

Language is a behavior that receives significant amounts of practice. Records of Adam and Eve at between two and three years with their respective mothers reveal 642 and 486 utterances per hour, including both mothers' and children's utterances (Moerk 1983: 134). The presence of the tape recorder may have elevated these figures, but even half this amount is still sizeable. The amount of rehearsal is especially sizeable when the limited range of language constructions being acquired at the time is considered—three basic sentence frames (SVO, N is N, N is ADJ), a few prepositions and noun phrases, and a vocabulary of at most about 1000 words.

Another aspect of practice at least superficially seems not to fit the facts of language acquisition. Learning theory would predict that the greater the practice of a particular language form, the more solidly would it be established as a language habit. Yet the phenomenon of overregularization (see Chapter 4) contradicts this prediction. In overregularization, well-practiced correct irregular forms are replaced temporarily by incorrect forms that follow regular rules but have not previously been heard or produced. Clearly a simple "practice makes perfect" model is inadequate.

Imitation

Children have been observed spontaneously imitating new words that they hear (Bloom et al. 1974). Adults probably also do this, though often very quietly or subvocally. I once attended a meeting in which a lecture was being given in ASL to an audience which included many deaf people. When a sign for "curriculum" was used, it was obvious that it was a new sign for many in the audience, for from my vantage point on the side of the meeting room I saw many people covertly rehearsing the sign in their laps.

The same type of rehearsal does not appear to occur in response to hearing a syntactic construction not yet learned by the child. In fact, when specifically asked to imitate such constructions, children produce reduced versions corresponding to the level of syntax they are at (Slobin & Welsh 1968). Furthermore, elicited imitation has been studied as a technique for language enhancement. Pre- and posttesting of Black disadvantaged youth showed no benefit of such training (Ammon & Ammon 1971). In any case, imitation cannot account for children's production of novel utterances, such as *Allgone outside.*

While imitation does occur spontaneously in response to new vocabulary, remembering and later comprehension are not necessarily tied to such behavior. This is shown by people who cannot use speech because of physical handicaps who nevertheless learn to comprehend language. Nevertheless, imitation is used as the basis of speech sound and word production training, and is considered to be one of the more powerful language training tools (Bricker & Bricker 1972, 1974; Mac-Auley 1968; Raymore & MacLean 1972). Elicited imitation is also used as a testing device for determining the language production errors of young children (e.g., Scott & Milisen 1954; M.W. Smith & Ainsworth 1967).

Frequency

Children's attempts at new constructions, or old constructions with new vocabulary items, often occur after repeated successive use of those constructions by the adult. Constructions employed three or more times by Eve's mother during the first six recording sessions were found to be used three times more often by Eve than those constructions that were used by her mother only once or twice. Eve used the more frequently heard constructions correctly five times more often (Moerk 1980).

Instructional techniques

About half of the utterances of Adam's and Eve's mothers can be described as instructional. These include, in order of frequency: self-repetitions; syntactic analyses across partners; imitations; initiating models—naming or describing a referent; vocabulary rehearsal; expansions; overt correction; conditioned positive reinforcement—praise or acceptance; conditioned negative reinforcement—criticism or rejection (Moerk 1983: 137). Some of these techniques, such as expansion, have been shown to be effective in experimental situations, as discussed in Chapter 3. From the point of view of general learning theory, however, the most relevant concept is that of reinforcement.

Reinforcement

A simple notion of reinforcement would be that when a child produces a syntactically correct utterance, the caregiver positively reinforces the child by saying *good* or giving other signs of approval. Such reinforcement would not be

For Better or for Worse (© 1977 by Lynn Johnston. Reprinted by permission of Meadowbrook Press and Simon & Schuster, Inc.)

forthcoming if the child's utterance were syntactically incorrect. However, caregivers do not do this, but rather ignore the grammatical aspects of the children's
utterances and respond to their truth value or pragmatic appropriateness (R. Brown
et al. 1969). In fact, children at the one-word stage whose mothers do engage in
selective reinforcement for good pronunciation and word choice actually develop
more slowly than children of mothers who do this only rarely (Ka. Nelson 1973a).

When children use syntactically or phonologically primitive utterances, one
would suppose that they would find they are less well understood than they would
be if they used more adultlike language. One could postulate that a differential
response to more-primitive versus less-primitive utterances might provide the reinforcement for language learning postulated by learning theorists. This hypothesis
has been investigated. Continuation of the conversation on the same topic was
considered to be positive reinforcement, while misunderstandings, introducing new
topics, failure to respond, and communication repair attempts such as *What did you
say?* were considered negative reinforcement. There was no difference in the frequencies of the two types of responses to more- versus less-primitive utterances, so
this hypothesis appeared to be unimportant to language acquisition (Brown &
Hanlon 1970). However, later research indicates that mothers are more inclined to
repeat two-year-olds' ungrammatical sentences than grammatical ones. Thus there
is a differential response which children may make use of (Hirsh-Pasek et al. 1984).

Nevertheless, many mother-child-mother interactions can be viewed as variations of a Stimulus—Response—Reinforcement paradigm. How high a rate
depends upon which responses can be considered reinforcement. According to a
restricted definition, reinforcement consists either of overt reinforcement or imitation of the preceding utterance. A broader definition might include expansion and
vocabulary repetition. Whatever definition one uses, it appears that some children—
for example, Eve—receive considerably more of this type of interaction than others—for example, Adam—and that such children may develop language faster
(Moerk 1983).

Behavior modification

Behavior modification describes intervention programs developed by psychologists to modify the behavior of their clients. The primary technique is known

as **shaping.** Shaping involves laying out the desired complex behavior as a sequence of small managable steps. At first the client is reinforced for the first small step. When that step is mastered, the client is rewarded only if both the first and second step are performed, and so on until the entire complex behavior is mastered.

This approach has been applied to language. First, receptive vocabulary is taught by rewarding identification of correct referents and not rewarding incorrect ones. Later, vocal imitative behavior is used to convert this to productive vocabulary. This is followed by relating the vocal behavior to the referents in labelling tasks. Still later, two-word responses are required for reinforcement, and so on.[15] While it may not be the total answer, it is not unreasonable to expect that such strategies might give some language-retarded children enough of a start to get the natural language acquisition process rolling.

A major problem for behavior modification advocates is to determine what constitutes the prerequisite small steps on which the more general language behavior is based. For example, if the child tests out low on the number of digits he or she can repeat, will training in this task have any effect on the child's memory for or understanding of sentences? Planning for a language or communication program must proceed in the context of a theory of the language production and comprehension mechanism. The psycholinguistic information helps determine the content of instruction, while the behavior management techniques provide the procedures that teach content most effectively (J. F. Miller & Yoder 1974: 507).

Language and cognitive development

The Piagetian position is that the infant does not acquire language by means of a set of innate linguistic universals, but rather that innate cognitive functions will ultimately result in universal structures of thought. These structures of thought are universal not because they are inborn, but because they are the inevitable result of "autoregulation factors" and "equilibration processes." Any aspects of language that turn out to be universal are the result of universal thought structures, not separate from them (Sinclair 1971).

While people without language, such as very young children and deaf people who have not been exposed to ASL, can think, mentally retarded people seem inevitably retarded in language as well. This may be taken as evidence of the nature of the relationship between language and thought. Language is a manifestation of the general human capacity for symbolic representation (Sinclair 1975).

It follows that a program for early language intervention might profitably include sensory and motor activity not directly related to language, but rather intended to further those aspects of general cognitive development thought to be prerequisite to language acquisition. Before children can manipulate a symbolic system such as language, they must be able to manipulate the objects represented by the symbols, according to cognitive developmentalists (e.g., Bruner 1966; Piaget & Inhelder 1969). Despite the contradictory evidence that children with severe muscular dysfunction can still learn language, it has been found that training programs involving such concrete manipulation can be effective with mentally retarded children (Bricker & Bricker 1974).

The same people who subscribe to this point of view also believe that the basic organization of cognitive information changes as children progress through their various cognitive stages (e.g., Bruner et al. 1966; Inhelder & Piaget 1958; Vygotsky 1934). If language is a special case of cognition, then one would expect to find evidence of reorganization in language as well. For example, one might expect that the set of referents associated with each word might start out as loose associations, and at a particular stage of development might be reorganized into more systematic collections. Those who have looked for such systematic shifts (e.g., Greenfield et al. 1972; Sinclair-de Zwart 1969, 1973a, 1973b) have found only very weak evidence in favor of them.[16]

If no such systematic reorganizations are found, it does not necessarily mean that language and cognition are separate. An alternative explanation is that there may not be a basic reorganization of cognition as many cognitive developmental theorists claim (see Rice 1983 for further discussion).

TOWARD AN ADEQUATE THEORY OF LANGUAGE ACQUISITION

The previous sections have reviewed the status of many of the prominent attempts at understanding how children acquire language. Most of us would agree that no theories currently in existence are adequate. What might an adequate theory look like? This section presents my own speculations on this matter.

Computational adequacy

An adequate model should be so explicit that its principles could be represented on a computer and, given reasonable interaction with adult language users, such a computer would be able to learn language.

Representation of initial and final state

A model of language acquisition will build structure. Before one can develop a model of acquisition, one must decide how the final state is to be represented and what the initial state will be—that is, how much structure is present at birth and the form of the structure that must be learned.

One of the major problems in developing a language acquisition model is that many of those attempting such a model have assumed that the end state must be something like a transformational grammar. However, it is known that without severe additional constraints, a grammar in transformational form is in principle unlearnable.

Three ways out of this dilemma are being explored by theorists. One way is to assume that infants are born with most of the structure built in. A second approach is to attempt to impose constraints on transformational grammars in such a way that they become learnable. A third approach is to reject the hypothesis that transformational grammar rules are the most appropriate way to represent language structure.

I prefer the third approach. A number of theoreticians in psychology, computer science, and linguistics are converging upon the representation of information in network form. Processing does not involve the form of rewriting partially formed language structure, but rather involves signals, or activation, moving from one node to another. Linguistic information can be shown to be storable efficiently in such a network (Reich 1970a; 1970b).

A concept that is a powerful one when applied to network models is that of **spreading activation.**[17] The idea is that when one node is activated, that activation spreads to neighboring nodes. Using this concept one can model language production phenomena such as slips of the tongue (Dell & Reich 1977, 1980a, 1980b, 1981), unintended puns (Reich 1985), and word choice. It can be used to model language comprehension phenomena such as disambiguation (Hirst 1983, 1984). It can also account for some language memory phenomena. I suggest that spreading activation can be used to account for meaning assignment in language acquisition.

Learning rules

Assuming the representation of language information in network form, the form that learning rules would take becomes clearer. Acquisition involves change of the language information. Learning rules are processes that modify the network of information in specified ways under specified conditions. For example, if a referent were active in the sense that, for example, an adult somehow drew the child's attention to the referent and uttered a sequence of sounds for which the child had assigned no previous referent, the child would connect its representation of the concept of the referent with its representation of as much of the phonological form as it could process (Reich 1970c).

Such a learning rule could be stated purely in terms of concurrent activity in neighboring areas of a network, and thus such a rule would be generally applicable not only in the area of meaning, but also in perception, phonology, syntax, or in any other area that is describable in network form. If the network representation system were powerful enough to handle language, cognitive, perceptual, and motor information, then the same learning rules might account for acquisition in all these areas.

Rules of the type just discussed are necessary to a model of language acquisition, but they are not sufficient. They are not sufficient because they are automatic, passively invoked by incoming data. However, as has been described, there are seemingly willful differences among children. Different children appear to invoke different strategies, even though the input language appears to be comparable, as in the case of siblings. The choice of strategies appears to be related not only to the language environment, but also to basic personality differences. The model must accommodate this aspect as well.

Data acceptance and rejection

Children control their linguistic input in two ways. Through the feedback they give to their caregivers, they push the caregivers to use simpler language. This control is not totally successful, so the second method they use is to 'tune out.' The tuning out is recognizable to most sensitive adults and is the signal they respond to, so the two aspects of control are closely related.

One aspect that a model should be able to predict, therefore, given a child's grammar and a particular input, is what parts of that input would be absorbed and what would be tuned out. Some principle explaining the concept of moderate novelty is appropriate, though probably not as an independent principle, but rather as a result of failure of the ability of the acquisition rules to derive meaning from the language and context input.

Production, comprehension, and acquisition

A complete model of a language user must include the three major aspects of language behavior—language production, language comprehension, and language acquisition. I doubt that a theory that accounts for less than all three aspects will be viable. Although children who cannot control the muscle movements of their oral articulators can learn language without speaking, most children speak quite a lot, and the feedback they get seems likely to be useful. Therefore, a computer-implemented acquisition model should be able to talk and understand as well.

If the language acquisition mechanism remains intact through adulthood, one might wonder how it is used by those of us who are not world travellers, constantly learning new languages. I believe it is because language acquisition is not essentially different from comprehension. The act of comprehension of new information presented linguistically or otherwise involves making new connections in a person's cognitive network. If the cognitive network is similar in nature to the network that stores linguistic information, then the same learning rules that are used for comprehension would also be used for acquisition. I would argue that what seems to be two distinct aspects of language behavior, namely acquisition and comprehension, are in fact one and the same thing.

Turning the argument around, if language acquisition is the same thing as language comprehension, this would explain why we do not lose our ability to acquire language after puberty.

SUMMARY

In this chapter we have surveyed the points of view of people who attempt to understand how children acquire language by proposing theories and/or specific models of what is going on as a child learns to talk. The arguments that language behavior is unique and not related to other learning have been analyzed in detail—especially the critical-period hypothesis. In general, these arguments have been found to be fallacious and/or unsupported by empirical fact. The specific theories looked at are founded upon empirical fact, but are not general enough to encompass language behavior at all levels, from phonological to semantic. The models of acquisition that attempt to tie language learning to general cognitive behavior are broader, but vague and incomplete, and thus are also inadequate. None of the theories is explicit enough to be turned into a computer simulation and tested to see if it is adequate to the task.

Having faced the reader with a dismal picture of failed argumentation and inadequate theories, I have attempted to shed a ray of hope by looking into my crystal ball and describing what the adequate theory will look like, once it is developed. Such a theory will not only help us understand natural language but also lead to computers—robots?—that can learn languages and gain understanding by engaging in spoken conversation.

SUGGESTED FURTHER STUDY

ATKINSON, MARTIN (1982)   *Explanations in the study of child language development.* Cambridge: Cambridge University Press.

BAKER, C. L. & J. J. MCCARTHY, eds. (1981)   *The logical problem of language acquisition.* Cambridge, Mass.: MIT Press.

BLACHE, STEPHEN E. (1978)   *The acquisition of distinctive features.* Baltimore, Md.: University Park Press.

DERWING, BRUCE L. (1973)   *Transformational grammar as a theory of language acquisition.* Cambridge: Cambridge University Press.

MALSON, LUCIEN (1972)   *Wolf children and the problem of human nature.* New York: Monthly Review Press.

STAATS, A.W. (1974)   Behaviorism and cognitive theory in the study of language: A neo-psycholinguistics. In Richard L. Schiefelbusch & L. L. Lloyd, eds., *Language perspectives—Acquisition, retardation, and intervention,* Baltimore: University Park Press, 1974, 615-646.

WEXLER, KEN & P. W. CULICOVER (1980)   *Formal principles of language acquisition.* Cambridge, Mass.: MIT Press.

NOTES

[1]For example, Jenkins & Palermo 1964; MacCorquodale 1969; Mower 1954; Osgood 1963; Palermo 1971; Piaget 1923; Sinclair 1971; Sinclair-de Zwart 1973a; Skinner 1957; Staats 1971. See especially Staats 1974.

[2]For additional coverage of this approach to language, see DeVito 1970: 57-78; Herriot 1970: 79-101; Hörmann 1971: 174-213; Houston 1972: 46-137.

[3]For additional coverage see Flavell 1963; Ginsberg & Opper 1969.

[4]See B. & A. Gardner 1980 for more discussion of this point.

[5]If the maze were hard enough and the motivation great enough, I'm sure humans could beat rats by engaging in more systematic exploration. Consider the myth of Theseus and the Minotaur.

[6]Chomsky does not make this strong a claim. See N. Chomsky 1965: 207 fn 32.

[7]See the next section for estimates of the time it takes.

[8]See the Hungarian-Serbo-Croatian, Egyptian Arabic, and Japanese-English examples in Chapter 4.

[9]Schiefflin 1980 suggested that some alternative paths to language are possible and practiced among some peoples.

[10]The average age of those with no disfluency was in fact lower, but the difference is not statistically significant.

[11]Such as Sturge-Weber's syndrome—see, for example, Menkes 1980: 533-535.

[12]Also known as: the law of cumulative complexity (R. Brown 1973); derivational simplicity (E. Clark 1973c: 587); the first principle of hypothesis formation (Roeper et al. 1981).

[13]See Leonard 1976: Appendix B for a quick review of some of these systems.

[14]Also called the missing feature theory (Su. Carey 1978b: 275).

[15]See Guess et al. 1974 for a review of some of these programs.

[16]For discussion, see Bowerman 1974; Su. Carey 1982: 381-383.

[17]Collins & Loftus 1975. In computer science, it is sometimes called **marker passing;** e.g., Charniak 1983.

REFERENCES

ABRAHAMS, ROGER D. (1969) *Jumprope rhymes: A dictionary.* American Folklore Society Bibliographical & Special Series, vol. 20. Austin: University of Texas Press.

ACKERMAN, B.P. (1978) Children's understanding of speech acts in unconventional directive frames. *Child Development* **49,** 311-318.

ADLER, ALFRED (1946) *The practice and theory of individual psychology.* London: Kegan Paul, Trench, Trubner.

AINSWORTH, M. & S. BELL (1977) Infant crying and maternal responsiveness. *Child Development* **48,** 1200-1207.

AITCHISON, JEAN (1976) *The articulate mammal: An introduction to psycholonguistics.* London: Hutchinson & Co.

AKIYAMA, M.M. (1979) Yes-no answering systems in young children. *Cognitive Psychology* **11,** 485-504.

AKSU, A. (1973) Unpublished paper. Berkeley, California. Cited in Ervin-Tripp 1977, 176 as: The development of request forms in Turkish children. Cited in Bates 1976b, 448 as: Request forms used by Turkish children.

ALAJOUANINE, T. & F. L'HERMITTE (1965) Acquired aphasia in children. *Brain* **88,** 653-662.

ALATIS, JAMES E., ED. (1970) *Report of the twenty-first annual round table meeting on linguistics and language studies: Bilingualism and language contract.* Washington, D.C.: Georgetown University Press. Note: libraries sometimes list this as: Georgetown University Institute (or School) of Languages and Linguistics (corporate author) (1970) *Monograph Series on Language and Linguistics* **23.**

ALBERT, MARTIN L. & L.K. OBLER (1978) *The bilingual brain: Neuropsychological and neurolinguistic aspects of bilingualism.* New York: Academic Press.

ALBRIGHT, R.W. & J.B. ALBRIGHT (1956) The phonology of a two-year-old child. *Word* **12,** 382-390.

ALDRICH, C.A., C. SUNG & C. KNOP (1945) The crying of newly born babies: I. The community phase. *Journal of Paediatrics* **26,** 313-326.

ALLER, S.K. (1977) The acquisition of relative constructions in Arabic. Paper presented at the 6th Annual University of Wisconsin-Milwaukee Linguistics Symposium, March. Cited in Bowerman 1979, 289, 293.

ALLER, W.K., S.K. ALLER & L. MALOUF-SAAD (1979) The acquisition of ask and tell structures by Arabic-speaking children. In Fred R. Eckman & A.J. Hastings, *Studies in first and second language acquisition,* Rowley, Mass.: Newbury House, 1979, 117-133.

ALVY, K.T. (1968) Relation of age to children's egocentric and cooperative communication. *Journal of Genetic Psychology* **112,** 275-286.

AMENT, WILHELM (1899) *Die Entwicklung von Sprechen und Denken beim Kinde.* Leipzig: Wunderlich. Cited in Werner & Kaplan 1963, 108.

AMERICAN NATIONAL STANDARDS INSTITUTE (1969) *Methods for calculation of the articulation index.* ANSI S3.5-1969. New York: American National Standards Institute.

AMES, L.B. (1937) The sequential patterning of prone progression in the human infant. *Genetic Psychology Monographs* **19**, 409-460.

AMIDON, A. (1976) Children's understanding of sentences with contingent relations: Why are temporal and conditional connectives so difficult? *Journal of Experimental Child Psychology* **22**, 423-437.

AMIDON, A. & P. CAREY (1972) Why five-year-olds can't understand *before* and *after*. *Journal of Verbal Learning and Verbal Behavior* **11**, 417-423.

AMMON, P.R. & M.S. AMMON (1971) Effects of training Black preschool children in vocabulary vs. sentence construction. *Journal of Educational Psychology* **62**, 421-426.

ANDERSON, B., P. VIETZE & P. DOKECKI (1977) Reciprocity on vocal interactions of mothers and intants. *Child Development* **48**, 1676-1681.

ANDERSON, E.S. (1975) Cups and glasses: Learning that boundaries are vague. *Journal of Child Language* **2**, 79-103.

ANDERSON, J. & M.L. WHEALDON (1941) A study of the blood group distribution among stutterers. *Journal of Speech Disorders* **6**, 23-28.

ANDREWS, G., A. CRAIG, A.-M. FEYER, S. HODDINOTT, P. HOWIE & M. NEILSON (1983) Stuttering: A review of research findings and theories circa 1982. *Journal of Speech and Hearing Disorders* **48**, 226-246.

ANDREWS, GAVIN & M. HARRIS (1964) *The syndrome of stuttering*. Clinics in Developmental Medicine 17. London: Spastics Society Medical and Information Unit, in association with Wm. Heinemann Medical Books.

ANDREWS, G., P.M. HOWIE, M. DOZSA & B.E. GUITAR (1982) Stuttering: Speech pattern characteristics under fluency-inducing conditions. *Journal of Speech and Hearing Research* **25**, 208-216.

ANGLIN, JEREMY M. (1977) *Word, object, and conceptual development*. New York: Norton.

ANISFELD, M. & G.R. TUCKER (1968) English pluralization rules of six-year-old children. *Child Development* **38**, 1201-1217. Reprinted in Ferguson & Slobin 1973, 211-226.

ANTINUCCI, F. & V. VOLTERRA (1975) Lo sviluppo della negazione nel linguaggio infantile: Un studio pragmatico. *Lingua e Stile* **10**, 231-260. Cited in H. Clark & Clark 1977, 315.

ARAM, D.M. & J.E. NATION (1980) Preschool language disorders and subsequent language and academic difficulties. *Journal of Communication Disorders* **13**, 159-190.

ARCHER, L.A. (1977) Blissymbolics—a nonverbal communication system. *Journal of Speech and Hearing Disorders* **42**, 568-579.

ARMEN, JEAN-CLAUDE (1971) *L'Enfant sauvage de Grand Désert*. Newchatel, Switzerland: Delachaux et Niestlé. Translation: *Gazelle-boy: A child brought up by gazelles in the Sahara Desert*, S. Hardman, tr., London: The Bodley Head, 1974.

ARONSON, E. & S. ROSENBLOOM (1971) Space perception in early infancy: Perception within a common auditory visual space. *Science* **172**, 1161-1163.

ASHA COMMITTEE ON THE MIDCENTURY WHITE HOUSE CONFERENCE (1952): Speech disorders and speech correction. *Journal of Speech and Hearing Disorders* **17**, 2, 129-137.

ASHER, J.J. (1972) Children's first language as a model for second language learning. *Modern Language Journal* **56**, 133-139.

ASSOCIATION FOR SPINA BIFIDA AND HYDROCEPHALUS (no date) *Children with spina bifida at school*. Sussex: Association for Spina Bifida and Hydrocephalus.

ATKINSON, K., B. McWHINNEY & C. STOEL (1970) An experiment on the recognition of babbling. *Papers and Reports on Child Language Development* **1**.

ATKINSON, MARTIN (1982) *Explanations in the study of child language development*. Cambridge: Cambridge University Press.

AUSTERLITZ, R. (1956) Gilak nursery words. *Word* **12**, 260-279.

BACHI, R. (1956) A statistical analysis of the revival of Hebrew in Israel. *Scripta Hierosolymitana* **3**, 179-247. Cited in Braine 1971.

BACHI, ROBERTO (1974) *The population of Israel*. (Committee for International Coordination of National Research in Demography) Jerusalem, Israel: Scientific Translations International.

BACKUS, O. (1938) Incidence of stuttering among the deaf. *Annals of Otolaryngology, Rhinology and Laryngology* **47**, 632-635.

BAGÚ, A. (1969) On the rim of belonging. *The Center Forum*, **4**, 13. New York: Center for Urban Education.

BAILEY, N., C. MADDEN & S.D. KRASHEN (1974) Is there a 'natural sequence' in adult second language learning? *Language Learning* **24**, 235-243.

BAIRD, R. (1972) On the role of chance in imitation-comprehension-production test results. *Journal of Verbal Learning and Verbal Behavior* **11**, 474-477.

BAKER, C.L. & J.J. McCARTHY, eds. (1981) *The logical problem of language acquisition*. Cambridge, Mass.: MIT Press.

BALDIE, B.J. (1976) The acquisition of the passive voice. *Journal of Child Language* **3**, 331-348.

BALLANTYNE, JOHN (1977) *Deafness*. Third edition. Edinborough: Churchill Livingstone.

BAR-ADON, A. (1971) Primary syntactic structure in Hebrew child language. In Bar-Adon & Leopold 1971, 433-472.

BAR-ADON, AARON & W.F. LEOPOLD, eds. (1971) *Child language: A book of readings*. Englewood Cliffs, N.J.: Prentice-Hall.

BARBER, V. (1940) Studies in the psychology of stuttering: XVI. Rhythm as a distraction in stuttering. *Journal of Speech Disorders* **5**, 29-42.

BARD, E.G. & A.H. ANDERSON (1983) The unintelligibility of speech to children. *Journal of Child Language* **10**, 265-292.

BARIK, H.C. & M. SWAIN (1974)   English-French bilingual education in the early grades: The Elgin study. *The Modern Language Journal* **58**, 392-403.

BARIK, H.C. & M. SWAIN (1975)   Three-year evaluation of a large scale early grade French immersion program. The Ottawa study. *Language Learning* **25**, 1-30.

BARIK, H.C. & M. SWAIN (1976a)   A Canadian experiment in bilingual education at the grade eight and nine levels: The Peel study. *Foreign Language Annals* **9**, 465-479.

BARIK, H.C. & M. SWAIN (1976b)   Primary grade French immersion in a unilingual English Canadian setting: The Toronto study through grade two. *Canadian Journal of Education* **1**, 39-58.

BARIK, H.C., M. SWAIN & V. GUADINO (1976)   A Canadian experiment in bilingual education in the senior grades: The Peel study through grade two. *International Review of Applied Psychology* **25**, 99-113.

BARNET, A. & A. GOODWIN (1965)   Averaged evoked electroencephalographic responses to clicks in the human newborn. *Electroencephalography and Clinical Neurophysiology* **18**, 441-450.

BARRETT, M.D. (1978)   Lexical development and overextension in child language. *Journal of Child Language* **5**, 205-219.

BARRIE-BLACKLEY, S. (1973)   Six-year-old children's understanding of sentences adjoined with time adverbs. *Journal of Psycholinguistic Research* **2**, 153-165.

BARTLETT, ELSA J. (1974)   How young children comprehend some relational terms and comparative sentences. Ed.D. dissertation. Harvard University. Cited in De Villiers & De Villiers 1978, 137.

BARTLETT, E.J. (1976)   Sizing things up: The acquisition of the meaning of dimensional adjectives. *Journal of Child Language* **3**, 205-219.

BARTOLUCCI, G., S. PIERCE, D. STREINER & P. EPPEL (1976)   Phonological investigation of verbal autistic and mentally retarded subjects. *Journal of Autism and Childhood Schizophrenia* **6**, 303-316.

BARTON, D. (1975)   Statistical significance in phonemic perception experiments. *Journal of Child Language* **2**, 297-298.

BARTOSHUK, A. (1962)   Human neonatal cardiac acceleration to sound: Habituations and dishabituation. *Perceptual and Motor Skills* **15**, 15-27.

BASSER, L.S. (1962)   Hemiplegia of early onset and the faculty of speech with special reference to the effects of hemispherectomy. *Brain* **85**, 427-460.

BAST, THEODORE H. & B.J. ANSON (1949)   *The temporal bone and the ear.* Springfield, Mass.: Thomas.

BATEMAN, W.G. (1914)   A child's progress in speech, with detailed vocabularies. *Journal of Educational Psychology* **5**, 307-320.

BATES, E. (1974)   Acquisition of pragmatic competence. *Journal of Child Language* **1**, 277-281.

BATES, ELIZABETH (1976a)   *Language and context: The acquisition of pragmatics.* New York: Academic Press.

BATES, E. (1976b)   Pragmatics and sociolinguistics in child language. In Morehead & Morehead 1976, 411-463.

BATES, E., L. CAMAIONI & V. VOLTERRA (1975)   The acquisition of performatives prior to speech. *Merrill-Palmer Quarterly* **21**, 205-226.

BATES, E. & B. McWHINNEY (1982)   Functionalist approaches to grammar. In Wanner & Gleitman 1982, 173-218.

BATES, E. & J. RANKIN (1979)   Morphological development in Italian: Connotation and denotation. *Journal of Child Language* **6**, 29-52.

BATES, ROBIN & G. MASSEY, producers. (1976)   *Benjamin.* Program in BBC Horizon series (In the U.S.: Nova; in Canada: Vista).

BATESON, M. (1975)   Mother-infant exchanges: The epigenesis of conversational interactions. *Annals of the New York Academy of Sciences* **263**, 101-113.

BATTISON, ROBBIN M. (1978)   *Lexical borrowing in American Sign Language.* Silver Springs, Md.: Linstok.

BATTISON, R.M. & I.K. JORDAN (1976)   Cross-cultural communication with foreign signers: Fact and fancy. *Sign Language Studies* **10**, 53-68.

BAYLEY, N. (1969)   *Bayley scales of infant development.* New York: The Psychological Corporation.

BEARISON, D.J. & L.M. LEVEY (1977)   Children's comprehension of referential communication: Decoding ambiguous messages. *Child Development* **48**, 716-720.

BELKIN, A. (1975)   *Investigation of the functions and forms of children's negative utterances.* Ph.D. dissertation. New York City: Columbia University. Cited in Bloom & Lahey 1978.

BELL, R.Q. (1968)   A reinterpretation of the direction of effects in studies of socialization. *Psychological Review* **75**, 81-95.

BELL, R.Q. (1971)   Stimulus control of parent or caretaker behavior by offspring. *Developmental Psychology* **4**, 63-72.

BELL, S. & M. AINSWORTH (1972)   Infant crying and maternal responsiveness. *Child Development* **43**, 1171-1190.

BELLINGER, D. (1980)   Consistency in the pattern of change in mothers' speech: Some discriminant analyses. *Journal of Child Language* **7**, 469-487.

BELLUGI, U. (1965)   The development of interrogative structures in children's speech. In Klaus Riegel, ed., The development of language functions, Ann Arbor: University of Michigan Language Development Program, Report No. 8, 1965, 103-138.

BELLUGI, U. (1971)   Simplifications in children's language. In Huxley & Ingram 1971, 95-117.

BELLUGI, U. (1982)   The acquisition of a visual-spatial language. Paper presented at a conference on Gestures, Cultures and Communication, Toronto, May 29.

BELLUGI, URSULA & R. BROWN, eds. (1964)   The acquisition of language. *Monographs of the Society for Research in Child Development* **29**, Serial 92.

BELLUGI, U. & E. KLIMA (1982)   From gesture to sign: Deixis in a visual-gestural language. In R.J. Jarvella & W. Klein, eds., *Speech, place and action: Studies in deixis and related topics*, Sussex: John Wiley & Sons.

BENCH, J. (1969)   Audio-frequency and audio-intensity discrimination in the human neonate. *International Audiology* **8**, 615-625.

BENEDICT, H. (1975)   The role of repetition in early language comprehension. Paper presented at the Biennial Meeting of the Society for Research in Child Development, Denver, Colorado. Cited in Tannock 1980.

BENEDICT, H. (1979)   Early lexical development: Comprehension and production. *Journal of Child Language* **6**, 183-200.

BENNETT, S. (1971)   Infant-caretaker interactions. *American Academy of Child Psychiatry Journal* **10**, 321-335.

BENTON, R.A. (1978)   Problems and prospects for indigenous languages and bilingual education in New Zealand and Oceania. In Spolsky & Cooper 1978, 126-166.

BERGSTROM, L., W.G. HEMENWAY & M.P. DOWNS (1971)   A high risk registry to find congenital deafness. *Otolaryngologic Clinics of North America* **4**, 369-399.

BERKO, J. (1958)   The child's learning of English morphology. *Word* **14**, 150-177. Reprinted in: Bar-Adon & Leopold 1971, 153-167; Bloom 1978, 39-59; Saporta 1961, 359-375. Page numbers refer to Saporta version.

BERKO, J. & R. BROWN (1960)   Psycholinguistic research methods. In Paul H. Mussen, ed., *Handbook of research methods in child development*, New York: Wiley, 1960, 517-557.

BERLIN, C.I., L.F. HUGHES, S.S. BOWE-BELL & H.L. BERLIN (1973)   Dichotic right ear advantage in children 5-13. *Cortex* **9**, 393-401.

BERNAL, J. (1972)   Crying during the first 10 days of life and maternal responses. *Developmental Medicine and Child Neurology* **14**, 362-372.

BERNARD, J. & L. SONTAG (1947)   Fetal reactivity to tonal stimulation: A preliminary report. *Journal of Genetic Psychology* **70**, 205-210.

BERNINGER, G. & C. GARVEY (1981)   Questions and the allocation, construction, and timing of turns in child discourse. *Journal of Psycholinguistic Research* **10**, 375-402.

BERRY, M.F. (1938a)   A common denominator in twinning and stuttering. *Journal of Speech Disorders* **3**, 51-57.

BERRY, M.F. (1938b)   Developmental history of stuttering children. *Journal of Pediatrics* **12**, 209-217.

BERRY, MILDRED & J. EISENSON (1956)   *Speech disorders: Principles and practices of therapy*. New York: Appleton-Century-Crofts.

BERWICK, N.H. (1955)   Stuttering in response to photographs of selected listeners. In W. Johnson & Leutenegger 1955, 275-277.

BETTELHEIM, B. (1959)   Feral children and autistic children. *American Journal of Sociology* **64**, 455-467.

BEVER, T.G. (1970)   The cognitive basis for linguistic structures. In Hayes 1970, 279-362.

BEVER, T.G. (1971)   The nature of cerebral dominance in speech behavior in the child and adult. In Huxley & Ingram 1971, 231-261.

BEVER, T.G., J.M. CARROLL & R. HURTIG (1976)   Analogy *or* Ungrammatical sequences that are utterable and comprehensible are the origins of new grammars in language acquisition and linguistic evolution. In Thomas G. Bever, J.J. Katz & D.T. Langendoen, 1976, *An integrated theory of linguistic ability*, New York: Thomas Y. Crowell, 149-182.

BEVER, T.G., J.A. FODOR & W. WEKSEL (1965a)   On the acquisition of syntax: A critique of "contextual generalization." *Psychological Review* **72**, 467-482. Reprinted in: Bar-Adon & Leopold 1971, 264-278; Jakobovits & Miron 1967, 257-273.

BEVER, T.G., J.A. FODOR & W. WEKSEL (1965b)   Is linguistics empirical? *Psychological Review* **72**, 493-500. Reprinted in Jakobovits & Miron 1967, 285-293.

BIERWISCH, M. (1967)   Some semantic universals of German adjectivals. *Foundations of Language* **3**, 1-36.

BLACHE, STEPHEN E. (1978)   *The acquisition of distinctive features*. Baltimore, Maryland: University Park Press.

BLAIR, R.G. (1965)   Vagitis uterinus: Crying in utero. *Lancet* **2**, 1164.

BLANK, M., M. GESSNER & A. ESPOSITO (1979)   Language without communication: A case study. *Journal of Child Language* **6**, 329-352.

BLANTON, M. (1917)   The behavior of the human infant during the first thirty days of life. *Psychological Review* **24**, 456-483.

BLANTON, MARGARET G. & S. BLANTON (1919)   *Speech training for children*. New York: Century: Cited in M.M. Nice, A child who would not talk. *The Pedagogical Seminary (Journal of Genetic Psychology)*, 1925, **32**, 105-142 (Nice excerpt reprinted as: The child as language creator, in Blumenthal 1970, 107-112; Blanton & Blanton citation on p. 110).

BLISS, CHARLES K. (1965)   *Semantography (Blissymbolics), 2nd ed.* Sydney, Australia: Semantography (Blissymbolics) Publications.

BLOODSTEIN, O. (1960)   The development of stuttering: I. Changes in nine basic features. *Journal of Speech and Hearing Disorders* **25**, 219-237.

BLOODSTEIN, OLIVER (1975)   *A handbook on stuttering, revised ed.* Chicago: National Easter Seal Society for Crippled Children and Adults.

BLOODSTEIN, O., J. ALPER & P.K. ZISK (1965)   Stuttering as an outgrowth of normal disfluency. In Dominic A. Barbara, ed., *New directions in stuttering: Theory and practice*, Springfield, Ill.: Charles C. Thomas, 1965, 531-543.

BLOODSTEIN, O. & B.F. GANTWERK (1967)   Grammatical function in relation to stuttering in young children. *Journal of Speech and Hearing Research* **10**, 786-789.

BLOOM, L. (1967) A comment on Lee's "Developmental sentence types: A method for comparing normal and deviant syntactic development." *Journal of Speech and Hearing Disorders* **32**, 294-296.

BLOOM, LOIS (1970) *Language development: Form and function in emerging grammars.* Cambridge, Mass., M.I.T. Press.

BLOOM, LOIS (1973) *One word at a time.* The Hague: Mouton. Excerpt in Bloom 1978, 161-165.

BLOOM, L. (1974) Talking, understanding, and thinking. In Schiefelbusch & Lloyd 1974, 285-311.

BLOOM, LOIS, ed. (1978) *Readings in language development.* New York: John Wiley & Sons.

BLOOM, L. (1984) Review of M. Atkinson, 'Explanations in the study of child language development.' *Journal of Child Language* **11**, 215-222.

BLOOM, L., L. HOOD & P. LIGHTBOWN (1974) Imitation in language development: If, when and why. *Cognitive Psychology* **6**, 380-420.

BLOOM, LOIS & M. LAHEY (1978) *Language development and language disorders.* New York: Wiley.

BLOOM, L., P. LIGHTBOWN & L. HOOD (1975a) Structure and variation in child language. *Monographs of the Society for Research in Child Development* **40.** Excerpt in Bloom 1978, 231-238.

BLOOM, L., S. MERKIN & J. WOOTEN (1982) Wh-questions: Linguistic factors that contribute to the sequence of acquisition. *Child Development* **53**, 1084-1092.

BLOOM, L.P. MILLER & L. HOOD (1975b) Variation and reduction as aspects of competence in language development. In Anne D. Pick, ed., *Minnesota symposia on child psychology, vol. 9,* Minneapolis: University of Minnesota Press, 1975, 3-55. Reprinted in Bloom 1978, 169-216.

BLOOM, L., L. ROCISSANO & L. HOOD (1976) Adult-child discourse: Developmental interaction between information processing and linguistic knowledge. *Cognitive Psychology* **8**, 521-552.

BLOUNT, B.G. (1969) *Acquisition of language by Luo children.* Ph.D. dissertation. Berkeley: University of California. Cited in R. Brown 1973.

BLOUNT, B.G. (1972) Parental speech and language acquisition: Some Luo and Samoan examplex. *Anthropological Linguistics* **14**, 119-130.

BLOUNT, B.G. & E.J. PADGUG (1977) Prosodic, paralinguistic, and interactional features in parent-child speech: English and Spanish. *Journal of Child Language* **4**, 67-86.

BLUMENTHAL, ARTHUR L. (1970) *Language and psychology.* New York: Wiley.

BOHANNON, J.L. III & A.L. MARQUIS (1977) Children's control of adult speech. *Child Development* **48**, 1002-1008.

BOHME, G. (1968) Stammering and cerebral lesions in early childhood. Examinations of 802 children and adults with cerebral lesions. *Folia Phoniatrica* **20**, 239-249.

BONVILLIAN, J.D. & K.E. NELSON (1978) Sign language acquisition in a mute autistic boy. *Journal of Speech and Hearing Disorders* **41**, 339-347. Reprinted in Lahey 1978, 409-417.

BONVILLIAN, J.D. & K.E. NELSON (1978) Development of sign language in autistic children and other language-handicapped individuals. In Siple 1978, 187-212.

BORDLEY, J.E. & W.G. HARDY (1951) The etiology of deafness in young children. *Acta Otolaryngolica* **40**, 72-79.

BORNSTEIN, HARRY & K.L. SAULNIER (1969) *The comprehensive Signed English dictionary.* Washington, D.C.: Gallaudet College Press.

BOUKYDIS, C.F.Z. & R.L. BURGESS (1982) Adult physiological response to infant cries: Effects of temperament of infant, parental status, and gender. *Child Development* **53**, 1291-1298.

BOVET, P. (1932) *Bilinguisme et education.* Report fait pour la Commission du Bilinguisme, Geneve. Cited in Engle 1975.

BOWERMAN, MELISSA (1973a) *Early syntactic development: A cross-linguistic study with special reference to Finnish.* Cambridge: Cambridge University Press.

BOWERMAN, M. (1973b) Structural relationships in children's utterances: Syntactic or semantic? In Moore 1973, 197-213. Reprinted in expanded form in Bloom 1978, 217-230.

BOWERMAN, M. (1974) Discussion summary—Development of concepts underlying language. In Schiefelbusch & Lloyd 1974, 191-209.

BOWERMAN, M. (1976) Semantic factors in the acquisition of rules for word use and sentence construction. In Morehead & Morehead 1976, 99-179.

BOWERMAN, M. (1978) The acquisition of word meaning: An investigation into some current conflicts. In Waterson & Snow 1978, 263-287.

BOWERMAN, M. (1979) The acquisition of complex sentences. In Fletcher & Garman 1979, 285-305.

BOWERMAN, M. (1982) Reorganizational processes in lexical and syntactic development. In Wanner & Gleitman 1982, 319-346.

BOWEY, J.A. (1982) The structural processing of the truncated passive in children and adults. *Journal of Psycholinguistic Research* **11**, 417-436.

BOWLBY, JOHN (1960) Grief and mourning in infancy and early childhood. *Psychoanalytic Study of the Child* **15**, 9-52.

BOYD, P.A. (1975) The development of grammar categories in Spanish by Anglo children learning a second language. *TESOL Quarterly* **9**, 125-135.

BOYD, W. (1914) The development of a child's vocabulary. *Pedagogical Seminary* **21**, 95-124.

BRADBURY, B. & E.A. LUNZER (1972) The learning of grammatical inflexions in normal and subnormal children. *Journal of Child Psychology and Psychiatry* **13**, 239-248.

BRAINE, M.D.S. (1963a)   The ontogeny of English phrase structure: The first phase. *Language* **39,** 1-14. Reprinted in: Bar-Adon & Leopold 1971, 279-289; Bloom 1978, 60-73.

BRAINE, M.D.S. (1963b)   On learning the grammatical order of words. *Psychological Review* **70,** 323-348. Reprinted in: Bar-Adon & Leopold 1971, 242-263; Jakobovits & Miron 1967, 232-256.

BRAINE, M.D.S. (1965)   On the basis of phrase structure: A reply to Bever, Fodor & Weksel. *Psychological Review* **72,** 483-492. Reprinted in Jakobovits & Miron 1967, 274-284.

BRAINE, M.D.S. (1971)   The acquisition of language in infant and child. In Carroll E. Reed, ed., *The learning of language,* New York: Appleton-Century-Crofts, 1971, 7-96.

BRAINE, M.D.S. (1976)   Children's first word combinations. *Monographs of the society for Research in Child Development* **41,** Serial 164.

BRAINERD, C.J. & M. PRESSLEY, eds. (1982)   *Verbal processes in children: Progress in cognitive development research.* New York: Springer-Verlag.

BRAM, S., M. MEYER & P. SUTHERLAND (1977)   A relationship between motor control and language development in an autistic child. *Journal of Autism and Childhood Schizophrenia* **7,** 57-67.

BRANIGAN, G. (1976)   Sequences of single words as structural units. *Papers and Reports on Child Language Development* **11,** 60-70.

BRANIGAN, G. (1979)   Some reasons why successive single word utterances are not. *Journal of Child Language* **6,** 411-421.

BRASEL, K.E. & S.P. QUIGLEY (1977)   Influence of certain language and communication environments in early childhood on the development of language in deaf individuals. *Journal of Speech and Hearing Research* **20,** 95-107.

BRAUNWALD, S.R. (1978)   Context, word and meaning: Towards a communicational analysis of lexical acquisition. In Lock 1978, 485-527.

BRAZELTON, T.B. (1962)   Crying in infancy. *Pediatrics* **29,** 579-588.

BRENER, R. (1983)   Learning the deictic meaning of third person pronouns. *Journal of Psycholinguistic Research* **12,** 235-262.

BRENNEIS, D. & LEIN (1977)   "You fruithead": A sociolinguistic approach to children's dispute settlement. In Ervin-Tripp & Mitchell-Kernan 1977, 49-65.

BREWER, W.F. & J.B. STONE (1975)   Acquisition of spatial antonym pairs. *Journal of Experimental Child Psychology* **19,** 299-307.

BRICKER, W.A. & D.D. BRICKER (1972)   Assessment and modification of verbal imitation with low-functioning retarded children. *Journal of Speech and Hearing Research* **15,** 690-698.

BRICKER, W.A. & D.D. BRICKER (1974)   An early language training strategy. In Scheifelbusch & Lloyd 1974, 431-468.

BRIDGER, W. (1961)   Sensory habituation and discrimination in the human neonate. *American Journal of Psychiatry* **117,** 991-996.

BRIFFAULT, ROBERT (1927)   *The mothers.* New York: Macmillan.

BRITISH NATIONAL UNIFORM TYPE COMMITTEE, ed. (1971)   *Standard English Braille—Grades I and II.* London: Royal National Institute for the Blind.

BRODBECK, A. & O. IRWIN (1946)   The speech behavior of infants without families. *Child Development* **17,** 145-156.

BROEN, P. (1972)   The verbal environment of the language-learning child. *American Speech and Hearing Association Monographs* **14.**

BROWN, E. (1978)   *Aids for visually handicapped people: What there is and where to get it.* Ontario: Canadian National Institute for the Blind.

BROWN, H.D. (1971)   Children's comprehension of relativized English sentences. *Child Development* **42,** 1923-1926.

BROWN, K.S. (1969)   Genetic and environmental factors in profound prelingual deafness. *The Medical Clinics of North America* **53,** 741-772.

BROWN, R. (1957)   Linguistic determinism and the part of speech. *Journal of Abnormal and Social Psychology* **55,** 1-5. Reprinted in R. Brown 1970b, 16-27; Saporta 1961, 503-509.

BROWN, R. (1968)   The development of wh-questions in child speech. *Journal of Verbal Learning and Verbal Behavior* **7,** 279-290. Reprinted in Bloom 1978, 239-253.

BROWN, R. (1970a)   The first sentences of child and chimpanzee. In R. Brown 1970b, 208-231. Reprinted in: Ferguson & Slobin 1973, 445-462; Sebeok & Umiker-Sebeok 1980, 85-101.

BROWN, ROGER (1970b)   *Psycholinguistics.* New York: Free Press.

BROWN, ROGER (1973)   *A first language: The early stages.* Cambridge, Mass.: Harvard University Press.

BROWN, R. & U. BELLUGI (1964)   Three processes in the child's acquisition of syntax. *Harvard Educational Review* **33,** 133-157. Reprinted in: Bar-Adon & Leopold 1971, 307-318; R. Brown 1970b, 75-99; Paul H. Mussen, J.J. Conger & J. Kagan, eds., *Readings in child development and personality, 2nd ed.,* New York: Harper & Row, 1970, 211-227.

BROWN, R., C. CAZDEN & U. BELLUGI (1969)   The child's grammar from I to III. In John P. Hill, ed., *Minnesota Symposia on Child Psychology, vol. II,* Minneapolis: University of Minnesota Press, 1969, 28-73. Reprinted in: Bar-Adon & Leopold 1971, 382-412; R. Brown 1970b, 100-154; Ferguson & Slobin 1973, 295-333.

BROWN, R. & C. FRASER (1963)   The acquisition of syntax. In Charles N. Cofer & B. Musgrave, eds., *Verbal behavior and learning: Problems and processes,* New York: McGraw-Hill, 1963, 158-201. Reprinted in Bellugi & Brown 1964, 43-79.

BROWN, R. & C. HANLON (1970) Derivational complexity and order of acquisition in child speech. In Hayes 1970, 11-53. Reprinted in R. Brown 1970b, 155-207.

BROWN, S.F. (1937) The influence of grammatical function on the incidence of stuttering. *Journal of Speech Disorders* **2**, 207-215.

BROWN, S.F. (1938) Stuttering with relation to word accent and word position. *Journal of Abnormal and Social Psychology* **33**, 112-120.

BROWN, S.F. & A. MOREN (1942) The frequency of stuttering in relation to word length during oral reading. *Journal of Speech Disorders* **7**, 153-159.

BRUCK, M., W.E. LAMBERT & G.R. TUCKER (1976) Cognitive consequences of bilingual schooling: The St. Lambert project through grade six. *International Journal of Psycholinguistics* **6**, 13-33.

BRUNER, J.S. (1966) *Toward a theory of instruction.* New York: Norton.

BRUNER, J.S. (1974/75) From communication to language—A psychological perspective. *Cognition* **3**, 255-287.

BRUNER, JEROME S., R. OLVER & P. GREENFIELD (1966) *Studies in cognitive growth.* New York: Wiley.

BRYDEN, M.P. (1970) Laterality effects in dichotic listening: Relations with handedness and reading ability in children. *Neuropsychologia* **8**.

BRYDEN, M.P. & F. ALLARD (1978) Dichotic listening and the development of linguistic processes. In Marcel Kinsbourne, ed., *The assymetrical function of the brain.* New York: Cambridge University Press, 1978, 392-404.

BUBENIK, V. (1978) The acquisition of Czech in the English environment. In Paradis 1978, 3-12.

BÜHLER, CHARLOTTE (1931) *Kindheit und Jugend, 3rd ed.* Leipzig: Hirzel. Cited in McCarthy 1954, 568.

BÜHLER, URS B. (1972) *Empirische und lernpsychologische Beiträge zur Wahl des Zeitpunktes für den Fremdsprachunterrichtsbeginn; Lernpsychologisch interpretierte Leistungsmessungen im Frage Französischunterricht an Primarschulen des Kantons Zürich.* Zürich: Orel Füssli. Cited in McLaughlin 1978, 57.

BULLEN, A.K. (1945) A cross-cultural approach to the problem of stuttering. *Child Development* **16**, 1-88.

BULLOWA, MARGARET, ed. (1979) *Before speech; The beginning of interpersonal communication.* Cambridge: Cambridge University Press.

BURKE, S.J. (1974) Language acquisition, language learning, and language teaching. *International Review of Applied Linguistics in Language Teaching* **12**, 53-68.

BURLESON, B.R. (1982) The development of comforting communication skills in childhood and adolescence. *Child Development* **53**, 1578-1588.

BURLING, R. (1959) Language development of a Garo- and English-speaking child. *Word* **15**, 45-68. Reprinted in: Bar-Adon & Leopold 1971, 170-185; Ferguson & Slobin 1973, 69-90; Hatch 1978, 54-75.

BURROUGHS, E.R. (1912) Tarzan of the Apes. *All-Story Magazine,* October.

BURTT, H.E. (1941) An experimental study of early childhood memory. *Journal of Genetic Psychology* **58**, 435-439.

BUSTAMANTE, H., M. VAN OVERBEKE & A. VERDOODT (1978) Bilingual education in Belgium. In Spolsky & Coomer 1978, 3-21

BYRNE, LIONER S.R. & E.L. CHURCHILL (1950) *A comprehensive French Grammar with classified vocabularies.* Oxford: Basil Blackwell.

CAIRNS, HELEN S. & C.E. CAIRNS (1976) *Psycholinguistics: A cognitive view of language.* New York: Holt, Rinehart & Winston.

CALCULATOR, S. & C. DOLLAGHAN (1982) The use of communication boards in a residential setting: An evaluation. *Journal of Speech and Hearing Disorders* **47**, 281-287.

CALCULATOR, S. & C.D'A. LUCHKO (1983) Evaluating the effectiveness of a communication board training program. *Journal of Speech and Hearing Disorders* **48**, 185-191.

CAMBON, J. & H. SINCLAIR (1974) Relations between syntax and semantics: Are they 'easy to see'? *British Journal of Psychology* **65**, 133-140.

CAMPBELL, ROBIN N. & P.T. SMITH, eds. (1978a) *Recent advances in the psychology of language: Language development and the mother-child interaction, vol. 4a.* New York: Plenum.

CAMPBELL-JONES, SUSAN (1974) *The first signs of Washoe.* Film of television show in NOVA series. Boston: WGBH-TV.

CANCINO, H., E.J. ROSANSKY & J.H. SCHUMANN (1974) Testing hypotheses about second language acquisition: The copula and the negative in three subjects. *Working Papers in Bilingualism* **3**, 80-96.

CANCINO, H., E.J., ROSANSKY & J.H. SCHUMANN (1975) The acquisition of the English auxiliary by native Spanish speakers. *TESOL Quarterly* **9**, 421-430.

CAPREZ, G., H. SINCLAIR & B. STUDER (1971) Endwicklung der passiveform im schweizerdeutschen. *Archives de Psychologie* **41**, 23-52.

CARAMAZZA, A. & R.S. BERNDT (1978) Semantic and syntactic processes in aphasia: A review of the literature. *Psychological Bulletin* **85**, 898-918.

CAREY, SUSAN (n.d.) Research cited by de Villiers & de Villiers 1978, 135.

CAREY, SUSAN (1978a) Less may never mean more. In Campbell & Smith 1978a, 109-132.

CAREY, SUSAN (1978b) The child as word learner. In Halle et al. 1978, 264-293.

CAREY, SUSAN (1982) Semantic development: The state of the art. In Wanner & Gleitman 1982, 347-389.

CAREY, SUSAN & T. CONSIDINE (1973) The domain of comparative adjectives. Unpublished paper. Cambridge, Mass.: M.I.T. Cited in de Villiers & de Villiers 1978, 137.

CAREY, SUSAN & M. POTTER (1976) The representation of size: Conceptual and lexical development. Paper presented at the New England Child Language Association, Boston University. Cited in Susan Carey 1978b, 279.

CARMICHAEL, LEONARD (1946a)   The onset and early development of behavior. In Carmichael 1946b, 43-166.
CARMICHAEL, LEONARD (1946b)   *Manual of child psychology.* New York: Wiley.
CARPENTER, G. (1973)   Mother-stranger discrimination in the early weeks of life. Paper presented at the meeting of the Society for Research in Child Development. Philadelphia, March. Cited in Lyons-Ruth 1977.
CARRELL, P.L. (1981)   Children's understanding of indirect requests: Comparing child and adult comprehension. *Journal of Child Language* **8**, 329-345.
CARROLL, JOHN B. (1964)   *Language and thought.* Englewood Cliffs, N.J.: Prentice-Hall.
CARROLL, JOHN B. (1967)   *The foreign language attainment of language majors in the senior year: A survey conducted in United States colleges and universities.* Cambridge, Mass.: Harvard Univesity. Cited in W.E. Lambert, The language laboratory: Other alternatives?, in Louis J. Chatagnier & G. Taggart, eds., *Language laboratory learning: New directions,* Montreal: Aquila, 1971, 73-78.
CARROW, E. (1971)   Comprehension of English and Spanish by preschool Mexican-American children. *Modern Language Journal* **55**, 299-307.
CARTER, A. (1978)   From Sensori-motor vocalizations to words: A case study of the evolution of attention-directing communication in the second year. In Lock 1978, 310-349.
CASAGRANDE, J.B. (1948)   Comanche baby language. *International Journal of American Linguistics* **14**, 11-14. Reprinted in Dell Hymes, ed., *Language in culture and society,* New York: Harper & Row, 1964, 245-250.
CAUDILL, W. & H. WEINSTEIN (1969)   Maternal care and infant behavior in Japan and America. *Psychiatry* **32**, 12-43.
CAZDEN, C.B. (1965)   *Environmental assistance to the child's acquisition of grammar.* Ph.D. dissertation. Cambridge, Mass.: Harvard University.
CAZDEN, C.B. (1968)   The acquisition of noun and verb inflections. *Child Development* **39**, 433-448. Reprinted in Ferguson & Slobin 1973, 226-240. Page references are to this version.
CAZDEN, COURTNEY (1972)   *Child language and education.* New York: Holt, Rinehart & Winston.
CELCE-MURCIA, M. (1978)   The simultaneous acquisition of English and French in a two-year-old child. In Hatch 1978, 38-53.
CENTRAL OFFICE OF INFORMATION (1981)   *Britain 1981: An official handbook.* London: Her Majesty's Stationery Office.
CHAMBERS, J.C. JR. & N. TAVUCHIS (1976)   Kids and kin: Children's understanding of American kin terms. *Journal of Child Language* **3**, 63-80.
CHAO, Y.R. (1951)   The Cantian idiolect: An analysis of the Chinese spoken by a twenty-eight-months-old child. In Walter J. Fishel, ed., *Semitic and Oriental studies,* University of California Publications in Semitic Philosophy XI, Berkeley & Los Angeles: University of California Press, 1951. Reprinted in Bar-Adon & Leopold 1971, 116-130.
CHAPMAN, A.H. & E.B. COOPER (1973)   Nature of stuttering in a mentally retarded population. *American Journal of Mental Deficiency* **78**, 153-157.
CHAPMAN, K., L.B. LEONARD, L.E. ROWAN & A.L. WEISS (1983)   Inappropriate word extensions in the speech of young language-disordered children. *Journal of Speech and Hearing Disorders* **48**, 55-62.
CHAPMAN, R.S. & J.R. MILLER (1975)   Word order in early two and three word utterances: Does production precede comprehension? *Journal of Speech and Hearing Research* **18**, 355-371. Reprinted in Bloom 1978, 329-346.
CHARLTON, M. (1964)   Aphasia in bilingual and polyglot patients—a neurological and psychological study. *Journal of Speech and Hearing Disorders* **29**, 307-311.
CHARNEY, R. (1979)   The comprehension of 'here' and 'there'. *Journal of Child Language* **6**, 69-80.
CHARNIAK, E. (1983)   Passing markers: A theory of contextual influence in language comprehension. *Cognitive Science* **7**, 171-190.
CHEN, H.P. (1942)   *Speech sounds of infants: The newborn period.* Ph.D. thesis. Iowa City: State University of Iowa. Cited in Irwin 1957.
CHOMSKY, CAROL S. (1969)   *The acquisition of syntax in children from 5 to 10.* Cambridge, Mass.: MIT Press.
CHOMSKY, NOAM (1957)   *Syntactic structures.* The Hague: Mouton.
CHOMSKY, N. (1959)   Review of B.F. Skinner's *Verbal behavior. Language* **35**, 26-58. Reprinted in: John P. DeCecco, ed., *The psychology of language, thought and instruction,* New York: Holt Rinehart & Winston, 1967, 325-339; Fodor & Katz 1964, 547-578; Jakobovits & Miron 1967, 142-171.
CHOMSKY, N. (1962)   The logical basis of linguistic theory. In Horace G. Lunt, ed., *Proceedings of the Ninth International Congress of Linguists, Cambridge, Mass., Aug 27-31, 1962,* The Hague: Mouton, 1964, 914-978, with discussion to 1008. See Chomsky 1964.
CHOMSKY, N. (1964)   Current issues in linguistic theory. In Fodor & Katz 1964, 50-118. Almost identical version published the same year under the same title as a separate monograph by Mouton. Revised version of Chomsky 1962.
CHOMSKY, NOAM (1965)   *Aspects of the theory of syntax.* Cambridge, Mass.: MIT Press.
CHOMSKY, NOAM (1966)   *Cartesian linguistics.* New York: Harper & Row.
CHOMSKY, N. (1967)   The formal nature of language. Appendix to Lenneberg 1967, 397-442.
CHOMSKY, N. (1968)   *Language and mind.* New York: Harcourt, Brace and World.
CHOMSKY, NOAM (1975)   *Reflections on language.* New York: Pantheon Books.
CHOMSKY, NOAM & M. HALLE (1968)   *The sound pattern of English.* New York: Harper & Row.

CHRISMAN, O. (1893)   Secret language of children. *Science* **22**, 303-305.

CHRISTOPHERSON, P. (1939)   *The articles: A study of their theory and use in English.* London: Oxford University Press.

CHUN, R.W., R. PAWSAT & F.M. FORSTER (1960)   Sound localization in infancy. *Journal of Nervous and Mental Disease* **130**, 472-476.

CICOUREL, A.V. & R.J. BOESE (1972)   Sign language acquisition and the teaching of deaf children. In Courtney Cazden & D. Hymes, eds., *Functions of language in the classroom,* New York: Teacher's College Press, 1972, 32-62.

CLANCY, P., T. JACOBSON & M. SILVA (1976)   The acquisition of conjunction: A cross-linguistic study. *Papers and Reports on Child Language Development* **12**, 71-80.

CLARK, E.V. (1971)   On the acquisition of the meaning of *before* and *after. Journal of Verbal Learning and Verbal Behavior* **10**, 266-275. Reprinted in E. Clark 1979, 133-147.

CLARK, E.V. (1972)   On the child's acquisition of antonyms in two semantic fields. *Journal of Verbal Learning and Verbal Behavior* **11**, 750-758. Reprinted in E. Clark 1979, 148-160.

CLARK, E.V. (1973a)   What's in a word? On the child's acquisition of semantics in his first language. In T. Moore 1973, 65-110. Reprinted in E. Clark 1979, 12-62.

CLARK, E.V. (1973b)   Non-linguistic strategies and the acquisition of word meanings. *Cognition* **2**, 161-182. Reprinted in: Bloom 1978, 433-451; E. Clark 1979, 161-183.

CLARK, E.V. (1973c)   How children describe time and order. In Ferguson & Slobin 1973, 585-606. Reprinted in E. Clark 1979, 110-132.

CLARK, E.V. (1974)   Some aspects of the conceptual basis for first language acquisition. In Schiefelbush & Lloyd 1974, 105-128. Also appeared in *Papers and Reports on Child Language Development,* 1974, **7.**

CLARK, E.V. (1977)   Universal categories: On the semantics of classifiers and children's early word meanings. In Alphonse Julliand, ed., *Linguistic studies offered to Joseph Greenberg: On the occasion of his sixtieth birthday,* Saratoga, Ca.: Anma Libri, 1977, 449-462. Reprinted in Clark 1979, 253-267.

CLARK, E.V. (1978)   From gesture to word: On the natural history of deixis in language acquisition. In Jerome S. Bruner & A. Garten, ed., *Human growth and development: Wolfson College lectures 1976,* Oxford: Clarendon Press, 1978, 85-120.

CLARK, EVE V., ed. (1979)   *The ontogenesis of meaning.* Wiesbaden: Akademische Verlagsgesellschaft Athenaion.

CLARK, E.V. (1980)   Lexical innovations: How children learn to create new words. *Papers and Reports on Child Language Development* **18**, 1-24.

CLARK, E.V. & O.K. GARNICA (1974)   Is he coming or going? On the acquisition of deiotic verbs. *Journal of Verbal Behavior* **13**, 559-572. Reprinted in E. Clark 1979, 206-224.

CLARK, E.V., S.A. GELMAN & N.M. LANE (1985)   Compound nouns and category structure in young children. *Child Development* **56**, 84-94.

CLARK, E.V. & C.J. SENGUL (1978)   Strategies in the acquisition of deixis. *Journal of Child Language* **5**, 457-475. Reprinted in E. Clark 1979, 184-205.

CLARK, H.H. (1973)   Space, time, semantics, and the child. In T. Moore 1973, 27-63.

CLARK, HERBERT H. & E.V. CLARK (1977)   *Psychology and language.* New York: Harcourt Brace Jovanovich.

CLARK, H.H. & S. HAVILAND (1977)   Comprehension and the given-new contract. In Roy O. Freedle, ed., *Discourse production and comprehension,* Norwood, N.J.: Ablex, 1977, 1-40.

CLARK, R., S. HUTCHESON & P. VAN BUREN (1974)   Comprehension and production in language acquisition. *Journal of Linguistics* **10**, 39-54.

CLARKE, B.R. & D. LING (1976)   The effects of using Cued Speech: A follow-up study. *Volta Review* **78**, 23-34.

CLEMENTS, M. (1977)   Observations on certain aspects of neonatal behavior in response to auditory stimuli. Paper presented at the 5th International Congress of Psychosomatic Obstetrics and Gynecology, Rome. Cited in Verny & Kelly 1981, 39.

COGGINS, R. (1976)   *The classification of relational meanings expressed in the early two-word utterances of Downs Syndrome children.* Ph.D. dissertation. Madison: University of Wisconsin. Cited in J. de Villiers & de Villiers 1978, 253.

COHEN, A.D. (1976a)   The acquisition of Spanish grammar through immersion: Some findings after four years. *Canadian Modern Language Review* **32**, 562-574.

COHEN, A.D. (1976b)   The case for partial or total immersion education. In A. Simões, ed., 1976, 65-89.

COHEN, A.D. & L.M. LAOSA (1976)   Second language instruction: Some research considerations. *Curriculum Studies* **8**, 149-165.

COKER, P.L. (1978)   Syntactic and semantic factors in *before* and *after. Journal of Child Language* **5**, 261-277.

COKER, P. & S. LEGUM (1974)   An empirical test of semantic hypotheses relevant to the language of young children. TM 2-74-07 SWRL Educational Research and Development, Los Alamitos, California. Cited in Goodz 1982.

COLEMAN, L. & P. KAY (1981)   Prototype semantics: The English word *lie. Language* **57**, 26-44.

COLLINS, A.M. & E.F. LOFTUS (1975)   A spreading-activation theory of semantic processing. *Psychological Review* **82**, 407-428.

COLLINS-AHLGREN, M. (1975)   Language development of two deaf children. *American Annals of the Deaf* **120: 6,** 524-539.

COLLIS, G.M. (1977)   Visual co-orientation and maternal speech. In Schaffer 1977, 355-378.

COMMITTEE ON PROSTHETICS RESEARCH AND DEVELOPMENT, ASSEMBLY OF LIFE SCIENCES (1975) *Communication and sensory aids for the deaf-blind, Report of a Workshop.* Washington, D.C.: National Research Council, National Academy of Sciences.

CONDON, W.S. (1975) Multiple response to sound in dysfunctional children. *Journal of Autism and Childhood Schizophrenia* **5,** 37-56.

CONDON, W.S. & L.W. SANDER (1974) Neonate movement is synchronized with adult speech: Interactional participation and language acquisition. *Science* **183,** 99-101.

CONKLIN, H.C. (1956) Tagalog speech disguise. *Language* **32,** 136-139.

CONNORS, K., N. MÉNARD & R. SINGH (1978) Testing linquistic and functional competence in immersion programs. In M. Paradis 1978, 65-75.

CONWAY, J.K. & B. QUARRINGTON (1963) Positional effects in the stuttering of contextually organized verbal material. *Journal of Abnormal and Social Psychology* **67,** 299-303.

COOK, V.J. (1973) The comparison of language development in native children and foreign adults. *International Review of Applied Linguistics in Language Teaching* **11,** 13-29.

COOLEY, C.H. (1908) A study of the early use of self-words by a child. *Psychological Review* **15,** 339-357.

CORNETT, O. (1969) In answer to Dr. Moores. *American Annals of the Deaf* **114,** 27-29.

CORNETT, R.O. (1967) Cued Speech. *American Annals of the Deaf* **112,** 3-13.

COSGROVE, J.M. & C.J. PATTERSON (1977) Plans and the development of listener skills. *Developmental Psychology* **13,** 557-564.

COSGROVE, J.M. & C.J. PATTERSON (1978) Generalization of training for children's listener skills. *Child Development* **49,** 513-516.

COURTRIGHT, J.A. & I.C. COURTRIGHT (1983) The perception of nonverbal vocal cues of emotional meaning by language-disordered and normal children. *Journal of Speech and Hearing Research* **26,** 412-417.

COWAN, N. & L.A. LEAVITT (1982) Talking backward: Exceptional speech play in late childhood. *Journal of Child Language* **9,** 481-495.

COWAN, N., L.A. LEAVITT, D.W. MASSARO & R.D. KENT (1982) A fluent backward talker. *Journal of Speech and Hearing Research* **25,** 48-53.

COX, M.V. (1979) Young children's understanding of 'in front of' and 'behind' in the placement of objects. *Journal of Child Language* **6,** 371-374.

CRAIG, H.K. & T.M. GALLAGHER (1982) Gaze and proximity as nonverbal turn regulators within three-party and two-party conversations. *Journal of Speech and Hearing Research* **25,** *32-42.*

CRITCHLEY, E. (1967) Language development of hearing children in a deaf environment. *Journal of Developmental Medicine and Child Neurology* **9,** 274-280.

CROMER, R.F. (1968) *The development of temporal reference during the acquisition of language.* Ph.D. dissertation. Cambridge, Mass.: Harvard University. Cited in Bowerman 1979.

CROMER, R.F. (1970) 'Children are nice to understand': Surface structure clues for the recovery of a deep structure. *British Journal of Psychology* **61,** 397-408.

CROMER, R.F. (1974) Receptive language in the mentally retarded: Processes and diagnostic distinctions. In Schiefelbusch & Lloyd 1974, 237-267.

CROMER, R.F. (1975) Are subnormals linguistic adults? In O'Connor 1975, 169-187.

CROSBY, F. (1976) Early discourse agreement. *Journal of Child Language* **3,** 125-126.

CROSS, T.G. (1975) Some relationships between mothers and linguistic level in accelerated children. *Papers and Reports on Child Language Development* **10,** 117-135.

CROSS, T.G. & J.E. MORRIS (1980) Linguistic feedback and maternal speech: Comparisons of mothers addressing infants, one-year-olds and two-year-olds. *First Language* **1,** 98-121.

CRUTTENDEN, A. (1970) A phonetic study of babbling. *British Journal of Disorders of Communications* **5,** 110-117.

CRUTTENDEN, ALAN (1979) *Language in infancy and childhood.* Manchester: Manchester University Press.

CRYSTAL, D. (1974) Review of Brown 1973. *Journal of Child Language* **1,** 289-334.

CSAPO, M. & B.R. CLARKE (1974) Deaf-blind children in Canada. *New Outlook for the Blind* **68,** 315-319.

CURTISS, SUSAN (1977) *Genie: A psycholinguistic study of a modern-day 'wild child'.* New York: Academic Press.

CUTSFORTH, T. (1932) The unreality of words to the blind. *Teachers Forum* **4,** 48-53.

CUTSFORTH, T. (1951) *The blind in school and society.* New York: American Federation for the Blind.

DALE, PHILIP S. (1976) *Language development: Structure and function, 2nd ed.* New York: Holt Rinehart & Winston.

D'ANGLEJAN, A. & G.R. TUCKER (1975) The acquisition of complex English structures by adult learners. *Language Learning* **25,** 281-293.

DANILOFF, J.K., L.L. LLOYD & M. FRISTOE (1983) Amer-Ind transparency. *Journal of Speech and Hearing Disorders* **48,** 103-110.

DANISH, J.M. & M. LEVITAN (1967) Changing aspects of deafness in school-age children. *Archives of Otolaryngology* **86,** 166-171.

DANISH, J.M., J.K. TILLSON & M. LEVITAN (1963) Multiple anomalies in congenitally deaf children. *Eugenics Quarterly* **10,** 12-21.

DANZGER, M. & H. HALPERN (1973) Relation of stuttering to word abstraction, part of speech, word length, and word frequency. *Perceptual and Motor Skills* **37,** 959-962.

DANZIGER, K. (1957) The child's understanding of kinship terms: A study in the development of relational concepts. *Journal of Genetic Psychology* **91,** 213-232.

DARWIN, C. (1877) A biographical sketch of an infant. *Mind* **2**, 285-294. Excerpt reprinted in Bar-Adon & Leopold 1971, 27-28.

DATO, DANIEL P. (1970) *American children's acquisition of Spanish syntax in the Madrid environment, preliminary edition.* U.S. Office of Education. Institute of International Studies. Project 3036, contract OEC 2-7-002637. Cited in McLaughlin 1978.

DATO, D.P. (1971) The development of the Spanish verb phrase in children's second-language learning. In Paul Pimsleur & T. Quinn, eds., *The psychology of second language learning: Papers from the Second International Congress of Applied Linguistics,* Cambridge: Cambridge University Press, 1971, 19-33.

DATO, DANIEL P., ed (1975) *Developmental psycholinguistics: Theory and applications.* Georgetown University Round Table on Languages and Linguistics **26.** Washington, D.C.: Georgetown University Press. See comment in Alatis reference.

DATO, D.P (1978) Development of Spanish interrogatives in children's second language learning. In Honsa & Hardman-de-Bautista 1978, 11-38.

DAVIS, D.M. (1937) *The development of linguistic skill in twins, singletons, and only children from age five to ten years.* Institute of Child Welfare Monograph Series 14. Minneapolis: University of Minnesota Press.

DAY, HERBERT E., I. FUSFELD & R. PINTER (1928) *A survey of American schools for the deaf.* Washington, D.C.: National Research Council. Cited by Moores 1974, 406.

DE BOYSSON-BARDIES, B. (1972) *L'etude de la négation: Aspects syntaxiques et lexicaux.* Ph.D. dissertation. L'Université de Paris. Cited in Bloom & Lahey 1978.

DE BOYSSON-BARDIES, B., L. SAGART & C. DURAND (1984) Discernible differences in the babbling of infants according to target language. *Journal of Child Language* **11,** 1-16.

DEESE, JAMES (1970) *Psycholinguistics.* Boston: Allyn & Bacon.

DEFOE, DANIEL (1719) *The life and strange surprising adventures of Robinson Crusoe.* London: Taylor.

DELACK, J.B. (1976) Aspects of infant speech development in the first year of life. *Canadian Journal of Linguistics* **21,** 17-37. Reprinted in Bloom 1978, 94-114.

DELL, G.S. & P.A. REICH (1977) A model of slips of the tongue. In Robert J. DiPietro & E.L. Blansitt, Jr., eds., *The third LACUS forum,* Columbia, S.C., Hornbeam Press, 1977, 448-455.

DELL, G.S. & P.A. REICH (1980a) Slips of the tongue: The facts and a stratificational model. In James E. Copeland & P.W. Davis, eds., *Papers in cognitive-stratificational linguistics,* Houston: Rice University Studies **66:2,** 1980, 19-34.

DELL, G.S. & P.A. REICH (1980b) Toward a unified model of slips of the tongue. In Victoria A. Fronkin, ed., *Errors in linguistic performance: Slips of the tongue, ear, pen, and hand,* New York: Academic Press, 1980, 273-286.

DELL, G.S. & P.A. REICH (1981) Stages in sentence production: An analysis of speech error data. *Journal of Verbal Learning and Verbal Behavior* **20,** 611-629.

DEMEYER, M. (1979) *Parents and children in autism.* Washington: V.H. Winston & Sons.

DEMOTT, R. (1972) Verbalism and affective meaning for the blind, severely visually impaired, and normally sighted children. *New Outlook for the Blind* **66:1,** 1-8, 25.

DENNIS, M. & B. KOHN (1975) Comprehension of syntax in infantile hemiplegics after cerebral hemidecortication: Left hemisphere superiority. *Brain and Language* **2,** 472-482.

DENNIS, M., J. SUGAR & H.A. WHITAKER (1982) The acquisition of tag questions. *Child Development* **53,** 1254-1257.

DEOSARAN, RAMESH, E. WRIGHT & T. KANE (1976) *The 1975 every student survey: Student's background and its relationship to program placement.* Toronto: The Board of Education for the City of Toronto, Research Department, 138.

DEPAULO, B.M. & D.D. BONVILLIAN (1978) The effect on language development of the special characteristics of speech addressed to children. *Journal of Psycholinguistic Research* **7,** 189-211.

DERWING, BRUCE L. (1973) *Transformational grammar as a theory of language acquisition.* Cambridge: Cambridge University Press.

DERWING, B.L. & W.J. BAKER (1977) The psychological basis for morphological rules. In John Macnamara, ed., *Language learning and thought,* New York: Academic Press, 1977, 87-110.

DERWING, B.L. & W.J. BAKER (1979) Recent research on the acquisition of English morphology In Fletcher & Garman 1979, 209-223.

DEVER, R.B. & W.I. GARDNER (1970) Performance of normal and retarded boys on Berko's test of morphology. *Language and Speech* **13,** 162-181.

DE VILLIERS, J.G. & P.A. DE VILLIERS (1973a) Development of the use of word order in comprehension. *Journal of Psycholinguistic Research* **2,** 331-341.

DE VILLIERS, J.G. & P.A. DE VILLIERS (1973b) A cross-sectional study of the acquisition of grammatical morphemes in child speech. *Journal of Psycholinguistic Research* **2,** 267-278. Reprinted in Bloom 1978, 74-84.

DE VILLIERS, JILL G. & PETER A. DE VILLIERS (1978) *Language acquisition.* Cambridge, Mass.: Harvard University Press.

DE VILLIERS, J.G., H.B. TAGER-FLUSBERG & K. HAKUTA (1976) The roots of coordination in child speech. Paper presented at the First Annual Boston University Conference on Language Development. Cited in J. de Villiers & de Villiers 1978, 110-111.

DE VILLIERS, J.G., H.B. TAGER-FLUSBERG, K. HAKUTA & M. COHEN (1979) Children's comprehension of relative clauses. *Journal of Psycholinguistic Research* **8,** 499-518.

DE VILLIERS, P.A. & J.G. DE VILLIERS (1974)   On this, that and the other: Nonegocentrism in very young children. *Journal of Experimental Child Psychology* **18**, 438-447.

DEVITO, JOSEPH (1970)   *The psychology of speech and language: An introduction to psycholinguistics.* New York: Random House.

DEVORE, I. & M. KONNER (1974)   Infancy in a hunter-gatherer life: An ethological perspective. In Norman White, ed., *Ethology and psychiatry,* Toronto: University of Toronto Press, 1974.

DEVRIES, JOHN & F.G. VALLEE (1980)   *Language use in Canada.* Ottawa: Statistics Canada.

DICKSON, S. (1971)   Incipient stuttering and spontaneous remission of stuttered speech. *Journal of Communication Disorders* **4**, 99-110.

DICKSON, W. PATRICK, ed. (1981a)   *Children's oral communication skills.* New York: Academic Press.

DICKSON, W.P. (1981b)   Referential communication activities in research and in the curriculum: A metaanalysis. In W. Dickson 1981a, 189-204.

DICKSON, W.P. (1982)   Two decades of referential communication research: A review and a meta-analysis. In Brainerd & Pressley 1982, 1-33.

DODD, BARBARA (1974)   *The phonological development of abnormal children.* Ph.D. dissertation. London: University of London. Cited in: Cromer 1974, 255; N. Smith 1975, 63-64.

DODD, B. (1975)   Children's understanding of their own phonological forms. *Quarterly Journal of Experimental Psychology* **27**, 165-172.

DODD, B. (1979)   Lip reading in infants: Attention to speech presented in- and out-of-synchrony. *Cognition* **11**, 478-484.

D'ODORICO, L. (1984)   Non-segmental features in prelinguistic communications: An analysis of some types of infant cry and non-cry vocalizations. *Journal of Child Language* **11**, 17-28.

DOKECKI, P. (1966)   Verbalism and the blind: A critical review of the concept and the literature. *Exceptional Children* **32**, 525-530.

DONALDSON, M. & G. BALFOUR (1968)   Less is more: A study of language comprehension in children. *British Journal of Psychology* **59**, 461-472.

DONALDSON, M. & R.J. WALES (1970)   On the acquisition of some relational terms. In Hayes 1970, 235-268.

DONNAN, G.A. (1979)   Stuttering as a manifestation of stroke. *Medical Journal of Australia* **1**, 44-45.

DONOGHUE, MILDRED R. (1968)   *Foreign languages and the elementary school child.* Iowa: William C. Brown.

DOOLEY, J. (1976)   *Language acquisition and Down's syndrome: A study of early semantics and syntax.* Ph.D. dissertation. Cambridge, Mass.: Harvard University. Cited in J. de Villiers & de Villiers 1978, 253-256.

DORE, J. (1973)   *The development of speech acts.* Ph.D. dissertation. City University of New York.

DORE, J. (1975)   Holophrases, speech acts and language universals. *Journal of Child Language* **2**, 21-40.

DORE, J. (1977)   "Oh them sheriff": A pragmatic analysis of children's responses to questions. In Ervin-Tripp & Mitchell-Kernan 1977, 139-163.

DORE, J., M.B. FRANKLIN, R.T. MILLER & A.L. RAMER (1976)   Transitional phenomena in early language acquisition. *Journal of Child Language* **3**, 13-28.

DRACH, K.M. (1969)   The language of the parent: A pilot study. In *The structure of linguistic input to children.* Language Behavior Research Laboratory, Working Paper 14, University of California, Berkeley. ERIC ED 138109.

DREIFUSS, F. (1961)   Observations on aphasia in a polyglot poet. *Acta Psychiatrica Scandinavia* **36**, 91-97. Cited in Albert & Obler 1978, 96.

DULAY, H.C. & M.K. BURT (1973)   Should we teach children syntax? *Language Learning* **23**, 245-258.

DULAY, H.C. & M.K. BURT (1974)   A new perspective on the creative construction process in child second language acquisition. *Language Learning* **24**, 253-278.

DULAY, H.C. & M.K. BURT (1978)   *Why bilingual education? A summary of research findings, 2nd edition.* San Francisco: Bloomsbury West.

DUNLEA, A.D. (1978)   Observations on the acquisition of definiteness and indefiniteness. *Papers and Reports on Child Language Development* **15**, 78-87.

DUNN, LLOYD M. (1959)   *Peabody Picture Vocabulary Test.* Circle Pines, Minn.: American Guidance Service.

EDWARDS, D. (1978)   Social relations and early language. In Lock 1978, 449-469.

EDWARDS, H.P. & F. SMYTH (1976)   Alternatives to early immersion programs for the acquisition of French as a second language. *The Canadian Modern Language Review* **32**, 524-533.

EDWARDS, M.L. (1974)   Perception and production in child phonology: The testing of four hypotheses. *Journal of Child Language* **1**, 205-219.

EILERS, R.E., W.J. GAVIN & D.K. OLLER (1982)   Cross-linguistic perception in infancy: Early effects of linguistic experience. *Journal of Child Language* **9**, 289-302.

EILERS, R.E., W.J. GAVIN & W.R. WILSON (1979a)   Linguistic experience and phonemic perception in infancy: A crosslinguistic study. *Child Development* **50**, 14-18.

EILERS, R.E. & F.D. MINIFIE (1975)   Fricative discrimination in early infancy. *Journal of Speech and Hearing Research* **18**, 158-167.

EILERS, R.E., K.K. OLLER & J. ELLINGTON (1974)   The acquisition of word meaning for dimensional adjectives: The long and the short of it. *Journal of Child Language* **1**, 195-204.

EILERS, R.E., W.R. WILSON & J.M. MOORE (1979b)   Speech discrimination in the language-wise: A study in the perception of voice onset time. *Journal of Child Language* **6**, 1-18.

EIMAS, P. (1974)   Linguistic processing of speech by young infants. In Schiefelbusch & Lloyd 1974, 55-73.

EIMAS, P. (1975a)   Speech perception in early infancy. In Leslie B. Cohen & P. Salapatek, eds., *Infant perception: From sensation to cognition, vol II: Perception of space, speech, and sound.* New York: Academic Press, 1975, 193-231.

EIMAS, P. (1975b)   Auditory and phonetic coding of the cues for speech: Discrimination of the [r-l] distinction by young infants. *Perception and psychophysics* **18**, 341-347.

EIMAS. P., E. SIQUELAND, P. JUSCZYK & J. VIGORITO (1971)   Speech perception in infants. *Science* **171**, 303-306. Reprinted in Bloom 1978, 87-93.

EISENBERG, L. (1956)   The autistic child in adolescence. *American Journal of Psychiatry* **112**, 607-612.

EISENSON, JON (1972)   *Aphasia in children.* New York: Harper & Row.

EISENSON, J. & E. HOROWITZ (1945)   The influence of propositionality on stuttering. *Journal of Speech Disorders* **10**, 193-197.

EISENSON, J. & C WELLS (1942)   A study of the influence of communicative responsibility in a choral speech situation for stutterers. *Journal of Speech Disorders* **7**, 259-262.

ELKIND, D. (1962)   Children's conceptions of brother and sister. *Journal of Genetic Psychology* **100**, 129-136.

ELLIOT, ALISON J. (1981)   *Child language.* Cambridge: Cambridge University Press.

ELWERT, W. THEODOR (1960)   *Das zweisprachige Individuum: ein Selbstzeugnis.* Wiesbaden: Steiner. Cited in McLaughlin 1978, 96.

EMRICH, L. (1938)   Beobachtungen über Zweisprachigkeit im ihrem Anfangsstadium. *Deutschtum im Ausland* **21**, 419-424. Cited in McLaughlin 1978.

EMSLIE, H.C. & R.J. STEVENSON (1981)   Pre-school children's use of the articles in definite and indefinite referring expressions. *Journal of Child Language* **8**, 313-328.

ENGLE, P. (1975)   Language medium in early school years for minority language groups. *Review of Educational Research* **45**, 283-325.

ERIKSON, E.H. (1959)   Identity and the life cycle: Selected papers. *Psychological Issues* **1**, 1-171.

ERREICH, A. (1980)   'Why you won't play with me?': Non-inversion errors in wh- questions. Paper presented at the 5th annual Boston University Conference on Language Development, October.

ERVIN-TRIPP, S. (1970a)   Discourse agreement: How children answer questions. In Hayes 1970, 79-107.

ERVIN-TRIPP, S. (1970b)   Structure and process in language acquisition. In Alatis 1970, 313-344.

ERVIN-TRIPP, S. (1973)   Some strategies for the first two years. In T. Moore 1973, 261-286. Revised version of Ervin-Tripp 1978.

ERVIN-TRIPP, S. (1974)   Is second language learning like the first? *TESOL Quarterly* **8**, 111-127.

ERVIN-TRIPP, S. (1976)   Is Sybil there? The structure of some American English directives. *Language in Society* **5**, 25-66.

ERVIN-TRIPP, S. (1977)   Wait for me, roler skate! In Ervin-Tripp & Mitchell-Kernan 1977, 165-188.

ERVIN-TRIPP, S. (1978)   The onset of grammar. In Honsa & Hardman-de-Bautista 1978, 71-91. See Ervin-Tripp 1973.

ERVIN-TRIPP, S. (1979)   Children's verbal turn-taking. In Elinor Ochs & B.B. Schieffelin, eds., *Developmental pragmatics,* New York: Academic Press, 1979, 391-414.

ERVIN-TRIPP, SUSAN & C. MITCHELL-KERNAN, eds. (1977)   *Child Discourse.* New York: Academic Press.

ESCALONA, S.K. (1973)   Basic modes of social interaction: Their emergence and patterning during the first two years of life. *Merrill-Palmer Quarterly* **19**, 205-232.

ESON, M.E. & A.S. SHAPIRO (1982)   When 'don't' means 'do': Pragmatic and cognitive development in understanding an indirect imperative. *First Language* **3**, 83-91.

ESPY, WILLARD R. (1971)   *The game of words.* London: Wolfe.

FANT, LOUIE J. JR. (1972)   *Ameslan: An introduction to American Sign Language.* Silver Spring, Md.: National Association of the Deaf.

FATHMAN, A.K. (1975)   Age, language background, and the order of acquisition of English structures. Paper presented at the annual TESOL conference, Los Angeles.

FAY, W.H. & B.V. BUTLER (1968)   Echolalia, I.Q. and the developmental dichotomy of speech and language systems. *Journal of Speech and Hearing Research* **11**, 365-371.

FEAGANS, L. (1980a)   Children's understanding of some temporal terms denoting order, duration, and simultaneity. *Journal of Psycholinguistic Research* **9**, 41-57.

FEAGANS, L. (1980b)   How to make sense of temporal/spatial 'before' and 'after.' *Journal of Child Language* **7**, 529-537.

FELIX, S. (1976)   Wh-pronouns and second language acquisition. *Linguistische Berichte* **44**, 52-64.

FERGUSON, C.A. (1964)   Baby talk in six languages. *American Anthropology* **66**, 103-114.

FERGUSON, C.A. (1977a)   Learning to pronounce: The earliest stages of phonological development in the child. In Fred D. Minifie & L.L. Lloyd, eds., *Communication and cognitive abilities: Early behavioral assessment,* Cambridge: Cambridge University Press, 1977, 273-297.

FERGUSON, C.A. (1977b)   Baby talk as a simplified register. In Snow & Ferguson 1977, 209-235.

FERGUSON, C.A.(1978)   Fricatives in child language acquisition. In Honsa & Hardman-de-Bautista 1978, 93-115.
FERGUSON, C.A. & C.B. FARWELL (1975)   Words and sounds in early language acquisition. *Language* **51**, 419-439.
FERGUSON, C.A. & O.K. GARNICA (1975)   Theories of phonological development. In Lenneberg & Lenneberg 1975a, 153-180.
FERGUSON, CHARLES A. & D.I. SLOBIN, eds. (1973)   *Studies of child language development.* New York: Holt, Rinehart & Winston.
FERGUSON, J. (1970)   *The religions of the Roman Empire.* London: Camelot Press.
FERNALD, C.D. (1972)   Control of grammar in imitation, comprehension, and production: Problems of replication. *Journal of Verbal Learning and Verbal Behavior* **11**, 606-613.
FERREIRO, E. & H. SINCLAIR (1971)   Temporal relationships in language. *International Journal of Psycholinguistics* **6**, 39-47.
FILLMORE, C. (1968)   The case for case. In Emmon Bach & R. Harms, eds., *Universals in linguistic theory,* New York: Holt, Rinehart & Winston, 1968, 1-90.
FILLMORE, C. (1971)   Lectures on deixis. Unpublished paper, Summer Program in Linguistics. Santa Cruz: University of California. Cited in Richards 1976, 655.
FILLMORE, L.W. (1976)   *The second time around: Cognitive and social strategies in second-language acquisition.* Ph.D. dissertation. Stanford: Cal.: Stanford University. Cited in McLaughlin 1978.
FINCHER, B.H. (1978)   Bilingualism in contemporary China: The coexistence of oral diversity and written uniformity. In Spolsky & Cooper 1978, 72-87.
FINE, J. (1978)   Conversation, cohesive and thematic patterning in children's dialogues. *Discourse Processes* **1**, 247-266.
FISCHER, S.D. (1974)   The ontogenetic development of language. In Erwin W. Straus, ed., *Language and language disturbances: The fifth Lexington conference on pure and applied phenomenology,* Pittsburgh: Duquesne University Press, 1974, 22-43.
FISHER, S. & B. GOUGH (1978)   Verbs in ASL. *Sign Language Studies* **18**, 17-48.
FISHER, M.S. (1934)   Language patterns of preschool children. *Child Development Monographs* **15**.
FISHMAN, JOSHUA, V.C. NAHIRNY, J.E. HOFMAN & R.G. HAYDEN (1966)   *Language loyalty in the United States.* The Hague: Mouton.
FLAVELL, JOHN H. (1963)   *The developmental psychology of Jean Piaget.* Princeton, N.J.: Van Nostrand.
FLAVELL, J.H., D.R. BEACH & J.N. CHINSKY (1966)   Spontaneous verbal rehearsal in a memory task as a function of age. *Child Development* **37**, 283-299.
FLAVELL, J.H., J.B. HIGGINS & W. KLEIN (1963)   Interview study on the speech of self of a sample of faculty children. Manuscript. Cited in Kohlberg et al. 1968, 701.
FLEMING, C.P. (1968)   The verbal behavior of hydrocephalic children. *Developmental Medicine and Child Neurology* **15 Supplement,** 74-82.
FLETCHER, P. (1979)   The development of the verb phrase. In Fletcher & Garman 1979, 261-284.
FLETCHER, PAUL & M. GARMAN, eds. (1979)   *Language acquisition: Studies in first language development.* Cambridge: Cambridge University Press.
FLORES D'ARCAIS, GIOVANNI D. & W.J.M. LEVELT, eds. (1970)   *Advances in psycholinguistics.* Amsterdam: North Holland Publishing.
FODOR, J.A. (1966)   How to learn to talk: Some simple ways. In F. Smith & Miller 1966, 105-122.
FODOR, JERRY A., T.G. BEVER & M.F. GARRETT (1974)   *The psychology of language: An introduction to psycholinguistics and generative grammar.* New York: McGraw-Hill.
FODOR, JERRY A. & J.J. KATZ (1964)   *The structure of language: Readings in the philosophy of language.* Englewood Cliffs, N.J.: Prentice-Hall.
FORMBY, D. (1967)   Maternal recognition of infant's cry. *Developmental Medicine and Child Neurology* **9**, 293-298.
FOSS, DONALD J. & D.T. HAKES (1978)   *Psycholinguistics: An introduction to the psychology of language.* Englewood Cliffs, N.J.: Prentice-Hall.
FOSTER, KATE A. (1926)   *Our Canadian Mosaic.* Cited in Gibbon 1938.
FOULKE, E., C. AMSTER, C. NOLAN & R. BIXLER (1962)   The comprehension of rapid speech by the blind. *Exceptional Children* **29**, 134-141.
FOUTS, R.S., D.H. FOUTS & D. SCHOENFELD (1984)   Sign language conversational interaction between chimpanzees. *Sign Language Studies* **42**, 1-12.
FRAIBERG, SELMA (1977)   *Insights from the blind: Comparative studies of blind and sighted infants.* New York: Meridan.
FRAIBERG, S. & S. ADELSON (1973)   Self-representation in language and play. *Psychoanalytic Quarterly* **42**, 539-562.
FRANCESCATO, G. (1969)   Appunti teorico-pratici sul bilinguismo infantile. *Lingua e Stile* **4**, 445-458. Cited in McLaughlin 1978.
FRASER, C. & N. ROBERTS (1975)   Mothers' speech to children of four different ages. *Journal of Psycholinguistic Research* **4**, 9-16.
FRASER, C.J., U. BELLUGI & R. BROWN (1963)   Control of grammar in imitation, comprehension and production. *Journal of Verbal Learning and Verbal Behavior* **2**, 121-135. Reprinted in R. Brown 1970b, 28-55.
FREMGEN, A. & D. FAY (1980)   Overextensions in production and comprehension: A methodological clarification. *Journal of Child Language* **7**, 205-211.

FRENCH, L.A. & A.L. BROWN (1977) Comprehension of *before* and *after* in logical and arbitrary sequences. *Journal of Child Language* **4**, 247-256.

FRIEDLANDER, B.Z. (1968) The effect of speaker identity, voice inflection, vocabulary, and message redundancy on infants' selection of vocal reinforcement. *Journal of Experimental Child Psychology* **6**, 443-459.

FRIEDLANDER, B.Z. (1970) Receptive language development in infancy: Issues and problems. *Merrill-Palmer Quarterly* **16**, 7-51.

FRIEDLANDER, B.Z., A.C. JACOBS, B.B. DAVIS & H.S. WETSTONE (1972) Time sampling analysis of infants' natural language environments in the home. *Child Development* **43**, 730-740.

FRISTOE, M. & L.L LLOYD (1979) Nonspeech communication. In Norman R. Ellis, ed., *Handbook of mental deficiency, 2nd ed.*, Hillsdale, N.J.: Lawrence Erlbaum, 1979, 401-430.

FRITH, U. (1972) Cognitive mechanisms in autism: Experiments with color and tone sequence production. *Journal of Autism and Childhood Schizophrenia* **2**, 160-173.

FROMKIN, V., S. KRASHEN, S. CURTISS, D. RIGLER & M. RIGLER (1974) The development of language in Genie: A case of language acquisition beyond the 'critical period.' *Brain and Language* **1**, 81-107. Reprinted in Lahey 1978, 287-309.

FRY, D.B. & E. WHETNALL (1954) The auditory approach to the training of deaf children. *Lancet* **1**, 583.

FULWILER, R.L. & R.S. FOUTS (1976) Acquisition of American Sign Language by a noncommunicating autistic child. *Journal of Autism and Childhood Schizophrenia* **6**, 43-51.

GAER, E.P. (1969) Children's understanding and production of sentences. *Journal of Verbal Learning and Verbal Behavior* **8**, 289-294.

GALLIGAN, ROSLYN F. (1981) *Individual differences in learning to speak: A study of the use of whole phrases, jargon and intonation.* Ph.D. dissertation. Toronto, Ont.: University of Toronto.

GALLAGHER, T.M. (1977) Revision behaviors in the speech of normal children developing language. *Journal of Speech and Hearing Research* **20**, 303-318.

GALLAGHER, T.M. & H.K. CRAIG (1978) Structural characteristics of monologues in the speech of normal children: Semantic and conversational aspects. *Journal of Speech and Hearing Research* **21**, 103-117.

GALLAGHER, T.M. & H.K. CRAIG (1982) An investigation of overlap in children's speech. *Journal of Psycholinguistic Research* **11**, 63-75.

GALLAGHER, T.M. & B.A. DARNTON (1978) Conversational aspects of the speech of language-disordered children: Revision behaviors. *Journal of Speech and Hearing Research* **21**, 118-135.

GANNON, JACK R. (1981) *Deaf heritage: A narrative history of deaf America.* Silver Spring, Md: National Association of the Deaf.

GARDINER, W., L. KARNOSH, C. MCCLURE & A. GARDINER (1955) Residual function following hemispherectomy for tumor and infantile hemiplegia. *Brain* **78**, 487-502.

GARDNER, B.T. & R.A. GARDNER (1974) *Behavioral development of the chimpanzee, Washoe.* Film. State College, Pa.: Psychological Cinema Register.

GARDNER, B.T. & R.A. GARDNER (1980) Two comparative psychologists look at language acquisition. In Ke. Nelson 1980, 331-369.

GARDNER, R. ALLEN & B.T. GARDNER (1969) Teaching sign language to a chimpanzee. *Science* **165**, 664-672.

GARDNER, R.A. & B.T. GARDNER (1972) Communications with a young chimpanzee: Washoe's vocabulary. In Rémy Chauvin, ed., *Modeles animaux du comportement humain,* Paris: Centre National de la Recerche Scientifique, 1972, 16-26.

GARDNER, R.A. & B.T. GARDNER (1973) *Teaching sign language to the chimpanzee Washoe.* Film. State College, Pa.: Psychological Cinema Register.

GARMAN, M. (1979) Early grammatical development. In Fletcher & Garman 1979, 177-208.

GARNICA, O.K. (1973) The development of phonemic speech perception. In Morse 1973, 215-222.

GARNICA, O.K. (1977) Some prosodic and paralinguistic features of speech to young children. In Snow & Ferguson 1977, 63-68.

GARTON, A.F. (1983) An approach to the study of determiners in early language development. *Journal of Psycholinguistic Research* **12**, 513-525.

GARVEY, C. (1975) Requests and responses in children's speech. *Journal of Child Language* **2**, 41-63. Reprinted in Bloom, 1978, 292-313.

GARVEY, C. (1977) The contingent query: A dependent act in conversation. In M. Lewis & Rosenblum 1977, 63-93.

GARVEY, C. & M. BENDEBBA (1978) An experimental investigation of contingent query sequences. *Discourse Processes* **1**, 36-50.

GARVEY, C. & G. BERINGER (1981) Timing and turn-taking in children's conversations. *Discourse Processes* **4**, 27-57.

GARVEY, C. & R. HOGAN (1973) Social speech and social interaction: Egocentrism revisited. *Child Development* **44**, 562-568.

GEFFNER, D.S. & M.F. DORMAN (1976) Hemispheric specialization for speech perception in four-year-old children from low and middle socioeconomic classes. *Cortex* **1**, 71-73.

GEISSLER, HEINREICH (1938) *Zweisprachigkeit deutscher Kinder im Ausland.* Stuttgart: Kohlhammer. Cited in McLaughlin 1978.

GENESEE, F. (1976) The suitability of immersion programs for all children. *The Canadian Modern Language Review* **32**, 494-515.

GENESEE, F. (1978) Second language learning and language attitudes. *Working Papers on Bilingualism* **16**, 19-42.

GENESEE, F. (1979)   Acquisition of reading skills in immersion programs. *Foreign Language Annals* **12,** 71-77.

GENESEE, F. (1981)   A comparison of early and late second language learning. *Canadian Journal of Behavioral Sciences* **13,** 115-127.

GENESEE, F. (1983)   Bilingual education of majority-language children: The immersion experiments in review. *Applied Psycholinguistics* **4,** 1-46.

GENESEE, F. & W.E. LAMBERT (1983)   Trilingual education for majority-language children. *Child Development* **54,** 105-114.

GENESEE, F., E. POLICK & M.H. STANLEY (1977)   An experimental French immersion program at the secondary school level—1969-1974. *Canadian Modern Language Review* **33,** 318-332.

GENESEE, F. & M.H. STANLEY (1976)   The development of English writing skills in French immersion programs. *Canadian Journal of Education* **3,** 1-18.

GENESEE, F., G.R. TUCKER & W.E. LAMBERT (1975)   Communication skills of bilingual children. *Child Development* **46,** 1010-1014.

GENESEE, F., E. SHEINER, G.R. TUCKER & W.E. LAMBERT (1976)   An experiment in trilingual education. *The Canadian Modern Language Review* **32,** 115-128.

GENIESSE, H. (1935)   Stuttering. *Science* **82,** 518.

GERANKINA, A. (1972)   *Practical work in sign language.* Moscow: Institute of Defectology. Cited in Moores 1982, 162.

GESCHWIND, N. & W. LEVITSKY (1968)   Human brain: Left-right assymmetries in temporal speech region. *Science* **161,** 186-187.

GESELL, ARNOLD & C.S. AMATRUDA (1941)   *Developmental diagnosis: Normal and abnormal child development.* New York: Hoeber.

GESELL, ARNOLD, H.M. HALVERSON, H. THOMPSON, F.L. ILG, B. COSTNER, L.B. AMES & C.S. AMATRUDA (1940)   *The first five years of life: A guide to the study of the preschool child.* New York: Harper & Row.

GEWIRTZ, J.L. & E.F. BOYD (1977)   Does maternal responding imply reduced crying? A critique of the 1972 Bell and Ainsworth report. *Child Development* **48,** 1200-1207.

GIBBON, JOHN M. (1938)   *Canadian mosaic: The making of a northern nation.* Toronto: McClelland & Stewart.

GIBSON, E.J. & R.R. WALK (1960)   The 'visual cliff'. *Scientific American* **202: 4 (April),** 64-71.

GIBSON, WILLIAM (1957)   *The miracle worker.* New York: Knopf.

GILBERT, JEANNE G. & E. RUBIN (1965)   Evaluating the intellect of blind children. *New Outlook for the Blind* **59,** 238-240.

GILBERT, JOHN H.V. (1982)   Babbling and the deaf child: A commentary on Lenneberg et al. 1965 and Lenneberg 1967. *Journal of Child Language* **9,** 511-515.

GINSBURG, HERBERT & S. OPPER (1969)   *Piaget's theory of intellectual development.* Englewood Cliffs, N.J.: Prentice-hall.

GLASNER, P.J. & D. ROSENTHAL (1957)   Parental diagnosis of stuttering in young children. *Journal of Speech and Hearing Disorders* **22,** 288-295.

GLEASON, HENRY A. (1961)   *An introduction to descriptive linguistics.* New York: Holt, Rinehart & Winston.

GLEASON, J.B. (1973)   Code switching in children's language. In Moore 1973, 159-167. Reprinted in E. Mavis Hetherington & R.D. Parke, eds., *Contemporary readings in child psychology,* New York: McGraw-Hill, 1981, 134-138.

GLEASON, J.B. (1975)   Fathers and other strangers: Their speech to young children. In Dato 1975, 289-297.

GLEASON, J.B. (1977)   Talking to children: Some notes on feedback. In Snow & Ferguson 1977, 199-205.

GLEASON, J.B. & S. WEINTRAUB (1978)   Input language and the acquisition of communicative competence. In Keith E. Nelson, ed., *Children's language, vol. 1,* New York: Gardner, 1978, 171-222.

GLEITMAN, L.R., H. GLEITMAN & E.F. SHIPLEY (1972)   The emergence of the child as a grammarian. *Cognition* **1,** 137-164.

GLEITMAN, L., E.L. NEWPORT & H. GLEITMAN (1984)   The current status of the motherese hypothesis. *Journal of Child Language* **11,** 43-80.

GLUCKSBERG, SAM & J.H. DANKS (1975)   *Experimental psycholinguistics: An introduction.* Hillsdale, N.J.: Lawrence Erlbaum Associates.

GLUCKSBERG, S. & R.M. KRAUSS (1967)   What do people say after they have learned to talk? Studies of the development of referential communication. *Merrill-Palmer Quarterly* **13,** 309-316.

GLUCKSBERG, S., R.M. KRAUSS & R. WEISBERG (1966)   Referential communication in nursery school children: Method and some preliminary findings. *Journal of Experimental Child Psychology* **3,** 333-342.

GOLDFISH, L. & H. TAYLOR (1974)   The Optacon: A valuable device for blind persons. *New Outlook for the Blind* **68: 2,** 49-56.

GOLDIN-MEADOW, S. (1982)   The resilience of recursion: A study of a communication system developed without a conventional language model. In Wanner & Gleitman 1982, 51-77.

GOLINKOFF, R.M. & G.J. AMES (1979)   A comparison of fathers' and mothers' speech with their young children. *Child Development* **50,** 28-32.

GOMEZ, ANTONIO (1968)   What am I about. *Con Safos* **1,** 8-9. (198-99)

GOODGLASS, H. (1973)   Developmental comparison of vowels and consonants in dichotic listening. *Journal of Speech and Hearing Research* **16,** 744-752.

GOODSTEIN, L. (1961)   Intellectual impairment in children with cleft palates. *Journal of Speech and Hearing Research* **4,** 287-297.

GOODZ, N.S. (1982)   Is before really easier to understand than after? *Child Development* **53,** 822-825.

GORDON, A. (1972) *Psychological and linguistic complexity in child language.* Ph.D. dissertation, Stanford, Cal.: Stanford University. Cited in Bowerman 1979.

GORDON, H.W. (1974) Auditory specialization of the right and left hemispheres. In Marcel Kinsbourne & W.L. Smith, eds., *Hemispheric disconnection and cerebral function,* Springfield, Ill.: Charles C. Thomas, 1974, 126-136.

GORDON, J. (1885) Deaf-mutes and the public schools from 1815 to the present day. *American Annals of the Deaf* **30,** 121-143. Cited by Moores 1982, 49.

GORDON, OAKLEY J., K.M. ENGER & D.R. SHUPE (1963) *Challenging the superior student by making the study of Russian available in the elementary school curriculum via television.* U.S. Office of Education Grant 7-54-0050-024. Salt Lake City: University of Utah.

GOSSEN, G.H. (1976) Verbal Dueling in Chamula. In Kirshenblatt-Gimblett 1976, 121-146.

GRAF, O.I. (1955) Incidence of stuttering among twins. In W. Johnson & Leutenneger 1955, 381-386.

GRAHAM, F.K. & J.C. JACKSON (1970) Arousal systems and infant heart rate responses. In Lewis Lipsitt & H.W. Reese, eds., *Advances in child development and behavior, vol. 5,* New York: Academic Press, 1970, 54-117.

GRAHAM, J.K. (1966) A neurologic and electroencephalographic study of adult stutterers and matched normal speakers. *Speech Monographs* **33,** 290. Abstract. Cited in Bloodstein 1975, 118.

GRAHAM, J.T. & L.W. GRAHAM (1971) Language behavior of the mentally retarded: syntactic characteristics. *American Journal of Mental Deficiency* **75,** 623-629.

GRANT, J.R. (1915) A child's vocabulary and its growth. *Pedagogical Seminary* **22,** 183-203.

GRAVES, Z. (1980) The effect of context on mother-child interaction. Paper presented at the 5th annual Boston University Conference on Language Development, October.

GRAY, M. (1940) The X family: A clinical and laboratory study of a "stuttering" family. *Journal of Speech Disorders* **5,** 343-348.

GREENE, JUDITH (1972) *Psycholinguistics: Chomsky and psychology.* Middlesex, England: Penguin Books.

GREENFIELD, P.M., K. NELSON & E. SALTZMAN (1972) The development of rulebound strategies for manipulating seriated cups: A parallel between action and grammar. *Cognitive Psychology* **3,** 291-310.

GREENFIELD, PATRICIA M. & J. SMITH (1976) *The structure of communication in early language development.* New York: Academic Press.

GREENLEE, M. (1974) Interacting processes in the child's acquisition of stop-liquid clusters. *Papers and Reports on Child Language Development* **7,** 85-100.

GRÉGOIRE, ANTOINE (1937) *L'apprentissage du language, vol. I.* Paris: Droz. Cited in Werner & Kaplan 1963.

GREVISSE, MAURICE (1964) *Le bon usage.* Paris: Hatier. Cited in Tucker et al. 1968.

GRIDER, R.E., A. OTOMO & W. TOYOTA (1961) Comparison between second, third, and fourth grade children in the audio lingual learning of Japanese as a second language. Research report. Honolulu: University of Hawaii. Cited in McLaughlin 1978, 70.

GRIEVE, R., R. HOOGENRAAD & D. MURRAY (1977) On the young child's use of the lexis and syntax in understanding locative instructions. *Cognition* **5,** 235-250.

GRIFFITHS, P. (1974) That there deixis I: that. Unpublished paper, University of York. Cited in E. Clark & Sengul 1978, 460; Edwards 1978.

GRIMM, HANNELORE (1973) *Strukturanalytische Untersuchung der Kindersprache.* Bern: Verlag Huber. Cited in H. Clark & Clark 1977.

GROF, STANISLAV (1976) *Realms of the human unconscious.* New York: E.P. Dutton. Cited in Verny & Kelly 1981, 42.

GUDSCHINSKY, S.C. (1971) Literacy in the mother tongue and second language learning. Paper presented at the Conference on Child Language, Chicago, November 22-24. Cited in Engle 1975, 309.

GUESS, D., W. SAILOR & D.M. BAER (1974) To teach language to retarded children. In Schiefelbusch & Lloyd 1974, 529-563.

GUILLAUME, P. (1927) Les débuts de la phrase dans le langage de l'enfant. *Journal de Psychologie* **24,** 1-25. Translations: First stages of sentence formation in children's speech, E.V. Clark, tr., in Ferguson & Slobin 1973, 522-541; reprinted in Bloom 1978, 131-148. Excerpt: The emergence of the sentence, A.L. Blumenthal & J. Goodman, tr., in Blumenthal 1970, 117-127.

GUILLEMEAU, JACQUES (1635) *Childbirth; or The happy delivery of Vvomen, vherein is set downe the government of vvomen. In the time of their breeding childe, of their travaile, both naturall and contrary to nature, and of their lying in. Together with the diseases which happen to vvomen in those times and the meanes to helpe them. Vvith a treatise for the nursing of children. To vvhich is added a treatise of the diseases of infants, and young children; with the cure of them, and also of the small pox.* London: Norton & Whitaker.

GUSTASON, GERILEE, D. PFETZING & E. ZAWOLKOW (1972) *Signing Exact English.* Los Alamitos, Calif.: Modern Signs Press.

GUTZMANN, H. (1911) Beobachtungen der ersten sprachlichen und stimmlichen Entwicklung eines Kindes. *Medizinischpädagogische Monatsschrift für die gesamte Sprachheilkunde* **11,** 1-28. Cited in Werner & Kaplan 1963.

GVOZDEV, A.N. (1948) *Usvoyeniye rebenkom zvukovoy storony russkovo yazyka.* Moscow: Akademiya Pedagogicheskikh Nauk RSFSR. Cited in: D.N. Bogoyavlenskiy, *Psikhologiya usvoyeniya orfografii,* Moskow: Akademiya Pedagogicheskikh Nauk RFSR, 1957 (translated excerpt: The acquisition of Russian inflections, G. Slobin, tr., in Ferguson & Slobin 1973, 284-292); Dale 1976: 46-47; Slobin 1966.

GVOZDEV, A.N. (1949) *Formirovaniye u rebenka grammaticheskogo stroya russkogo yazyka.* Moscow: Akademiya Pedagogichesikh Nauk RSFSR. Cited in Slobin 1966.

HAHN, E.F. (1942)   A study of the relationship between stuttering occurrence and phonetic factors in oral reading. *Journal of Speech Disorders* **7,** 143-151.

HAKUTA, K. (1974a)   A preliminary report on the development of grammatical morphemes in a Japanese girl learning English as a second language. *Working papers in Bilingualism* **4: 3,** 18-44. Reprinted as: A report on the development of grammatical morphemes in a Japanese girl learning English as a second language. In Hatch 1978, 132-147.

HAKUTA, K. (1974b)   Prefabricated patterns and the emergence of structure in second language acquisition. *Language Learning* **24,** 287-297.

HAKUTA, K. (1975)   Learning to speak a second language: What exactly does the child learn? In Dato 1975, 193-208.

HAKUTA, K. (1976a)   A case study of a Japanese child learning English as a second language. *Language Learning* **26,** 321-351.

HAKUTA, K. (1976b)   The role of word order in children's acquisition of Japanese. Paper presented at the New England Child Language Association, Brown University, December. Cited in Bowerman 1979.

HALE, H. (1887)   The origin of language and the antiquity of speaking man. *Transactions of the American Association for the Advancement of Science* **35,** 279-323.

HALL, P.K. & J.B. TOMBLIN (1978)   A followup study of children with articulation and language disorders. *Journal of Speech and Hearing Disorders* **43,** 227-241.

HALLE, MORRIS, J. BRESNAN, & G.A. MILLER, eds. (1978)   *Linguistic theory and psychological reality.* Cambridge, Mass.: MIT Press.

HALLIDAY, M.A.K. (1967a)   Notes on transitivity and theme in English, part 1. *Journal of Linguistics* **3,** 37-81.

HALLIDAY, M.A.K. (1967b)   Notes on transitivity and theme in English, part 2. *Journal of Linguistics* **3,** 199-244.

HALLIDAY, MICHAEL A.K. (1975)   *Learning how to mean: Explorations in the development of language.* London: Edward Arnold.

HALLIDAY, MICHAEL A.K. & J.R. MARTIN (1981)   *Readings in systemic linguistics.* London: Batsford Academic and Educational Ltd.

HAMRE, C.E. & M.E. WINGATE (1973)   Stuttering consistency in varied contexts. *Journal of Speech and Hearing Research* **16,** 238-247.

HANSEN, B. (1975)   Varieties in Danish Sign Language and grammatical features of the original sign language. *Sign Language Studies* **8,** 249-256.

HANSEN, H.P. (1956)   The effect of a measured audience reaction on stuttering behavior patterns. *Speech Monographs* **23,** 144. Abstract.

HARLEY, R. (1963)   *Verbalism among blind children.* Research Series 10, American Foundation for the Blind.

HARMS, M.A. & J.Y. MALONE (1939)   The relationship of hearing acuity to stammering. *Journal of Speech Disorders* **4,** 363-370.

HARRIS, F.N. & J.A. FLORA (1982)   Children's use of *get* passives. *Journal of Psycholinguistic Research* **11,** 297-312.

HARRIS, L.J. & E.A. STROMMEN (1972)   The role of front-back features in children's "front," "back," and "beside" placement of objects. *Merrill-Palmer Quarterly* **18,** 259-271.

HARRISON, R. & B. PHILIPS (1971)   Observations on hearing levels of preschool cleft palate children. *Journal of Speech and Hearing Disorders* **36,** 252-256.

HARWOOD, F.W. (1959)   Quantitative study of the speech of Australian children. *Language and Speech* **2,** 237-271.

HATCH, E.M. (1971)   The young child's comprehension of time connectives. *Child Development* **42,** 2111-2113.

HATCH, EVELYN M., ed. (1978)   *Second language acquisition: A book of readings.* Rowley, Mass.: Newbury House.

HAUGEN, G.M. & R.W. MCINTIRE (1972)   Comparisons of vocal imitation, tactile stimulation, and food as reinforcers for infant vocalizations. *Developmental Psychology* **6,** 201-209.

HAVILAND, S.E. & E.V. CLARK (1974)   'This man's father is my father's son': A study of the acquisition of English kin terms. *Journal of Child Language.* **1,** 23-47. Reprinted in E. Clark 1979, 225-252.

HAVILAND, S.E. & H.H. CLARK (1974)   What's new? Acquiring new information as a process of comprehension. *Journal of Verbal Learning and Verbal Behavior* **13,** 512-521.

HAYES, JOHN R., ED. (1970)   *Cognition and the development of language.* New York: Wiley.

HAYHURST, H. (1967)   Some errors of young children in producing passive sentences. *Journal of Verbal Learning and Verbal Behavior* **6,** 654-660.

HAYNES, H., B.L. WHITE & R. HELD (1965)   Visual accomodation in human infants. *Science* **148,** 528-538.

HAYWOOD, VICTORIA (1922)   *Romantic Canada.* Toronto: Macmillan.

HEBB, DONALD O. (1949)   *The organization of behavior.* New York: Wiley.

HÉCAEN, H., G. MAZARS, A. RAMIER, M. GOLDBLUM & L. MERIENNE (1971)   Aphasie croisée chez un sujet droitier bilingue (Vietnamien—français). *Reviue Neurologique* **124,** 319-323. Cited in Albert & Obler 1978, 107.

HEHNER, BARBARA, compiler & ed. (1980)   *Blissymbols for use.* Toronto, Ontario: Blissymbolics Communication Institute.

HEJNA, R.F. (1972)   The relationship between accent or stress and stuttering during spontaneous speech. *ASHA: A Journal of the American Speech and Hearing Association* **14,** 479. Abstract.

HELFMAN, ELIZABETH S. (1981)   *Blissymbolics: speaking without speech.* New York: Elsevier-Dutton.

HELM, N.A., R.B. BUTLER & D.F. BENSON (1978)   Acquired stuttering. *Neurology* **28,** 1159-1165.

HELMERS, H. (1965) *Sprache and Humor des Kindes*. Stuttgart: Ernst Klett Verlag. Cited in P.E. McGhee, The development of the humor response: A review of the literature, *Psychological Bulletin* **76**, 328-348, 1971.

HELMREICH, H.G. & O. BLOODSTEIN (1973) The grammatical factor in childhood disfluency in relation to the continuity hypothesis. *Journal of Speech and Hearing Research* **16**, 731-738.

HERODOTUS (5th century B.C.) *The histories*. A. de Selincourt, tr. Middlesex: Penguin, 1954. Book 2, paragraph 3.

HERRIOT PETER (1970) *An introduction to the psychology of language*. London: Methuen.

HERVAS Y PANDURO, LORENZO (1785) *Origine, formazione, meccanismo, ed armonia degl'idiomi. Opera dell'abbate Don Lorenzo Hervas*. Cesena: G. Biasini. Cited in F. Müller 1877, 395.

HIGGINS, E. (1973) An analysis of the comprehensibility of three communication methods used with hearing impaired students. *American Annals of the Deaf* **118**, 46-49.

HILDRETH, G. (1958) Learning a foreign language. *French Review* **31**, 307-316.

HILDYARD, A. & D.R. OLSON (1978) Memory and inference in the comprehension of oral and written discourse. *Discourse Processes* **1**, 91-117.

HILL, H. (1944) Stuttering: II. A review and integration of physiological data. *Journal of Speech Disorders* **9**, 289-324.

HILLIER, W. (1954) Total left hemispherectomy for malignant glioma. *Neurology* **4**, 718-721.

HIRSH-PASEK, K., R. TREIMAN & M. SCHNEIDERMAN (1984) Brown & Hanlon revisited: Mothers' sensitivity to ungrammatical forms. *Journal of Child Language* **11**, 81-88.

HIRST, GRAEME (1983) *Semantic interpretation against ambiguity*. Ph.D. dissertation. Department of Computer Science Technical Report CS-83-25. Providence, R.I.: Brown University.

HIRST, G. (1984) Jumping to conclusions: Psychological reality and unreality in a word disambiguation program. Paper presented at annual meeting of the Cognitive Science Society, Boulder, Colo., June. To appear in the Proceedings.

HOCKETT, C.F. (1967) Where the tongue slips, there slip I. In *To honor Roman Jakobson: Essays on the occasion of his seventieth birthday*, The Hague: Mouton, 1967. Reprinted in Victoria A. Fromkin, ed., *Speech errors as linguistic evidence*, The Hague: Mouton, 1973, 93-119. Page numbers refer to this version.

HOCKETT, CHARLES F. (1968) *State of the art*. The Hague: Mouton.

HOEMANN, H.W. (1975) The transparency of meaning of sign language gestures. *Sign Language Studies* **7**, 151-161.

HOEMANN, HARRY W., E. OATES & S. A. HOEMANN, eds. (1981) *The sign language of Brazil*. Mill Neck, N.Y.: Mill Neck Foundation.

HOLLAND, V.M. & D.S. PALERMO (1975) On learning "less": Language and cognitive development. *Child Development* **46**, 437-443.

HOLMES, K.M. & D.W. HOLMES (1980) Signed and spoken language development in a hearing child of hearing parents. *Sign Language Studies* **28**, 239-254.

HOLZMAN, M. (1972) The use of interrogative forms in the verbal interaction of three mothers and their children. *Journal of Psycholinguistic Research* **1**, 311-336.

HOLZMAN, MATILDA (1983) *The language of children: Development in home and school*. Englewood Cliffs, N.J.: Prentice-Hall.

HONSA, VLADIMIR & M.J. HARDMAN-DE-BAUTISTA, eds. (1978) *Papers in Linguistics and Child Language: Ruth Hirsch Weir Memorial Volume*. The Hague: Mouton.

HOOD, S.B. (1975) Effect of communicative stress on the frequency and form-types of disfluent behavior in adult stutterers. *Journal of Fluency Disorders* **1**, 36-47.

HOPKINS, K. & L. MCGUIRE (1966) Mental measurement of the blind: The validity of the Wechsler Intelligence Scale for Children. *International Journal for the Education of the Blind*. **15**: 3, 65-73.

HOPKINS, L.A. (1954) Heredity and deafness. *Eugenics Quarterly* **1**, 193-199.

HORGAN, D. (1978) The development of the full passive. *Journal of Child Language* **5**, 65-80.

HÖRMANN, HANS (1971) *Psycholinguistics: An introduction to research and theory*. H. Stern, tr. New York: Springer-Verlag.

HORTON, D. (1976) Linguistic knowledge at early stage I: Evidence from successive single word utterances. *Papers and Reports on Child Language Development* **12**, 116-126.

HOUSEHOLDER, FRED. W. (1971) *Linguistic speculations*. London: Cambridge University Press.

HOUSTON, SUSAN H. (1972) *A survey of psycholinguistics*. The Hague: Mouton.

HOWE, C.J. (1980) Learning language from mothers' replies. *First Language* **1**, 83-97.

HOWIE, P.M. (1976) The role of genetic factors in stuttering: A twin study. Paper presented at the 1976 ASHA meeting. Abstract in *ASHA: A Journal of the American Speech and Hearing Association* **18**, 656. Cited in Sheehan & Costley 1977, 55.

HOWIE, P.M. (1981) Concordance for stuttering in monozygotic and dizygotic twin pairs. *Journal of Speech and Hearing Research* **24**, 317-321.

HOYER, A.E. & G. HOYER (1924) Über die Lallsprache eines Kindes. *Zeitschrift für angewandte Psychologie* **24**, 363-384. Cited in McLaughlin 1978.

HUMMEL, D.D. (1982) Syntactic and conversational characteristics of fathers' speech. *Journal of Psycholinguistic Research* **11**, 465-483.

HUTTENLOCHER, J. (1974) The origins of language comprehension. In Robert L. Solso, ed., *Theories in cognitive psychology: The Loyola symposium*, Potomac, Md.: Lawrence Erlbaum, 1974, 331-368.

HUXLEY, R. (1970)   The development of the correct use of subject personal pronouns in two children. In Flores D'Arcais & Levelt 1970, 141-165.

HUXLEY, RENIRA & E. INGRAM, eds. (1971)   *Methods and models in language acquisition.* New York: Academic Press.

ILLINGWORTH, R.S. (1955)   Crying in infants and children. *British Medical Journal* 1, 75-78.

IMEDADZE, N.V. (1960)   K psikhologicheskoy prirode rannego dvuyazychiya. *Voprosy psikhologii* 6, 60-69. Cited in McLaughlin 1978.

IMEDADZE, N.V. (1967)   On the psychological nature of child speech formation under conditions of exposure to two languages. *International Journal of Psychology* 2, 129-132. Reprinted in Hatch 1978, 23-32.

INDUSTRIAL HOME FOR THE BLIND (1959)   *Rehabilitation of deaf-blind persons, vol. 2: Communication—A key to service for deaf-blind men and women.* Brooklyn: Industrial Home for the Blind.

INGRAM, D. (1971)   Transitivity in child language. *Language* 47, 888-910.

INGRAM, D. (1974a)   Phonological rules in young children. *Journal of Child Language* 1, 49-64.

INGRAM, D. (1974b)   Fronting in child phonology. *Journal of Child Language* 1, 233-241.

INGRAM, D. (1975)   Surface contrast in children's speech. *Journal of Child Language* 2, 287-792.

INGRAM, DAVID (1976)   *Phonological disability in children.* London: Edward Arnold.

INGRAM, D. (1978)   Sensori-motor intelligence and language development. In Lock 1978, 261-290.

INGRAM, D. & D. TYACK (1979)   Inversion of subject NP and aux in children's questions. *Journal of Psycholinguistic Research* 8, 333-341.

INGRAM, R.S. (1963)   Late and poor talkers. In M. Bax, ed., *The child who does not talk.* London: Heinemann/ Spastic Society.

INGRAM, T.T.S. (1972)   The classification of speech and language disorders in young children. In Rutter & Martin 1972, 13-32.

INHELDER, BARBEL & J. PIAGET (1958)   *The growth of logical thinking from childhood to adolescence.* New York: Harper & Row.

IRONSMITH, M. & G.J. WHITEHURST (1978)   The development of listener abilities in communication: How children deal with ambiguous information. *Child Development* 49, 348-352.

IRWIN, O.C. (1942)   The developmental status of speech sounds of ten feeble-minded children. *Child Development* 13, 29-39.

IRWIN, O.C. (1947a)   Infant speech: Consonant sounds according to place of articulation. *Journal of Speech Disorders* 12, 397-401.

IRWIN, O.C. (1947b)   Infant speech: Consonant sounds according to manner of articulation. *Journal of Speech Disorders* 12, 402-404.

IRWIN, O.C. (1948a)   Infant speech: Development of vowel sounds. *Journal of Speech and Hearing Disorders* 13, 31-34.

IRWIN, O.C. (1948b)   Infant speech: The effect of family occupational status and of age on use of sound types. *Journal of Speech and Hearing Disorders* 13, 224-226.

IRWIN, O.C. (1952)   Speech development in the young child. 2. Some factors related to the speech development of the infant and the young child. *Journal of Speech and Hearing Disorders* 17, 269-279.

IRWIN, O.C. (1957)   Phonetical description of speech development in childhood. In Louise Kaiser, ed. *Manual of phonetics,* Amsterdam: North-Holland, 1957, 403-425.

IRWIN, O.C. & T. CURRY (1941)   Vowel elements in the crying vocalization of infants under ten days of age. *Child Development* 12, 99-109.

ITOH, H. & E. HATCH (1978)   Second language acquisition: A case study. In Hatch 1978, 76-88.

JACOBSON, J.J., D.C. BOERSMA, R.B. FIELDS & K.L. OLSON (1983)   Paralinguistic features of adult speech to infants and small children. *Child Development* 54, 436-442.

JAKOBOVITS, LEON A. & M.S. MIRON, eds. (1967)   *Readings in the psychology of language.* Englewood Cliffs, N.J.: Prentice-Hall.

JAKOBSON, R. (1939)   Les lois phoniques du langage enfantin et leur place dans la phonologie générale. Supplement to N.S. Trubetzkoy, *principes de phonologie,* Paris, 1949. Reprinted in Roman Jakobson, *Selected writings,* Mouton: The Hague, 1962, 1971: vol. 1, 317-327. Translation: The sound laws of child language and their place in general phonology, in Bar-Adon & Leopold 1971: 75-82.

JAKOBSON, ROMAN (1941)   *Child language, aphasia, and phonological universals.* The Hague: Mouton. Translation 1968.

JAKOBSON, R. (1962)   Anthony's contribution to linguistic theory. Forward to Weir 1962, 18-20.

JAKOBSON, ROMAN & M. HALLE (1956)   *Fundamentals of language.* The Hague: Mouton.

JAMES, S. & M.A. SEEBACH (1982)   The pragmatic function of children's questions. *Journal of Speech and Hearing Research* 25, 2-11.

JAMES, WILLIAM (1890)   *The principles of psychology, vol. II.* New York: Holt, Rinehart and Winston.

JENKINS, J. & D. PALERMO (1964)   Mediation processes and the acquisition of linguistic structure. In Bellugi & Brown 1964, 141-169.

JESPERSON, OTTO (1922)   *Language, its nature, development, and origin.* London: Allen & Unwin.

JESPERSON, OTTO (1925)   *Language,* New York: Holt, Rinehart & Winston.

JOCIĆ, M. (1976)   Types of adaptations in adult speech when communicating with a child. In Waterson & Snow 1976, 159-171.

JOHNSON, C.E., J.S. FLORES & F.P. ELLISON (1963)   The effect of foreign language instruction on basic learning in elementary schools. *The Modern Language Journal* **47**, 8-11.

JOHNSON, E.H. (1948)   Ability of pupils in a school for the deaf to understand various methods of communication. *American Annals of the Deaf* **93**, 194-213, 258-314.

JOHNSON, H.L. (1975)   The meaning of *before* and *after* for pre-school children. *Journal of Experimental Child Psychology* **19**, 88-99.

JOHNSON, W. (1944)   The Indians have no word for it. I. Stuttering in children. *Quarterly Journal of Speech* **30**, 330-337.

JOHNSON, WENDELL, (1961)   *Stuttering and what you can do about it.* Minneapolis: University of Minnesota Press.

JOHNSON, WENDELL & ASSOCIATES (1959)   *The onset of stuttering.* Minneapolis: University of Minnesota Press.

JOHNSON, WENDELL ET AL. (1967)   *Speech handicapped school children, 3rd ed.* New York: Harper & Row.

JOHNSON, W. & S.F. BROWN (1935)   Stuttering in relation to various speech sounds. *Quarterly Journal of Speech* **21**, 481-496.

JOHNSON, W. & A. KING (1942)   An angle board and hand usage study of stutterers and non-stutterers. *Journal of Experimental Psychology* **31**, 293-311.

JOHNSON, W. & J.R. KNOTT (1937)   Studies in the psychology of stuttering: I. The distribution of moments of stuttering in successive readings of the same material. *Journal of Speech Disorders* **2**, 17-19.

JOHNSON, WENDELL & R.R. LEUTENNEGGER, eds. (1955)   *Stuttering in children and adults.* Minneapolis: University of Minnesota Press.

JOHNSON, W. & L. ROSEN (1937)   Studies in the psychology of stuttering: VII. Effect of certain changes in speech pattern upon frequency of stuttering. *Journal of Speech Disorders* **2**, 105-109.

JOHNSON, W. & A. SOLOMON (1937)   Studies in the psychology of stuttering: IV. A quantitative study of expectation of stuttering as a process involving a low degree of consciousness. *Journal of Speech Disorders* **2**, 95-97.

JOHNSTON, J.R. & T.K. SCHERY (1976)   The use of grammatical morphemes by children with commuicative disorders. In Morehead & Morehead 1976, 239-258.

JONES, S.A. & H.A. MOSS (1971)   Age, state, and maternal behavior associated with infant vocalizations. *Child Development* **42**, 1038-1051.

JORDAN, I.K. & R. BATTISON (1976)   A referential communication experiment with foreign signers. *Sign Language Studies* **10**, 69-80.

JORDAN, I.K., G. GUSTASON & R. ROSEN (1979)   An update on communication trends at programs for the deaf. *American Annals of the Deaf* **124**, 350-357.

JUSCZYK, P., B. ROSNER, J. CUTTING, C. FOARD & L. SMITH (1977)   Categorical perception of nonspeech sounds by two-month-old-infants. *Perception and Psychophysics* **27**, 50-54.

KAGAN, JEROME, R. KEARSLEY & P. ZELAZO (1978)   *Infancy: Its place in human development.* Cambridge, Mass.: Harvard University Press.

KANNER, L. (1943)   Autistic disturbances of affective contact. *Nervous Child* **2**, 217-250. Reprinted in Lahey 1978, 145-153.

KANNER, L. (1946)   Irrelevant and metaphorical language in early infant autism. *American Journal of Psychiatry* **103**, 242-246.

KAPER, W. (1959)   *Kindersprachforschung mit Hilfe des Kindes.* Groningen: Wolters. Cited in Werner & Kaplan 1963: 127.

KAPLAN, E. & G. KAPLAN (1971)   The prelinguistic child. In John Eliot, ed., *Human development and cognitive processes,* New York: Holt, Rinehart & Winston, 1971, 358-381.

KARLIN, I.W. & A.E. SOBEL (1940)   A comparative study of the blood chemistry of stutterers and non-stutterers. *Speech Monographs* **7**, 75-84.

KARLIN, I.W. & M. STRAZZULA (1952)   Speech and language problems of mentally deficient children. *Journal of Speech and Hearing Disorders* **17**, 286-294.

KARMILOFF-SMITH, ANNETTE (1979)   *A functional approach to child language: A study of determiners and reference.* Cambridge: Cambridge University Press.

KATZ, JERROLD J. (1966)   *The philosophy of language.* New York: Harper & Row.

KATZ, N., E. BAKER & J. McNAMARA (1974)   What's in a name? A study of how children learn common and proper names. *Child Development* **45**, 469-473.

KAUFMAN, BARRY N. (1975)   *Son-rise.* New York: Harper & Row.

KAVANAUGH, R.B. (1979)   Observations on the role of logically constrained sentences in the comprehension of 'before' and 'after'. *Journal of Child Language* **6**, 353-357.

KAYE, K. (1976)   Infants' effects upon mothers' teaching strategies. In John C. Glidewell, ed., *The social context of learning and development,* New York: Gardiner Press, 1977, 173-206.

KAYE, K. (1980)   Why we don't talk 'baby talk' to babies. *Journal of Child Language* **7**, 489-507.

KEATING, RAYMOND F. (1963)   *A study of the effectiveness of language laboratories.* New York: The Institute of Administrative Research.

KEENAN, E.O. (1974a)   Again and again: The pragmatics of imitation in child language. Paper presented at the 73rd Annual Meeting of the American Anthropoligical Association, Mexico City. Cited in H. Clark & Clark 1977.

KEENAN, E.O. (1974b)   Conversational competence in children. *Journal of Child Language* **1**, 163-183.
KEENEY, T.J. & J. WOLFE (1972)   The acquisition of agreement in English. *Journal of Verbal Learning and Verbal Behavior* **11**, 698-705.
KELKAR, A. (1964)   Marathi baby talk. *Word* **20**, 40-54.
KELLER, HELEN (1903)   *The story of my life.* New York: Doubleday.
KELLER, HELEN (1908)   *The world I live in.* New York: J.F. Taply.
KENDON, A. (1980)   A description of deaf-mute sign language from the Enga Province of Papau New Guinea with some comparative discussion. Part 1: The formational properties of Enga signs. *Semiotica* **31**, 1-34. Part 2: The semiotic functioning of Enga signs. *Semiotica* **32**, 81-117. Part 3: Aspects of utterance construction. *Semiotica* **32**, 245-313.
KENYERES, A. (1938)   Comment une petite Hongroise de sept ans apprehend le français. *Archives de Psychologie* **26**, 321-366.
KERNAN, K.T. (1969)   *The acquisition of language by Samoan children.* Ph.D. dissertation. Berkeley: University of California. Cited in R. Brown 1973.
KESS, JOSEPH F. (1976)   *Psycholinguistics: Introductory perspectives.* New York: Academic Press.
KESSEL, F.S. (1970)   The role of syntax in children's comprehension from ages six to twelve. *Monographs of the Society for Research in Child Development.* **35: 6.**
KESSLER, C. (1972)   Syntactic contrasts in child bilingualism. *Language Learning* **22**, 221-233.
KESSLER, C. & I. IDAR (1977)   The acquisition of English syntactic structures by a Vietnamese child. Paper presented at the 2nd Language Research Forum, UCLA, February.
KHUBCHANDANI, L.M. (1978)   Multilingual education in India. In Spolsky & Cooper 1978, 88-125.
KIMURA, D. (1963)   Speech lateralization in young children as determined by an auditory test. *Journal of Comparative Physiological Psychology* **56**, 899-902.
KIMURA, D. (1967)   Functional asymmetry of the brain in dichotic listening. *Cortex* **3**, 163-178.
KING, H.L. & G.A. BOURGEOIS (1947)   *Bulletin of the United States Army Medical Department* **7**, 147. Cited in Illingworth 1955, 75.
KINSBOURNE, M. (1980)   Disorders of mental development. In Menkes 1980, 636-666.
KIPLING, RUDYARD (1894)   *The jungle book.* London: Macmillan, 1961.
KIRBY, J. (1978)   Blissymbols and an aphasic patient. *Alberta Speech and Hearing Association Journal* **3**, 4.
KIRSHENBLATT-GIMBLETT, BARBARA, ed. (1976)   *Speech play.* Philadelphia: University of Pennsylvania Press.
KLEIN, W.L. (1963)   *An investigation of the spontaneous speech of children during problem solving.* Ph.D. dissertation. Rochester, N.Y.: University of Rochester. Cited in Kohlberg et al. 1968.
KLIMA, E.S. & U. BELLUGI (1966)   Syntactic regularities in the speech of children. In John Lyons & R.J. Wales, eds., *Psycholinguistic papers,* Edinburgh: Edinburgh University Press, 1966, 183-208. Reprinted in: Bar-Adon & Leopold 1971, 412-424; David A. Reibel & S.A. Schane, eds., *Modern studies in English,* Englewood Cliffs, N.J.: Prentice-Hall, 1969, 448-466.
KLIMA, EDWARD & U. BELLUGI (1979)   *The signs of language.* Cambridge, Mass.: Harvard University Press.
KLIMA, E., U. BELLUGI & E. LENTZ (1979)   Wit and play on signs. In Klima & Bellugi 1979, 319-339.
KLOPPING, H.W. (1972)   Language understanding of deaf students under three auditory-visual stimulus conditions. *American Annals of the Deaf.* **117**, 389-396.
KLOSS, HEINZ & G.D. McCONNELL, eds. (1978)   *Linguistic composition of the nations of the world, vol. 2: North America.* Quebec City: Les Presses de L'Université Laval.
KLOSS, HEINZ & G.D. McCONNELL, eds. (1979)   *Linguistic composition of the nations of the world, vol. 3: Central and South America.* Quebec City: Les Presses de L'Université Laval.
KNAPP, HERBERT & MARY KNAPP (1976)   *One potato, two potato: The secret education of American children.* New York: W.W. Norton.
KNOTT, J.R., W. JOHNSON & W.J. WEBSTER (1937)   Studies in the psychology of stuttering: II. A quantitative evaluation of expectation of stuttering in relation to the occurrence of stuttering. *Journal of Speech Disorders* **2**, 20-22.
KOBASHIGAWA, B. (1969)   Repetitions in a mother's speech to her child. In *The structure of linguistic input to children.* Working Paper 14. Language Behavior Research Laboratory, University of California, Berkeley. ERIC ED138109.
KOHL, H. (1979)   The strange ones. *The Canadian Magazine,* April 7, 10-14.
KOHLBERG, L., J. YAEGER & E. HJERTHOLM (1968)   Private speech: Four studies and a review of theories. *Child Development* **39**, 691-736.
KONIGSMARK, B. (1972a)   *Genetic hearing loss with no associated abnormalities: A Review.* Maico Audiological Library Series XI: 6. Cited in Moores 1982.
KONIGSMARK, B. (1972b)   *Genetic hearing loss with no associated abnormalities: A review.* Maico Audiological Library Series XI: 7. Cited in Moores 1982.
KONSTANTAREAS, M.M., J. OXMAN, D. TAYLOR & T. RICHARDS (1977a)   *Say it with signs.* Film. Also in ¾″ videotape. Toronto: Clarke Institute of Psychiatry.
KONSTANTAREAS, M.M., J. OXMAN & C.D. WEBSTER (1977b)   Simultaneous communication with autistic and other severely dysfunctional children. *Journal of Communication Disorders* **10**, 267-282.
KRAMER, P.E., E. KOFF & Z. LURIA (1972)   The development of competence in an exceptional structure in older children and young adults. *Child Development* **43**, 121-130.
KRASHEN, S.D. (1973)   Lateralization, language learning, and the critical period: Some new evidence. *Language Learning* **23**, 63-74.

KRASHEN, S.D. (1975) The development of cerebral dominance and language learning: More new evidence. In Dato 1975, 179-192.

KRASHEN, D.S., V. SFERLAZZA, L. FELDMAN & A.K. FATHMAN (1976) Adult performance on the SLOPE test: More evidence for a natural sequence in adult language acquisition. *Language Learning* **26,** 145-151.

KUCZAJ, S.A. II (1978) Why do children fail to overgeneralize the progressive inflection? *Journal of Child Language* **5,** 167-171.

KUCZAJ, S.A. II & A.R. LEDERBERG (1977) Height, age, and function: Differing influences on children's comprehension of ''younger'' and ''older.'' *Journal of Child Language* **4,** 395-416.

KUCZAJ, S.A. II & M.P. MARATSOS (1975) On the acquisition of *front, back,* and *side. Child Development* **46,** 202-210.

KUHL, P.A. & J.D. MILLER (1975) Speech perception by the chinchilla: Voiced-voiceless distinction in alveolar-plosive consonants. *Science* **190,** 69-72.

KURSHEV, V.A. (1968) Issledovanie vnerechenovo dykhaniya u zaikayushchikhsya. *Zhurnal Nevropatologii i Psikhiatrii Imeni S.S. Korsakova (Moskva)* **68,** 1840-1841. Cited in Bloodstein 1975, 105.

KUSCHEL, R. (1973) The silent inventor: The creation of a sign language by the only deaf-mute on a Polynesian island. *Sign Language Studies* **3,** 1-27.

KUSSMAUL, ADOLF (1885) *De Störungen der Sprache.* Leipzig: F.C.W. Vogel. Cited in Werner & Kaplan 1963, 105.

KUUSINEN, J. & E. SALIN (1971) Children's learning of unfamiliar phonological sequences. *Perceptual and Motor Skills* **33,** 559-562.

LABOV, W. (1973) The boundary of words and their meanings. In Charles-James N. Bailey & R. Shuy, eds., *New ways of analyzing variation in English,* Washington, D.C.: Georgetown University Press, 1973, 340-373.

LABOV, W. & T. LABOV (1978) Learning the syntax of questions. In Robin N. Campbell & P.T. Smith, eds., *Recent advances in the psychology of language: Formal and experimental approaches, vol. 4b,* New York: Plenum, 1978, 1-44.

LACKNER, J.R. (1968) A developmental study of language behavior in retarded children. *Neuropsychologia* **6,** 301-320. Reprinted in: Lahey 1978, 19-42; Morehead & Morehead 1976, 181-208.

LACZKOWSKI, A. (1965) Urine investigations in children with speech defects. *De Therapia Vocis et Loquelae, vol. 1.* XIII Congress of the International Society of Logopaediae et Phoniatriae.

LADEFOGED, PETER, R. GLICK & C. CRIPER (1968) *Language in Uganda.* London: Oxford University Press.

LAHEY, M. (1974) Use of prosody and syntactic markers in children's comprehension of spoken sentences. *Journal of Speech and Hearing Research* **17,** 656-668.

LAHEY, MARGARET, ed. (1978) *Readings in childhood language disorders.* New York: Wiley.

LAMB, M. (1977) Influence of the child on marital quality and family interaction during the prenatal, perinatal, and infancy periods. Paper presented at the Conference on the Contribution of the Child to Marital Quality and Family Interaction through the Life Span, Pennsylvania State University, April. Cited in Murray 1979, 207.

LAMB, M.M., F.B. WILSON & H.A. LEEPER (1972) A comparison of selected cleft palate children and their siblings on the variables of intelligence, hearing loss, and visual-perceptual-motor abilities. *Cleft Palate Journal* **9,** 218-228.

LAMBERT, W.E. (1967) A social psychology of bilingualism. *Journal of Social Issues* **23,** 91-109.

LAMBERT, W.E., H. GILES & O. PICARD (1975) Language attitudes in a French-American community. *International Journal of the Sociology of Language* **4,** 127-152.

LAMBERT, WALLACE E. & G.R. TUCKER (1972) *Bilingual education of children: The St. Lambert experiment.* Rowley, Mass.: Newbury House.

LAMSON, MARY S. (1881) *Life and education of Laura Dewey Bridgman (the deaf, dumb and blind girl).* New York: Arno, 1975.

LANE, HARLAN (1976) *The wild boy of Aveyron.* Cambridge, Mass: Harvard University Press.

LANE, HARLAN & FRANCIS GROSJEAN (1980) *Recent perspectives on American Sign Language.* Hillsdale, N.J.: Lawrence Erlbaum.

LANE, HARLAN & R. PILLARD (1978) *The wild boy of Burundi: A study of an outcast child.* New York: Random House.

LANE, V.W. & J.M. SAMPLES (1981) Facilitating communication skills in adult apraxics: Application of Blissymbols in a group setting. *Journal of Communication Disorders* **14,** 157-167.

LANGE, S. & K. LARSSON (1973) Syntactical development of a Swedish girl Embla, between 20 and 42 months of age, I: Age 20-25 months. Report 1, Project Child Language Syntax, Institutionem for Nordiska Sprak, Stockholm Universitet. Cited in E. Clark & Sengul 1978.

LANGOVÁ, J & L. ŠVÁB (1973) Reduction of stuttering under experimental social isolation. The role of the adaption effect. *Folia Phoniatica* **25,** 17-22.

LANSDELL, H. (1969) Verbal non-verbal factors in right-hemisphere speech: Relation to early neurological history. *Journal of Comparative and Physiological Psychology* **69,** 734-738.

LANYON, R. (1969) Speech: Relation of nonfluency to information value. *Science* **164,** 451-452.

LARSEN-FREEMAN, D. (1976) An explanation for the morpheme acquisition order of second language learners. *Language Learning* **26,** 125-134.

LASKY, R.E., A. SYRDAL-LASKY & R.E. KLEIN (1975) VOT discrimination by four to six and a half month old infants from Spanish environments. *Journal of Experimental Child Psychology* **20,** 215-225.

LASS, NORMAN J., ed. (1979) *Speech and language: Advances in basic research and practice, vol. 2.* New York: Academic Press.

LAUERMAN, C. (1981) Is U.S. getting lost in the translation? *Chicago Tribune,* August 26, Sect. 2, 1-3.

LECOURS, A.R. (1975) Myelogenetic correlates of the development of speech and language. In Lenneberg & Lenneberg 1975a, 121-135.

LEE, L. (1966) Developmental sentence types: A Method for comparing normal and deviant syntactic development. *Journal of Speech and Hearing Disorders* **31**, 311-330.

LEINO, WALTER B. & L.B. HAAK (1963) *The teaching of Spanish in the elementary school and the effect on achievement in other selected subject areas.* U.S. Office of Education Contract SAE 9515. St. Paul, Minn.: Public Schools.

LEMERT, E.M. (1953) Some Indians who stutter. *Journal of Speech and Hearing Disorders* **18**, 168-174.

LEMPERS, J., E.L. FLAVELL & J.H. FLAVELL (1977) The development in very young children of tacit knowledge concerning visual perception. *Genetic Psychology Monographs* **95**, 3-53.

LEMPERT, H. (1978) Extrasyntactic factors affecting passive sentence comprehension by young children. *Child Development* **49**, 694-699.

LENNEBERG, E.H. (1962) Understanding language without ability to speak: A case report. *Journal of Abnormal and Social Psychology* **65**, 419-425. Reprinted in Norman S. Endler, L.R. Boulter & H. Ossler, eds., *Contemporary issues in developmental psychology*, New York: Holt Rinehart & Winston.

LENNEBERG, E.H. (1964) Language disorders in childhood. *Harvard Educational Review* **34**, 152-177.

LENNEBERG, ERIC H. (1967) *Biological foundations of language.* New York: Wiley.

LENNEBERG, ERIC H. & E. LENNEBERG, eds. (1975) *Foundations of language development: A multidisciplinary approach, vol. 1.* New York: Academic Press.

LENNEBERG, E.H., I.A. NICHOLS & E.R. ROSENBERGER (1964) Primative stages of language development in mongolism. *Disorders of Communication* **42**, 119-137.

LENNEBERG, E.H., F.G. REBELSY & I.A. NICHOLS (1965) The vocalization of infants born to deaf and to hearing parents. *Vita Humana (Human Development)* **8**, 23-37.

LEONARD, L.B. (1972) What is deviant language? *Journal of Speech and Hearing Disorders* **37**, 427-447.

LEONARD, LAURENCE B. (1976) *Meaning in child language.* New York: Grune & Stratton.

LEONARD, L.B. & M.E. FEY (1979) The early lexicons of normal and language-disordered children: Developmental and training considerations. In Lass 1979, 113-147.

LEONARD, L.B. & R.G. SCHWARTZ (1978) Focus characteristics of single-word utterences after syntax. *Journal of Child Language* **5**, 151-158.

LEONARD, L.B., R.G. SCHWARTZ, K. CHAPMAN, L.E. ROWAN, P.A. PRELOCK, B. TERRELL, A.L. WEISS & C. MESSICK (1982) Early lexical acquisition in children with specific language impairment *Journal of Speech and Hearing Research* **25**, 554-564.

LEOPOLD, WERNER (1939) *Speech development of bilingual child: A linguist's record, vol. 1: Vocabulary growth in the first two years.* Evanston, Ill.: Northwestern University Press. Excerpt in Bloom 1978, 4-30.

LEOPOLD, WERNER (1974) *Speech development of a bilingual child: A linguist's record, vol. 2: Sound-learning in the first two years.* Evanston, Ill.: Northwestern University Press.

LEOPOLD, WERNER (1949a) *Speech development of a bilingual child: A linguist's record, vol. 3: Grammar and general problems in the first two years.* Evanston, Ill.: Northwestern University Press.

LEOPOLD, WERNER (1949b) *Speech development of a bilingual child: A linguist's record, vol. 4: Diary from age two.* Evanston, Ill.: Northwestern University Press.

LEOPOLD, W. (1956-57) Ein Kind lernt zwei Sprachen. *Sprachforum* **2**, 248-252.

LEWIS, E.G. (1978) Bilingual education and social change in the Soviet Union. In Spolsky & Cooper 1978, 203-248.

LEWIS, MICHAEL & L.A. ROSENBLUM, eds. (1977) *Interaction, conversation, and the development of language.* New York: Wiley.

LEWIS, MORRIS M. (1936) *Infant speech.* New York: Harcourt Brace Jovanovich.

LEWIS, M.M. (1938) The beginning and early functions of questions in a child's speech. *British Journal of Educational Psychology* **8**, 150-171.

LEWIS, MORRIS M. (1957) *How children learn to speak.* London: Harrap. Republished: New York: Basic Books. Page numbers refer to this edition.

LEWIS, MORRIS M. (1963) *Language, thought and personality.* New York: Basic Books.

L'HERMITTE, R., H. HÉCAEN, J. DUBOIS, A. CULIOLI & A. TABOURET-KELLER (1966) Le probleme de l'aphasie des polyglottes: Remarques sur quelques observations. *Neuropsycologia* **4**, 315-329. Cited in Albert & Obler 1978, 107.

LIBERMAN, A.M., F.S. COOPER, D. SHANKWEILER & M. STUDDERT-KENNEDY (1967) Perception of the speech code. *Psychological Review* **74**, 431-461.

LIDDELL, S.K. (1978) Nonmanual signals and relative clauses in ASL. In Siple 1978, 59-90.

LIEBERMAN, PHILIP (1967) *Intonation, perception, and language.* Cambridge, Mass.: MIT Press.

LIGHTBOWN, P.M. (1978) Question form and question function in the speech of young French L2 learners. In Paradis 1978, 21-43.

LILEY, A. (1972) The fetus as a personality. *The Australian and New Zealand Journal of Psychiatry* **6**, 99-105. Cited in Verny & Kelly 1981, 37.

LIMBER, J. (1973) The genesis of complex sentences. In T. Moore 1973, 169-185.

LIMBER, J. (1977) Language in child and chimp? *American Psychologist* **32**, 280-295. Reprinted in Sebeok & Umiker-Sebeok 1980, 197-220.

LING, D. (1972)   Acoustic stimulus duration in relation to behavioral responses of newborn infants. *Journal of Speech and Hearing Research* **15**, 567-571.

LING, D. (1977)   Statement made in *Across the silence barrier,* film for television, NOVA series, WGBH-TV, producer, New York: Time-Life Films.

LING, D. & B.R. CLARKE (1975)   Cued Speech: An evaluative study. *American Annals of the Deaf* **120**, 480-488.

LING, DANIEL & AGNES LING (1978)   *Aural habilitation: The foundations of verbal learning in hearing-impaired children.* Washington: The Alexander Graham Bell Association for the Deaf.

LISKER, L. & A.S. ABRAMSON (1970)   The voicing dimension: Some experiments in comparative phonetics. In B. Hala, M. Romportl & P. Janota, eds., *Proceedings of the Sixth International Congress of Phonetic Sciences (Prague, 1967),* Prague: Academia Publishing House of the Czechoslovak Academy of Sciences, 1970, 563-573.

LIVINGSTON, S. (1983)   Levels of development in the language of deaf children. *Sign Language Studies* **40**, 193-286.

LOCK, ANDREW, ed. (1978)   *Action, gesture and symbol: The emergence of language.* New York: Academic Press.

LOCK, A. (1980)   *The guided reinvention of language.* New York: Academic Press.

LOCKE, J.L. (1979)   Homonomy and sound change in the child's acquisition of phonology. In Lass 1979, 257-282.

LOCKWOOD, DAVID (1972)   *Introduction to stratificational grammar.* New York: Harcourt Brace Jovanovich.

LOPATO, E.W. (1963)   FLES and academic achievement. *The French Review* **36**, 499-506.

LORENZ, KONRAD (1952)   *King Solomon's ring.* London: Methuen.

LOTTER, V. (1966)   Services for a group of autistic children in Middlesex. In Wing 1966, 241-255.

LOVAAS, O.I. (1966)   A program for the establishment of speech in psychotic children. In J. Wing 1966, 115-144.

LOVAAS, O.I. & R. KOEGEL, J.Q. SIMMONS & J.S. LONG (1973)   Some generalization and follow-up measures on autistic children in behavior therapy. *Journal of Applied Behavior Analysis* **6**, 131-166.

LOVAAS, O.I., R. SCHREIBMAN, R. KOEGEL & R. REHM (1971)   Selective responding by autistic children to multiple sensory input. *Journal of Abnormal Psychology* **77**, 211-222. Reprinted in Lahey 1978, 219-234.

LOVAAS, O.I., J.W. VARNI, R.L. KOEGEL & N. LORSCH (1977)   Some observations on the nonextinguishability of children's speech. *Child Development* **48**, 1121-1127.

LOVELL, K. & B. BRADBURY (1967)   The learning of English morphology in educationally subnormal special school children. *American Journal of Mental Deficiency.* **71**, 609-615.

LOVELL, K. & E.M. DIXON (1965)   The growth and control of grammar in imitation, comprehension, and production. *Journal of Child Psychology and Psychiatry and Allied Disciplines* **5**, 1-9.

LUCHSINGER, R. (1959)   Die Vererbung von Sprach- und Stimmstörungen. *Folia Phoniatica* **11**, 7-64. Cited in Bloodstein 1975, 90.

LUFTIG, R.L. & L.L. LLOYD (1981)   Manual sign translucency and referential concreteness in the learning of signs. *Sign Language Studies* **30**, 49-60.

LYONS-RUTH, K. (1975)   Integration of auditory and visual spatial information during early infancy. Paper presented at the meeting of the Society for Research in Child Development, Denver, April. Cited in Lyons-Ruth 1977.

LYONS-RUTH, K. (1977)   Bimodal perception in infancy: Response to auditory-visual incongruity. *Child Development* **48**, 820-827.

MACAULEY, B.D. (1968)   A program for teaching speech and beginning reading to nonverbal retardates. In H.N. Sloane & B.D. MacAuley, eds., *Operant procedures in remedial speech and language training,* Boston: Houghton Mifflin.

MACCORQUODALE, K. (1969)   B.F. Skinner's *Verbal behavior:* A retrospective appreciation. *Journal of the Experimental Analysis of Behavior* **12**, 831-841.

MACE, L.L. & E.R. KEISLAR (1965)   Reversibility of stimulus and response terms following discrimination learning of French phonemes. *Journal of Educational Psychology* **56**, 46-49.

MACKEY, WILLIAM F. (1967)   *Bilingualism as a world problem.* Montreal, Que.: Harvest House.

MACKEY, WILLIAM F. (1972)   *Bilingual education in a binational school: A study of equal language maintenance through free alternation.* Rowley, Mass.: Newbury House.

MACLEAN, CHARLES (1978)   *The wolf children.* London: Allen Lane.

MACNAMARA, JOHN (1966)   *Bilingualism in primary education.* Edinburgh: Edinburgh University Press.

MACNAMARA, J. (1974)   Nurseries as models for language classrooms. In Stephen Carey, ed., *Bilingualism, biculturalism, and education,* Edmonton: University of Alberta Press, 1974, 91-94.

MACNAMARA, J., J. SVARC & S. HORNER (1976)   Attending a primary school of the other language in Montreal. In Simões 1976, 113-131.

MACRAE, A.J. (1976)   Movement and location in the acquisition of deictic verbs. *Journal of Child Language* **3**, 191-204.

MALHERBE, E.G. (1978)   Bilingual education in the Republic of South Africa. In Spolsky & Cooper 1978, 167-202.

MALMBERG, B. (1945)   Drag ur en fyråarig finsk flinchas språkliga utvectling. *Nordisk Tidskrift för Vetenskap* **21**, 170-181.

MALONE, M.J. & R.F. GUY (1982)   A comparison of mothers' and fathers' speech to their 3-year-old sons. *Journal of Psycholinguistic Research* **11**, 599-608.

MALSON, LUCIEN (1972)   *Wolf children and the problem of human nature.* New York: Monthly Review Press.

MANDELBAUM, D.G. (1943)   Wolf-child histories from India. *Journal of Social Psychology* **17**, 25-44.

MARATSOS, M.P. (1973a)   Decrease in the understanding of the word 'big' in preschool children. *Child Development* **44**, 747-752.

MARATSOS, M. (1973b)   Nonegocentric communication abilities in preschool children. *Child Development* **44**, 697-700.

MARATSOS, M.P. (1974a)   Children who get worse at understanding the passive: A replication of Bever. *Journal of Psycholinguistic Research* **3**, 65-74.

MARATSOS, M.P. (1974b)   How preschool children understand missing complement sentences. *Child Development* **45**, 700-706.

MARATSOS, M.P. (1974c)   Preschool children's use of definite and indefinite articles. *Child Development* **45**, 446-455.

MARATSOS, MICHAEL P. (1976)   *The use of definite and indefinite references in young children: An experimental study of semantic acquisition.* Cambridge: Cambridge University Press.

MARATSOS, M. (1978)   New models in linguistics and language acquisition. In Halle et al. 1978, 246-263.

MARATSOS, M.P. (1979)   Learning how and when to use pronouns and determiners. In Fletcher & Garman 1979, 225-240.

MARATSOS, M.P. & R. ABRAMOVITCH (1975)   How children understand full, truncated, and anomalous passives. *Journal of Verbal Learning and Verbal Behavior* **14**, 145-157.

MARLER, P. (1970)   A comparative approach to vocal learning: Song development in white-crowned sparrows. *Journal of Comparative and Physiological Psychology* **71: 2 part 2**, 1-25. Monograph.

MARLER, P. (1977)   Sensory templates, vocal perception, and development: A comparative view. In M. Lewis & Rosenblum 1977, 95-114.

MARLER, PETER & W.J. HAMILTON (1966)   *Mechanisms of animal behavior.* New York: Wiley.

MARTLEW, M., K. CONNOLY & C. MCCLEOD (1978)   Language use, role and context in a five-year-old. *Journal of Child Language* **5**, 81-99.

MARTYN, M.M., J.G. SHEEHAN & K. SLUTZ (1969)   Incidence of stuttering and other speech disorders among the retarded. *American Journal of Mental Deficiency* **74**, 206-211.

MAYBERRY, R. (1976)   An assessment of some oral and manual language skills of hearing children of deaf parents. *American Annals of the Deaf* **121**, 501-512.

McCARTHY, D. (1930)   *The language development of the preschool child.* Institute of Child Welfare Monograph Series, No. 4. Minneapolis: University of Minnesota Press.

McCARTHY, D. (1954)   Language development in children. In Leonard Carmichael, *Manual of child psychology*, 2nd ed., New York: Wiley, 1954, 492-630.

McCLURE, W. (1969)   Historical perspectives in the education of the deaf. In Jerry Griffith, ed., *Persons with hearing loss*, Springfield, Ill.: Charles C. Thomas, 1969, 3-30.

McCROSKEY, R.L. (1957)   Effect of speech on metabolism: A comparison between stutterers and non-stutterers. *Journal of Speech and Hearing Disorders* **22**, 46-52.

McDONALD, EUGENE T. (1980)   *Teaching and using Blissymbolics.* Toronto: Blissymbolics Communication Instutute.

McGUIRE, L. & C. MEYERS (1971)   Early personality in the congenitally blind child. *New Outlook for the Blind* **65**, 137-143.

McGURK, H. & J. McDONALD (1976)   Hearing lips and seeing voices: A new illusion. *Nature* (London) **264**, 746-748.

McGURK, H., C. TURNURE & S.J. CREIGHTON (1977)   Auditory-visual coordination in neonates. *Child Development* **48**, 183-143.

McINTIRE, M.L. (1977)   The acquisition of American Sign Language hand configuration. *Sign Language Studies* **16**, 247-266.

McLAUGHLIN, B. (1977)   Second-language learning in children. *Psychological Bulletin* **84**, 438-459.

McLAUGHLIN, BARRY   (1978) *Second-language acquisition in childhood.* New York: Wiley.

McLAUGHLIN, B., D. WHITE., T. McDEVITT & R. RASKIN (1983)   Mothers' and fathers' speech to their young children: Similar or different? *Journal of Child Language* **10**, 245-252.

McNEILL, D. (1966)   Developmental psycholinguistics. In F. Smith & Miller 1966, 15-84.

McNEILL, DAVID (1970)   *The acquisition of language: The study of developmental psycholinguistics.* New York: Harper & Row.

McNEILL, D. & N.B. McNEILL (1968)   What does a child mean when he says 'no'? In Eric Zale, ed., *Proceedings of the conference on language and language behavior*, New York: Appleton-Century-Crofts, 1968, 51-62. Reprinted in Ferguson & Slobin 1973, 619-627.

McWHIRTER, NORRIS, ed. (1978)   *The Guinness book of answers.* Middlesex: Guinness Superlatives.

MEAD, M. & N. NEWTON (1967)   Cultural patterning of perinatal behavior. In Stephen Richardson & A. Guttmacher, eds., *Childbearing: Its social and psychological aspects*, Baltimore, Md.: Williams & Wilkins, 1967, 142-244.

MEADOW, K. (1966)   *The effect of early manual communication and family climate on the deaf child's development.* Ph.D. dissertation. Berkeley: University of California. Cited by Moores 1982.

MEISSNER, J. & H. APTHORP (1976)   Nonegocentrism and communication mode switching in Black preschool children. *Developmental Psychology* **12**, 245-249.

MENIG-PETERSON, C. (1975)   The modification of communicative behavior in preschool-aged children as a function of the listener's perspective. *Child Development* **46**, 1015-1018.

MENKES, JOHN H. (1980) *Textbook of child neurology, 2nd ed.* Philadelphia: Lea & Febiger.
MENN, L. (1975) Counter example to 'fronting' as a universal of child phonology. *Journal of Child Language* **2**, 293-296.
MENN, L. (1977) Phonotactic rules in beginning speech. *Lingua* **26**, 225-251.
MENYUK, P. (1963a) Syntactic structures in the language of children. *Child Development* **34**, 407-422, Reprinted in Bar–Adon & Leopold 1971, 290-299.
MENYUK, P. (1963b) A preliminary evaluation of grammatical capacity in children. *Journal of Verbal Learning and Verbal Behavior* **2**, 429-439.
MENYUK, P. (1964) Comparison of grammar of children with functionally deviant and normal speech. *Journal of Speech and Hearing Research* **7**, 109-121.
MENYUK, PAULA (1969) *Sentences children use.* Cambridge, Mass.: MIT Press.
MENYUK, PAULA (1971) *The acquisition and development of language,* Englewood Cliffs, N.J.: Prentice-Hall.
MENYUK, P. & P.L. LOONEY (1972) A problem of language disorder. Length versus structure. *Journal of Speech and Hearing Research* **15**, 264-279. Reprinted in Morehead & Morehead 1976, 259-279.
MENZEL, E.W. (1973) Leadership and communication in young chimpanzees. In E.W. Menzel, ed., *Symposia of the Fourth International Congress of Primatology, vol. 1: Precultural primate behaviour.* Basel: Karger Press.
MENZEL, E.W. (1975) Natural language of young chimpanzees. *New Scientist* **65**, 127-130.
MENZEL, E.W. (1978) Implications of chimpanzee language-training experiments for primate field research—and vice versa. In D. Chivers, ed., *Recent advances in primatology, vol. 1: Primate behavior,* New York: Academic Press, 1978.
MERVIS, C.B. & C.A. MERVIS (1982) Leopards are kitty-cats: Object labeling by mothers for their thirteen-month-olds. *Child Development* **53**, 267-273.
MESSER, D.J. (1978) The integration of mothers' referential speech with joint play. *Child Development* **49**, 781-787.
METRAUX, R.W. (1965) Study of bilingualism among children of U.S.-French parents. *French Review* **38**, 650-665.
METROPOLITAN SEPARATE SCHOOL BOARD· (1981) Metropolitan Separate School Board: Distribution of children by country and language. Computer printout, June 30.
MEUMANN, ERNST (1902) *Die Entstehung der ersten Wortbedeutungen beim Kinde.* Leipzig: Engelmann. Cited in Werner & Kaplan 1963.
MICHELSSON, K. & O. WASZ-HÖCKERT (1980) The value of cry analysis in neonatology and early infancy. In Thomas Murry & J. Murry, eds., *Infant communication: Cry and early speech,* Houston: College-Hill Press, 1980, 152-182.
MIKEŠ, M. (1967) Acquisition des categories grammaticales dan le langage de l'enfant. *Enfance* **20**, 289-298.
MIKEŠ, M. & P. VLAHOVIĆ (1966) Razvoj gramatickih kategorija u decjem govoru. *Prilozi Proucavanjy jesika* **2**. Novi Sad, Yugoslavia.
MILBERG, ALAN (1976) *Street games.* New York: McGraw-Hill Ryerson.
MILES, L.W. (1978) Language acquisition in apes and children, In Fred C.C. Peng, ed., *Sign language and language acquisition in man and ape: New dimensions in comparative pedolinguistics,* American Association for the Advancement of Science Selected Symposium 16. Boulder, Colo.: Westview, 1978, 103-120.
MILISEN, R. (1938) Frequency of stuttering with anticipation of stuttering controlled. *Journal of Speech Disorders* **3**, 207-214.
MILISEN, R. & W. JOHNSON (1936) A comparative study of stutterers, former stutterers and normal speakers whose handedness has been changed. *Archives of Speech* **1**, 61-86.
MILLER, A. & E. MILLER (1973) Cognitive-developmental training with elevated boards and sign language. *Journal of Autism and Childhood Schizophrenia* **3**, 65-85. Reprinted in Lahey 1978, 392-408.
MILLER, G.A. & P. NICELY (1955) An analysis of perceptual confusions among some English consonants. *Journal of the Acoustical Society of America* **27**, 338-352. Reprinted in Saporta 1961, 153–175.
MILLER, J. (1970) Oralism. *Volta Review* **72**, 211-217.
MILLER, J.F. & R.S. CHAPMAN (1979) The relation between age and mean length of utterance in morphemes. Unpublished paper. Madison: University of Wisconsin. Cited in Jon F. Mlller, *Assessing language production in children. Experimental procedures,* Baltimore, Md.: University Park Press, 1981.
MILLER, J.F. & D.E. YODER (1974) An ontogenetic language teaching strategy for retarded children. In Schiefelbusch & Lloyd 1974, 505-528.
MILLER, W.R. & S.M. ERVIN (1964) The development of grammar in child language. In Bellugi & Brown 1964, 9-33. Reprinted in: Bar-Adon & Leopold 1971, 321-339; Ferguson & Slobin 1973, 355-380.
MILNER, B., C. BRANCH & T. RASMUSSEN (1964) Observations on cerebral dominance. In Anthony V.S. DeReuck & M.O. O'Connor, eds., *Disorders of language: A CIBA foundation symposium,* London: J. & A. Churchill 1964, 200-214. Reprinted in Richard C. Oldfield & J.C. Marshall, eds., *Language,* Middlesex, England: Penguin, 1968, 366-378. Page numbers refer to this version.
MILON, J.P. (1974) The development of negation in English by a second language learner. *TESOL Quarterly* **8**, 137-143.
MINKOWSKI, M. (1922) Über frühzeitige Bewegungen. Reflexe und muskülare Reaktionan beim menschlichen Fötus und ihre Beziehungen zum fötalen Nerven- und Muskuelsystem. *Schweizerische Medizinische Wochenschrift* **52**, 721-724, 751-755. Cited in Carmichael 1946a, 117.
MODIANO, N. (1968) Bilingual education for children of linguistic minorities. *America Indigena* **28**, 405-414.
MODIANO, NANCY (1973) *Indian education in the Chiapas Highland.* New York: Holt, Rinehart & Winston.

MOERK, E.L. (1972)   Principles of interaction in language learning. *Merrill-Palmer Quarterly* **18**, 229-257.
MOERK, E.L. (1974)   Changes in verbal child-mother interactions with increasing language skills of the child. *Journal of Psycholinguistic Research* **3**, 101-116.
MOERK, E.L. (1980)   Relationships between parental input frequencies and children's language acquisition: A reanalysis of Brown's data. *Journal of Child Language* **7**, 105-118.
MOERK, E.L. (1983)   A behavioral analysis of controversial topics in first language acquisition: Reinforcements, corrections, modeling, input frequencies, and the three-term contingency pattern. *Journal of Psycholinguistic Research* **12**, 129-156.
MOLFESE, D.L., R.B. FREEMAN & D.S. PALERMO (1975)   The ontogeny of brain lateralization for speech and nonspeech stimuli. *Brain and Language* **2**, 356-368.
MONCUR, J.P. (1952)   Parental domination in stuttering. *Journal of Speech and Hearing Disorders* **17**, 155-165.
MONOD, PROF. (1945)   The life of Sidi Mohamed Ould Sidia with the ostriches for ten years, related by himself. In M. Cournarie, ed., *Notes Africaines*, **26.** Excerpt in Armen 1971, 119-122.
MOORE, TIMOTHY E., ed. (1973)   *Cognitive development and the acquisition of language*. New York: Academic Press.
MOORE, W.E. (1938)   A conditioned reflex study of stuttering. *Journal of Speech Disorders* **3**, 168-183.
MOORES, D.F. (1969a)   Cued speech: Some practical and theoretical considerations. *American Annals of the Deaf* **114**, 23-27.
MOORES, D.F. (1969b)   A question of accuracy and sufficiency. *American Annals of the Deaf* **114**, 29-32.
MOORES, D.F. (1974)   Nonvocal systems of verbal behavior. In Schiefelbusch & Lloyd 1974, 377-417.
MOORES, DONALD F. (1982)   *Educating the deaf: Psychology, principles, and practices, 2nd ed.* Boston: Houghton Mifflin.
MOORES, D.F. & S. QUIGLEY (1967)   Cloze procedures in assessment of language skills of deaf persons. In *A century of oral education in the United States, 1867-1967. Proceedings of the International Conference on Oral Education of the Deaf, Northampton, Mass., and New York City, 1967*, Washington, D.C.: Alexander Graham Bell Association for the Deaf, 1967, 1363-1395.
MOORES, D.F., K. WEISS & M. GOODWIN (1973)   Receptive abilities of deaf children across five modes of communication. *Exceptional Children* **39**, 22-28.
MOORES, J.M (1980)   Early linguistic environment: Interactions of deaf parents with their infants. *Sign Language Studies* **26**, 1-13.
MOREHEAD, D.M. (1975)   The study of linguistically deficient children. In Sadanand Singh, ed., *Measurement procedures in speech, hearing, and language*, Baltimore: University Park Press, 1975, 19-53.
MOREHEAD, D.M. & D. INGRAM (1973)   The development of base syntax in normally and linguistically deviant children. *Journal of Speech and Hearing Research* **16**, 330-352. Reprinted in: Lahey 1978, 43-66; Morehead & Morehead 1976, 209-238.
MOREHEAD, DONALD M. & A.E. MOREHEAD, eds. (1976)   *Normal and deficient child language*. Baltimore: University Park Press.
MORGENSTERN, J.J. (1953)   *Psychological and social factors in children's stammering*. Ph.D. dissertation. Edinburgh: University of Edinburgh. Cited in W. Johnson et al. 1967, 244ff.
MORGENSTERN, J.J. (1956)   Socio-economic factors in stuttering. *Journal of Speech and Hearing Disorders* **21**, 25-33.
MORI, K. & S.D. MOESER (1983)   The role of syntax markers and semantic referents in learning an artificial language. *Journal of Verbal Learning and Verbal Behavior* **22**, 701-718.
MORISON, ELTING E., ed. (1954)   *The letters of Theodore Roosevelt, vol. 8*. Cambridge, Mass.: Harvard University Press.
MOROZOVA, NATAL'YA G. (1954)   Development of the theory of preschool education of the deaf. Moscow: Institute of Defectology. Cited in D. Moores 1982, 244.
MORSBACH, G. & P.M. STEEL (1976)   'John is easy to see' reinvestigated. *Journal of Child Language* **3**, 443-447.
MORSE, P.A. (1972)   The discrimination of speech and nonspeech stimuli in early infancy. *Journal of Experimental Child Psychology* **14**, 477-492.
MORSE, P.A. (1974)   Infant speech perception: A preliminary model and a review of the literature. In Schiefelbusch & Lloyd 1974, 19-53.
MORSE, P.A. & C.T. SNOWDEN (1975)   An investigation of categorical speech discrimination by rhesus monkeys. *Perception and Psychophysics* **17**, 9-16.
MOSCOVITCH, M. (1977)   The development of lateralization of language functions and its relation to cognitive and linguistic development: A review and some theoretical speculations. In Sidney Segalowitz & F. Gruber, eds., *Language development and neurological theory*, New York: Academic Press, 1977, 193-211.
MOSKOWITZ, A.I. (1970)   The two-year-stage in the acquisition of English phonology. *Language* **46**, 426-441.
MOSKOWTIZ, A.I. (1973)   The acquisition of phonology and syntax: A preliminary study. In Kaarlo J.J. Hintikka, J.M. Moravcsik & P. Suppes, ed., *Approaches to natural language*, Dordrecht, Holland: Reidel, 1973, 48-84.
MOSS, H. & K. ROBSON (1968)   The role of protest behavior in the development of mother-infant attachment. Paper presented at the meeting of the American Psychological Association, San Francisco, August-September. Cited in Murray 1979, 200.
MOWER, O.H. (1954)   The psychologist looks at language. *The American Psychologist* **9**, 660-694. Reprinted in Jakobovits & Miron 1967, 6-50.

MUELLER, E. (1972) The maintenance of verbal exchanges between young children. *Child Development* **43**, 930-938.

MUELLER, E., M. BLEIER, J. KRAKOW, K. HEGEDUS & P. COURNOYER (1977) The development of peer verbal interaction among two-year-old boys. *Child Development* **48**, 284-287.

MÜLLER, E., H. HOLLIEN & T. MURRY (1974) Perceptual responses to infant crying: Identification of cry types. *Journal of Child Language.* **1**, 89-95.

MÜLLER, F. MAX (1877) *Lectures on the science of language, vol. 1., 9th ed.* London: Longmans, Green.

MUIR, D. & J. FIELD (1979) Newborn infants orient to sounds. *Child Development* **50**, 431-436.

MUNRO, J.K. & R.J. WALES (1982) Changes in the child's comprehension of simultaneity and sequence. *Journal of Verbal Learning and Verbal Behavior* **21**, 175-185.

MURAI, J.-I. (1960) Speech development of infants. *Psychologia* **3**, 27-35.

MUROOKA, HAJIME (1974) *Lullaby from the womb.* Capital Records, ST-11421.

MURPHY, C.M. & D.J. MESSER (1977) Mothers, infants, and pointing: A study of a gesture. In H. Schaffer 1977, 325-354.

MURRAY, A.D. (1979) Infant crying as an elicitor of parental behavior: An examination of two models. *Psychological Bulletin* **85**, 191-215.

MURRELL, M. (1966) Language acquisition in a trilingual environment: Notes from a case study. *Studia Linguistica* **20**, 9-35.

NAIR, K.R. & V. VIRMANI (1973) Speech and language disturbances in hemiplegics. *Indian Journal of Medical Research* **61**, 1395-1403. Cited in Albert & Obler 1978, 107.

NAMIR, L. & I.M. SCHLESINGER (1978) The grammar of sign language. In I.M. Schlesinger & L. Namir, eds., *Sign language of the deaf: Psychological, linguistic, and sociological perspectives,* New York: Academic Press, 1978, 97-140.

NATIONAL SOCIETY FOR THE STUDY OF EDUCATION (1929) Preschool and parental education. *Yearbook of the National Society of Studies in Education* **28**, 495-568. Cited in McCarthy 1954.

NEELLY, J.N. & R.J. TIMMONS (1967) Adaption and consistency in the disfluent speech behavior of young stutterers and non-stutterers. *Journal of Speech and Hearing Research* **10**, 250-256.

NELSON, KATHERINE (1973a) Structure and strategy in learning to talk. *Monographs of the Society for Research in Child Development* **38**, 149.

NELSON, KATHERINE (1973b) Some evidence for the cognitive primacy of categorization and its functional basis. *Merrill-Palmer Quarterly of Behavior and Development* **19**, 21-39.

NELSON, KATHERINE (1974) Concept, word and sentence: Interrelations in acquisition and development. *Psychological Review* **81**, 267-285.

NELSON, KATHERINE (1975) The nominal shift in semantic-syntactic development. *Cognitive Psychology* **7**, 461-479.

NELSON, KATHERINE (1979) Features, contrasts and the FCH: Some comments on Barrett's lexical development hypothesis. *Journal of Child Language* **6**, 139-146.

NELSON, KEITH E., ed. (1980) *Children's language, vol. 2.* New York: Gardner.

NELSON, KEITH E., G. CARSKADDON & J.D. BONVILLIAN (1973) Syntax acquisition: Impact of experimental variation in adult verbal interaction with the child. *Child Development* **44**, 479-504.

NELSON, S.E., N. HUNTER & M. WALTER (1945) Stuttering in twin types. *Journal of Speech Disorders* **10**, 335-343.

NEUGEBAUER, H. (1915) Aus der Sprachentwicklung meines Sohnes. *Zeitschrift für angewandte Psychologie un Psychologische Sammelforschung* **9**, 298-306.

NEWBY, HAYES A. (1972) *Audiology, 3rd ed.* Englewood Cliffs, N.J.: Prentice-Hall.

NEWCOMB, N. & M. ZASLOW (1981) Do 2½-year olds hint? A study of directive forms in the speech of 2½-year-old children to adults. *Discourse Processes* **4**, 239-252.

NEWELL, W. (1978) A study of the ability of day-class deaf adolescents to comprehend factual information using four communication modalities. *American Annals of the Deaf* **123**, 558-562.

NEWFIELD, M.U. & B.B. SCHLANGER (1968) The acquisition of English morphology by normal and educable mentally retarded children. *Journal of Speech and Hearing Research* **11**, 693-706.

NEWPORT, E.L. (1976) Motherese: The speech of mothers to young children. In N. John Castellan, D. Pisoni & G. Potts, eds., *Cognitive theory,* New York: Wiley, 1976, 177-210.

NEWPORT, E.L., L.R. GLEITMAN & H. GLEITMAN (1977) Mother, I'd rather do it myself: Some effects and non-effects of maternal speech style. In Snow & Ferguson 1977, 109-149.

NICE, M.M. (1915) The development of a child's vocabulary in relation to environment. *Pedagogical Seminary* **22**, 35-64.

NICHOLLS, G.H. & D. LING (1982) Cued Speech and the reception of spoken language. *Journal of Speech and Hearing Research* **25**, 262-269.

NORTON, S.J., M.C. SCHULTY, C.M. REED, L.D. BRAIDA, N.I. DURLACH, W.M. RABINOWITZ & C. CHOMSKY (1977) Analytic study of the Tadoma method: Background and preliminary results. *Journal of Speech and Hearing Research* **20**, 574-595.

O'CONNELL, B.A. (1974) Request forms as a measure of social context. Unpublished paper. Berkeley, Calif. Cited by Ervin-Tripp 1977, 176.

O'CONNOR, NEIL, ed. (1975) *Language, cognitive deficits, and retardation.* London: Butterworth.

OFFENHEIM, SANDY (1978)   *Are we there yet?* Record album. Ber 9041. Berandol Music Limited, 11 St. Joseph Street, Toronto, Ontario M4Y 1J8.

OGBURN, W.F. (1959)   The wild boy of Agra. *American Journal of Sociology* **64**, 449-454.

OKADA, A. (1969)   *Psychology of language education.* Tokyo: Sinkokaku Shoten. In Japanese. Cited in Taylor 1976, 347.

OKASHA, A., Z. BISHRY, M. KAMEL & A.H. HASSAN (1974)   Psychosocial study of stammering in Egyptian children. *British Journal of Psychiatry* **124**, 531-533.

OKSAAR, E. (1970)   Zum Spracherwerb des Kindes in zweisprachiger Umgebung. *Folia Linguistica* **4**, 330-358. Cited in McLaughlin 1978.

OLLER, D.K. & R.E. EILERS (1982)   Similarity of babbling in Spanish- and English-learning babies. *Journal of Child Language* **9**, 565-577.

OLLER, D.K., R.E. EILERS (1983)   Speech identification in Spanish- and English-learning 2-year-olds. *Journal of Speech and Hearing Research* **26, 50-53.**

OLLER, D.K. & L.A. WIEMAN, W.J. DOYLE & C. ROSS (1976)   Infant babbling and speech. *Journal of Child Language* **3**, 1-11.

OLLER, J.W. JR. & E.Z. REDDING (1971)   Article usage and other language skills. *Language Learning* **21**, 85-95.

OLMSTED, DAVID L. (1971)   *Out of the mouth of babes.* The Hague: Mouton.

OLNEY, R.A. & E.K. SCHOLNICK (1976)   Adult judgements of age and linguistic differences in infant vocalization. *Journal of Child Language* **3**, 145-155.

OLSON, L.L. & S.J. SAMUELS (1973)   The relationship between age and accuracy of foreign language pronunciation. *Journal of Educational Research* **66**, 263-268.

OMAR, MARGARET K. (1973)   *The acquisition of Egyptian Arabic as a native language.* The Hague: Mouton.

OPIE, IONA & PETER OPIE (1959)   *The lore and language of school-children.* Oxford: Oxford University Press.

ORMEROD, F.C. (1960)   The pathology of congential deafness in the child. In Alexander Ewing, ed., *The modern educational treatment of deafness,* Manchester University Press, 1960. Cited in Morse 1974, 49.

OSGOOD, C.E. (1963)   On understanding and creating sentences. *American Psychologist* **18**, 735-751. Reprinted in Jakobovits & Miron 1967, 104-127.

OSTWALD, P. (1972)   The sounds of infancy. *Developmental Medicine and Child Neurology* **14**, 350-361.

OWENS, ROBERT E. JR. (1984)   *Language development.* Columbus, Ohio: Charles E. Merrill.

OXMAN, J., C.D. WEBSTER & M.M. KONSTANTAREAS (1978a)   Condon's multiple-response phenomenon in severely dysfunctional children: An attempt at replication. *Journal of Autism and Childhood Schizophrenia* **8**, 395-402.

OXMAN, J., C.D. WEBSTER & M.M. KONSTANTAREAS (1978b)   The perception and processing of information by severely dysfunctional nonverbal children: A rationale for the use of manual communication. *Sign Language Studies* **21**, 289-316.

PAIVIO, ALLAN & I. BEGG (1981)   *Psychology of language.* Englewood Cliffs, N.J.: Prentice-Hall.

PALERMO, D.S. (1971)   On learning to talk: Are principles derived from the learning laboratory applicable? In Slobin 1971b, 41-62.

PALERMO, D.S. (1973)   More about less: A study of language comprehension. *Journal of Verbal Learning and Verbal Behavior* **12**, 211-221.

PALERMO, D.S. (1974)   Still more about the comprehension of "less." *Developmental Psychology* **10**, 827-829.

PANAGL, O. (1977)   Aspekte der kindersprachlichen Wortbuildung. In G. Drachman, ed., *Akten der 3. Salzburger Jarestagung für Linguistik (Psycholinguistik),* Salzburg: Verlag Wolfgang Neugebauer, 1977. Cited in S. Lewandowsky & G. Braschel, Acquisition of word formation skills in German speaking children, Unpublished paper, Psychology Department, University of Toronto, 1982.

PARADIS, M. (1977)   Bilingualism and aphasia. In Haiganoosh Whitaker & H.A. Whitaker, eds., *Studies in neurolinguistics, vol. 3,* New York: Academic Press, 1977, 65-121.

PARADIS, MICHEL, ed. (1978)   *Aspects of bilingualism.* Columbia, S.C.: Hornbeam.

PARADISE, J., C. BLUESTONE & H. FELDER (1969)   The universality of otitis media in 50 infants with cleft palate. *Pediatrics* **44**, 35-42.

PARASNIS, I. (1983)   Effects of parental deafness and early exposure to manual communication on the cognitive skills, English language skill, and field independence of young deaf adults. *Journal of Speech and Hearing Research* **26**, 588-594.

PARK, T. (1970a)   The acquisition of German syntax. Unpublished paper. University of Bern, Switzerland. Cited in R. Brown 1973.

PARK, T. (1970b)   Language acquisition in a Korean child. Unpublished paper. University of Bern, Switzerland. Cited in R. Brown 1973.

PARK, T. (1971)   The acquisition of German morphology. Unpublished paper. Psychological Institute, Bern. Cited in Maratsos 1979, 233.

PARVIAINEN, S. (1949)   [Title not given in source] *Annales Chirurgiae et Gynaecologiae Fenniae Supplement* **3: 38**, 330. Cited in Illingworth 1955, 75.

PATTERSON, C.J. & M.C. KISTER (1981)   The development of listener skills for referential communication. In Dickson 1981a, 143-166.

PATTERSON, FRANCINE & E. LINDEN (1981)   *The education of Koko.* New York: Holt, Rinehart & Winston.

PAVLOVITCH, MILIVOIE (1920)   *Le langage enfantin: Acquisition du serbe et due français par un enfant serbe.* Paris: Champion. Library of Congress transliteration of name: Milivoje Pavlović.

PEET, H. (1851)   Memoir on origin and early history of the art of instructing the deaf and dumb. *American Annals of the Deaf* **3**, 129-161. Cited in Moores 1982, 31-42.

PEIPER, A. (1925)   Sinnesempfindungen des Kindes vor seiner Geburt. *Monatsschrift für Kinderheilkunde* **29**, 236. Cited in Carmichael 1946a.

PELLEGRINI, A. (1967)   The deaf child: Diagnosis and cause of deafness. *International Audiology* **6**, 127-129.

PENG, F. (1974)   Kinship signs in Japanese Sign Language. *Sign Language Studies* **5**, 31-47.

PETERSON, C., F. DANNER & J. FLAVELL (1972)   Developmental stages in children's response to three indicators of communicative failure. *Child Development* **43**, 1463-1468.

PHILLIPS, J.R. (1970)   *Formal characteristics of speech which mothers address to their young children.* Ph.D. dissertation. Baltimore: John Hopkins University. Cited in DePaulo & Bonvillian 1978; Phillips 1973.

PHILLIPS, J.R. (1973)   Syntax and vocabulary of mothers' speech to young children: Age and sex comparisons. *Child Development* **44**, 182-185.

PIAGET, JEAN (1923)   *Le langage et la pensée chez l'enfant.* Neuchâtel-Paris: Delachaux & Niestlé. English title: *The language and thought of the child.* Translations: M. Wardon, tr., New York: Routledge & Kegan Paul, 1926, excerpt reprinted in Bar-Adon & Leopold 1971, 60-63; M. Gabain, tr., Cleveland: Meridan Books, 1955. Page numbers refer to Meridan version.

PIAGET, JEAN (1928)   *Judgement and reasoning in the child.* New York: Harcourt, Brace.

PIAGET, JEAN & B. INHELDER (1969)   *The psychology of the child.* New York: Basic Books.

PICKERT, S.M. (1981)   Imaginative dialogues. *First language* **2**, 5-20.

PIERCE, S. & G. BARTOLUCCI (1977)   A syntactic investigation of verbal autistic, mentally retarded, and normal children. *Journal of Autism and Childhood Schizophrenia* **7**, 121-134.

PIKE, KENNETH & E.G. PIKE (1980)   *Grammatical Analysis.* Dallas: Summer Institute of Linguistics and the University of Texas at Arlington.

PILLET, R.A. (1968)   The impact of FLES: An appraisal. *Modern Language Journal* **52**, 486-490.

PLANTE, A.J. (1977)   Connecticut pairing model proves effective in bilingual bicultural education. *Phi Delta Kappa* **58**, 427.

POKROVSKII, A.I. (1953)   On the development of visual perceptions and judgements in the post-operative newly seeing in the light of the words of I.P. Pavlov. *Vestnik Oftalmologii* **32**, 6-17. Translation: A Russian report on the post-operative newly seeing. I. Loadon, tr. *American Journal of Psychology*, 1960, **73**, 478-482.

POLITZER, R.L. (1974)   Developmental sentence scoring as a method of measuring second language acquisition. *Modern Language Journal* **58**, 245-250.

POPE, E. (1973)   Question answering system. *Papers from the 9th regional meeting of the Chicago Linguistic Society*, 482-492.

POPOVA, M.I. (1958)   Grammaticheskiye elementy yazyka v rechi detey preddoshkol'nogo vozrasta. *Voprosy psikhologii* **4**, 106-117. Translation: Grammatical elements of language in the speech of preschool children. In Ferguson & Slobin 1973, 269-284.

PORFERT, W. & D. ROSENFIELD (1978)   Prevalence of stuttering. *Journal of Neurology* **41**, 954-956.

PORGES, IRWIN (1975)   *Edgar Rice Burroughs: The man who created Tarzan.* Provo, Utah: Brigham Young University Press.

PORTER, H. V. K. (1939)   Studies in the psychology of stuttering: XIV. Stuttering phenomena in relation to size and personnel of audience. *Journal of Speech Disorders* **4**, 323-333.

POZZI-ESCOT, I. (1972)   Report on the research carried out by the linguistics development plan of the National University of San Marcos. Paper presented at Seminar on Bilingual Education, Lima, Peru. Cited by Engle 1975.

PRATT, K.C. (1946)   The neonate. In Carmichael 1946b, 190-254. Reprinted in Carmichael 1954, 215-291.

PRATT, M., S. SCRIBNER & M. COLE (1977)   Children as teachers: Developmental studies of instructional communication. *Child Development* **48**, 1475-1481.

PREMACK, DAVID (1976)   *Intelligence in ape and man.* Hillsdale, N.J.: Lawrence Erlbaum Associates.

PRESIDENT'S PANEL ON MENTAL RETARDATION (1962)   *A proposed program for national action to combat mental retardation.* Washington, D.C.: U.S. Government Printing Office.

PREUS, A. (1972)   Stuttering in Down's Syndrome. *Scandinavian Journal of Educational Research* **16**, 89-104.

PREYER, WILHELM (1882)   *Die Seele des Kindes.* Leipzig: Greiben.

PREYER, WILHELM (1888)   *The senses and the will.* Translation of the first part of the 2nd ed. of *Die Seele des Kindes.* H.W. Brown, tr. New York: Appleton.

PREYER, WILHELM (1889)   *The development of the intellect.* Translation of the second part of the 2nd ed. of *Die Seele des Kindes.* H.W. Brown, tr. New York: Appleton.

PRICE, E. (1968)   Early bilingualism. In Charles J. Dodson, E. Price & L.T. Williams, eds., *Toward bilingualism,* Cardiff: University of Wales Press, 1968.

PRICE, R. & S. PRICE (1976)   Secret play languages in Saramaka: Linguistic disguise in a Caribbean Creole. In Kirshenblatt-Gimblett 1976, 37-50.

PRINS, D. (1972)   Personality, stuttering severity, and age. *Journal of Speech and Hearing Research* **15**, 148-154.

PRINZ, P.M. & L.J. FERRIER (1983)   ''Can you give me that one?'': The comprehension, production and judgement of directives in language-impaired children. *Journal of Speech and Hearing Disorders* **48**, 44-54.

PRINZ, P. & E. PRINZ (1979)   Simultaneous acquistion of ASL and spoken English (in a hearing child of a deaf mother and hearing father): Phase I, Early lexical development. *Sign Language Studies* **25**, 283-296. Also appears as: Acquisition of ASL and spoken English in a hearing child of a deaf mother and hearing father: Phase I, Early lexical development. *Papers and Reports on Child Language Development* **17**, 139-146.

PRINZ, P. & E. PRINZ (1981)   Acquisition of ASL and spoken English by a hearing child of a deaf mother and a hearing father: Phase II, Early combinatorial patterns. *Sign Language Studies* **30**, 78-88.

PROCTOR, C.A. & B. PROCTOR (1967)   Understanding hereditary nerve deafness. *Archives of Otolaryngology* **85**, 23-40.

PRONOVOST, W. (1951)   A survey of services for speech and hearing handicapped in New England. *Journal of Speech Disorders* **16**, 148-156. Cited in Taylor 1976, 333.

PRONOVOST, W., M. WAKSTEIN & D. WAKSTEIN (1966)   A longitudinal study of the speech behavior and language comprehension of fourteen children diagnosed atypical or autistic. *Exceptional Children* **33**, 19-26.

QUARRINGTON, B. (1965)   Stuttering as a function of the information value and sentence position of words. *Journal of Abnormal Psychology* **70**, 221-224.

QUARRINGTON, B. (1974)   The parents of stuttering children: The literature re-examined. *Canadian Psychiatric Association Journal* **19**, 103-110.

QUARRINGTON, B., J. CONWAY & N. SIEGEL (1962)   An experimental study of some properties of stuttered words. *Journal of Speech and Hearing Research* **5**, 387-394.

QUIGLEY, STEPHEN (1969)   *The influence of fingerspelling on the development of language, communication and educational achievement of deaf children.* Urbana: University of Illinois.

QUIGLEY, STEPHEN & D. FRISINA (1961)   *Institutionalization and psycho-educational development of deaf children.* Washington, D.C.: Council for Exceptional Children.

QUINN, P.T. (1971)   Stuttering: Some observations on speaking when alone. *Journal of the Australian College of Speech Therapists* **21**, 92-94.

RAMIG, P. & M.R. ADAMS (1980)   Rate reduction strategies used by stutterers and nonstutterers during high- and low-pitched speech. *Journal of Fluency Disorders* **5**, 27-41.

RAMOS, M., J.V. AGUILAR & B.F. SIBAYAN (1967)   The determination and implementation of language policy. *Philippine Center for Language Study Monograph Series* **2**. Quezon City, Philippines: Alemar/Phoenix. Cited in Engle 1975.

RASMUSSEN, T. (1964)   Discussion of Zangwill 1964. *Research Publications—Association for Research in Nervous and Mental Disease* **42**, 105-113. Cited in Krashen 1973.

RAVEM, R. (1968)   Language acquisition in a second language environment. *International Review of Applied Linguistics in Language Teaching* **6**, 175-185. Reprinted in J.W. Oller, Jr. & J.C. Richards, eds., *Focus on the learner,* Rowley, Mass.: Newbury House, 1973, 136-144.

RAVEM, R. (1974)   The development of Wh- questions in 1st and 2nd language learners. In Richards 1974, 134-155. Reprinted in John Schumann & N. Stenson, eds., *New frontiers in second language learning,* Rowley, Mass.: Newbury House, 1975, 153-175.

RAVEM, R. (1978)   Two Norwegian children's acquisition of English syntax. In Hatch 1978, 148-154.

RAWLINGS, B. (1973)   *Characteristics of hearing impaired students by hearing status, United States: 1907-1971.* Series D. No. 10. Washington, D.C.: Office of Demographic Studies, Gallaudet College.

RAYMORE, S. & J.E. McLEAN (1972)   A clinical program for carry-over of articulation therapy with retarded children. In J.E. McLean, D.E. Yoder & R.L. Schiefelbusch, eds., *Language intervention with the retarded,* Baltimore, Md.: University Park Press.

READ, B.K. & L.J. CHERRY (1978)   Preschool children's production of directive forms. *Discourse Processes* **1**, 233-245.

READ, CHARLES (1971)   Pre-school children's knowledge of English phonology. *Harvard Educational Review* **41**, 1-34.

READ, CHARLES (1975)   Lessons to be learned from the preschool orthographer. In Eric H. Lenneberg & E. Lenneberg, eds., *Foundations of language development: A multidisciplinary approach, vol. 2,* New York: Academic Press, 1975b, 329-346.

REED, CHARLOTTE M., M.J. DOHERTY, L.D. BRAIDA & N.I. DURLACH (1982b)   Analytic study of the Tadoma method: Further experiments with inexperienced observers. *Journal of Speech and Hearing Research* **25**, 216-223.

REED, CHARLOTTE, M., N.I. DURLACH, L.D. BRAIDA & M.C. SCHULTZ (1982a)   Analytic study of the Tadoma method: Identification of consonants and vowels by an experienced Tadoma user. *Journal of Speech and Hearing Research* **25**, 108-116.

REED, CHARLOTTE M., S.I. RUBIN, L.D. BRAIDA & N.I. DURLACH (1978)   Analytic study of the Tadoma method: Discrimination ability of untrained observers. *Journal of Speech and Hearing Research* **21**, 625-637.

REEDER, K. (1980)   The emergence of illocutionary skills. *Journal of Child Language* **7**, 13-28.

REES, N.S. (1978)   Pragmatics of language. In Richard L. Schiefelbusch, ed., *Bases of language intervention,* Baltimore: University Park Press, 1978, 191-268.

REICH, C., D. HAMBLETON & B.K. HOULDIN (1977)   The integration of hearing impaired children in regular classrooms. *American Annals of the Deaf* **122**, 534-543.

REICH, P.A. (1970a)   Relational networks. *Canadian Journal of Linguistics* **15**, 95-110.

REICH, P.A. (1970b)   The English auxiliaries: A relational network description. *Canadian Journal of Linguistics* **16**, 18-50.

REICH, P.A. (1970c) Language acquisition. In Peter A. Reich, *A relational network model of language behavior.* Ph.D. dissertation. Ann Arbor: University of Michigan.
REICH, P.A. (1975) Visible distinctive features. In Adam Makkai & V.B. Makkai, eds., *The first LACUS forum,* Columbia, S.C. Hornbeam Press, 1975, 348-356.
REICH, P.A. (1976) The early acquisition of word meaning. *Journal of Child Language* 3, 117-123.
REICH, P.A. (1985) Unintended puns. In Robert A. Hall, Jr., ed. *The eleventh LACUS forum 1984,* Columbia, S.C.: Hornbeam Press, 314-322.
REICH, P.A. & M. BICK (1976) An empirical investigation of some claims made in support of Visible English. *American Annals of the Deaf* 121, 573-577.
REICH, P.A. & M. BICK (1977) How visible is Visible English? *Sign Language Studies* 14, 59-72.
REICH, PETER A. & C.M. REICH (1974) *A follow-up study of the deaf.* Toronto: Board of Education Research Department.
REMICK, H. (1976) Maternal speech to children during language acquisition. In von Raffler-Engle & Lebrun 1976, 223-233.
RICE, M. (1978) *The effect of children's prior nonverbal color concepts on the learning of color words.* Ph.D. dissertation. Lawrence: University of Kansas. Cited in Carey 1982, 380.
RICE, M.L. (1983) Contemporary acounts of the cognition/language relationship: Implications for speech-language clinicians. *Journal of Speech and Hearing Disorders* 48, 347-359.
RICHARDS, JACK, C., ed. (1974) *Error analysis: Perspectives on second language acquisition.* London: Longmans.
RICHARDS, M.M. (1976) Come and go reconsidered: Children's use of deictic verbs in contrived situations. *Journal of Verbal Learning and Verbal Behavior* 15, 655-665.
RICHARDS, M.M. (1979) Sorting out what's in a word from what's not: Evaluating Clark's semantic features acquisition theory. *Journal of Experimental Child Psychology* 27, 1-47.
RICHMAN, L.C. (1976) Behavior and achievement of cleft palate children. *Cleft Palate Journal* 16, 81-85.
RICKS, D. & L. WING (1975) Language, communication, and the use of symbols in normal and autistic children. *Journal of Autism and Childhood Schizophrenia* 5, 191-221.
RIEKEHOF, LOTTIE L. (1978) The joy of signing. Springfield, Mo.: Gospel Publishing House.
RIESTRA, M.A. & C.E. JOHNSON (1964) Changes in attitudes of elementary school pupils toward foreign speaking peoples resulting from the study of a foreign language. *Journal of Experimental Education* 33, 65-72.
RIMLAND, BERNARD (1964) *Infantile autism.* New York: Appleton-Century-Crofts.
RINGEL, R.L. & D.D. KLUPPEL (1964) Neonatal crying: A normative study. *Folia Phoniatrica* 16, 1-9.
RINGLER, N. (1978) A Longitudinal study of mothers' language. In Waterson & Snow 1978, 151-158.
RITZMAN, C.H. (1943) A cardiovascular and metabolic study of stutterers and non-stutterers. *Journal of Speech Disorders* 8, 161-182.
ROBINSON, E.J. & W.P. ROBINSON (1977a) Children's explanations of failure and the inadequacy of the misunderstood message. *Developmental Psychology* 13, 151-161.
ROBINSON, E.J. & W.P. ROBINSON (1977b) Development in the understanding of causes of success and failure in verbal communication. *Cognition* 5, 363-378.
RODGON, MARIS M. (1976) *Single word usage, cognitive development and the beginnings of combinatorial speech.* Cambridge: Cambridge University Press.
ROEPER, T., S. LAPOINTE, J. BING & S. TAVAKOLIAN (1981) A lexical approach to language acquisition. In Susan L. Tavakolian, ed., *Language acquisition and linguistic theory,* Cambridge, Mass.: MIT Press, 1981, 35-58.
ROGERS, WOODES (1712) *A cruising voyage round the world.* London: Bell and Lintot. Cited in Lane 1976, 179.
ROM, A. & L.S. BLISS (1981) A comparison of verbal communicative skills of language impaired and normal speaking children. *Journal of Communication Disorders* 14, 133-140.
RONDAL, J.A. (1980) Fathers' and mothers' speech in early language development. *Journal of Child Language* 7, 353-369.
RONJAT, JULES (1913) *Le développement du langage observé chez un enfant bilingue.* Paris: Champion. Cited in McLaughlin 1978.
ROSCH, E.R. (1973) On the internal structure of perceptual and semantic categories. In T. Moore 1973, 111-144.
ROSE, S., P.M. CONNEALLY & W.E. NANCE (1977) Genetic analysis of childhood deafness. In Fred Bess, ed., *Childhood deafness: Causation, assessment and management,* New York: Grune & Stratton, 1977, 19-35.
ROSENBAUM, PETER (1967) *The grammar of English predicate constructions.* Cambridge, Mass.: MIT Press.
ROSENBECK, J., B. MESSERT, M. COLLINS & R.T. WERTZ (1978) Stuttering following brain damage. *Brain and Language* 6, 82-96.
ROSIER, P. & M. FARELLA (1976) Bilingual education at Rock Point—Some early results. *TESOL Quarterly* 10, 379-388.
RUBIN, J. (1968) *National bilingualism in Paraguay.* The Hague: Mouton. Excerpt: Acquisition and proficiency, in John B. Pride & J. Holmes, eds., *Sociolinguistics: Selected readings,* Middlesex, England: Penguin, 1972, 350-366.
RŪĶE-DRAVIŅA, V. (1959) Zur entstehung der Flexion in der Kindersprache: Ein Bietrag auf der Grundlage des lettischen Sprachmaterials. *International Journal of Slavic Linguistics and Poetics* 1/2, 201-222. Translation: On the emergence of inflection in child language: A contribution based on Latvian speech data. R. Sayre, tr. In Ferguson & Slobin 1973, 252-267.

RŪĶE-DRAVIŅA, V. (1965)   The process of acquisition of apical /r/ and uvular /R/ in the speech of children. *Linguistics* **17**, 56-68. Reprinted in Ferguson & Slobin 1973, 158-167.

RŪĶE-DRAVIŅA, VELTA (1967)   Mehrsprachigkeit im Vorschulalter. Lund: Gleerup. Cited in McLaughlin 1978.

RŪĶE-DRAVIŅA, V. (1977)   Modifications of speech addressed to young children in Latvian. In Snow & Ferguson 1977, 237-253.

RUMBAUGH, DUANE M., ed. (1977)   *Language learning by a chimpanzee: The LANA project.* New York: Academic Press.

RUSSELL, WILLIAM R. & M. ESPIR (1961)   *Traumatic aphasia.* Oxford University Press.

RUTHERFORD, B (1956)   *Give them a chance to talk.* Minneapolis: Burgess.

RUTTER, M. (1972)   Psychiatric causes of language retardation. In Rutter & Martin 1972, 147-160.

RUTTER, M. & L. LOCKYER (1967)   A five to fifteen year follow-up study of infantile psychosis: I. Description of sample. *British Journal of Psychiatry* **113**, 1169-1182.

RUTTER, MICHAEL & J.A.M. MARTIN (1972)   *The child with delayed speech.* London: William Heinemann.

RYDEN, INGEGARD (1971)   A Swedish child in the beginning of syntactic development and some cross-linguistic comparisons. Unpublished paper. Cited in R. Brown 1973.

SACHS, J., B. BARD & M.L. JOHNSON (1981)   Language learning with restricted input: Case studies of two hearing children of deaf parents. *Applied Psycholinguistics* **2**, 33-54.

SACHS, J., R. BROWN & R.A. SALERNO (1976)   Adults' speech to children. In von Raffler-Engel & Lebrun 1976, 240-245.

SACHS, J. & J. DEVLIN (1976)   Young children's use of age-appropriate speech styles in social interaction and role-playing. *Journal of Child Language* **3**, 81-98.

SACHS, J. & L. TRUSWELL (1976)   Comprehension of two-word instructions by children in the one-word stage. *Papers and Reports on Child Language Development* **12**, 212-220.

SAGI, A. & M. HOFFMAN (1976)   Emphatic distress in the newborn. *Developmental Psychology* **12**, 175-176.

SALIMBENE (13TH CENTURY)   *Cronica, vol. 1.* Manuscript. The Vatican. First published in *Monumenta Historica, vol. 3: 1-6,* Parma: P. Fiaccadorii, 1857. Translated excerpt: The Emperor Frederick II, in James Ross & M.M. McLaughlin, eds., *The portable medieval reader,* New York: Viking, 1949, 362-368.

SALK, L. (1962)   Mother's heartbeat as an imprinting stimulus. *Annals of the New York Academy of Sciences* **24**, 753-763.

SALLAGOÏTY, P. (1975)   The sign language of southern France. *Sign Language Studies* **7**, 181-202.

SALMON, PETER J. (1970)   *Out of the shadows.* New York: National Center for Deaf-Blind Youths and Adults.

SAMARIN, WILLIAM J. (1972)   *Tongues of men and angels.* New York: Macmillan.

SAMUELS, D.D. & R.J. GRIFFONE (1979)   The Plattsburg French language immersion program: Its influence on intelligence and self esteem. *Language Learning* **29**, 45-52.

SANCHES, M. & B. KIRSHENBLATT-GIMBLETT (1976)   Children's traditional speech play and child language. In Kirshenblatt-Gimblett 1976, 65-110.

SANDER, E.K. (1972)   When are speech sounds learned? *Journal of Speech and Hearing Disorders* **37**, 55-63.

SAN DIEGO CITY SCHOOLS (1982)   *Bilingual demonstration project.* April.

SANK, D. & F. KALLMAN (1963)   The role of heredity in early total deafness. *Volta Review* **65**, 461-476.

SANTIN, S. & J. SIMMONS (1977)   Problems in the conservation of reality in congenitally blind children. *Journal of Visual Impairment and Blindness* **71**, 425-429.

SAPORTA, SOL (1961)   *Psycholinguistics: A book of readings.* New York: Holt, Rinehart and Winston.

SAVAGE-RUMBAUGH, S., D. RUMBAUGH & S. BOYSEN (1980)   Do apes use language? *American Scientist* **68**, 49-61.

SAVIĆ, S. (1974)   One form of imitation and creation in child speech among young children. *Pedagagy* (Belgrade) **3**, 147-160. Cited in E. Clark 1978.

SAVIĆ, S. (1975)   Aspects of adult-child communication: The problem of question acquisition. *Journal of Child Language* **2**, 251-260.

SAYA, M.J. (1978)   Bliss and the adult aphasic. *Alberta Speech and Hearing Association Journal* **3**, 8.

SAYLES, D.G. (1971)   Cortical excitability, perseveration, and stuttering. *Journal of Speech and Hearing Research* **14**, 462-475.

SCAIFE, B.K. & J.S. BRUNER (1975)   The capacity for joint visual attention in the infant. *Nature* **253**, 265-6.

SCHAEFFER, M. & W. SHEARER (1968)   A survey of mentally retarded stutterers. *Mental Retardation* **6**, 44-45.

SCHAFFER, A. & M. AVERY (1977)   *Diseases of the newborn, 4th ed.* Philadelphia: W.B. Saunders.

SCHAFFER, H. RUDOLPH, ed. (1977)   *Studies in mother-infant interaction.* New York: Academic Press.

SCHERER, GEORGE A. & M. WERTHEIMER (1964)   *A psycholinguistic experiment in foreign-language teaching.* New York: McGraw-Hill.

SCHIEFELBUSCH, RICHARD L. & L.L. LLOYD, eds. (1974)   *Language perspectives—Acquisition, retardation, and intervention.* Baltimore: University Park Press.

SCHIEFFELIN, B. (1980)   Cultural dimensions of language acquisition. Paper presented at the Developmental Pragmatics Symposium, Buffalo, N.Y.

SCHIFF, N. & I.M. VENTRY (1976)   Communication problems in hearing children of deaf parents. *Journal of Speech and Hearing Disorders* **41**, 348-358.

SCHINDLER, M.D. (1955)   A study of educational adjustments of stuttering and non-stuttering children. In W. Johnson & Leutenegger 1955, 348-357.

SCHLANGER, B.B. (1953)   Speech examination of a group of institutionalized mentally handicapped children. *Journal of Speech and Hearing Disorders* **18**, 339-349.

SCHLESINGER, H. (1972)   Language acquisition in four deaf children. In H. Schlesinger & Meadow 1972, 45-87.

SCHLESINGER, HILDA S. & K.P. MEADOW (1972) *Sound and sign*. Berkely: University of California Press.

SCHLESINGER, I.M. (1967) A note on the relationship between psychological and linguistic theories. *Foundations of Language* **3**, 397-402.

SCHLESINGER, I.M. (1971) The grammar of sign language and the problem of language universals. In John Morton, ed., *Biological and social factors in psycholinguistics,* London: Logos, 1971, 98-121.

SCHLESINGER, I.M., R. MELKMAN & R. LEVY (1966) Word length and frequency and determinants of stuttering. *Psychonomic Science* **6**, 255-256.

SCHNITZER, M.L. (1978) Cerebral lateralization and plasticity: Their relevance to language acquisition. In Paradis 1978, 149-155.

SCHUMANN, J.H. (1975) Affective factors and the problem of age in second language acquisition. *Language Learning* **25**, 209-235.

SCHWARTZ, R.G. & L.B. LEONARD (1982) Do children pick and choose? An examination of phonological selection and avoidance in early lexical acquisition. *Journal of Child Language* **9**, 319-336.

SCOLLON, R.T. (1974) *One child's language from one to two: The origins of construction*. Ph.D. dissertation. Honolulu: University of Hawaii. Cited in H. Clark & Clark 1977.

SCOTT, D.A. & R. MILISEN (1954) The effectiveness of combined visual-auditory stimulation in improving articulation. *Journal of Speech and Hearing Disorders* **4**, 51-56.

SCOVEL, T. (1969) Foreign accents, language acquisition, and cerebral dominance. *Language Learning* **19**, 245-253.

SCUPIN, ERNST & G. SCUPIN (1907) *Bubis erste Kindheit*. Leipzig: Grieben. Cited in Werner & Kaplan 1963.

SCUPIN, ERNST & G. SCUPIN (1910) *Bubi im vierten bis sechsten Lebensjahr*. Leipzig: Greiben. Cited in Werner & Kaplan 1963.

SEARLE, J.R. (1975) Indirect speech acts. In P. Cole & J.L. Morgan, eds., *Syntax and semantics, Vol. 3: Speech acts,* New York: Seminar Press, 1975, 59-82.

SEBEOK, THOMAS A. & J. UMIKER-SEBEOK (1980) *Speaking of apes: A critical anthology of two-way communication with man*. New York: Plenum.

SEIDEL, A., R.B. WEINSTEIN & O. BLOODSTEIN (1973) The effect of interposed conditions on the consistency of stuttering. *Journal of Speech and Hearing Research* **16**, 62-66.

SEIDENBERG, M.S. & L.A. PETITTO (1979) Signing behavior in apes: A critical review. *Cognition* **7**, 177-215.

SHAMES, G.H. & H. BEAMS (1956) Incidence of stuttering in older age groups. *Journal of Speech and Hearing Disorders* **21**, 313-316.

SHARLESS, E.A. (1974) *Children's acquisition of personal pronouns*. Ph.D. dissertation. New York: Columbia University. Cited in E. Clark 1978.

SHATZ, M. (1978a) Children's comprehension of their mothers' question-directives. *Journal of Child Language* **5**, 39-46.

SHATZ, M. (1978b) On the development of communicative understandings: An early strategy for interpreting and responding to messages. *Cognitive Psychology* **10**, 271-301.

SHATZ, M. & R. GELMAN (1973) The development of communication skills: Modifications in the speech of young children as a function of the listener. *Monographs of the Society for Research in Child Development* **152, 38, 5.**

SHEARER, W.M. & J.D. WILLIAMS (1965) Self-recovery from stuttering. *Journal of Speech and Hearing Disorders* **30**, 288-290.

SHEEHAN, J.G. & M.S. COSTLEY (1977) Heredity in stuttering. *Journal of Speech and Hearing Disorders* **47**, 47-59.

SHEEHAN, J.G., R. HADLEY & E. GOULD (1967) Impact of authority on stuttering. *Journal of Abnormal Psychology* **72**, 290-293.

SHEEHAN, J.G. & M.M. MARTYN (1970) Stuttering and its disappearance. *Journal of Speech and Hearing Research* **13**, 279-289.

SHEEHAN, J.G., M.M. MARTYN & K.L. KILBURN (1968) Speech disorders in retardation. *American Journal of Mental Deficiency* **73**, 251-256.

SHELDON, A. (1974) The role of parallel function in the acquisition of relative clauses in English. *Journal of Verbal Learning and Verbal Behavior* **13**, 272-281.

SHEPPARD, W.C. & H.L. LANE (1968) Development of prosodic features of infant vocalizing. *Journal of Speech and Hearing Research* **11**, 94-108.

SHERMAN, M. (1927) The differentiation of emotional responses in infants. II. The ability of observers to judge the emotional characteristics of the crying of infants, and of the voice of an adult. *Journal of Comparative Psychology* **7**, 335-351.

SHERROD, K., S. FRIEDMAN, S. CRAWLEY, D. DRAKE & J. DEVIEUX (1977) Maternal language to prelinguistic infants: Syntactic aspects. *Child Development* **48**, 1662-1665.

SHERZER, J. (1970) Talking backwards in Cuna: The sociological reality of phonological descriptions. *Southwestern Journal of Anthropology* **26**, 343-353.

SHERZER, J. (1976) Play languages: Implications for (socio) linguistics. In Kirshenblatt-Gimblett 1976, 19-36.

SHIPLEY, E.F. & T.E. SHIPLEY (1969) Quaker children's use of thee: A relational analysis. *Journal of Verbal Learning and Verbal Behavior.* 8, 112-117.

SHIPLEY, E.F., C.S. SMITH & L.R. GLEITMAN (1969) A study of the acquisition of language: Free responses to commands. *Language* **45**, 322-342. Reprinted in Bloom 1978, 347-370.

SHIRE, M.L. (1945) *The relation of certain linguistic factors to reading achievement in first grade children*. Ph.D. dissertation. New York: Fordham University. Cited in McCarthy 1954.

SHIRLEY, M. (1933) *The first two years: A study of twenty-five babies*. Minneapolis: University of Minnesota Press.

SHULTZ, T.R. (1974)   Development of the appreciation of riddles. *Child Development* **45**, 100-105.
SHULTZ, T.R. & R. PILON (1973)   Development of the ability to detect linguistic ambiguity. *Child Development* **44**, 728-733.
SHVACHKIN, N. (1948)   Razvitiye fonematicheskogo vospriyatiya rechi v rannem vozraste. *Izvestiya Akademii Pedagogicheskikh Nauk RSFSR* **13**, 101-132. Translation: The development of phonemic speech perception in early childhood, E. Dernbach, tr., in Ferguson & Slobin 1973, 911-127. Page numbers refer to this version.
SIEGEL, G.M. & D. HAUGEN (1964)   Audience size and variations in stuttering behavior. *Journal of Speech and Hearing Research* **7**, 381-388.
SILVA, P.A. (1980)   The prevalence, stability and significance of developmental language delay in preschool children. *Developmental Medicine and Child Neurology* **22**, 768-777.
SILVERMAN, E.M. (1974)   Word position and grammatical function in relation to preschoolers' speech disfluency. *Perceptual and Motor Skills* **39**, 267-272.
SILVERMAN, F.H. (1972)   Disfluency and word length. *Journal of Speech and Hearing Research* **15**, 788-791.
SILVERMAN, F.H. & D.E. WILLIAMS (1972)   Prediction of stuttering by school-age stutterers. *Journal of Speech and Hearing Research* **15**, 189-193.
SIMNER, M.L. (1971)   Newborn's response to the cry of another infant. *Developmental Psychology* **5**, 136-150.
SIMÕES, ANTÓNIO, ed. (1976)   *The bilingual child: Research and analysis of existing educational themes.* New York: Academic Press.
SIMÕES, M.C.P. & C. STOEL-GAMMON (1979)   The acquisition of inflections in Portuguese: A study of the development of person markers on verbs. *Journal of Child Language* **6**, 53-67.
SIMON, N. (1975)   Echolalic speech in childhood autism: Consideration of possible underlying loci of brain damage. *Archives of General Psychiatry* **32**, 1439-1446.
SINCLAIR, A., H. SINCLAIR & O. DE MARCELLUS (1971)   Young children's comprehension and production of passive sentences. *Archives de psychologie* **161**, 1-22.
SINCLAIR-DE-ZWART, H. (1969)   Developmental psycholinguistics. In David Elkind & J.H. Flavell, eds., *Studies in cognitive development: Essays in honor of Jean Piaget,* New York: Oxford University Press, 1969, 315-336.
SINCLAIR, H. (1971)   Sensorimotor action patterns as a condition for the acquisition of syntax. In Huxley & Ingram 1971, 121-135.
SINCLAIR-DE-ZWART, H. (1973a)   Language acquisition and cognitive development. In T. Moore 1973, 9-25.
SINCLAIR-DE-ZWART, H. (1973b)   Some remarks on the Genevan point of view on learning with special reference to language learning. In L.L. Hinde & H.C. Hinde, eds., *Constraints on learning,* New York: Academic Press, 1973.
SINCLAIR, H. (1975)   The role of cognitive structures in language acquisition. In Lenneberg & Lenneberg 1975, 223-238.
SINCLAIR, H. & E. FERREIRO (1970)   Etude génétique de la compréhension, production et répétition des phrases au mode passif. *Archives de Psychologie* **40**, 1-42. Cited in Karmiloff-Smith 1979.
SINGH, JOSEPH A.L. & R.M. ZINGG (1942)   *Wolf-children and feral man.* New York: Harper & Brothers.
SIPLE, PATRICIA, ED. (1978)   *Understanding language through sign language research.* New York: Academic Press.
SIQUELAND, E.R. & C. DE LUCIA (1969)   Visual reinforcement of nonnutritive sucking in human infants. *Science* **165**, 1144-1146.
SKELLY, MADGE (1979)   *Amer-Ind gestural code based on universal American Indian hand talk.* New York: Elsevier.
SKELLY, M., L. SCHINSKY, R. SMITH, R. DONALDSON & P. GRIFFIN (1975)   American Indian sign: A gestural communication for the speechless. *Archives of Physical and Rehabilitative Medicine* **56**, 156-160.
SKINNER, B.F. (1957)   *Verbal behavior.* New York: Appleton-Century-Crofts.
SKUTNABB-KANGAS, T. & P. TOUKOMAA (1976)   *Teaching migrant children's mother tongue and learning the language of the host country in the context of the socio-cultural situation of the migrant family.* Helsinki: The Finnish National Commission for UNESCO.
SLOBIN, D.I. (1966)   The acquisition of Russian as a native language. In F. Smith & Miller 1966, 129-148.
SLOBIN, D.I. (1968)   Recall of full and truncated passive sentences in connected discourse. *Journal of Verbal Learning and Verbal Behavior* **7**, 876-881.
SLOBIN, D.I. (1970)   Universals of grammatical development in children. In Flores d'Arcais & Levelt 1970, 174-186.
SLOBIN, D.I. (1971a)   Developmental psycholinguistics. In William O. Dingwall, ed., *A survey of linguistic science,* College Park, M.D.: Linguistics Department, University of Maryland, 1971, 298-400. Discussion of paper: 401-410. Expanded version of Slobin 1978.
SLOBIN, DAN I. ed. (1971b)   *The ontogenesis of grammar: A theoretical symposium.* New York: Academic Press.
SLOBIN, D.I. (1973)   Cognitive prerequisites for the development of grammar. In Ferguson & Slobin 1973, 175-208. Reprinted in Bloom 1978, 407-432.
SLOBIN, D.I. (1978)   Suggested universals in the ontogenesis of grammar. In Honsa & Hardman-de-Bautista 1978, 249-264. See Slobin 1971a.
SLOBIN, DAN I. (1979)   *Psycholinguistics, 2nd ed.* Glenview, Ill.: Scott, Foresman.
SLOBIN, D.I. & C.A. WELSH (1968)   Elicited imitation as a research tool in developmental psycholinguistics. Working paper 10. Language-Behavior Research Laboratory. Berkeley: University of California. Also printed in Celia S. Lavatelli, ed., *Language training in early childhood education,* Urbana: University of Illinois Press, 1971, 170-185. Reprinted in Ferguson & Slobin 1973, 485-497. Page numbers refer to this version.

SMITH, A. (1966)   Speech and other functions after left (dominant) hemispherectomy. *Journal of Neurology, Neurosurgery and Psychiatry* **29**, 467-471.

SMITH, B.L. & C. STOEL-GAMMON (1983)   A longitudinal study of the development of stop consonant production in normal and Down's Syndrome children. *Journal of Speech and Hearing Disorders* **48**, 114-118.

SMITH, FRANK & G.A. MILLER, eds. (1966)   *The genesis of language*. Cambridge, Mass.: MIT Press.

SMITH, M.D. (1974)   Relative clause formation between 29-36 months: A preliminary report. *Papers and Reports on Child Language Development* **8**, 104-110.

SMITH, M.E. (1926)   An investigation of the development of the sentence and the extent of vocabulary in young children. *University of Iowa Studies in Child Welfare* **3**, 5. Cited in McCarthy 1954, 496.

SMITH, M.E. (1933)   The influence of age, sex, and situation on the frequency, form, and function of questions asked by preschool children. *Child Development* **4**, 201-213.

SMITH, M.E. (1935a)   A study of some factors influencing the development of the sentence in preschool children. *Journal of Genetic Psychology* **46**, 182-212.

SMITH, M.E. (1935b)   A study of the speech of eight bilingual children of the same family. *Child Development* **6**, 19-25.

SMITH, M.W. & S. AINSWORTH (1967)   The effects of three types of stimulation of articulatory testing results. *Journal of Speech and Hearing Disorders* **10**, 348-353.

SMITH, NEILSON V. (1973)   *The acquisition of phonology: A case study*. Cambridge: Cambridge University Press.

SMITH, N.V. (1975)   Universal tendencies in the child's acquisition of phonology. In O'Connor 1975, 47-65.

SMITH, R. & B.J. McWILLIAMS (1968)   Psycholinguistic abilities of children with clefts. *Cleft Palate Journal* **5**, 238-249.

SMITH, W. (1976)   Taiwan sign language. Unpublished paper. Northridge: California State University. Cited in Stokoe 1980.

SMYTHE, P.C., R.G. STENNET & R.C. GARDNER (1975)   The best age for foreign-language training: Issues, options and facts. *Canadian Modern Language Review* **32**, 10-23.

SNIDECOR, J.C. (1947)   Why the Indian does not stutter. *Quarterly Journal of Speech* **33**, 493-495.

SNOW, C.E. (1971)   *Language acquisition and mothers' speech to children*. Ph.D. dissertation. Montreal: McGill University. Cited in J. de Villiers & de Villiers 1978.

SNOW, C.E. (1972a)   Mothers' speech to children learning language. *Child development* **43**, 549-565. Reprinted in Bloom 1978, 489-502.

SNOW, C.E. (1972b)   Young children's responses to adult sentences of varying complexity. Paper presented to the third International Congress of Applied Linguistics, Copenhagen. Cited in Dale 1976.

SNOW, C.E. (1978)   The conversational context of language acquisition. In Campbell & Smith 1978a, 253-270.

SNOW, C.E., A. ARLMAN-RUPP, Y. HASSING, J. JOBSE, J. JOOKSEN & J. VORSTER (1976)   Mothers' speech in three social classes. *Journal of Psycholinguistic Research* **5**, 1-19.

SNOW, CATHERINE E. & C.A. FERGUSON, eds. (1977)   *Talking to children: Language input and acquisition*. New York: Cambridge University Press.

SNOW, C.E., A. DE BLAUW & G. VAN ROOSMALEN (1979)   Talking and playing with babies: The role of ideologies of child-rearing. In Bullowa 1979, 269-288.

SNOW, C.E. & M. HOEFNAGEL-HÖHLE (1978)   The critical period for language acquisition: Evidence from second language learning. *Child Development* **49**, 1114-1128.

SNOW, C.E., N.S.H. SMITH & M. HOEFNAGEL-HÖHLE (1980)   The acquisition of some Dutch morphological rules. *Journal of Child Language* **7**, 539-553.

SODERBERG, G.A. (1962)   Phonetic influences upon stuttering. *Journal of Speech and Hearing Research* **5**, 315-320.

SODERBERG, G.A. (1966)   The relations of stuttering to word length and word frequency. *Journal of Speech and Hearing Research* **9**, 584-598.

SODERBERG, G.A. (1967)   Linguistic factors in stuttering. *Journal of Speech and Hearing Research* **10**, 801-810.

SODERBERG, G.A. (1971)   Relations of word information and word length to stuttering disfluencies. *Journal of Communication Disorders* **4**, 9-14.

SOLAN, L. & T. ROEPER (1978)   Children's use of syntactic structure in interpreting relative clauses. In Helen Goodluck & L. Solan, eds., *Papers in the structure and development of child language*, University of Massachusetts, Occasional Papers in Linguistics IV, 1978. Cited in Bowerman 1979.

SONET, ÉDOUARD & G. SHORTLIFFE (1954)   *Review of standard French*. New York: Harcourt, Brace & World.

SORENSON, R. (1975)   Indications of regular syntax in deaf Danish school children's sign language. *Sign Language Studies* **8**, 257-263.

SPADINO, E.J. (1941)   *Writing and laterality characteristics of stuttering children*. New York City: Columbia University Teachers College.

SPELKE, E. (1976)   Infants' intermodal perception of events. *Cognitive Psychology* **8**, 553-560.

SPELT, D.K. (1948)   The conditioning of the human fetus in utero. *Journal of Experimental Psychology* **38**, 338-346.

SPILTON, D. & L.C. LEE (1977)   Some determinants of effective communication in four-year-olds. *Child Development* **48, 968-977.**

SPOCK, BENJAMIN (1957)   *Baby and child care*. New York: Pocket Books.

SPOLSKY, BARNARD & R.L. COOPER, eds. (1978)   *Case studies in bilingual education*. Rowley, Mass.: Newbury House.

SPRING, D.R. (1974)   Effects of style of maternal speech of infants' selection of vocal reinforcement. Unpublished paper. Seattle: University of Washington. Cited in Dale 1976.

SPRING, D.R. & P.S. DALE (1977) Discrimination of linguistic stress in early infancy. *Journal of Speech and Hearing Research* **20**, 224-231.

STAATS, A.W. (1971) Linguistic-mentalistic theory versus an explanatory S-R learning theory of language development. In Slobin 1971b, 103-150.

STAATS, A.W. (1974) Behaviorism and cognitive theory in the study of language: A neopsycholinguistics. In Scheifelbusch & Lloyd 1974, 615-646.

STARK, R.E. (1978) Features of infant sounds: The emergence of cooing. *Journal of Child Language* **5**, 379-390.

STARK, R.E. (1979) Prespeech segmental features development. In Fletcher & Garman 1979, 15-32.

STARK, R.E., S.N. ROSE & M. McLAGEN (1975) Features of infant sounds. *Journal of Child Language* **2**, 205-221.

STEELE, B. & C. POLLOCK (1968) A psychiatric study of parents who abuse infants and small children. In R. Helfer & C. Kempe, eds., *The battered child*, Chicago: University of Chicago Press, 1968.

STEER, M.D. & W. JOHNSON (1936) An objective study of the relationship between psychological factors and the severity of stuttering. *Journal of Abnormal and Social Psychology* **31**, 36-46.

STEFANKIEWICZ, S.P. & O. BLOODSTEIN (1974) The effect of a four-week interval on the consistency of stuttering. *Journal of Speech and Hearing Research* **17**, 141-145.

STEFFENSEN, M.S. (1978) Satisfying inquisitive adults: Some simple methods of answering yes/no questions. *Journal of Child Language* **5**, 221-236.

STEINSCHNEIDER, A. (1968) Sound intensity and respiratory responses in the neonate. *Psychosomatic Medicine* **30**, 534-541

STEINSCHNEIDER, A., E.L. LIPTON & J.B. RICHMOND (1966) Auditory sensitivity in the infant: Effect of intensity on cardiac and motor responsivity. *Child Development* **37**, 233-252.

STERN, CLARA & W. STERN (1907) *Die Kindersprache: Eine psychologische und sprachtheoretische Untersuchung.* Leipzig: Barth. Excerpt: The language of children. J. Lyon & A.L. Blumenthal, tr., in Blumenthal 1970, 86-100.

STERN, CLARA & W. STERN (1928) *Die Kindersprache, Eine Psychologische und sprachtheoretische Untersuchung.* Revised edition. Leipzig: Barth. Cited extensively in Werner & Kaplan 1963.

STERN, D.N., J. JAFFE, B. BEEBE & S.L. BENNETT (1975) Vocalizing in unison and in alternation: Two modes of communication within the mother-infant dyad. *Annals of the New York Academy of Sciences* **263**, 89-100. Reprinted in Bloom 1978, 115-127.

STERN, W. (1914) *Psychologie der frühen Kindheit.* Leipzig: Quelle & Meyer. Translation: *Psychology of Early Childhood,* A. Barwell, tr., London: George Allen & Unwin, 1924. Excerpt: The chief periods of further speech development, in Bar-Adon & Leopold 1971, 45-52. Page numbers refer to excerpt.

STEVENSON, E. (1964) A study of the educational achievement of deaf children of deaf parents. *California News* **80**, 143. Cited by D. Moores 1982: 220.

STINCHFIELD, SARA M. E.H. YOUNG (1938) *Children with delayed and defective speech.* London: Oxford University Press.

STOCKMAN, I.J., D.R. WOODS & A. TISHMAN (1981) Listener agreement on phonetic segments in early infant vocalization. *Journal of Psycholinguistic Research* **10**, 593-617.

STOCKWELL, ROBERT, P. SCHACHTER & B. PARTEE (1973) *The major syntactic structures of English.* New York: Holt, Rinehart & Winston.

STOEL-GAMMON, C. & J.A. COOPER (1984) Patterns of early lexical and phonological development. *Journal of Child Language* **11**, 247-271.

STOKOE, WILLIAM C. (1972) *Semiotics and human sign language.* The Hague: Mouton.

STOKOE, W.C. (1980) Sign language structure. *Annual Review of Anthropology* **9**, 365-390.

STRATTON, P.M. (1970) The use of heart rate for the study of habituation in the neonate. *Psychophysiology* **7**, 44-56.

STROHNER, H. & K.E. NELSON (1974) The young child's development of sentence comprehension: Influence of event probability, nonverbal context, syntactic form, and strategies. *Child Development* **45**, 567-576.

STUBBS, E.M. (1934) The effect of the factors of duration, intensity, and pitch of sound stimuli on the responses of newborn infants. *University of Iowa Studies on Child Welfare* **9:4**, 75-135. Cited in Pratt 1946.

STUCKLESS, E. & J. BIRCH (1966) The influence of early manual communication on the linguistic development of deaf children. *American Annals of the Deaf* **111**, 452-460, 499-504.

STUMPF, C. (1901) Eigenartige sprachliche Entwicklung eines Kindes. *Zeitschrift für Pädagogische Psychologie und Yugendkunde* **3**, 419-444. Cited in Werner & Kaplan 1963.

SULLY, J. (1896) *Studies of childhood.* New York: Appleton. Cited by: E. Clark 1978; Huxley 1970.

SUPALLA, T. & E. NEWPORT (1978) How many seats in a chair? The derivation of nouns and verbs in American Sign Language. In Siple 1978, 91-159.

SUPPES, P., M. LÉVEILLE & R.L. SMITH (1974) Developmental models of a child's French syntax. Technical report 243. Stanford: Institute for Mathematical Studies in the Social Sciences. Cited in DePaolo & Bonvillian 1978, 207.

SUTTON-SMITH, B. (1976) A developmental structural account of riddles. In Kirshenblatt-Gimblett 1976, 111-119.

SWAIN, M. (1971) Bilingualism, monolingualism and code acquisition. Paper presented at the Child Language Conference, Boston. Cited in McLaughlin 1978.

SWAIN, M. (1974) French immersion programs across Canada: Research findings. *Canadian Modern Language Review* **31**, 117-129.

SWAIN, M. (1976) Bibliography: Research on immersion education for the majority child. *The Canadian Modern Language Review* **32**, 592-596.

SWAIN, M. (1978) Home-school language switching. In Richards 1974, 238-250.

SWAIN, M., H. BARIK & E. NWANUNOBI (1973) Bilingual education project: Evaluation of Elgin County Board of Education partial immersion program for grades one, two and three, Spring 1973. Unpublished paper. Toronto: Ontario Institute for Studies in Education.

SWAIN, M. & S. LAPKIN (1982) *Evaluating bilingual education: A Canadian case study.* Clevedon, England: Multilingual Matters.

TABOURET-KELLER, A. (1962) L'acquisition du langage parlé chez un petit enfant en milieu bilingue. *Problemes de Psycholinguistique* **8**, 205-219. Cited in McLaughlin 1978.

TAMIR, L. (1980) Interrogatives in dialogue: Case study of mother and child 16-19 months. *Journal of Psycholinguistic Research* **9**, 407-424.

TANNOCK, R. (1980) Communication patterns between mothers and preschool-aged children. M.A. thesis. Toronto: Ontario Institute for Studies in Education.

TANZ, CHRISTINE (1980) *Studies in the acquisition of deictic terms.* Cambridge: Cambridge University Press.

TASHIRO, L. (1971) On the acquisition of some non-comparative terms. B.A. thesis. Stanford, Cal.: Stanford University. Cited in J. de Villiers & de Villiers 1978, 137.

TAVAKOLIAN, S.L. (1977) *Structure and function in child language.* Ph.D. dissertation. Amherst: University of Massachusetts. Cited in Bowerman 1979.

TAYLOR, I.K. (1966) The properties of stuttered words. *Journal of Verbal Learning and Verbal Behavior* **5**, 112-118.

TAYLOR, INSUP K. (1976) *Introduction to psycholinguistics.* New York: Holt, Rinehart & Winston.

TEITELBAUM, H. & R.J. HILLER (1977) The legal perspective. In *Bilingual education: Current perspectives (Law), vol. 3,* 1-64. Arlington, Va.: Center for Applied Linguistics.

TEMERLIN, MAURICE K. (1975) *Lucy: Growing up human.* Palo Alto, Calif.: Science & Behavior Books.

TEMPLIN, M. (1953) *The development and interrelations of language skills in children.* Institute of Child Welfare Monograph Series. Minneapolis: University of Minnesota Press.

TEMPLIN, MILDRED (1957) *Certain language skills in children: Their development and interrelationship.* Minneapolis: University of Minnesota Press.

TERMAN, LEWIS M. & M. ODEN (1947) *The gifted child grows up.* Stanford University Press.

TERMAN, LEWIS M. & M. ODEN (1959) *The gifted group at mid-life.* Stanford University Press.

TERRACE, HERBERT S. (1979) *Nim.* New York: Knopf. Paperback: Washington Square Press/Pocket Books.

TERRACE, H.S., L.A. PETITTO, R.J. SANDERS & T.G. BEVER (1980) On the grammatical capacities of apes. In Ke. Nelson 1980, 371-495.

THOMAN, E.B., A.F. KORNER & L. BEASON-WILLIAMS (1977) Modification of responsiveness to maternal vocalization in the neonate. *Child Development* **48**, 563-569.

THORNDIKE, EDWARD L. & I. LORGE (1944) *The teacher's word book of 30,000 words.* New York: Teachers College Press.

TIBBITS, D.F. (1980) Oral production of linguistically complex sentences with meaning relationships of time. *Journal of Psycholinguistic Research* **9**, 545-564.

TILLMAN, M. (1967) The performance of blind and sighted children on the Wechsler Intelligence Scale for Children: Study I. *International Journal for the Education of the Blind* **16: 3**, 65-74.

TILNEY, F. (1929) A comparative sensory analysis of Helen Keller and Laura Bridgman. *Archives of Neurology and Psychiatry* **21**, 1227-1269.

TISCHLER, H. (1957) Schreien, Lallen und erstes Sprechen in der Entwicklung des Säuglings. *Zeitschrift für Psychologie* **160**, 209-263. Cited in Werner & Kaplan 1963.

TITONE, R. (1973) Some factors underlying second-language learning. *English Language Teaching* **27**, 110-120.

TITS, DÉSIRÉ (1948) Le mécanisme de l'acquisition d'une langue se substituent à la langue maternellechez une enfant espagnole âgée de six-ans. Brussels: Veldeman. Cited in McLaughlin 1978, 102.

TODD, P.H. (1975) A case of structural interference across sensory modalities in second language learning. *Word* **27**, 102-118.

TODD, P.H. & J. AITCHISON (1980) Learning language the hard way. *First Language* **1**, 122-140.

TONKOVA-YAMPOL'SKAYA, R.V. (1968) Razvitiye rechevoy intonatsii u detey pervykh dvukh let zhizni. *Voprosy psikhologii* **14**, 94-101. Translation: Development of speech intonation in infants during the first two years of life. M. Vale, tr. *Soviet Psychology,* 1969, **7**, 48-54. Reprinted in Ferguson & Slobin 1973, 128-138.

TOTTEN, G.O. (1960) Bringing up children bilingually. *American Scandinavian Review* **48**, 42-50.

TOWNSEND, D.J. (1974) Children's comprehension of comparative forms. *Journal of Experimental Child Psychology* **18**, 293-303.

TOWNSEND, D.J. (1976) Do children interpret "marked" comparative adjectives as their opposites? *Journal of Child Language* **3**, 385-396.

TOWNSEND, D.J. & M. ERB (1975) Children's strategies for interpreting complex comparative questions. *Journal of Child Language* **2**, 1-7.

TREHUB, S.E. (1973) Infant's sensitivity to vowel and tonal contrasts. *Developmental Psychology* **9**, 91-96.

TREHUB, S.E. (1976) The discrimination of foreign speech contrasts by infants and adults. *Child Development* **47**, 466-472.

TREHUB, S.E. & R. ABRAMOVITCH (1978) Less is not more: Further observations on nonlinguistic strategies. *Journal of Experimental Child Psychology* **25**, 160-167.

TREHUB, S.E. & M.S. RABINOVITCH (1972) Auditory-linguistic sensitivity in early infancy. *Developmental Psychology* **6**, 74-77.

TREVARTHEN, C. (1974) Conversations with a two-month-old. *New Scientist* **62**, 230-235.

TREVARTHEN, C. (1979) Communication and cooperation in early infancy: A description of prinamy intersubjectivity. In Bullowa 1979, 321-347.

TROIKE, R.C. (1978) Research evidence for the effectiveness of bilingual education. *National Association for Bilingual Education Journal* **3**, 13-24.

TROSBORG, A. (1982) Children's comprehension of 'before' and 'after' reinvestigated. *Journal of Child Language* **9**, 381-402.

TROTTER, W.D. & F.H. SILVERMAN (1974) Does the effect of pacing speech with a miniature metronome on stuttering wear off? *Perceptual & Motor Skills* **39**, 429-430.

TUCKER, G.R. (1977) The linguistic perspective. In *Bilingual education: Current perspectives (Linguistics), vol. 2*, 1-40. Arlington Va.: Center for Applied Linguistics.

TUCKER, G.R. & T.C. GRAY (1980) The pursuit of equal opportunity. *Language and Society* **2**, 5-8.

TUCKER, G.R., W.E. LAMBERT, A. RIGAULT & N. SEGALOWITZ (1968) A psychological investigation of French speakers' skill with grammatical gender. *Journal of Verbal Learning and Verbal Behavior* **7**, 312-316.

TUCKER, G.R., F.T. OTANES & B.P. SIBAYAN (1970) An alternate days approach to bilingual education. In Alatis 1970, 281-295.

TYACK, D. & D. INGRAM (1977) Children's production and comprehension of questions. *Journal of Child Language* **4**, 211-224.

USUDA, S. & T. KOIZUMI (1981) Children with abnormal speech development—loss of early speech. In Dale & Ingram 1981, 353-372.

VALENTE, M. & K. DE JONGE (1981) High frequency amplification. *Audecibel* Fall, 168-177.

VALETTE, R.M. (1964) Some reflections on second-language learning in young children. *Language Learning* **14**, 91-98.

VALIAN, V.V., J. CAPLAN & A.M. DESCIORA (1976) Children's use of abstract linguistic knowledge in an everyday speech situation. Paper presented at the First Annual Boston University Conference on Language Development. Cited in J. de Villiers & de Villiers 1978, 112-113.

VALIAN, V.V. & R.J. WALES (1976) What's what: Talkers help listeners hear and understand by clarifying sentential relations. *Cognition* **4**, 155-176.

VAN DER GEEST, TON (1974) *Evaluation of theories on child grammars*. The Hague: Mouton.

VAN DER GEEST, T. (1975) *Some aspects of communicative competence and their implications for language acquisition*. Amsterdam: Van Gorcum.

VAN RIPER, C. (1936) Study of the thoracic breathing of stutterers during expectancy and occurrence of stuttering spasm. *Journal of Speech Disorders* **1**, 61-72.

VAN RIPER, CHARLES (1950) *Teaching your child to talk*. New York: Harper & Brothers.

VAN RIPER, CHARLES (1971) *The nature of stuttering*. Englewood Cliffs, N.J.: Prentice-Hall.

VAN RIPER, CHARLES (1972) *Speech correction: Principles and methods, 5th ed*. Englewood Cliffs, N.J.: Prentice-Hall.

VELTEN, H.V. (1943) The growth of phonemic and lexical patterns in infant language. *Language* **19**, 281-292. Reprinted in Bar-Adon & Leopold 1971, 82-91.

VERNON, M. (1973) Overview of Usher's syndrome: Congenital deafness and progressive loss of vision. In *Symposium on Usher's syndrome*. Washington, D.C.: Gallaudet College, 1-11.

VERNON, M. (1974) Effects of parents' deafness on hearing children. In Peter J. Fine, ed., *Deafness in infancy and early childhood*, New York: Medcom, 1974, 219-224.

VERNON, M. & S. KOH (1979) Effects of manual communication on deaf children's educational achievement, linguistic competence, oral skills, and psychological development. *American Annals of the Deaf* **115**, 527-536.

VERNY, THOMAS, & J. KELLY (1981) *The secret life of the unborn child*. Toronto: Collins.

VIHMAN, M.M. & B. MCLAUGHLIN (1982) Bilingualism and second language acquisition in preschool children. In Brainerd & Pressley 1982, 35-58.

VILDOMEC, VĚRBOJ (1963) *Multilingualism: General linguistics and psychology of speech*. Leyden: A.W. Sijthoff. Excerpt reprinted in Bar-Adon & Leopold 1981, 300-301.

VOCOLO, J.M. (1967) The effect of foreign language study in the elementary school upon achievement in the same language in high school. *Modern Language Journal* **51**, 463-469.

VOEGELIN, C.F. & F.M. ROBINETT (1954) "Mother language" in Hidatsa. *International Journal of American Linguistics* **20**, 65-70.

VOLTERRA, V. (1972) Il "no": Prime fasi dello sviluppo della negazione nel linguaggio infantile. *Archivio de Psicologia, Neurologia e Psichiatria* **33**, 16-53. Cited in: H. Clark & Clark 1977; Bloom & Lahey 1978.

VOLTERRA, V. & T. TAESCHNER (1978) The acquisition and development of language by bilingual children. *Journal of Child Language* **5**, 311-326.

VON MALTITZ, FRANCES (1975) *Living and learning in two languages: Bilingual-bicultural education in the United States*. New York: McGraw-Hill.

VON RAFFLER-ENGEL, W. (1965) Del bilinguismo infantile. *Archivio Glottologico Italiano* **50**, 175-180. Cited in McLaughlin 1978.

VON RAFFLER-ENGEL, WALBURGA & Y. LEBRUN, eds. (1976) *Baby talk and infant speech*. Amsterdam: Swets & Zeitlinger.

VON SENDEN, MARIUS (1932) *Raum- und Gestaltauffassung bei operierten Blindgeborenen vor und nach der Operation*. Leipzig: J.A. Barth. Cited in Hebb 1949, 29.

VYGOTSKY, LEV S. (1934) *Myshleniye i rech'*. Moscow: Sotzegiz. Translation: *Language and thought*, E. Hanfmann & G. Vaker, tr., Cambridge, Mass.: MIT Press, 1962. Page numbers refer to this version. Excerpts in: Saporta 1961, 509-535; *Psychiatry*, 1939, *2*, 29-54.

VYGOTSKY, L. & A. LURIA (1930) The function and fate of egocentric speech. In Edwin S. Boring, ed., *Proceedings of the Ninth International Congress of Pscyhology (New Haven, 1929)*, Princeton: Psychological Review Company, 1930, 464-465.

WADA, J.A., R. CLARK & A. HAMM (1975) Cerebral hemispheric asymmetry in humans: Cortical speech zones in 100 adult and 100 infant brains. *Archives of Neurology* **32**, 239-246.

WALES, R.J. (1974) The child's sentences make sense of the world. In François Bresson, ed., *Problèms actuels en psycholinguistique/Current problems in psycholinguistics*, Paris: Editions du Centre National de la Recherche Scientifique, 1974, 89-97.

WALES, R.J. (1979) Deixis. In Fletcher & Garmaan 1979, 241-260.

WALES, R.J. & R. CAMPBELL (1970) On the development of comparison and the comparison of development. In Flores D'Arcais & Levelt 1970, 373-396.

WALKER, S.T. & J.M. WALKER (1973) Differences in heart-rate variability between stutterers and nonstutterers following arousal. *Perceptual and Motor Skills* **36**, 926.

WANNEMACHER, J.T. & M.L. RYAN (1978) "Less" is not "more": A study of children's comprehension of "less" in various task contexts. *Child Development* **49**, 660-668.

WANNER, E. & L.R. GLEITMAN (1982) *Language acquisition: The state of the art.* Cambridge: Cambridge University Press.

WARDEN, D.A. (1976) The influence of context on children's use of identifying expressions and references. *British Journal of Psychology* **67**, 101-112. Reprinted in Bloom 1978, 314-326.

WARDEN, D.A. (1977) Review of Maratsos 1976. *Journal of Child Language* **4**, 123-127.

WASHABAUGH, W., J. WOODWARD & S. DE SANTIS (1978) Providence Island sign language: A context-dependent language. *Anthropological Linguistics* **20: 3**, 95-109.

WASHBURN, A. (1971) *Seeing Essential English.* Community College of Denver.

WASZ-HÖCKERT, OLE, J. LIND, V. VUORENKOSKI, T. PARTANEN & E. VALANNE (1968) *The infant cry: A spectrographic and auditory analysis.* London: Heinemann.

WATERS, R.S. & W.A. WILSON JR. (1976) Speech perception by rhesis monkeys: The voicing distinction in synthesized labial and velar stop consonants. *Perception and Psychophysics* **19**, 285-289.

WATERSON, NATALIE & C. SNOW, eds. (1978) *The development of communication.* New York: Wiley.

WATT, W. (1970) On two hypotheses concerning psycholinguistics. In Hayes 1970, 137-220.

WEBB, P.A. & A.A. ABRAHAMSON (1976) Stages of egocentrism in children's use of 'this' and 'that': A different point of view. *Journal of Child Language* **3**, 349-367.

WEBER-OLSEN, M. & K. RUDER (1980) Acquisition and generalization of Japanese locatives by English-speakers. *Applied Psycholinguistics* **1**, 183-198.

WEBSTER, C.D., H. McPHERSON, L. SLOMAN, M.A. EVANS & E. KUCHAR (1973) Communication with an autisitic boy by gestures. *Journal of Autism and Childhood Schizophrenia* **3**, 337-346.

WEBSTER, C.D., M.M. KONSTANTAREAS, J. OXMAN, S. DESROCHERS & T. MARWOOD (1975) *Come dance with me: Simultaneous communication procedures with severely dysfunctional children.* Film. Toronto: Clarke Institute of Psychiatry.

WECHSLER, D. (1952) *Wechsler intelligence scale for children.* New York: The Psychological Corporation.

WEDENBERG, E. & B. JOHANSSON (1970) When the fetus isn't listening. *Medical World News.* April 10, 28-29. Cited in Verny & Kelly 1981, 38.

WEEKS, T. (1971) Speech registers in children. *Child Development* **42**, 1119-1131.

WEIL, J. & K. STENNING (1978) A comparison of young children's comprehension & memory for statements of temporal relations. In Campbell & Smith 1978a, 395-409.

WEINBERG, B. (1964) Stuttering among blind and partially sighted children. *Journal of Speech and Hearing Disorders* **29**, 322-326.

WEIR, RUTH H. (1962) *Language in the crib.* The Hague: Mouton. Excerpt in Bar-Adon & Leopold 1971, 235-241.

WEISS, A.L., L.B. LEONARD, L.E. ROWAN & K. CHAPMAN (1983) Linguistic and nonlinguistic features of style in normal and language-impaired children. *Journal of Speech and Hearing Disorders* **48**, 154-164.

WEISS, CURTIS, E. & H.S. LILLYWHITE (1981) *Communication disorders: A handbook for prevention and early intervention, 2nd ed.* St. Louis: Mosby.

WEIST, R.M. & B. KRUPPE (1977) Parent and sibling comprehension of children's speech. *Journal of Psycholinguistic Research* **6**, 49-58.

WEIST, R.M. & P. STEBBINS (1972) Adult perception of children's speech. *Psychonomic Science* **27**, 359-360.

WELLEN, C. (1985) Effects of older siblings on the language young children hear and produce. *Journal of Speech and Hearing Disorders* **50**, 84-99.

WELLMAN, H.M. & J.D. LEMPERS (1977) The naturalistic communicative abilities of two-year-olds. *Child Development* **48**, 1052-1057.

WEPMAN, J.M. (1939a) Familial incidence in stammering. *Journal of Speech Disorders* **4**, 199-204.

WEPMAN, J.M. (1939b) Familial incidence of stammering. *Journal of Heredity* **30**, 207-210.

WERNER, HEINZ (1948) *Comparative psychology of mental development.* New York: Science Editions.

WERNER, HEINZ & B. KAPLAN (1963) *Symbol formation.* New York: Wiley.

WERTHEIMER, M. (1951) Hebb and Senden on the role of learning in perception. *American Journal of Psychology* **64**, 133-137.

WERTHEIMER, M. (1961) Psychomotor coordination of auditory and visual space at birth. *Science* **134**, 1692.

WEST, R. (1931) The phenomenology of stuttering. In Robert W. West, ed., *A symposium on stuttering*, Madison, Wisc.: College Typing Co., 1931.

WEST, R., S. NELSON & M.F. BERRY (1939) The heredity of stuttering. *Quarterly Journal of Speech* **25**, 23-30.

WEXLER, KEN & P.W. CULICOVER (1980)   *Formal principles of language acquisition.* Cambridge, Mass.: MIT Press.

WHETNALL, EDITH & D.B. FRY (1964)   *The deaf child.* London: William Heinemann.

WHETSTONE, H.S. & B.Z. FRIEDLANDER (1973)   The effect of word order on young children's responses to simple questions and commands. *Child Development* **44,** 734-740.

WHITAKER, HARRY A. (1973)   Comments on the innateness of language. In Roger W. Shuy, ed., *Some new directions in linguistics,* Washington, D.C.: Georgetown University Press, 1973, 95-120.

WHITE, H. (1961)   Cerebral hemispherectomy in the treatment of infantile hemiplegia. *Confinia Neurologica* **21,** 1-50.

WHITE HOUSE CONFERENCE COMMITTEE REPORT ON CHILD HEALTH AND PROTECTION, SECTION III;   *"Special education: The handicapped and the gifted."* New York: D. Appleton Century.

WHITE, R.W. (1960)   Competence and the psychosexual stages of development. In Marshall Jones, ed., *Nebraska symposium on motivation,* Lincoln: University of Nebraska Press, 1960, 97-141.

WHITEHURST, G.J. & A.E. MERKUR (1977)   The development of communication: Modeling and contrast failure. *Child Development* **48,** 993-1001.

WICKELGREN, L.W. (1969)   The ocular response of human newborns to intermittent visual movement. *Journal of Experimental Child Psychology* **8,** 469-482.

WIDD, THOMAS (1886)   *The deaf and dumb and blind deaf-mutes.* Toronto: Norman V. Lewis.

WIEMAN, L.A. (1976)   Stress patterns of early child language. *Journal of Child Language* **3,** 283-286.

WIGGLESWORTH, VINCENT B. (1953)   *Principles of insect physiology.* London: Methuen.

WILCOX, S. & D.S. PALERMO (1974)   "In", "on", and "under" revisited. *Cognition* **3,** 245-254.

WILKINSON, L.C., S. CALCULATOR & C. DOLLAGHAN (1982)   Ya wanna trade—just for awhile: Children's requests and responses to peers. *Discourse Processes* **5,** 161-176.

WILLIAMS, D.E., F.H. SILVERMAN & J.A. KOOLS (1969)   Disfluency behavior of elementary-school stutterers and nonstutterers: The consistency effect. *Journal of Speech and Hearing Research* **12,** 301-307.

WILLIAMS, R.N. & M.L. MATTSON (1942)   The effect of social groupings upon the language of preschool children. *Child Development* **13,** 233-245.

WILSON, P.J. (1970)   Cerebral hemispherectomy for infantile hemiplegia. *Brain* **93,** 147.

WING, JOHN K., ed. (1966)   *Early childhood autism: Clinical educational and social aspects.* London: Pergamon.

WING, L. (1969)   The handicaps of autistic children—A comparative study. *Journal of Child Psychology and Psychiatry* **10,** 1-40.

WING, L. (1971)   Perceptual and language development in autistic children: A comparative study. In Michael Rutter, ed., *Infantile autism: Concepts, characteristics and treatment,* London: Churchill Livingstone, 1971, 173-197.

WINGATE, M.E. (1962)   Personality needs of stutterers. *Logos* **5,** 35-37.

WINGATE, M.E. (1964)   Recovery from stuttering. *Journal of Speech and Hearing Disorders* **29,** 312-321.

WINGATE, M.E. (1967)   Stuttering and word length. *Journal of Speech and Hearing Research* **10,** 146-152.

WINITZ, H. (1969)   *Articulatory acquisition and behavior.* New York: Appleton-Century-Crofts.

WINZEMER, J.A. (1980)   A lexical-expectation model for children's comprehension of wh-questions. Paper presented at the 5th Annual Boston University Conference on Language Development, October.

WITELSON, S.F. & W. PALLIE (1973)   Left hemisphere specialization assymmetry. *Brain* **96,** 641-647.

WODE, H. (1976)   Developmental principles in naturalistic L1 acquisition. *Arbeitspapiere zum Spracherwerb* **16.** Keil University. Cited in McLaughlin 1978.

WOLF, E.G. & B. RUTTENBERG (1967)   Communication therapy for the autistic child. *Journal of Speech and Hearing Disorders* **32,** 331-335.

WOLF, M.W., T. RISLEY & H. MEES (1964)   Application of operant conditioning procedures to the behavior problems of an autistic boy. *Behavior Research and Therapy* **1,** 305-312.

WOLFF, P.H. (1969)   The natural history of crying and other vocalizations in early infancy. In Brian M. Foss, ed., *Determinants of infant behaviour IV. Proceedings of the fourth Tavistock Study Group on Mother-Infant Interaction,* 1969, 81-109.

WOLL, BENCIE, J. KYLE & M. DEUCHAR, eds. (1981)   *Perspectives on British sign language and deafness.* London: Croon Helm.

WYATT, G.L. (1958)   A developmental crisis theory of stuttering. *Language and Speech* **1,** 250-264.

WYATT, GERTRUDE L. (1969)   *Language learning and communication disorders in children.* New York: Free Press.

YAIRI, E. (1983)   The onset of stuttering in two- and three-year old children: A preliminary report. *Journal of Speech and Hearing Disorders* **48,** 171-177.

YAU, S.C. (1977)   *The Chinese signs.* Ed. Lang. Croises. Hong Kong: Chui Ming. Cited in Stokoe 1980.

ZAKHAROVA, A.V. (1958)   Usvoyeniye doshkol'nitani padezhnykh form. *Dokl. Akad. Pedag. Nauk RSFFR* **2:3,** 81-84. Translation by Greta Slobin: Acquisition of forms of grammatical case by preschool children. In C. Ferguson & Slobin 1973, 281-284.

ZANGWILL, O. (1964)   The current status of cerebral dominance. *Research publications—Association for Research in Nervous and Mental Disease* **42,** 105-113.

ZANGWILL, ISRAEL (1909)   *The melting pot, drama in four acts.* New York: Macmillan.

ZAREBA, A. (1953)   Hezyk polski w szwecji. *Jezyk Polski* **33,** 29-31, 98-111. Cited in McLaughlin 1978.

ZEHLER, A.M. & W.F. BREWER (1982)   Sequence and principles in article system use: An examination of *a, the,* and *null* acquisition. *Child Development* **53,** 1268-1274.

ZESKIND, P. & B. LESTER (1978) Acoustic features and auditory perceptions of the cries of newborns with prenatal and perinatal complications. *Child Development* **49,** 580-589.

ZIMMERMANN, G., S. LILJEBLAD, A. FRANK & C. CLEELAND (1983) The Indians have many terms for it: Stuttering among the Bannock-Shoshoni. *Journal of Speech and Hearing Research* **26,** 315-318.

ZINGG, R.M. (1940) Feral man and extreme cases of isolation. *American Journal of Psychology* **52,** 487-517.

AUTHOR INDEX

SUBJECT INDEX